God, Huma

God, Humanity and the Cosmos

Second Edition
Revised and Expanded
as

A Companion to the Science–Religion Debate

CHRISTOPHER SOUTHGATE
JOHN HEDLEY BROOKE
CELIA DEANE-DRUMMOND
PAUL D. MURRAY
MICHAEL ROBERT NEGUS
LAWRENCE OSBORN
MICHAEL POOLE
ANDREW ROBINSON
JACQUI STEWART
FRASER WATTS
DAVID WILKINSON

T & T CLARK INTERNATIONAL
A Continuum imprint
LONDON • NEW YORK

Published by T&T Clark International
A Continuum imprint
The Tower Building, 11 York Road, London SE1 7NX
15 East 26th Street, Suite 1703, New York, NY 10010

www.tandtclark.com

First Published 1999
Reprinted 2003
Second edition, revised and expanded 2005

British Library Cataloguing-in-Publication Data
A catalogue record for this book is available from the British Library

Library of Congress Cataloging-in-Publication Data
God, humanity, and the cosmos / Christopher Southgate ... [et al.].–2nd ed., rev. and expanded as a companion to the science-religion debate.
        p. cm.
    Includes bibliographical references (p.) and index.
    ISBN 0-567-04144-1 – ISBN 0-567-03016-4 (pbk.)
        1. Religion and science–Textbooks.   I. Southgate, Christopher, 1953-

    BL240.3.G62 2005
    201′.65–dc22   200505068

Typeset by YHT Ltd, London
Printed on acid-free paper in Great Britain by MPG Books Ltd, Cornwall

ISBN 0567030164 (paperback)
        0567041441 (hardback)

Contents

BOOK ONE

1. An introduction to the debate between science and religion

3

Christopher Southgate and Michael Poole

Section A: Outlines of the debate (1.1–1.11)
1.1 Two views of the conversation between science and religion – 1.2 Important sources, figures and developments – 1.3 Typologies of the relationship – 1.3.1 Natural theology vs theology of nature – 1.4 Further typologies – 1.5 Two crucial points – 1.5.1 Science and religion, or science and *theology*? – 1.6 The metaphor of the maps – 1.7 Critical realism in science – 1.8 Critical realism in theology – 1.9 The central role of model and metaphor – 1.10 Consonances – 1.11 Was religion necessary to the rise of science?

Section B: Three historical examples of tensions as science and theology developed (1.12–1.15)
1.12 Copernicanism and the Galileo Affair – 1.13 The love affair gone wrong: the eighteenth century – 1.14 A contemporary instance of interplay between consonance and conflict – 1.15 The Big Bang and the beginning of the universe

Section C: Key principles for developing theology in the light of science (1.16–1.20)
1.16 Different types of causation and explanation – 1.17 Determinism, indeterminism and their implications – 1.18 Developing theology in the light of science – 1.18.1 The interdependence of different aspects of a model – 1.19 Three attributes of models of God, humanity and the cosmos – 1.20 Questions of value

1.21 Conclusion

BOOK TWO

BOOK THREE

agency – 10.7.1 The mind and the brain – 10.7.2 The mind–brain debate – 10.8 Views of God's action – 10.9 The causal joint – 10.10 Peacocke and Polkinghorne compared – 10.11 Process schemes and double agency – 10.12 Conclusion to the debate on special divine action – 10.12.1 The contribution of Robert J. Russell

Section B: What God has done: the history of the universe (10.13–10.19)
10.13 The Big Bang and 'before' – 10.14 Anthropic considerations – 10.15 The early universe – 10.16 The origin of life – 10.17 The evolutionary development of life – 10.18 Questions of theodicy in respect of evolution – 10.18.1 The probability of self-conscious beings – 10.19 Possible theologies of divine action in respect of evolution

Section C: What God will do (10.20)
10.20 Eschatology

10.21 Conclusion

BOOK FOUR

11. Science and education   303
Michael Poole

11.1 Introduction to Book Four – 11.2 Science education and the science–religion debate – 11.3 Meeting-points – 11.3.1 The content of science – 11.3.2 The nature of science – 11.3.3 The applications of science – 11.3.4 How science operates as a social activity – 11.4 Some educational questions – 11.5 A *modus operandi* – 11.6.1 One way for science education to make a contribution – 11.6.2 A second way – 11.6.3 A third way – 11.7 Recent developments in England – 11.7.1 Primary education – 11.7.2 Secondary education – 11.7.3 Tertiary education

12. Islam and science   321
Michael Robert Negus

12.1 Introduction – 12.2 The concept of God – 12.3 The religious dimensions of Islam – 12.4 The universe and its Creator – 12.5 The Golden Age of Islam – 12.6 The Islamic paradigm of the universe – 12.7 Islam and modern science – 12.8 Identifying problems and recognizing points of agreement – 12.9 Proposals for the regulation and Islamization of science – 12.10 Islam and Darwinism

12.11 Conclusion

13. Technology and Christianity   340
Jacqui Stewart

13.1 Introduction – 13.2 What is technology? – 13.3 Is technology good or bad? – 13.4 Technology and Christianity in the history of Western Europe –

BOOK FIVE

Figures

Tables

Exercises

Contributors

DR CHRISTOPHER SOUTHGATE, the Coordinating Editor, trained originally in research biochemistry at Cambridge. He is now a poet, editor and theologian based at the University of Exeter, where he is Honorary University Fellow in Theology. He won a Hawthornden Fellowship in 1999, and is the author of four books of poetry and around sixty other articles and reviews, scientific, literary and theological.

PROFESSOR JOHN HEDLEY BROOKE is the Andreas Idreos Professor of Science and Religion and Director of the Ian Ramsey Centre at the University of Oxford, where he is also a Fellow of Harris Manchester College. A former President of the British Society for the History of Science, he gave the Gifford Lectures, jointly with Professor Geoffrey Cantor, at the University of Glasgow in 1995. From 2001 to 2004 he was Co-ordinator of the European Science Foundation Network on Science and Human Values and is a founding member of the Oxford Centre for the Science of Mind.

PROFESSOR CELIA DEANE-DRUMMOND FRSA qualified originally as a plant scientist at Cambridge, gaining an honours degree in Natural Sciences, followed by a doctorate in plant physiology from Reading University. She then taught in the Botany Department at Durham University. She has published over thirty articles in international scientific journals. She holds an honours degree and a doctorate in theology from Manchester University, and she received a personal Chair in theology and the biological sciences at University College Chester in 2000. She is currently chairperson of the Science and Religion Forum, and first director of the Centre for Religion and the Biosciences at University College Chester.

DR PAUL D. MURRAY is currently Lecturer in Systematic Theology at the University of Durham. He is a married lay Roman Catholic theologian who holds degrees from the Universities of Durham and Cambridge. He has previously held posts at St Cuthbert's Seminary, Ushaw College, Durham, and at Newman College, Birmingham. He has published a number of essays in edited volumes and leading journals in the areas of theology and science, philosophy and theology and contemporary Roman Catholic theology. His first monograph is *Reason, Truth and Theology in Pragmatist Perspective* (Leuven: Peeters, 2005).

DR MICHAEL ROBERT NEGUS, a biologist, was until 2001 the Head of Science at Newman College, Birmingham. He holds qualifications in Computer Science and Islamic Studies. He is now retired from academic teaching. His recent publications are in the areas of science and scientists in Islam.

DR LAWRENCE OSBORN lives and works in Glasgow as a freelance editor, writer and practical theologian. He is a former holder of the Templeton Fellowship in Science, Religion and Humility Theology.

MICHAEL POOLE is currently Visiting Research Fellow in Science and Religion in the Department of Education and Professional Studies at King's College London. With a background in science education, his research interests have centred on the interplay between science and religion with special reference to its educational context. He is the author of several books and some seventy articles and papers on the topic.

DR ANDREW ROBINSON is a General Practitioner in Newton Abbot, Devon, and Honorary University Fellow in Theology at the University of Exeter. He holds degrees in physiology and medicine, and a doctorate in theology. He is interested in evolutionary biology, trinitarian theology and philosophical theories of meaning.

DR JACQUI STEWART has a Ph.D. in population genetics and held a lectureship in that subject until 1990. Since then she has worked in theology, gaining a second Ph.D. in that area. She is presently Senior Lecturer in Theology at the University of Leeds. Her research interests include the works of Pannenberg and Ellul.

THE REVD DR FRASER WATTS is Reader in Theology and Science at the University of Cambridge, Fellow of Queens' College, Vice-President of the International Society for Science and Religion, and Vicar-Chaplain of St Edward King and Martyr, Cambridge. He was formerly at the MRC Applied Psychology Unit, working on cognitive aspects of emotional disorders, and has been President of the British Psychological Society.

THE REVD DR DAVID WILKINSON is Wesley Research Lecturer in Theology and Science in the Department of Theology and Religion, University of Durham. He has Ph.D.s in theoretical astrophysics and systematic theology and is a Fellow of the Royal Astronomical Society. His most recent books are *God, Time and Stephen Hawking* (Monarch, 2001) and *Creation* (IVP, 2002).

How to use this book

This book is intended both as a companion to the debate for the general reader, and as a resource for teachers and students on undergraduate-level courses. No scientific background is presumed. Where a technical theological term is used for the first time an explanation is provided. The index enables the reader to refer to these definitions.

The book is designed to be read as a whole or to be used in its individual sections, or its individual chapters:

BOOK ONE introduces the science and religion debate, giving key historical examples (Chapter 1), and then provides a survey of what it has meant, in the Christian tradition, to talk of God as Creator (Chapter 2), an examination of the lessons history offers re the science–religion debate (Chapter 3), and a philosophical analysis of science and theology as related rational enterprises (Chapter 4).

BOOK TWO proceeds to a detailed examination of how three types of science – physics (Chapter 5), evolutionary biology (Chapter 6) and psychology (Chapter 7) – interact with theological and religious claims.

BOOK THREE explores further the relevant theological resources available within contemporary Christian theology (Chapter 8) and deriving from a range of other traditions (Chapter 9). Chapter 10 considers what the foregoing material implies for a description of divine action in the light of contemporary science.

BOOK FOUR takes up the question of science's place in society. First we look at science education and the role it can play in relating science to values, social and religious (Chapter 11). Then we consider the Islamic tradition and how that can give rise to a different perspective on the place of science (Chapter 12). Science has also been a major contributory factor in the development of technology. We review this historically and theologically in Chapter 13. Chapter 14 concentrates on 'biotechnology' – genetic modification and cloning – considered theologically and ethically.

Finally in BOOK FIVE we speculate on how the debate between science and religion is likely to develop (Chapter 15).

The sections within each chapter

These are all numbered. The main sections carry the number of the chapter and the number of the section – e.g. '10.7 Personal agency'. Sections going into a particular issue in more detail are shown by a three-digit number, e.g. '10.7.1 The mind and the brain'. An initial skip-read of a chapter, or a summary reading for revision purposes, might concentrate on the two-numbered sections. More detailed work would include the three-numbered sections.

Bibliographical references

Wherever possible actual page references have been given. So section 1.4 introduces Ted Peters' classification of possible relations between science and religion, to be found in pages 650–4 of Peters, 1997a, which the main Bibliography shows to be Peters' article in *The Modern Theologians*, edited by David Ford and published in Oxford by Blackwell.

Foreword

In one sense, of course, issues of 'faith and culture', 'faith and reason' and 'science and religion' are as old as the Christian faith itself. Many have discovered this with surprise, indeed a sense of déjà vu, as they have gone back in time to try and grasp the ever-evolving intellectual process that has defined these crucial issues so differently in different epochs.

But those of us who have been part of the developing conversation about theology and science during the past fifteen years now find ourselves in the middle of shifts in paradigm and intellectual changes so profound that suddenly the whole world looks different.

Not so long ago the troubled relationship between religion and science could still be seen as the specialized, and often inaccessible, domain of a privileged few intellectuals who cared passionately about these two very diverse and often conflicting cultural forces. Today, however, everything has changed: not only has the 'theology and science' debate come to symbolize much more comprehensively the face of today's 'faith and culture' and 'faith and reason' debates, but what was formerly a private and specialized conversation has now burst onto the public scene in ways which would once have been unthinkable. Not only is the science-and-religion debate alive and well in many parts of the world, but a number of centres and societies have sprung up, and the debate is finding a permanent place in schools and colleges as well as in seminaries and universities. This highly visible public profile is further enhanced by a veritable explosion of books, papers and conferences on this fascinating topic.

This amazing phenomenon is still of course embedded in the complexity of our Western culture, with its ambivalence not only about the status of the debate, but about what we mean by 'science' and 'theology'. Most of us accept today that we have inherited from modernity a troubling and challenging dichotomy in which 'science' is taken to have emerged triumphantly as a superior form of rational thinking, and 'religion' is taken to have faded into a rather privatized form of subjective (if not irrational) experience. The ramifications of this modernist heritage have been all-consuming, and certainly devastating for religion: the divisions between science and religion (and theology, as a reflection on religious practice) led to sharp distinctions between objective descriptions and subjective experiences, between scientific and symbolic uses of language, between scientific truth and religious opinion, and finally to an all-consuming worldview in which science was taken to be more enduringly true precisely because it is empirically based on observation and repeatable experimentation. In the face of this superior paradigm of human rationality, which steadily accumulates knowledge, and even aspires to a 'theory of everything' which might even yield a complete account of all that is genuinely knowable, religion has often been forced to retreat into symbol and art as expressions of personal and communal experience.

This dichotomy left theology still firmly embedded in the stark modernist separation between knowledge and opinion, explanation and understanding, natural and human sciences, epistemology and hermeneutics. Part of the complexity and ambivalence of our culture's appropriation of the 'theology and science' issue has therefore been precisely the image of an enduring 'conflict' between science and religion. This conflict image extended to some stark differences and hostilities on philosophical and historical issues, as well as on issues of content.

Theologians and believing scientists to this day try to resolve these differences through attempts to construct wide-ranging typologies – trying to 'name' the sort of relationship one might want to see between these dominant and apparently conflicting forces in our culture. The ongoing conversation about the relationship between religion and science is also, however, revealing some important nuances in this age-old relationship: it has become increasingly clear that, contrary to some popular misconceptions, the dialogue is not only about conflict and dissensus. The image of perpetual conflict is increasingly seen as an invention of the late nineteenth century, and scholars in the field are realizing that the truth about the historical relationship has always been much more complex (cf. Gregersen and van Huyssteen, 1998:1ff.; Watts, 1998c:2f., and Chapters 1 and 3 of *God, Humanity and the Cosmos*). Moreover, for many participants in this discussion the whole idea of a 'conflict' has become something of a moot issue, given that science and religion often seem to be answering such different questions rather than giving different and conflicting answers to the same questions (cf. Watts, 1998c:2).

While an important part of the current ambivalent state of affairs represents the enduring attempt to maintain science's alleged priority as the paradigmatic way of establishing true knowledge, the continuing embeddedness of our contemporary culture in modernist epistemic values is by no means the entire story. Our culture is being radically redefined and challenged by a new, all-pervasive mood which we have come to know as postmodernity. The confusing co-presence in our intellectual culture of both superior (modernist) notions of natural scientific rationality and pluralist postmodern views which radically reject all notions of scientific superiority has emerged as the defining challenge to anyone trying to come to terms with the values that shape the rationality of theological and scientific reflection today. Postmodernity has given us a cultural context which has been deeply affected by what many see as the complete fragmentation of knowledge, and even as rampant pluralism and relativism.

This gives new urgency to the question whether a more affirmative reading of postmodernity might leave scope for an intelligible, cross-disciplinary conversation between theology and the sciences today. Some postmodernists consider conventional definitions of academic disciplines simply as remnants of modernity and directly question the viability of strict boundaries between the natural sciences, social sciences, humanities, art, literature and religious reflection. Even more important, though, is that the reasons, arguments and value judgments employed by the community of scientists – like those of communities of theologians – are now seen to be fundamentally grounded in social practices. The very criteria and norms that traditionally guided and defined scientific and theological activities thus become open and vulnerable to criticism. In what seems to be a complete loss of any meta-standpoints from which to reflect on a possible interdisciplinary relationship between theology and science, all our interpretations of theology and science now seem to be reduced to the local context within which we operate. At the end of the day the postmodern challenge seems to leave theology in just the same place where modernity left it – isolated, and out in the cold.

In a provocative paper by John Bowker this radical contemporary revisioning of the theology and science question is anticipated in an intriguing way. Bowker asks: what would happen if we looked at the relationship between science and religion in an entirely different way? He then proceeds to argue that this relationship looks entirely different when one realizes that the really persistent issue between religion and science is not so much about different kinds of knowledge claims, but rather one of power (cf. Bowker, 1998:116f.). Although he never identifies this important shift as a postmodern one, it is clear what some of the ramifications of this epistemic shift might imply for a possible interdisciplinary relationship between theology and science. For Bowker the real challenge of science to religion and theology is not so much a conflict of competing propositions and worldviews, but rather a ruthless challenge to the independence of religion's own authority. In doing this, science is taking over areas where religion traditionally had its authority and control.

Against the background of this argument Mary Hesse has asked whether science and technology in some sense represent 'the new religion' (Hesse, 1998:120ff.). By asking this Hesse too wants to alert us to issues of power and authority as crucial for thinkers trying to rescue a sense that religion has an essential function in human life (a function which cannot be allowed to be taken over by the increasing power of scientism). The power of science today is certainly overwhelmingly present in the technology without which our society would almost certainly collapse. But the focus of the power of science is certainly still found – in spite of the postmodern mood – in its claims to rational authority (cf. Hesse, 1998:122).

In addition, of course, postmodern pluralism makes it almost impossible to speak generically about 'science', 'religion', and 'theology' today. Both postmodernity's epistemic pluralism as well as modernity's marginalization of religious meaning have therefore been very successful in deconstructing our attempts to find a space for meaningful dialogue between disciplines as diverse and different as theology and science.

I have argued elsewhere that the only way out of the confusing 'double challenge' presented by modernist as well as postmodernist themes in contemporary culture is to probe the interdisciplinary possibilities and shared resources of the ongoing conversation between theology and the sciences (cf. van Huyssteen, 1998). It is precisely on this point that Chris Southgate and his excellent and capable team of co-authors have been so remarkably successful. They have together produced a textbook on the current theology and science dialogue which is very different from other works currently available.

Not only is *God, Humanity and the Cosmos* directly addressed to teachers and students, and as such manages to be remarkably accessible; it also carefully addresses all the contemporary issues in the field, but in such a way that it moves the theology and science debate to the cutting edge of the current conversation, and in so doing brings their readers to the frontier of one of the most exciting explorations of our time.

This book represents a strong and quite remarkable move beyond some of the ubiquitous generalities of the religion and science dialogue. It is the living proof that the theology and science conversation 'works' if we contextualize it to specific issues in specific sciences and specific kinds of theologies in specific religions. In this sense the book will appeal to those of us with qualified postmodern sensibilities, and goes beyond much of what is out there in the current literature. The student and teacher using this work will very soon learn the far-reaching educational impact of the fact that the evolving relationship between different sciences and any one religion will be different at any given time, and will keep changing through history.

Moving beyond stereotypes of 'science' and 'the scientific method' the authors of this book also acknowledge the complexity of both scientific practice and theological discourse. What is developed clearly is that any focus on science is always a focus on practice and reflection, with all-important implications for science education. Similarly any focus on theology is, or should be, a focus on the models, the metaphors and the propositions that give theology its rational framework – these always, however, deeply embedded in religious practice. What emerges from this is the book's most important leitmotif: scientific and theological descriptions of our (one) world are like different maps of reality, maps which can rightly claim a profound degree of independence, but which are fundamentally interrelated because even as radically different discourses they share the resources of human rationality. The authors of this book thus succeed eminently in creating a space for true interdisciplinary reflection, and in doing that give a strong answer to both modernist and postmodernist challenges to the ongoing dialogue between theology and the sciences.

In reading this book students will quickly learn that both theology and the sciences are to be seen as more complex activities than merely a realist search for progressively truer data. At the same time the authors very convincingly show how science – on this point remarkably like theology – needs to be seen as exemplifying the activities of communities of motivated believers, holding core assumptions, and testing out new possibilities. Even more importantly, though, an awareness is created of just what kind of theology is being done in the light of contemporary science. One of the most important themes of this book emerges precisely around a sustained argument against any cultural or epistemic isolation of theology as a discipline. On this view a pattern emerges which finds a careful balance between highlighting the public voice of theology, on the one hand, while at the same time never just narrowly focusing on theological reflection as a mere acquisition of knowledge; the Christian faith, and Christian theological reflection, is also, indeed first and foremost, about conformity to Christ. An integrating force in this book is, therefore, the holding together of the reflection on epistemological issues of theory and belief with an analysis of how these theories and belief grow out of, and are permanently embedded in, practice. This leaves us with a strong sense of how the continually evolving Christian tradition unfolds in new and creative ways as a direct response to a culture so definitively shaped today by science and technology.

The basic thrust underlying the central argument of the book is therefore found in the strong conviction of the various authors that it is both possible and fruitful to seek to bring the insights and concerns of the sciences and religion together in a mutually constructive interchange. As such it boldly addresses interdisciplinary issues and even moves them into the more complex field of interreligious dialogue, while at the same time pointing to what the future may hold for the ongoing dialogue between religion, science and technology. What unfolds from this is a clear and unambiguous answer to the ambivalent cultural challenge to theology and science today: nothing in our world – even in our science and technologies – has been understood adequately until it has been understood from within its relationship to God as Creator of that world.

J. WENTZEL VAN HUYSSTEEN
James I. McCord Professor of Theology and Science
Princeton Theological Seminary

Editor's note and acknowledgements

This book is unusual among the many emerging on the science–religion dialogue in that:

- it offers a depth of exploration between popular accounts and specialized research publications;
- it presumes little background knowledge, but signposts students to the forefront of the debate;
- it draws on the expertise of 11 different authors, all experienced teachers and researchers.

Five of the authors (Christopher Southgate, Paul D. Murray, Michael Robert Negus, Lawrence Osborn and Michael Poole) formed the core editorial team that shaped the first edition of the book.

As Coordinating Editor I take this opportunity to thank all my colleagues for the patience and diligence with which they went about this complex collaboration – also Professor Wentzel van Huyssteen who kindly contributed the Foreword. Other scholars helped us in various ways. The Revd Dr Arthur Peacocke was a great encouragement in the early stages of the project. He, and Drs Bob Russell and Janet Martin Soskice, kindly supplied manuscripts of material not yet published. Professor Mary Midgley kindly sent information on 'the metaphor of the maps' (Section 1.6).

Much of the critical comment came from within the editorial team itself, but we would also like to thank Dr Walter Moberly of Durham University and Professor Jeff Astley of the North of England Institute for Christian Education for comments on Chapter 2, Dr John Martin of King's College, London, for comments on Chapter 5, Revd David Moss and Dr Louise Hickman for comments on Chapter 8, and Dr R.W.J. Austin, formerly of Durham University, for checking (for the first edition) the specialized Islamic material in Chapter 12. Dr Cherryl Hunt and Ms Kate Davies kindly acted as readers of early drafts. Richard Skinner valiantly checked the whole proof of the first edition. More general thanks go to the many winners of Templeton Foundation Course Awards who offered comments on an early synopsis of the book.

We thank also the John Templeton Foundation itself, which generously provided a grant towards the costs of the work on the first edition.

Finally it is a pleasure to thank the publishers for their painstaking and ever-courteous help in seeing the manuscript through the press.

Copyright permissions. We acknowledge the following: the Association for Science Education, in whose journal Figure 1.3 first appeared; Dr Jonathan Kingdon for permission to reproduce Figures 6.1(a) and (b); University Science Books for permission to reproduce Figures 6.2 and 6.3.

BOOK ONE

Chapter 1

An introduction to the debate between science and religion

Christopher Southgate and Michael Poole[1]

SECTION A
OUTLINES OF THE DEBATE (1.1–1.11)

1.1 Two views of the conversation between science and religion

> Whenever theology touches science, it gets burned. In the sixteenth century
> astronomy, in the seventeenth microbiology, in the eighteenth geology and
> paleontology, in the nineteenth Darwin's biology all grotesquely extended
> the world-frame and sent churchmen scurrying for cover in ever smaller,
> more shadowy nooks, little gloomy ambiguous caves in the psyche where
> even now neurology is cruelly harrying them, gouging them out from the
> multifolded brain like wood lice from under the lumber pile. (Updike,
> 1986:32)

> By encouraging openness between the Church and the scientific commu-
> nities, we are not envisioning a disciplinary unity between theology and
> science like that which exists within a given scientific field or within
> theology proper. As dialogue and common searching continue, there will be
> growth towards mutual understanding and a gradual uncovering of com-
> mon concerns which will provide the basis for future research and discus-
> sion. Exactly what form that will take must be left to the future. What is
> important, as we have already stressed, is that the dialogue should continue
> and grow in depth and scope. In the process we must overcome every
> regressive tendency to a unilateral reductionism, to fear, and to self-imposed
> isolation. (John Paul II, 1988:M7)

A caricature, crisply phrased by a leading novelist, and an excerpt from a papal
letter to the Director of the Vatican Observatory. We begin with this juxtapos-
ition, because these two extreme viewpoints will be with us throughout this look
at the interactions between the sciences and religion.

The character in Updike's novel talks of theology in progressive and inevitable
retreat before the dominance of science. There is a conflict in which one subject is
overwhelming the other, forcing it off its territory.[2] The tone of the Pope's letter
is very different, implying a common territory on which may take place

exploration and dialogue. He renounces the idea that theology might seek to preserve itself from the 'harryings' of science (*qua* Updike) by seeking isolation.

1.2 Important sources, figures and developments in the field of science and religion

The Pope's letter was published at the beginning of the proceedings of a Vatican Conference held at Castelgandolfo in 1987, marking the tercentenary of the publication of Newton's *Principia*.[3] Since then a series of conferences have offered leading articulators of the debate between science and religion an intensive opportunity to compare positions. The resultant proceedings, edited by Robert John Russell and others (Russell *et al.*, 1988; 1993; 1995; 1998; 1999; 2001; 2005), are invaluable guides to the cutting-edge of the debate, particularly on the vexed question of God's action in the world science describes. We take up that question in Chapter 10. Another landmark in the field was the publication of *The Encyclopedia of Science and Religion*, edited by J. Wentzel van Huyssteen, in 2003.

Much of the literature in this field builds on the pioneering work of **Ian Barbour**, who brought out *Issues in Science and Religion* in 1966 and *Myths, Models and Paradigms* in 1974. His Gifford Lectures of 1990, published as *Religion in an Age of Science*[4] and *Ethics in an Age of Technology*, gave a valuable overview of the field.[5] The extent of Barbour's contribution may be gauged from the festschrift in his honour (Russell, 2004). His name is often linked with those of the British scientist-theologians **Arthur Peacocke** and **John Polkinghorne**,[6] but the contribution of the American philosopher **Holmes Rolston III** has been of comparable stature. All emerged from a background in 'hard' sciences – Peacocke in physical biochemistry, the other three in physics itself. Peacocke's groundbreaking Bampton Lectures of 1978, *Creation and the World of Science*, were reissued in 2004, and his work is summarized in his *Paths from Science to God* (2001a). Polkinghorne, former Professor of Mathematical Physics at Cambridge and since then a vigorous and articulate apologist for Christianity in dialogue with science, has brought out an extraordinary number of books, of which arguably the most adventurous and important is his *Science and Providence* (1989). He re-explored a number of his key positions in *Faith, Science and Understanding* (2000). His *Science and the Trinity* (2004) is important for his coverage of eschatology[7] (see **10.20**), and his *Science and Theology* (1998) remains an excellent introductory text.[8] Holmes Rolston's Gifford Lectures *Genes, Genesis and God* (1999) mark a major investigation of value in natural and human history – as such they build on his pioneering work in environmental ethics (see e.g. Rolston, 1988; 1994).

Just as the development of the Zygon Center for Religion and Science at Chicago (founded by Philip Hefner) and the Center for Theology and the Natural Sciences at Berkeley (founded and still directed by Robert J. Russell) were most valuable in establishing the academic integrity of the science–religion debate, so the endowment of the James I. McCord Chair at Princeton Seminary (1990), the Starbridge Lectureship at Cambridge (1994), and the Andreas Idreos Chair at Oxford (1999) marked other important landmarks in the debate's development. The McCord Professor, Wentzel van Huyssteen, contributes our Foreword, Fraser

Watts, the first Starbridge post-holder, our Chapter 7, and John Hedley Brooke, the Andreas Idreos Professor, our Chapter 3.

Two other figures not normally thought of as theologians have also done a great deal to stimulate the debate. The first is the physicist Paul Davies, who has been drawn towards theism by the directions he has seen his scientific field take, and who has written of this journey in books such as *God and the New Physics* and *The Mind of God* (Davies, 1990; 1993). The second is the biologist Richard Dawkins, whose vigorous dismissals of the claims of religion (see **6.13.4**) have had a most stimulating effect on believers interested in dialogue with science. Had Dawkins not existed, the Christian Church might have found it necessary to invent him.

One of the ways sometimes used to try and characterize the relations between science and religion is to interview practitioners in the different fields. Two short but rewarding books in this area are *Science and Wonders* (Stannard, 1996)[9] and *Faith in Science* (Richardson and Slack, 2001). Two others well worth consulting are *Cosmos, Bios, Theos* (Margenau and Varghese, 1992) and *Cosmic Beginnings and Human Ends* (Matthews and Varghese, 1995). Very many other books have emerged in the last ten years which are important in particular areas – these are cited at the relevant points in the text. *For convenience there is a single alphabetical list of references and bibliography at the back of the book – though it might seem large and daunting, readers are urged to make use of it.* It is of the nature of this book that it functions quite largely as a signpost to more specialized material.

To produce a companion to this field, which draws on so many areas in philosophy and theology as well as on the material of a number of different sciences, is a massive task. Hence this volume draws on the expertise of 11 authors. However, even such a team is very reliant on the best of what has been written by others. We highlighted above four great figures in the field. Two outstanding books which appeared in 1996 and still merit close attention are *Religion and Science: History, Method, Dialogue*, an important collection of research positions edited by W. Mark Richardson and Wesley J. Wildman, and Willem B. Drees' *Religion, Science and Naturalism* (Drees, 1996). Drees applies an intensely intelligent, theologically sceptical approach to a wide variety of topics.

However, the present authors consider that more can be said of the positive overlap between scientific and theological positions than Drees allows. We write from within a Western Christian perspective, which we clarify in more detail below. The book, however, also surveys a wide variety of Christian thought in Chapter 8, and outlines some very different patterns of thought, deriving from Judaism, Taoism, Hinduism and Buddhism, in Chapter 9. Chapter 12 is devoted to Islam, a monotheism in some ways closely related to Christianity but leading to a very different set of relations with the world of science.

We have mentioned the great explosion of work there has been in this area, much facilitated in various ways by the work of the John Templeton Foundation. The Foundation has commissioned lecture series, funded courses and sponsored workshops which have greatly furthered dialogue between educators working in the field. It is in considerable part due to Templeton funding that there are several hundred courses running in this interdisciplinary subject area in the USA, and probably almost as many again in universities in the rest of the world.

1.3 Typologies of the relationship between science and religion

One of the features of this movement has been a search for typologies of the relationships between science and religion. Again Barbour has taken a lead, proposing a fourfold scheme with subdivisions (Figure 1.1).

Figure 1.1 Ian Barbour's typology of the relations between science and religion. This is a slight revision of the scheme in his 1990 Gifford Lectures, and is thoroughly discussed in Barbour, 1998: ch. 4. Here we merely note a distinction within his Category IV.

1.3.1 An important distinction – natural theology vs theology of nature

What does Barbour mean by these two similar terms?

- *Natural theology* is traditionally understood as the consideration of what can be known about God without the aid of revelation, i.e. from consideration of the created world in general, aided by reason. Whereas
- Barbour's *theology of nature* 'starts from a religious tradition based on

religious experience and historical revelation. But it holds that some traditional doctrines need to be reformulated in the light of current science' (Barbour, 1998:100). The framing of a theology of nature is in fact what most of the contemporary writers in the science-and-religion field are engaged upon, and what this book will encourage its readers also to attempt (see **1.18–1.19** and **8.4.3** on models of God, humanity and the cosmos).

Most Christian natural theology has stemmed in one way or other from the work of Thomas Aquinas (1224/5–74).[10] Two of his arguments for the existence of God have stimulated particular interest among those concerned with science: *the cosmological argument* (that all change must stem from a necessary, self-existent being who is the First Cause of all phenomena in the universe) and *the teleological argument* (that order and intelligibility and apparent purpose in nature imply a rational designer). Much of the science done in the late seventeenth and the eighteenth centuries was motivated by a desire to learn more of the nature of this ordering designer-divinity (see **1.13** below, also Brooke and Cantor, 1998:ch. 5). However, the teleological argument was the subject of a devastating attack by David Hume (1711–76), who pointed out, for example, that our experience of the world does not rule out its order having arisen by chance, or indeed there being not one but many designers, and so forth. Arguments for the existence of God from apparent design in nature persisted, but were finally laid to rest by the work of Darwin (see **6.6–6.7** – also Brooke, 1991:181–9, 192–225).[11] The cosmological argument has also received much critical scrutiny from the time of Immanuel Kant (1724–1804), and it must be accepted that what we know about the universe can never demonstrate whether it has a cause, or whether its existence is ultimately inexplicable.

The demise of natural theology, and its partial rebirth as 'a philosophical theology or new style natural theology' are well analysed by Macquarrie (1977: ch. 2). The central point to note is that those authors claiming to revive natural theology tend to do so in a way which is 'descriptive instead of deductive' (Macquarrie, 1977:56). A good example concerns the 'anthropic balances' which will be discussed in **5.20–5.24** and **10.14**. Commenting on the notion that the universe appears to be fine-tuned so as to produce life, Polkinghorne calls this not a demonstration of the existence or the nature of God but merely 'a fact of interest calling for an explanation' (1991:78).

The boldest attempt to reinvoke natural theology in our own time is that of Richard Swinburne, who claims not that what we know of the universe demonstrates God, but that it renders theism more *probable* than not. We analyse Swinburne's approach in **4.5**.

1.4 Further typologies

Barbour's scheme at least maps out the territory, but in practice students often experience a lot of difficulty in applying his categories with any precision, or aligning themselves wholeheartedly with any particular one. A related scheme is that of John Haught, who in his ingenious book *Science and Religion: From Conflict to Conversation* (1995) addresses a series of key issues from the standpoints of *conflict, contrast, contact* and *confirmation*. This is a more helpful approach than Barbour's because the categories are not simply mapped out in the abstract, but applied to particular questions. Ted Peters offers eight possibilities for under-standing the relation between science and religion, varying 'from pitched battle to an uneasy truce' (Peters, 1997a:650). His categories are:

- *scientism* – religion is outdated, science tells us all we need to know;
- *scientific imperialism* – science can give us good information even about what were formerly religious questions (see, for example, Tipler's 'phy-sical eschatology' mentioned at 5.23–5.23.1 and 7.7);
- *ecclesiastical authoritarianism* – the Church should have authority over science (effectively the Roman Catholic Church claimed this until the Second Vatican Council in the early 1960s);
- *scientific creationism* – geological and biological data attest to biblical truth. Peters points out that creationists are usually seen as anti-science, but scientific creationists see themselves as within science;
- *the two-language theory* – 'peace through separation' – the two disciplines speak in their own discourse and shared understanding is impossible;
- *hypothetical consonance* – the two disciplines do raise questions of concern to the other, and should be open to subjecting their assertions to further investigation (see also 1.10);
- *ethical overlap* – theology has a vital role in speaking to questions of value raised by science and technology, especially in respect of the ecological crisis (see 1.20, Chapter 8 *passim*, 13.8–13.11, 14.9–14.10);
- *New Age spirituality* – a term covering certain recent attempts to fuse science and spirituality (see 9.9).

(cf. Peters, 1997a:650–4)[12]

Oddly, Peters' scheme does not develop the nuances of the crucial area between 'two-languages' (Barbour's 'independence'), and 'hypothetical consonance' (Bar-bour's 'dialogue/integration'). Peters does, however, clarify the nature of positions at the extremes. A further survey of science–religion relationships is offered by Mikael Stenmark (2004), who proposes a threefold typology: independence, contact and monism (Stenmark, 2004:9, see also 2004:250–9 for a comparison of his position with Barbour's).

Near the end of his career the eminent biologist Stephen Jay Gould (1941–2002) published a book entitled *Rocks of Ages* (Gould, 2002), in which he articulated his theory of 'non-overlapping magisteria'. Science and religion need have no conflict if each sticks to its own area of expertise, the area where it 'holds the appropriate tools for meaningful discourse and resolution' (Gould, 2002:5). This looks at first sight like 'peace through separation', but, as Stenmark notes, Gould restricts the domain of authority to which religion can lay claim. For example, 'religious believers cannot properly claim that God's action sometimes results in the occurrence of a miracle' (Stenmark, 2004:3).[13] Gould offers a valuable cautionary response to the arrogance of some of his biologist colleagues (see 6.13.1–6.13.4) but at the expense of denying space for dialogue on questions of shared interest, perhaps most strikingly the issue of God's providential action in the world (see Chapter 10).

1.5 Two crucial points about the science–religion relationship

Any investigation of the possible relations between science and religion – and a consideration of what relation is most appropriate – must take account of two most important points:

(i) *The relations between different sciences and any one religion – even any one branch of any religion – will be different at any given time, and will alter through history.* That a given science can dramatically alter its character is shown by the sense some physicists had in the 1870s that the subject was coming to an end – the young Max Planck was advised against doing physics on the grounds that everything to be discovered would shortly have been discovered.[14] Fifty years later (partly because Planck ignored the advice) the subject underwent such changes that there was a golden age of conceptual advance, a time 'when second-rate men did first-rate work' (Paul Dirac, quoted in Polkinghorne, 1990:14).

Clearly the self-image of a scientific community will have enormous effect on its attitude to theological claims which seem to relate to its subject area. The 'cruelly harrying' effect of neurology as described by Updike (1.1) – instanced by the sense evinced by such scientists as Francis Crick that it will be possible at some stage to describe all human activities in neurophysiological terms – this effect is testimony to a science whose experimental techniques are rapidly expanding its database (especially through positron emission tomography and magnetic resonance scanning). The effect of Darwinism on 'the world-frame' of biology, especially when coupled first with Mendelian genetics and then with molecular biology (see 6.6, 6.8–6.9), has led to a science which is still expanding under the influence of a great unifying set of ideas – much as physics did in the two hundred years after Newton. We look at some resultant reductionisms in 6.11–6.13.4.

Contemporary cosmological physics seems to be in a rather different place – very conscious of limits both to its experimental and its theoretical purchase on the ultimate questions which it tends to raise. As we shall see in 1.15, the most ingenious quantum-cosmological speculations, going far beyond what could ever be tested experimentally, cannot answer the metaphysical question as to whether the universe had an underlying cause – why, in other words, there is something and not nothing. But the fundamental structure of the universe has led some physicists like Paul Davies to express themselves in quasi-religious terms, as here:

> I belong to the group of scientists who do not subscribe to a conventional religion but nevertheless deny that the universe is a purposeless accident. Through my scientific work I have come to believe more and more strongly that the physical universe is put together with an ingenuity so astonishing that I cannot accept it merely as brute fact. There must, it seems to me, be a deeper level of explanation. Whether one wishes to call that deeper level

'God' is a matter of taste and definition. (Davies, 1993:16 – see also Davies quoted in 5.24)

Psychology is in a different place again in relation to religion (see Chapter 7). So John Brooke's conclusion is of the first importance:

There is no such thing as *the* relationship between science and religion. It is what different individuals and communities have made of it in a plethora of different contexts. Not only has the problematic interface between them shifted over time, but there is also a high degree of artificiality in abstracting from the science and religion of earlier centuries to see how they were related. (Brooke, 1991:321)

The special relationship

Some of the 'discoveries' of the appropriate relation between science and religion proposed in recent years are reminiscent of the 'special relationship' 'that has always existed between our two countries' invented by Winston Churchill in his efforts to woo the USA into the war with Hitler. Indeed there had been all sorts of relationships between Britain and the United States in the preceding two hundred years: empire–colony, empire–rebellion, naval powers at war, distant economic power awaiting the result of civil war, belated allies against the Kaiser. And indeed there has always been a relationship of a special kind between the advance of different types of knowledge of the natural world and religious understandings. But this 'special relationship' has been just as diverse and as ambiguous as the one Churchill invoked!

(ii) In their important collection of papers referred to above Richardson and Wildman write:

At times it has seemed as if theology and science had nothing in common at all. At other times they have been regarded as only partially distinguishable aspects of a single kind of intellectual inquiry. (Richardson and Wildman, 1996:84)

That last sentence reflects the fact that our understanding of the relation between science and religion will depend on our understanding of what it is that human enquiry, human rationality *consists of*. That understanding has itself been subject to major changes even within the last fifty years. These we examine in Chapter 4.

1.5.1 Is the important relation that between science and religion, or science and <u>theology</u>?

One of the most important analyses of the relation between science and religion is that of Drees in *Religion, Science and Naturalism* (1996). Drees stresses two points which have received too little attention in the debate:

(a) That religion contains a number of elements other than the cognitive-propositional (the effort to express in conceptual and analysable terms understandings of the nature of reality). In particular much of the content of religion rests on *religious experience* (which we consider in more depth in 7.8–7.12) and *tradition*. So Drees proposes a much wider scheme of 'areas of discussion concerning the relationship of religion and science' (Table 1.1).

Table 1.1

CHALLENGE POSED BY SCIENCE	CHARACTER OF RELIGION		
	1. Cognitive	*2. Experience*	*3. Tradition*
(a) New knowledge	(1a) Content: i Conflicts ii Separation iii Partial adaptation iv Integration	(2a) Opportunities for experiential religion? Religious experience and the brain.	(3a) Religious traditions as products of evolution.
(b) New views of knowledge	(1b) Philosophy of science and opportunities for theology.	(2b) Philosophical defences of religious experiences as data.	(3b) Criticism and development of religions as 'language games'.
(c) Appreciation of the world.	(1c) A new covenant between humans and the Universe?	(2c) Ambivalence of the world and implications for the concept of God.	(3c) A basis for hope? Or religions as local traditions without universal claim?

(Drees, 1996:45)

This broadens the debate helpfully, and shows that the categories that have received most attention, Drees' '1a. Content', form only one aspect of a complex matrix. These categories concern science's propositional claims and the way they impinge upon the cognitive claims developed by *theologies*. Drees shows that these interactions do not exhaust the content of science's interaction with *religions*, or the challenges science poses to them.

Where Drees' analysis is itself too limited is in not acknowledging that the 'science' which gives rise to challenges to religions has itself all sorts of different components. Sciences themselves have their traditions. As well as their cognitive claims they have imaginative, indeed aesthetic, components which are important in the generation and evaluation of novel hypotheses and models. Drees himself in an earlier book mused that 'a metaphysics informed by a religious perspective might determine the criteria for theory development and appraisal' (Drees, 1990:7). The matrix of interaction, then, has extra dimensions beyond those represented in Table 1.1, which only concern the *challenge* of science (viewed as a homogeneous whole) to various aspects of religion.

While this present volume is predominantly concerned with Christianity, indeed with Christian theology as an enterprise of rational exploration within a Christian commitment, we recognize that other traditions have much to contribute to the debate. We show in 9.3–9.6.1 how the scriptural teachings of Eastern religions offer radically different ways of thinking about divinity and the cosmos – some of which may prove to be a source of new models and metaphors within science. We also consider in Chapter 12 the framework of Islamic thought, in which the challenges posed by scientific theories (such as evolution) may receive a very different theological reception from that which is typical of the relation between the sciences and Western Christianity.

(b) Drees also recognizes clearly that *religion is itself a phenomenon in the evolution of human culture.* As such it is an object of scientific study.[15] We show in 6.13.3–6.13.4 that seeing religion as an aspect of human evolution has led some to dismiss its truth-claims, whereas Drees himself recognizes that this inference need not be drawn. A significant study which sees religion as an evolved phenomenon is Gerd Theissen's *Biblical Faith: An Evolutionary Approach* (1984). This book is important not least for a fine 'history-of-religions' account of the rise of Hebrew monotheism, but even within that account one can see the problems associated with Theissen's attempt to hold to an evolutionary epistemology,[16] to knowledge as a form of adaptation to reality. Within such a scheme, a religious or scientific explanation is only more or less successful than its competitors. But when he reaches the climax of his description of the evolution of Hebrew religion, Theissen cannot forbear to speak of 'the *discovery* of the one and only God' (1984:64, emphasis ours). Two pages later he has reverted to 'the *development* of the one and only God, [with which] a radically new environment opened up with completely new "demands for adaptation"' (1984:66, emphasis ours). But *either* such a God in some sense *constituted* the ultimate environment of human culture and the physical world alike, and was, however partially and provisionally, 'discovered', *or* there is not and never has been such a God, and the belief merely 'developed'. As van Huyssteen shows, Theissen is actually putting forward the former view, a 'critical-realist epistemology'[17] under the guise of his evolutionary descriptions (van Huyssteen, 1997: ch. 10).

Theissen's difficulties with terminology reflect the fact that the evaluation of scientific descriptions of religion as an evolved phenomenon will necessarily depend on the religious position of the evaluator. It is easy to concede a point made years ago by D.T. Campbell (1976:167–208): religion *may* have served to facilitate the transition from a human society dominated by biological evolution to one in which tribes were knitted together by holding certain common propositions about reality. Cultural, rather than biological, evolution then became dominant.[18] But the belief that religion is also able to anticipate future possibilities to which cultural evolution has not yet attained, because it represents a process of adaptation to the-way-things-really-are, is a much more contentious one. It will be held inside believing communities, but will be largely opaque to those outside.

Our concern throughout most of the present volume will be with *theology* – with the network of models, metaphors and propositions which give a religion its rational framework. But in examining in Chapter 4 the respects in which that framework is related to that of a scientific community we also indicate how theology must be integrally related to religious praxis (how a believing community acts out its faith within society). Indeed we see theology, ethics and action as intimately bound up together with an understanding of the world as the natural and social sciences describe it, as in Figure 1.2.

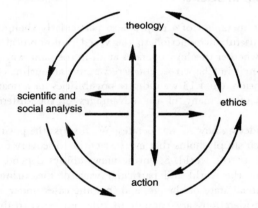

Figure 1.2 The 'Bossey Circle'. A World Council of Churches diagram, taken here from Gosling, 1992:65

1.6 The metaphor of the maps

It will be clear from the preceding sections that we recommend abandoning the search for any sort of 'philosopher's stone' of a definition of a perfectly appropriate relation between science and religion. A more helpful way to think of the relationship might be in terms of the metaphor of different 'maps' of the one world. Mary Midgley has used this in arguing for an approach to consciousness which is neither reductionist nor dualist.[19] She argues that different sorts of mental phenomena – and aspects of humanity dependent on our consciousness, such as society – can be described using the analogy of different maps (political, demographic, climatic, etc.) – of the (one) world. These different maps are no less accurate or genuine than the 'physical' maps of that world in terms of atoms and forces.

Furthermore, Midgley insists that consciousness, and indeed society and politics and the like, *are not any less real* than the atoms of which they are made, and the maps drawn of them should not be regarded as inferior. 'Neither houses nor quarks . . . are more real than mental items' (Midgley, 1996a:513).

The image of different maps of reality has been used by a number of philosophers – Midgley (1996b:58) mentions the discussion by John Ziman in *Reliable Knowledge* (1978), but suspects the idea goes back to Wittgenstein. It seems to us a most appropriate metaphor for the ways scientific and theological descriptions of the (one) world operate. It connotes a degree of independence, and yet a degree of relationship. It allows for the possibility of dialogue, and the likelihood of 'border disputes'. And as we have noted above, each science will have its own map, and its own relation to the maps theologians draw (of which there will be a diversity even within one religious tradition[20]).

1.7 Critical realism in science

Consideration of the metaphor of a map is also particularly thought-provoking, since it provides a useful introduction to the vexed philosophical debate about what science *is* and whether theology operates at all in the same way. This we take up in much more detail in Chapter 4, but here we give an outline of some of the main areas of contention. (In 4.13 we indicate possibilities for a nuanced position which we consider offers many of the advantages of the different positions described here.)

We start by considering how *science* operates. We dismiss the position known as 'naive realism', which simply holds that every scientific discovery directly corresponds to a truth about the world. Scientific views always depend on particular preconceptions about the world and particular ways of measuring it; they are moreover in a continual state of change, and in some cases undergo radical correction – these considerations are enough to rule out naive realism. Equally, however, the success of the various sciences seems to suggest that they *do* manage to articulate something of the complexity of reality, in a way which is open to ever-new discoveries. So we rule out also any of the more extreme forms of 'idealism' which promote the notion that mental concepts are somehow more real than the physical world.

We revert to assessing a more sophisticated form of realism, frequently referred to as 'critical realism'. The critical realist recognizes that we hold our views of reality *provisionally*, that we cannot simply read off the nature of the world from scientific data. The theories and presuppositions with which we approach our studies are acknowledged to affect our selection of what data we count as important to collect, as well as the ways in which we interpret these data. For example, simple *measurements* using something as basic as an electricity meter *rest upon commitments to theories* about interactions between current-carrying conductors and magnetic fields. Experimental data are never other than *theory-laden, and there are never enough data totally to demonstrate every element of a theory*. Other reasons for adopting a critical approach take into account the fact that observations themselves affect the character of an entity as it is observed (most markedly in quantum mechanics, see 5.10–5.14).

Although it is unclear how we could be sure whether we had arrived at the best fit between scientific data and reality, it is widely agreed that there are criteria for our theories which can be taken as pointers to such a fit. They are:

- the *comprehensiveness* of the theory in taking account of all known data deemed relevant;
- the *consistency* of the theory – being devoid of internal contradictions;
- the *compactness* of the theory – its economy in not doing 'with more what can be done with fewer', a principle known as Ockham's razor.

These three can be seen as interrelated aspects of a 'coherence-based' approach to the assessment of truth (see 4.12, note 17). A fourth criterion should be added – that of whether a theory possesses a quality of 'comeliness' – 'elegance' would be a better word though it doesn't begin with 'c'! Scientists are often influenced by a sense of the neatness and elegance, indeed the sheer beauty, of a particular formulation (cf. Derkse, 1993, also Barrett, 2000).

An alternative to a *realist* position is the claim made by what is referred to as the 'strong programme' of the sociology of science – that science is simply a social construction, rather than an attempt to describe a real world. Such a claim appears to suffer from major defects. For one thing it runs counter to what almost all practising scientists think they are doing. Its main problem, however, is that of *reflexivity*. If it *were* the case, then no human analysis could be more than a social construction, so the social scientists who made this claim would have to face up to the implication that *their* analyses and conclusions suffered from the same problem of being socially constructed. These analyses would not be saying anything true about how the world is or about what scientists are actually doing, but only reflecting the results of the sociologists' own social conditioning. (To reject the validity of a thorough-going relativism is not, however, to decry the importance of social and political factors in determining the course of science, not least in determining what research will be funded. See 4.10 on Thomas Kuhn's work for a fuller exploration of this.)

The most profound challenge to critical realism in science comes from views falling under headings such as 'instrumentalism' or 'constructivism'. These focus on the impossibility, already mentioned, of detaching data from the instrumental and experimental design which produced them. Given that we can neither think nor speak nor engage with the world at all except through language, theory and concept, there can be no way to step beyond our theoretical frameworks and assess directly how adequate any particular theory is to the complexity of reality. It should be noted moreover that science undergoes major periods of change in which old theories are discarded and radically new ones adopted. Consequently many philosophers of science have argued that it is better to make no realist claims at all, but merely to regard scientific data as, however successfully, a function of the instrumentation, and of the conceptual constructs, by which science functions. To return to our starting metaphor, this view would hold that our map gets us about on the particular contrived journey that is science (just as a map of the

London Underground gets us around the city) but we have no real idea what the streets are like which surround our path.

- The major problems, then, for realists, even critical realists, are *the theory-ladenness of data, the underdetermination of theory by experiment*, and in particular *scientific revolutions* in which supposed points of reference to reality have to be discarded because a radically new 'paradigm' takes over within a science (see **4.10**).
- The major problem for instrumentalists is *the sheer success and apparent progressiveness of science*. Its maps seem to work, in general, astonishingly well. It is hard to credit that an electron is an instrumental fiction, even though no one has ever seen one directly, since so many phenomena have been observed in accordance with the behaviour and properties of electrons.

To follow this debate in more detail see in particular Laudan (1977) and Banner (1990). Particularly important to critical realism is the concept of *inference to the best explanation*. Granted that we cannot be sure that data correspond in any simple way to reality, we can nevertheless consider a variety of explanations of the data, and elicit the one that best fits our criteria of comprehensiveness, consistency and compactness. For a defence of inference to the best explanation see Clayton (1997b).

1.8 Critical realism in theology

A very influential array of scientist-theologians[21] have argued that theology is also a critical realist discipline, which considers data, draws inferences to explanations, and submits these to testing closely analogous to that outlined for a scientific hypothesis. This is a problematic claim. What are the 'data' of a religion which correspond to those of a science? Some might argue that they are the scriptures of that faith, others the liturgy, others religious experience. Again, can it be said that there is a genuine critical element which can lead to theories being discarded, or are religious data privileged against falsification?

Willem B. Drees dismisses the claim of theology to be regarded as a realist discipline like the sciences. In his view theology shows no parallel with the spectacular success of science. With the science of the last three hundred years there is a cumulative success, an ongoing fertility in the development of new theories, which is simply absent from theology (cf. Drees, 1996:141–2). Polkinghorne concedes that 'One could not assert that (theology) has been characterised by the same power of its community to reach conclusions, which is such an impressive feature of the cumulative advance of science' (1996a:17). He points out that 'Theology depends for its moments of transparency to the divine upon events and people that are unrepeatably unique' (1996a:18). So its data are going to be more precarious and less testable for that reason alone.

Working from the proposals of Imre Lakatos (see **4.12**), Nancey Murphy wants to claim strong parallels between science and theology as rational explorations.

But she rejects critical realism in theology, on the grounds that it makes too great a claim as to our knowledge of elements of reality beyond our ordinary human ways of knowing (Murphy, 1990:197). Van Huyssteen, however, takes issue with Murphy, claiming in effect that we can make inferences to the best explanation even in matters close to the core beliefs of theism (1997:48–51). Roger Trigg dismisses critical realism as no more than 'a vague umbrella concept' (1998:86).

Critical realism, then, as a way of thinking about the claims of either science and theology, or science alone, is a position towards which many in the field are drawn. Its philosophical usefulness remains a matter of keen debate.

We can understand more about the similarities and differences between claims to realism in science and in theology by looking at the role played by model and metaphor in these two rationalities.

1.9 The central role of model and metaphor

One of Ian Barbour's great contributions to the science-and-religion debate was to indicate as long ago as 1974 in *Myths, Models and Paradigms* how central to both scientific and religious frameworks is the role of models (Barbour, 1974: chs 3 and 4; 1998: ch. 5). A model in science can be thought of as a means whereby the human imagination can engage with and depict the aspect of nature under investigation. A good example is the one Barbour himself uses (1998:116) – the picture of the atom developed by Niels Bohr. At a time at which atomic structure was proving very baffling, Bohr produced a model in which the negatively charged electrons orbited the positively charged nucleus in a way which was like – and yet not like – the way the planets orbit the sun (see 5.10.3). The model proved a fruitful heuristic device – that is to say, it promoted further exploration, and allowed various predictions to be made and tested. As a result of that work, earlier models – from Democritus to Rutherford – have long since been discarded. A refined form of the Bohr model is still a valid way of imagining the atom for certain restricted purposes. But a new structure of concepts and theories – based on the Schrödinger Equation – overtook the Bohr model. This mathematical formulation, though much harder to picture, is now the basis on which predictions about the atom are made.

If we now consider as an example of a model in Christian theology one of Augustine's 'psychological' models of the Trinity – the relationship between Father, Son and Spirit being seen as like – but yet not like – the relation between memory, understanding and will in the human mind – we can see all sorts of similarities with the part models play in science. The model emerged in a situation of difficulty and controversy – this time over how to imagine God. Augustine's was one of a number of attempts to picture how God might be like – but yet not like – three co-equal entities in relationship. Again, it was a model which greatly stimulated theological debate and led ultimately to a new conceptual framework.[22]

But these similarities should not be allowed to disguise differences. Augustine's model remains just one of a range of ways of stretching the imagination towards the mystery of the Trinity. No great advance has superseded it, yet it does not hold sway. More importantly, a whole range of *earlier* understandings of the relationship between Father, Son and Spirit remains alive for the Christian community through the Scriptures. The whole spectrum of titles for Jesus remains just as important as it was before the work of the Fathers of the fourth and fifth centuries.

As well as Barbour, Janet Martin Soskice and Sallie McFague have written importantly on model and metaphor in religion (Soskice, 1985; McFague, 1982; 1987). McFague in particular stresses the role of metaphor in the development of imaginative formulations – all metaphor contains an is/is not – in some respects a crafty statesman may 'be' an old fox, in other respects he clearly is not. In the foregoing paragraphs we saw the 'is/is not' operating in the Bohr atom and Augustine's Trinity. Theology, for McFague, operates between poetry and philosophy, so metaphor is indispensable. A model, for her, is 'a metaphor with "staying power"', a pattern which allows relatively comprehensive and coherent (though still exploratory and open-ended) explanation (McFague, 1987:ch. 2). Both in science and religion human exploration requires both the imaginative and metaphorical on the one hand and the conceptual and systematic on the other. Models are what connects them. They are necessarily provisional and heuristic in character.

Polkinghorne, a former theoretical particle physicist, wants to draw a sharper distinction than many between model and metaphor. He writes: 'In my opinion, when scientists use apparently metaphorical language – as in talk of "black holes" or the "genetic code" – they are using these terms as picturesque shorthand for ideas they can more readily and more adequately convey in precise scientific language, and they are not using them as imaginative resources for the generation of ideas in a truly metaphorical way' (1996a:20). This remark is an important corrective to an over-romantic view of science, but does not do justice to the way metaphors determine what can and cannot be thought, even in a highly mathematical science such as physics. We discuss what can and cannot be thought in science when we look at Kuhn's concept of a 'paradigm' – see **4.10**. One of Kuhn's points is particularly relevant here – he notes that a science does not teach its students, to any great extent, the classic texts of the past, however seminal they might have been (Kuhn, 1970b:165). In a religious tradition old models and the metaphors that inform them remain part of the currency of the tradition. And whatever metaphors or narratives continue to inform the worship of a religious community will continue to influence its theology, in a way which has no parallel in science.

We argue in Chapter 4 that theology has to be seen as a more complex activity than merely a realist search for progressively truer data, and at the same time we are able to show how science, like theology, needs to be seen as the activity of a community of motivated believers, holding core assumptions and testing out new possibilities. On realism this will bring us out close to the position defended by van Huyssteen, a so-called 'weak form of critical realism' (van Huyssteen, 1997:51). Addressing reality is the goal of the rational explorations of sciences and religions, but our *confidence* as to which elements of our models do refer to real entities will vary across a discipline and over time. What we do retain is a strong sense of the ultimately *practical* nature of theological work. For example, for the believing Christian theologian the work is not only weighing the world in the light of Christ but also living within it in the power of the Spirit. This is the stance of the present authors, though we also explore other emphases within Christianity and those of various other faiths.

1.10 Consonances

We noted above parallels between the methods of exploration in science and theology, but methodological parallels do not of themselves establish any particular relationship as to *content*. However, we also suggested that both disciplines manifest a sort of realism – however tentatively they expect their concepts to *refer* to elements of reality. To return to our previous metaphor (1.6) the disciplines are maps of the same world. We might therefore expect that 'following the coastlines', as Mary Midgley suggests (1996b:57), might enable us to see 'consonances' – places where the descriptions of reality offered by the two types of mapping seem to show a particularly close relation, when they (to change the metaphor) 'chime together'. For Ernan McMullin the Christian '*must* strive to make his theology and his ... cosmology consonant in the contributions they make to (this) world-view' (quoted in Drees, 1990:26).

At once this notion sounds certain 'warning-bells', as follows:

(i) in respect of the history of natural theology (see 1.3.1 and 1.13). If science fails to 'show us God' by matching a piece of coastline with that drawn by theology, or if a piece of science we took for a sign of God loses its consonance (see 1.15), does that make God non-existent, or less probable?

(ii) the claims made by sciences and religions must both be recognized as a function of their cultural contexts, as being in some sense 'constructed' by those contexts. So as Drees has emphasized, consonances are also constructs (1990:29).

Polkinghorne has also discussed consonance (see his 1991:80–4). He is clear that the position is complex in respect of Big Bang cosmology (see 1.15). He finds a more rewarding consonance in respect of the physical world being shaped by an interplay between chance and physical law (see 10.3.1). (Note, however, that Jacques Monod places a very different construct on the presence of so much chance (see 6.13.2).) Concerning eschatology there seems to be no consonance – scientific cosmology predicts that the universe will end in a state devoid of structure or meaning; Christianity cherishes a final hope of redemption (see 10.20).[23]

In our view Peters has assessed the situation correctly when he writes:

'Consonance' in the strong sense means accord, harmony. Accord or harmony might be a treasure we hope to find, but we have not found it yet. Where we find ourselves now is working with consonance in a weak sense – that is – by identifying common domains of question-asking. (Peters, 1997a:652)

Indeed even if we find from time to time glints of the 'treasure' we may not be able to glimpse them for long, since both the sciences and theology move on. Even McMullin, an early proponent of consonance, recognized that it would be 'in constant slight shift' (quoted in Drees, 1990:26). What consonance often seems to mean in practice is that theology is asked to redraw its map in order to fit its coastlines to new scientific understandings (as we shall see in **6.3.2** in respect of the doctrine of the Fall).

But if the scientific cartographers are the powerful ones now, it is often claimed that they could not have acquired this power except in the context of a theistic society. So we turn now to look at the history of the 'special relationship', beginning with the question as to whether religion was necessary to the rise of science, and going on to examine occasions when the map-makers have been in conflict. A fuller reflection on the role of history in the debate is found in Chapter 3.

1.11 Was religion necessary to the rise of science?

It is often claimed, particularly by those who want to emphasize the positive relations between science and religion, that Western science could only have arisen in the context of the three great monotheisms, Judaism, Christianity and Islam. This is a very complex issue, but it is possible to set down certain markers. For example:

- The first thinkers ever to ask, in anything like their modern form, such radical and demythologized questions as 'What is the world made of?' and 'How does it change?' were the Pre-Socratic philosophers of Ancient Greece (operating between roughly 600 and 400 BCE). Their intellectual ingenuity and daring remains one of the great landmarks in human achievement. It gave rise to an atomic theory, Pythagoras' Theorem, and geometric techniques good enough to obtain a reasonable estimate of the circumference of a (spherical) Earth. *Nevertheless the Greeks did not go on to invent experimental science.*[24] This is partly because their philosophy became dominated by two patterns of thinking, both extremely ingenious, but neither propitious for science:
    - (i) Plato's idealism, the conviction that a perfect abstraction is more real and worthier of study than a physical entity which may crudely imitate the abstraction; and
    - (ii) Aristotle's complex theory of causation, which included not only material causes (what things are made of) and efficient causes (what past events affected them) but also formal causes (to what pattern the matter in them conforms) and final causes (towards what purpose or end are things being attracted).
- To say that Plato and Aristotle of themselves do not lead to experimental science is not, however, to deny their enormous contribution in framing and training the patterns of thought of the Western world from their own time until now. For instance, Aristotle's texts on logic,

metaphysics[25] and the structure of the world were a major spur to intellectual development in the late Middle Ages.

- These great Aristotelian texts *entered Western Europe through the work of Islamic commentators*. We explore in Chapter 12 the relation between science and Islam, and note some tensions which may have prevented the Golden Age of Islamic enquiry into the world from going on to give rise to a scientific tradition such as the one that flowered with Galileo and Newton.
- A *belief that the world is fundamentally ordered and reliable is essential to science*. It seems clear that, of different kinds of religious beliefs about creation, the conviction found in the Hebrew Scriptures that the world is 'good' in itself – the work of one God, a Creator who does not keep changing the rules – is very favourable to a belief in an ordered world.
- The *belief that God brought the world out of nothing as an act of free creation*, which is the main line of the Christian doctrine of creation, *implies (a) that the world is not itself part of God, and is not therefore itself holy, and (b) that God could have created a different world*. Hence in order to discover what harmonious, faithful and ordered work God did do – a plausible task for natural theology and philosophy – *it is both permissible and necessary to 'put the world to the test'* in Francis Bacon's memorable phrase – to conduct experiments.

Beyond this, seventeenth-century Puritanism may have provided the perfect climate for science to grow, since, as Janet Martin Soskice has pointed out, both Puritanism and natural science appealed to living experience rather than merely accepting received tradition, and both drew on sources they considered had been neglected (in the one case Scripture, in the other experiment) (Soskice, 1993a). She goes on to claim that the relationship between science and religion in Britain in the seventeenth and eighteenth centuries was 'almost a rapturous love affair' (1993a:71).

We have come a long way from the quotation from John Updike with which we began! But we would want to stop short of the trite conclusion that Christianity was both a necessary and a sufficient condition for the rise of science (see also 3.5.2). After all, the 'experiment' of the rise of Western science has only run once. Sweeping hypotheses about the history of thought neglect the complexity and contingency of history. To what extent, for instance, did the final cohering of the scientific tradition depend on the particular genius of Galileo, the first man to bring together mathematics, observation and experiment in a combination such as modern science employs? To what extent was the history of the world changed by the fact that the precocious and almost entirely self-taught genius of Newton was able to come to fruition in a country at peace?

Mention of 'rapturous love affairs' should not blind us, moreover, to the tensions that *have* existed. These we examine in the next few sections. The irony is that the two most famous conflicts – between Galileo and the Catholic Church of the early seventeenth century and between the early Darwinists and certain members of the Anglican Church in the mid-nineteenth – have both occurred when the relevant branch of the Christian Church was taking a vigorous role in promoting the type of scientific research in question.

Newton's post at Cambridge was for many years under threat because of his beliefs. This, however, was not a reflection of his science – rather of the non-Trinitarian theological schemes to which he devoted much of his time. More famously and significantly, Galileo spent the last years of his life under house arrest, and this *did* stem from his convictions about the structure of the solar system.

SECTION B
THREE HISTORICAL EXAMPLES OF TENSIONS AS SCIENCE AND THEOLOGY DEVELOPED (1.12–1.15)

1.12 Copernicanism and the Galileo Affair[26]

The origin of Galileo's notorious dispute with the papal authorities came long before the Italian astronomer's birth. Aristotle had placed the Earth at the centre of the universe, not because it was the most important place, but because it was the coldest, most impure place in the cosmos and it would therefore fall as far as it could – to the centre. The celestial bodies were made out of a very pure and perfect element and travelled on the surface of spheres, the most perfect geometric shape.[27] The mediaeval Church adopted this system, and for Christians the Earth was central as being of the place of the salvation of the cosmos. Not surprisingly astronomical observation of the planets fitted only erratically with this Earth-centred (geocentric) scheme, and complicated explanations were devised to overcome these anomalies. These were refinements on the general system of Ptolemy (second century CE) (Figure 1.3(a)). In the 1530s the Polish mathematician Nicolaus Copernicus (1473–1543) began to challenge the Ptolemaic model and suggest a sun-centred (heliocentric) model (Figure 1.3(c)); this was only published as Copernicus was dying (in his *De Revolutionibus* of 1543).

There followed a period of what Kuhn has called 'paradigm shift', a crisis in the (newly developing) scientific community, in which two radically different models were in competition. Nor was it clear that Copernicus was right – his circular orbits gave no better fit than its best geocentric competitor – that of the Imperial mathematician Tycho Brahe (Figure 1.3(b)).[28] This is because the planetary orbits are in fact ellipses, a model first proposed by Johannes Kepler (1571–1630), who was one of the very few thinkers other than Galileo to adopt Copernicanism before 1600.

Enter then Galileo Galilei, whose career can be briefly summarized as follows:

1564   Born in Pisa.
1592–   Taught mathematics in Padua, a city under the protection of Venice. Convinced from early on of the truth of Copernicanism.
1609   Obtained the principles of the telescope, constructed his own, and observed the craters of the Moon, the phases of Venus and the moons of Jupiter, none of which was predicted by the Ptolemaic model.

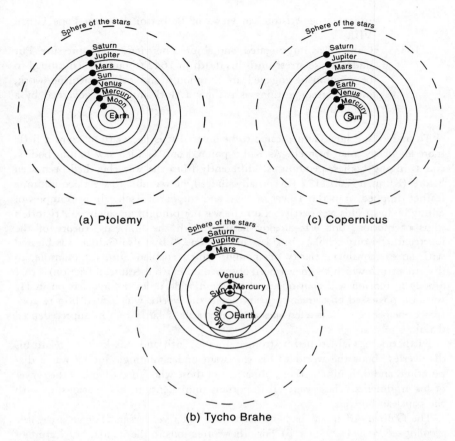

Figure 1.3   Three competing models of the solar system (early seventeenth century)
from Poole (1995:105).

1610   Went to work for Cosimo de' Medici in Florence, insisting on the
       title 'first philosopher and mathematician'.[29]
1613   Wrote to Benedetto Castelli about the compatibility of Coperni-
       canism with Scripture – this letter later developed into 'The Letter
       to the Grand Duchess Christina' (1615).
1616   Cautioned by Cardinal Bellarmine in Rome not to teach Coperni-
       canism as a *fact*, though *De Revolutionibus* was republished in 1620
       with the heliocentric view treated as a *hypothesis*. Cardinal Maffeo
       Barberini of Florence was instrumental in ensuring the book's
       republication.
1632   Galileo published his *Dialogue Concerning the Two Chief World Systems
       – Ptolemaic and Copernican*. This passed the ecclesiastical censors, and
       indeed did nominally present the systems as alternatives, but
       actually it was heavily pro-Copernican. Moreover, it appeared to

> ridicule the Aristotelian views of Barberini, by then Pope Urban VIII.
>
> 1633   Galileo was interrogated, and abjured his views under pressure. Put under house arrest until his death in 1642 (though he continued to be vigorously engaged in astronomy and other scientific work, including suggestions as to how a clock might be governed by a pendulum).

To understand how Galileo came to be on trial it is necessary to know a little more about the man himself. As Kuhn pointed out, Galileo saw falling bodies, and swinging bodies, pendulums, 'differently from the way they had been seen before' (Kuhn, 1970b:119). (Eventually, indeed, he was able to see a pendulum, a feather dropped from the Tower of Pisa, and the Earth itself, all as examples of falling bodies.) This was partly because he was not brought up solely on Aristotle's ideas of motion, but was already familiar with the 'impetus' theory of the fourteenth-century scholars Buridan and Oresme.[30] But also Galileo was blessed with an extraordinary clarity of thought which enabled him, for example, to discern a truth which had never been observed on Earth (because of friction) – that a body in motion will continue in the same motion unless a force acts on it. He was also possessed of a great curiosity about the world, which fired him to construct one of the earliest telescopes and observe the solar system in unprecedented detail.

Furthermore, Galileo had a strong religious faith and was keen to relate his discoveries about the world to his Christian understanding. But he was a disputatious and difficult character, impatient of those who failed to follow the power of his arguments. These were all important ingredients in his relationship with the papal authorities.

The Galileo Affair has had intensive study in recent years. For an accessible account see Poole (1995: ch. 6). For other corrections to the standard caricature of the merely blinkered Church against the noble scientist, see Brooke and Cantor (1998: ch. 4), Drees (1996:55–63), Brooke (1991:82–105), or Gingerich (1982). For more specialized investigations see Finocchiaro (1989) or Fantoli (1996).

One of the most important documents in the case is Galileo's letter eventually issued as 'The Letter to the Grand Duchess Christina'. Howell (1996) has analysed the type of case Galileo was making, drawing a parallel with the arguments of Augustine about the reading of the book of Genesis, as follows:

> (i)   distinguishing matters of science from matters of faith – Galileo begins from the dictum that Scripture was given to show how to go to heaven rather than how the heavens go. But if it is not conceded that science and biblical interpretation are separate, Galileo's fallback is
>
> (ii) that the interpretation of Scripture should not go against demonstrated truths in science. But if his opponents will not concede either that Copernicanism is a demonstrated truth, or that such truths can oppose a scriptural text (such as the description in the book of Joshua of the sun standing still only by the mighty action of God) and still be true, then Galileo has a second fallback, that

(iii) actually Copernicanism is closer to literal Scripture than the Ptolemaic model.

So Galileo's own position was multifaceted, and very much rooted in the hermeneutics[31] of one of the great doctors of the Church. We have seen too that Pope Urban had defended Copernicus' book despite disagreeing with it. Moreover Cardinal Bellarmine, chiefly responsible for dealing with Galileo for the Vatican until his death in 1621, was not a bigoted cleric either, but an open and thoughtful one, keenly concerned with astronomy. His approach emerges in passages like this one from a letter to Foscarini:

> I say that if there were a true demonstration that the sun is at the centre of the world and the earth in the third heaven, and that the sun does not circle the earth but the earth circles the sun, then one would have to proceed with great caution in explaining the Scriptures that appear contrary, and say rather that we do not understand them than that what is demonstrated is false. (Quoted in Finocchiaro, 1989:68)

This complex affair, then, was influenced by a number of factors:

- the scientific, yes, but it is worth pointing out that because Galileo ignored Kepler's work his model still fitted the data no better than its best geocentric competitor. It also suffered from the great problem that it predicted stellar parallax, which had not then been observed;[32]
- the epistemological – what, in the terms of the passage quoted above from Bellarmine, constitutes a 'demonstration'? How should Bible-reading astronomers understand their data, and their Bibles, in the interim phase when a scientific model has been proposed but is not yet established?[33]
- the hermeneutical – how should Scripture be read, how should that reading affect or be affected by science? Above all, who should have the authority to determine the range of permitted readings?[34]
- the political – it was a stage in the Counter-Reformation at which the Vatican felt the need to assert its central authority.
- the personal – Galileo pursued his cause with an arrogant lack of tact and diplomacy which in the end forfeited the patience even of those inclined to sympathize with his view.

Small wonder that when the trial is 'rerun' in classes on science and religion Galileo is often the loser!

The utter triumph of heliocentrism that followed ended forever any prospect that a Christian group could exercise the sort of hegemony over an area of scientific enquiry that the Vatican tried to assert in suppressing Galileo. It showed moreover that a scientific theory could *gradually* gain in comprehensiveness and coherence until it displaced another, without requiring a strict *logical* demonstration.

1.13 The love affair gone wrong: the eighteenth century

We noted above (1.3.1) that the period from around 1680 to 1800 saw the great flourishing of natural theology. The great explanatory power of the new science, especially of Newtonian mechanics, was pressed into service to investigate how the Creator had worked and was working. In the process more and more purely scientific explanations were given of natural phenomena.[35] At first this was not in tension with a strongly theistic position – Newton himself regarded God as directly mediating the force of gravity. Newton's successors developed the idea of the mechanical universe which accepted action-at-a-distance without the need for divine mediation, but neither was this necessarily in tension with the narrative of God's creative action. Rather the mechanical model was regarded as constituting the 'how' of the great Architect's work, and was therefore a source of understanding of God's character. The 'Book of Nature' could be read alongside the 'Book of Scripture'.

The great irony of this period is that as Brooke puts it: 'the God *known* through science would prove most vulnerable to being *overthrown* in the name of science' (1996:10). The atheist Anthony Collins remarked that it would never have occurred to anyone to doubt the existence of God if theologians had not tried so hard to prove it. Mechanistic explanations of natural phenomena, not involving miraculous intervention, were suggestive of true objectivity. They were celebrated by Robert Boyle and his successors, the 'physicotheologians', as descriptions of the Creator's activity. But they were equally attractive to 'deists', who confined God's work to the initial establishment of the created order, and highly prized by the new movement of atheists which developed from the 1740s. Moreover the 'Book of Nature' could only give rise to generalized theistic conclusions about creation; over-focus on this aspect of theology tended to cut natural theologians off from the great strengths of Christianity in giving an account of redemption. Pascal had described seeing in his famous vision the '"God of Abraham, of Isaac and of Jacob", not of philosophers and scholars' (Pascal, 1966:309) – a God who had been in saving relation to humans throughout history – but this perspective tended to be lost. For further exploration of this period see Chapter 3.

1.14 A contemporary instance of the interplay between claims of consonance and claims of conflict

Today the hegemony lies with the scientific community. Science is a rational enterprise of unparalleled success (by its own lights – those of providing understanding of the physical universe – if not necessarily those of furnishing humans with wisdom as to how to live). Theissen claims that 'Nowadays religion is on the opposition benches and science forms the government. It would be good if religion could find a way out of its role as a smouldering opposition, and if science were less arrogant as the government' (Theissen, 1984:40). The Bossey Circle (Figure 1.2) all too often looks like one-way traffic – science sets the parameters for what can be believed about the world, religious doctrines have to fall in line. In later chapters we discuss the idea of a historical Fall (6.3.2), the possibility of resurrection and virginal conception (10.10(v)), and the ultimate fate of the universe (5.17, 10.20). We shall show that in some cases, such as the Fall, science has restricted what it seems appropriate to believe, but in other cases, such as the end of the universe, it seems essential for theology to continue to assert hopes to which astrophysics is in no position to give support.

1.15 The Big Bang and the beginning of the universe

One particular case will be helpfully illustrative of a number of these themes, namely the question of the origin of the universe in a 'Big Bang'. We describe in 5.16 and 5.18 the development of the theory, and how it prevailed over the competing 'steady-state' theory of Bondi, Gold and Hoyle. Interestingly, one of Hoyle's motivations was aversion to the Genesis-like connotations of the Big Bang. He wrote: 'Unlike the modern school of cosmologists, who in conformity with Judaeo-Christian theologians believe the whole universe to have been created out of nothing, my beliefs accord with those of Democritus who remarked "Nothing is created out of nothing" ' (Hoyle, 1982:2f.). *Here, then, we have an important example, albeit a negative one, of theory selection in science being influenced by theological stance!*

The Big Bang survived Hoyle's counter-proposal, and *it seemed to have a most pleasing consonance with the opening of Genesis, the dramatic beginning of the universe in an event of vast mystery.* For a study of this controversy within science, see Kragh, 1996.

Intriguingly, an early proponent of Big Bang thinking, George Lemaître, had written in a speculative paper years before: 'I think that everyone who believes in a supreme being supporting every being and every acting, believes also that God is essentially hidden and may be glad to see how present physics provides a veil hiding the creation' (quoted in Kragh, 1996:48–9). In other words, *Lemaître, a Catholic priest, hoped that newly emerging science would confirm the hiddenness of God.* Others, however, were less cautious, and celebrated the beauty of the consonance with Genesis. Pope Pius XII claimed that 'modern scholars in these fields [astronomy and physics] regard the idea of creation as quite compatible with scientific conceptions, and ... they are even led naturally to such a conclusion by their researches' (quoted in Kragh, 1996:257). This may be compared with John Paul II's warning against 'making uncritical and overhasty use for apologetic purposes of such recent theories as that of the "Big Bang" in cosmology' (John Paul II, 1988:M11–12, see also 5.18). John Paul was aware that, in Rolston's words, 'the religion that is married to science today is a widow tomorrow, while the religion that is divorced from science leaves no offspring tomorrow' (Rolston 1990:87). What followed in cosmological physics shows the wisdom of this saying on 'widowhood'.

Since around 1980 cosmological interest has shifted to the first ten million, billion, billion, billion, billionth of a second (10^{-43} second) of the universe's history, when the developing universe was so small as to be significantly affected by quantum theory. Stephen Hawking records that he was at a conference at the Vatican in 1981 at the end of which:

the participants were granted an audience with the Pope [John Paul II]. He told us that it was all right to study the evolution of the universe after the big bang, but we should not inquire into the big bang itself because that was the moment of Creation and therefore the work of God. I was glad then that he did not know the subject of the talk I had just given at the conference – the possibility that space–time was finite but had no boundary, which means that it had no beginning, no moment of Creation. (Hawking, 1988:116)

The physicist continues, ironically, 'I had no wish to share the fate of Galileo ...' However, Hawking has ventured various theological comments much more extreme than any uttered by Galileo, most famously that:

So long as the universe had a beginning, we could suppose that it had a creator. But if the universe is really completely self-contained, having no boundary or edge, it would have neither beginning nor end: it would simply be. What place, then, for a creator? (Hawking, 1988:140–1)

Hawking is referring to his proposal, with Jim Hartle, about the very early universe. There is very substantial agreement as to the development of the universe from the first 10^{-43} second on (see Figure 1.4a). Traditional Big Bang theory allowed the space–time diagram to arise from a point, like an ice-cream cone (Figure 1.4b). This point was then a so-called 'singularity' at which values such as the density of the universe would go to infinity and the laws of physics could not hold. The Hawking–Hartle proposal allows the time dimension, the vertical axis of the diagram, to 'fade away', to be subsumed into the space dimensions. The diagram therefore originates not from a point but from a curved surface with no boundary or edge, like the surface of the Earth at one of the poles (Figure 1.4c).

Hawking and Hartle's proposal is the most ingenious of the quantum-cosmological speculations which aim to overcome the problem of the singularity. These speculations as they stood at the end of the 1980s were reviewed by Drees (1990:ch. 2). He points out that indeed at this early stage in the development of these theories a physicist *might* be influenced as to which one to pursue by a sense of their theological connotations (1990:67–8).

However, theologians of science are uniform in their rejection of the last-quoted comment of Hawking's. They also reject as the militantly atheistic programme of P.W. Atkins to the effect that: 'The only way of explaining the creation is to show that the creator had absolutely no job at all to do, and so might as well not have existed' (Atkins, 1981:17).

Atkins draws comfort from the notion that quantum cosmology has shifted away from the 'blue touch-paper' model, in which everything arose from a single inexplicable moment, towards various types of proposal in which space–time arises by chance out of a simpler state – Hawking's boundariless space, or a quantum vacuum, or some such.

Such views seem to show consonance not so much with theistic creation as in Genesis as with the view that the universe arose by some transition which had no purpose or meaning.

Keith Ward has rightly taken issue with the suggestion that quantum

Figure 1.4   Space–time diagrams of the early universe

Figure 1.4a   The Development of the Universe

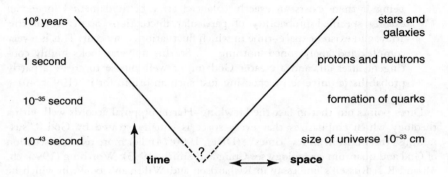

10^9 years	stars and galaxies
1 second	protons and neutrons
10^{-35} second	formation of quarks
10^{-43} second	size of universe 10^{-33} cm

time   ?   space

Figure 1.4b   Origin of the universe in a singularity

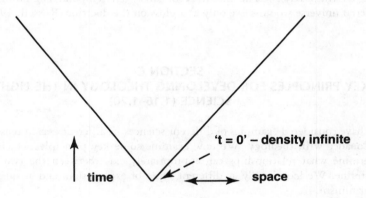

't = 0' – density infinite

time   space

Figure 1.4c   The Hawking–Hartle proposal – no 't = 0'

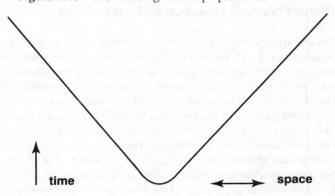

time   space

cosmology implies that the *reason* for the universe is pure chance (1996b:ch. 2). He writes:

> On the quantum fluctuation hypothesis, the universe will only come into being if there exists an exactly balanced array of fundamental forces, an exactly specified probability of particular fluctuations occurring in this array, and existent space–time in which fluctuations can occur. This is a very complex and finely tuned 'nothing' ... So this universe looks highly contingent after all, and a creator God might well choose to create a partly probabilistic universe by choosing just such an origin for it. (1996b:40)

Drees points out that in fact the Hawking–Hartle proposal accords well with a theology which emphasizes that every space is equally created by God, ' "sustaining" the world in all its "times" ' (Drees, 1990:74). For more recent discussion of God and quantum cosmology see Craig and Smith (1993); Worthing (1996: ch. 3); and R.J. Russell's fine essay in Richardson and Wildman's book, in which he shows that at the core of the doctrine of *creatio ex nihilo* (divine creation out of absolutely nothing) is the principle of ontological dependence (see also 2.5.1 and 4.12 on this essay).[36] The discovery of an actual temporal beginning to this material universe would serve only as a gloss on the doctrine (Russell, 1996:201–24).

SECTION C
KEY PRINCIPLES FOR DEVELOPING THEOLOGY IN THE LIGHT OF SCIENCE (1.16–1.20)

We have considered examples of different sciences in different eras in tension or in consonance with theology. We now examine some key principles which help to determine what relationships can appropriately exist between the two types of discipline. We look briefly at different types of explanation, and at questions of determinism.

1.16 Different types of causation and explanation

We saw in discussing Aristotle that he had devised a very sophisticated fourfold pattern of causation (1.11). However, Western physical science only developed in its present form by refusing to discuss final causation – the ultimate purpose or end towards which an entity was attracted. A cannonball (or a feather) dropped off the Leaning Tower of Pisa is considered to fall not because it is seeking its natural end or *telos* in being united to the Earth but because there is a net force acting on it – that of gravity. The force, mathematically characterized and operative throughout the universe, is the efficient cause of the motion. This shift in understanding also resulted, eventually, in the removal of a divine purposing agent from any scientific explanation. Science deals in *non-teleological* explanations, which do not invoke some purpose acting from outside the system concerned.

Poole points out that:

> ...an object such as a thermostat might have a number of **compatible** explanations:
>
> *An interpretive explanation* A thermostat is a device for maintaining a constant temperature.
>
> *A descriptive explanation* A (particular) thermostat consists of a bi-metallic strip in close proximity to an electrical contact.
>
> *A reason-giving (scientific) explanation* Constant temperature is maintained because, when the temperature falls, the bi-metal strip bends, so making electrical contact. It switches on a heater which operates until, at a pre-determined temperature, the bi-metal strip bends away from the contact, thereby breaking the circuit.
>
> *A reason-giving (motives) explanation* An agent wished to be able to maintain enclosures at constant temperatures to enable people to work comfortably, ovens to cook evenly, and chickens to hatch successfully.
>
> ...It needs to be understood that there is no logical conflict between reason-giving explanations which concern mechanisms, and reason-giving explanations which concern the plans and purposes of an agent, human or divine.
>
> (Poole, 1994:48–9, see also Poole, 2002)

The success of science has been based on restricting itself to particular forms of non-teleological explanation – reason-giving (scientific) in the classification above. We saw above that natural theology went into retreat because such explanations of natural phenomena displaced explanations (for instance of how gravity could act) which relied on divine mediation. Science has also succeeded by concentrating as much as possible on measurable behaviour which can be reproduced by a range of different observers – on what Galileo called 'the primary qualities' of mass and motion, rather than 'secondary qualities' such as taste and smell (see 5.2).[37]

In considering types of explanation it is important to clarify reason-giving explanations in biology. Biologists will often describe the 'purpose' of a particular entity – for example, the prehensile tails of some monkeys are 'designed' to enable them to swing through trees. By this, however, biologists are not giving a 'motives' explanation about the activity of a conscious, designing agent (though as Poole points out, motives explanations can coexist with scientific explanations). Rather they are saying that the tails of these monkeys have evolved a property which helps the organisms survive and reproduce (by extending their mobility in their habitat). Descriptions of the extent to which a biological property fits an organism for its environment and 'improves its design' constitute a special category of description known as the 'teleonomic'.

1.17 Determinism, indeterminism and their implications

The physics of Newton proved an enormously powerful way of describing moving bodies (see 5.2–5.4). A century later Pierre Simon de Laplace (1749–1827) showed among other things how the solar system could have arisen without divine intervention.[38] He went on to claim that an 'intelligence' possessing complete knowledge of the position and momentum of every body in the universe would be able to predict all future states of that universe. In other words, that the cosmos is *deterministic*. Laplace's 'intelligence' was a mathematical fiction. But it illustrated the problem of determinism, which challenges our instinct that we ourselves as humans are able to make choices about the future, that we are to some extent 'free' agents. Indeed determinism raises problems as to how God could either enter into any sort of real relationship with humans, or indeed guide the material world towards divine purposes.

We explore this in more detail in Chapter 10, together with 'compatibilist' positions which hold that free will can coexist with determinism. It is enough to note here the conviction of many thinkers in this field that this is not a wholly determined world, but one in which the laws and processes God has created can give rise to novel structures through the operation of chance, and that God can cooperate with those developments, and relate to the conscious beings to which evolution has ultimately given rise. So Ward writes:

> there can only be an open future if there is a degree of indeterminism. There can only be the sort of freedom that is morally important if there is an open future, at least sometimes. So indeterminism is a necessary condition of the later development of morally important freedom in rational beings. (Ward, 1996b:20)

1.18 Developing theology in the light of science

We are now beginning to see the sort of theology that is being done in the light of contemporary science. It is theology which treats scientific principles with great respect, while recognizing how their emphasis may shift (see **1.15** above on the origin of the universe). It expects that there will be consonances between two disciplines which are both 'mapping' the same territory, albeit in different ways, but it handles these consonances gently, using them to ask further questions rather than celebrating them in themselves.

It is one aim of this book to enable students *to do such theology for themselves*. It is too often overlooked that one task of theology is to generate new, vital and creative ways of speaking about the relationship of God to human beings and the non-human creation, and students should feel free to generate such ideas. As we indicated above, we ourselves see this task as one of starting within a religious tradition (in our case the Christian, rooted in Scripture, tradition, reason and religious experience) and seeking to renew and refresh that tradition by contact with the methods and descriptions of science. We pursue, then, a 'theology of nature' in Barbour's sense (see 1.3.1). We would encourage students to embark on that same model-making process – whether rooted in a particular tradition, or having no especial allegiance – and to do so creatively and imaginatively. (The corollary is that they also need to learn the skills of defending the rationality of their models.)

It cannot be stressed too strongly that such a model is always provisional, exploratory. A student should never be put off from beginning a model on the grounds that every position taken must be precisely accurate. The tradition of 'apophaticism' or 'negative theology' acts as a corrective to any precise attempt to describe God or the divine in relation to any other entity. (Apophaticism stresses that whatever description we assign to any aspect of God's nature, however coherent in itself, falls vastly short of encompassing that aspect of God.) But models of God, humanity and the cosmos, informed by the insights of contemporary science, remain a valuable heuristic tool. Such models would be expected also to be fruitful in terms of proposals for ethics and praxis (see Figure 1.2).

1.18.1 The interdependence of different aspects of a model

This will be familiar to those who have studied, for example, Christology and atonement theory. 'High' Christologies stressing the divinity of Jesus drew much of their momentum from the perception that only God could save human sinners – hence they tend to be found in company with objective theories of Christ's atoning passion and with eschatologies centred on the conviction that in the divine Christ all things will ultimately be reconciled (Colossians 1.20). Likewise an Abelardian picture of the crucified Jesus as the supreme exemplar of love *can* (though it need not necessarily) be held with 'lower' Christologies of Jesus the God-centred man. One doctrinal choice will affect a number of others.

We can extrapolate this into a more general model of the relation between God and humanity. Much will depend on the attitude taken to human beings. Are they to be viewed, initially, as 'little lower than the angels' (Psalm 8), the God-commissioned organism *par excellence*, vice-regent of creation, or is the starting point for thinking of humans to be that they are exceptionally highly culturally developed anthropoids, in whom the habit of worship and ritual practice has developed to a very marked extent? (See 6.2–6.3.2 for more on the evolution of humanity.) Once such a choice has been made as to which picture of humans the model will start from, then that picture has to be meshed with the chosen model of God (see Chapter 8). From there the model-maker must consider how the *relationship* between God and humans is to be characterized. Since humans are part of the creation, made out of elementary particles like all other entities, this relationship will in turn be affected by what stance is taken on the relationship of the divine to the material world. And so on. The exercise is exploratory, and each element in the model will be affected by understandings of what claims theology and science make in general, and what are the particular claims of different sciences in areas of special concern to theologians.

Chapter 2 gives an indication of the range of resources available in the Christian theological tradition for thinking about God as Creator of the world. Chapter 3 examines how an understanding of history enables us to look cautiously at what are supposedly classic examples of conflict (or yet harmony) between religious and scientific thought. Chapter 4 gives a background to how scientific rationality works, and various ways in which theology has responded, culminating in a proposal as to a way in which they may be seen to operate in parallel. Chapters 5–7 look at some of the key questions which touch on major narratives in different sciences and in theology – the origin, functioning and end of the physical universe, the origin and development of life and humanity, the nature of mentality and religious experience.[39] Chapter 8 provides an opportunity for students to look at a wide variety of models derived from Christian theologians, which is complemented in Chapter 9 by exploration of examples from Jewish and Eastern thought. Chapter 10 provides an opportunity to test out models students may be developing on a theology of divine action. But it is helpful to stress three aspects of models at this stage.

1.19 Three attributes of models of God, humanity and the cosmos

(i) As we indicated above, different elements in the model will be *interdependent* – the effect of one choice has to be evaluated in terms of its coherence with the other proposals that are being made. Thus a model of God as intimately and vulnerably related to every entity in the non-human creation would sit distinctly oddly with an ethic which allowed humans to do whatever they chose to the environment.

(ii) Models may *derive from different metaphysical positions* – they may for example be critically realist with respect to both science and theology (see 1.7), critically realist with respect to science and non-realist in respect of theology (see 4.3), or instrumentalist (see 1.7) with respect to both. Those who wish to propose models which involve no divine entity should not feel excluded from the exercise – they have still the task of giving an account of origins and ends, of the nature and significance of humanity and of human relationships to the environment. (Furthermore, just as theists have to face the problem of evil – see 8.3, 10.5 and 10.18 – so atheists have to face 'the problem of goodness' and address questions about the surprising existence of beauty and intelligibility in the universe – also about the (much disputed) phenomenon of altruism.[40])

(iii) As will be clear from the above, models *are expected to give rise to ethics*, possibly indeed to proposals for action (see the Bossey Circle, Figure 1.2). Here Chapters 11–14 of this book are particularly important, since they indicate among other things ways in which the effects of science are manifest in society, and areas where science might or might not be regulated to meet theological and ethical concerns. Here we begin that exploration by looking briefly at questions of value.

1.20 Questions of value

What humans count as valuable involves their *thinking*, their *feeling* and their *willing* – the *cognitive, affective* and *volitional* domains of their lives. The values humans hold because of their beliefs are often referred to as their dispositions or their commitments. These may arise from beliefs about major matters like the meaning – or otherwise – of life; values may also be attached to factors like the quality of objects as works of art, their irreplaceability and sale value, the stability given to society by traditional customs, the sanctity of life and so forth.

With a vast array of possible values, *value judgements have to be made*. These may be between the relative values of objects or organisms, or they might be between alternative courses of action in science or technology. If for instance we want to say that a piece of rainforest has value, we have to be able to say why. The sciences can provide certain data on rare species, biodiversity, etc. but they cannot of themselves provide the ethical basis for attaching value to an organism or a system. Likewise science and technology can help humans to judge the likely outcomes of particular courses of action, but cannot tell us whether those courses of action ought or ought not to be pursued.

However, the scientific community *does* continually make decisions as to value, by selecting different priorities for research, and different methods of carrying it out. These selections, then, need to be a matter of public concern. Religious beliefs about right and wrong provide a source of these moral *oughts*, as do non-religious stances for living. Such beliefs are continually seen to interact with both science and technology, over matters like deciding whether to clone human beings, how long to keep patients who are in a persistent vegetative state on life-support machines, or indeed how much countryside is to be used up for roads.

Even a brief list of issues like this highlights one logical point: '*ought*' implies '*can*'. It would sound odd to say that the doctors *ought* to have saved the patient's life, if the illness was one for which there was no known cure. However, the converse, '*can* implies *ought*' is not true. Just because science and technology make something possible does not imply that it ought to be done. One only has to remember some of the bizarre experiments performed by Nazi concentration-camp doctors to see a grim illustration of that point.

As we indicate in Chapter 14, the possibilities presented by science and technology need to be assessed within a view of the world which seeks for *wisdom*. Daniel Hardy has written:

> wisdom designates more than the wisdom of human beings. It is the domain in which the dynamics of fundamental dimensions of the world and God are placed relative to each other, the domain ... of relativities. Wisdom is therefore the *configuration* of insight – both theoretical and practical – into the multi-dimensionality of the world and God, *not only how they are related but how they should be related* [this emphasis ours] ... Anyone who tried to understand how the world and God are related, and therefore how they are best approached, or how the various disciplines of human understanding are best related to each other, is involved in the search for, and finding of, wisdom. (Hardy, 1998:137)

In other words the making of models such as we have proposed, with their emphasis on relationality and on the ethical reflection that should result as to the *appropriate* relationships between God, humanity and the cosmos, is an aspect of a new search for wisdom, which humans so urgently seem to need.

1.21 Conclusion

In this chapter we have indicated the importance of moving beyond the trite caricature that science simply displaces religion from every aspect of life where the two meet. We have indicated important sources for exploring the 'special relationship', both historically and in the contemporary world. We considered, and moved beyond, some of the main efforts to narrow the relationship to a typological scheme. The metaphor of different maps of the same reality led us into a discussion of the claims of critical realism in science and theology, which prepares for our examination of their historical and philosophical backgrounds in Chapters 2–4. We then considered whether religion was necessary to the rise of science, and some of the classic cases where conflict has been real. Clarification of different types of explanation, and of the importance of questions of determinism and value, enables the reader to tackle the suggested task of making her or his own model of God, humanity and the cosmos.

Notes

1   Sections 1.7, 1.16 and 1.20 were drafted or part-drafted by MP; all other sections, and 2005 editing, by CS.

2   The conflict or warfare hypothesis was much furthered by two books originating in the 1870s: *History of the Conflict Between Religion and Science* by John William Draper and *A History of the Warfare of Science with Theology in Christendom* by Andrew Dickson White. See 3.5.1 and Welch, 1996, for a discussion of these.

3   On the significance of Newton's work see 5.2–5.4.

4   Republished in an enlarged form as *Religion and Science* (Barbour, 1998).

5   For a series of articles on Barbour and his Gifford Lectures see *Zygon* 31 (1) (1996).

6   Polkinghorne has surveyed the contributions made by himself, Peacocke and Barbour in *Scientists as Theologians* (Polkinghorne, 1996a).

7   For the benefit of non-theologians we define key technical terms as they arise. *Eschatology*, literally the study of the last things, is the area of theology concerned with God's final consummation of the world, the transformation of the first creation into whatever is pictured as being the new creation.

8   Another very useful introduction is that of Peters and Bennett (2002), which also gives an account of a range of religions in conversation with science.

9   Stannard interviews both Dawkins and another arch-opponent of theism, the Oxford chemist Peter Atkins.

10   For more discussion of 'Thomist' theology – that based on the thought of Aquinas, see 2.5.2.

11   Arguments for a different sort of divine designer then developed, but they were arguments *from* presuppositions about God, rather than attempts to *prove* God's existence or character (see Brooke, 1991:310–17).

12   See also Peters, 1998.

13   For a study of miracle see 10.10(iv).

14   See 5.4 *re* Lord Kelvin's similar advice and the two 'clouds' he noted on the horizon of classical physics.

15   It is less evident, though equally important, to note that the activities of scientific communities are properly the subject of theological and ethical critique. What

values do the communities *actually* evince? Are they committed to disinterested enquiry, or merely to a self-perpetuating search for funding? Does their source of funding constrain what results they can admit to obtaining (as in the case of those epidemiologists employed by the tobacco industry, or those climatologists employed by oil companies)? We look further into this in 1.20, and in Chapter 11.

16   *Epistemology* is the study of the nature of knowledge – how and to what extent we possess different kinds of knowledge. For a further exploration of evolutionary epistemology see van Huyssteen's 2003–4 Gifford Lectures (van Huyssteen, 2006).

17   We take up the issue of critical realism in 1.7.

18   For more developed discussion of these themes see 6.3.1, 6.13.3–6.13.5, van Huyssteen, 2003, and Bowker, 1995: chs 1–14.

19   Midgley (1996a and b). For an analysis of reductionism see 6.11–6.13.4. For a rejection of dualism between mind and brain see 7.4.

20   See our study of two closely related Anglican theologies, those of Arthur Peacocke and John Polkinghorne, in 10.10.

21   Such as Barbour (1998:118–20), Polkinghorne (1991: ch. 1), Peacocke (1993:11–19) and Bowker (1995:42–6). For a summary of the debate between the first three, see Polkinghorne, 1996a: ch. 2.

22   Mackey points out that Aquinas (in his great thirteenth-century system) 'did little more … than systematize Augustinian thought on this matter' (Mackey, 1983:586).

23   R.J. Russell has called attention to this as an example of *dissonance* (Peters, 1997a:662).

24   See Luscombe, 2000:16–19.

25   The very term *metaphysics* was originally the title given to the books of Aristotle which followed his *Physics*. It refers to questions about reality which 'lie beyond or behind those capable of being tackled by the methods of science' (Blackburn, 1994:240).

26   See also 3.2.1.

27   These conclusions of Aristotle's about the shape of the cosmos and the place of the Earth are fine examples of the most characteristic type of Ancient Greek reasoning – *deductive* from general principles (some of them philosophical and aesthetic rather than astronomical in the ordinary sense) rather than *inductive* from observations to theories.

28   Brahe (1546–1601) had proposed a scheme in which the planets revolved around the sun, but the sun itself revolved around a stationary Earth (Figure 1.3(b)).

29   This was an important addition to his status (and hence to the weight of influence perceived to be carried by his views) – mathematicians were technicians; philosophers were those who could establish truth.

30   By which 'the continuing motion of a heavy body is due to an internal power implanted in it by the projector which initiated its motion' (Kuhn, 1970b:119).

31   *Hermeneutics* is a study of the principles of interpreting the meaning of written texts. It includes the whole question of how a particular text is 'received', especially considerations such as discerning the author's intentions as well as understanding the social context and the thought-forms of the period.

32   The reason for this, as Copernicus had guessed, is that the solar system is a relatively tiny place enormously far from even the nearest stars. Stellar parallax is therefore very small. It was not observed until 1832.

33 Gingerich has shown moreover that Galileo's own logic was not always of the soundest in his efforts to demonstrate his case (Gingerich, 1982).

34 The Council of Trent, in tightening the structures of the Roman Church, had ruled in 1546 that 'no one should dare to interpret Scripture "contrary to the unanimous consensus of the Fathers"' (Brooke, 1991:97). (Though as we have seen Galileo did in fact follow the hermeneutical method of Augustine.)

35 As Kaiser makes clear this was a process which had been going on at least since the twelfth century (Kaiser, 1996:185–97).

36 *Ontology* is the study of being, of how reality is in itself, as opposed to how we might have knowledge of it (epistemology). Ontological dependence implies that all creation owes its being, from moment to moment, absolutely and utterly to God.

37 However, this latter success has tended to privilege physics, the science most concerned with fundamental forces, at the expense of biology. Some recent thinkers, such as Brian Goodwin (see his 1995:215–20), have called for a less mechanistic approach, especially in biology.

38 When Napoleon remarked to him the absence of God in his models, legend has it that Laplace said he 'had no need of that hypothesis'. The mathematician was nevertheless a practising Catholic.

39 It may be asked why chemistry seems to have been omitted from our sequence of sciences! Chemistry finds mention only insofar as it forms part of consideration of one of the particularly acute questions for the interface between science and theology listed above. *Historically*, chemistry has of course had a vastly important part to play in the growth of human understanding. For some fine descriptions of relevant incidents in the history of chemistry see Russell, C.A., 1994.

40 See Irons (1996) and Hefner (1996) for a fascinating exchange on altruism.

Further reading

BARBOUR, I.G. (1998) *Religion and Science: Historical and Contemporary Issues* (London: SCM Press)

PEACOCKE, A. (2004) *Creation in a World of Science: The Re-shaping of Belief* (Oxford: Oxford University Press)

PETERS, T. and BENNETT, G. (eds) (2002) *Bridging Science and Theology* (London: SCM Press)

POLKINGHORNE, J. (2000) *Faith, Science and Understanding* (London: SPCK)

POOLE, M.W. (1995) *Beliefs and Values in Science Education* (Buckingham: Open University Press)

RICHARDSON, W.M. and WILDMAN, W.J. (1996) *Religion and Science: History, Method, Dialogue* (London and New York: Routledge)

ROLSTON, HOLMES, III (1999) *Genes, Genesis and God: Values and their Origins in Natural and Human History* (Cambridge: Cambridge University Press)

STANNARD, R. (1996) *Science and Wonders: Conversations about Science and Belief* (London: Faber & Faber)

STENMARK, MIKAEL (2004) *How to Relate Science and Religion: A Multidimensional Model* (Grand Rapids, MI, and Cambridge: Eerdmans)

VAN HUYSSTEEN, J.W. (1998) *Duet or Duel? Theology and Science in a Postmodern World* (London: SCM Press)

WATTS, F. (ed.) (1998) *Science Meets Faith* (London: SPCK)

Chapter 2

The significance of the theology of creation within Christian tradition: systematic considerations

Paul D. Murray and David Wilkinson

2.1 What do we mean by the theology of creation?

The title of this book is bold: *God, Humanity and the Cosmos* covers a huge sweep of issues, not least in the area of theological thinking. The word 'cosmos' figures here as a shorthand reference for the totality of finite reality, animate and inanimate. So, a key aspect of *God, Humanity and the Cosmos* is to explore how the relation between God and all-that-is-not-God is diversely understood and what it means to live within such understanding. Within Judaeo-Christian understanding this relation has traditionally been spoken of in terms of creation – all that is not God as being related to God as created to creator.

There is an important sense, therefore, in which the entire book is concerned with the theology of creation – with the question, that is, How might it be possible in the contemporary world to articulate an understanding of the world as created? With this, what does it mean to live as self-conscious creatures? Indeed, is it meaningful to speak in terms of creation at all? Of course, in order to make sense of such questions we need to explore a wide diversity of insights. This is one of the integrating themes of the book and of the various particular explorations that are pursued here. Frequently, however, this integrating concern operates in the background with other windows more obviously to the fore. Thus, the purpose of this chapter is to focus directly on the theology of creation in order to inform these various other specific explorations. The aim is to give an initial sense of what the theology of creation is all about; to identify more specifically the key aspects of classical Judaeo-Christian theology of creation and their implications and, with this, to highlight the significance of this material for the science and religion interface.

Staying with the title of this book for a moment, the huge sweep says something about the immense range of interests and systematic concerns that are at work not just in the theology of creation specifically but in the search for theological understanding more generally. Science, for its part, is not just an amalgam of various bits and pieces but the concern for coherent understanding of the entirety of the natural world in naturalistic perspective.[1] So also theology, classically understood, does not simply represent a vague collection of different bits and pieces of religious data but the concern to understand all things in relation to God. Aquinas spoke in this regard of theology as the study both of God and of all particular things in relation to God as their 'origin and end' (Aquinas, 1964a:1a.1.7, p. 27).

This grand ambition at the heart of both science and theology *can* (but does not necessarily have to!) lead to their treading on each other's toes. Alternatively, it can lead to the view that science and theology are correctly to be seen as each taking a narrower and a broader perspective respectively on the one reality, in a way that allows for mutual interaction. In this way of thinking, science can be thought of as raising questions that only theology can tackle. In turn, it might be maintained that a necessary aspect of asking after the theological significance of anything, for example contemporary cosmology, is to seek also to understand it in naturalistic terms.

This view of theology in general and of the theology of creation in particular as concerned with the big picture – with understanding the relation between God and all that is not God, and what it means to live such an understanding – contrasts with the common assumption that creation simply concerns the origins and beginning of things. Controversies between evolutionary theory and theology on the one hand and cosmology and theology on the other have frequently served to reinforce this assumption by making it seem that what is at stake is simply differing accounts of the origins of things. However, in classical Christian theology of creation 'being created' is a phrase with past, present and future force. Not only does it claim that all things have their origin in God, it further claims that they are held in being by God and destined to find their flourishing in God. In an important sense, a biblical theology of creation stretches from the first words of the book of Genesis through to the closing vision of the book of Revelation and is at issue on every page in between. Aquinas even went so far as to say that creation refers first and foremost not to the claim that the world depends upon God as its originator but to the claim that all things depend upon God moment by moment of their existence (Aquinas, 1967:1a.46.2, p. 81). Even with an everlasting world, he reasoned, it would be necessary to think of God as creator. Don Page, a cosmologist and collaborator of Stephen Hawking, makes a similar point about the Judaeo-Christian theology of creation:

> God creates and sustains the entire Universe rather than just the beginning. Whether or not the Universe has a beginning has no relevance to the question of its creation, just as whether an artist's line has a beginning and an end, or instead forms a circle with no end, has no relevance to the question of its being drawn. (Page, 1998:742–3)

So, the doctrine of creation says something about the story of the world being a God-given, God-held and God-orientated story. The challenge at issue in this book is to explore whether it is still possible to view the world as God-narrated given the stories of things to be found in the natural sciences and, if so, how this might most fruitfully be done.

2.2 Telling the story of creation

The language of story and of seeking to view things within the perspective of a God-given, God-directed story is quite a helpful way into what theology is about. Story or narrative is a fundamental part of human life. We are continually re-telling our own stories and as we do so we are concerned not just for the bare facts and sequence of events but for the meaning, order and purpose that we perceive in these facts and events.

More generally, story or narrative is almost a basic form of writing and pre-sentation in the sense that, regardless of context, we always seek an orderly rather than confused presentation of the relevant material. An orderly presentation, moreover, that goes beyond the level of mere description in order to draw out the significance of things – think of a synopsis of legal proceedings, or a laboratory report, or an essay on recent movements in contemporary philosophy or theology. We tell stories of communities, groups and nations and celebrate such stories in festival: whether it be Christmas, Passover or Thanksgiving. Again, the sciences tell us stories of the natural order of things as perceived within an entirely naturalistic perspective. For their part, religious traditions tell us stories of the meaning and purpose of things as perceived in relation to God and what the practical implications of this might be.

In the study of theology this underlying narrative structure is sometimes transparently obvious, such as in the New Testament Gospels, or the story of Israel as recounted in the Hebrew Scriptures. Indeed, a cursory reading of Genesis chapters 1 to 3 gives you the clear impression of narrative structure. At other times, the narrative structure of theology is less obvious, for example when we are exploring a doctrinal issue such as whether the universe was created out of nothing – generally referred to as the doctrine of creation *ex nihilo*. Such issues can sound very conceptual and unrelated to matters of story. It is important to recognize, however, that even such explicitly conceptual, doctrinal issues flow from the attempt to draw out the implications of claiming that the world is to be viewed as a God-given, God-sustained, God-directed story in which we are participants.

The telling of creation stories is of course not unique to the Judaeo-Christian tradition. On the contrary, the telling of stories concerned to communicate a sense of the meaning and value of things in their totality ('Why?') and not simply to identify the causal sequence of how things got to be how they are ('How?') seems to be a universal human phenomenon. Modern scientific accounts are distinctive in prioritizing the how question over the why question. But even here, such nar-ratives are frequently used in a way that goes beyond their strictly scientific focus in order to convey certain assumptions about the order and value of things – for example, a sense of deep unity in and through diversity and, for some, materialist nihilism.

Many stories of creation find their origin in the ancient Near East. Indeed, the context in which the Genesis narratives were produced was steeped in such creation stories (Lambert, 1965:294). Such stories are less to be seen as attempts in primitive science and more as explanations as to why things are as they are experienced to be ('aetiology'). One of the most famous of these is the *Enuma Elish* story deriving from Babylonia somewhere between the mid- to late second millennium BCE and the sixth century BCE. It is worth reflecting that given that Israel's patriarchal background is associated with this region (Abraham is regarded as deriving from Ur of the Chaldeans) and that Israel was taken into exile in Babylonia in the mid-sixth century, it is entirely likely that the biblical writers would have been aware of this story.

Against this background, it is fruitful to turn to examine the early chapters of Genesis. As we do so it is worth bearing the following questions in mind. What is being suggested about the character of the Creator? What about the character of reality? What is being said about the material world? What about human vocation? What kind of view of society is being suggested?

2.3 The creation narratives of Genesis 1–3

It is important to recognize that the Genesis narratives represent inspired scripture for living faith communities. For such communities they are not simply a source of academic or, indeed, historical discussion but are valued as a means of God speaking in the world. But under this broad notion there can be significant diversity in interpretation, both with regard to the nature of inspiration and with regard to the nature of the text.

For example, some Christians view the Genesis text as a disclosure of *how* exactly creation came into existence and not simply *why*. Such approaches are collectively referred to as 'Creationism'. However, even here, it is important to recognize that there is a diversity of such creationist approaches (see Numbers, 1992, also Peters and Hewlett, 2003: ch. 4). Some believe in a creation that is only thousands of years old. Some view just the earth itself as being only thousands of years old but think of the universe in its totality as being much older. Others believe that the universe *appears* to be billions of years old but is in fact only thousands of years old. Thus God creates an 'old' universe with fossils already in the rocks.

In these views contemporary science is seen to be misleading compared to the evidence of Scripture. Such views are dependent on seeing the Genesis text as a scientific history of God's creative acts. However, the current scientific picture of a universe which is billions of years old cannot be dismissed lightly. The theories of modern science have gathered a very considerable consensus around them with a very considerable body of supporting evidence in their favour. Moreover, many of the scientists who explore the history of the universe in this way are devout Christians and Jews. Nor is this simply a scientific problem but also a theological one, for if God is the creator of all then creation should surely disclose something of God? God as creator, it might be reasoned, has authored 'the book of nature' as well as 'the book of scripture'. It is odd, therefore, on theological grounds to think of the book of nature and the book of scripture as standing in fundamental conflict with each other.

Other approaches to the Genesis text share the concern to preserve the biblical account of the sequence in which creation came about but seek to express this in the light of the accounts to be found in contemporary cosmology and evolutionary theory. Some, for example, have suggested a gap between the original creation and a subsequent restorative creation after the fall of Satan, and others have interpreted the biblical days as periods of time rather then 24-hour days.

Another approach, again, is to pay careful attention to the different kinds of literature represented in the Genesis texts (see Lucas, 2001). This means noting immediately the differences in style between Genesis 1.1–2.4a and Genesis 2.4b–3.24, and beginning to ask questions as to whether they are meant to be read as scientific accounts. On this basis, some will maintain a mode of direct inspiration for the author of Genesis, but a revelation that is much more concerned with theological questions than scientific ones. Others, however, will think of a mode of inspiration that works more indirectly, in and through people's natural capacities, enhancing them and bringing them to fulfilment. This would allow for the inspiration of scriptural writings as a process over time with texts coming to be reverenced, prayed, lived and even adapted before finding their final form.

Such an approach is, therefore, compatible with viewing different parts of the Genesis narratives as having different origins in different phases of the community's life, while allowing for a reworking of them into a final coherent narrative. It is also compatible with saying that whatever pre-scientific, pre-historical interests may also have been at work in the shaping of these stories, their primary purpose is not to provide a primitive scientific account of the world's origins but to articulate how Hebrew faith understood the meaning, purpose and order of things as God-given, God-held and God-directed. As Galileo would later express it, the point of the scriptures is not to tell us how the heavens go but how to get to heaven (see 1.12, 3.2.1).

Further, it is important to recognize that this is not some kind of new, modern approach without precedent in the history of the Church. Early church fathers such as Gregory of Nyssa (*c.*335–95) and Augustine of Hippo (354–430) pointed out very clearly some of the problems that exist with taking the seven days of Genesis 1 literally, for example the fact that night and day are spoken of before the creation of sun and moon. We might also point to the differences between the first creation narrative in Genesis (Genesis 1.1–2.4a) and the second (Genesis 2.4b–2.25). Augustine here introduced an interesting and important principle to the effect that, with regard to matters of natural order that do not impinge on the heart of revelation, scriptural interpretation should bow to the findings of natural reason and adopt a symbolic interpretation of the text. Indeed, viewed in this way it is in fact strictly literal readings of Scripture that are the modern novelty. When we bring this concern for the literary nature of scriptural writings to our reading of Genesis 1.1–2.4a, two important themes emerge.

2.3.1 The sovereignty of God in creation

This passage is generally assigned to the 'Priestly' strand within the Pentateuch, the first five books of the Hebrew Bible. Here the command of God is central. It displays a concern for order and worship evocative in turn of the good order of well-being marked out in the Torah, the Jewish law, and the reverencing of God as creator that lay at the heart of Temple liturgy and architecture. For example, the structure and constant repetition within the passage is itself not unlike a hymn to the Creator, or even an act of worship. Some have even speculated that we are dealing here with a liturgical text that was used in an annual festival of creation celebrating, submitting to and invoking the blessed order of things that God intends.

There are certain possible parallels with the Babylonian *Enuma Elish* story – for example, both accounts start with either water or chaos at the beginning, followed by the creation of the firmament, of dry land, of the heavenly bodies and of people in that order. Beyond such structural similarities, however, the parallels cease and it is the differences that are significant. In direct contrast to the Babylonian account, creation is not depicted here as the result of a violent struggle between opposed forces, with the material world being made out of the slain corpse of a defeated deity. There may be in other parts of the Hebrew scriptures an allusion to creation involving the overcoming of water chaos (as we see in Psalm 74.13–14) but there is no sense of there being an independent power that might stand in the way of the Creator. As Walter Zimmerli writes:

> Whatever mythical power may originally have resided in the individual elements, they have here become mere material for the creator to work with. At God's command, everything takes shape, starting with the foundations of the cosmos (the firmament of heaven, the earth, the sea, the stars). (Zimmerli, 1978:34)

This demythologizing of the cosmic elements is shown most clearly in the purely functional references to the lesser and greater lights in order to avoid the mythologically laden proper names 'sun' and 'moon'. In keeping, then, with the characteristic emphasis of the Hebrew Scriptures on the distinction between creator and creature, the emphasis is placed in Genesis 1 upon the sovereignty and independence of God. In creating there is no struggle. Creation is a free, unconstrained act of God's Word, flowing from nothing other than the unopposed command of God that it should be so (cf. Psalm 33.9, 'He spoke and it took place; he commanded and it stood there'; Psalm 148.5, 'He commanded and they were created'; Isaiah 48.13; Genesis 6.22).

It is worth us pausing for a moment in order to consider what is going on here. Some scholars suggest that this passage reflects something of Israel's devastating experience of the Babylonian exile, during which Israelites would have been exposed to the Babylonian stories of creation. In this light, Genesis 1 can be viewed as a vehicle for asserting Israel's own distinctive belief in God's absolute power over chaos and, with this, in the fundamental goodness of what God creates and in God's ability and commitment to redeem the mess we make of things (Hasel, 1974:81–102). Viewed in this way, the key purpose of this account is the rekindling of confidence in the God of Israel as the creator and redeemer of all – and the celebration of this as lived truly within Torah and Temple. Indeed, something like this has been characteristic of the theology of creation in Jewish and Christian thought in many different contexts. That is, rather than being a purely academic discussion of beginnings, the theology of creation has been a way of exploring and reasserting the power and purposes of God not just for the present but also for the future.

Further, it is interesting to note that this key insight – of God freely creating the universe in an orderly way – has been recognized by some to be fundamental to the growth of science (see **1.11, 3.5.2**). In particular, this notion of the fundamental ordering of the world by God led to the rise of the concepts of the laws of science (see Zilsel, 1942; Oakley, 1961) and engendered a positive attitude towards the study of nature in theologians otherwise as different as Thomas Aquinas and John Calvin.

2.3.2 The place of human beings in creation

While the main focus of Genesis 1.1–2.4a is on God the Creator, the passage also focuses significantly on human beings in relation to the Creator. The phrase referring to humankind being in the 'image and likeness' of God (Genesis 1.26–7) combines the concrete term *ṣelem*, referring typically to a physical likeness, with the more abstract form *dᵉmût*, meaning 'similarity'. This combination has given rise to wide-ranging speculation in Jewish and Christian thought as to what might be intended. Image and likeness were contrasted in differences between 'natural qualities' such as reason and 'supernatural graces' such as spiritual qualities (Irenaeus *c.*130–*c.*200), or humanity after the fall and human nature after its perfection at final consummation (Origen *c.*185–*c.*254). Tertullian (*c.*160–*c.*220) suggested that the image of God was retained after sinning, while the lost likeness was restored through the renewing activity of the Spirit after conversion. However, there is little support for such exegetical distinctions. Image and likeness are used interchangeably (Gen. 5.3), and the majority of recent scholars see 'likeness' used here simply to qualify 'image' in order to stress that humans are not identical to God while being a real reflection of God. The meaning of 'image' itself has caused even more difficulty (see Clines, 1998). Different suggestions have included: that God is physically embodied and human beings are physically the image of God, or that the image denotes human reason, or freedom, or our moral sense. Yet none of these interpretations does justice to the biblical material (see also 6.3.1 on the image of God).

Studies in the language and context of the ancient Near East lead to a different understanding of image as not so much a part of the human constitution as a pointer to the distinctive place of humanity within the created order. It is less about something we have or do and more about relationship (see Westermann, 1984:158). In contrast to the Babylonian account where the role of humans is simply one of serving the gods, humanity is viewed here, in distinction from the rest of creaturely reality, as enjoying a relationship of unique conscious intimacy with God. Or, perhaps better, humanity is that part of creation that is capable of being conscious of and responsive in its relationship to the Creator. In fact, within Christian theology Athanasius (*c.*296–373) spoke of the image of God as the capacity to relate to and partake in the life of God, while the twentieth-century theologian Emil Brunner (1889–1966) spoke of it as 'existence for love' (Brunner, 1952:57). Or as David Fergusson more recently put it, 'The image of God is thus to be understood not substantively in terms of the possession of an immortal soul, but relationally in terms of the role that human beings play before God and before the rest of creation' (Fergusson, 1998:14).

Furthermore, as this already implies, this relationship involves responsibility. In particular, there is a close connection in the text between being made in the image of God and God's command to humans to exercise dominion over the natural world (Genesis 1.26–8). This is to be understood as a call to share in the creative, sustaining dominion of God and so act as the visible representatives of God's benevolent care for creation. This, in turn, relates to the vexed question as to whether the dominion granted to human beings is objectionable on ecological grounds. The historian Lynn White Jr, speaking at the American Association for the Advancement of Science in 1967, argued that our ability to harness natural resources was marred by the deep-rooted assumption that, 'we are superior to nature, contemptuous of it, willing to use it for our slightest whim', and proceeded to claim pointedly that:

> We shall continue to have a worsening ecological crisis until we reject the Christian axiom that nature has no reason for existence but to serve man ... Both our present science and our present technology are so tinctured with orthodox Christian arrogance towards nature that no solution for our ecological crisis can be expected from them alone. (White, 1967:1203)[2]

Thus, Christianity, it is claimed, bears 'a huge burden of guilt' for the environmental crisis (see also 8.4).

If, however, the representative role of humans is taken seriously as suggested here, it implies that an authentic theology of creation in Judaeo-Christian perspective would promote attitudes not of aggressive exploitation but of responsible stewardship. That is, the unique role given to humans is better understood here, as Fergusson writes, 'in terms of a relationship to care for and to preserve the creation', rather than to dominate it. In this regard, it is striking that the Genesis 1 narrative reaches fulfilment not in the creation of Adam and Eve but in the sabbath day on which 'the whole creation glorifies its maker' (Fergusson, 1998:17). This provides further perspective on the distinctive role of humans within the created order as that of priests giving voice to creation's praise. That is, resting in, rejoicing in and living out of the sabbath praise of God is regarded here as the very pinnacle of what created reality and human reality in particular is called to. Viewed in this way, we humans are called not just to 'use' material reality for our own ends, but to hallow it, to reverence it as God's gift, to work for its flourishing and, in this manner, be viceroys of God's gracious generative sovereignty in God's good world.

Once again we encounter here a significant theological foundation for science (see Foster, 1934). Christians have understood this responsibility of stewardship as God's encouragement to develop science and technology for the good of all.[3] It goes against those views that see science as inherently evil. Rather than being banned from 'interfering with nature' we are actively encouraged to do good. In this regard, the theologian Philip Hefner coins the term 'created co-creators' to describe human beings made in the image of God (Hefner, 1993). God gives us responsibility and ability not only to care but also to innovate within the context of his creation and his will. Reijer Hooykaas comments that this biblical understanding of human beings in relation to both creation and Creator liberated us from 'the naturalistic bonds of Greek religiosity and philosophy and gave a religious sanction to the development of technology, that is, to the dominion of nature by human art' (1972:67).

In summary, then, it is authentic to the Christian theology of creation both to affirm technology and to question how it is used (see Chapters 13 and 14). Humanity's power, dominion and sovereignty are properly to be conceived not in terms of a controlling, destructive force and threat of violence, but in terms of a God-given and God-revealing generative capacity to create and to sustain life in well-being. With this, it is significant that in Christian tradition it is Jesus of Nazareth who is *the* disclosure *par excellence* of true divine power in a manner profoundly subversive of common expectations and, likewise, Jesus who is regarded as truly being in the 'image of God'. This is an insight that Karl Barth (1886–1968) emphasized perhaps more clearly than any other theologian in the modern period. For Barth the image of God is in turn reflected in man and woman created as the sign of hope of the coming Son of Man.

2.4 From Alpha to Omega: the theology of creation in the broader Scriptural narrative

As the above suggests, it is a major mistake to view Christian theology of creation as built simply on the first chapters of the book of Genesis. Not only in terms of the image of God, but more broadly in terms of God's relationship with the universe, Jewish and Christian thinkers have been influenced by many other passages in the Hebrew Scriptures and the New Testament. Genesis needs to be seen alongside passages such as Proverbs 8.22–36 and Job 38.1–42.17 which stress the wisdom of God in creation, passages which celebrate the glory and majesty of God (Psalms 8, 19, 148; Isaiah 40.9–31), and passages which look forward to new creation (Isaiah 65.17–25; Romans 8.18–27; 2 Peter 3.3–13; Revelation 21.1–8) (see Wilkinson, 2002). In this latter regard, of course, central to the New Testament is the role of Christ in creation (John 1.1–18; Colossians 1.15–20; Hebrews 1.1–14), regarded as the word or wisdom of God through whom all was spoken and in whom all are destined to find their authentic voice. In all of these passages, it is clear that creation is not the subject of pure intellectual speculation, but is used to convey a message about God and God's relationship with the world. Here cosmology is rarely of interest for its own sake.

While the interest of the modern world may be on how the theology of creation relates to scientific cosmology, the biblical writers were concerned with something very different – with the meaning of things in God's providential plan. As has been noted, Karl Barth reflected this very clearly in his own theological thinking about creation. He expressed it in terms of the covenant being the 'internal basis of creation' (its inner rationale) and of creation being the 'external basis of the covenant' (the context within which covenant could be initiated and brought to consummation). By so doing, he attempted to reorientate the discussion away from creation and cosmology to God's relationship with creation and humanity in particular. For Barth it is quite clear, God creates not out of any necessity on God's behalf but in order to draw creation into covenant in Christ. As such, for Barth, God's self-disclosure in Jesus of Nazareth is, somewhat controversially, essential even to understanding aright even what it means to view God as creator. In his own words:

> I believe in Jesus Christ, God's Son our Lord, in order to perceive and to understand that God the Almighty, the Father, is Creator of heaven and earth. If I did not believe the former, I could not perceive and understand the latter. (Barth, 1958:29)

As is explored further in Chapter 4, this conviction underpinned Barth's hostility to any idea of natural theology which starts outside of revelation and is not a result of grace. For many other theologians Barth pushes his argument too far at this point in denying that humans have the ability to see something of the Creator in creation itself and in appearing not to value the physical creation as anything other than backdrop or context for the covenant to unfold. Even within the terms of Barth's theological vision, it might be argued that if creation really is intrinsically Christ-shaped and Christ-orientated, then should it not be expected that something at least of God's truth in Christ can be known, albeit in partial and confused form, by looking truly at the created order? This being said, it equally needs to be acknowledged that Barth's emphasis on the relationship between Christ and creation reflects well a core conviction of the New Testament writings.

Take, for example, the depiction of Christ at the heart of creation in Colossians 1.15–20. Here we find applied to Jesus everything that could be said of the figure of 'wisdom' in creation (Proverbs 8.22) (Burney, 1925–6). The implication is that at the heart of creation is not simply a divine attribute but a divine personality. Christ is proclaimed here as 'the first born over all creation' (v. 15), signifying supreme rank or that he is prior in importance. Nor is Christ simply a part of the created order, 'for by him all things were created' (v. 16). Creation, in this view, is the activity of God the Father in the Son: not only do all things have their origin in Christ, 'in him all things hold together' (v. 17). The verb is in the perfect tense indicating that 'everything' has held together in him and continues to do so, that through him the world is sustained and prevented from falling into chaos. The source of the universe's unity, order and consistency is to be found, Colossians is suggesting, in the continuing work of God in Christ.

Far, then, from science and technology being necessarily 'unChristian', or in conflict with Christian faith, they are properly affirmed by Christian theology given that the whole of the created order is thought of as owing its origin, purpose and continued existence to Christ. Indeed, in this way of thinking, the exploration or use of the order in the universe is only possible because of Christ.

Further Colossians 1.15–20 emphasizes that the God of creation is also the God of new creation by placing these ideas in parallel. Contrary to the deist-like assumption that God's work stops at the end of the first chapter of Genesis, Christian theology views God as both creator and redeemer. This reflects and extends the Jewish conviction that Israel's God, the one who delivered them from Egypt, is also the creator of the whole universe (Isaiah 40.12–31). The parallel here is expressed in the phrase 'first born'. It is used as 'over all creation' (Colossians 1.15) and then 'from the dead' (v. 18). Christ is not only the beginning of creation, he is also the beginning of the new creation, as demonstrated for the writer of Colossians by his resurrection. One of the key aspects of this new creation is reconciliation, not just of sinful men and women but of 'all things'. The canvas is of cosmic proportions and has the sense of bringing the entire universe into a new order and harmony. Indeed, within other passages of the New Testament, God's purposes are seen to go beyond this universe into a 'new heaven and new earth' (Revelation 21).

Thus, a Christian theology of creation maintains that this creation really is good, while also looking forward in the purposes of God to a new creation. This hope of a new creation is not of God completely starting again, or the hope for some kind of disembodied immaterial state, but the hope for the transfiguring fulfilment of this present creation into all that it was called into being to be. Given this combination of identity and transformation, the present created order is not to be written off as evil or unimportant, but is, rather, to be cared for, respected, enjoyed and delighted in.

2.5 The development of the theology of creation within Christian tradition

In turn, neither did Christian understanding of creation cease with the biblical writers. As Christian faith negotiated its encounter with different historical contexts, so theologians began to apply, reappraise and build upon what they had received from the biblical writers. In this process, a number of key areas emerged.

2.5.1 *Creatio ex nihilo*

What is the relationship between God and creation? In what sense does creation depend upon God? Aristotle (384–322 BCE) had argued for the eternity of the world (*Physics* I.9; *On the Heavens* I.3). In contrast, as we have seen, the biblical material stresses the universe's dependence on God for its origin and its continued existence. This, however, leaves open the question as to whether God simply shaped the universe from pre-existing matter, somewhat like an architect imposing order on matter that was ready to hand. This view, reflected in Plato's *Timaeus*, also appeared in Gnostic writers and was, in turn, used for apologetic purposes by Christian apologists such as Justin Martyr, who was executed in 165.

As has been noted, Genesis 1 polemically affirmed that God has no competitors to overcome in creation. We find a clear hint at the notion of creation out of nothing in Jewish thought in 2 Maccabees 7.28, 'I beg you, my child, to look at the heaven and the earth and see everything that is in them, and recognize that God did not make them out of things that existed.' But does Genesis 1 itself reflect such an understanding or does it see God as working with pre-existing matter? The opening image of the primordial water over which God's spirit hovered and into which God's word was spoken would seem to suggest the second option. Some have consequently claimed that the notion of 'creation out of nothing' is at best ambiguous in Genesis and only came to clear articulation as Christian faith encountered and responded to the questions and challenges of Greek philosophy and Gnostic thought (May, 1994; Young, 1991).

While recognizing, however, that the writer of Genesis 1 was much more concerned to proclaim the divinely ordained order of things than to speculate on their absolute origin, it is important to be clear that for the biblical writers there was no significant dualism of God and matter (cf. Westermann, 1984:109). On the contrary, the emergence of the doctrine of *creatio ex nihilo* in Christian writers of the second and third centuries such as Theophilus of Antioch, Irenaeus and Tertullian was driven precisely by the concern to maintain the biblical affirmations of the basic goodness of the world and of God's utterly unopposed freedom in creating. As Irenaeus expressed it, countering Gnostic dualism in *Against the Heresies*, 'God, in the exercise of his will and pleasure, formed all things ... out of what did not previously exist' (Irenaeus, 1967:II.x.2, p. 370). In turn, writing against the Manichaeans, Augustine later clarified that this meant that God created out of nothing at all (Augustine, 1961:XII.7, p. 284). In T.F. Torrance's terms:

> The creation of the universe out of nothing does not mean the creation of the universe out of something that is nothing, but out of nothing at all. It is not created out of anything – it came into being through the absolute fiat of God's word. (Torrance, 1996:207)

The profoundly scriptural point at issue here is that all that exists has its source in nothing other than the limitless possibilities for life that God is and that, as such, there is nothing that lies utterly beyond the capacity of God's creative-transforming action. Consequently, as Osborn maintained, while the actual words 'creation out of nothing' may not be found in the Bible, the concept itself resonates with the deep assertions to be found there (cf. Osborn, E., 2001:65–8). Or as Mark Worthing puts it, the doctrine is 'biblical in its seminal form, if not indeed in its full expression' (1996:76).

Torrance further argues, significantly, that this doctrine and the associated rejection of Gnosticism was important for the development of the natural sciences on account of the affirmation of the fundamental goodness of creation it represents. Creation is distinct *from* God but dependent for its existence *on* God. As such, creation is both to be valued, rather than to be escaped, and free to be investigated rather than worshipped. Along with this, God was not constrained in creating by the limitations of pre-existing matter but could create freely. Thus, to fully understand the God-given order of the universe it was necessary to observe it – the basic principle of empirical science.

This in turn prompts the question as to whether the doctrine of *creatio ex nihilo* favours particular scientific models of the origin of the universe. For example, does it favour the temporal beginning commonly associated with Big Bang models over against the eternal universe of the steady-state model proposed by Hoyle, Bondi and Gold? In this regard, R.J. Russell suggests that the notion of a historical origination of the universe provides an important corroborative meaning for the logically prior notion of the ontological origination of the universe – the belief that all that exists depends on God regardless of whether or not it had a beginning – although it is not essential to it (Russell, R.J., 1993:293–329). The relationship between historical and ontological origin lies in the concept of finitude. The fact that the universe has a finite history is not trivial, in the sense that a temporal origination of the universe can provide confirming but not conclusive or essential evidence for ontological origination. As Aquinas also recognized, at the core of the doctrine of *creatio ex nihilo* is the principle of ontological dependence, and the discovery of an actual temporal beginning to the universe would serve only as a gloss on this (Russell, R.J., 1996; cf. Aquinas, 1967:1a.46.2, p. 81). However, if *creatio ex nihilo* was viewed as a hypothesis to understand the universe then a temporal beginning could be used as confirming evidence alongside other things.

2.5.2 Aquinas, causes and design

Thomas Aquinas (*c.*1225–74) moved the theology of creation forward in a number of key ways, from the use of reflection on creation to demonstrate the reasonableness of belief in the existence of God, to the identification of natural law and its implication for human societies.

In his 'Five Ways' he famously attempted to demonstrate the existence of the transcendent cause of the world, 'to which everyone gives the name "God"' (Aquinas, 1964b:1a.2.3, pp. 13–17). This approach was based on the premiss that by examining known features of the world (e.g. causal sequences or the appearance of order), it is possible to draw universal conclusions about the relation of world and Creator. Relying on Aristotelian science, he argued that the order observable in nature is due to universal and objectively real forms that determine the nature of things. Thus, one can arrive at universally accessible truths about nature through a method which is strictly logical and argumentative, rather than depending explicitly on biblical revelation. This being said, it is important to recognize that, since he was a Dominican preacher, reflection on Scripture and the desire to give cogent expression to the world it evokes is what guided Aquinas throughout all of his theological work (see Healy, 2003). Indeed, even his high regard for human reason was guided by the conviction that, as created, the world could be assumed to be impressed with the mark of its Creator, an idea that received formal articulation in his 'analogy of being'.

While the relationships and differences between the 'Five Ways' are still debated, in broad outline we may note that where the first three ways argue to the necessary cause of the existence of the world and are varieties of the so-called 'cosmological argument', the final two lay more stress on the order and purpose in the world and are variations of the so-called 'design argument' or 'teleological argument'.

In the first way, Aquinas focuses on the fact that the world is in the process of change. This basic dynamism must, as with all change, he reasoned, have a cause. In turn, this requires a single fundamental cause, or 'first mover', since an infinite chain of movers is, he claimed, impossible or, perhaps better, less reasonable and satisfying as an explanation. Whatever this fundamental cause is, however it is to be understood, it is, Aquinas claimed, what people mean when they speak of God.

Similarly, in the second way Aquinas observed a network of cause–effect relations, or 'efficient causes' in his Aristotelian terminology, each the consequence of preceding causes. As before, he argues there must be something on which this entire causal order in turn depends for its existence. For Aquinas, God is this first cause who makes things to be and sets them in motion and which motion in turn makes other things happen. This being said, it is important to note again that for Aquinas the strict idea of a temporal beginning of creation – as distinct from its eternal dependence on God as first cause – cannot be derived on the basis of human reason, but must, rather, come from revelation. In turn, the third way differentiates between necessary and contingent beings. Human beings, for example, are contingent beings which come into existence and which can cease to exist. But contingent beings, Aquinas argues, can only come into existence if they are caused so to do by an original cause of being whose existence is there as a matter of necessity. As before, Aquinas claims that this idea of a necessary being is what people refer to when speaking of God.

The fourth way observes values in human beings such as goodness, beauty and truth. Where do such things come from, Aquinas asks. In reply he argues that the existence of such values implies that something must exist that is the most good, beautiful and true and that brings these human values into existence. That something is in fact God who is the perfect and original cause of these values. Finally, the fifth way sees intelligent design in the world, that is, things seem to be adapted with certain purposes in mind. The source of this design or natural ordering must, Aquinas reasons, in turn be some intelligent being – God – who works out God's purposes in creation.

Despite the authority that eventually came to be accorded to Aquinas' work, he was by no means without his critics in the Middle Ages, in particular Duns Scotus (1255/6–1308) and William of Ockham (1280/5–1349). For such thinkers, it was not clear that a sequence of cause and effect had to stop at a first cause. Again, why should the arguments lead inevitably to just one god rather than a number of gods. Ockham even suggested that Aquinas' arguments do not rule out that God as first cause may have started things off, but then ceased to exist.

Such disputes have, of course, continued into modern times. Most famously, Immanuel Kant (1724–1804) argued that all arguments for the existence of God ultimately depend on the truth of the failed ontological argument that Aquinas himself had rejected – the argument, that is, associated with Anselm of Canterbury (1033–1109) to the effect that the definition of God as necessary being *logically requires* the actual existence of God.

More recently, the Big Bang model of the universe has encouraged some to reconsider the cosmological argument. For example, encouraged by the work of Roman Catholic cosmologists such as Whitaker, Pope Pius XII in 1951 stated on the basis of the Big Bang model:

> Thus with that concreteness which is characteristic of physical proofs, it [science] has confirmed the contingency of the universe and also the well founded deduction as to the epoch [some five billion years ago] when the cosmos came forth from the hands of the Creator. Hence, creation took place in time. Therefore, there is a Creator. (quoted in Jaki, 1980:19)

Some distinguish here the cosmological argument used by Aquinas, from a temporal form of the argument, the so-called 'kalam argument', which derives from an Arabic school of philosophy in the early Middle Ages (see Fergusson, 1998:36–9). This argument, which clearly extends cause and effect back in time, arguing for a temporal first cause to the Big Bang, is, however, faced with a number of significant objections. First, it is not clear in terms of the nature of time whether cause and effect observed within the universe can be extended to the whole universe. Second, the spectre of what Charles Coulson called 'the god of the gaps' (Coulson, 1958:41) is always in the background of such an argument. Coulson cautioned that theologians should be cautious that if a gap exists in science, then it is dangerous to insert God into the gap. The danger is that tomorrow's science may fill in today's gaps, with the result that God is pushed out into obscurity (see 1.13, 10.3, 10.16).

Likewise, as the next chapter explores more fully, the design argument became very popular following the scientific revolution. Newton's universal law of gravitation and laws of motion suggested a mechanistic universe, carefully crafted with a purpose in mind. Careful observation of the biological world compounded this sense of design in the natural world, as it came to expression most famously in William Paley's (1743–1805) analogy of a watch. Yet its weaknesses were exposed philosophically (a) by David Hume (1711–76), who pointed to the degree of disorder or natural evil in the world as a significant countervailing fact, and (b) by Charles Darwin when he provided an alternative explanation of the apparent 'design' of the natural world in his theory of evolution by natural selection (see 6.6, 6.7). In the light of this, it is interesting that a significant element of the science–religion dialogue in the past few decades has been a revival of the design argument, particularly in the area of cosmology with the observation of anthropic balances in the laws and circumstance of the universe essential to intelligent life. Whatever might be made of such arguments viewed philosophically, it is notable in theological terms that when dislocated from Aquinas' prior concern to witness to revelation, they have often served to promote a merely deistic view of God. In fact, the rise of deism in the late seventeenth century was itself intertwined with the development of such rational arguments for the existence of God (see Buckley, 1987). Within such a perspective, the Creator is viewed as remote in the sense of having created the mechanism of the universe but then having nothing more to do with it.

Aquinas' own view, of course, was far from deism. He highlights the attempt to conceive the way in which God was thought to act in creating that had become widespread in the Christian community from the early centuries on under the influence of Neoplatonic philosophy. The central metaphor here is that of 'emanation', of all that exists as coming forth from the being of God.[4] This idea had already been used by early Christian writers with reference to the image of light or heat emanating from the Sun. It suggests a close connection between creation and Creator, such that creation is thought of as really participating in the being of the Creator.[5] With this, it suggests that creation in all its diverse particularity manifests something of the inexhaustible abundance of God's being (Aquinas, 1967:1a.47.1, p. 95) and, therefore, that by inspecting creation it should be possible to discern something of the truth of God.

Unless qualified, however, the metaphor of emanation could also imply a lack of personal intention by God in creation, as though creation simply flowed forth from God with an unwilled inevitability. In this regard, it is notable that Aquinas does indeed significantly qualify his use of the metaphor such that he thinks not in terms of 'mere overflow' but of a freely willed and gracious (i.e. unowed) overflow of the infinite richness of God's being in order to draw something other than God into existence to share in this richness of being (Aquinas, 1967:1a.46.1, p. 69). Viewed in this way, God literally has no need of creation. In keeping with God's nature as love and the infinite richness of the Trinitarian God's being in which there is no lack, creation is for creation's good, not God's (Aquinas, 1965:1a.32.1, p. 109). Further, far from disabling God from the possibility of any real concern for creation, as some have charged, this lack of need and self-interest means that God is free to be genuinely interested in creation for its own sake (Williams, R., 2000:63–78). God's will, it follows, can always be trusted as being genuinely in our best interests, rather than feared as the demands of an ultimately self-serving despot.

Alongside an emphasis on the gracious, willed character of the creative overflow of God's being, Aquinas further qualifies the metaphor of emanation by using it in conjunction with other metaphors such as that of God as artisan (Aquinas, 1964d:1a.14.8, p. 31). This is a much more personal metaphor, stressing the creative initiative of the Creator and the resulting beauty of creation. However, if the notion of emanation suffers from the potential suggestion of a sub-personal mode of creation, artisan imagery – along with a third widespread metaphor, that of construction – can tend, if unqualified, to suggest again the idea of creation from pre-existing matter. More positively, however, both the artisan image and the image of construction give clear emphasis to the intentional order of creation that is fundamental alike to the biblical witness and to Aquinas' Aristotelian-influenced view of the natural order.

For Aquinas, the ongoing relation between God and the created order is viewed both in terms of God as first cause, holding in being a hierarchically structured set of secondary causes and God as final cause, or *telos*, towards which all created secondary causes are orientated as their fulfilment which they strive to attain. In one sense, the entire created order and all that happens is within the will, or *fiat* of God. More particularly, however, the will of God is actualized to the degree that secondary causes, brought into being and held in being by God, act in accordance with their natural orientation to their supernatural end under the guidance of the Holy Spirit. This represents Aquinas' understanding of providence (see 10.9(iii)(a)). In this way God governs and sustains the world. Without God's sustaining activity everything would fall into nothingness. Without God's gracious inspiring-transformative activity nothing would reach its end.

Previously, Augustine had asserted that creation is an instantaneous act, in that everything appears the moment God brings the universe into being. However, creation continues to be completely dependent on God for its existence while being given the opportunity to pursue with a degree of independence the potential that God has granted it. For Augustine time was part of creation with the consequence, he concluded, that the universe was created not *in* time but *with* time. With such an understanding he viewed the Genesis account not as scientific history but as a revelation fitted to the limited powers of its recipients (see van Till, 1996:30). In a similar way, Aquinas saw creation as both depending on God for its existence at every moment, but as also having been granted its own integrity to unfold according to its God-given nature through the action of secondary causes striving, under the inspiring-transforming draw of God's Spirit, to achieve their desired end and fulfilment in God.

With this, along with his arguments for the existence of God, Aquinas developed the concept that nature had purposes deriving from God's design. Not only did these purposes provide evidence of God, they also gave a natural reve-lation of the end of creation. Thus God's eternal law is revealed in divine law through the scriptures and in natural law, reflected in the nature of the creation itself. If every part of creation naturally tends to seek its natural end or good, in the case of human beings this takes particular form in the search to know God and to build an ordered society reflecting the well-being of God's good order. In building such a society, in addition to the biblical commands, natural law means that human beings can identify universal and eternal moral standards. Human law is therefore built on these moral standards, and indeed the natural law provides a framework for laws in specific situations. The strength of this is that it gives the possibility of agreement on international law across different countries and cul-tures, as is evidenced in the role it played in developing concepts such as just war theory.

2.5.3 The Reformation and the growth of science

It should be clear that, with the theology of creation within the Judaeo-Christian tradition and the development of that tradition by thinkers such as Aquinas, the foundations for modern science were in place. This is evidenced, for example, in the widespread and innovative use of technology within monastic culture (see 13.4). The role of reason and search for the laws of nature built upon the origins of science from the Greeks with considerable contributions from Chinese and Muslim scholars. Combined with this was the necessary regard for the world as both good – and, therefore, to be appropriately valued and taken seriously – and contingent, or dependent on God for its order which consequently requires investigation rather than mere theorizing.

In turn, the Reformation seems to have had its own contribution to make. Certainly, in the seventeenth century it was the Protestant areas of Europe that dominated the emerging scientific revolution (Gingerich, 1982). Some have suggested that it was the criticism of scholasticism's Aristotelian-based science and the placing of emphasis on the direct observation of nature that fed through into the rapid growth of science. Others argue that the Reformation created a climate of openness to new ideas. Relevant also, particularly within the realm of technology, is Weber's famous thesis as to the relationship between the rise of capitalism and the Protestant work ethic. The history is of course complex, and it is both significant and somewhat disheartening to note that claims for the respective contributions of mediaeval and Reformation thought to the rise of science all too frequently follow strictly confessional lines of interpretation.[6] On surer ground, whatever might be said about the rise of science, it is uncontroversially the case that the theology of creation was affirmed, critiqued and built upon in Reformed theology.

Calvin (1509–64), for example, reacted trenchantly against any understanding of God on the basis of the world that was utterly independent of God's revelation. At the same time, he also reacted against the monastic tendency to renounce the world. He wanted to affirm the world, and did so by stressing both the world as created good and the world as fallen and in need of redemption. Thus, while Calvin allowed for the possibility of some knowledge of God in creation, describing it even as a theatre or mirror for displaying knowledge of God, alongside this was the qualification that such a natural knowledge of God is imperfect and confused because of sin, even to the point of contradiction – all of which, it should be noted, Aquinas also maintained, albeit in lower register. Therefore Calvin is positive about reason, logic and experience, while stressing that saving knowledge of God has to be through Christ and the regenerating work of the Holy Spirit. For Calvin, Christ is the mediator of creation, at the dual levels of both general and special providence:

> Calvin makes room in his doctrine of creation for: the Logos who orders existence and its intelligibility, and the Word incarnate through whom alone life reaches its goal; the providence which preserves all life, even after the perfidy of human sin, and the providence which especially guards the community of the elect; a humanity which bears God's image as qualities of excellence engraved by a loving hand, and a humanity which can truly mirror God's excellence and goodness only as remade in the image of Christ. (Wyatt, 1996:81)

In clearer contrast to Aquinas, however, Calvin plays down the role of secondary causes in natural processes and instead emphasizes God's immediate primary activity in creation. He argued that the immediate agency of God was to be seen not just in sustaining but in every act in the universe. For example, in the Heidelberg Catechism of 1563 the traditional threefold distinction of God's providential work into conservation, *concursus* and *gubernatio* was conflated into a view that all things come directly from the hand of God the Father. Indeed, this is also the case for new creation. The effect of sin on creation means that it has to wait for its future restoration by the redemptive activity of Christ, the saviour as well as the creator (McGrath, 2001:174–5).

Luther (1483–1546) for his part, like Calvin, affirmed the reality and goodness of creation. But like Aquinas also, he was much more impressed by God's sustaining of the universe rather than by the initial act of creation, remarking that many people have the energy to start something but few to continue it. He commented that God had 'not created the world like a carpenter builds a house and then leaves it ... but he stays with it and sustains it the way he has made it, otherwise it would not remain' (Luther, 1983:VIII.25). God had ordered everything in the world from nature to humanity and although, as Aquinas had maintained, patterns for ideal relationships could be found in natural law, this did not have compelling power for us, because of sin. Perhaps most distinctively,

Luther interpreted the Genesis texts in a strongly Trinitarian fashion (1958:9), and, indeed, more generally there does seem to be in both Luther and Calvin a move away from the language of derived causality to one of divine personal action, understood in terms of Trinitarian mediation (see Gunton, 1998:153).

Again, Luther was clearly open to the authentic scientific advances of his age, including the value of engineering, medicine and astronomy. He accepted the claims of the astronomers who suggested that the moon was the smallest and closest of the stars. As with Augustine, he likewise interpreted the opening chapters of Genesis as God accommodating his revelation to the limited understanding of the readers (see Spitz, 1971:583–4). In the light of this, it is surprising to see Luther often portrayed as a fierce opponent of Copernicus (Kearny, 1971:103; Butterfield, 1965:68; Kuhn, 1957:196). This is in large part based on an offhand remark that he is alleged to have made about Copernicus in 1539. In Luther's defence, we need to note both that disputes exist about what was actually said on the occasion in question and that, in its historical context, opposition to Copernicus represented less an opposition to science *per se* and more the prevailing dominance of Aristotelian thought combined with the lack of evidence for the new theory (Burtt, 1954:38; Kobe, 1998:190–6).

Overall, the Reformation influence on the development of the theology of creation was generally very positive for science. This was strengthened by an understanding of the stewardship responsibility given to human beings. Luther and Calvin were adamant that work outside the church was as much a matter of Christian vocation as was that of the religious orders. As a consequence, scientific work was seen as serving God, revealing the glory of God in creation and using the scientific insights for the benefit of all (Barbour, 1966:48–9). For example, Kepler commented that he had turned away from a vocation as a theologian and that 'through my effort God is being celebrated in astronomy' (quoted in Gingerich, 1993:307).

2.5.4 The modern period

From the nineteenth century to the present day there have been a whole range of important theological insights, movements and thinkers who have further shaped the theology of creation within the Christian tradition. For example, Friedrich Schleiermacher (1768–1834) – oft referred to as the 'father of modern theology' – tended to read the doctrines of creation and conservation together, with the result that the emphasis shifted from the originating to the sustaining action of God. He conceived the relationship between creation and God as one of absolute dependence, but in such a fashion as has been judged by some to diminish the role of the Son and the Spirit in the mediation of creation. In reaction to this, we have already mentioned Barth's Christocentric understanding of creation. While it is beyond the scope of this chapter to give a detailed account of the many components of this development, it will be helpful briefly to sketch a number of significant questions in modern theology which are relevant to the dialogue of science and religion. Each of them will be picked up in greater detail in the following chapters.

First, how important is science to a theology of creation? Barth has not been the only theologian with an ambivalent attitude to science. Some have reacted to the controversies surrounding evolution by trying to distance any theology of creation from scientific insights. Nevertheless, in the modern period a number of theologians have attempted to build bridges with science. Moltmann continues to bemoan the lack of dialogue on this subject between scientists and theologians and pleads for a new 'natural theology' in which scientific findings tell us something about God, and theological insights tell us something about nature (Moltmann, 2003). In a similar way, Pannenberg argues that a theology of creation must be influenced by the insights of natural science or it will become irrelevant. Equally, however, he maintains that unless God is properly considered, a scientific theory cannot fully comprehend the world it seeks to explain, as the world is only properly viewed when understood as creation rather than a purely natural phenomenon. He wants to construct a 'theology of nature', preferring this term rather than 'creation', which he argues speaks to many people simply about the origins of things rather than God's continued sustaining of the entire creative process (Pannenberg, 1989, 1993).

Such concern to think the disciplines of science and theology through together comes to particular expression in the theology of Thomas Torrance (e.g. Torrance, 1969, 1980, 1985). Where Pannenberg reacts against what he perceives as Barth's revelatory positivism, Torrance's work has an explicitly Barthian feel to it. Using insights from special and general relativity, he argues that theology should not be trapped in the analytical and dualist ways of thinking of the Newtonian worldview. Just as science attends to the reality of the material order disclosed through empirical method and hypothesis, so theology as the science of God attends to the reality of God disclosed in Christ and the Holy Spirit. As with Barth, so for Torrance the reality of the Creator God is known as we are reconciled to God in Christ. In this way, while recognizing the differences and similarities between the methods of science and theology, Torrance saw a new synthesis emerging in which science could be situated in its properly theological context (see also 4.6). Following Torrance, Alister McGrath has been engaged on pursuing a closely related project (see McGrath, 2004 for a summary).

Alongside these theologians, there has been a significant amount of work done in the theology of creation by scientist-theologians, who trained and worked as professional scientists before subsequently moving to theological work, most notably John Polkinghorne, Ian Barbour and Arthur Peacocke.[7] Typical of their approach has been the concern to look at the various specific issues that modern science has raised, whether cosmology, evolution or complex systems, and then to ask what these insights might mean for the theology of creation (see e.g. Barbour, 2000; Peacocke, 2001a; Polkinghorne, 1998a).

Second, how does God act in the world? Since the time of Aquinas, the action of God in special and general providence has been the subject of much theological debate. Dominating the concerns of some have been the difficulties posed to any notion of God acting in the world by the now outdated Newtonian worldview (so Bultmann, 1983). Others, seeking to respond to the problem of evil, have viewed God as only acting in the creating and sustaining of the world (so Wiles, 1986). Others again have built on the philosophy of Whitehead to produce a process view of God within which God is thought of as working through persuasion rather than coercion (Cobb and Griffin, 1976). While Gilkey could complain that providence had been demoted to the level of a footnote in twentieth-century theology (Gilkey, 1963), the last 40 years have seen a growth of interest. This goes beyond the simple use of the language of providence in situations of crisis that continues to play a significant role in Christian spirituality. Beyond the level of Christian piety and ordinary theology there has been a serious attempt to understand the nature of providence in any theology of creation and to bring it into dialogue with insights from the world of science. Leading the way in this field has been a series of publications sponsored in part by the Vatican (Russell, R.J. *et al.*, 1993, 1995, 1998, 1999, 2001, 2005 – for a full discussion see Chapter 10).

Third, what is God's relationship to time? This issue of God's knowledge of our future and God's relationship to time has provoked controversy among theologians. Some defend God's omniscience and foreknowledge in a classical sense (Kvanvig, 1986; Plantinga, 1987; Craig, 1991). Others argue that God cannot be totally separated from time, if he is in some form of personal relationship with creatures and the universe which takes petitionary prayer and human responsibility seriously (see Pike, 1970; Davis, 1983; Brümmer, 1984; Padgett, 1992). Following the model of the dipolar God of process theology, some theologians have suggested that God has both eternal and temporal poles to God's nature. Others use the Trinity as a way of maintaining both God's eternal and temporal aspects. Yet others speculate that God is timeless without creation and temporal subsequent to it (Ward, 1996a; Wolterstorff, 2000).

Indeed, within mainstream theology since the work of Moltmann and Vanstone, it has been fashionable to view God's creative love as being accompanied by vulnerability (Vanstone, 1977; Moltmann, 1985). Within such contemporary theologies of kenosis,[8] God is thought of as limiting Godself and as giving to humans and the universe a degree of freedom to explore potentiality. Thus, God creates through an evolutionary process that includes chance to give human beings the possibility of development but with the consequent risk of suffering (so Ward, 1996a; Murphy and Ellis, 1996). While often accepted without much criticism in European theology, this notion of God as giving openness to the future has provoked major controversy in US evangelical circles. For example, Pinnock's and Sanders' arguments for it are situated against a bitter backlash from more conservative theologians (Sanders, 1998; Pinnock, 2001; Bray, 1998; Ware, 2000 – for further discussion see Chapter 8).

Fourth, what does the theology of creation mean for our care of the environment? Subsequent to Lynn White's charge that Christian theology of creation is complicit in the environmental crisis, Christian theology has responded to his call for a 'refocused Christianity', and has looked again at its theology of creation in order to make ecology an integrating concern across the theological spectrum from feminist to evangelical theology (see Chapter 8). Alongside this, there has been a significant body of work specifically aimed at a theology of animals, from their place in a theology of creation to the ethics of their care (e.g. Birch and Vischer, 1997; Linzey, 1994).

Fifth, how does the theology of creation relate to a theology of new creation? The eschatological concern to ask what it means to live in the present in the light of God's purposes for the future consummation of things has played centre stage in much recent contemporary theology due, in no small part, to the work of Jürgen Moltmann (see Moltmann 1967, 1996). While much of this thinking has concentrated on the future of human beings or even the Earth in terms of the environmental crisis, some theologians have begun to ask what it means for creation as a whole (see Ellis, 2002; Polkinghorne, 2002; Polkinghorne and Welker, 2000; also **10.20**). Theology of creation needs, it is maintained, to take account of the end as well as the beginning of the story. For Hardy, for example, creation is what both keeps the universe from ending, and 'brings it to its end' (Hardy, 1996:157). That is, there is an important relationship, we might say, between this creation and new creation, and each needs to be seen in the light of the other.

Sixth, what is the importance of the Trinity for the theology of creation? As has been noted, this is a tradition from the early church fathers through Aquinas, Luther, Calvin and Barth and has found varying re-emphasis in contemporary theologians such as Gunton, Lash, Pannenberg and Zizioulas.[9] The Nicene Creed declares, 'We believe in one God, the Father Almighty, maker of heaven and earth ... and in one Lord Jesus Christ, the only begotten Son of God, ... of one Being with the Father, through whom all things were made ... and in the Holy Spirit, the Lord and Giver of life.' The Father creates not in isolation but through the Son in the Spirit.

Within this purview, creation is thought of as flowing from and reflecting something of the Trinitarian communion of God in which it exists. God creates not out of any need to establish communion, but rather from the freely willed desire to share this life with that which is not God. This has two significant implications. First, creation in Trinitarian perspective is radically contingent rather than necessary. Second, the deep order of things reflects God's own dynamic good order, manifest, in Christian understanding, in the person of Jesus of Nazareth and promoted in the created order through the inspiring-transforming action of the Holy Spirit.

Seventh, what is the significance of human beings in creation? This is a crucial question for the theology of creation.[10] Christian theology has attempted at times to answer this question in terms of dualism. Augustine saw soul and body, after the fashion of Plato, as two separate substances held together in an uneasy union. Aquinas, by contrast, reflected a more holistic vision inspired by Aristotle. Here soul is seen as the substantial form, or animating principle, of the matter–form composite and, hence, not as a complete substance in its own right. In the contemporary period there are still a few voices in biblical studies who continue to argue that body/soul duality is embedded in the Bible (e.g. Barr, 1992), and, with them, a larger number of Christian philosophers who see the value of body/soul dualism in describing disembodied personal existence after death (Swinburne, 1997; Hasker, 1999; Cooper, 2001). It is recognized by others, however, that such views have tended to devalue the body and by implication the physicality of the creation.

Consequently, there has been a significant movement in near recent biblical theology towards seeing the human person as a psychosomatic unity (Berger, 2003; Green, 2002). Indeed dualism rather than monism has been the minority opinion among biblical scholars over the past century (so Chamberlain, 1993).

Thus, biblical scholars argue that the dominant view of the human person is that of ontological monism, and that the overall biblical picture presents 'the human person fundamentally in relational terms' (Green, 2004:85–100). Such ideas have, likewise, become increasingly popular within contemporary systematic and philosophical theology (cf. Pannenberg, 1991–4: vol. 2.182; Murphy, 2000:99–131; Miller, 2004; also **6.3.1**).

Alongside this, feminist theologians/thealogians in particular have pointed out the importance of the body and how it has often been devalued within Christian theology of creation. In particular, sexuality has been linked to sin, with this in turn reflecting a broader understanding that the soul is good but the flesh is evil (cf. Brown, 1993). In this context, a rediscovery of the goodness of sexuality and of the body more generally has been a valuable contribution to the theology of creation (so Parsons, 1996; Ross, 1998).

2.6 Conclusion

So then, what is meant by the theology of creation within Judaeo-Christian tradition? In this brief overview we have seen that it says something about God's freedom and unique sovereignty in creating, in turn implying something about the fundamental goodness, or God-wardness, of all that exists and the consequent possibility of God's redeeming or transforming of situations. Again, we have seen that the theology of creation is not simply a conceptual belief but a code of practice, an ethic of living in the world as gift to be cherished and nurtured.

In the writings of Irenaeus, Augustine and their later successors, one finds the essential features of the historic theology of creation spelled out: creation originates in the will of the Triune Creator, is made out of nothing, and is a continuing process, the product of the outpouring of God's goodness and love and the object of God's providential care. Creation, in obedient response to God's command but in accordance with the autonomy and integrity of powers and processes graciously bestowed upon it, brings into existence over time the various forms and capacities displayed by the manifold creatures that populate the cosmos. It is a theology ready for dialogue with science. It has provided the basis for the growth of that science and, in as much as it is committed to the common reality of God's creation, should be eager to hear from and contribute to the insights of science. It is to this dialogue itself that we now turn, first historically (Chapter 3), then philosophically (Chapter 4), then with reference to specific sciences (Chapters 5–7).

Notes

1   Naturalism is an approach to explaining the world without recourse to explanations running counter to the framework of the sciences.
2   White's article is reprinted in Berry, R.J., 2000:31–42.
3   For more on stewardship see **8.6.3**.
4   Aquinas, 1964c:1a.13.11, pp. 91–3 (p. 93); also 1967:1a.45.3, pp. 35–9 (p. 37);

and 1a.45.4, pp. 39–43 (p. 41). For commentary on this and what follows, see Burrell, 2004:27–44.

5   See Aquinas, 1967:1a.44.1, pp. 5–9; and 1a.45.5, pp. 43–51 (p. 47); also 1964b:1a.3.4, pp. 31–5 (p. 33).

6   For example, where Hooykaas strongly argues for the distinctive contribution of his own Reformed tradition, the Catholic Stanley Jaki resolutely maintains the essential role of medieval theology in laying the foundations for modern science, see Jaki (1978) and Hooykaas (1972).

7   For a comparative study see Polkinghorne, 1996a.

8   The mainspring of Christian reflection on suffering comes from the suffering of Christ, and in particular the concept that Jesus 'emptied himself, taking the form of a servant' (Philippians 2.7). The word for 'self-emptied', *ekenosen*, has given theology the term 'kenosis'. For a range of applications of this concept to the theology of creation see Polkinghorne (ed.), 2001.

9   See e.g. Gunton, 1998; Lash, 1992; Pannenberg, 1991–4; Zizioulas, 1989.

10 See e.g. Gregersen *et al.* (2000); Myers and Jeeves, 2002; Barbour, 2002; Green, 2004; also **6.3.1–6.3.2** and **10.19**.

Suggested Further Reading

ASTLEY, J., BROWN, D. and LOADES, A. (eds) (2003) *Problems in Theology, 1: Creation: A Reader* (London and New York: T&T Clark)

BURRELL, D.B. (1993) *Freedom and Creation in Three Traditions* (Notre Dame: University of Notre Dame Press)

(2004) 'Act of creation with its theological consequences', in *Aquinas on Doctrine: A Critical Introduction*, ed. T.G. Weinandy, D.A. Keating and J.P. Yocum, (Edinburgh: T&T Clark International)

FERGUSSON, D.A.S. (1998) *The Cosmos and the Creator: An Introduction to the Theology of Creation* (London: SPCK)

KAISER, C. (1991) *Creation and the History of Science* (London and Grand Rapids: Marshall Pickering and W.B. Eerdmans)

WILKINSON, D. (2002) *The Message of Creation: Encountering the Lord of the Universe* (Leicester: IVP)

Chapter 3

Learning from the past

John Hedley Brooke

3.1 Introduction

It is sometimes said that the one thing we learn from history is that we never learn from history. We are apt to close our eyes to what the past might teach, pre-occupied as we inevitably are with the present and with our priorities for the future. It is of course convenient to shut out the past: there has been a lot of it, and much that seems remote from the pressing concerns of today. Scientific progress may itself contribute to a mindset in which the beliefs of past generations, having been superseded, are no longer of interest. A moment's reflection, however, shows that the present cannot so easily be dislocated from the past. Today will be history tomorrow; the beliefs and practices associated with many world religions are rooted in events that occurred centuries ago; and the acquisition of scientific knowledge has a rich and fascinating history. There has been no linear, triumphal march to a 'truth' rendered sacrosanct by virtue of its belonging to the present. In any exploration of scientific and religious views about the cosmos, it would therefore be unfortunate, even dangerous, to overlook the lessons of the past and the questions they pose.

Every generation has reflected on the big issues concerning the place of humanity in the cosmos, the meaning of human life and the possibility of higher purposes at work in the universe. Deeply divisive answers have been given in different times and places by different religious authorities, by different representatives of the same religion, and by different scientific thinkers, many of whom have tried to extract cultural and philosophical meanings from their science. In Western traditions alone there has been a rich tapestry of controversy and debate. One of the lessons of history is that many of these controversies cannot be forced into a single mould, such as the popular assumption of constant 'conflict between science and religion'.

The aim of this chapter is to see what difference a historical perspective might make to our understanding. How have the relations between scientific and religious beliefs been constructed and understood? It is an important question because those relations have often been constructed for apologetic, political or polemical purposes. In eighteenth-century England, for example, the dissenting minister and scientist Joseph Priestley (1733–1804) championed the cause of scientific progress, arguing that it would help to reduce the political power of the Anglican Church. But he also championed the cause of Unitarian religion, arguing that true

Christianity must be shorn of its irrational elements, which included the doctrine of the Trinity. It was then possible for him to say that true science and true religion were fighting on the same side against popular superstition. Priestley paid a heavy price for his radicalism when, following the French Revolution with which he had political sympathies, his house and laboratory were destroyed by a reactionary Birmingham mob. His conviction that there was no conflict between science and a purified Christianity nevertheless presents a rather different picture of the relations between science and religion than more familiar constructs.

Can historical analysis do more than open up alternative possibilities? We shall suggest an affirmative answer by surveying the several respects in which it can surprise and instruct. It will then be necessary to consider a problem that arises in any historical study: what are the criteria that guide the choice of examples? At least four master-narratives have traditionally shaped discussion of the inter-penetration of science and religion:

- the thesis of essential conflict
- the thesis of essential harmony
- the thesis that advances in science and technology have fuelled processes of secularization
- the thesis that certain developments in twentieth-century science created new spaces for human spirituality.

Each of these will be examined briefly before exploring in more detail how theological assumptions could be, and have been, relevant to the sciences. Finally, we shall return to our main question: what are the lessons from history and how might they shape our questions about God, humanity and the cosmos?

3.2 Why history?

A powerful justification for the study of philosophy is that it helps to correct bad philosophy. The study of history has a comparable justification in the opportunity it affords to correct bad history. Popular literature on science and religion is full of myths and misperceptions that are often passed uncritically from one author to another. Examples might be that Galileo was imprisoned for believing the Earth to be round, a proposition one hears from time to time. Or that the triumph of science over religion was secured in 1860 when, at a meeting of the British Association for the Advancement of Science in Oxford, Charles Darwin's 'bulldog', Thomas Henry Huxley, scored a resounding victory over an ignorant and impertinent Bishop, Samuel Wilberforce. Or again that science and religion coexisted peacefully in the West until very recently; or conversely that they were at war until very recently when a peaceful coexistence finally became possible. The contradiction between these last two propositions calls into question the very attempt to make such sweeping generalizations.

3.2.1 Myths and misconceptions: the Galileo Affair

In correcting mythologies, it would be necessary of course to observe that the issue in the Galileo Affair (see 1.12) was not the rotundity of the earth but its rotation about its axis and its annual revolution around the sun. Galileo's trial in 1633 for his vigorous defence of the Copernican system was indeed a suppression of freedom (though it led to house arrest not imprisonment); but his clash with Pope Urban VIII, who had earlier shown him respect, arose not so much from an inherent conflict between 'science' and 'religion' as from a constellation of philosophical disagreements and political circumstances. Whereas Galileo used the phenomenon of the tides to argue for the real motion of the earth, Urban VIII considered the conclusion premature because it would surely be possible for an omnipotent God to have devised other mechanisms to produce the tidal oscillations? If the conflict was unavoidable, its inevitability arose largely from the fact that the Roman Catholic Church had endorsed the natural philosophy of Aristotle with its common-sense arguments for the earth's immobility. It was the sun one saw moving and it was difficult to understand why, if the earth were in motion, an object dropped from the top of a tower should land at its foot rather than some way behind.

3.2.2 Myths and misconceptions: the Darwinian controversies

The legend of Huxley's triumph over Wilberforce (3.2) makes a marvellous anecdote. The Bishop had taunted Huxley: would he prefer to think of himself descended from an ape on his grandfather's or grandmother's side? Huxley's famous retort was that he would not mind an animal ancestry but that he *would* mind having for an ancestor a person who used his intelligence and privileged position to introduce ridicule into the discussion of a serious matter. The implication was obvious and Huxley is often reported as having said that he would rather have an ape for an ancestor than a bishop. The event has come to symbolize the victory of professional science over clerical amateurism. But corrections to the mythology are again necessary. Even Huxley's son Leonard, who made the story famous more than thirty years after the event, conceded that his father had not won a victory. A majority of the audience would have been on the bishop's side. Nor was Wilberforce such an ignoramus on scientific matters. He had studied with the celebrated anatomist and palaeontologist Richard Owen and, in an extensive review of Darwin's *Origin of Species*, he put the spotlight on the weakest parts of the argument. Darwin himself described the review as 'uncommonly clever' (Darwin, 1860).[1] And just as the Catholic Church in Counter-Reformation Italy could appeal to earlier scientific authorities to justify its stance towards Galileo, so Wilberforce was able to appeal to scientists of the calibre of Owen and Charles Lyell to underline what he saw as a lack of rigour in Darwin's bold hypothesizing. Huxley undoubtedly showed courage in deflating the Bishop so publicly, but the latest research suggests that the event left few traces during the ensuing thirty years. Ironically, instead of anti-Darwinians being converted by Huxley, at least one Darwinian was de-converted in the debate. This was Henry

Baker Tristram, who, in studying the darker colour of desert larks in North Africa, had been one of the first to apply Darwin's principle of natural selection. The darker birds, Tristram had suggested, would be less visible to desert predators. But we are told that, during the Wilberforce–Huxley debate, he 'waxed exceedingly wroth as the discussion went on and declared himself more and more anti-Darwinian' (Cohen, 1985:589–607).

Anecdotes about apes and angels abound in the post-Darwinian debates, but the historical reality was far richer than a simple opposition between evolutionary science and conservative religion. One of the valuable features of historical research is that it reveals the middle positions, the efforts at mediation, the refusal on the part of cultivated minds to accept the polarities that so often structure unsophisticated debate. The anatomist and palaeontologist Richard Owen, to whom Wilberforce deferred, makes a striking example of an eminent scientist who refused to concur either with Darwin's mechanism of natural selection or with a theory of supernatural acts of creation. Owen, who coined the word 'dinosaur' and who was the prime mover behind the Natural History Museum in London, interpreted the history of life on earth as the unfolding of a divine plan, effected through 'natural' causes. The process was one of continuous creation: an archetypal idea in the mind of God (an idealized vertebrate skeleton) was instantiated in each living vertebrate. The point here is not whether Owen turned out to be correct but that such intermediate positions were available to those engaged in controversy. It was not that difficult in Victorian Britain to see evolution as a method of creation. Darwin himself had referred to a Creator creating 'through laws', and he was pleased to find clergymen such as Charles Kingsley and Frederick Temple among his early converts (see 6.7).

3.3 The concept of science, viewed historically

When speaking of 'science' and 'religion' it is a common mistake to imagine that these two words have meanings that are timeless – as if there were a defining essence of each and therefore of the relationship between them. The challenge that history poses arises from the fact that the theoretical content of the sciences has changed with time and that religious principles have undergone reformation and reformulation. It is a challenge that runs deeper still because the meanings of the word 'science' and of the word 'religion' have changed over time. 'Science' once meant any organized body of knowledge, making it possible to see theology as a science, even as 'queen of the sciences' for some medieval thinkers. During the period from the middle of the sixteenth century to the end of the seventeenth, when what it is often called the 'scientific revolution' occurred, reference was often made to the principles of 'natural philosophy', a discipline that for Isaac Newton (1642–1727) included reference to the attributes of God. The task of natural philosophy, as Newton saw it, was to deduce causes from their effects until one arrived at the great First Cause, on which all ultimately depended. The important lesson is that it can be anachronistic to ask how the scientists of the past 'reconciled' their faith with their science. The question assumes there would necessarily have been a need for reconciliation when possibly none existed. It also assumes a clear separation of scientific and theological discourse before such a divorce had been achieved. It was certainly not achieved by Newton, for whom space was constituted by the omnipresence of God and for whom the mathematical principles underlying the orderly motions of the planets pointed to a deity no less skilled in mechanics and geometry than Newton himself (Newton, 1713).

Historical examples also bring the humanity back into science; for scientists, like everyone else, have their hopes and fears, their hunches and their disappointments, their beautiful theories and cherished beliefs. Such beliefs can of course be secular, atheistic or agnostic; they can also be 'religious' in the sense of belonging to particular faith traditions. On this point historical analysis has even more to teach, because a person's beliefs may change with time. Could so wonderful a universe as this be the product of chance alone? Darwin thought not and denied that he had ever been an atheist. But he did become increasingly agnostic as he grew older. This means there is no simple answer to questions such as 'What did Newton, or Darwin or Einstein believe about the relation of God to the cosmos?' Even as an agnostic, Darwin admitted that his beliefs often fluctuated (Desmond and Moore, 1991:622–37).

At the heart of modern scientific culture is the belief that the personal beliefs of the scientist, whether religious or political, must not be allowed to influence the interpretation of data. The disinterestedness of scientific knowledge has been one of its self-commending virtues. There is something of an asymmetry here, because it is not uncommon to find popularizers of science using current scientific thinking to attack or defend ideological beliefs. Darwin's theory of evolution would be an obvious example of a resource used to attack the Christian faith (see 6.7, 6.13.1–6.13.4). It is often implied in such polemics that, once one understands the science, certain metaphysical or theological conclusions must follow – as if they are logically entailed by the theory or facts in question. Historical sensitivity is particularly valuable here because many examples would show the ambivalence of scientific theories as a cultural resource. Rarely do they *entail* a metaphysical conclusion. The mechanistic universe of the seventeenth century, in which nature was compared to the cathedral clock of Strasbourg, might be used to promote the view that nature is autonomous and can run by itself. But this was far from being the only possible conclusion. Even if the universe ran like clockwork, it might be thought to indicate a transcendent designer since clocks are not the kind of things that design and make themselves. Clocks are also made for a purpose, so the analogy could be used to support theistic conclusions about a divine purpose pervading the cosmos. In short, history should make us more critical, and a little humbler, when assessing the cultural implications of science. It brings to light the existence of predispositions in those who presume to dictate what the implications are.

3.4 The problem of selectivity

References to a scientific or to a religious understanding of the cosmos face an immediate difficulty. Whose science and whose religion do we have in mind? Can we even assume an overarching unity among the sciences themselves? Historically there have certainly been occasions when two or more scientific disciplines have diverged in their methods and conclusions, as when physicists, notably William Thomson (Lord Kelvin) (1824–1907), advocated a younger earth than most geologists, in the second half of the nineteenth century, required. Differences between the world's major religions have also manifested themselves in divergent accounts of divine activity in the cosmos. The voices of Jews, Christians and Muslims, Buddhists and Hindus were heard in reflections on the tsunami disaster of 26 December 2004 when at least 250,000 people lost their lives on the shores of the Indian Ocean. Many different responses were to be found within each tradition, but it is clear that some sentiments possible for a Muslim (that the event has to be ascribed to the inscrutable will of Allāh) might not be possible for a Buddhist. For a Jew the very attempt to rationalize might be inappropriate, one of the lessons of the book of Job. A Hindu might stress the spark of divinity in all human beings, visible in the compassionate global response. The irrepressible question why a merciful Creator should allow such appalling suffering is often answered by Christians with a denial that God is complicit in such 'natural' disasters and by affirming the loving presence of a God who, in the person of Christ, has also suffered. But this is scarcely a question for the Buddhist who takes suffering as a given and already denies the existence of a Creator.[2]

Such differences can have consequences for philosophies of nature and especially for the way in which the forces of nature have been understood. Because of his strong monotheism Newton would not concede that the principle of gravity was an innate property of matter. That would have been too materialistic a view. Rather, the law that the gravitational force obeyed had been freely chosen by the Creator. That the inverse square relation was simple, elegant and so prevalent in nature was testimony to a transcendent intelligence.

There is much work to be done to reveal the different contributions made to science by different religious cultures and the degree to which scientific knowledge has been valued by them. The need for discrimination was already clear to Newton at the end of the seventeenth century. In his opinion the natural sciences had prospered in monotheistic cultures, the belief in one God providing a rationale for the unity and intelligibility of the universe. With an appropriate selection of examples, this is a thesis that might still be rendered plausible. But how *should* we select our examples? Here we encounter a major problem because another of the lessons of history is that history itself can so easily be slanted to support a hidden agenda. It is not surprising that Christians often take a special interest in scientists such as Robert Boyle (1627–91), Michael Faraday (1791–1867) and James Clerk Maxwell (1831–79), who combined a Christian piety with innovative science. It is not surprising that Muslims wish to celebrate the advances in optics, algebra and astronomy made during the 'Golden Age' of Islam (see 12.5); nor that Jews might take a special delight in the scientific achievements of Jewish emigrants from Germany in the middle years of the twentieth century. Hindus might relish the fact that evolutionary motifs have featured in their philosophies of nature more perhaps than in other religious traditions.[3] Buddhists might be expected to enjoy the high profile given to their meditation techniques in recent brain-imaging experiments. The problem arises when a special relationship is claimed between one faith tradition and the sciences, such that the predispositions and contributions of other cultures are demeaned or obscured. Underlying that problem is another: when scientific practices can be discerned in a culture dominated by a particular religion, it may be difficult to show that the science was a consequence of the religion. It is true that science and monotheism have often gone hand in hand; but, in the modern period, so have science, materialism and atheism.

Is it then possible to write a dispassionate history, free from the personal bias of the historian? Almost certainly not. In the very issues chosen for discussion, preferences intrude. There is, however, a case for trying to stand back and at least being open to possibilities that one might not have considered. This is the exciting consequence of exposing oneself to serious scholarship in religious history and the history of science. There have been more things in heaven and earth than we are apt to dream of.

3.5 Four master narratives

3.5.1 The thesis of conflict

A common approach to the historical record is based on the premiss that *scientific and religious ways of thinking are not only different but also destined to collide*. Contrasts between them can be drawn in many ways, but they often boil down to the assertion that religious beliefs are less well grounded than those of science because they involve faith commitments and appeals to traditional sources of authority. New forms of science, especially if they pose a threat to sacred texts, are likely to produce conflict. And so they often have. In many contexts, radical science has clashed with conservative religion. And the conflict makes for a good story because the clashes have often been colourful. Galileo ridiculed as 'mental pygmies' those who would not take his science seriously. When Andrew Dickson White published his influential *History of the Warfare of Science with Theology in Christendom* (1896), he relished the opportunity to enumerate the many hapless bell-ringers across Europe who had met an unnecessary death because their churches had been slow to fit lightning rods. White implied that this unforgivable sloth derived from the belief that to use the new technology would be a presumptuous meddling with providence. There is little evidence that this was the case. After all there was rarely opposition to medical intervention on such grounds.

There are of course more solid reasons why the conflict model is difficult to dislodge. Scientific discoveries can be corrosive of a religious faith. In one of his early novels, *Two on a Tower*, Thomas Hardy exploited the vast number of stars, visible only through the telescope, to argue that because they could not have been made for humankind, nothing had been. This was not perhaps the most valid of arguments but it captured an important psychological consequence of new scientific knowledge. In so greatly expanded a universe and in one so greatly extended in time, was it not naive to imagine that on this speck of Earth were beings in whom a deity really took an interest? In other contexts the conflicts are less subtle: the contemporary movement known as young-earth creationism in the United States, with its depiction of Adam walking with the dinosaurs,

deliberately sets itself in opposition to an intellectual elite of evolutionary biologists who, unsurprisingly, find its 'science' derisory.

There are many reasons why the conflict narrative, though applicable to certain
issues, has proved unsatisfactory and inadequate as a guide to the richness of
debate. It does focus on the extreme positions, as one of its nineteenth-century
advocates, John Draper, admitted in the introduction to his *History of the Conflict
between Religion and Science* (1874). It has difficulty in accommodating the many
scientists who have seen their science and religion as complementary, rather than
contradictory, aspects of their lives. It also overlooks the vitality of a long tradition of natural theology (see 1.3.1), in which arguments for the existence and
attributes of God were reinforced with evidence from the latest science. The use of
Newton's science to combat atheism would be a telling example, Newton having
insisted that the ordered motions of the planets could never have emerged by
chance. In one of the classic works of this genre, William Paley's *Natural Theology*
(1802), the unity of the universe described by Newton, in which the law of
gravitation was deemed to be universal, was used to argue for the unity of God.
The intricate 'designs' of anatomical structures, the sometimes marvellous adaptation of living creatures to their environments, even the laws of nature themselves
were used by Paley and many others, before and after him, to celebrate divine
wisdom and ingenuity (see Brooke, 1991: ch. 6; and 6.10.5).

3.5.2 The thesis of harmony

Not surprisingly then, as a counterpoint to the conflict narratives, *the metaphor of
harmony* has been used to construct a quite different historical account. The
possibility outlined earlier of conciliatory middle positions, the realization that
many of the great scientists have held strong, if not always orthodox, religious
beliefs, and the fact that the study of nature can generate a sense of awe and
beauty, have fostered arguments to the effect that the practice of science can itself
be a religious activity. Such were the regular patterns seemingly imposed on
nature, and the seemingly exquisite craftsmanship discernible in the minutest of
creatures, that Boyle could say, in the seventeenth century, that only those who
had *not* studied nature could be atheists.

During the eighteenth century David Hume (1711–76) and Immanuel Kant
(1724–1804) demonstrated that the appearance of design in nature could not be
used to prove the existence, or establish the attributes, of a Creator. The argument
to a transcendent designer depended on the analogy between the universe and a
human artefact such as a clock, but Hume was able to show how fragile the
analogy was. One could just as easily compare the universe to an organism, in
which case the cause of the universe might not be a creator but an egg or seed.
And even if the universe did resemble a machine, this could not prove that it was
the product of one mind since in the construction of some machines, a ship for
example, many hands and minds were involved. In his critique Kant observed that
the most the argument could show was that there might have been a craftsman
working with pre-existing material. It could not show there was a Creator who
had made the world from nothing. The loss of a *proof* of God's existence does not,

however, necessitate the conclusion that science and religious faith could no longer be harmonized. In fact Kant acknowledged that belief in a designed and regulated universe had provided inspiration for scientific work.

The motif of an underlying harmony between science and religion has some-times led to the stronger claim that, when both are properly understood, there cannot or need not be a conflict at all. It has even produced a revisionist literature in which it is claimed that, without a doctrine of creation, there would have been no modern science. With greater specificity, but less plausibility, it has been claimed that without a *Christian* doctrine of creation there would have been no modern science. We shall examine this controversial claim more closely in the next section. Meanwhile we should note a problem with the harmonizing approach that will take us to the third metanarrative. The problem concerns the cumulative effect of successive attempts at harmonization. It is not difficult for the historian to show that for each new and challenging scientific disclosure there will be religious thinkers able to harmonize the innovation with their deepest beliefs. During the first half of the nineteenth century, for example, there was a sequence of revelations from the geological sciences, each of which provoked a readjustment (rarely a rejection) of Christian beliefs. A far older earth was harmonized with Scripture by exploiting the gap that could be found between 'In the beginning . . .' and the first 'day' of the Genesis narrative. The Oxford geologist William Buckland was attracted to this view for a while (see Brooke, 1991:272–3). When it transpired that new species had appeared sequentially, separated by larger intervals of time, a new harmony was found by regarding the Genesis days as symbols of long geological epochs. When it transpired that there had been death in the animal kingdom long before humans had appeared, and for which the 'fall' of Adam could not then be held responsible, other saving moves were found. When it was no longer possible to avoid the conclusion that the fossil record pointed to the disturbing and oppressive fact of extinction, yet another harmon-izing scheme appeared. This was the idea of progressive creation. At succeeding points in time the deity had arranged for the extermination of one set of creatures to make way for another. The old idea that God had made every creature it was possible to make was still preserved. It was just that they had not all coexisted simultaneously. Pointing to patterns of increasing complexity as one ascended the stratigraphical column, it was still possible to see evidence of providence at work. Many were the texts produced to show that the order of creation in Genesis matched, at least roughly, the findings of palaeontology. With each new step in geology, a new harmonization was achievable. But the cumulative effect of repeated readjustments could lead to a threshold beyond which one might sud-denly find oneself making a larger reorientation, perhaps even renouncing the whole attempt to find consonance between science and Scripture. By 1859, when Darwin published his theory of natural selection, critics of the various harmon-ization schemes were arguing that the best strategy for peaceful coexistence was to abandon any pretence that the Bible had authority in matters of natural science. This was the conclusion of one contributor to *Essays and Reviews* (1860), C.W. Goodwin, who declared that 'the spectacle of able and . . . conscientious writers engaged in attempting the impossible is painful and humiliating' (Goodwin, 1860:250). There is a danger that histories regulated by the idea of harmony might miss the longer-term effects of scientific change and the paradoxical consequences of too much harmonization.

3.5.3 The thesis of secularization

Not surprisingly then, a third kind of story is often told – one in which there is room for both conflict and harmony but where a longer perspective is offered on the effects of scientific progress and technological innovation. *The guiding concept here is that of secularization.* Put very simply, science and technology are seen as major contributors to the process whereby religious beliefs and institutions have been marginalized in the modern world. The sciences have led to a secularization of knowledge, new technologies have delivered such power over nature that their exponents are sometimes accused of 'playing God'. New medicines have removed that direct sense of dependence on God, which in times past found expression in doctrines of providence. If one source of religious belief was fear and ignorance of natural forces, as Thomas Hobbes supposed, then it would seem reasonable that the elimination of ignorance, through the sciences, would render religious beliefs more precarious. It is certainly part of the culture of science that, in seeking explanations for the hitherto inexplicable, only naturalistic explanations are to be tolerated. In the English-speaking world an aesthetic revulsion against the idea of supernatural intervention was gradually coming to dominate the sciences by the middle of the nineteenth century. Darwin expressed it succinctly when in his *Autobiography* he wrote that the more we learn of the fixed laws of nature, the more incredible do miracles become (Darwin, 1958:86).

One of the more important lessons of history is that it is actually quite difficult to pinpoint a time when the presupposition that nature was a closed inviolable system of causes and effects came to dominate intellectual life. This is because the timeframe varied from one European society to another and because there would always be some dissenting voices. In France explicitly atheistic philosophies of nature can be found by the middle of the eighteenth century, publicized by luminaries such as Denis Diderot and Baron d'Holbach. In Britain, the exclusion of divine intervention from the history of nature could still evoke animosity a hundred years later, as when the Edinburgh publisher Robert Chambers went into print, anonymously, with his *Vestiges of the Natural History of Creation* (1844). This contained an account of species transformation fifteen years before Darwin published, and was both reviled and widely read. It was condemned by the Cambridge geologist and cleric Adam Sedgwick as a work of 'base materialism', which turned 'morality into moonshine' (see also 6.5).

If this aspect of secularization is hard to pin down, it is nevertheless possible to identify shifts in sensibility, particularly during the eighteenth century, which could be said to reflect a growing desacralization of nature. At the close of the seventeenth century, Newton was still affirming the activity of God in both creating and maintaining the solar system. By the close of the eighteenth, Laplace (see 1.17) was explaining how the solar system could have originated from the condensation of a swirling nebular mass circling the sun. At the close of the seventeenth century Thomas Burnet composed a *Sacred History of the Earth*, in which events recorded in the Bible, such as Noah's flood, were deemed responsible for major physical changes. A hundred years later, in James Hutton's *Theory of the Earth* (1795), the word 'sacred' has disappeared and endless cycles of mountain-building and erosion obscure any evidence of a beginning. In seventeenth-century works of natural history, such as John Ray's *Wisdom of God manifested in the Works of Creation* (1691), the meaning of the word 'creation' included the notion that, from its inception, the Earth and its contents had remained essentially unchanged. A century later, Jean-Baptiste Lamarck (1744–1829), was proposing a systematic theory of evolution in which what had once been 'creatures' were described as products of nature. In the writings of a seventeenth-century chemist, Robert Boyle, there had still been a fascination with the spirit world and the belief that, in his mental life, there could be direct communication with a God capable of supplying 'pregnant hints' for his scientific work. By the end of the eighteenth century, Joseph Priestley had banished spirits from both chemistry and theology. And as for the idea that God could directly influence the human mind, this, for Priestley, was a prime example of superstition.

And so the story could be continued. During the first half of the nineteenth century, as we saw in introducing the secularization thesis, a science of geology was forged, gradually denuded of biblical reference. With the subsequent revolutions of thought associated with Darwin and Freud came further blows to human dignity. It all adds up to a plausible story in which the sciences have been primary agents of secularization. While there can be no doubt that gods devised to patch up scientific theories have been progressively marginalized by scientific progress; another of the lessons of history is that processes of secularization may not be entirely irreversible and that religious beliefs and institutions can be remarkably resilient. Advances in science have often been particularly welcomed by religious thinkers, as when Louis Pasteur (1822–95) was perceived to have disproved the spontaneous generation of living things. Even Darwin's theory of evolution has found favour with many Christian commentators because, on Darwin's own interpretation, it showed that all human races ultimately have a common origin. It also permitted more sophisticated models of divine creativity than the older models of divine intervention, which had made God something of a magician who had conjured up new species out of nothing.

The revival of religious movements and convictions in some of the technologically most advanced nations has also cast doubt on the secularization model.

3.5.4 The thesis that certain developments in twentieth-century science created new spaces for human spirituality

In a fourth kind of narrative something quite different is proposed – that developments in twentieth-century science, far from eroding religious belief, have created new spaces for the sacred. The argument has taken several forms, usually starting from the assertion that the new science of quantum mechanics became the basis for less deterministic models of nature at the sub-atomic level. Although it was still understood that one state of a physical system gave rise to the next, the fact that a quantum-mechanical description could not be given without reference to probabilities suggested that each state was only one of several possibilities permitted by its antecedent. This enabled Werner Heisenberg (1901–76) to say that the new physics had restored the concept of potentiality in nature. For some this could also mean a restoration of human freedom. The fact that it proved impossible to know simultaneously both the position and momentum of an electron sparked an enduring debate: is the limitation merely a limitation of the knowing subject or does it reflect something deep in the structure of nature (see 5.11)? It is a question that also arises in the context of recent chaos theory and our inability to predict the future states of systems that are highly sensitive to the values of the initial parameters (see 5.26, also 10.10(iii)). In quantum physics, the need for complementary wave and particle models to capture the behaviour of electrons encouraged some commentators to speak of the complementarity, not opposition, between scientific and religious perspectives. And the realization that, in making measurements at the quantum level, the observer affected the outcome encouraged more holistic understandings of our relationship to nature. For Niels Bohr, who along with Heisenberg developed what became known as the Copenhagen interpretation of quantum mechanics, there was an analogy between the way the subject disturbs the object when conducting experiments at the sub-atomic level and the way the subject disturbs the object when interrupting a stream of consciousness to 'observe' it through introspective analysis. Though attempts to reinstate divine activity in the world by postulating undetectable manipulation of quantum probabilities are deeply problematic (see 10.9(iv)(b), 10.12), there is no doubt that twentieth-century physics did expose the limitations of a purely mechanistic conception of nature.

An example of a popular and influential metanarrative based on the supposedly redeeming features of twentieth-century science would be Fritjof Capra's *The Tao of Physics* (1975). Capra's argument in a nutshell was that an older physics, derived from the mechanistic philosophies of Descartes and Newton, not only detached the human observer from the world under observation, but also encouraged the exploitation of natural resources in ways that led eventually to our ecological crises (see 8.4). In his view, the Christian religion had done little to mitigate the consequences. In the opinion of the historian Lynn White Jr it had actually made matters worse by emphasizing the unique privileges given to humanity according to the book of Genesis (see 8.4, also 2.3.2). The privilege of dominion over nature could easily translate into a principle of domination. Both White and Capra have been widely cited in New Age literature, Capra especially because of his additional claim that a holistic understanding of nature sits more comfortably with the insights of Eastern religions than with Hebraic and Christian models. These are issues that will not be pursued here since they are discussed elsewhere in the book, but it should be noted that Capra's story depends on a more or less complete discontinuity and disjunction between classical and quantum mechanics, a disjunction which can be shown to be exaggerated (Brooke and Cantor, 1998:77–101).[4]

3.6 Mapping mutual relevance

The four metanarratives summarized above by no means exhaust the possibilities. But enough has been said to show that no one model can capture a complex, multifaceted history. These various stories do, however, have one feature in common. They assume the mutual relevance and not the separate compartmentalizing of scientific and religious interests. It therefore becomes important to look more closely at some of the ways in which metaphysical and religious beliefs have been relevant to science. As a test case, let us return to the controversial claim that, without a Christian doctrine of creation, there would have been no modern science.

If the claim is that modern science was created by Christianity it is surely overstated. A more sophisticated formula would be that, during the seventeenth century in Europe, the Christian religion, in both Catholic and Protestant variants, provided a set of resources that could be appropriated and reinterpreted in ways that helped to justify scientific activity. This is not the same as saying that scientific investigation and Christianity were related as effects to a cause. There were, nevertheless, resources within Christendom that became relevant to the promotion of scientific activity, even if these have sometimes been exaggerated (Jaki, 1978; Hooykaas, 1972).

At the most basic level, the assumption of a divine Creator and lawgiver, whose will had been expressed in the order of nature, could provide a metaphysical guarantee that there were 'laws' to be discovered. The most mechanistic of the natural philosophers, René Descartes (1596–1650), described his scientific quest as a search for the laws that God had impressed upon matter. Two hundred years later Charles Darwin (1809–82) would still be using that same image, of a deity who had legislated for nature. One can of course identify regularities in nature without giving them theological meaning; but it is striking how many of the great names of seventeenth-century science presented their discoveries in theological language. When the astronomer Johannes Kepler (1571–1630) found an elegant mathematical correlation between the period of a planet's orbit and its mean distance from the sun he spoke ecstatically of the rapture he experienced at the spectacle of heavenly harmony. As with Copernicus before him and Newton later, he found great beauty in a planetary system focused on, and imaginatively viewed from, the sun.

One of the greatest diplomats for experimental science, Francis Bacon (1561–1626), found other resources within a Protestant Christianity. He was able to stress an analogy between God's two books – the book of God's word (the Bible) and the book of God's works (the world of nature). As there was a duty to study the former, there was a corresponding duty to study the latter. To celebrate the magnificence of creation could be a way of glorifying the Creator. An experimental method had the virtue of encouraging humility, which Bacon opposed to the dogmatism and sterility of scholastic philosophy. Precisely because God had been free to create whatever world God wished, the only way to discover which of the many possibilities had been instantiated was not to indulge in armchair reasoning but to conduct an empirical investigation. With a suitable reinterpretation Bacon even turned the doctrine of Adam's 'fall' to advantage. Bacon knew that the story of Adam and Eve in the Garden of Eden had been used as a morality tale to admonish those who were selfishly prying into the secrets of nature. But a science pursued for the glory of God and for the relief of man's estate was a very different matter. Sciences linked, for example, to the improvement of medicine and agriculture were surely permissible, promising a restoration of the dominion of nature that humanity had lost at the 'fall'.

The promotion of science in religious terms was not confined to Protestants. It has, however, been argued that Protestant readings of Scripture tended to be more literal, less symbolic and allegorical than before, with corresponding changes to the way the book of nature was read (Harrison, 1998). Instead of seeing objects in nature as religious symbols or emblems, it became more important to study the relationships between them and the uses to which they could be put. Even fleas were found to have a use – by their own form of blood-letting they spared the poor expensive medical attention. Protestant exegesis also tended to favour single unique meanings for biblical texts, a disposition that had its equivalent in Newton's quest for definitive interpretations of natural phenomena. At the same time, Catholic natural philosophers were at the forefront of the mechanization of nature: Mersenne and Descartes, Galileo and Gassendi contributed in different ways to a new worldview in which natural phenomena were explained by changing patterns of matter in motion (Brooke, 1991:117–51). Not all adopted an atomic theory of matter, but Gassendi, for example, did try to revive the atomic philosophy of Epicurus. The problem was that, in antiquity, atomism had been associated with atheism, with the view that worlds passed in and out of being by the chance collision of atoms. A Christian response to the problem was possible because one could argue that atoms left to their own devices could never produce an integrated world that had all the appearance of design. Without the ultimate control of a deity it was inconceivable that a viable cosmos could have resulted from random atomic motions. An emphasis on the reality of design helped to combat the atheistic connotations of atomism and the negative theology of Thomas Hobbes (1588–1679), who denied that it was possible to know anything of the deity through rational inference from nature. By emphasizing the designs of an original Creator, it was possible to justify the search for nature's hidden mechanisms. In England Boyle insisted that some at least of God's designs could be known: how could one doubt that the human eye had been made to see with? Not until Darwin did that rhetorical question lose its force, and even Darwin confessed that he shivered whenever he thought of the eye.[5]

During the formative period of European science theological concerns were frequently expressed in discussions of scientific method. We have already seen Bacon's adoption of a voluntarist theology of creation to justify an experimental approach.[6] Newton would also stress the freedom of the divine will when attacking the rationalism of Descartes. That all the planets circled the sun in the same direction was ultimately due to the free choice of the Creator who incorporated beauty into creation. References to beauty have recurred many times in the history of science because there is no doubt that theories have been especially valued when they have exhibited simplicity, elegance and beauty. They have to fit the facts, of course, and they are specially valued when they make fertile new predictions; but the ancillary epistemic virtues of economy, elegance and beauty have frequently been invoked in theory appraisal (cf. 1.7 and the 'aside' in 6.12). The appreciation of beauty in nature and in descriptions of nature does not compel one to ascribe the beauty to a deity; but the association has often been a strong one. It is perhaps best epitomized by a great scientist who was not a Christian: Albert Einstein. When presented with a new scientific theory, Einstein once remarked, he would ask himself whether, if he had been God, he would have made the world that way. A Christian geologist of the nineteenth century, the Scottish evangelical Hugh Miller (1802–56), was deeply impressed by the fact that the most beautiful forms of human architecture, such as the structures in Gothic cathedrals, were precisely those found among fossil forms, even though there had been no conscious imitation. For Miller this was corroboration of a Christian doctrine of creation according to which humans had been made in the image of God. Miller could share the same aesthetic appreciation with his Maker.

Connections such as these reveal something of the intimate relations between science and Christianity in the West. They undermine the view, sometimes heard from representatives of other faith traditions, that Christianity, unlike their religion, has been obstructive to the sciences. But do they show that science was the creation of Christianity? Not really. The complications are too great. What of the scientific achievements of antiquity, of Archimedes who so impressed Galileo with his application of mathematics to physical problems, or of Pythagoras who so impressed Newton with the mathematical ratios underlying musical intervals? What of the scientific learning of the Arabs, so respected by Roger Bacon in the thirteenth century? Studying the science of optics, Bacon was indebted to the research of Ibn al-Haytham (see 12.5), who had investigated the reflection and refraction of light and whose successor al-Farisi suggested that a glass globe filled with water could be used as a model for examining the passage of light through a raindrop – the very technique later used in the West by Descartes in a famous study of the rainbow. Many other examples could be given of Arabic initiatives in extending and not merely transmitting the science of the Greeks. They are discussed in Chapter 12.

While it is true that Christian teaching on the constancy of God could help to reinforce ideas about the order and uniformity of nature, popular Christian culture embraced a widespread belief in supernatural intervention that was distinctly less conducive to the search for nature's regularities. Another objection – that early scientists would naturally use theological language to avoid persecution – is too crude. Each case has to be assessed by examining the biography of the subject concerned. But it is true that statements affirming harmony between Christian teaching and the disclosures of science were sometimes a response to situations in which the scientist felt threatened or under suspicion. Galileo's argument that the language of Scripture had been accommodated to the needs of the common people, and should not therefore be used to contest the findings of technical science, was by no means uncommon. It had been commended earlier by John Calvin (1509–64), who had insisted that one should not look to the Bible for a grounding in astronomy. But this tactical appeal to biblical accommodation was employed by Galileo when he already knew that his academic enemies were invoking the authority of the Church against him. An important lesson of history is that there is a difference between motivation and justification. It is very difficult to prove that Christianity provided decisive motivation for particular scientific studies. That they could be *justified* by reference to Christian principles is a different matter and perfectly demonstrable. Recent research has shown that several seventeenth-century naturalists in England who were also clergymen were conscious that their scientific pursuits were being perceived as a self-indulgent digression from their professional duties (Feingold, 2002). They naturally sought arguments for the spiritually edifying character of science; and the familiar argument for design was one of them. As we have seen, it would remain a prominent feature of popular scientific culture until the time of Darwin and beyond.

A further objection to the thesis that science was the creation of Christianity draws attention to the importance of historical context. The sceptic might well ask why, if the Christian religion was so auspicious for the rise of science, did it take 1500 years for an enduring scientific movement to take off? A satisfactory answer would then have to identify a range of other preconditions for scientific activity to expand. These might include the availability of leisure time, patronage, the development of new technologies and instruments, the establishment of communication networks among those with similar interests and the eventual founding of scientific academies and societies. It could still be argued that these social and economic circumstances would not themselves suffice without an appropriate philosophy of nature; but the problem for those who wish to present seventeenth-century science as an organic outgrowth of the Christian faith, is that it took many different forms and was conducted under the aegis of many different metaphysical schemes. One of the most striking features of the early scientific societies such as the Paris Academy of Sciences and the Royal Society of London, both founded in the 1660s, was their exclusion of religious matters from discussion. The hope, not always realized, was that experimental science would lead to consensus, whereas religious disputes, especially during the Civil War in England, had been notorious for their divisiveness.

3.7 Lessons from the past

Does a historical approach to questions of science and religion have anything to offer religious thinkers whose goal is to defend the faith tradition to which they belong? It almost certainly does if there is a will to avoid mistakes that, with the privilege of hindsight, have proved damaging in the past. One such mistake has surfaced many times. This is when religious apologists build their arguments on what science cannot currently explain. It is perfectly true that some questions may remain unsolvable by scientific research. They have been called 'limit questions', which include one that is invariably adduced: why does anything exist at all? What ultimately makes possible a universe of possibilities?

The mistake, however, arises in contexts other than those set by the limit questions. Suppose, for example, one discovered that Darwin was unable to account for the origin of variations on which his mechanism of natural selection relied. It might be tempting to ascribe the production of variation to the activity of a God who ensured that beneficial variations appeared. Darwin's American correspondent Asa Gray adopted this line (Gray, 1860). But, with hindsight, the problem is obvious: once the mechanism becomes understood, in this case by reference to genetic mutation, the God invoked to complete the science becomes redundant.[7] Such a pattern has been repeated many times. Among contemporaries of Darwin who pointed out the danger was Frederick Temple (1821–1902), who eventually became Archbishop of Canterbury. As early as 1860, and during the same meeting of the British Association at which Wilberforce and Huxley had their exchange, Temple warned that theologians had too often tried to build their theology at the point where scientific knowledge gave out. Far better, he suggested, to celebrate what was known of God's creation.

Avoiding the one pitfall could, however, land one in another. Religious apologists have sometimes staked too much on what the current state of scientific knowledge (as distinct from ignorance) has been. Where the science has appeared supportive of theism, as in the astronomy of Kepler, the celestial mechanics of Newton, or the models of progressive creation superimposed on the fossil record in the nineteenth century, it is perfectly understandable that it should have been adopted for that purpose. One of the routes by which Newton's science was popularized was via the first set of Boyle Lectures given in the 1690s by the Reverend Richard Bentley (1662–1742), who clearly relished the opportunity to show he was abreast of the latest science.

The danger in this case is that the scientific theory on which the theology is built might turn out to be shifting sand as new, competing theories displace them. In antiquity, Augustine warned against making the exegesis of scriptural texts dependent upon as yet undemonstrated secular knowledge: if the science moved on, the authority of Scripture could so easily be compromised. One of the greatest scientific minds of the nineteenth century, James Clerk Maxwell, issued a similar warning, stressing the provisional status of scientific theories. Too intimate a fusion of science with theology could lead to embarrassment for another reason. A God whose attributes are redescribed through the categories of science becomes more sharply defined and a clearer target for secular critiques. In some ways this was the fate of Newton's God during the eighteenth century. Providential activity identified with the restabilizing of planetary orbits was compromised when it transpired that no such cosmic plumbing was necessary (see 1.17, 10.3).

3.8 Conclusion

In conclusion we must leave the dilemmas of the apologist and return to the most general message from historical scholarship. The crucial lesson is that *ideas, whether religious, political or scientific have to be placed in their contexts*. It is worth repeating that to understand the politics of the Galileo Affair, it is crucial to know that the events leading to the trial were taking place during the Counter-Reformation when the Catholic Church in Europe was seeking to re-establish its authority. Pope Urban VIII was under pressure from the Catholic authorities in Spain to take a harder line against heretics. He also felt that Galileo had betrayed his trust by positively advocating, rather than merely expounding, the Copernican system.

The fact that some of Galileo's friends, such as Paolo Sarpi who had led a revolt against the papacy from the Venetian state, were perceived as Protestants or crypto-Protestants could only make matters worse.

It is striking that two of the most significant scientific challenges to the Christian Churches, those springing from Copernican cosmology and from Darwinian evolution, each occurred in the midst of another crisis and added to the unease. In 1859, when Darwin published his *Origin of Species*, the Church in England was having to come to terms with critical methods of biblical scholarship, which assumed that the biblical writers had been men of their own times, fallible and with their own agendas. The importance of historical context was being discovered in the analysis of Scripture itself. The same Samuel Wilberforce who became embroiled with Huxley was far more indignant about historical criticism of Scripture than about Darwin because this, in his view, was a cancer growing from within the Church. To add to his troubles, as Bishop of Oxford he witnessed several members of his own family follow John Henry Newman in deserting the Anglican Church for the Church of Rome.

For historians of science and religion, such local events and circumstances can become full of significance. They have certainly had an effect on attitudes towards Darwinian evolution, attitudes that could differ markedly even within the same theological tradition. It has been observed that during the last quarter of the nineteenth century, leading Presbyterians in Northern Ireland were generally more hostile to evolutionary science than their brethren in Princeton, who included a leading advocate of theistic evolution, James McCosh. Part of the explanation appears to be the notorious occasion in 1874 when John Tyndall, in delivering his Presidential Address to the Belfast meeting of the British Association, used Darwin's theory in a scathing attack on the pretensions of theology to answer the big questions of cosmology (Livingstone, 1992). Tyndall's address provoked an adverse reaction because of aggressive remarks about the state of scientific education in Ireland and because his version of Darwinism was so uncompromisingly naturalistic. Darwin had chosen his words carefully when discussing the mystery behind the appearance of the first few living things, even on occasions using biblical language. In Tyndall's monistic philosophy of nature there was no room for any prevarication: 'Either let us open our doors freely to the conception of creative acts, or abandoning them, let us radically change our notions of matter' (Tyndall, 1874:182). Henceforward, in that locality, the name of Darwin was tarred with the brush of materialism and atheism.

To insist on the importance of local context as one of the primary lessons of history is not a dry academic point. It is relevant to each of us because it is salutary to ask about the contexts in which our own beliefs about God, humanity and the cosmos have been forged and the events that might have changed them.

Notes

1   For a review of the key elements of Darwin's work, and its theological implications, see 6.6–6.7.

2   See Chapter 10 for an exploration of the problem of divine action investigated

within Christian theology, and Chapter 12 for the Islamic understanding of God's action.

3 See 9.4 on Hindu metaphysics.
4 For more on Capra see **9.3 and 9.9**.
5 See **6.10.5–6.10.6** and Dawkins (1991) for further mention of the 'design' of the eye.
6 A voluntarist theology is one in which the will of God is regarded as the fundamental principle or dominant factor in the universe and which rejects the view that God, out of necessity, was obliged to make a universe with particular, rationally determinable features.
7 See **5.24, 10.3**, for further discussion of the 'God of the gaps'.

Further reading

BROOKE, J. (1991) *Science and Religion: Some Historical Perspectives* (Cambridge: Cambridge University Press)

BROOKE, J. and CANTOR, G. (1998) *Reconstructing Nature* (Edinburgh: T&T Clark; New York: Oxford University Press)

CANTOR, G. (1991) *Michael Faraday: Sandemanian and Scientist* (London: Macmillan)

DESMOND, A. (1997) *Huxley: From Devil's Disciple to Evolution's High Priest* (Reading, MA: Addison Wesley)

FANTOLI, A. (1996) *Galileo: For Copernicanism and for the Church*, trans. G. Coyne, 2nd edn (Vatican City: Vatican Observatory)

HARRISON, P. (1998) *The Bible, Protestantism and the Rise of Natural Science* (Cambridge: Cambridge University Press)

LINDBERG, D. (1992) *The Beginnings of Western Science* (Chicago: University of Chicago Press)

LINDBERG, D. and NUMBERS, R. (eds) (2003) *When Science and Christianity Meet* (Chicago: University of Chicago Press)

MOORE, J. (1979) *The Post-Darwinian Controversies: A Study of the Protestant Struggle to Come to Terms with Darwin in Great Britain and America, 1870–1900* (Cambridge: Cambridge University Press)

RUPKE, N. (1983) *The Great Chain of History: William Buckland and the English School of Geology, 1814–1849* (Oxford: Clarendon Press)

Chapter 4

Truth and reason in science and theology: points of tension, correlation and compatibility

Paul D. Murray

4.1 Introduction

In Chapters 1 and 3 we saw that the 'conflict' model of the relationship between science and religion is only one possibility among many, and not by any means necessarily at all typical. Indeed we saw that monotheistic religion, especially Christianity, had had an important role in nurturing the roots of Western science (see 1.11).

However, *it is still all too frequently the case that science and theology are thought of as two utterly distinct spheres of human interest with the relationship between them being viewed, at best, as one of uneasy tension.*

One might note the respective ways in which the words 'science' and 'theology' function in popular usage. 'Science' and 'scientific' are frequently appealed to as a means of bestowing respectability on a subject, bringing with them connotations of rationality, reliability and utility. How often in the media do we encounter the authoritative 'Science tells us ...'? Interviewees when pressed riposte with 'We need to be scientific about this ...', and advertisers attract us with such phrases as 'The appliance of science', 'The science diet' and all manner of goods which come with a supposedly scientific seal of approval.

In contrast 'theology' and 'theological' have, for some at least, taken the place of the once popular 'metaphysical abstraction' as the standard terms of derogation: 'Theological nonsense' cries an MP across the floor of the British House of Commons, implying irrationality, confusion and irrelevance.

The theological problems occasioned by the rise of science extend then, it would seem, beyond particular disputes to a more pervasive sense that science stands as the measure of all valid knowledge – in a way which calls into question the notion that theology is a route to truth. This belief can take many forms:

- science is a truly modern form of knowing, while theology represents a pre-modern throwback;
- science is useful, whereas theology promotes a disengagement from reality;

- science is value-free, whereas theology is compromised by personal commitment;
- science is open to falsification and renewal, whereas theology is dogmatically entrenched;
- science is based upon empirical data, whereas theology is a matter of pure speculation;
- in short, science seeks after objective truth, whereas theology deals only in subjective meaning.

We consider these assumptions to be as untrue to the reality of science as to the practice of theology. The present chapter explores the relevant philosophical background before considering the more constructive possibilities opened up by recent thought. As such, the chapter falls into three broad sections (A, B and C): the first is concerned to trace the high-water mark of scientistic rationalism in the logical positivism of the early part of the twentieth century, the constraints which this imposed on Christian theology, and the relative merits of some attempted responses; the second traces the unravelling of positivism in the middle part of the century; and the third explores more recent post-positivist accounts of science and their theological relevance – particular attention is given here to Nicholas Rescher's thought.

SECTION A
EARLY TWENTIETH CENTURY: THE CHALLENGE OF LOGICAL POSITIVISM (4.2–4.6)

4.2 The verificationist criterion of meaning

In the early part of the twentieth century a group centred upon the University of Vienna articulated a formal theory of knowledge which established scientific propositions as the measure of all truth in a way which condemned all other kinds of propositions as meaningless. Heirs to the traditions of scientific positivism and British empiricism alike, the 'Vienna Circle's' views are generally referred to under the labels 'logical positivism' or 'logical empiricism'. A.J. Ayer's *Language, Truth and Logic* (first published 1936) is the standard English-language presentation of their thought.

Following the lead of Kant, the logical positivists drew a distinction between 'analytic' and 'synthetic' statements. Under the category of the analytic they included statements of definition (e.g. 'All bachelors are unmarried', '2 + 2 = 4') and statements of logic (e.g. 'Something cannot be both true and false in the same respect at the same time') – statements the truth of which can be uncontroversially ascertained without recourse to empirical reality. In turn, the category of the synthetic included all statements which go beyond logic and definition alone to exert claims concerning what reality is actually like (e.g. 'The swan on the lake is white', 'There is a God'). According to the logical positivists' characteristic 'verificationist' principle of meaning, the class of meaningful propositions consists of analytic propositions, which are true by definition, and synthetic propositions which can be verified in a similarly empirical manner as was presumed to be the case with scientific propositions.[1] In the face of any given synthetic proposition, the logical positivists asked for the sensory data which might serve to verify the truth of that proposition. If no such data could be adduced then the proposition was to be classed as meaningless on the grounds that there was no means of distinguishing its truth from its falsity.

Whether the verification principle is actually capable of supporting scientific explanations (which are less concerned with particular descriptions than with general laws) is a moot point (see 4.7). What is apparent, however, is that its rigorous application would condemn vast swathes of discourse as meaningless – in particular metaphysics, religion, aesthetics and ethics (Ayer, 1971:42). Take ethics as an example. Given that it is impossible to verify value statements in an uncontentious manner, the logical positivists concluded that they could not be classed as meaningful in any literal sense. At most they can be ascribed an emotive or evaluative meaning in the sense of expressing the preferences of those stating them – statements such as 'Theft is wrong' being understood along the lines of 'We reject the practice of stealing.' Likewise it was claimed that statements concerning the being of God cannot even be discussed, let alone affirmed, in any meaningful manner (Ayer, 1971:152).

As we discuss in 4.9, the two central presuppositions of the logical positivist agenda (i.e. the analytic/synthetic distinction and the assumption that it is possible to verify propositions in a discrete manner) have each been subjected to rigorous challenge in subsequent philosophy. As a result the focus of contemporary interaction between theology and the philosophy of science has shifted to other very different places (see 4.10–4.13). Nevertheless, the assumptions which logical positivism formalized continue to ripple through popular consciousness. It will therefore be helpful to pause in order to consider the range of possible theological responses. We will focus upon four. Whereas the first and third represent differing attempts to *accommodate* theology to the positivist challenge, the second and fourth represent differing attempts to *isolate* theology from it. The critical comments that we offer lay down certain markers for the more constructive case which will follow later (see 4.13 in particular).

4.3 Strict accommodation: non-cognitive accounts of religious belief

1955 saw the publication of R.B. Braithwaite's lecture 'An empiricist's view of the nature of religious belief' in which he sought to defend the meaningfulness of religious discourse while embracing a positivist perspective. He did this by evacuating religious assertions of any cognitive content concerning the nature of reality (i.e. of any claim to convey conceptual *knowledge* of reality) and then treating them as statements of purely ethical intent embroidered with illustrative stories. His argument hinges around two claims: first that 'Unless religious principles are moral principles, it makes no sense to speak of putting them into practice' and second that while 'A religious assertion will ... have a propositional element which is lacking in a purely moral assertion ... it is not necessary ... to believe in the truth of the story involved' (Braithwaite, 1971:81, 84–5). The point of this was to suggest that religious assertions are to be accorded the kind of evocative or evaluative meaning attributed to ethical statements in a verificationist perspective rather than the more literal kind of meaning reserved for analytic and empirically testable propositions (p. 86).

R.M. Hare had already published a similar account of religious belief in 1951. For Hare as for Braithwaite, religious beliefs do not count as cognitive claims about the nature of reality. Rather they are to be understood as constituting what he terms a '*blik*', or overarching principle, which guides believers' lives and their interpretation of their experience.

The most obvious problem facing such strategies is the fact that their response to the positivist challenge is bought at the cost of an account of religious belief which few adherents would either recognize or wish to endorse. With regard to Braithwaite's proposed identification of religious and ethical statements, while most if not all theological statements can indeed be held to have practical implications, this is somewhat different from claiming that they are ethical statements without remainder. Within the Christian tradition, for example, it is widely held that the true force of Christian living consists not in the stoic observance of ethical codes but in a process of grace-filled conversion and conformity of life to the transforming reality of God in Christ and the Holy Spirit. This is certainly what we find in the epistles of Paul and again in Augustine's dispute with Pelagius. For each of them Christian life is rooted in convictions about the action of God and not simply the ethical intentions and imaginative faculties of humans. As such, there is an inescapably cognitive dimension to Christian faith which makes the strategy espoused by Hare and Braithwaite appear odd to say the least.

This point could be pressed further. Implicit within the claim that Christian faith is centred upon the action of God is the recognition that we do not, of ourselves, have the wherewithal to sort out the intractable messiness of the human condition and that hence, any genuine hope of transformation must be grounded in something more than human resources alone. Indeed, in a context where belief in God has ceased to have any literal meaning it could be argued that Camus' *La Peste*, with its portrayal of the heroic refusal of Dr Rieux to be overwhelmed by the futility of his actions, represents a more appropriate narrative ethic than does the kind of transposition of Christian stories advocated by Hare and Braithwaite.[2]

4.4 Strict isolation: Christian existentialism

The second of our four possible theological responses to logical positivism seeks to identify a realm of significant discourse quite different to the scientific, and hence distinct from anything that would figure under a positivist epistemology, with a view to claiming that this constitutes the true locus for a meaningful use of religious language. The key text is Rudolph Bultmann's 1941 essay 'New Testament and mythology', in which he claimed that scientific understanding had shown the need for what he referred to as the 'mythical world picture of the New Testament' to be demythologized if it is to speak to twentieth-century men and women. By this he did not simply mean the traces of the ancient three-storey picture of the cosmos which can be found there. He referred equally to the basic notion of the Earth as 'a theatre for the working of supernatural powers' (Bultmann, 1985:1). As he expressed it in particularly sharp form at one point, 'We cannot use electric lights and radios and, in the event of illness, avail ourselves of modern medical and clinical means and at the same time believe in the spirit and wonder world of the New Testament' (1985:4).[3]

The larger point at issue here – as to the possibilities for making sense of a real divine action in the natural order within the context of contemporary scientific understanding – will be discussed in Chapter 10. We see Bultmann as having allowed his theological agenda to be dictated by an overly deterministic worldview which such developments as quantum theory (see 5.11–5.14) were already placing in question at the time that he was writing. Bultmann's response to this situation was to draw a sharp distinction between the kind of empirical knowledge supposedly at issue in science and the more existential style of knowledge which he believed to lie at the heart of Christian faith. Where the former is concerned with causal connections in the world, the latter is concerned with questions of personal meaning and significance. For Bultmann, any attempt to link God-talk with talk about physical happenings in the natural order confuses the categories of causality and existential significance in the way in which a mythical worldview did previously. Faced with such confusion, the task is to seek to demythologize the language concerned by extracting the underlying message from the imagery in which it is expressed. As he put it:

> The real point of myth is not to give an objective world picture; what is expressed in it, rather, is how we human beings understand ourselves in our world. Thus, myth does not want to be interpreted in cosmological terms but in anthropological terms – or, better, in existentialist terms. (1985:9)

Accordingly Bultmann reinterpreted all talk of God's action in particular events in terms of the way in which they open up new possibilities for understanding human existence when perceived with the eyes of faith. God's action is confined to the inner level of personal address and existential challenge rather than to the external level of factual explanation. Most notoriously, the resurrection narratives are understood as testimonies to the continuing possibility of finding faith and personal meaning in Jesus rather than as witnesses to the fact of God actually having raised the dead Jesus to a new state of life. To this extent, similar fault lines run through Bultmann's position as have been identified in the work of noncognitivists such as Braithwaite and Hare. With them he shares the basic positivist assumption that the realm of facts is to be distinguished from the realm of values, with religious belief being placed firmly on the latter side of the divide. But as Nancey Murphy observes, 'If theological meanings are not grounded in theological facts – facts about the character and acts of God, in particular, then they are mere fairy tales, however comforting they may be' (Murphy, 1996:153).

In fairness to Bultmann it has to be acknowledged that he, unlike Hare and Braithwaite, did genuinely wish to think in terms of God's acting at the level of personal address in order to initiate the believer's transformed vision of things. Nevertheless Bultmann severely curtails the scope of divine transformative action when compared with traditional Christian claims concerning God's action in and through particular events in the historical order, most notably those surrounding the life, death and resurrection of Jesus. As such it would be as difficult to preserve the necessary cognitive dimension to such aspects of Christian faith on the basis of Bultmann's account of things, as it would on the basis of either Hare's or Braithwaite's. It would therefore be equally difficult to present an account of Christian faith which is capable of speaking to the depths of human need.

Finally, it could further be argued that Bultmann's attempt to immunize Christian faith from the challenge of scientific positivism is itself self-defeating. Implicit in Bultmann's strategy is the assumption that whereas an action of God within the external world would necessitate God's intervening in the continuum of natural causality, God can be thought of as acting in the inner life of the believer without any such problems arising. But such an assumption is by no means beyond question. If, as will be argued in 7.2–7.4, mental states and neuronal activity are necessarily interrelated, then God's inspiring of altered mental states must be thought of as having a neuronal component to it also. Bultmann has not solved the problem of God's action so much as merely shifted it to a different level. As such his existentialist version of Christian faith appears to be as inadequate to the positivistic worldview which it assumes as it is to the tradition of faith that it espouses.

4.5 Relative accommodation: on the possible verification of Christian faith

Whereas our first possible strategy of theological response to the challenge of logical positivism (see 4.3) shared the positivist assumption that religious belief is in principle unverifiable, a polar opposite strategy (but still one of accommodation) would be to claim that it is indeed open to such verification, or at least a form thereof. Two quite different forms of this strategy will be considered: the first, espoused by John Hick, appeals to the possible 'eschatological verification' of religious belief after death; the second attempts to reclaim something of the tradition of natural theology.[4]

Taking verification in its broadest sense as 'the ascertaining of truth by the removal of grounds for rational doubt', Hick noted that the fulfilment of predictions has a particular role to play (Hick, 1971:54–5). He told a parable (pp. 59–60): two men walk together along the same road but with radically different beliefs about the road's terminus – one believes that it leads towards a Celestial City, the other that it leads nowhere (comparable to the positions of the theist and the atheist respectively). The point for Hick is that while neither of these interpretative frameworks gives rise to any testable predictions about events *in the course of* the journey, the controverted claim that the road leads to a Celestial City does itself represent a potentially verifiable prediction. To this extent there are matters of real substance at issue in the counter-claims of the 'believer' and the 'non-believer' in such a manner as makes it utterly inappropriate to think of them as non-cognitive *bliks* (4.3 **para** 2) lacking in any real content. Likewise, he argued that Christian faith is correctly to be viewed as having a cognitive dimension to it which is open to potential, albeit eschatological, verification in such manner as renders it meaningful even within the strict terms of the verification principle (1971:65–71).

Where Hick settled for the modest task of establishing that Christian faith could, on account of its *potential* verifiability, be meaningfully discussed within a positivist perspective, the second possible verificationist approach to religious belief would attempt the more ambitious task of establishing that such belief is open to actual verification *in this order*. More precisely, by exploiting a distinction which Ayer himself drew between 'strong' and 'weak' forms of the verification principle it might be claimed:

- first, that experience which renders a given proposition probable, rather than absolutely certain, is sufficient to verify it in the 'weak' sense (Ayer, 1971:50–1);
- second, that religious beliefs are indeed open to being verified in just such a 'weak' probabilistic manner (Swinburne, 1993:182).

In support of this latter claim, appeal might be made to certain implications deriving from the belief in God as Creator. This belief, in the Christian view, is more concerned to maintain the absolute and continuing dependence of all that is upon the creative and sustaining hand of God than it is merely to exert a claim about temporal origins (Aquinas, 1967:77–85; see **1.15**, **2.5.1**). More precisely, the belief in God as Creator is concerned to maintain that everything that exists (a) is brought into being through the Logos or self-reflected reason of God and (b) is sustained in being by the generative and transforming Spirit of God. As such, it implies that all that exists reflects in very diverse and particular ways something of the rationality and being of God (Soskice, 1993a:71; Aquinas, 1967:95). Such a stance readily lends itself to being employed in support of the claim that the observable data of the natural order bear the impress of the hand of the Creator within them. This in turn makes it possible to interpret them as indirect evidence for the existence of God.

Complementing this it might equally be argued that science itself provokes the need for a broader explanatory framework by raising questions which cannot be answered purely within its own terms (Murphy and Ellis, 1996:5, 15–18, 59–62, 250–1). For example, science has yielded unparalleled effective knowledge concerning imminent causal relations within the world, but is incapable of answering the question which this almost inevitably raises as to the possible ultimate cause of the entire causal order taken as a whole. This remains the case no matter how far cosmology penetrates into the first milliseconds of the cosmos, or even if it concludes that the origins of all that is lie in a boundariless singularity (see **1.15**). Still the question remains as to the possible cause lying behind even this – why is there something rather than nothing?

Putting this together, where a doctrine of creation might be taken as supporting the belief that there is evidence for the existence of God to be discerned within the world, the limits of scientific explanation might be taken as creating an opportunity for just such a conversation to occur. These two assumptions form the twin pillars supporting the attempt here being considered to ground religious belief on the basis of observation and experience. Where this approach differs from the eighteenth-century Anglican tradition of natural theology is that *it forgoes any hope of articulating a definitive proof of God's existence* and settles instead for *seeking to establish the greater probability of God's existence than not.*

Richard Swinburne is probably the best-known advocate of this approach.[5] His thesis is that the various arguments are best taken jointly rather than individually, as together contributing to a many-sided cumulative, or inductive, case which serves, through the application of probability theory, to establish that the exist-ence of God is more likely than not (1979:13–14, 277–91). Basil Mitchell had already commended the benefits of a 'cumulative case' approach to the justification of religious belief.[6] The application of probabilistic confirmation theory is, however, Swinburne's own distinctive contribution to the task. This determines the particular form that his argument takes and lends to it an appearance of rational clarity and logical rigour which, he believes, serves to set it on a par with the examination of large-scale scientific theories (1979:2–3). However, while appearing attractive to those looking for a robust defence of theistic belief, to others it represents an inappropriate form of argumentation.

Much of the force of Swinburne's case lies in his adoption of an apparently neutral starting point. He presents an account shorn of rhetorical flourish and 'written in deep conviction of the possibility of reaching fairly well justified conclusions by rational argument' – the implication being that any rational person should be swayed by the case which he presents (1979:1). The problem is, however, that the underlying notion of a pure, neutral rationality untainted by perspective and commitment is now widely thought of as an elusive ideal at best and an unhelpful illusion at worst (see 4.7–4.13). We are all always embedded in linguistic and conceptual frameworks, cognitive and evaluative commitments and shared practices which, rather than acting as an obstacle to rationality, actually constitute the contexts within which human reason appropriately functions. *Consequently, we each bring differing perspectives to the process of rational reflection in such a manner as rules out any chance of there being arguments which are equally persuasive for all.*

For example, pivotal to Swinburne's argument is the claim that 'the intrinsic probability of there being a universe such as ours and no God is very much lower than . . . the intrinsic probability of there being a God' (1979:288). But this is by no means an uncontentious claim. One sharing a different set of presuppositions to Swinburne could legitimately challenge his case at numerous points and arrive rationally at a different conclusion (Mackie, 1982). The broader issue, as Michael Banner has pointed out, is that probabilistic confirmation theory can at best offer 'a means whereby one encodes one's prior judgements in a more technical form' rather than a precise formula for neutral theory choice (Banner, 1990:144; see also Putnam, 1981:189–93). It would seem then that not only is there no possibility of articulating a deductively certain proof of God's existence; there is no possibility either of presenting a probabilistic inductive case to which all people should feel themselves compelled to submit. Indeed the best writing in this tradition already recognizes this fact (Mitchell, 1973:21–41, 59; compare Aquinas, 1964a:1a.1.8, pp. 29–33). The most that arguments such as Swinburne's can do is establish that, given certain presuppositions, a rational case can be made demonstrating a fit between belief in God and other aspects of human knowledge and experience. Reflecting this we suggest that rather than being articulated from a position of supposed neutrality, they are most appropriately set within an explicit faith context. Further, there are sound theological rather than merely philosophical reasons why this is so.

Intrinsic to Swinburne's case is the prioritizing of what are presumed to be the common perceptions of general human reason over the particular commitments of Christian faith, the latter being relegated to the point of arrival rather than departure. As he has expressed it himself: 'In all my works on the philosophy of religion my approach has been to start from where secular humanity stands, develop a philosophy of that area of thought, and then show how that philosophy leads to a Christian understanding of things in some respect' (1993:197–8). The problem with this from a theological point of view is that it runs the risk of allowing the terms of the debate to be set without any reference to that which is distinctive about the Christian understanding of God (i.e. the belief that the character of God's presence and action in the world is demonstrated most clearly in and indeed is actually identified with the particular living unto death of the crucified and risen Christ).

More precisely, Swinburne starts out with the confident assertion that 'God is by definition an omnipotent (that is, infinitely powerful), omniscient (that is, all-knowing) and perfectly free person ...' (1993:192; 1979:8). He thus displays no concern to wrestle with the difficult question as to whether this widely assumed philosophical concept actually matches with what is alleged by Christians to be revealed of God in the life, death and resurrection of Jesus. As such, Swinburne's case appears more as a defence of the 'God of the philosophers' than it does a justification of Christian faith itself. Indeed, some have argued that a related strategy was actually responsible for paving the way for modern atheism. Their claim is that it was the very shift in focus of theological reflection to general cosmological speculation which in turn provoked the naturalistic response which saw no need to invoke God in the chain of causal explanation (see 1.13, also Buckley, 1987; Brooke, 1996:14–17; Jüngel, 1983).

4.6 Relative isolation: the Barthian emphasis upon the primacy of God's self-revealed Word

In Chapter 2 we looked briefly at some of the great contributions made by Karl Barth to the Christian theology of creation (see 2.3.2, 2.4, 2.5.4). Horrified first by the support given to the Kaiser's war policy by liberal theologians in 1914 and then again by the ready submission of German Christianity to the allure of the Third Reich in the 1930s, Barth denounced all attempts to establish Christian faith upon the basis of prevailing secular reason. For Barth such attempts inevitably serve to compromise the true focus of Christian theology (i.e. the absolutely free God revealed in Jesus as capable of challenging and transforming the created order) by conflating it with the terms of contemporary culture in such a manner as dulls its critical edge. From the publication of his epochal commentary on *The Epistle to the Romans* (particularly the 1922 second edition) onwards, Barth took it as axiomatic that Christian theology should be shaped exclusively in accordance with the 'wholly other' self-revelation of God in the life, death and resurrection of Jesus.[7] The force which this methodological tenet exerted over his theology is most evident in the complex spiralling form of the *Church Dogmatics* in which each interlocking theme is continually related back to what God has supposedly shown of God's self in the person of Christ (Hunsinger, 1991:28–9).[8]

Donald MacKinnon has pointed to a certain parallelism here between Barth's trenchant emphasis upon the particular givenness of Christ as the self-disclosure of God and the positivists' emphasis upon the 'given' of empirical data as the privileged disclosure of natural reality.[9] This could be pressed further and used to justify the claim that while science represents the appropriate means of gaining knowledge about the natural world on the basis of empirical observation, this does not raise any problems for theology which, as the 'science' of God, is focused upon the reality of God's dealings with the world as known through the scriptural witness to God's self-revelation in the person of Christ.

While such a strategy would support a far more full-blooded version of theological truth than is at work in Bultmann's programme (in as much as it would resist the reduction of God's being in action in Christ and the Spirit to the purely 'interior' level of personal address), it would nevertheless stand with that project in espousing what amounts to a strategy of isolation. As with Bultmann the implicit claim would be that science and theology are focused upon different dimensions of reality and that, provided their boundaries are respected, there can be no undue conflict. In this regard it is significant to note that when Barth turned to the doctrine of creation in Volume III of the *Church Dogmatics*, he showed no apparent concern to reflect upon the theological significance of contemporary scientific thinking. The entire discussion, extending to well over two thousand pages in the English translation, is given over exclusively to the significance of the created order as viewed within a Christocentric perspective. As such, it exemplifies both Barth's overriding concern to forgo all attempts to found Christian theology on the basis of general human reason – and the limitations in this project as Barth himself pursued it.

On the one hand we believe there to be something of lasting significance in Barth's concern to shape Christian theology in radical accordance with the disclosed truth of God in Christ, particularly so in the light of the now-widespread consensus that there is no possibility of attaining to a perspectiveless neutrality in human reason (see 4.5 and 4.10–4.13). Put bluntly the point could be expressed as follows: if the hope for neutrality is illusory then why should theologians feel obliged to chase after it when it only serves to skew what is distinctive about Christian faith anyway?

On the other hand, however, we would equally claim that this legitimate Barthian sense of priorities requires to be matched by a more explicit concern to expose the particular commitments of Christian faith to the refreshing challenge of other traditions of thought and practice. Unless some such attempt is continually made then Christian faith is in danger of closing in upon itself in such a manner as would threaten to reduce the supposedly objective truth of God's self-disclosure to the level of a mere communal *blik*. As Wentzel van Huyssteen has put it:

> A positivistic theology of revelation that adopts a highly esoteric method
> makes it extremely difficult to convince others that the basic tenets of
> theology – God, revelation, Holy Scripture, inspiration, etc. – are not the
> basic constructs of subjective whim, whether personal or directed by an
> influential tradition. (van Huyssteen, 1989:22)

Somewhat more positively, it could be argued that Barth's re-articulation of the
belief that the entire created order relates to Christ itself suggests a need in
Christian theology. This is the need to adopt a constant self-critical exposure to
the challenge and refreshment of other traditions of thought and practice. The
point is that if the deepest significance of all things is Christological in orientation, then it is possible that *there are things to be learned about the reality of God in
Christ which can only be learned by allowing the insights of other aspects of human
understanding to refresh and renew the perspective of Christian faith.*

The contemporary renaissance in Barthian studies has revealed the extent to
which Barth himself acknowledged that his Christocentric focus and starting
point in Christian theology was by no means in tension with a recognition as to
there being truth (what he referred to as 'other lights') outside the sphere of
Christian faith (Barth, 1961:106–9, 114–25, 139–43, 151–4, 156–65; Hunsinger, 1991:234–80). Further, the fact that this was no mere late aberration on
his behalf can be seen by looking again at the first Article of the Barmen
Declaration cited earlier (see note 7 in this chapter):

> Jesus Christ, as He is attested to us in Holy Scripture, is the one Word of
> God, whom we have to hear and whom we have to trust and obey in life and
> in death. We condemn the false doctrine that the Church can and must
> recognise as God's revelation other events and powers, forms and truths,
> apart from and alongside this one Word of God. (Barth, 1957:172)

Upon which he later commented:

> We may notice that it does not deny the existence of other events and
> powers, forms and truths alongside the one Word of God, and that therefore
> throughout it does not deny the possibility of a natural theology as such. On
> the contrary, it presupposes that there are such things. But it does deny and
> designate as false doctrine the assertion that all these things can be the
> source of Church proclamation, a second source alongside and apart from the
> one Word of God. It excludes natural theology from Church proclamation.
> (Barth, 1957:178)

Indeed, the tension which this discloses can be held to have characterized
Barth's line of argument throughout (McCormack, 1995). As early as the very first
part of the first volume of the *Church Dogmatics* we find surprisingly 'un-Barthian'
quips about God speaking through Russian communism, blossoming shrubs and
even dead dogs (Barth, 1936:60). Earlier still in *Romans* he had already referred to
the 'faithfulness of God' as 'the divine patience according to which He provides, at
sundry times and at many divers points in human history, occasions and

possibilities and witnesses of the knowledge of His righteousness' (Barth, 1968:96). Immediately following this he referred to Jesus not as the *exclusive* locus of the knowledge of God but rather as 'the point at which it can be seen that all the other points form one line of supreme significance. He is the point at which is perceived the crimson thread which runs through all history.'

It seems then that the Barthian project is open to being extended into just the kind of rooted yet expansively self-critical theological rationality that is required. Given the uncompromising tones he adopted in the face of crisis and the relative lack of attention that he himself paid to the task of explicitly exposing the Christian tradition to the refreshment of other perspectives, it is not entirely surprising that Barth has frequently been interpreted as rejecting all possibility of such critical interaction (Pannenberg, 1976:265–76). More significant, however, is the fact that Thomas F. Torrance, drawing upon the post-positivist, or 'post-critical', understanding of scientific knowledge articulated by Michael Polanyi (1890–1976), could not only expand the Barthian project in order to take explicit account of the findings of contemporary science but could do so with Barth's full support (Torrance, 1969; 1976:ix–xiii; 1985).[10]

For Polanyi, far from personal commitment necessarily preventing the possibility of objective knowledge – as the positivist mindset assumes – it is the prior personal, even passionate, involvement of the knower with the known, in ways extending beyond the level of explicit conceptual knowledge to more 'tacit' dimensions, that makes all knowledge, even scientific knowledge, possible (Polanyi, 1958; 1967). In turn, for Torrance, where the natural sciences represent the personally committed concern to understand the natural world as disclosed through empirical observation, theology represents the responsibly committed concern to understand the reality of God in the light of God's self-revelation in Christ and the Spirit. In the course of the present section we have already anticipated certain points which will feature as component elements in the approach to theological rationality that we ourselves most strongly favour. It will be readily apparent that our own sympathies lie far more with the claim that there is a great deal more to reason and truth than the positivists allowed for than it does with attempts to fit theology to the positivist agenda (see **4.5** in particular). This being said, however, it equally needs to be stated that, far from siding uncritically with any of the attempts which have been made to argue for a strict demarcation between rationality in the scientific and the theological domains (see **4.4** and our comments above on Barth), we see the need rather to hold these two spheres in tension and to seek for what Wittgenstein might have referred to as certain 'family resemblances' between them (Wittgenstein, 1967:32[e], 46[e]; 1969:17). In order to show something of the possibility of doing so, we turn in the next section to follow the unravelling of the logical positivist agenda in the middle part of the twentieth century. Along with this went the breaking of the stranglehold which it had exerted over both the philosophy of science in particular and the concept of rationality more generally. Before doing so, it may be helpful for you to pause awhile in order to reflect upon your own reactions to the material under discussion.

> **EXERCISE 4.1**
>
> 1. Restate in your own words the essential challenge that logical positivism posed to claims for the rationality and truth of religious beliefs.
> 2. What is your assessment of the adequacy of the verificationist principle as a criterion of meaning and/or truth?
> 3. Outline the key differences between the four strategies here explored of possible theological response to the challenge of logical positivism.
> 4. Assess the respective strengths and weaknesses of these differing strategies. Which of them are you personally most in sympathy with and why?
> 5. What questions does all of this raise for you?

SECTION B
MID-TWENTIETH CENTURY: THE UNRAVELLING OF THE POSITIVIST AGENDA (4.7–4.9)

4.7 The problem of induction and Popperian falsificationism

While the likes of Hare, Braithwaite, Bultmann and Barth were each writing against the backdrop of positivist accounts of science, philosophy of science was itself coming to view such an account as inadequate to the true character of scientific explanation. The problem, it was realized, is that while the available set of observations against which a proposition may be verified is always finite in extent, the propositions which most truly characterize the task of scientific explanation (i.e. all-embracing laws) are themselves universal in scope – they are more of the form 'All x's are y' than of the form 'This x is y' (Popper, 1959:93–5). Even were it possible to extend the range of observations to include all actual cases of the relevant kind, this would still be insufficient for universal propositions, the scope of which extends to embrace not only the actual but also the hypothetical and hence as yet unobservable.

The irony then is that *a rigorous application of the verificationist criterion would have the effect of condemning the core language of science itself to meaninglessness* (Ayer, 1971:50–1). Alternatively stated, the 'strong' verificationist agenda founders on the problem of induction – that is, the question as to how one might validly move from a finite number of observations to the articulation of universal laws.

It was in response to this problem that Karl Popper (1902–94) articulated his falsificationist account of scientific rationality, at the heart of which is the belief that while any number of confirming instances of a given law still fall short of strict verification, even one counter-instance falsifies it in just the way that it took only one sighting of a black swan to falsify the belief that all swans are white. For Popper it follows that while it is impossible to verify proffered laws beyond all possibility of future refutation on the basis of empirical observation, it is at least possible to distinguish between those which can be shown to be false and those which show themselves resilient in the face of all attempts to falsify them (Popper, 1959:42). This represents a reversal in the way in which scientific rationality is to be thought of as proceeding. Rather than moving inductively from observations to generalizations, the suggested way of proceeding is by deducing predictions from the available theories and then testing for them with a view to the possible refutation of the theory in question (1959:27–30; 1963:82). For Popper it is this falsificationist manner of proceeding which serves to demarcate science from non-science (1963:33–7).

More generally Popper's reversal of theory and observation marks a significant step in twentieth-century philosophy of science. It opened the way to a recovery of the more radical insight of Pierre Duhem to the effect that theory not only precedes the concern for empirical observation but actually helps to determine the character of what is observed in any given situation (Duhem, 1954, originally published in French in 1906). For example, one trained in the theory and practice of X-ray plate interpretation observes something different when examining such a plate than does someone else without such training (Hanson, 1958). Nor was this general point lost on Popper. In *Objective Knowledge* he wrote:

> In science it is *observation* rather than perception which plays the decisive part. But observation is a process in which we play an intensely *active* part. An observation is a perception but one which is planned and prepared. We do not 'have' an observation (as we may 'have' a sense experience) but we 'make' an observation ... An observation is always preceded by a particular interest, a question, or a problem – in short, by something theoretical. (Popper, 1972:342)

We will return to the broader significance of this point a little later (see 4.9). For the time being it is necessary to explore the possible theological implications of Popper's thought. At the outset it is important to note that while Popper used his falsificationist approach in order to distinguish science from non-science, he did not intend thereby to condemn all non-science to meaninglessness in the way in which the logical positivists had done (Popper, 1963:38).

4.8 Falsifiability, fallibility and theology

Whatever Popper's own intentions were in adopting falsification as a means of demarcating science from non-science, Anthony Flew in a famous essay first published in 1950 proceeded to draw the conclusion that theological statements were to be condemned as meaningless on account of their failing to meet the principle of falsification. His argument in effect was that believers normally respond to any potentially falsifying evidence by continually qualifying the expression which they give to their belief in a way which tends to evacuate their belief of any meaningful content.

Flew illustrated his point with reference to an extended version of a parable, first introduced by John Wisdom, concerning the differing reactions of two explorers upon encountering a clearing in which is growing a profusion of flowers.

One is adamant that this must be the work of a gardener, the other sees no need to explain it in such terms. In the face of each piece of apparently disconfirming evidence (e.g. the lack of sight, sound and smell of any gardener) the believer continually makes some qualification to his belief in order to avoid having to abandon it, to the point of eventually provoking the reaction from his sceptical colleague: 'But what remains of your original assertion? Just how does what you call an invisible, intangible, eternally elusive gardener differ from an imaginary gardener or even from no gardener at all?' (Flew, 1955:96). Likewise:

> Now it often seems to people who are not religious as if there was no conceivable event or series of events the occurrence of which would be admitted by sophisticated religious people to be a sufficient reason for conceding 'There wasn't a God after all' or 'God does not really love us then' ... Some qualification is made – God's love is 'not a merely human love' or it is 'an inscrutable love' ... But then perhaps we ask: what is this assurance of God's (appropriately qualified) love worth, what is this apparent guarantee really a guarantee against? (1955:98–9)

Two points can be made in response to Flew, one concerning the character of theology in particular and the other concerning the way in which our theories and beliefs confront the bar of experience more generally.

To take the specifically theological point first: implicit throughout Flew's discussion is the assumption that it would be utterly contrary to the practice of theology for it to adopt a genuinely falsificationist or, perhaps better, fallibilist approach to matters of religious belief. This assumption is, however, by no means beyond question. More precisely, while Flew is indeed on solid ground in claiming that the theologian is concerned to scrutinize potentially falsifying arguments with a view to examining whether any credible responses might be made, the point is that this is only *part* of the task of theology. Equally important, as Nicholas Lash reminds us, is the task of acting as the bad conscience of faith – concerned to apply the tools of historical, philosophical and literary analysis to the realities of faith in a spirit of constant criticism, even to the point of their possible destruction (Lash, 1986:116; 1979:45–59). J.L. Mackie presses further in claiming that the fact and extent of evil in the world does indeed serve to falsify religious belief in such a manner as satisfies the falsificationist criteria of meaning (Mackie, 1971:92–104; 1982). Contrary to Flew then, there is no reason either *in principle* or *in practice* why theology should not be fallibilist in spirit and indeed every reason why it should be so (see 4.13).

Granted this, Flew does seem to be correct in maintaining that individual theological propositions cannot be falsified in the straightforward manner presupposed in the falsification principle. It is always possible to salvage a particular theological proposition by making adjustments in the total framework of beliefs within which it is set (e.g. 'God's love is "not a merely human love" or it is "an inscrutable love"'). But perhaps this suggests more about the inadequacy of the falsification principle as a criterion of meaning than it does about the meaninglessness of theological propositions. This brings us to the second, more general, point that can be made in response to Flew, concerning the way in which our theories and beliefs face the bar of experience.

4.9 The Duhem–Quine rejection of thesis fallibilism

According to a thesis originally propounded by Duhem and later popularized by Willard Van Orman Quine it is no more true of scientific theories that they face the bar of experience in a discrete manner than it is of theological propositions. Rather they confront experience as an interrelated system of mutually supportive theories and auxiliary hypotheses. In Quine's terms: 'our statements about the external world face the tribunal of sense experience not individually but only as a corporate body' (Quine, 1953:41). And again, 'Taken collectively, science has its double dependence upon language and experience; but this duality is not significantly traceable into the statements of science taken one by one . . . The unit of empirical significance is the whole of science' (p. 42). Consequently it is never possible to point to one crucial experiment which serves to falsify a theory in a straightforward fashion for it is always possible to salvage it by making adjustments elsewhere in the overall framework of beliefs. It is worth quoting Quine's argument at length:

> The totality of our so-called knowledge or beliefs, from the most casual matters of geography and history to the profoundest laws of atomic physics or even of pure mathematics and logic, is a man-made fabric which impinges on experience only along the edges. Or, to change the figure, total science is like a field of force whose boundary conditions are experience. A conflict with experience at the periphery occasions readjustments in the interior of the field . . . Reevaluation of some statements entails reevaluation of others, because of their logical interconnections . . . But the total field is so underdetermined by its boundary conditions, experience, that there is much latitude of choice as to what statements to reevaluate in the light of any single contrary experience. No particular experiences are linked with any particular statements in the interior of the field, except indirectly through considerations of equilibrium affecting the field as a whole. (1953:42–3)

In the light of this, the following conclusion is drawn, 'Any statement can be held true come what may, if we make drastic enough adjustments elsewhere in the system.' Likewise, 'no statement is immune to revision' and for this reason it is even 'folly to seek a boundary between synthetic statements, which hold contingently on experience, and analytic statements, which hold come what may'. In short, *in place of the image of knowledge as a superstructure erected on the basis of firm empirical foundations* (the strength of which can be tested in a piecemeal fashion), *the Duhem–Quine thesis suggests a non-foundational or post-foundational*[11] *image of knowledge as a complex flexible net (or web) the value of which must be determined in a more holistic way.* This points to what is arguably the most serious weakness in Popper's falsificationist account of scientific reason (and, along with this, in Flew's elevation of falsifiability to the level of a criterion of meaning): while Popper rejected the verificationist criterion of meaning, he continued to hold with the underlying positivist assumption that it is possible to confirm the negation of a proposition *in a discrete manner*.[12] With this in view we turn in Section C to explore the work of philosophers who have sought to articulate genuinely post-positivistic accounts of scientific reason and to reflect upon the possible theological relevance of their work. Before doing so, however, it may again be helpful for you to pause in order to take stock of the material which has been under discussion in the present section.

EXERCISE 4.2

1(a) Can you summarize the weakness which Popper pointed to in the verificationist criterion of meaning?

1(b) What alternative strategy did Popper himself propose in place of verification?

1(c) To what extent do these differing approaches represent a contrast between inductive and deductive forms of argumentation?

2(a) How significant in your opinion is Flew's argument concerning the unfalsifiability of religious belief?

2(b) How important do you consider it to be that the discipline of theology should promote an active regard for the fragility and potential fallibility of all religious thought and practice?

3(a) How does the Duhem–Quine notion that our beliefs face the bar of experience collectively rather than discretely challenge the assumptions at work in both verificationist and falsificationist forms of positivism?

3(b) What is your reaction to the claim that it is not possible to identify any absolutely sure, certain and universally adequate 'foundations' for human knowledge?

3(c) Some assume that the lack of firm foundations makes all concern for knowledge and truth futile. Others believe that it helpfully promotes a more realistic understanding of the way in which the valid search for knowledge is always rooted, partial and fragile and hence constantly requiring to be renewed. With which of these positions do you at present find yourself most in sympathy and why?

3(d) Do you think that religious belief and the discipline of theology have more to gain or to lose from the shift to a post-foundationalist image of human knowledge? Why?

SECTION C
LATTER PART OF THE TWENTIETH CENTURY: REVOLUTION, ANARCHY AND RESISTANCE IN SCIENTIFIC THEORY CHANGE, AND THE NEED FOR TEMPERED POST-FOUNDATIONALIST ACCOUNTS OF SCIENTIFIC AND THEOLOGICAL RATIONALITY (4.10–4.13)

4.10 Thomas Kuhn's revolutionary account of scientific theory change

We have seen that while Popper replaced the overly confident image of science as dealing in proven truths with the more modest image of it as dealing in potentially refutable conjectures, he nevertheless left intact the assumption that science makes steady progress through the piecemeal testing of discrete hypotheses and theories. It is this widely held assumption that was in turn radically called into question in 1962 by the publication of Thomas Kuhn's *The Structure of Scientific Revolutions*, one of the most influential books in recent intellectual history.

Kuhn's central thesis is that scientific 'progress' over the long term shows more a pattern of occasional dramatic and total transformations in our understanding of the world (what he refers to as 'paradigm' shifts) than it does one of steady development within an enduring framework of understanding. The shift from the Ptolemaic geocentric view of the cosmos to the Copernican heliocentric worldview (see 1.12) is one of Kuhn's favourite examples – another is the shift from Newtonian to relativistic physics (see 5.6–5.7). According to Kuhn the effects of such paradigm shifts are so total as to be spoken of in revolutionary terms (Kuhn, 1962:92–110). Further, there seems to be no strictly logical or *reasonable* way (to continue with the image of revolutionary overthrow) in which to move from one paradigm to another (p. 94). As he wrote in his Postscript to the second edition of *The Structure of Scientific Revolutions*, 'There is no neutral algorithm for theory-choice, no systematic decision procedure which, properly applied, must lead each individual in the group to the same decision' (Kuhn, 1970b:200; see also 1970c:260). Each move from one paradigm to another is 'a conversion experience which cannot be forced' involving a total switch from one way of viewing the world to another, with no apparent middle state in between (Kuhn, 1962:151, 111–12, 85, 150).

Kuhn even went as far as talking of the subscribers to competing paradigms as working in different worlds with no possibility of direct communication between them (1962:121, 150; 1970c:275–6). By this he meant that they cannot even reach common agreement as to what the relevant data is, since the data itself is perceived differently within the competing paradigms (1962:94, 148–9; 1970b:199–200; 1970c:266–7). To take the case of a ball rolling along a flat surface and gradually slowing to stationary: while the Aristotelian philosopher perceives in this the natural propensity of a moving object to come to rest, the Newtonian physicist, in contrast, perceives the effects of friction impeding the natural propensity of a moving object to continue at uniform velocity in a straight line. Kuhn referred here to the *'incommensurability'* of competing paradigms – by which he meant that while they are not utterly incomparable, it is nevertheless impossible to compare them in any direct one-to-one manner.[13]

For Kuhn it is precisely this determining effect of paradigms over observation which renders them resistant to straightforward Popperian falsification. Indeed, rather than thinking of science as focused always upon the potential falsification of current paradigms, he viewed it, in its 'normal' state at least, as operating within the terms of an accepted paradigm, seeking to solve problems, explain apparent anomalies and extend the scope of its application (1962:23–42). Only when the number of anomalies reaches a critical level will a new paradigm begin to stand a chance of being widely accepted (1962:52–65). Even at this point there is likely to be much resistance (1962:150–2, 81); a resistance which will be compounded, moreover, by extra-rational factors such as formative training, personal investment of time and reputation, peer loyalty, professional patronage and the influence of ideological presuppositions, commitments and interests deriving from the broader socio-cultural milieu. For example, for an age which interpreted Scripture in a particular way and which was steeped in a metaphysic which placed the creation of humans at the centre of its cosmic story, it is not surprising that so many were initially opposed to the counter-intuitive idea that the Earth revolves around the sun (rather than vice versa).

For Kuhn it is impossible for scientists ever to distance themselves completely from such factors and hence impossible for them to assess competing paradigms in a neutral fashion. To play upon the title of Thomas Nagel's book, there are for Kuhn no 'views from nowhere', only particular views from somewhere (cf. Nagel, 1986). The most that is possible is for scientists to seek to be aware of the anomalies in their own favoured paradigms and to be open to the task of applying commonly held values such as simplicity, coherency and empirical fruitfulness to the task of assessing, from their own standpoint, the relative merits of competing paradigms (Kuhn, 1970b:199; 1970c:261–2). As such, scientific theory change is held to come about less by strict rational proof than by a combination of growing discontent with the inadequacies of one theory and gradual persuasion, operating on a number of levels, that another offers a more fruitful way of looking at things.

4.11 Feyerabendian anarchism and the need for tempered post-foundationalist accounts of rationality

As Janet Martin Soskice has noted, there is a common assumption, shared both by those committed to the tenets of positivism and by those who espouse a thoroughgoing relativism, to the effect that the concern for rationality is inextricably linked with the hope of attaining to a purely objective, strictly neutral standpoint.[14] Where positivists believe that such a hope can indeed be realized, at least with regard to the empirical data of the hard sciences, relativists forgo all such hopes as both illusory and oppressive and point instead to the myriad different ways in which humans creatively construe the world in word and deed (Rorty, 1979).

For those caught in this bind, Kuhn's challenge to the positivist agenda and his espousal of a holistic approach to 'paradigm' change readily located him among the relativists (e.g. Scheffler, 1967). The assumption was that if there is no neutral standard against which to judge the relative adequacy of competing paradigms then all is a matter of mere subjective preference. This situation was further exacerbated with the publication in 1975 of Paul Feyerabend's ominously entitled *Against Method: Outline of an Anarchistic Theory of Knowledge.*

Where Kuhn had challenged the image of science as progressing through gradual refinement and consolidation, Feyerabend challenged the more pervasive notion of there being any such thing as *the* scientific method which can be taken as the model for all human rationality. In place of this assumption Feyerabend spoke in flamboyant rhetorical tone of the history of science displaying a methodological 'anarchism' in which practically 'anything goes' which happens to contribute to the handling of specific problems (Feyerabend, 1993:27–8). Whether or not Feyerabend meant these words literally – he has since denied that he did (1993:vii, 231) – he was widely taken as claiming not simply that scientists find inspiration for their theories in the most surprising of places (cf. Popper, 1959:32), or even that all judgements are value-laden, contextual and hence partial (cf. Kuhn); more than this Feyerabend was assumed to be denying that reason and criticism perform any legitimate role at all in the practice of science and that, in contrast, all is a matter of ideological bias and perceived utility.

Throughout the controversy that has been generated by the combined effects of Kuhn's revolutionary account of scientific theory change and Feyerabend's dismissal of the notion of there being one uniquely successful and precisely definable method for organizing our dealings with the world, Kuhn has consistently maintained that it represents a fundamental misinterpretation of their work to view either of them as abandoning all concern for rationality *per se* (Kuhn, 1970b:174–210; 1970c:231–78). Rather, they are to be seen as challenging an overly circumscribed model of rationality – one that does not fit even the practice of science – and as calling for it to be readjusted and changed in order 'to explain why science works as it does' (Kuhn, 1970c:264). That is, they are to be seen as pointing to the need for what we have referred to as viable post-foundationalist[15] accounts of rationality which are capable, in Bernstein's terms, of opening a way beyond the false dichotomy of a narrow objectivism on the one hand and an unconstrained relativism on the other (Bernstein, 1983). In Kuhn's own words:

> if history or any other empirical discipline leads us to believe that the development of science depends essentially on behaviour that we have previously thought to be irrational, then we should conclude not that science is irrational but that our notion of rationality needs adjustment here and there. (Kuhn, 1971:144)

We have already seen the need for a comparable revisioning of theological rationality (see 4.6). What is required is a way of holding together on the one hand a sense of the perspectively particular character of Christian faith with, on the other hand, a recognition of the need for that faith to be constantly exposed to the challenge and refreshment of other insights. Indeed we claimed that without such a concern Christian faith is in danger of appearing as a self-enclosed communal *blik* which is incapable of supporting its traditional claim to represent *the* perspective within which all aspects of reality can truly be set (cf. Aquinas, 1964a:5–9, 25–7). More particularly we claimed that the central Christian beliefs concerning God's action in Christ and the Spirit require constant rethinking in dialogue with the best of contemporary scientific understanding of the processes operative in the natural order if they are not to degenerate to the level of merely inspirational myths (see 4.3 and 4.4).

The main limitation of Kuhn's work, and even more so of Feyerabend's, is that while they have exposed the inadequacies of narrowly objectivist accounts of rationality, neither of them has really complemented this with a more positive account of how rationality might actually function in the more fragile, humble and partial mode which they point to. Accordingly in 4.12 and 4.13 respectively we turn to explore two such attempts to reconfigure human rationality in the light of the post-empiricist, post-foundationalist perspective which we have seen to have been opened up by the work of Quine, Kuhn, Feyerabend and others. In each case we are equally as concerned to reflect upon the possible theological relevance of the particular approach to rationality that is in view, as we are to address the question of its relevance to the scientific context.

EXERCISE 4.3

1. In what ways have the respective discussions of Kuhn's and Feyerabend's work furthered your understanding of some of the challenges which can be levelled at foundationalist/objectivist accounts of human reason?
2. What is your reaction to these challenges?
3. How might concerns to continue with a rational quest for truth best be taken forward in this context?

4.12 Imre Lakatos' account of the methodology of scientific research programmes and Nancey Murphy's theological appropriation of Lakatos

As a former student of Karl Popper and a friend of Paul Feyerabend, Imre Lakatos was well placed to seek to achieve the kind of dialectical overcoming of the objectivist–relativist dichotomy called for above. His concern was to take full account of the thesis-holism espoused by the likes of Quine and Kuhn, while seeking to tie this in to a much stronger emphasis upon the rationality of scientific theory change than he found in Kuhn's language of incommensurable paradigms and scientific revolutions.

In place of Kuhn's somewhat vague notion of competing scientific paradigms, Lakatos set the central concept of differing collaborative 'research programmes' enduring through time and guiding the practice of different communities of scientists. *At the heart of each such research programme is a 'hard core' theory which determines its shape and identity.* While revision of this 'hard core' is by no means inconceivable, such revision would amount to the abandonment of the particular research programme in question. *Surrounding the hard core and protecting it from premature abandonment is a safety belt of lower-level 'auxiliary hypotheses'* which mediate between the hard core and what is deemed to count as relevant data within the purview of a particular research programme. In one direction the auxiliary hypotheses serve to define and to support the core theory and are themselves explained with reference to that core; in the other direction they guide the interpretation of appropriate data.[16]

As with Quine's account the image which suggests itself is that of an inter-related web of theories, some of which are more firmly embedded than others (the 'hard core') but none of which is open to discrete verification or falsification. It is the web as a whole which hangs together with the data that it interprets. Like Quine, Lakatos emphasized that potentially falsifying data can be accommodated within research programmes by making appropriate adjustments in the protective belt of auxiliary hypotheses in such manner as allows the central core to remain intact (Lakatos, 1970:133). The important thing for Lakatos, however, is that while this ability to preserve the hard core of any given research programme serves to slow the pace of change between competing programmes, it does not make of such changes the kind of irrational affairs which he presumed Feyerabend and Kuhn to imply. The key for Lakatos here is the fact that *research programmes do not represent mere ways of interpreting the world. Rather, they represent programmes of action which seek both to explain the available data and to guide future research*. More spe-cifically they make predictions which can in turn be tested. On this basis he allowed a distinction to be drawn between what he referred to as 'progressive' and 'degenerative' programmes of research (1970:118).

According to Lakatos a programme is to be deemed progressive if the auxiliary hypotheses that are adopted not only serve to defend the hard core against some potentially falsifying data (what he refers to as the 'negative heuristic') but also allow for the prediction of hitherto unexpected 'novel facts'. In contrast, a pro-gramme is degenerative if all or most of the auxiliary hypotheses are added in a purely ad hoc manner with a view to avoiding potential disconfirmation and without themselves predicting any new facts. For Lakatos a research programme can be thought of as being pursued rationally to the degree to which it yields predictions which either are actually confirmed, or which hold out the realistic possibility of finding some significant confirmation following further investiga-tion of new data (or the reinvestigation of existing data).

The most obvious objection that could be raised against Lakatos' position is that he nowhere specified how long it is appropriate to seek to hold to an apparently degenerating programme in the hope that further research might yield some new significant data. Without this it becomes more difficult to distinguish between progressive and supposedly degenerating programmes in any clear and unambiguous manner. One of Lakatos' own favoured examples itself illustrates this point. Prout formulated as early as 1815 his theory to the effect that the atomic weights of all chemical elements are whole numbers. There followed, however, a considerable stretch of time during which there were periods when, in Lakatosian terms, it could easily have been abandoned as degenerative. Indeed, it was only on account of the perseverance and tenacity of its advocates that it eventually succeeded in establishing itself (Lakatos, 1970:138–40). This point could be pressed further: the attraction of Lakatos' approach is that it appears to point to a mechanism for rational adjudication between competing research programmes; on closer inspection, however, it becomes apparent that Lakatos no more provides a precise formula for rational theory choice than is to be found in the work of Kuhn or Feyerabend.

In response it could be argued that to find Lakatos wanting in this regard is to miss the real point of what he was seeking to do. It is clear from the role that he attributed to 'auxiliary hypotheses' in the interpretation of 'data' that he fully accepted that research programme adoption, adaptation and potential rebuttal is a matter of holistic judgement rather than precise formulation. As such he is best viewed not as one searching for a guaranteed algorithm with which to escape the ambiguity of judgement but rather as one seeking to expand the range of resources available for guiding this process in a rational manner. His own particular contribution was to argue that the somewhat negative move of adapting a research programme in the face of potentially disconfirming data can be complemented by the more positive move of seeking for a progressive coherence with 'novel facts' which it can be held to predict. As such he has made a significant contribution to the search for a viable post-foundationalist or post-empiricist rationality.

For this reason, were it possible to transpose Lakatos' thought into the theological sphere, then it might be expected to make an equally significant contribution there as it has already been found to make in the scientific sphere. At the very least such a transposition would show that there are significant family resemblances between the ways in which rationality functions in the respective domains of science and theology, and hence good reasons for believing that the insights and concerns of these two disciplines can be brought together in a mutually constructive interchange.

In this regard, it is significant to note that Robert J. Russell's approach – already explored in 1.15 and 2.5.1 – to analysing the relationship between *creatio ex nihilo* and the question of the temporal finitude of the cosmos draws explicitly upon Lakatosian imagery. For Russell, the equating of *creatio ex nihilo* with the ontological dependence of all that exists on God represents the core hypothesis at issue in the doctrine of creation. That in turn makes contact with empirical reality through a number of auxiliary hypotheses of varying levels of importance and openness to adaptation (1996:214–17). In this way, he seeks to show that it is entirely possible for theologians to negotiate claims deriving from quantum cosmology, to the effect that finitude does not require temporal beginning, without relinquishing the core claim for the ontological dependence of all things on God (1996:217–20).

More substantially still, Nancey Murphy has pursued a thoroughgoing theological transposition of Lakatos' thought in what has for a number of years now been developing as one of the most exciting 'research programmes' in the contemporary theology-and-science landscape. The most extended presentation of this position is to be found in her 1990 work *Theology in the Age of Scientific Reasoning*. Murphy's strategy is twofold: first, to indicate the theological relevance of Lakatos' basic account of the structure of science by pointing to examples of 'coherent series of theories in theology that have the formal properties of a research programme' and second, to claim that some of these can be deemed empirically progressive in a manner comparable to that intended by Lakatos (Murphy, 1990:86, 183–92). For Murphy, talk of there being a 'hard core' to theological research programmes is best thought of along the lines of David Kelsey's notion of a ' "single, synoptic, imaginative judgement" regarding what Christianity is all about' which serves to give a particular theological project its distinctive shape and focus (Murphy, 1990:184). Where 'God is the God of the oppressed' might be taken as the 'hard core' of liberation theology, Murphy's own inclination at the time of writing *Theology in the Age of Scientific Reasoning* was to identify the hard core of Christian belief with the doctrine of the Trinity (1990:184; 1994:106). She has since given this a more practical slant by pushing it back to the more fundamental notion of the self-giving, kenotic character of God's being in action as revealed in Jesus (Murphy and Ellis, 1996).

Howsoever the hard core of Christian belief is defined, once it has been identified the next step in a Lakatosian theology is to evaluate the extent to which all other significant aspects of theology mediate successfully between the hard core on the one hand and what is judged to be the total range of relevant data on the other hand (Murphy, 1990:186–98). The rationale here is that where some of these lower-level doctrines might appear almost exclusively concerned with the further conceptual clarification of the hard core – as does, for example, the *homoousion* ('of one substance') clause in Christology – others, most notably the doctrines of revelation and the Holy Spirit, relate equally closely to the identification, interpretation and discrimination of potentially relevant theological data. For example, a sufficiently broad doctrine of revelation would support the treating of data from practically any source whatsoever as being of potential theological significance. Murphy's own preference is to focus, in the main, upon data arising from the interpretation of Scripture and the discernment of God's presence and address in the life of the believing community (1990:188–9).

More precisely, she argues that theories of scriptural interpretation and of spiritual discernment function within theology in a manner comparable to the role performed by theories of instrumentation in the scientific context (1990:130–73; 1994:107–22). Indeed, in what is undoubtedly the most original part of her argument, she claims that such theories can be put to work in order to yield significant new data against which it is possible to test the accuracy of certain predictions arising from particular theological programmes. For example she signals that the claim that it is appropriate to address the Holy Spirit as *she* might be tested against a widespread process of communal Christian discernment as to whether or not this is indeed the will of God (1990:167–8). More generally, the image which this suggests is one of Christian communities as living laboratories in which theological hypotheses can be put to the test (1990:166; 1994:121).

Murphy's Lakatosian account undoubtedly makes a significant contribution to the search for a viable post-foundational approach to theological rationality. As with Lakatos, her particular contribution is to extend an essentially coherence-based approach to rational judgement[17] beyond the mere concern to maintain overall coherence in the face of potentially disconfirming data. Her approach complements this with the need also for progressive coherence with certain predicted 'novel facts'. Vital though it is, however, the rational testing of theological positions by no means constitutes the entirety of theological activity and hence cannot be thought of as an exhaustive account of theological rationality. The point is that the testing of theological positions presupposes their prior articulation. In this regard Christian theology is constantly facing new challenges and new situations (e.g. the challenge posed by the rise of feminism) which require the tradition to be rethought and reworked (see Chapter 8). Further, this reworking does not represent a merely reactionary concern to maintain the tradition at all costs; rather it goes to the very heart of the Christian understanding of the truth of God in Christ and the Holy Spirit as a living truth which continues to impact on new situations in ever new ways.

When viewed in this light, the task of Christian theology is seen to be rightly focused as much upon an expansive exploration of what possibilities are open for the refreshment, renewal and rearticulation of the tradition, as it is upon a rigorous testing of the ensuing proffered positions. Accounts of theological rationality must therefore attend to each of these aspects of theological work. Accordingly, we believe that Murphy's proposal, valuable though it is, requires to be set within a more rounded account of theological rationality as a whole; one that pays equal attention to both the constructive and the critical/evaluative moments in Christian theology. Related to this, we believe that it also needs to be complemented by a more explicit appreciation for the essentially practical focus of theological work. Our earlier dismissal of non-cognitivist accounts of Christian faith was rooted in the conviction that at the heart of the Christian tradition is the reality of God's action rather than a set of merely human ideas or ethical ideals (see 4.3). It was suggested there that *Christianity consists neither in a mere way of looking at the world, nor simply in a way of living within it, but in a lived process of deepening conformity to the transforming action of God in Christ and the Holy Spirit.*

This point has direct bearing upon the function of theology within the Christian tradition, for it suggests that the constructive dimension of theological work referred to above should never be driven by a mere concern to renew Christian *concepts* alone (as opposed, more fundamentally, to Christian living also) in the light of contemporary ways of *thinking*. Rather it should be driven by the ultimately practical concern always to understand better how to respond to, and so manifest more cogently, the living truth of God. As Murphy herself states, 'The point of being a Christian is not first of all to acquire knowledge, but rather to be obedient to Christ' (1990:196). Again, as is clear from the impact of feminist theory on Christian circles, the task of theological analysis in both its constructive and its evaluative modes must be held in close relationship with the need for constant ecclesial renewal. Anything less threatens to reduce Christian belief to the level of a mere ideology detached from material reality.

When viewed in these terms, Murphy's otherwise excellent application of Lakatosian methodology to the rational assessment of theological programmes appears – in its 1990 articulation at least – somewhat truncated as an account of theological rationality in the round. While she acknowledges that Christian faith is more about conformity to Christ than it is the mere acquisition of knowledge, when she turns her attention in *Theology in the Age of Scientific Reasoning* to the task of theology she defines it purely in terms of the analysis of beliefs. As she states, 'I suggest that theology is a *rational reconstruction* of the beliefs of a Christian community. Its job is to examine the community's belief system in order to display the relations among its parts and its justification relative to whatever else there is' (1990:196). While this is right, in so far as it goes, the problem is that it does not go far enough. The notion of Christian theology as being focused upon the rational assessment of beliefs requires complementing with a more explicit emphasis upon the way in which such beliefs may already be called into question by live issues concerning the adequacy of the practices which they promote. *What is required is a model of rationality which is capable of holding together the assessment of theory and belief on the one hand with the analysis and evaluation of practice on the other.*

Alternatively stated, what this points to is the need for a broader account of theological rationality than can be supported by a transposition of Lakatosian methodology alone. Lakatos stands with the majority of philosophers of science in assuming a more or less strict demarcation between the question as to the rational justification of theoretical frameworks on the one hand and the ethical evaluation of their potential applications on the other. Consequently, for all the contribution which he made to the rational assessment of competing research programmes in a post-foundationalist perspective, his work offers little or no help with the larger and arguably prior task of assessing the value of such programmes (i.e. whether they should be pursued at all)[18] in terms of the practices which they support.

Somewhat in contrast to this received view, Chapter 13 explores the work of philosophers who argue for the recontextualization of science and technology within a prior, explicitly ethical debate. Indeed it is to be noted that, subsequent to *Theology in the Age of Scientific Reasoning*, Murphy has herself moved to arguing, conjointly with George Ellis, for just such a prior location of science within a wider context of explicitly ethical concern (see Murphy and Ellis 1996; also Murphy 1997). The implication is that there is just as much need for the kind of extended vision of rationality in the scientific context as we have pointed to in the theological: that is, one which combines the standard *cognitive* concern for the assessment of theory and belief with an *ethical* concern for the analysis and evaluation of practice, and which pursues each of these concerns in a genuinely post-foundationalist manner. The work of the Pittsburgh-based philosopher Nicholas Rescher presents us with just such an account of rationality.

EXERCISE 4.4

1. How helpful do you find Lakatos' account of scientific research pro-grammes as a contribution to the task of seeking to articulate a con-structive post-foundationalist account of human rationality?
2. What questions and difficulties does it raise for you?
3. What new insights does it open up?
4. How helpful do you find Murphy's attempted theological appropriation? Again, seek to identify the specific questions and/or new insights which it prompts for you.

4.13 Nicholas Rescher's pragmatic-idealist account of human rationality and its theological significance

According to Rescher, one of the best ways to gain an initial understanding of a philosopher's work is to know who his or her philosophical heroes are. For

Rescher, three stand out from among the many lesser others whose combined influence contributes to the distinctive combination of expansive *coherentism*, conceptual *idealism* and tempered *pragmatism* which characterizes his work.[19] They are the German thinkers Gottfried Wilhelm Leibniz (1646–1716) and Immanuel Kant (1724–1804) and the American philosopher Charles Sanders Peirce (1839–1914).

Leibniz's influence manifests itself both in a commitment to the role of formal logic in the elucidation of philosophical problems, and also in an expansive, architectonic vision which views the task of philosophy as consisting in an ever-renewed attempt to present a coherent, systematic account of the way in which, in Wilfrid Sellars' words, 'things in the broadest possible sense of the term hang together in the broadest possible sense of the term' (Sellars, 1963:1). For Rescher, there is nothing that is ultimately irrelevant to this task; there is no sense in which the expansive, systematic urge of philosophy can be thought of as being brought to a point of stasis and irreformable finality.

In turn, Kant's influence is at its clearest in Rescher's espousal of the idealist claim that our ways of understanding the world really are *our* ways; ways, that is, which might be quite different were our own composition in turn different to the way in which it in fact is. However, Rescher does not view this constructive role of the mind as operating without all constraint. Rather, *he views our conceptual frameworks and human rationality more generally, as being shaped by a process of successful evolutionary interaction with a world that is really there*, with the implication that they can generally be trusted as being at least partially adequate to their task. To this extent, Rescher's pragmatic idealism might be viewed as a sophisticated, or critical, form of realism (see 1.7). This being said, Rescher stands fully with the force both of Sellars' attack on 'the myth of the given' and Wittgenstein's analysis of language to the effect that there is no possibility of our attaining to a pre-conceptual, pre-linguistic understanding of reality and, hence, no possibility either of our successfully pursuing a foundationalist approach to rationality.

What marks Rescher out as significant for present purposes is the fact that he by no means equates this with a fundamental disavowal of rationality and truth *per se*. Rather his concern is to seek an approach to rationality and truth that is genuinely fitted to the exigencies of this situation. It is here that the influence of Charles Sanders Peirce is at its most evident. Like Peirce, Rescher intends to maintain a firm grasp on the cognitive dimension of truth. While he accepts that truth cannot be directly assessed in terms of correspondential accuracy, he equally maintains that it should continue to be defined in such terms and this regardless of the fact that it must always function as an ideal to be aspired towards, rather than as a terminus at which one can know that one has arrived. Again like Peirce, Rescher looks to practical considerations as providing a reality principle against which it is possible to test the strength of our truth claims.

More precisely, while Rescher accepts that pragmatic benefit cannot be taken as a direct indicator of cognitive truth at the level of individual theses – false theses can after all support desirable consequences[20] – he maintains that it can be legitimately applied at the methodological level as a measure of whether or not a particular method is effective for the purposes for which it is intended. When it is recalled that our purposes in seeking after truth are both cognitive (i.e. to gain understanding) and practical (i.e. to better organize our dealings with reality), Rescher is left in no doubt that it is consistently the findings of coherentist methods of truth assessment which show such methods to be the most effective means of seeking after truth. More precisely, for Rescher, while the adoption of a coherentist approach to truth assessment cannot guarantee the attainment of truth, it does at least guarantee that one is moving in the direction in which truth (and that as traditionally defined in terms of correspondential accuracy) is best sought. So truth is to be *defined* in correspondential terms, but *assessed* in terms of the coherence of the rational framework which attempts both to describe reality and to indicate ways to respond authentically to that reality.

This brings us to the very heart of Rescher's approach to truth and rationality. For Rescher, pure objective neutrality and unassailable certainty are each impossible to attain. We are always already engaged in value-laden practices of knowing the world, the veracity of which are constantly called into question by the existence of other differently value-laden practices. Again, while Rescher's aforementioned emphasis upon the evolutionary adaptation of human reason to reality helps to reassure us, against radical sceptical concerns, that our value-laden practices of knowing do indeed have some hold on reality, the fact that he views truth as an ideal state which always eludes full and final attainment should equally serve to counteract any complacency concerning the adequacy of current states of knowledge. In contrast, it should act as a constant reminder of the partial, fragile, value-laden nature of all human knowing and of the consequent need for current states of knowledge to be constantly exposed to potential revision. For Rescher, it is precisely such an expansive, recursive, fallibilistic model of rationality which is in mind in his advocacy of coherentist approaches to truth assessment.

Thus far attention has been concentrated upon Rescher's treatment of the cognitive dimension of human rationality. Since the late 1970s he has progressively complemented this with a more adequate treatment of the evaluative and practical dimensions of rationality also. The result is that Rescher's mature thought presents an integrated and genuinely post-foundationalist account of the complex interweaving of human rationality in its cognitive, evaluative and practical dimensions. It is an account which retains a concern for the cognitive dimension of truth while setting this within the context of a strong sense of the human knowing subject as first and foremost an engaged agent in the world.

For such reasons the hope is raised that a theological appropriation of Rescher's thought will support just the kind of contextually rooted, yet dynamically expansive account of theological reason that was earlier held to be required by an authentic understanding of Christian truth and tradition (see 4.12).[21] In the light of what has emerged in the course of the present chapter, however, any such appropriation will have to be clearly distinguished from what in present terms would appear as a theologically inappropriate and philosophically incoherent attempt to establish Christian theology on the basis of Rescher's post-foundationalist account of rationality. In other words, theologically speaking, the most appropriate kind of interaction between philosophical work, on the one hand, and the Christian tradition, on the other hand, will be one that unfolds as a subsequent drawing of Rescherian insights into an enriching conversation with resonant emphases already widely acknowledged as being intrinsic to the Christian tradition; the purpose being to seek by so doing to grant these emphases clearer voice in such a manner as will extend their shaping power over the practice of theology more generally.

Perhaps paramount here is the traditional emphasis upon the unknowability of God. As Rescher himself notes, it is the very reality of the object that is at issue in faith (i.e. the inexhaustibly rich mystery that is God) which itself serves to place in permanent question the adequacy of any attempt to give truthful expression to it (Rescher, 1993b:131). However, while this features as a traditional tenet of Christian belief, at the level of theological practice it is all too frequently smothered by a somewhat less humble tone rather more at home with certainties than it is with open questions. A theologically focused engagement with Rescher's recursively expansive and determinedly fallibilist account of rationality at this point will help to restore something of the ethic of continual conversion and renewal by which Christian theology, as with the entirety of Christian living, should be distinguished.

Likewise, a theologically engaged reflection upon Rescher's vision of rationality as a dynamic interweaving of cognitive, evaluative and practical concerns (as prompted by specific questions and occurrences) will in turn promote a heightened sense of the ultimately practical focus of theological work. More precisely, it will promote a heightened sense of the way in which the theological concern to understand God, the world and the relationship between the two is most appropriately set within the prior context of the dual practical concern to weigh the world in the light of Christ and to live within it in the transforming power of the Spirit. Taken in conjunction with the previous point, it will promote the view of Christian tradition as not just a conservative, retrospective force but as equally a creative, prospective impulse which continues to unfold ever anew in diverse situations. Such an emphasis by no means excludes the possibility of certain parameters of thought and patterns of action becoming recognized as essential to the authentic continuance of Christian identity. Indeed correctly understood it can be held to require it. Nevertheless, it does represent a recovery of the sense in which the promised infallibility of the Church should serve to encourage Christian communities to risk discerning new answers to new questions and not merely to root them in what they inherit.

Alternatively stated, it suggests that the appropriate grounding of Christian thought and practice in what have become recognized as the distinctive patterns of Christian faith should never be allowed to justify the petrifying of theology into a self-enclosed discourse – a discourse which feels assured of its full and final adequacy, and which is immune from all challenge and criticism from without. On the contrary, the cosmic scope of the belief in the risen Christ's universally particular presence to all of created reality should itself impel Christian communities to adopt as expansive a vision in the theological sphere as Rescher advocates in the philosophical. This in turn holds implications for the range of contexts in which, and people by whom, this process of continuously renewed reflection upon the nature of Christian identity is properly pursued in a way which serves significantly to blur any supposed boundary between the *ecclesia docens* (the 'teaching Church') and the *ecclesia discens* (the 'listening Church'). While all of this reintroduces an element of risk to the practice of Christian theology, sustaining it throughout should be the memory that the central Christian narratives themselves identify the very truth and purpose of God with the creative embrace of such risk and vulnerability.

EXERCISE 4.5

1. How helpful do you find the kind of approach to rationality that Rescher advocates?
2. What is your reaction to the claims made here for its potential relevance to the theological sphere?

4.14 Summary and conclusion

The present chapter started out with the caricatured assumption that science stands as *the* model of rationality in such a manner as leaves no place for theology to be understood as a rational discipline. This assumption was examined more closely in the guise of logical positivism, as also were the strengths and weaknesses of four differing theological strategies for responding to the challenge which it posed. The central section of the chapter traced the unravelling of the positivist agenda in the middle part of the twentieth century and the shift towards a more modest account of scientific rationality in the work of Karl Popper. This story was continued into the final section where we traced the rise of holistic accounts of scientific rationality in the work of Quine and Kuhn and the final disavowal, in the work of Paul Feyerabend, of the claim that there is any such thing as *the* scientific method which defines the essence of rationality.

Emergent from this discussion was the realization that while the demise of positivism and the move beyond philosophical foundationalism served to reopen the possibility of taking seriously explicitly tradition-bound discourses such as theology, such a move equally requires complementing with viable accounts of how rationality should function in post-foundationalist perspective. Without such accounts, the move beyond foundationalistic objectivism appears simply to sanction a collapse into unconstrained relativism (Bernstein, 1983). In the hope of finding some guidance we turned in the final two subsections of the chapter to consider the work of Imre Lakatos and Nicholas Rescher respectively, each time with a view to the potential theological relevance of their work. We found that while they each make a real contribution to the search for a viable post-empiricist, post-foundationalist account of rationality, Lakatos' approach to the assessment of theoretical frameworks requires to be set within the broader vision of rationality espoused by Rescher.

In short, where the chapter started out with the positivistic assumption as to the exemplary rational character of science and the corresponding irrationality of theology, it drew to a close with two examples of the family resemblances which can be traced between the operation of rationality in each of these contexts when viewed within a post-foundationalist perspective (4.12 and 4.13 respectively). *This in turn lends weight to the assumption underlying the entirety of this book: that it is both possible and fruitful to seek to bring the insights and concerns of these two perspectively distinct disciplines together in a mutually constructive interchange.* Indeed, the necessary self-critical openness to other traditions of thought and practice which has been seen to be such an essential feature of rationality in a post-foundationalist perspective itself demands such a mutual interchange.

Going beyond this, the present chapter has already highlighted certain aspects of science and theology which themselves prompt the need for a mutually constructive interchange. On the one hand, we have seen that while science is quite appropriately methodologically agnostic or naturalistic (in the sense that it leaves questions about the ultimate origin and end of things out of account), it nevertheless serves to raise questions which cannot be answered within its own perspective, in such a manner as itself suggests the need for them to be set within the broader perspectives of metaphysical and theological reflection (see 4.5). Again, we have seen the need for science to be set within a prior context of explicitly ethical debate in such a manner as provides renewed impetus to the need for constructive dialogue between science and religious traditions (see 4.12).

On the other hand, we have seen that the distinctiveness of Christian theology consists not in its treating of God *as opposed* to any of the things which constitute the furniture of the world but rather in its treating of all that is within the perspective of God as its 'origin and end' (see 4.5 and 4.6; Aquinas, 1964a:27, 9). For this reason Christian theology must, by its very nature, be concerned with what can be known of creaturely reality on the basis of other disciplines. In accordance with this, it has been claimed that the openness to challenge, refreshment and renewal which this necessitates goes to the very heart of the character of God's continuing impact in Christ and the Holy Spirit on the diverse particularities of created reality. In turn, and related to this, it has been indicated that the credibility of these central claims concerning the reality of God's act in Christ and the Holy Spirit itself requires those claims to be thought through in dialogue with what can be known of the processes operative in the world in the purview of the natural sciences (see 4.3 and 4.4). Each of these points will be treated more fully in subsequent chapters.

Notes

1   As Ayer put it: 'We say that a sentence is factually significant to any given person, if, and only if, he knows how to verify the proposition which it purports to express – that is, if he knows what observations would lead him, under certain conditions, to accept the proposition as being true, or reject it as being false' (Ayer, 1971:48).

2   As Nicholas Lash has commented in a somewhat different context, '... there are surely less cumbersome ways of being an atheist than to use the paraphernalia of Christian language and imagery simply to express the form of our alienation?' (1986:117). Substantially the same charge could be levelled against the more recent and more vigorous non-realism of writers such as Mark C. Taylor and Don Cupitt (see Murray, 2005:10–11).

3   See 10.3 to locate this position in a spectrum of view on divine action.

4   See 1.3.1 for an introduction to natural theology and the problems it faces.

5   His 1979 *The Existence of God* stands as the classic text. In the Introduction he

describes the book as 'concerned with whether the claim [that there is a God] is true; it is concerned to assess the weight of arguments from experience for and against this claim, and to reach a conclusion about whether on balance the arguments indicate that there is a God or that there is not' (1979:1; see also Swinburne, 1993:188).

6   In *The Justification of Religious Belief* (1973).

7   This principle received classic statement in the first article of the Barmen Declaration in 1934: 'Jesus Christ, as He is attested to us in Holy Scripture, is the one Word of God, whom we have to hear and whom we have to trust and obey in life and in death. We condemn the false doctrine that the Church can and must recognise as God's revelation other events and powers, forms and truths, apart from and alongside this one Word of God' (Barth, 1957:172).

8   For a theory of the roots of Barth's suspicion of natural theology in the history of the Genevan tradition see McGrath, 2001:268–79.

9   See MacKinnon (1968:66–9); for a related point see also Hunsinger (1991:32–5). For further discussion of the particular use which MacKinnon himself makes of Barth's Christocentric particularity, see Murray (2005: particularly 178–84).

10   See also McGrath, 2001:279–86 on Torrance's Barth-influenced approach to natural theology.

11   'Foundationalism represents the assumption that it is both necessary and possible to identify certain sure foundations for human knowledge (i.e. claims of knowledge the truth of which is absolutely certain) which underpin the rest of human knowledge by providing a firm basis upon which the ensuing edifice of human reason can be securely established' (Murray, 2005:5). Correlatively, post-foundationalism refers to the now widespread assumption that such indubitable foundations are simply not available for real human knowing which is always rooted in and shaped, to some degree at least, by the particular contexts (historical, socio-political, psychological, linguistic, etc.) within which it operates (see Murray, 2005:3–6 and *passim*).

12   For the sake of accuracy it should be noted that at one point Popper does add the following rider to his thesis: 'In point of fact, no conclusive disproof of a theory can ever be produced; for it is always possible to say that the experimental results are not reliable, or that the discrepancies which are asserted to exist between the experimental results and the theory are only apparent and that they will disappear with the advance of our understanding' (Popper, 1959:50). However, the broader implications of this statement do not figure in Popper's overall argument. Thomas Kuhn seems to be correct in stating: 'Having barred conclusive disproof, he has provided no substitute for it, and the relation he does employ remains that of logical falsification. Though he is not a naïve falsificationist, Sir Karl may, I suggest, legitimately be treated as one' (Kuhn, 1970a:14).

13   Cf. Kuhn, 1962:103, 112, 148; 1970c:267. The most helpful reading of what Kuhn did and did not intend in introducing this vexed notion is to be found in Richard Bernstein's *Beyond Objectivism and Relativism* (1983:20–5, 51–71, 79–93; see also Poole, 1995:44f.).

14   Soskice, 1993b:49; 1985:119–26. Bernard Williams has referred in this regard to the notion of an 'absolute conception of reality' (Williams, 1978:65–7 and *passim*).

15   See note 11 above. Mary Hesse has termed this type of account of rationality 'post-empiricist'. For her account see Hesse (1980:167–86). Likewise, Michael Polanyi spoke in this regard of the need for a 'post-critical' understanding of human knowledge, see 4.6 here.

16   This is particularly so in the case of what Lakatos referred to as 'theories of

instrumentation', by which he meant theories which are involved, either implicitly or explicitly, in the construction, use and interpretation of data-gathering
instruments.

17   As the name suggests, coherence-based approaches to truth and reason typically
emphasize the relevance of the degree of overall coherence which pertains within a
given body of beliefs to questions concerning the truth-status of that body of
beliefs. See 1.7 for coherence as an overall term for a variety of criteria of theory-
comparison. Where some would view truth as actually consisting in propositional
coherence, others settle for viewing such coherence as the most reliable means of
testing for truth as correspondence to reality (see 4.13, also Barbour, 1998:109–
10; Rescher, 1973).

18   See 1.5.1 note 15, 1.20.

19   Even more so than is the case with the term 'coherentism' (see note 17 in this
chapter), 'idealism' and 'pragmatism' are terms used variously to refer to a wide
range of differing yet related positions. Where the central integrating assumption
at work in all forms of idealism is that reality is somehow mind-dependent or
'mind-coordinated' (for more on this, see Rescher, 1992a:187–91), the central idea
throughout the various shades of pragmatism is that questions of truth require to
be held together with considerations of practical efficacy (for more on this, see
Rescher, 1995:710–13). The combined influence respectively of coherentist,
pragmatist and idealist emphases on Rescher's thought is signalled by the overall
title that he gave to his three-volume *magnum opus* – he calls his work in its vast
interconnected entirety *A System of Pragmatic Idealism* (see Rescher, 1992b; 1993a;
1994). For focused discussion of the relevance of realist, idealist, coherentist and
pragmatist concerns to the science–religion interface, see Murray, 2003:266–8.
For an essay-length critical exposition of Rescher's understanding of human
rationality, see Murray, 2005:91–130.

20   Such as for example the thesis that 'unless conserved, all the Earth's non-renewable
resources will be exhausted by 2020' or that 'enemies always give up their hate if
they know themselves loved'.

21   Some of what follows in the remainder of this section has already been published
in Murray, 1998a:167–8. We acknowledge with thanks permission from *The Way*
to reproduce the relevant material here (for a fuller discussion, see Murray, 2005:
133–8, 152–61, 13–16).

Further reading

BANNER, M.C. (1990) *The Justification of Science and the Rationality of Religious Belief*
(Oxford: Clarendon Press)

BERNSTEIN, R.J. (1983) *Beyond Objectivism and Relativism: Science, Hermeneutics and Praxis*
(Oxford: Blackwell)

MURPHY, N. (1994) 'What has theology to learn from scientific methodology?' in *Science
and Theology: Questions at the Interface*, ed. M. Rae, H. Regan and J. Stenhouse
(Edinburgh: T&T Clark), 101–26

MURRAY, P.D. (2005) *Reason, Truth and Theology in Pragmatist Perspective* (Leuven: Peeters)

SOSKICE, J.M. (1993) 'Bad language in science and religion', in *Explorations in Science and
Theology: The Templeton London Lectures at the RSA* (London: RSA), 69–78

—— (1993) 'The truth looks different from here, or: on seeking the unity of truth from a
diversity of perspectives', in *Christ in Context: The Confrontation Between Gospel and
Culture*, ed. Hilary D. Regan and Alan J. Torrance (Edinburgh: T&T Clark), 43–59

RESCHER, N. (1992) *A System of Pragmatic Idealism, Volume 1: Human Knowledge in Idealist Perspective* (Princeton, NJ: Princeton University Press)

STENMARK, M. (2004) *How to Relate Science and Religion: A Multidimensional Model* (Grand Rapids, MI: Eerdmans)

VAN HUYSSTEEN, J.W. (1999) *The Shaping of Rationality: Towards Interdisciplinarity in Theology and Science* (Grand Rapids, MI: Eerdmans)

BOOK TWO

Chapter 5

Theology and the New Physics

Lawrence Osborn

5.1 Introduction

In this chapter we shall look first of all at the powerful (and continuing) influence of Newtonian thinking (Section A). Then we shall consider two ways in which physics has parted company with the Newtonian worldview: through the rediscovery of time (Section B), and the rediscovery of the observer (Section C) – noting some theological implications. We go on to look at issues in modern cosmology – the beginning and end of the universe (Section D) and the possible rediscovery of purpose (Section E). Finally we consider the new science of chaos and complexity (Section F).

SECTION A
CLASSICAL PHYSICS AND THE NEWTONIAN WORLDVIEW (5.2–5.4)

5.2 The scientific revolution

The century and a half from the middle of the sixteenth century to the end of the seventeenth is, with some justification, regarded as a watershed in the development of the natural sciences. Beginning with the publication of Nicolaus Copernicus' *De revolutionibus* (*On the Revolutions of the Celestial Spheres*) in 1543 and culminating in the appearance of Isaac Newton's *Principia mathematica* (*Mathematical Principles of Natural Philosophy*) in 1687, a succession of radical thinkers revolutionized the disciplined study of the physical world. Among the main achievements of these early scientists were the establishment of a potentially simpler heliocentric model of the solar system in preference to the geocentric model favoured at the time (Copernicus, 1473–1543); the application of experimental method and mathematical analysis to the study of motion (Galileo, 1564–1642); the refinement and mathematization of the heliocentric model (Kepler, 1571–1630); and the grand synthesis of these elements to show that all the situations under consideration, whether Earthbound or celestial, could be explained in terms of three mathematical laws of motion and a law of universal gravitation (Newton, 1642–1727).

Certain common assumptions regarding the nature of the physical world may be gleaned from this body of scientific work. Natural phenomena appear to be unimaginably complex, but the founders of modern physics were committed to the view that underlying this complexity the world was rational and simple. In pursuit of this simplicity, they rejected the qualitative approach of traditional Aristotelian physics in favour of an emphasis on measurement. This reinforced a tendency (traceable back as far as the Ancient Greek philosopher Democritus) to distinguish between primary and secondary qualities. The former (mass, extension and duration) can be quantified and measured accurately, and were thought to be characteristic of an object in itself. They were, therefore, amenable to the combination of experimentation and mathematical analysis adopted by classical physics. Secondary qualities (such as colour, temperature and hardness), by contrast, could not be measured accurately and were, at that time, dismissed as subjective. The world envisaged by early modern science was well ordered, stable and predictable. Indeed subsequent generations of classical physicists were prepared to argue that, in principle, the future motion of every particle in the universe is predictable given an accurate knowledge of their positions, masses and velocities at some arbitrary point in time (see our discussion of Laplace in 1.17).

5.3 From method to worldview

This Newtonian paradigm had an impact that extended far beyond the methods of the virtuosi and the doors of the learned societies. According to Holton and Roller,

> So impressive were the victories of Newtonian mechanics that, in the early part of the 18th Century, there spread a mechanistic world-view which asserted that man's confident intellect could eventually reduce *all* phenomena and problems to the level of mechanical interpretations. The development of this new view through the extrapolation of the findings of science to philosophy was carried out mainly by philosophers, and it had important effects on economics, the 'science of man', religion, and political theory. (Holton and Roller, 1958:207)

However, in order to understand why something as far removed from practical concerns as a law of gravity should so catch the public imagination, we must recall that science does not exist in a vacuum. The peculiar attraction of Newtonian mechanics becomes much clearer when it is set in its wider cultural context (a task which is dealt with in detail by Toulmin, 1990:45–87).

Europe had been divided on religious lines after the Reformation. After an initial period of hostility, efforts at reconciliation (or, at least, at finding some way for divided communities to coexist) began during the sixteenth century, which proved to be a brief golden age during which the arts, the sciences and indeed a revived magical practice all flourished. However, efforts at reconciliation between Roman Catholic and Protestant failed. The first two decades of the seventeenth century were marked by growing intolerance, culminating with the opening shots of the Thirty Years War in 1618. In the wake of war came severe economic instability, famine and disease. Not surprisingly, apocalyptic speculation was rife, with Christ's return widely expected to occur before the end of the century.

This anarchy inevitably generated a desire for order and stability. But where were these to be found? Religion had been tried in the fires of the Thirty Years War and found seriously wanting. The cultural and political leadership of Europe began to seek elsewhere for a secure basis for social order. A crucial part of their answer was the rationalistic philosophy of René Descartes (1596–1650). Perhaps human reason could succeed where religious tradition and authority had failed.

Rationalism offered the scientists of the seventeenth century a powerful device for underwriting the reliability and universality of their assertions. The mental discipline of subjecting their interpretations of nature to reason distinguished early modern science from competing ways of viewing the natural world. Classical physics, in turn, provided the exercise of reason (in conjunction with experimentation) with an early success story. The Newtonian paradigm in physics represented the successful adaptation of science to the new emphasis on universal truths of reason. And it did for the natural world what Cartesian rationalism promised to do for human society – it ushered in a new era of order and stability.

In the exhaustion that followed the Peace of Westphalia (1648), Descartes and Newton offered the intellectuals of Europe the hope of a new way forward. Within half a century their ideas dominated Western philosophy and science. The despair and hopelessness that led the intellectuals of 1650 to speculate about the imminent end of the world were swept away. In their place was a new vision – of a just society empowered by human reason, progressing towards an undefined goal in the future.

The success of the Newtonian paradigm in physics encouraged others to emulate it in other spheres. In particular, it offered the ruling elites a new and authoritative image for the ideal society. The modern nation state as it began to emerge in the eighteenth century was modelled upon the world of Newtonian astronomy. Like the solar system, it was centralized – a central authority (whether it be *le Roi Soleil*, a constitutional monarch, or a democratically elected government) wielding authority over successive circles of subjects, all of whom knew their places. On a smaller scale this centralized pattern was reflected in the paternalistic family. Social Newtonians (notably Newton's staunch advocate Samuel Clarke) insisted that the order of nature indicated the rightness of the social order – that we should be content with our rulers and with our station in life. This is the outlook enshrined in that politically incorrect verse from 'All things bright and beautiful' by Cecil Alexander (1818–95):

> The rich man in his castle,
>   The poor man at his gate,
> God made them high and lowly
>   And ordered their estate.

According to Margaret Wertheim,

> The Newtonian society, like the Newtonian cosmos, was a lawful, stable, immutable, and supposedly God-given order. Just as the planets remained

fixed in their respective orbits, human beings were to remain fixed in their respective 'stations' . . . It was thus humanity's moral duty to emulate in the social realm the order Newton had discovered in nature. And so, . . . Newtonian science in the eighteenth [century] was enlisted to justify the status quo. (Wertheim, 1995:132)

5.4 Change and continuity in the physical sciences

In the nineteenth century Newton's laws of motion were successfully used to describe the motion of charged particles in electromagnetic fields, raising hopes that a complete description of the physical world could be achieved within the Newtonian paradigm. Indeed one of the most eminent physicists of the nineteenth century, Lord Kelvin, was so convinced of the completeness of Newtonian physics that in 1900 he told the British Association for the Advancement of Science, 'There is nothing new to be discovered in physics now. All that remains is more and more precise measurement.' In the same year he told the Royal Institution that only two clouds remained to obscure the 'beauty and clearness' of Newtonian physics.

The first of those clouds was the failure of the Michelson–Morley Experiment to detect the motion of the Earth through the aether (the medium through which it was assumed light must be propagated). The other was the failure of classical physics to account for the colour of hot objects – the spectrum of black-body radiation. Kelvin may have dismissed them as clouds, but within a few years of his death they had grown into great storms. One gave rise ultimately to relativity theory; the other to quantum theory. Together these new theories amounted to a revolution in our understanding of the physical world.

However, while the content of the physical sciences may have changed radically, there remain underlying continuities. These continuities are highlighted by the marginal place of the new physics in elementary science education. Critics sometimes deplore the fact that very little of the new physics appears in the average school science syllabus. But such criticisms betray a superficial under-standing of science. Content is less important than method and attitude. For today's physics students, the role models are still men like Galileo, Kepler, Newton, Joule, Coulomb, Faraday, Maxwell and Kelvin. Einstein and Hawking may have become icons of science in the popular mind but they have so far had little impact on attitudes and methods. As for great women physicists, Marie Curie stands alone as a romantic figure in the popular mind – and her contribution to physics is still undervalued by a physics establishment that perpetuates the sexist myth that her husband Pierre was the creative member of the partnership.[1]

The formative assumptions of physics may be enumerated in a variety of ways. One example would be Coulson's account of the scientific method in his *Science and Christian Belief* (1958:42–83). He presents an idealized vision of the scientist as one who comes to his task with honesty, integrity, hope, enthusiasm, humility, singleness of mind, willingness to cooperate with others, patience and critical judgement – the gifts of the scientific spirit. Furthermore he highlights certain assumptions without which science would make little headway and reminds us of their roots in the Judaeo-Christian worldview:

> that common search for a common truth; that unexamined belief that facts are correlatable ... that unprovable assumption that there is an 'order and constancy in Nature,' without which the patient effort of the scientist would be only so much incoherent babbling and his publication of it in a scientific journal for all to read pure hypocrisy; all of it is a legacy from religious conviction. (Coulson, 1958:75)

Specifically, it is a legacy of the mediaeval synthesis, the worldview that informed Christendom. That the legacy continued to influence physics in the twentieth century will be a theme of the next section.

SECTION B
THE REDISCOVERY OF TIME (5.5–5.9)

5.5 Classical physics and the exorcism of time

At first sight, classical physics appears to lend support to the common-sense view of time – that only present events exist; past events have ceased to exist, and future ones do not yet exist. In Newtonian physics time is linear and uniform with physical reality restricted to present events and things.

However, on closer examination we find that classical physics treats time as entirely external to and independent of the physical world. In spite of its apparent ontological priority, the present has no special status in the Newtonian scheme. Indeed, far from explaining or integrating time into its theories, the first priority of classical physics appears to have been to eliminate it from consideration. Classical physics is characterized by the quest for laws that do not vary with time (or make no reference to time). This bias amounts to what Ilya Prigogine has described as an exorcism of time (Prigogine and Stengers, 1984:291f.) from classical physics.

This is not to suggest that physicists made a conscious decision to exclude time from consideration. Rather such an exclusion follows naturally (and unconsciously) from certain philosophical and theological assumptions that were widespread in seventeenth- and eighteenth-century Europe.

One of these assumptions was the sharp division of reality into two incommensurable realms. On the one hand, there is *res cogitans*: the intelligible realm, the province of subjectivity, of mind, soul and spirit (and, hence, of religion and supernature). On the other hand, there is *res extensa*: the material realm, the province of nature and science. According to Descartes, the entities of *res extensa* possessed no other properties besides spatial extension. It was a passive world amenable to the physicists' ideal of quantification.

The significance of this dualism for a physical account of time becomes clear in the light of the very close association between time and mind. As Genevieve Lloyd puts it, 'we cannot think consciousness without thinking time, or time without thinking consciousness . . . if we take away the thought of consciousness, time also vanishes' (Lloyd, 1993:2). The Cartesian elimination of mind from physical reality could only result in a similar elimination of time or, at least, its reduction to an external parameter. As a result, classical physics became the observation of a world characterized only by extension from the vantage point of a quasi-divine spectator, namely, from eternity.

Another factor affecting the classical physical treatment of time was the dominant interpretation of eternity in Christian theology. This tended to be treated either as timelessness or as a present that does not pass away. Typical is the following passage from Boethius (470–5–524):

> Embracing the infinite lengths of past and future, it [God's knowledge] considers everything as if it were going on now in a simple mode of awareness. So, if you want to weigh the presentness with which he discerns everything, you will more rightly judge it to be not a foreknowledge as of the future, but the knowledge of a never failing instant. Hence it is called pro-vidence rather than pre-vision, because it looks forth from a position far removed from things below as if from the highest summit of things. (Quoted in Sorabji, 1983:256)

Boethius portrays God's view of history as that of an observer on a mountain-top viewing the countryside all laid out equally below. Time is likened to space. From God's (true) perspective there is no passage of time in creation. And it was to these heights that the classical physicist aspired.

5.6 Relativity and the rediscovery of time

As physicists became more confident of their ability to model the world, they set their sights beyond the very simple mechanical phenomena that had been the foundation of Newtonian dynamics. Thus the idea of unvarying or time-free physical laws began to come under pressure during the nineteenth century with the development of thermodynamics. The more complex phenomena associated with heat transfer were simply not amenable to the same treatment as, say, a simple pendulum. As the Ancients realized, *ignis mutat res* – fire changes things. And change is a fundamental aspect of the common-sense view of time.

However, it is not thermodynamics that is commonly associated with the rediscovery of time in physics but Einstein's theory of relativity – the answer to the first of Lord Kelvin's clouds. Published in 1905, Albert Einstein's innocuously entitled paper 'On the electrodynamics of moving bodies' was first and foremost an attempt to explain anomalies arising from attempts to apply Maxwell's Theory of Electromagnetism to moving bodies. The velocity of light appears in that theory as a universal constant – but relative to what: the source, the intervening medium or the observer?

Drawing on our experience of objects moving at low speeds, we might expect the velocity of light to be constant relative to its source. However, this is not borne out by observation (e.g. it would significantly affect observations of binary star orbits). Thus attention turned to the second option: the velocity of light is constant relative to the intervening medium – absolute space – the aether. If so, it should be possible to detect the aether by looking for variations in the velocity of light caused by the Earth's motion relative to the aether. Failure to do so was one of the clouds that worried Lord Kelvin.

Einstein's extraordinary proposal was to treat the velocity of light as constant relative to the observer while, at the same time, insisting that 'the same laws of electrodynamics and optics will be valid for all frames of reference for which the equations of mechanics hold good' (Einstein, 1923:37f.) – his *principle of relativity*. These apparently irreconcilable postulates allowed Einstein to develop an alternative to Newton's laws of motion that effectively dissolved the anomalies that had troubled his predecessors.[2]

However, the new theory required a redefinition of the concept of simultaneity. In a Newtonian world there would be universal agreement that two events had occurred simultaneously. According to Einstein, one observer moving relative to another would not agree with the second that the two events were simultaneous. A corollary of this disagreement is that there can be *no universal present moment* – what is present to me may be past to one observer and still to come for another! Thus the principle of relativity rules out the possibility of a Newtonian universal 'now'. The universe may not be thought of as a succession of instantaneous spaces. Space and time are simply not separable in the manner envisaged by Newtonian physics.

5.7 Relativity and the spatialization of time

Ironically, Einstein's revolution in our treatment of space and time is often interpreted as supporting the classical view of temporal passage as extraneous to physics. Many physicists maintain that the connection between time and space established by Einstein is of such a kind that time should be thought of as analogous to space – a fourth spatial dimension. For them, reality consists of the entire collection of events that ever have been or ever will be – past, present and future taken together in a static block (sometimes called the stasis theory of time). If so, our perception of time as passing is an artefact of human psychology rather than a physical reality. The following quotations are typical:

> The objective world simply is. It does not happen. Only to the gaze of my consciousness crawling upward along the lifeline of my body does a section of this world come to life as a fleeting image. (Weyl, 1949:166)

> relativity physics has shifted the moving present out from the super-structure of the universe, into the minds of human beings, where it belongs. (Davies, 1974:2f.)

> [The physicist] does not regard time as a sequence of events which *happen*. Instead, all of past and future are simply there, and time extends in either direction from any given moment in much the same way as space stretches away from any particular place. (Davies, 1990:124)

What these assertions (and many others like them) fail to make clear is that this is an *interpretation* of the special theory of relativity. It is not that relativity theory has somehow proven Boethius' analogy between time and space to be the case. Rather these physicists are reading relativity in the light of that analogy. Indeed it is an interpretation about which Einstein himself was ambivalent. On occasions he certainly wrote in a similar vein. However, when faced with Meyerson's critique of this interpretation, Einstein agreed that 'The element of spatial distance and the element of duration remain distinct in nature, distinct even in the formula giving the square of the world interval of two infinitely near events' (Einstein (1928) quoted in Capek, 1976:366f.).

5.8 Time and space

What are the implications of accepting a strong analogy between time and space?

It would, to say the least, be odd to entertain the notion that the things and events located in some regions of space were somehow more real than those located elsewhere. By analogy, then, we must deny that present events are more real than past or future events. In other words, events at every temporal location must be equally real. All things and events coexist timelessly. I am ignorant of the events of 2010 only because of my location in 2004 (just as I am ignorant of events in Exeter while revising this chapter in Glasgow). All future events are there to be read off as and when we reach the right spatio-temporal location. Nor do past events pass away into oblivion — they remain (timelessly) in spatio-temporal locations to which I (the conscious observer moving through spacetime) no longer have access.

If this is so, then we must admit the validity of certain strange locutions. For example, few people living in November 2004 would quibble with the assertion that 'Tony Blair is alive and well, and living in Downing Street'. But the theory that all entities and events exist timelessly (a 'stasis' view of time) requires us also to accept such assertions as 'John F. Kennedy is (timelessly) alive and well and living in 1958.' Of course, oddity does not imply that this is invalid. However, it does highlight the fact that this view of time is strongly counterintuitive.

5.8.1 Spacelike time and determinism

We generally believe the past to be determinate. For example, we may not have access to all the details of the Napoleonic Wars but we do know that a joint Anglo-Prussian force finally defeated Napoleon's army at the Battle of Waterloo. It simply is the case that this happened — nothing can change the fact (not even the most inspired historical reinterpretation). Conversely it is our experience that the future is not determinate in this sense. We do not know what the future will bring. However, we can make predictions based upon past trends and present knowledge. Our predictions generally take the form of a range of possibilities. We further believe that in certain cases it is possible to influence the outcome by acting in certain ways.

In direct contradiction of our experience of past and future, the spatial treatment of time asserts that future events are determinate in precisely the same way as past events. Advocates of this approach are quick to point out the mind-dependence of the experience described above. They argue that the apparent indeterminacy of the future is entirely explicable in terms of our psychological limitations. There is a *merely psychological* arrow of time that denies us access to knowledge of events which are located at spatio-temporal locations later than our own.

However, this has interesting physical implications. As we shall discuss in 5.11–5.14, quantum mechanics is usually taken to imply indeterminacy – future states of the universe cannot be totally predicted, even in theory, from the present state.[3] But on a 'stasis' view where all future events are (timelessly) determinate, the most obvious candidate for an adequate interpretation of quantum mechanics would be some kind of hidden-variables theory, one in which the apparent indeterminacy of the quantum world is underpinned by a more fundamental determinism (see 5.13 (ii)). Thus all uncertainty about the future is merely a product of our ignorance. Alternatively, we may opt for a many-worlds interpretation in which all possible future events are equally real but isolated from each other in parallel universes (see 5.13 (iii)).

5.8.2 Spacelike time and causality

To say that A causes B is to say that A has some (significant) role in bringing B into existence. In our common understanding (with its implicit dependence upon a process theory of time), temporal location is usually implicated in such statements. A temporal relation of 'earlier than' is generally assumed to be a necessary but not sufficient condition for asserting a causal relation. Thus, when faced with the challenge to 'Discuss the influence of James Joyce upon William Shakespeare', an English undergraduate will either lapse into blank incomprehension or reinterpret it in postmodern terms as a request to explore the impact of Joyce's work upon all *subsequent* readings of Shakespeare.

If the stasis theory is correct, there is no warrant for our habit of attempting to explain the present in terms of the past. Temporal location should have no more significance for our investigations of causes than spatial location. And, if there really were a strong analogy between time and space, we might expect the cause of some event to lie in one particular direction rather than another!

In reality, of course, we observe a systematic distinction between past, present and future that is quite unlike the characteristics of space. On the face of it, time and space are distinct even though intimately related.

However, the difficulties created by a spacelike view of time are by no means insuperable. One way out might be to assert the timelessness of all causal relations. There is clear precedent for such a move in the classical understanding of divine causality. Another (possibly preferable) option might be to relate causality not to temporal location as such but rather to the physical factors that lead to the apparent distinctions between past and future.

5.9 Space, time and theology

Is time essentially spacelike with all that implies for our understanding of freedom and causation? Or is it the fundamental determinant of being and non-being? *Contrary to popular belief, the new physics does not adjudicate between the rival interpretations of time that have been touched on in this section.*

Both interpretations are open to theologians. Indeed both have appeared in Christian theology, albeit under very different guises. By and large theologians have tended to adopt a more or less common-sense view of created time. Thus Emil Brunner is typical when he comments that,

> Everyone knows that time passes away. Everyone knows that the moment which was just now and is now gone never more returns. What men of all times and countries have been conscious of as the painful experience of time is the unceasing flow of the time stream, transience, the irreversibility and inexorability of this movement from the 'not yet' to the 'now' and onwards to the 'no longer' ... The flow of time is inseparably bound up with transience, mortality, the not lingering, the not being able to return to what has once been, and just that constitutes the linearity of time. (Brunner, 1953:43)

However, when the same theologians try to imagine what the passage of created time might look like from God's perspective, the answer they often come up with is akin to the stasis theory of time described above, as though God were looking down on the four-dimensional space–time diagram that relativistic physicists draw. Polkinghorne has repeatedly rejected this view of God, insisting that there is a temporality to the divine experience (1989:ch. 7; 2004:104–10). Willem B. Drees, however, questions whether relativity offers any time that could be thought of as God's time (1996:261–6). The debate over the nature of time initiated by contemporary interpretations of relativity theory reveals a long-standing inconsistency in Christian theology with respect to time. For further discussion of different theories of time, especially of 'the block universe', a technical term for the 'stasis' view we have described, see Isham and Polkinghorne (1993:135–44) and DeWeese (2004).

EXERCISE 5.1

Consult the papers by Isham and Polkinghorne on this subject (Isham and Polkinghorne 1993:135–44), and then consider your own view of time in relation to the universe and to God.

SECTION C
THE REDISCOVERY OF THE OBSERVER (5.10–5.14)

5.10 The observational basis of quantum theory

Einstein's explanation of the null result of the Michelson–Morley (5.4) experiment led to a radical revision of our understanding of space and time. If anything, the explanation for Lord Kelvin's other 'cloud' – the spectrum of black-body radiation – has led to even more radical changes in our understanding of the world.

5.10.1 The ultraviolet catastrophe

In line with Kelvin's warning, the first crack in the edifice of classical physics came with attempts to explain the colour of hot objects using classical physics and electromagnetism. The light from these objects is a mixture of different frequencies (colours). Observations reveal that such objects have a distinctive spectrum (pattern of energy distribution at different frequencies). However, attempts to explain this in classical terms failed abjectly – they predicted instead that the amount of energy would tend towards infinity at the high-energy (violet) end of the spectrum – an ultraviolet catastrophe.

Enter Max Planck. In 1900 he suggested that physics should abandon the assumption that electromagnetic energy is continuous and wave-like. If, instead, energy can only be absorbed and emitted in discrete packets (or quanta), theory can be made to fit observations exactly. However, while his suggestion certainly gave the right answer, its abandonment of a cherished assumption of classical physics gave it an air of contrivance that led to its relative neglect for several years.

5.10.2 The photoelectric effect

Another anomaly that concerned physicists at the beginning of the twentieth century was the ability of light to eject electrons from metal. The principle is simple – the light imparts energy to electrons which then effectively 'evaporate' from the surface of the metal. The classical analogy with the evaporation of water suggests that some degree of evaporation should occur regardless of the frequency of the light, provided it is sufficiently intense. In reality, there is a clear threshold frequency, which varies from metal to metal, below which the effect will not occur.

It was Einstein who, in 1905, rehabilitated Planck's quantum theory and explained this anomaly by assuming that the energy imparted by the light is packaged (quantized) in a manner that is related to the frequency of the light rather than spread evenly over the wavefront. Furthermore, he assumed that the way in which electrons absorbed that energy is also quantized – so that they can only acquire the energy necessary to escape if the light is of sufficiently high frequency. Light of frequencies lower than this threshold has no effect regardless of the intensity of the light source.

5.10.3 Collapsing atoms and spectral lines

In 1898 Antoine-Henri Becquerel had discovered an entirely new physical phenomenon – radioactivity. This growth area in physics rapidly led to the realization that atoms were not simply inert billiard balls. On the contrary, they have an internal structure. By the end of the first decade of the twentieth century sufficient research had accumulated for physicists to be able to begin making models of this structure. It was clear that atoms had a very small, dense, positively charged nucleus surrounded by negatively charged electrons.

Ernest Rutherford proposed a planetary model for the atom – electrons in orbit around a nucleus like planets around a star. The fly in the ointment was electromagnetism. An electric charge moving in a circle emits energy. If electrons were classical particles emitting energy in this way, they would very rapidly dissipate all their energy and fall into the nucleus.

A solution was offered by a young Danish physicist, Niels Bohr, whose model of the atom was mentioned in 1.9. Again the key was the abandonment of continuity in favour of quantization. Bohr simply ruled out the possibility of electrons occupying every possible orbit. Instead they are confined to certain discrete energy levels. Although outlandish, his suggestion had the added attraction that it explained another anomaly – the fact that the light emitted by hot gases is emitted only at certain frequencies (spectral lines).

5.10.4 When is a particle a wave?

The above phenomena indicated that under certain circumstances light can behave in a particle-like manner rather than its usual wave-like manner. The next step in the development of a quantum view of the world was due to an aristocratic French physicist, Prince Louis de Broglie. In his 1924 doctoral thesis, de Broglie proposed that, under certain circumstances, particles might be observed behaving in a wave-like manner. His prediction was confirmed in 1927 by Clinton Davisson and Lester Germer. They found that low-energy electrons fired at a nickel surface were deflected into a series of low- and high-intensity beams. In other words, diffraction – a characteristic property of waves – occurred.

Similarly, if you take a beam of electrons and pass it through a pair of slits (a classical wave experiment), you get diffraction and interference – properties characteristic of a wave rather than a particle. If you reduce the intensity of the electron beam to a single electron at a time, the detector on the other side of the slits will still gradually accumulate a trace that looks like an interference pattern (see Figure 5.1). Explaining this in classical terms is impossible – if the electrons go through one slit or the other the pattern would look quite different.[4] The ability of quantum particles also to behave as waves is known as 'wave-particle duality'.

5.11 The quantum revolution

By the early 1920s, these anomalies had grown into a gaping hole in the fabric of physics. At the same time, the explanations proffered by physicists such as

source of electrons

detector screen

pattern on detector with one slit open

number of impacts

pattern on detector with both slits open

Figure 5.1 The double-slit experiment, used to illustrate wave–particle duality. If only one slit is open a scatter pattern, characteristic of particles, is observed. If both slits are open the interference pattern characteristic of a wave is observed. Even if only one 'particle' is in the apparatus, faced with two slits it still 'divides itself' to give wave behaviour. Quantum particles, then, can exhibit two radically different behaviours depending only on how they are observed.

Einstein and Bohr held out the promise of a radical reconstruction. The task of integrating these insights into a coherent theory of sub-atomic physics fell to Werner Heisenberg and Erwin Schrödinger. Although they were working independently, their approaches were sufficiently similar to be formally merged into quantum mechanics. This new theory constituted a radical shift in the conceptual foundations of physics. We mention here three key aspects of quantum mechanics.

(i) The Schrödinger Equation and the importance of probability

Wave–particle duality is one of the properties enshrined in the fundamental equation of quantum mechanics, the Schrödinger wave equation – so-called because it takes a mathematical form characteristic of classical wave equations. However, *this equation does not refer to physical waves but rather to probabilities, e.g. the probability of finding an electron in one location rather than another.* The final outcome may be determinate (an electron in a particular location), but the probability distribution of the possible outcomes has the mathematical form of a wave. This peculiar feature of a very successful equation has led to the intractable problem of how we should interpret quantum mechanics (see 5.13).

(ii) Uncertainty

Uncertainty is one of the best-known implications of quantum mechanics. In 1927 Heisenberg argued that key physical quantities (e.g. position and momentum) are paired up in quantum theory. As a result, they cannot be measured simultaneously to any desired degree of accuracy. Attempts to increase the precision of one measurement result in less precise measures of the other member of the pair.

Take an electron, for example. We might try to determine its position by using electromagnetic radiation. Because electrons are so small, radiation of very short wavelength would be necessary to locate it accurately. However, shorter wavelengths correspond to higher energies. The higher the energy of radiation used, the more the momentum of the electron is altered. Thus any attempt to determine the location accurately will change the velocity of the electron. Conversely, techniques for accurately measuring the velocity of the electron will leave us in ignorance about its precise location. Looked at conservatively, this is an epistemological issue: quantum uncertainty is a principle of ignorance inherent in any measuring technique used on such a small scale. *However, Heisenberg himself took a more radical view – he saw this limitation as a property of nature rather than an artefact of experimentation. This radical interpretation of uncertainty as an ontological principle of indeterminism implies that quantum mechanics is inherently statistical – it deals with probabilities rather than well-defined classical trajectories. Such a view is clearly inimical to classical determinism.* Equally clearly, this is a metaphysical interpretation that goes beyond what is required by the mathematics of the Uncertainty Principle.

(iii) Radical interdependence

In spite of his crucial role in the early development of quantum mechanics, Einstein was very uneasy about its implications and, in later years, organized a rearguard action against it. His aphorism 'God does not play dice' highlights the depths of his distaste for quantum uncertainty. His strongest counter-argument was to call attention to a paradoxical implication of quantum mechanics now known as the Einstein–Podolsky–Rosen (EPR) Paradox.

Take, for example, a pair of protons whose quantum spins cancel out. Now separate them and measure the spin of one proton. Because they were paired, they had a combined wave equation. Measuring the spin of one proton 'collapses' that wave equation and determines the spin of the other. It appears that a measurement in one place can have an instantaneous effect on something that may be light years away.

For Einstein this was proof that quantum mechanics must be incomplete. To him this result only made sense if the spins were determinate (but unknown to us) before the protons were separated. In this case, measurement would merely tell what was always the case. But, according to the orthodox interpretation of quantum mechanics, it is not merely a matter of ignorance. The spin is not determined until it has been measured. In other words, the pair of protons cannot be regarded as separate entities until the measurement has been made.

Some years later, a quantum logician turned this paradox into a testable prediction that now bears his name – Bell's Inequality. This is an equation which should be true if two principles (assumed by Einstein and his colleagues in formulating the EPR Paradox) hold in the world:

> The principle of reality: *that we can predict a physical quantity with certainty without disturbing the system*; and

> The locality principle: *that a measurement in one of two isolated systems can produce no real change in the other*.

Taken together, these principles imply an upper limit to the degree of cooperation that is possible between isolated systems. In 1982 a team of physicists at the University of Paris led by Alain Aspect demonstrated experimentally that this limit is exceeded in nature. In other words, our physical descriptions of the world in which we live cannot be both real and local in the above sense.

What this means in practice is a greater emphasis on describing quantum-mechanical systems as a *whole*. This runs counter to the tendency of classical physics towards 'bottom-up thinking' – treating systems as collections of separate entities, and trying to reduce their properties to the individual properties of the simplest possible components. The quantum world, which deals with the simplest entities we know, seems to resist this reduction – it is in Karl Popper's famous phrase 'a world of clouds' as well as 'clocks' (quoted in Polkinghorne, 1991:44). 'Bottom-up' thinking has served science extremely well, we simply indicate here that it has its limitations.[5]

5.12 Shaking the foundations

The quantum view of the world departs from classical assumptions in four main ways.

1. Determinism has given way to an emphasis on *probabilities*. We simply do not have access to enough information to make deterministic predictions. And this is widely held to be a feature of the world rather than an observational limitation.
2. Reductionism has given way to a more *holistic* approach to physical systems.
3. Closely allied to this, locality (the impossibility of information being propagated instantaneously) has given way to *correlation-at-a-distance*.
4. Most basic of all, the classical assumptions of continuity and divisibility (that between any two points there is an infinite number of

intermediate values) have given way to *quantization* – for certain physical quantities, the range of permissible values is severely restricted.

5.13 Schrödinger's cat and the meaning of quantum theory

The EPR Paradox described in 5.11(iii) introduces us to one of the basic problems of quantum mechanics – the relationship between measurement and reality. This is highlighted by a famous thought-experiment involving a hapless cat. The cat is in a box together with a canister of poisonous gas connected to a radioactive device. If an atom in the device decays, the canister is opened and the cat dies. Suppose that there is a 50–50 chance of this happening. Clearly when we open the box we will observe a cat that is either alive or dead. But is the cat alive or dead prior to the opening of the box?

Interpretation (i) Quantum orthodoxy (Copenhagen interpretation)

The dominant view in quantum mechanics is that quantum probabilities become determinate on measurement – that the wave function is collapsed by the intervention of classical measuring apparatus. This means that the cat is neither alive nor dead until the box is opened. The cat is in an indeterminate state.

This interpretation is usually allied with a tendency to extreme instrumentalism (see 1.7). On such a view the probabilities generated by the Schrödinger wave equation do not correspond to any physical reality. There simply is no reality to be described until an act of measurement collapses the wave function. Quantum mechanics is merely a useful calculating device for predicting the possible outcomes of such acts of measurement.

In spite of its dominance in the textbooks, this interpretation is hardly satisfactory. To begin with, it may be regarded as proposing a dualism in physical reality: two worlds – an indeterminate quantum world and a determinate classical world. Then there is the problem of what constitutes classical measuring apparatus. At what level does the wave function actually collapse?

The act of measurement that collapses the wave function cannot be limited to scientific instruments. After all, why should we assume that *our* scientific measurements are solely responsible for collapsing the wave function? This would give rise to a most peculiar world – one that was indeterminate until the evolution of hominids.

Some physicists, e.g. Wigner and Wheeler, have identified the classical measuring apparatus of the Copenhagen interpretation with consciousness. If so, they must be using a much broader definition of consciousness than is usual. What level of consciousness would be needed to make something determinate? Is the cat sufficiently conscious to determine the outcome of the experiment? Would earthworms do? What about viruses? The effect of pursuing this line of enquiry is to move towards a form of panpsychism – the doctrine that every part of the natural world, no matter how humble, is in some sense conscious!

An alternative might be to postulate a transcendent world observer – a divine mind whose observations collapse the wave functions on our behalf. In effect this would be the quantum-mechanical version of Bishop Berkeley's idealism.[6] This is memorably summarized in a couple of limericks:

> There was once a man who said 'God
>   Must think it exceedingly odd
> If he finds that this tree
>   Continues to be
> When there's no one about in the quad.'

And the reply:

> Dear Sir, Your astonishment's odd:
>   *I* am always about in the quad.
> And that's why the tree
>   Will continue to be,
> Since observed by Yours faithfully, God.

The problem with this attractive solution to the measurement problem is that it proves too much. Invoking a divine observer leads to the question of why there should be any quantum measurement problem at all. Why should anything be left indeterminate for us to determine by our measurements? Is God only interested in those aspects of creation that are above a certain size?

Returning to the classical measuring apparatus, perhaps we should put the emphasis on 'classical' rather than 'measuring' – stressing not so much our *intervention* in the system as a *transition* from the world of the very small, in which quantum principles operate, to the everyday world of classical physics. This neo-Copenhagen interpretation has the merit that it avoids the absurdities of the consciousness-based approaches. However, we are still faced with the difficulty of identifying an acceptable transition point. How small is small? (There is now evidence that a molecule of fullerene containing around seventy carbon atoms can exhibit wave–particle duality.) One suggestion is that we choose the level at which physical phenomena become so complex that they are irreversible. Another, from Roger Penrose, is that gravity provides the key (Penrose, 1994:ch. 6; 1997:ch. 2).

Interpretation (ii) Hidden variables (neo-realism)

Einstein was not alone in finding this interpretation of quantum mechanics objectionable. A few physicists have persisted in arguing that the statistical nature of quantum mechanics implies that it is only really applicable to ensembles of particles (just as an opinion poll is only meaningful if a reasonable sample of the population has been polled). In other words, quantum mechanics is an incomplete description of reality. They maintain that underlying this level of indeterminacy there is an objective foundation.

The best-known hidden-variables theory is that of the physicist and philosopher David Bohm (see Bohm, 1980). What Bohm did was to distinguish between the quantum particle, e.g. an electron, and a hidden 'guiding wave' that governs its motion. Thus, in this theory electrons are quite clearly particles. When you perform a two-slit experiment, they go through one slit rather than the other. However, their choice of slit is not random but is governed by the guiding wave, resulting in the wave pattern that is observed.

The main weakness of Bohm's theory is that it looks contrived – which it is. It was deliberately designed to give predictions that are in all details identical to conventional quantum mechanics. His aim was not to make a serious counter-proposal but simply to demonstrate that hidden-variables theories are indeed possible.

It is sometimes suggested that hidden-variables theories have been ruled out by the Aspect experiment (5.11(iii)). This is a misunderstanding of the experiment. What it did was to show that attempts to explain quantum phenomena cannot be both deterministic and local. Hidden-variables theories, with their underlying determinism, must be non-local, maintaining the existence of instantaneous causal relations between physically separated entities. Such a view contradicts the simple location of events in both classical atomism and relativity theory. It points to a more holistic view of the quantum world. Indeed Bohm himself stressed the holistic aspect of quantum theory in his later years, after his conversion from Marxism to theosophy.

Interpretation (iii) the many-worlds interpretation

The third main class of interpretations starts from the assumption that scientific theories ought to be self-interpreting. The Schrödinger wave equation in quantum mechanics is smooth, continuous and deterministic. There is nothing in it that corresponds to the collapse of the wave function.

In 1957 Hugh Everett surprised his more conventional colleagues by proposing that the Schrödinger wave equation as a whole *is* an accurate description of reality. There is no collapse of the wave function. Whenever there is a choice of experimental outcomes, all the possibilities are realized. Somewhere Schrödinger's cat will be really dead and somewhere it will be really alive. With each decision at the quantum level the universe splits into a number of isolated domains, each corresponding to a different outcome. In one universe the cat dies, in another it lives.

Most physicists find this extremely unattractive. One of the most venerable assumptions of the scientific method is Ockham's razor – *non sunt multiplicanda entia praeter necessitatem*; i.e. entities are not to be multiplied beyond necessity. In practice this leads to a very strong aesthetic bias in favour of the simplest possible explanation.

Only quantum cosmologists beg to differ. They attempt to apply quantum mechanics to the entire universe. Clearly this leaves no room for a separate classical measuring apparatus. In this context, a many-universes approach such as was described above may seem an attractive non-theistic alternative to the notion of a transcendent world observer. But one wonders which option requires the larger act of faith!

5.14 Quantum consciousness

In classical mechanics, with its close association with Cartesian dualism, the physical world was neatly divorced from the realm of consciousness. As far as classically minded materialists were concerned, the latter was a mere side effect of biochemical interactions. However, as noted above, the dominant Copenhagen interpretation of quantum mechanics envisages a greatly expanded role for the observer. Granted the traditional association of temporal perception with consciousness, the rediscovery of time by modern physics may point in the same direction.

Such considerations have given rise to the suggestion that consciousness itself may be interpreted as a quantum phenomenon. Perhaps the best-known proponent of a quantum explanation of consciousness is Roger Penrose (1989; 1994; 1997). He rejects the currently popular view that human consciousness is essentially computational (that minds are analogous to computer programs) because, in his opinion, this model fails to account for intuitive problem-solving. The brain must be non-algorithmic (i.e. it does not operate by mechanically following a fixed set of procedures in the manner of a computer). Further he argues that classical physics is inherently algorithmic in its nature. Thus consciousness is not explicable in classical terms.

The obvious candidate for a non-algorithmic process in physics is the quantum-mechanical collapse of the wave function. Penrose suggests that the brain uses quantum collapse to solve problems non-algorithmically. But by what means? He pins his hopes on structures called microtubules that occur within cells, speculating that quantum effects within the microtubules may be coordinated across groups of neurones to provide the basis for such intuitive processes. However, as many physicists and neurophysiologists have pointed out, this is *highly* speculative – a weakness that Penrose himself acknowledges.

SECTION D
MODERN COSMOLOGY AND UNIVERSAL HISTORY (5.15–5.19)

5.15 The beginnings of scientific cosmology

The first step towards a scientific cosmology was taken in 1823 when the German astronomer Wilhelm Olbers discussed a paradox that has subsequently been associated with his name. He simply asked 'Why is the sky dark at night?' The paradox becomes apparent when you calculate the brightness that should be expected given the assumptions that were current about the overall structure of the universe. If the universe is infinitely large, Euclidean (i.e. the shortest distance between two points is a straight line) and stars (or galaxies) are distributed evenly throughout it, the sky should not be dark at all but as bright as the surface of the average star!

This might have been explained by arguing that the universe is relatively young so that light from distant stars has not had time to reach us. However, by the nineteenth century it was widely accepted that the Earth (and, hence, the universe) was very old. Thus a more popular explanation was that the universe consisted of a finite number of stars concentrated into a finite region of an infinite space – the island universe model of cosmology in which the Milky Way (our own galaxy) constituted a unique island of matter and energy in an infinite void.

In the 1920s astronomers were able to show that some nebulae (clouds of luminous gas and dust) were too far away to be part of the Milky Way – they were island universes or galaxies in their own right. One of the discoverers of extragalactic objects, Edwin Hubble, went a stage further. In 1924 he announced the discovery that light from distant galaxies was systematically redder than light from nearby galaxies and that the degree of red shift was proportional to the distance. This provides a simple explanation for Olbers' Paradox: if light from distant galaxies is redder, it contributes less energy to the overall brightness of the night sky than light from nearby galaxies. Eventually there comes a point where a galaxy is so distant that it is simply invisible (the 'event horizon').

The simplest explanation for this red shift is that it is a case of the Doppler effect. This is the phenomenon that causes the pitch of a train whistle to vary as the train approaches or recedes. According to this explanation, the light is reddened because the galaxies are moving away from us. Since the degree of reddening is also a measure of the speed of recession, Hubble was able to show that more distant galaxies are receding from us faster than nearby ones.

5.16 The Big Bang

At first sight this observation might suggest that the Earth was located at the centre of some cosmic explosion. However, the fact that all motion is relative implies that observers elsewhere in the universe would make similar observations. This observation is consistent with an expanding universe. To illustrate this one might paint spots on a balloon and blow it up. As the balloon expands, the spots recede from each other and more distantly separated spots recede more rapidly.

Extrapolating backwards in time from the observation that the universe is expanding leads to the suggestion that there might have been a time in the distant past (between 10 and 20 billion years ago) when the entire universe was concentrated into a single point. This point would be unimaginably hot and dense. At this 't = 0' the universe would begin to expand rapidly, if not violently. As it expands and cools, matter as we now know it begins to appear. Small variations in the density of that matter lead to condensation and the eventual formation of stars, galaxies and planets. Gradually the mutual gravitational attraction of matter slows the expansion of the universe. The result is the basic picture of the universe as portrayed by modern cosmology.

5.16.1 Evidence for a Big Bang?

Taking the Big Bang as our educated guess about the origin of the universe, we naturally ask what would such a universe look like? Can we deduce potential observations from the hypothesis of a primordial fireball? The answer is 'yes'.

Since light travels at a finite velocity, observations of distant objects are also observations of conditions in the past. In the distant past, the universe was smaller and therefore denser than it is today. We would therefore expect distant objects to be closer together than those nearby – there is some evidence from radio astronomy that this is the case. We would also expect observations of very distant objects to be consistent with a younger, hotter universe.

In an effort to discredit this theory, Fred Hoyle and some colleagues calculated the chemical composition of a Big Bang universe. This is relatively straightforward since the bulk of the chemical elements would be generated in the first couple of seconds of violent expansion and cooling. Much to their surprise, the outcome of their predictions was very similar to the observed chemical composition of the universe (about 80 per cent hydrogen and 20 per cent helium – all the rest is a mere trace explicable as the result of supernova explosions at the end of the first generation of stellar evolution).

But the most convincing evidence for the Big Bang came from an accidental discovery in 1965. Two young American astronomers, Penzias and Wilson, were attempting to pioneer astronomy in the microwave part of the spectrum. They picked up a very faint signal which seemed to be coming from every part of the sky. At first they thought it was a problem with the telescope. Only when they had thoroughly checked all their equipment did the full significance of their observation became apparent. In the 1940s, George Gamow had predicted that the Big Bang should have left a trace of itself in the form of microwave radiation spread evenly across the sky. Furthermore, the predicted strength of this radiation was comparable with observed results.

5.17 The shape of things to come

The fact that mutual gravitational attraction is causing the expansion of the universe to slow down suggests three possible future scenarios, depending on how much matter there is in the universe. The more matter, the greater the gravitational attraction and the more rapidly the expansion of the universe will slow down. If there is sufficient matter, the gravitational attraction will eventually overcome the expansion and the universe will begin to collapse again. This leads to a family of so-called *closed* cosmological models. If the total mass of the universe is less than that critical mass, expansion will continue indefinitely – an *open* universe. At the critical mass itself, the expansion will cease in the infinitely far future.

But what is the mass of the universe? Direct observations of luminous objects suggest a mass that is only a tiny fraction of the critical mass. This would suggest an open universe. However, studies of galaxy clusters reveal that their masses are much greater than what we might expect from their luminosity. In other words, much of the mass of the universe is in the form of 'dark matter' that is observable only through its gravitational effects. Estimates of the amount of dark matter vary but many sources suggest that it is sufficient for the actual mass of the universe to be quite close to the critical mass.[7] We discuss the implications of these predictions for theology in 10.20.

5.18 Is the Big Bang a moment of creation?

Strictly speaking the point associated with the Big Bang itself is a singularity – a point at which our laws of physics break down. In itself, this does not imply an absolute beginning. Nevertheless, it is tempting to read the Big Bang as having theological significance. After all, it does seem remarkably like a moment of creation.

This temptation received strong papal endorsement in 1951. Pope Pius XII announced that 'everything seems to indicate that the universe has in finite times a mighty beginning'. He went on to claim that unprejudiced scientific thinking indicated that the universe is a 'work of creative omnipotence, whose power set in motion by the mighty *fiat* pronounced billions of years ago by the Creating Spirit, spread out over the universe'. To be fair, he did also admit that 'the facts established up to the present time are not an absolute proof of creation in time'.

Such pronouncements are guaranteed to provoke controversy. Even members of the Pontifical Academy of Sciences were divided over the wisdom of the Pope's remarks. While Sir Edmund Whittaker could agree that the Big Bang might 'perhaps without impropriety' be referred to as the Creation, George Lemaître, one of the pioneers of the Big Bang theory, felt strongly that this was a misuse of his hypothesis (see 1.15).

Beyond the Christian community there was even greater unease. One of the fundamental assumptions of modern science is that every physical event can be sufficiently explained solely in terms of preceding physical causes. Quite apart from its possible status as the moment of creation, the Big Bang singularity is an offence to this basic assumption. Thus some philosophers of science have opposed the very idea of the Big Bang as irrational and untestable.

One popular way to evade the suggestion of an absolute beginning has been to argue that the universe must be closed. If it will eventually return to a singular point, why should it not then 'bounce'? This is the so-called *cyclic* universe (see 5.22). Other astronomers opposed to the Big Bang, proposed instead a *steady-state* theory. Fred Hoyle took a lead in this proposal. As we indicated in 1.15, his motives were explicitly theological. The steady-state theory argued that, in spite of appearances, the universe was infinitely old and did not evolve over time. Although defended by some very able scientists, this theory suffered a number of major setbacks which led to its demise. In order to maintain a steady state in the face of universal expansion it was necessary to postulate the continuous creation of matter from negative energy – ingenious, but contrived. There was the embarrassment of Hoyle's failed attempt to show that the Big Bang could not account for the chemical composition of the universe (5.16.1). Finally, the steady-state theory was not able to accommodate the new data that appeared – particularly the existence of the microwave background (5.16.1).

5.19 From Big Bang to inflation

The Big Bang theory has been very effective in predicting phenomena that have subsequently been observed by astronomers (5.16.1). However, the theory also raises a number of questions that it is unable to answer.

One of these questions is the so-called 'horizon problem'. Observations reveal that above a certain scale (about 10^{24} metres[8]) the universe is highly uniform in structure. However, this degree of uniformity is an embarrassment to cosmologists. According to relativity theory, there should be no causal connection between points separated by distances greater than c multiplied by t (where c is the velocity of light and t is the age of the universe). Extrapolating this back to the Big Bang suggests that the primordial universe was partitioned into about 10^{80} causally separate regions (Barrow and Tipler, 1986:420). Nevertheless, all these disconnected regions had to expand at the same rate to maintain the observed degree of uniformity!

Equally embarrassing for conventional Big Bang theory is the fact that although the universe is highly uniform it is not perfectly uniform. According to current theories, galaxy formation depends upon the existence of small initial irregularities in the Big Bang itself. These are amplified by cosmic expansion to the point where gravitation can begin the process of stellar condensation (Barrow and Tipler, 1986:417). If the initial irregularities are too large, the result is the rapid and widespread formation of black holes instead of stars. If the initial irregularities are sufficiently small, the precise expansion rate of the cosmos becomes critical – too rapid and the irregularities will not be amplified enough for galaxy formation to occur; too slow and the cosmos will be closed with a lifetime too short to permit biological evolution. Evidence of the existence of such irregularities in the early universe has been supplied by the COBE (COsmic Background Explorer) satellite's observations of small irregularities in the cosmic microwave background. There is no mechanism within conventional Big Bang theory to account for these primordial irregularities. This is often called the 'fine-tuning problem'.

The widespread expectation among cosmologists that the actual mass of the universe is close to the critical mass (5.17) is a further problem for Big Bang theory in that it offers no explanation of this coincidence. Yet another difficulty arises from the fact that, according to particle physics, the cooling of the early universe after the Big Bang should lead to the production of topological anomalies, particularly magnetic monopoles. Indeed, monopoles should be the dominant matter in the universe. And yet, no monopole has ever been observed, directly or indirectly.

In the 1980s dissatisfaction with these shortcomings of conventional Big Bang theory led Alan Guth to propose an alternative – the inflationary universe theory. According to this theory, in the earliest moments of its existence the region we now think of as the universe contained an excited state known as a false vacuum. This false vacuum possessed a repulsive force that caused this region to expand far more rapidly than would be possible in conventional Big Bang theory. In an unimaginably short period (perhaps 10^{-37} seconds) this region doubled in size at least 100 times. However, due to the peculiar properties of false vacuum, its energy density remained unchanged. In other words, the total energy contained in the region grew enormously. This false-vacuum state is extraordinarily difficult to imagine, but the best non-mathematical account available is provided by Brian Greene (2004: chs 9–10).

The period of inflation must have been extremely short because the false vacuum is unstable. A false vacuum 'decays' into other forms of matter, converting its energy into a tremendously hot gas of elementary particles; essentially the same conditions as are predicted by conventional Big Bang theory for the period before the formation of the first atoms of hydrogen and helium. However, the inflationary phase means that the universe was originally much smaller than had previously been thought (perhaps a billion times smaller than a proton); small enough for it to have become uniform before inflation began. This primordial uniformity would then have been preserved during the inflationary phase and beyond, thus solving the horizon problem. Again unlike conventional Big Bang theory, the inflationary approach leads to an explanation of why the actual mass of the universe is close to the critical mass. Inflationary models may also account for the fine-tuning problem, if the irregularities in the cosmic background are understood as quantum fluctuations blown up by inflation (Greene, 2004:305–10).

Guth's original version of inflation was later shown to be unsatisfactory, but this approach has spawned an entire family of inflationary models. One popular version is that developed by Andrei Linde. In this 'chaotic' version, different regions of the false vacuum decay at different times; each region becoming a separate 'bubble universe'. However, because the false vacuum as a whole is expanding at an exponential rate, it is outgrowing the decay process. In other words, it is spawning 'bubble universes' *ad infinitum*. For comment on the relation of inflationary models to the problem of God's action, see **10.15**. Greene is one of those working on a 'superstring' account of the early universe, using descriptions in eleven dimensions. This approach shows some promise, but also reflects just how difficult it is to devise experimental tests of phenomena which only occur in the very special conditions of the early universe (see Greene 2004:chs 12–13).

SECTION E
MODERN COSMOLOGY AND THE REDISCOVERY OF PURPOSE?
(5.20–5.24)

5.20 Some contemporary cosmological enigmas

Modern cosmology offers us mathematical models of the possible large-scale structure of the universe. Like any other mathematical model, the actual features depend on the numbers that we choose to put in the equations. Thus in **5.17** we noted that different values of the total mass of the universe will give rise to very different cosmological models. In general, the overall structure of many physical systems is strongly influenced by the numerical values of a relatively small number of universal constants (e.g. the gravitational constant). Since the 1970s physicists have become increasingly aware that *the physical conditions that enable life to exist are* *very sensitive to the values of a number of these constants. If they had been only slightly different, life as we know it could not have evolved.*

5.20.1 The chemical composition of the universe

As we noted in 5.16.1, the overall chemical composition of the universe was determined by physical conditions during the first seconds of the Big Bang. However, the elements on which life depends (such as carbon, nitrogen, oxygen, sulphur and iron) are the product of nuclear reactions within stars. In both situations the processes by which the chemical elements are formed are governed very precisely by the strengths of four fundamental physical interactions: gravitation, electromagnetism, and the weak and strong nuclear interactions.

If the relative strengths of these forces were different, the resultant universe would also be different. For example, increasing the strong nuclear interaction by 3 per cent relative to the electromagnetic interaction gives a cosmological model in which none of the known chemical elements could form. Conversely, decreasing it by 1 per cent gives a model in which carbon atoms would be unstable. Both scenarios would preclude carbon-based life. Other tiny variations in these forces might have given rise to a universe which was 100 per cent helium or one in which supernova explosions could not occur (since these explosions are thought to be the chief way in which the chemicals necessary for life are ejected from stars, this too would preclude the evolution of life).

5.20.2 'Anthropic' features

The actual chemical composition of the universe is just one way in which the universe appears to have been finely tuned to permit the evolution of life. Until their explanation by inflationary cosmology (5.19), the horizon and fine-tuning problems were also seen in this light by many physicists, and there are still elements within inflation which look fine-tuned (Craig, 2003:158–61). The various unexplained factors that have been perceived as necessary for the emergence of life have come to be known as 'anthropic' features (or coincidences).

5.21 Possible responses to the 'anthropic' coincidences

There is no obvious physical reason why the parameters mentioned in 5.20.1 should have the observed values. However, very small changes in any of these key parameters would have resulted in a grossly different universe; one in which life as we know it would almost certainly be precluded. The set of life-permitting cosmological models is a vanishingly small subset of the set of all theoretically possible cosmological models. How should the scientist-theologian respond? Murphy and Ellis provide a list of possibilities (1996:49–59).

One response to these enigmas might be to adopt a hard-nosed empiricism and say, 'So what? It is meaningless to speak of our existence as improbable after the event.' However, few cosmologists seem prepared to ignore these cosmological coincidences in this fashion.

Another possible response would be to deny the contingency of physical laws and parameters. For example, some physicists speculate about possible developments in physics that would demonstrate that only this precise set of laws and parameters is possible. This is the approach that leads Drees to be cautious about drawing any inferences from the coincidences (1996:269–72).

An important further caution is provided by philosophers who question whether we can really apply the formal measure of probability to a range of possibilities about the universe of which we know so little (see Manson, 2000; McGrew *et al.*, 2003). Nevertheless, however vaguely defined, the coincidences remain striking and seem to call for some explanation.

A third type of response is to invoke some form of anthropic 'principle'.

5.22 The Weak Anthropic Principle

The approach which does the least violence to conventional modes of scientific thought is to invoke a *Weak Anthropic Principle* (WAP). Barrow and Tipler describe it thus:

> The observed values of all physical and cosmological quantities are not equally probable but they take on values restricted by the requirement that there exist sites where carbon-based life can evolve and by the requirement that the Universe be old enough for it to have already done so. (Barrow and Tipler, 1986:16)

In other words, our existence as observers functions as a cosmological selection effect. There can be no observations without observers. Our observations must satisfy the conditions necessary for our existence.

However, the WAP does not take us very far towards an explanation of the observed coincidences. In conjunction with a conventional Big Bang cosmology, it still gives the impression that our existence is an accident of vanishingly small probability. *Thus, in practice, it usually appears in conjunction with a cosmological model that suggests that there is a sense in which all possible universes actually exist*. Three such strategies are to be found in the literature.

The first is to extend the closed Big Bang model to permit an endless series of expansions and contractions: the so-called *cyclic Big Bang* (see 5.18). Each passage through a singularity is supposed to randomize the physical parameters that give rise to the anthropic features. Advocates of this approach argue that in an infinite series of closed universes there will certainly be a subset whose physical features permit the evolution of life, and the function of the WAP is to remind us that only in such an atypical subclass of universes could life evolve. The main difficulty faced by this scenario is justifying the assumption that, while the singularity randomizes the laws and constants of nature, it leaves the geometry of spacetime untouched. If, as seems reasonable, passage through a singularity also affects the geometry of the universe, we should expect an open Big Bang after a finite number of cycles, thus putting an end to any hope of an infinite sequence of universes.

A second approach would be to opt for Linde's version of inflationary cosmology (see **5.19**). In an *infinite chaotic universe* in which an infinite number of 'bubble' universes are created by the decay of the false vacuum, we should expect every possible stable state to appear an infinite number of times. Again the WAP is a reminder of the atypical nature of the universe in which we find ourselves.

The third and, currently, most popular strategy for relaxing the uniqueness of our universe is to adopt a *many-worlds interpretation of quantum mechanics* (**5.13(iii)**). Again it is sufficient to invoke the WAP to 'explain' our atypical cosmos.

5.23 The Strong Anthropic Principle

For some cosmologists the WAP does not go far enough. Their response is to invoke the existence of rational carbon-based life forms as an *explanation* of the anthropic features of the universe. Barrow and Tipler formulate a general version of the *Strong Anthropic Principle* (SAP) thus: 'The Universe must have those properties which allow life to develop within it at some stage in its history' (Barrow and Tipler, 1986:21).

One version of the SAP is Wheeler's *Participatory Anthropic Principle* (PAP). This asserts that the existence of the cosmos and the detailed course of its evolution are dependent on the existence of rational observers at some epoch. In his own words, 'Observership is a prerequisite of genesis' (Wheeler, 1977:7). It is essentially an extension of his own particular interpretation of quantum mechanics (see **5.13(i)**). All properties, including the very existence of the universe, are brought about by the inter-subjective agreement of observers. Thus the universe may be likened to a self-excited circuit. Past and future events are so coupled as to obviate any need for a first cause.

Against the PAP, Barrow and Tipler point out that the capacity of human observers to 'create' in this way is very limited indeed (Barrow and Tipler, 1986:470). Thus the PAP seems to entail the present or future existence of a community of beings with a 'higher degree of consciousness' than our own. They suggest that the process by which the appropriate kind of inter-subjective agreement is reached is the sequential coordination of separate sequences of observations, 'until all sequences of observations by all observers of all intelligent species that have ever existed and ever will exist, of all events that have ever occurred and will ever occur are finally joined together by the Final Observation by the Ultimate Observer' (Barrow and Tipler, 1986:471). The theistic implications of such a statement are obvious.[9] However, Barrow and Tipler avoid such a theistic conclusion by modifying the PAP into their *Final Anthropic Principle* (FAP).

They state the FAP in the following terms: 'Intelligent information-processing must come into existence in the Universe, and, once it comes into existence, it will never die out' (Barrow and Tipler, 1986:23). In other words, intelligent life-forms have cosmological significance by virtue of their future capacity to understand and manipulate matter on a cosmic scale.

This belief leads them to develop a non-theistic 'physical eschatology'. Tipler has amplified this further in his *The Physics of Immortality* (1995).[10] Humankind may not exist forever but human culture will persist, being preserved and developed by self-replicating intelligent machines. The transfer of our cultural software to alternative forms of hardware is one factor in encouraging the indefinite growth of the capacity to process information and to manipulate matter. They envisage the inevitable expansion of human culture to the point where it engulfs the entire cosmos. But let them have the final word:

> if life evolves in all of the many universes in a quantum cosmology, and if life continues to exist in all of these universes, then all of these universes, which include all possible histories among them, will approach the Omega Point. At the instant the Omega Point is reached, life will have gained control of all matter and forces not only in a single universe, but in all universes whose existence is logically possible; life will have spread into all spatial regions in all universes which could logically exist, and will have stored an infinite amount of information, including all bits of knowledge which it is logically possible to know. And this is the end. (Barrow and Tipler, 1986:676f.)

And, in a footnote, they add, 'A modern-day theologian might wish to say that the totality of life at the Omega Point is omnipotent, omnipresent, and omniscient!' (Barrow and Tipler, 1986:682 note 123).

In spite of the metaphysical tone of much of their discussion, Barrow and Tipler stress that the FAP makes clear predictions about the kind of universe we can expect to observe. Most importantly, they argue that, in order for life literally to engulf the universe, the universe must be closed. It must eventually begin to collapse under its own gravitation toward a final singularity.

5.23.1 Is it science?

Implicit in Barrow and Tipler's insistence on the predictive power of the Anthropic Principles is a claim that they be accorded scientific status. Predictive capacity is a keystone of Popper's well-known Criterion of Falsifiability. But what sort of scientific status is being claimed?

The SAP claims that the statement, 'Observers exist', in some sense constitutes a scientific explanation of the anthropic features of the cosmos. Two ways of interpreting this are possible.

It may be a claim that rational observers are the efficient cause of the universe. However, this would imply that time reversal is a reality on a cosmic scale and that in a very strong sense intelligent observers have (will have?) created their own reality.

Alternatively, the SAP may be read as a denial of the sufficiency of efficient causes as scientific explanations of certain physical problems. This implication of the SAP has caused some scientists and philosophers to reject it out of hand. However, it should be recalled that it was only with the rise of the mechanical model of the world that efficient causes were accepted as complete explanations in physics. Furthermore, the biological sciences have proved remarkably resistant to this view of scientific explanation.

By contrast, the WAP does not claim to be explanatory: it is merely a selection effect. However, like the SAP, it has a covert content. It is pointless unless it is used in conjunction with a cosmological model which postulates an ensemble of universes. Thus it functions as a way of commending to the scientific establishment certain speculative cosmologies which have so far failed to convince when restricted to more conventional forms of scientific argumentation.

5.24 Anthropic design arguments

> It is hard to resist the impression of something – some influence capable of transcending spacetime and the confinement of relativistic causality – possessing an overview of the entire cosmos at the instant of its creation, and manipulating all the causally disconnected parts to go bang with almost exactly the same vigour at the same time, and yet not so exactly co-ordinated as to preclude the small scale, slight irregularities that eventually formed the galaxies, and us. (Davies, 1982:95)[11]

As this quotation from Paul Davies suggests, the apparent fine-tuning of the cosmos is a rich source of material for new forms of design argument for the existence of God. Several such design arguments appear in recent theological (and scientific) literature.

Anthropic design arguments use aspects of cosmic fine-tuning as evidence that the universe was *designed* to permit (or, in stronger forms, to necessitate) the evolution of rational carbon-based life forms. There can be little doubt that, from the perspective of Christian faith, such features are suggestive of design. However, design arguments based on these features make certain assumptions that may make one cautious about placing too much reliance on them.

To begin with, they assume that the anthropic features of the cosmos are, in themselves, improbable. However, quite apart from the difficulties of assigning probabilities to these parameters, such an assumption is far from proven. As we noted earlier (5.21), it is conceivable that future developments in physics might render these very features quasi-necessary. In such a situation, this entire class of design argument would collapse. There is a hint of the God of the gaps about such arguments:[12] the universe appears to be a highly improbable structure: we cannot give a rational explanation of these cosmological features: therefore, they constitute evidence of an intelligent designer. And, like the God of the gaps, the role of this deity shrinks with the expansion of scientific understanding. This shrinkage is illustrated neatly by the above quotation from Davies, which refers to the horizon problem now explained by inflationary cosmology.

A second assumption of anthropic design arguments is that the ultimate goal of creation is the existence of rational carbon-based life forms (i.e. humankind). This is in agreement with the dominant view of Western Christian theology. However, it is arguable that the anthropocentricity of Western Christianity is derived from sources other than the Christian revelation. For example, instead of presenting humankind as the end of creation, Genesis 1 may be read as insisting that the end of God's creative activity is his Sabbath rest in the presence of all his creation. A move towards less anthropocentric readings of the Bible (and Christian tradition) is a common feature of contemporary theologies of creation (see Chapter 8). This change of emphasis involves rethinking these arguments and recognizing that 'anthropic' is an unfortunate term. What is remarkable is that the universe arose in a way fruitful for the formation of carbon-based life. Conditions permitting the simplest colonies of bacteria to arise would still be extremely remarkable.

As we discuss in 10.14–10.15, it is important to distinguish arguments about the initial character of the universe, the 'settings of the dials', from arguments about how it happened that, roughly ten billion years later, there arose a 'Goldilocks planet' like Earth, a rocky planet at the appropriate sort of distance from the appropriate sort of star to allow life to arise. Anthropic arguments as they are usually understood apply to discussion of the initial 'settings' of the universe. The major positions at present are:

(a) versions of the many-universes position combined with the WAP (5.22)
(b) the fine-tuning of the universe attributed to some sort of designer entity.

The choice between these options will tend to be motivated by metaphysical presuppositions about the coherence of design arguments (see Polkinghorne 1998b:18–22).

EXERCISE 5.2

Consider which of the interpretations of the anthropic features you prefer, and why this might be. *Then* look at a recent assessment of the arguments, such as Manson, 2003:chs 7–10.

SECTION F
THE REDISCOVERY OF COMPLEXITY (5.25–5.28)

5.25 Introduction: 'Newtonian' limits to Newtonian physics

From the perspective of Newtonian physics, reality could be exhaustively understood in terms of particles moving in well-defined ways under the influence of certain forces. Of course it was recognized from the outset that real life was more complex than that. Many everyday situations involved too many factors to be amenable to such straightforward treatment. In such cases physicists had to be satisfied with approximations. Nevertheless it was assumed that, in principle, these awkward cases could be treated exactly.[13]

Take, for example, the motion of planets round the Sun. Using his laws of motion, Newton was able to provide an exact solution to the two-body problem – the case of two physical bodies interacting gravitationally but isolated from other influences. However, Newton's successors were unable to create exact solutions for larger ensembles of bodies (e.g. the Solar System or even just the Sun, Earth and Moon considered in isolation from all the rest – the three-body problem). Instead they had to adopt a method of approximations – beginning with the simple case, they asked how the presence of an additional element might perturb the orbits of the two bodies, then they calculated the effect of that change on the third body, then corrected the original calculations in the light of that, and so on to higher and higher degrees of accuracy.

It was not until the end of the nineteenth century that astronomers finally abandoned the search for an exact solution to the three-body problem. In 1889 a young mathematical physicist, Henri Poincaré, won a competition sponsored by the King of Sweden with an essay demonstrating the impossibility of such a solution.

5.26 Recognizing chaos

Poincaré may justly be called the father of chaos theory. In addition to demonstrating that there were physical systems which could not be precisely analysed using Newtonian physics, he was among the first physicists to comment on the extreme sensitivity of many physical systems to small variations in initial conditions. Little notice was taken of his remarks when he made them in 1903 but, since then, physicists have become much more conscious of the extent to which such chaotic behaviour is to be found in the physical world. This new awareness of chaos and complexity is not so much a recent discovery as a gradually changing perception resulting from a range of factors.

The research that has resulted from Poincaré's own work on perturbation theory is one of these factors. This has revealed the existence of chaotic behaviour in simple isolated systems. Take, for example, the motion of balls on a snooker table. It can be shown that their motion is so sensitive to external factors that in order to predict the position of the cue ball after a minute of motion (and collisions), one would have to take into account the gravitational attraction of electrons on the far side of the galaxy! Even something as apparently simple as the tossing of a coin or the motion of a water droplet on a convex surface is so sensitive to minute variations in the environment as to be unpredictable.

A second area of research that has encouraged physicists to take chaos more seriously is that of turbulent flow in fluids. Its relevance to engineering and meteorology ensured that this was a growth area in research. Unlike the simple situations described above, turbulence is not merely a matter of uncertainties in the system created by random motion at the molecular level. That aspect of fluid dynamics can be handled statistically. The real issue is the sudden emergence of random motion on a macroscopic scale – eddies and currents involving large collections of molecules. Such situations are bounded but unstable – in many such cases we are now able to generate equations that tell us the boundaries within which the motion will take place. Inside those boundaries, however, the particles involved are subject to irregular fluctuations quite independent of any external perturbation.

A third aspect in the development of chaos theory has been the availability of more and more powerful electronic computers. They have allowed physicists to extend classical perturbation theory to situations that previously were too complicated to calculate. As a result more and more situations have been revealed to be chaotic.

Finally, the widespread acceptance of quantum theory may also have played an important part in changing the attitudes of physicists to unpredictable situations. This is not to suggest that quantum theory is directly relevant to chaos at an everyday level.[14] However, the acceptance of quantum uncertainties may have made it easier for physicists to accept a degree of unpredictability about the physical world at other levels.

5.27 Coming to terms with chaos

This new awareness of complexity implies a profound change in the way in which many physical scientists view the world, a new perception of the relation between freedom and necessity. This can be summarized in the apparently paradoxical statement that chaos is deterministic. The situations described above are not completely anarchic. On the contrary, we are dealing with ensembles of bodies moving at the everyday level where Newtonian laws of motion still hold sway. The behaviour of these chaotic situations is generated by fixed rules that do not involve any elements of chance. Many of the physicists of chaos would insist that, in principle, the future is still completely determined by the past in these situations. In an accessible introduction to the subject Alan Cook advocates that the term 'deterministic chaos' should always be used (Cook, 1998:31–41). However, these are situations which are so sensitive to the initial conditions that, in spite of the determinism of the associated physical laws, it is impossible to predict future behaviour. *Deterministic physics no longer has the power to impose a deterministic outcome.* According to one of the classic papers on the subject, 'There is order in chaos: underlying chaotic behaviour there are elegant geometric forms that create randomness in the same way as a card dealer shuffles a deck of cards or a blender mixes cake batter' (Crutchfield *et al.*, 1995:35).

At first glance this may seem entirely negative. The admission that chaos is far more widespread than previously realized appears to impose new fundamental limits on our ability to make predictions. If prediction and control are indeed fundamental to science then chaos is a serious matter. On the other hand, the deterministic element in these chaotic situations implies that many apparently random phenomena may be more predictable than had been thought. The exciting thing about chaos theory is the way in which, across many different sciences, researchers have been able to take a second look at apparently random information and, while not being able to predict exact outcomes, nevertheless explain the random behaviour in terms of simple laws. This is true of meteorology. It can also be applied to dripping taps or to many biological systems (e.g. the mathematical physics of a heart-beat).

5.28 Implications for the philosophy of science

As we have just hinted, the emergence of a science of chaos has profound implications for our understanding of what science is and can do.

One may disagree with the notion that the *raison d'être* of science is prediction and control. Nevertheless, prediction still retains a central place in the scientific method. How else are we to test our scientific models? The classical approach is to make predictions from the model and devise experiments to test those predictions. Here, however, we are faced with situations in which such predictions seem inherently impossible. In fact, what is required is that we take a more subtle approach to prediction. What we observe may well be random (or pseudo-random). However, the deterministic element in mathematical chaos implies that the random observations will be clustered into predictable patterns.

A second important implication of chaos theory has to do with the continuing tendency to reductionism in the sciences (see 6.11–6.11.1). Chaos and complexity highlight the fact that only in the very simple systems that formed the backbone of classical physics is it true that the whole is merely the sum of the parts. Chaotic systems simply cannot be understood by breaking them down into their component parts and seeing how they fit together again.

Closely allied to this challenge to reductionism is a question about the possibility of completeness in physics. The reality of chaos undermines the hope that such completeness can be achieved by an increasingly detailed understanding of fundamental physical forces and constituents. It also provides a physical basis for the concept of emergence that is so important in philosophical and theological perspectives on the life and human sciences. The behaviour of chaotic systems suggests that interaction of components at one level can lead to complex global behaviour at another level – behaviour that is not predictable from a knowledge of the component parts. Indeed some chaos scientists suggest that 'chaos provides a mechanism that allows for free will within a world governed by deterministic laws' (Crutchfield *et al.*, 1995:48).

However, we consider caution is needed at this point. Chaotic randomness is not complete randomness. True, we are unable to predict the detailed outcome of a chaotic scenario. However, the mathematics of chaos does permit us to predict the limits of the possible outcomes. This is randomness within constraints – deterministic constraints. In fact, chaos theory allows us to extend our physical understanding of the world into new areas specifically by applying deterministic covering laws to situations that were previously thought to be completely random. This could be taken as evidence that determinism really works.

On the other hand, the fact that the equations we use are deterministic does not necessarily mean that nature is deterministic. The equations are maps, not the reality. It could be that the apparent determinism is an artefact of the particular way in which we have chosen to map reality – in terms of mathematical physics. The idea that our equations are only approximations to the laws that govern the macroscopic world is an important part of Polkinghorne's position on divine action (see **10.9(iv)(a)**) and Polkinghorne, 1998a:64–6.

5.29 Conclusion

We have seen that, though Newtonianism remains very influential, in a number of areas modern physics has broken with the Newtonian paradigm. It has given rise to questions of interpretation which relate directly to theology – in the areas of quantum theory and chaos theory (*re* determinism), the Big Bang origin and final fate of the universe, and the question of evidence for design. A number of these areas will be considered again in our discussion of divine action in Chapter 10.

Notes

1   Wertheim (1995:173) cites comments to this effect made at a meeting of the American Physical Society in 1972.

2   Russell Stannard's *Black Holes and Uncle Albert* (Stannard, 1991), though aimed at children, provides a very good introduction to the strange implications of Einstein's theory.

3   See also 1.17 on the significance of indeterminacy.

4   For a discussion of the two-slit experiment in terms of quantum theory see Davies, 1990:108–11.

5   For a brief discussion of 'bottom-up' and 'top-down' thinking see Peacocke (1993:53–5). See also our 'note on emergence' in 6.11.1. We take up the question of 'top-down causation' in relation to divine action in 10.9(iii)(c).

6   George Berkeley (1685–1753) – a philosopher famous for his apparent denial of the reality of any external world.

7   At the moment of writing (August 2004) the prevailing view is that the so-called 'cosmological constant' which would accelerate the universe's expansion (see Guth, 1997:37–42 for the history of this term) may be non-zero, and sufficiently large to guarantee an ever-expanding universe.

8   The scientific convention for writing very big and very small numbers is used here. 10^2 is 10 multiplied by itself, or a hundred – 10^6 is ten multiplied by itself four more times, or a million. 10^{24} is 10 multiplied by itself twenty-three times, or a million million million million. Numbers less than 1 are written with negative indices – so 10^9 would be $1/10^9$ or one-billionth.

9   Barrow and Tipler see analogies between this Ultimate Observer and the God of Berkeleian idealism. An alternative analogy would be with the self-surpassing deity of process thought.

10   See also 7.7.

11   At the same time an inference to the existence of 'some influence capable of transcending spacetime and the confinement of relativistic causality' is very far from being an inference to belief in any established religion.

12   See 10.3 for more on 'the God of the gaps'.

13   See 1.17 on Laplace and the determinism of the Newtonian universe.

14   Except in that Heisenberg's Uncertainty Principle (5.11(ii)) sets a limit on the precision of our knowledge of *any* system.

Further reading

COOK, Alan (1998) 'Uncertainties of science', in *Science Meets Faith: Theology and Science in Conversation*, ed. Fraser Watts (London: SPCK), 25–41

DAVIES, P. (1990) *God and the New Physics* (Harmondsworth: Penguin)

—— (1995) *About Time* (London: Viking)

DEWEESE, G.J. (2004) *God and the Nature of Time* (Aldershot: Ashgate)

GLEICK, J. (1988) *Chaos: Making a New Science* (London: Cardinal)

GREENE, BRIAN (2004) *The Fabric of the Cosmos: Space, Time and the Texture of Reality* (Harmondsworth: Penguin)

MANSON, NEIL A. (ed.) (2003) *God and Design: The Teleological Argument and Modern Science* (London: Routledge)

POLKINGHORNE, J. (1989) *Science and Providence* (London: SPCK)

(1990) *The Quantum World* (Harmondsworth: Penguin)

(1998) *Belief in God in an Age of Science* (New Haven, CT: Yale University Press)

(2004) *Science and the Trinity: The Christian Encounter with Reality* (London: SPCK)

RUSSELL, R.J., CLAYTON, P., WEGTER-MCNELLY, K. and POLKINGHORNE, J. (eds) (2001) *Quantum Mechanics, Scientific Perspectives on Divine Action* 5 (Vatican City: Vatican Observatory; Berkeley, CA: Center for Theology and the Natural Sciences)

RUSSELL, R.J., MURPHY, N. and PEACOCKE, A.R. (1995) *Chaos and Complexity, Scientific Perspectives on Divine Action* (Vatican City: Vatican Observatory; Berkeley, CA: Center for Theology and the Natural Sciences)

WERTHEIM, M. (1995) *Pythagoras' Trousers: God, Physics and the Gender Wars* (New York, NY: Times Books)

WORTHING, M.W. (1996) *God, Creation and Contemporary Physics* (Minneapolis, MN: Fortress Press)

Chapter 6

Theology and evolutionary biology

Christopher Southgate, Michael Robert Negus and Andrew Robinson[1]

6.1 Introduction

We saw in the quotation from John Updike in 1.1 that the caricature of this relationship is one in which the development of evolutionary theory has been enough to sweep aside the claims of religion. In this chapter we shall begin by looking at the topic of human evolution. This will serve as an introduction to some of the themes to be explored further in the rest of the chapter. We will then review the science of biological evolution as it has developed since the pioneering work of Darwin. We shall indicate the challenges Darwinian thought posed to Christian theology of creation in the nineteenth century. We shall discuss how evolutionary theory has subsequently developed. Different phases through which evolutionary theory has passed present different questions and challenges for theology. We shall indicate how twentieth-century Darwinism produced new prophets of conflict: in particular we will consider Francis Crick, Richard Dawkins, Jacques Monod and E. O. Wilson. We will use the views of these authors to focus on one of the most important issues raised by evolutionary biology, namely the merits and limitations of different forms of reductionism. The challenge of synthesizing evolutionary and theological narratives will be taken up in more detail in Chapter 10.

SECTION A
HUMAN EVOLUTION (6.2–6.4)

6.2 The discovery of pre-history

In 1879, so the story goes, Don Marcelino Sanz de Sautuola was exploring a cave on his property on the northern Spanish coast. While he had his eyes fixed firmly on the floor, his young daughter Maria turned her gaze upwards to the ceiling. There her eyes lighted on the now famous bison paintings of the Altamira cavern.[2] Years later Picasso would say of these, the first examples of cave art to be discovered in the modern era, 'None of us could paint like that.'[3]

Over the following years many more examples of cave art were discovered in Europe (and subsequently in Africa, America and Australia). Sophisticated dating techniques are able to tell us that the oldest European examples were painted over 30,000 years ago (Tattersall, 1998:16). In some cases there is evidence that, prior to the discovery of these paintings in the late nineteenth century, relatively modern visitors to the caves must already have seen the images without realizing their significance. In one instance, some graffiti dated 1660 were inscribed less than a metre from large, well-preserved images of bison and ibex.

As Lewis-Williams points out (2002:19), the reason why de Sautuola appreciated the possible significance of his daughter Maria's discovery, whereas the seventeenth-century graffitist did not, is that until the nineteenth century Western thought had no concept of *pre-history* – the sheer extent of time that had passed before humans began to record their own stories. By the time the young Maria looked up at the ceiling of the Altamira cave the idea of pre-history was widely accepted. Charles Lyell had published his *Principles of Geology* (1830), establishing the antiquity of the Earth, and Charles Darwin had published *On the Origin of Species* (1859), establishing the antiquity of life. The story of the 'discovery' of Altamira is a good example of the theory-dependence of our observations – how what we see is influenced by our theories, as well as the other way round (see **1.7, 4.10**).

In the following sections (**6.2–6.4**) we will briefly outline some of the current state of knowledge about human evolution, and then ask how this may be interpreted in the light of the accounts given in the opening chapters of Genesis. This very brief sketch will serve as an introduction to the question of the relationship between evolutionary theory and theology, which will then be taken up in more detail in the rest of the chapter.

Our knowledge of the course of human evolution is derived principally from fossil evidence (combined with accurate dating techniques) and from studies of genetic data in living populations (which is able to give information about where and when current populations are likely to have originated). The key conclusions from combining these approaches are:

(i) Modern humans (*Homo sapiens*), i.e. people who were anatomically nearly indistinguishable from ourselves, originated about 200,000 years ago, almost certainly in Africa. It was modern humans who created the cave art mentioned above, together with virtually all the other sophisticated cultural artefacts of pre-history – complex tools, body decoration, jewellery, ritual (religious?) burials, etc. It is not known what suddenly enabled this astonishing burst of cultural activity around 40,000 years ago, or why it took so long to happen.[4]

(ii) For much of the time that modern humans have existed we shared the planet with another distinct human species, *Homo neanderthalis*.[5] The Neanderthals became extinct about 30,000 years ago, for reasons that are not known. They practised burial of the dead, even possibly with some ceremony.[6] In October 2004 bones were found on an Indonesian island suggesting that a previously unknown dwarf human species ('Flores man', *Homo floresiensis*) persisted there at least until 18,000 years ago (Brown *et al.*, 2004; see also Diamond, 2004 for a preliminary analysis). The inferences from this find have been contested,

The 'pagoda tree' of hominid evolution. The hominids in each storey diverge into regional/adaptive branches which also subdivide and diverge. The second storey may derive from more than one stem.

Modern grade: Very large brains, reduced brows, smaller teeth, jutting chin.

Heidelberg grade: Very large brains, rounded brows.

Erect grade: Relatively large brains, prominent bar-shaped brows, flared cheeks.

Handyman or Habiline grade: First sign of an increase in relative brain size.

Southern Ape or *Australopithecus* grade: Very ape-like heads in spite of being erect.

Savanna ape trunk.

Figure 6.1(a)   The 'pagoda tree' of hominid evolution. The hominids in each storey diverge into regional/adaptive branches which also subdivide and diverge. The second storey may derive from more than one stem. Reproduced with permission from Kingdon, 1993:34.

Figure 6.1(b) Four trees representing different assumptions about human evolution. A. Loring Brace in 1971 envisaged a single line extending over 15 million years. B. A typical 1960s 'main-line' stem with hominids distinct for 15 million years. C. A 2000 tree with more branches but still a single tree on a 5-million-year timescale. D. The Olson/Falk tree (1981–8), including apes on an 8- or 9-million-year timescale. Reproduced with permission from Kingdon, 2003:9.

but if substantiated they would sharpen questions as to God's (and our) relationship with our now extinct near relatives. The fact that at least one, and possibly more, closely related human species have coexisted with us in the past illustrates that the pattern of human evolution has been more like a branching tree (or perhaps a small shrub!) rather than a single progressive 'ascent' from less advanced ancestors.

(iii)   Moving back further into the past, before the origin of modern humans, we again find a branching pattern of evolution. Our closest living relatives are the chimpanzees. Genetic evidence suggests that humans and chimpanzees are both descended from a 'common ancestor' species which lived about 5 million years ago. The fossil record suggests that after the hominid (human family) branch diverged from the pongid branch (chimpanzee, gorilla and orang-utan family) there were several further branchings of the hominid branch, with several different hominid species coexisting with one another at various times. It was probably from a population of *Homo erectus*, which appeared about 2 million years ago and survived in some areas to as recently as 100,000 years ago, that modern humans descended. Although *Homo erectus* had a very wide global distribution the fossil and genetic evidence strongly supports the hypothesis that all current human populations are descended from a single population in Africa, followed by successive migrations. This view has very largely super-seded an alternative hypothesis, which was often propounded with distinctly racist overtones, that different contemporary human popu-lations descended from local varieties of *Homo erectus*, some of which may have already been more advanced than others.

6.3 Human evolution and the Genesis accounts of creation

6.3.1 Made in the image of God

Genesis 1.26 describes humans as made in the image and likeness of God. Since this is not said of other creatures the implication appears to be that there is a radical *discontinuity* between (modern?) humans and non-human animals. The evolutionary account, in contrast, tells the story of a continuous process of change with no sharp transition from the non-human to the human. Human distinc-tiveness, whatever it is understood to consist of, appears to have evolved gradually. This does not mean, however, that those who accept the fact that evolution has occurred in this way must necessarily abandon the idea of the *imago Dei*.

Instead, the way in which the *imago* is understood to be manifest in humans could be framed so as to avoid the assumption that it is something specially added to the physical/animal nature of humans. The possibilities would include, for example, understanding the *imago* in terms of:

(a) rationality (a traditional but questionable approach)
(b) dominion (another notoriously problematic strategy)
(c) morality
(d) creativity
(e) capacity for loving relationship.[7]

Alternatively, the *imago* may be best understood not in terms of something humans *possess*, or a description of our place in the order of creation, but as expressing a particular relationship and responsibility *to God*, such as that of being a representative or ambassador of God on earth (cf. Peacocke, 2004a:284), or a priest of creation (Peacocke 2004a:296, also Southgate, 2005). An understanding of the *imago Dei* in terms of relationship to God is certainly in tune with the notion that the divine image developed only when human culture developed a shared symbolic thought. J. Wentzel van Huyssteen has explored this theme, noting that the Cro-Magnons[8] were not simply more intelligent than their hominid forebears but 'differently intelligent' (2003:173), possessing a symbol-system as well as the cognitive fluidity that allowed the human brain to develop such rich imagination and culture (see Deacon, 1998; also Mithen, 1999). Religion may well have been a key aspect of the development of this symbolic intelligence.[9]

Such a reframing of the notion of the *imago Dei* in terms consistent with the evolutionary account need not be thought of as a capitulation on the part of theology. On the contrary, the scientific view might be regarded as pointing us back to the traditional Hebrew understanding of the psychosomatic unity of the human person: 'The LORD God formed man (*adam*) from the dust of the ground (*adamah*).'[10]

6.3.2 The Fall

If one expects that the evolutionary story will deliver a historical confirmation of the Genesis account, then the theological idea of the Fall presents a similar sort of problem to that of the *imago Dei*. There is no evidence that hominids ever lived in a suffering-free paradise.[11] Furthermore, it is clear from a scientific perspective that the condition of creation 'groaning' in pain (cf. Romans 8.22) long preceded the appearance of humans (for the timescales involved see 6.4). If anything, a historical doctrine of the Fall has tended to obscure the need for theological exploration of how a creation pronounced 'very good' by God (Gen. 1.31) can be the place of so much pain, suffering and evil (See **6.7(iv), 10.18, 10.19**). Of course, humans have increasingly become the cause of much of this suffering; as Peacocke puts it, the doctrine of the Fall has some 'prophetic if not ontological force' (2004a:286).

In the light of the evolutionary perspective the relevance of the Fall story must surely be that it describes that peculiar sense of alienation that seems to characterize human life; a sense that we cannot wholly settle in our ecological niche or network of relationships, a sense that we yearn for something which we cannot grasp. As Davies (2001:115) helpfully points out, when Adam and Eve's eyes are opened to their new existential situation, God's question to Adam is not, as Adam seems to interpret it, 'Where are you *hiding?*' (presumably God has no difficulty knowing where Adam is), but simply '*Where are you?*' in a deep, existential sense (so Genesis 3.7–10). As we shall see in the course of this chapter, evolutionary biology cannot be expected to answer this existential and religious question for us, but it may help us to hear the question in new ways.

6.4 The timescale of evolution

We noted above (6.3) that current evidence suggests that anatomically modern humans first appeared about 200,000 years ago. To understand how this timescale relates to the whole story of evolution on our planet it may help to consider an analogy of a 450-page book.[12] In such a book the 4,500-million year history of the Earth would be told at a rate of 10 million years per page. (Another two similar-sized volumes would be needed as a prequel if the story were to be told from the time of the Big Bang – see **5.16**.) According to this analogy, if the Earth were formed on page 1, modern humans would not appear until the *last line of the last page*. The period from the start of the narrative of the biblical patriarchs to the present (something over 3,000 years) would be compressed into the *last letter* of the last word on the last page.

Table 6.1[13]   Chronology of evolution (in terms of a book of 450 pages)

Earth formed	4,500 million years ago	Page 1
Origin of life	?3,800 million years ago	Page 70
First eukaryotic cells[14]	?2,000 million years ago	Page 250
First multicellular organisms	600 million years ago	Page 390
First dinosaurs and mammals	200 million years ago	Page 430
Extinction of dinosaurs	65 million years ago	Page 443
Origin of hominids	5 million years ago	Last half-page
Origin of modern humans	200,000 years ago	Last line
Abraham to the present	3,000–4,000 years	Last letter

Antagonists of the theory of evolution sometimes attempt to reject it on the basis that it is unprovable. It is true that the theory of evolution cannot be completely verified by direct observation of every part of the process. This is true of all theories that provide explanations for processes that involve immense periods of time. Peacocke (1986:35) comments: 'the postulate of past biological evolution cannot be falsified in the sense of Karl Popper,[15] by performing repeatable experiments whose outcomes are inconsistent with the postulate [that evolution has occurred] – nor can most theories of geology and of cosmology'. In this sense evolutionary biology, then, is akin to Big Bang cosmology, and much of astrophysics, in that it offers models to explain processes which are historically particular, and could never be duplicated in a laboratory. In the case of cosmology this is because the energies involved are too high; in the case of evolution, because the timescales are too long.

Nevertheless, it is important to note that although we can never completely 're-run the tape' of evolution, there are hypotheses which can be generated and tested in a Popperian sense. To imagine an extreme example, if evidence emerged of modern humans having lived 2,000 million years ago (the age of the single-celled organisms with internal structure) then evolutionary theory as a whole would be in serious trouble. For this reason evolution is not 'just a theory', as some people complain, but a robust and (as will shall see in the rest of this chapter) extremely fruitful scientific *research programme* (cf. 4.12). We turn, then, to begin to consider the basis of the evolutionary research programme that Charles Darwin (1803–82) initiated.

SECTION B
DARWIN AND DARWINISM (6.5–6.7)

6.5 Evolutionary ideas before Darwin[16]

When Darwin unveiled his theory of evolution in 1859 he was by no means the first person to have questioned the constancy of species. Naturalists were aware of the need to offer some explanation for the existence (known since the end of the eighteenth century) of fossils from species which no longer appeared to exist. Several different interpretations of the fossil evidence were offered, including:

(i) *Transmutation* – the idea that species are continuously transforming into new species on an upward escalator of progress. This was the view espoused by Jean-Baptiste Lamarck (1744–1829). Lamarck was reluctant to accept the possibility that species became *extinct* (as opposed to transformed into something else); possibly because he wanted his theory to cohere with the optimistic rationalism of the French Revolution.

(ii) *Progressive replacement* – the idea that as species become extinct they are replaced by progressively more advanced species, either by migration from elsewhere or by new acts of 'special creation'. This was the view championed by Lamarck's rival Georges Cuvier (1769–1832).

When Darwin's father sent the 16-year-old Charles to Edinburgh in 1825 to study medicine the city happened to be home to two British 'transmutationists', Robert Knox and Robert Grant. Darwin was miserable as a medical student and left in 1827, enrolling the following year at Cambridge to study for the Church. Before doing so, however, he enjoyed a brief but influential friendship with Grant, experiencing both the excitement of new ideas but also witnessing the hostility with which radical thinking tended to be regarded in 1820s Britain (Desmond and Moore 1991:33–44).[17] When an anonymous evolutionary treatise appeared in 1844 under the title *Vestiges of the Natural History of Creation*, Darwin had already completed a secret sketch of his theory. By this time, however, anti-evolutionism had gained the upper hand in both Britain and France. The scepticism with which the *Vestiges* was received by the scientific community was probably one reason for Darwin's famous delay (a further 15 years) before revealing his hand[18] (Browne, 1996:465).

6.6 Darwin's theory of evolution by natural selection

When in 1859 Darwin eventually dared to publish, the full title of his revolutionary book was *On the Origin of Species by Means of Natural Selection, or the Preservation of Favoured Races in the Struggle for Life*. Twenty-two years had passed since he first started a clandestine notebook on transmutation (Desmond and Moore, 1991:229).

In the *Origin* Darwin presented a compelling range of observations and arguments in favour of the idea that species arise by a process of evolution from earlier forms. In addition, as the title indicates, Darwin proposed a *mechanism*, which he called 'natural selection', to explain how this process could give rise over time to the vast variety of life-forms he had observed. The essential elements of this mechanism are:

(i) The existence of *variation* between the individuals of any species.
(ii) That some (not necessarily all) of the differences that distinguish one organism from another are *heritable* (i.e. may be passed from parent to offspring).
(iii) That some of this *heritable variation* (i.e. inherited difference) affects the individual's *fitness* or chances of *survival* (and hence the likelihood of producing its own offspring).

These three concepts – variation, heritability and differential survival – are the general requirements for a Darwinian process of evolution by natural selection. (In fact Darwin did not express his thinking in precisely this way, but it is widely accepted that these conditions express the logical structure of his concept of natural selection – see Endler, 1986.) Crucially, Darwin had realized that natural selection could work on small variations if applied over the very long timescales that the new geology had revealed to be available.

Interestingly, Darwin generally avoided using the word 'evolution', employing it only once in the *Origin* (Darwin, 1859:460; and cf. Ridley, 1993:8). The pre-Darwinian connotations of the word would have suggested a predictable unrolling of events, as seen for example in the processes of embryonic development. In contrast, Darwinian 'descent with modification' (Darwin's preferred phrase) is based on random variations – or, more accurately, variations which are *undirected* with respect to any subsequent effect on fitness. This is one reason (though not the only one) why the pattern of evolutionary change that can be inferred from the fossil record and from genetic evidence shows a disorderly branching pattern rather than a straight ladder of progress.

6.7 Scientific and theological responses to Darwin's theory

In Chapters 1 and 3 we discussed how caricatures of the 'conflict' between science and theology can obscure more subtle and revealing aspects of the relationship between the two. As we have seen, some commonly accepted accounts of the nineteenth-century reception of Darwinism exemplify this point (3.2.2). In reality, both the scientific and religious reactions to the *Origin* were mixed. On the scientific side, it was soon accepted that the evidence for evolution (descent with modification) was compelling. However, Darwin's arguments for his proposed mechanism of evolution, natural selection, were not generally found to be convincing. The principal reason for this was that the mechanisms of heredity were not yet understood, and it was therefore not clear why any heritable variation which happened to be beneficial to fitness would not simply be diluted away in subsequent generations. It was not until the 1930s–1940s that advances in the field of genetics would convince scientists that Darwin had been right about natural selection. We will pick up this story again in Section C.

On the theological side, reaction to the *Origin* was also mixed. Of course, some people found Darwin's ideas unsettling or repugnant. The wife of the Bishop of Worcester (her name is not handed down with the story, which may in any case be apocryphal) is reputed to have exclaimed, 'Descended from apes! My dear, let us hope it is not so; but if it is, that it does not become generally known.'[19] On the other hand, there were those Christian thinkers who immediately celebrated evolution. Frederick Temple, who preached the official sermon at the British Association Meeting in 1860, 'was … said by one observer to have espoused Darwin's ideas fully' (Brooke, 1991:41). Charles Kingsley found that it was 'just as noble a conception of Deity, to believe that He created primal forms capable of self development … as to believe that He required a fresh act of intervention to supply the lacunas which He Himself had made' (quoted in Desmond and Moore, 1991:477). Kingsley saw that the new science might redirect the all-important balance in Christian theology between God's transcendence and the divine indwelling of creation (immanence) in favour of a greater emphasis on immanence.

As we pointed out in Chapter 3, just as it is false to over-emphasize the conflicts between science and theology it is equally a mistake to impose an artificial harmony on the narrative of their relationship (3.5.2). It is therefore important to an understanding of the development of the 'special relationship' between evolutionary theory and theology to understand what it was about Darwin's scheme which challenged nineteenth-century theological descriptions. Four major issues may be identified:

> (i) Darwin's scheme refuted, virtually at a stroke, the notion that creatures had been individually designed by God, and hence any suggestion that one could argue *directly* from the ingenuity of their design, or the exquisite nature of their adaptation to their environment, to point to the existence or the ingenuity of such a Being.[20]
>
> (ii) It cohered with the geological proposal of Lyell that the Earth was very old, compared with the chronology suggested by Genesis, and that

therefore no literal reading of Scripture could accord with the scientific account (see 6.3).

(iii) It implied that apes and humans share a common ancestor; rather than humans arising by any distinct act of creation which might guarantee their theological uniqueness (see 6.2, 6.3.1). In fact Darwin prudently avoided anything more than a hint at the implications for our understanding of humanity in the *Origin*, simply noting in the Conclusion that: 'In the future I see open fields for far more important researches. . . . Much light will be thrown on the origin of man and his history.' He waited until the publication of *The Descent of Man* (1871) to extend his theory explicitly to human evolution.

(iv) It brought to the fore the theological difficulty of affirming the goodness of God in the face of suffering in the world (technically known as the problem of theodicy): evolution seems to contain such cruelty, waste and ugliness as to make it hard to defend as the means to a divine end. One of the strengths of Darwin's theory was that it explained, without the need for any ad hoc hypotheses, both aesthetically appealing adaptations, such as the beak of the woodpecker, and the 'ugliness' of species like the *ichneumonidae* – wasps whose larvae are implanted within the body of a caterpillar and eat it alive from the inside. We explore the extent of apparent disvalue in evolution as a continuing problem for theology in 10.18–10.19.

EXERCISE 6.1

Consider to what extent these challenges remain problems for a contemporary faith. How might Christian theological schemes address these problems?

It is important not to think of Christian theology at the time of Darwin in too static a way. As Welch points out, before 1850 Schleiermacher and those following him had already questioned whether the doctrine of creation implied any particular point of temporal origin (see 2.5.4), whether the Fall implied a particular event in early human history (see 6.3.2), and whether God was immutable in the traditional sense (Welch, 1996:34). Probably the greatest challenges to the mainstream of the Christian tradition in the nineteenth century came from biblical criticism rather than natural science. The controversy over Darwin's scheme is one of the great moments in the history of the 'special relationship' between scientific and religious thought. But it is *a* moment in history, albeit a complex one, as we saw in 3.2.2. It is not surprising, therefore, that Christian theology and evolutionary theory have likewise *both* undergone changes since the publication of the *Origin*.

SECTION C
DARWINISM EVOLVING[21] (6.8–6.10)

6.8 Genetic Darwinism: the neo-Darwinian synthesis

As we noted above (6.7) one of the problems with Darwin's theory was that he knew nothing of the mechanisms of heredity. He formulated a hypothesis (which subsequently proved to be wrong) that each cell in the body produced tiny particles which budded off from the cell and made their way to the reproductive cells (eggs and sperm). Darwin imagined that these tiny buds could contain information about the organism, including experiences that it had had in its lifetime, which could then be inherited by the organism's offspring. One of the reasons why the idea of natural selection was not widely accepted in Darwin's time is that it was not clear why characteristics passed on in this manner would not subsequently be diluted out in later generations. This was why, in addition to the *undirected* mechanism of natural selection, Darwin continued to think that another mechanism of evolution – *the inheritance of acquired characteristics* – must also operate. This was the mechanism that Lamarck had proposed to explain his own version of 'transmutationism' (see 6.5).[22]

Ironically, the experiments on the basis of heredity which would later form the cornerstone of genetics and vindicate Darwin's hypothesis had been begun by Gregor Mendel, an Augustinian monk in Brün, Moravia, three years before the publication of the *Origin*. Mendel's work on the inheritance of different characteristics (i.e. variations) in garden pea plants were published in 1866, sixteen years before Darwin died, but their significance was not recognized until Mendel's work was 'rediscovered' in the early twentieth century. One of the variations studied by Mendel was whether the seeds (peas) from a particular plant were smooth or wrinkly. Mendel showed that if he crossed (hybridized) a 'smooth' plant with a 'wrinkly' plant the next generation of plants did *not* have seeds that were halfway between smooth and wrinkly. Instead, the pattern of inheritance suggested that each plant possessed a pair of 'units of inheritance'. Different combinations of these 'smooth' or 'wrinkly' units of inheritance determined whether the plant had smooth or wrinkly seeds. The crucial thing about Mendel's experiments is that he had shown that heredity can be 'particulate'; in other words, what is passed from parent to offspring can be a discrete 'unit' of inheritance, which can be passed on unchanged and without dilution through successive generations.

When Mendel's work was rediscovered in the early twentieth century his 'unit-characters' of inheritance soon became known as 'genes' (the term was coined by the Danish botanist Wilhelm Johannsen in 1909). The first supporters of Mendelian genetics rejected Darwinian evolution, arguing that Darwin's proposed accumulation of minute variations were different from the much larger changes observed by Mendel. The breakthrough came with paper and pencil, rather in the laboratory, when the British mathematicians G.H. Hardy, R.A. Fisher and J.B.S. Haldane demonstrated the surprising power that natural selection could be expected to have when applied over successive generations, even when acting on variations with very small selective advantages (recall the key requirements for

Darwinian evolution listed in 6.6). This mathematical approach began to receive experimental support from geneticists in the United States, notably Sewall Wright and Russian émigré Theodosius Dobzhansky. The publication of Julian Huxley's book *Evolution: The Modern Synthesis* in 1942 signalled a new phase in Darwinism. This new phase is usually referred to as *the neo-Darwinian synthesis*, because it rested on the new union of genetics with Darwin's theory of evolution by natural selection.

6.9 DNA and the molecular revolution in biology

Further consolidation of the neo-Darwinian synthesis occurred as a result of the remarkable discovery in the 1950s and 1960s of the *molecular basis* of the genetic theories that had arisen out of Mendel's work, and it is to this that we now turn.

Most of the functional molecules in cells are proteins. For a long time it was therefore assumed that the material basis of inheritance was also likely to be based on protein biochemistry. During the 1940s, however, it became increasingly clear that DNA rather than proteins were going to turn out to be the key to heredity. In 1953, using X-ray diffraction photographs taken by Rosalind Franklin and Maurice Wilkins at King's College, London, Francis Crick and James Watson from Cambridge achieved the crucial step of deducing the structure of DNA.[23] A schematic representation of the elegant 'double helix' structure which they discovered is shown in Figure 6.2.

If you look carefully at the Figure in conjunction with the bullet points below you will be able to see how the copying and functioning of DNA contributes to *variation, heredity* and *differential survival* (recall again that these are three of the key ingredients of Darwinian evolution, listed in 6.7). It is helpful to understand the process in some detail.

- At the top part of the figure you can see that DNA is structured something like a spiral staircase, held together by rungs running crossways between the two strands of the helix. Each rung consists of a pair of chemical 'bases' (called 'nucleotide bases'), which may be one of four kinds: A, T, G or C. Because the bases are on the inside of the structure they are in a chemically very stable position. This is why DNA is able to function as a very stable resource in the function of cells and organisms, a resource which may be passed (almost) unchanged from generation to generation.
- Notice that of the four bases, C is always paired with G, and T is always paired with A. The reason for this is that each of these bases is a slightly different shape and can only fit within the structure if paired with its usual partner (the subtlety of the differences between the shapes of the bases is not reflected in the diagram). This complementary pairing of bases explains how DNA can be replicated so as to provide copies for other cells, which is required when cells divide during the growth and development of an organism. At the lower part of the figure you can see that the double helix has unfolded, so that each strand can be copied to

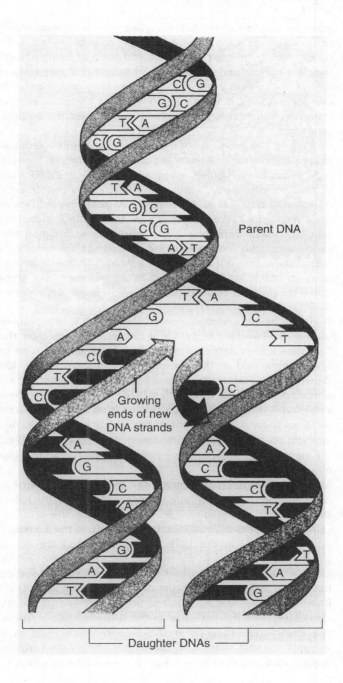

Figure 6.2   A replicating DNA molecule
(reproduced with permission from Berg and Singer, 1992:47)

generate two 'daughter' helices. When individual bases are brought up to the growing strands, each one can only be paired with the base complementary to itself. So the blacked-out base being paired with C on the right-hand strand in the Figure must be a G. When a strand is copied it gives rise to a copy with the *complementary* sequence (with Gs wherever there was a C in the parent, Ts wherever there was an A, and so on). When the daughter strand is subsequently copied the original sequence is restored.

- Looking up and down one of the strands of the helix you can see that the bases are arranged in a linear sequence. For example, reading from top right strand in the figure the sequence starts GCAGACGT. This sequence is the basis of genetic 'coding'. GCAGACGT has a different 'meaning' from AAGCCGTG, just as the word 'moonstone' has a different meaning from 'monotones'. Proteins, which are the usual functional molecules in cells, are made from long linear sequences of building blocks called amino-acids. The properties which give rise to the specific function of each protein derive from the way in which the line of amino-acids subsequently folds into a particular shape. Different DNA sequences can 'code' for proteins of different amino-acid sequence, and hence of different properties.

- There are twenty common types of amino-acid in living organisms, so as soon as the structure of DNA was discovered it was clear that a single DNA base (of which there are only four types) could not be specifying a single amino-acid in the corresponding protein. In the 1960s it was shown that the sequence of bases in DNA is a 'triplet code': each amino-acid is specified by a 'three-letter' DNA 'word'. As there are 64 possible three-letter 'words' that can be formed from A, T, C and G, some of the words code for more than one of the twenty amino-acids. All organisms on Earth use almost exactly the same genetic code, which is evidence for the view that all organisms are descended from the same group of primitive cells.

- Now look at Figure 6.3, showing the complex structure of animal and plant cells. In cells with a complex structure like this the most important DNA involved in heredity is in the nucleus of the cell. Many of the complex functions of proteins take place outside the nucleus. One of the discoveries made in the 1960s was that proteins are not synthesized directly from the DNA in the nucleus. Instead, the relevant sequence of bases in the DNA is 'transcribed' into complementary sequence of similar bases in a 'messenger' molecule called messenger RNA. The messenger RNA then leaves the nucleus and attaches to special structures called ribosomes. Here the 'message' in the RNA molecule is 'translated' into the amino-acid sequence of the protein which is to be made. For example, the RNA 'word' CGG codes for the amino-acid arginine, and the 'words' AAA and AAG both code for the amino-acid lysine.

Figure 6.3 A diagram of a typical cell from an animal (left) and a plant (right) (reproduced with permission from Berg and Singer, 1992:12)

Putting all of the above together, we can now understand the molecular basis of the genetic variation which underpins the neo-Darwinian view of evolution (6.8). Although DNA is chemically a very stable molecule the sequence of bases does occasionally become altered, or 'mutated'. The simplest form of mutation is a 'point' mutation where a single base of DNA is changed, like a single mistyped letter. If this changes the three-letter DNA word into a triplet that codes for a different amino-acid the mutation will result in the synthesis of a protein with a slightly different amino-acid sequence. Many such changes have little or no effect on the function of the protein, others may be ruinous. A few such changes may happen to improve the protein's function, or enhance another function that may later develop. This, then, is the basis of Darwinian (or neo-Darwinian) evolution at the *molecular* level, corresponding to the three requirements of evolution by natural selection identified in 6.7: **Variation** is caused by genetic mutations; these are random, in the sense of being *undirected* from the point of view of any benefit or harm to the organism. This variation is **heritable** because it occurs within the organism's DNA and will be faithfully replicated and passed on to future generations. Finally, this heritable variation can give rise to **differential fitness or survival** because it may affect the function of one of the organism's proteins, either for better or worse.

This molecular explanation also shows why evolution cannot occur by Lamarck's mechanism of the *inheritance of acquired characteristics* (6.8 and note 22). Mutations in DNA can lead to changes in proteins, but changes in proteins (i.e.

things that may happen to the proteins in our bodies) have no way of being passed back to DNA. This idea that information can pass from DNA to protein but not the other way round is known as the 'central dogma' of molecular biology.[24]

Perhaps *any* talk of a 'central dogma' should put us on our guard. The basic details of the above account of the molecular basis of evolution remain crucial to contemporary evolutionary theory. But some aspects or assumptions of the basic neo-Darwinian scheme have turned out to require revision, modification or expansion. In many ways, as we shall see in the following section, these developments of the Darwinian research programme allow for a more complex, multilayered view of evolution. According to this more expansive view we shall see that several key assumptions which tended to be associated with neo-Darwinism (even the 'central dogma') may be called into question once 'higher' levels of genetic function are taken into account.

6.10 Hard neo-Darwinism and expanded neo-Darwinism

6.10.1 The Darwinian research programme

The *details* of evolutionary theory are hotly debated. But it has developed from Darwin's original proposal into a theory of enormous explanatory power – it fits to a very marked degree Barbour's criteria for a successful scientific theory: agreement with data, coherence, scope and fertility (1998:113). It is for this reason that we do not consider here schemes which seek an alternative science in order to defend a literalist reading of Scripture.[25] However, there are vigorous debates within Darwinism; we outline some of the main ones in the paragraphs following.

Many of the current areas of debate in evolutionary theory may be regarded as revisions or expansions of the neo-Darwinian synthesis (6.9). Table 6.2 gives a summary of some of the differences between the original form of neo-Darwinism (which we refer to as 'hard' neo-Darwinism) and more recent developments (referred to as 'expanded neo-Darwinism'). For a detailed technical discussion of the development of Darwinism as a scientific research programme see Depew and Weber (1995).[26]

In the following sections we consider some of the main themes in which differences may be identified between neo-Darwinism and expanded neo-Darwinism. These are summarized in Table 6.2. The remainder of the chapter (Section D) is devoted to a more detailed exploration of issues related to *reductionism*.

Table 6.2 Evolutionary theory since the neo-Darwinian synthesis[27]

'HARD' NEO-DARWINISM	EXPANDED NEO-DARWINISM
Gradualism	
The rate of evolution is constant.	Periods of evolutionary stasis are followed by periods of (relatively) more rapid change (punctuated equilibrium).
Although genetic mutations are random, the overall effect is a systematic exploration of the possible ways of adapting to the environment.	Chance factors play a major role in determining which branches of the evolutionary tree survive.
Adaptationism	
All characteristics of organisms can be explained as adaptations.	Adaptation is one explanation among others, e.g. chance, self-organization.
Specific behaviours have specific adaptive explanations.	Specific behaviours can be manifestations of a general *biological potential*, rather than being the result of a tight *genetic determinism*.
Natural selection (rather than God) is the cosmic designer, ensuring the adaptation of organisms to their environment.	There is little room for the notion of design, either natural or divine.
Genetic reductionism	
Biology can be reduced to a single level of explanation: 'Selfish-gene theory' – the organism is just the gene's way of making more genes.	Biological explanations have to take account of complex relationships between different levels of organization.
	DNA sequences are only meaningful within the context of the whole functioning cell.
Genes provide 'instructions' or 'blue-prints' for making an organism.	Genes are not a central controller of development, but one developmental resource among many.
There is a simple one-to-one relationship between a gene and the characteristic that it 'codes' for.	There is rarely any such simple relationship. A single gene often has multiple effects, and many genes (together with environmental influences) are involved in the development of a single characteristic.

We now take up the issues for the Table in turn – gradualism in 6.10.2, adaptationism in 6.10.3, design in 6.10.5, and genetic reductionism in 6.12 as part of a larger treatment of reductionism.

6.10.2 Gradualism, punctuated equilibrium and radical contingency

The neo-Darwinian synthesis was formulated in the 1930s and 1940s. By the 1970s various features of neo-Darwinism began to come under pressure. The first such assumption to be questioned was that evolutionary changes occur at a constant rate. Darwin supposed that variation would involve very small changes that might be difficult to detect and would initially appear to have little significance for natural selection. The idea that evolution proceeds by such small steps and never makes jumps, is a key 'dogma' in neo-Darwinism. It is called *gradualism*. There have been some challenges to this belief but the most significant have been by Niels Eldredge and Stephen Jay Gould, stemming from a paper in 1972. They stated that there was strong evidence in the fossil record for long periods of *stasis*, during which virtually no evolution occurred. These long periods of several million years were *punctuated* by relatively short periods of rapid evolution, over periods of 5,000 to 50,000 years, which is very brief in geological time. This view has more or less been integrated into neo-Darwinism.

The work of Gould in particular remains important, through his resolute resistance to Dawkins' genetic reductionism (see below), his insistence that evolution cannot be equated with progress, and his emphasis on historical contingency. In 1989 Gould published *Wonderful Life*, a beautiful book on the fossil evidence of the Burgess Shale (a sediment in the Canadian Rockies). The Burgess Shale preserves not only the fossilized bones but even soft body parts of some of the extraordinary range of creatures that evolved in the so-called 'Cambrian explosion' (between 590 and 525 million years ago). Gould emphasizes that it would have been impossible, inspecting the range of organisms of 500 million years ago, to say which would survive into later eras, yet all the vertebrates[28] we know are thought to be descended from a single, insignificant-seeming type of worm called *Pikaia*. So, Gould holds, running the tape of life again would be very unlikely to give rise to creatures like ourselves (Gould, 1991: especially ch. 5).

The status of Gould's conclusions in *Wonderful Life* has recently been challenged by Simon Conway Morris in his *The Crucible of Creation* (1998) and *Life's Solution* (2003).[29] Conway Morris, one of the principal investigators of the Burgess Shale, takes issue in particular with one of Gould's main points – that the last 500 million years have been characterized much more by the 'grim reaper' of extinction than by the continual branching of the tree of life. Different analyses of the data can give a very different conclusion – that evolutionary innovation has persisted, and shown considerable evidence of convergence (the same characteristics arising by different evolutionary paths). Conway Morris infers from this that it was extremely likely that some form of complex life, resembling humanity in key features such as consciousness, would have evolved (1998:13–14, 199–205). For further discussion of these probabilities see 10.18.1.

6.10.3 Adaptation, self-organization and complexity

The first type of pressure on the neo-Darwinian synthesis which we considered above (6.10.2) concerns issues such as the *rate* of evolutionary development and the *shape* of the branching tree of evolution. The second type of pressure on the synthesis that we will discuss concerns the mechanisms behind evolutionary change. A key assumption of neo-Darwnism is that all evolutionary change is the result of the development, through the mechanism of natural selection, of new adaptations to a changing environment. This view is sometimes called 'adaptationism'. In the expanded form of neo-Darwinism that has developed since the 1970s there is much more room to allow that there may be other mechanisms of evolution. Natural selection is still considered to be an important mechanism, but it is no longer assumed to be the only cause of evolutionary change.

One way in which evolutionary theory has moved beyond a narrowly adaptationist perspective is the recognition of the concept of self-organization. Here an important figure is Stuart Kauffman, whose ideas are most accessibly presented in his *At Home in the Universe* (1995) and *Investigations* (2000). Kauffman's work stems principally out of his analysis of non-linear systems – the mathematics of chaos, as modelled on the modern computer and applied to biological systems.

Kauffman has made use of work by Ilya Prigogine on complex chemical systems held far from equilibrium. The surface of the early Earth contained many such systems (because energy was continually pouring in from the sun and upwards from the hot interior). It is now known that these systems are always likely to give rise to greater complexity.[30] So the particularly elaborate systems that are self-replicating cells were, Kauffman alleges, very likely to arise.[31] Not merely that, but such evolving systems will tend to move to a special ordered state near to 'the edge of chaos', representing the ideal balance between stability and propensity to explore change.[32] So one of the properties that organisms may be expected to evolve is 'evolvability' – the capacity to try out new properties without prematurely losing the benefit of the old. Although the course of evolution will always be influenced by selection and adaptation, and radically altered by any sudden climatic or geological change, it will be much influenced by the mathematics of self-organization. For a collection of essays on the scientific and theological issues raised by complexity theory see Gregersen and Görman, 2002.

6.10.4 The rhetoric of Darwinism

Stephen Jay Gould has suggested that Darwin deliberately stressed the reductionistic, physicalist aspects of his theory in order to eliminate any hint of the involvement of a designer or a vital force in his explanation of the development of living things (see Depew and Weber, 1985:253). Rather the rhetoric of Darwinism is of a 'force' (selection) acting upon essentially passive objects considered in isolation (organisms). It is the rhetoric of physics. And physics has also profoundly influenced molecular biology;[33] genes are described as strings of chemicals to which mutations happen.[34] It may be, however, that the rhetoric of evolution in the coming century will be much more in terms of Kauffman's work, of inter-dependent organisms exploring together the possibilities of greater complexity.

6.10.5 A note on natural theology and design

The tradition of 'natural theology' which developed from the seventeenth century onwards rested heavily on the idea that the intricately coordinated functioning parts of organisms could only be satisfactorily explained by reference to a divine designer. The idea was clearly expressed by Archdeacon William Paley in his thought-experiment involving finding a fully working watch while walking on a heath (Paley, 1802; see 3.5.1 and Dawkins, 1991: ch. 1). Paley argued that the existence of the watch entailed the existence of a watchmaker, and in the same way the complexity of living things ought to lead us to infer the existence of a divine designer. By the time of Darwin's *Origin of Species* there were already powerful philosophical criticisms of natural theology, and in particular the argument from design (see 1.3.1 and Brooke, 1991: chs 6–8). There is no doubt though, that the *Origin* was another nail in the coffin of Paley's watchmaker, since it offered an alternative agent of the apparent design, namely natural selection.

This is not nearly as serious a blow to theology as is often assumed. The idea of God as the almighty engineer had only arisen in an age in which the greatest human achievements were considered to be our technological advances. Eight-eenth-century deism (the idea that God sets the world in motion and then leaves it to its own devices) bears little resemblance to Hebrew or Christian ideas of the creator God in faithful loving relationship with their creation. Nowadays people often regard science and technology with considerable ambivalence. Theology in and after the twentieth century, grappling (among other horrors) with two World Wars and the Holocaust, has become much more willing to describe a God who suffers; a God whose continual creative activity takes place *within* a universe characterized by processes of law and chance; processes which God rarely, if ever, sets aside. The imagery of a transcendent purely rational God is now more often weighed against descriptions of God 'the fellow-sufferer who understands' (see Chapter 8, especially 8.2–8.3, 8.5.1–8.5.3).

As alluded to above, there is an interesting sense in which, even if Darwinism saw off the idea of a divine designer, the idea of design is retained. It is no accident that the book Darwin most admired while he was studying at Cambridge was Paley's *Evidences of Christianity*. Richard Dawkins's celebrated attack on theology in *The Blind Watchmaker* (1991) misses the mark for the reasons outlined above.[35] It illustrates, however, that even the 'hardest' neo-Darwinist will see design in nature – design achieved not by God but by the process of evolution by natural selection. Evolved adaptations often *look* designed.[36] We referred to this in 1.16 as 'teleonomy' as opposed to the action of a designer (teleology).

Developments in Darwinism since the neo-Darwinian synthesis may suggest a different emphasis (see Table 6.2 in Section 6.10.1). As Depew and Weber put it: '. . . there is no watchmaker, blind or sighted, *for the simple reason that there is no watch*. Natural organization is not an artefact, or anything like it, but instead a manifestation of the action of energy flows in informed systems poised between order and chaos' (1995:477–8, italics ours). In other words, in a fundamental sense 'self-organizing systems' are very different from the sorts of thing that humans have (so far) been able to design. This is a very interesting perspective on the nature of living things but we must emphasize that, for the theological reasons given above, the loss of the watch would not entail the non-existence of God.

6.10.6 Intelligent Design Theory

A further twist in the saga of design is the relatively recent emergence of an argument going by the name of Intelligent Design (ID) Theory (see for example Behe, 1996; Dembski, 1998). For a brief examination see Ruse, 2003: ch. 15; for more detail see Shanks, 2004; Peters and Hewlett, 2003: ch. 5. Behe's argument, in essence, is that certain biochemical and biological complexes are too complex and intricate to have arisen by chance evolution of their individual components.[37] Dembski takes this forward by discussion of what patterns might or might not be expected on the basis of a sequence of chances. Intelligent Design theorists tend to say that their ideas are scientific rather than theological, but one is left in little doubt that their ultimate motivation is to suggest the existence of (a Paley-esque) God. We would regard their position as flawed on scientific grounds – plausible evolutionary explanations for the relevant processes are possible, and also questionable theologically. For a confrontation between ID theory and its critics see Dembski and Ruse, 2004.

SECTION D
REDUCTION, REDUCTIONISM AND RELIGION (6.11–6.13)

6.11 An analysis of reduction and reductionism

As we have seen in this chapter, nature is organized in a hierarchy of 'levels' – for example, the hierarchy of molecule–cell–organism–species–ecosystem.[38] The concept of *reduction* refers to the project of attempting to describe all the *phenomena* in nature with reference to the *fewest* possible types of *entity* or *explanation*. The project of reduction is central to the scientific enterprise. For example, we have seen how the discovery of the structure of DNA in the 1950s was able to explain certain phenomena at higher levels of organization, including (some of) the variation between individuals, and (at least part of) the basis of heredity. Reduction, then, is a perfectly legitimate aim in science. However, debates arise as to whether a particular reduction has, in fact, achieved what it claims. For example, it will be obvious that not all the variation between individuals can be explained by variations in DNA – many differences between two people will be due to differences in their life-experiences, not their DNA. (Note that for Darwinian evolution to occur it is only necessary that *some* of the variation between individuals is heritable.) When an explanation appears to be claiming to have reduced the number of types of entity or explanation to *fewer* than the number that one thinks are required to adequately describe nature, then one might refer to the explanation as reduction*ist*. On the whole the terms reductionist or reductionism are used in a pejorative sense, indicating that one thinks that someone else's reduction is a 'greedy' reduction.[39]

Reduction can be applied to either entities, or explanations. A reduction can attempt to reduce the number of entities or explanations by looking 'horizontally' (across a chosen level of nature) or 'vertically' (between different levels of nature). This means that there are several different sorts of reduction, and much confusion has been caused in the past by a failure to recognize this. We therefore propose the following classification of types of reduction.[40]

> *ontological reduction*: the question of how many types of entity there are at any particular level of nature (not necessarily the lowest one). The aim is a horizontal reduction to the fewest possible distinct types of entity (for example, we might accept that at the level of physics there are certain types of force and certain types of matter).

> *constitutive reduction*: the question of whether the number of entities at a particular level of nature is any more than the number at the level below. The question is a vertical one, involving a comparison of the number of different sorts of entity that there are at different levels. A constitutive reduction has been achieved if it can be shown that there are *no more* entities at this level than at the level below. (And the conviction of contemporary science is indeed that biology does involve the same matter, and the same forces, as physics and chemistry.)

> *conceptual-explanatory reduction*: the question of whether we can explain (some of) the phenomena at one level of nature with reference only to explanations at another level of nature. The aim is a vertical reduction between different levels of nature. Note that for this to be a successful reduction the level of nature which 'does the explaining' can be either lower or higher than the level to be explained. For example molecular biology (6.9) is normally used to explain phenomena at a higher level, whereas the concept of self-organization (6.10.3) offers explanations of phenomena in a 'top-down' direction (cf. Peacocke, 1993:53–5; see also 10.9(iii)(c)).

> *cross-explanatory reduction*: the question of how many different types of explanation there are at any *particular* level of nature. The aim is a horizontal reduction to the fewest possible distinct types of explanation (in this respect it resembles ontological reduction). As we shall see below, this type of reduction is often the most contentious in debates about alleged conflicts between science and religion because what counts as a legitimate or distinct type of explanation is largely a matter of metaphysical preference or pre-supposition (see 6.13.2–6.13.4).

6.11.1 Notes on methodological issues in reduction, on emergence and on ontological naturalism

A note on methodological issues in reduction. Discussions of reductionism often refer to the concept of a 'methodological reduction'. We do not include this concept in our scheme because we do not think that it adds to the types of reduction listed above. The confusion is caused because there are *methodological issues* within *all* the types of reduction; indeed each type of reduction is characterized by a distinct kind of methodological question.

- For ontological reduction the methodological issue is, how do we detect the presence of different entities? Of course, there may be entities that exist but which we have no way (yet) of detecting.
- For constitutive reduction this issue is not so pressing because all we are doing is comparing the number of entities at different levels: if we subsequently discover a new sort of entity at one of these levels we will simply have to ask the constitutive reduction question again.
- For conceptual-explanatory reductions the methodological issue is, what is the best method of finding an explanation for this phenomenon? For example, one sort of phenomenon might be best approached by anatomical dissection, another by computer modelling. Deciding these questions is an important part of the practice of science.
- The methodological issue in cross-explanatory reduction is how we choose criteria for deciding what constitutes a legitimate sort of explanation. Note that this is not a question of choosing a *level* of explanation, but a *type* of explanation. We saw in section 1.16 that different sorts of explanation may often be entirely compatible with one another. What counts as a legitimate or distinct type of explanation is largely a matter of metaphysical preference or presupposition.[41] Therefore it is not surprising that cross-explanatory reduction gives rise to some heated debates at the interface of science and theology.

A note on 'emergence'. One way of expressing the idea of conceptual-explanatory non-reductionism is in the concept of *emergence*. An emergent phenomenon is one which occurs at a particular level of the hierarchical organization of nature and which cannot be fully described in terms of phenomena at lower levels. (Peacocke, 1986:28–9; also Ayala, 1985). A classical example would be that of an ecosystem. In order to understand what happens over time to populations of organisms coexisting together we need to employ concepts from the field of ecology, not just those of physics and chemistry. Likewise with the mind: although there is a successful constitutive reduction with respect to the entities which can be identified in the brain (there is no added ingredient that makes us distinct from other animals – 6.3.1). Nevertheless, consciousness is an *emergent* property which cannot be directly inferred from a knowledge of the electrical activity of brain cells. It is important to realize that the concept of emergence is simply an affirmation, with respect to a particular phenomenon, that a conceptual-explanatory reduction of that phenomenon to a lower level is not currently possible.[42] (It is necessary to say *not currently* because, as with all potential conceptual-explanatory reductions, this could change in the light of new knowledge.) Emergence is just another way of talking about conceptual-explanatory reductions, not a completely separate concept.

A note on 'ontological naturalism'. Our approach owes much to the helpful classification proposed by Drees. However, it differs from Drees's scheme in that (i) it explicitly distinguishes between horizontal and vertical reductions and (ii) it adds the category of cross-explanatory reduction. A further difference is that Drees includes the question of ontological naturalism, which he defines as the position which holds that:

> The natural world is the whole of reality that we know of and interact with; no supernatural or spiritual realm distinct from the natural world shows up *within* our natural world, not even in the mental life of humans. (Drees, 1996:12)

We suggest that this is one issue (among others) within the question of ontological reduction: i.e. are there supernatural entities, forces, or influences at any level of nature. As with the other methodological issues that apply to ontological reduction (see previous paragraph), the question here is one about the reliability of our 'apparatus' and the correct interpretation of results. For example, in order to determine whether a new sub-atomic particle has been detected a physicist might have to engage in debate with her colleagues about the significance of the results she has obtained using a particle accelerator. Similarly, the issue of ontological naturalism might revolve around the question of whether religious experiences show that we have the 'apparatus' to detect supernatural influences (see also 6.13.5).

6.12 Genetic reductionism[43]

It would be fair to say that advocates of 'hard' neo-Darwinism often tend towards a fairly strong version of reduction*ism*. We can see why the knowledge of genetics that emerged in the mid-twentieth century gives rise to vastly tempting forms of reduction. In the 1940s neo-Darwinism showed how powerful a genetic understanding of evolution by natural selection could be (6.8). Then in the 1950s the elegant structure of DNA was deduced (6.9), which provided an explanation of the particulate inheritance first discovered by Mendel almost a century earlier. In the 1960s the 'cracking' of the genetic code (6.9) held out the prospect that all the elements necessary to Darwinian evolution – variation, heritability and differential survival – could be explained by (*reduced to*) the level of changes in the sequence of the 'letters' in an organism's DNA.

We have noted earlier how Darwin could not convince his contemporaries of the importance of natural selection because he lacked an understanding of the basis of *heredity* (6.8). Given that he knew nothing of any of the advances outlined in the preceding paragraph it is perhaps remarkable that he was able, in 1859, to propose such a far-reaching evolutionary theory. However, it is instructive to consider what aspects of biology *we* may not understand adequately, equivalent to Darwin's ignorance of genetics.

Probably the most important such gap in our knowledge concerns the mechanisms which underlie *development*: what biologists call the question of ontogeny (the process of individual development from a fertilized egg), as distinct from phylogeny (the evolution of species over time). A simplistic (reductionist) view is that the development of the organism is 'programmed' in its genes, with the genes acting as a 'blueprint' or complete description of the whole organism. It has taken philosophers working in the field of biology to point out that there is no such 'representation' of the whole organism in its DNA (Oyama, 2000). A sequence of 'letters' in DNA may be thought of as 'coding for' a sequence of amino acids in a protein, but the further steps which connect genes to the characteristics of the organism, including the relationship between genes and development, are – with a few notable exceptions – not well understood. (The cases that allowed the basic mechanisms of genetics to be elucidated, such as Mendel's peas, were unusual cases in which there happens to be a one-to-one relationship between a gene and a characteristic of the organism.)

Since the cracking of the genetic code in 1967 genetics has, as is well known, become an extraordinarily fruitful field of research. It is often assumed that the culmination of this research has been the Human Genome Project, which led in February 2001 to the publication by two competing research groups of complete sequences of human DNA. However, bearing in mind the criticisms of genetic reductionism noted above, it will be evident that – by itself – knowledge of the order of all the 'letters' in human DNA is not necessarily as interesting as it sounds. It is certainly not the complete 'recipe' for making a human. In many respects the more interesting advances in genetics have been those that demonstrate the unexpected *complexity* of the function of the genome. Some examples are as follows:

- Promoters and enhancers – genes which act as 'switches' and 'volume' controls, influencing the 'expression' of the genes which code for proteins.
- Introns, exons and post-transcriptional splicing. Genes are not continuous stretches of DNA, but are composed of modules which may be cut and spliced at various stages of the process of gene expression – like putting together many different versions of a film: the 'director's cut'.
- The protein scaffolding around which DNA is folded (not shown in Figure 6.1) turns out to have an active regulatory function, hiding genes from the promoters and transcription factors by acting as a molecular 'chaperone'. The way in which this works seems to involve another chemical 'code', completely separate from the genetic code.
- Some of the bases (the C bases) in a DNA sequence can be chemically modified in a way that does not affect the underlying sequence but alters the way in which the gene functions. Therefore, to know the genetic make-up of an individual you need to know their individual pattern of these modifications (the epigenotype) as well as the DNA sequence

(genotype). Furthermore, since these modifications can be inherited they present a potential challenge to the 'central dogma' (6.9).[44]

Aside on elegance in biology and physics

One interesting feature of the development of molecular biology parallels that of particle physics. In 1932, with the discovery of the neutron, it was thought that there were precisely three sub-atomic particles. There are now thought to be in the region of 160. In 1964 there was thought to be a very simple relation between DNA sequence and functional protein in a cell, and that relationship is now known to be very complex and diverse (see above). Science *sometimes* gives rise to extraordinarily elegant, simplifying steps forward, but other phases render the picture of a subject more and more intricate. And scientists' sense of what *is* elegant also moves on with the subject.

Resumé: So far in this chapter we have introduced some themes in the relationship between evolutionary theory and biology as focused through the lens of the topic of human evolution (6.2–6.4) and the development of Darwinism from Darwin (6.5–6.7) to neo-Darwinism (6.8–6.9) and through to an expanded neo-Darwinism (6.10). Three key themes of theological interest emerged from the discussion of the differences between 'hard' neo-Darwinism and its more recent expansions (Table 6.2 in 6.10.1): (i) gradualism and the associated theme of evolutionary contingency (6.10.2); (ii) adaptationism and the associated issue of design (6.10.3, 6.10.5); and (iii) reductionism including the issue of genetic reductionism (6.11, 6.12).

Of these issues the issue of reductionism has been central to many of the apparent conflicts between theology and biology (though as we noted in 6.10.6 the issue of design has recently reappeared in a new guise). One of the best ways of engaging with new prophets of conflict at the interface of science and theology is to hear from them in their own words. It is to this task of critical listening that we now turn, in the course of which we will be able to illustrate and clarify the differences between the four types of reduction introduced in 6.11.

6.13 New prophets of conflict

6.13.1 Francis Crick and the 'ultimate aim' of biology

We have already come across Francis Crick, the co-discoverer of the structure of DNA. It was also Crick who coined the idea of the 'central dogma' of molecular biology (6.9). In his book *Of Molecules and Men*, he proclaimed that:

> 'The ultimate aim of the modern movement in biology is in fact to explain *all* biology in terms of physics and chemistry.'[45]

Let us consider what sorts of reductionism might be implied by this statement. Two questions may be asked to discover whether the type of project espoused by Crick has so far succeeded:

(i) are there any entities (particles, forces, or otherwise) that are present in living things which are not present at the level of physics or chemistry? (A *constitutive reduction* question, answer: no.)

(ii) are there any phenomena at the level of biology which cannot be explained purely by reference to phenomena at the level of physics and chemistry? (A *conceptual-explanatory* reduction question, answer: yes.)

Question (i) is a question about constitutive reduction. As we noted above, biology does involve the same matter, and the same forces, as physics and chemistry. Evolutionary biology has no place for old fashioned *vitalism* – the view that living things are animated by a special life-force.

Question (ii) is a question about conceptual-explanatory reduction. With regard to this question we can see that not everything in biology can be explained merely by reference to the interactions of atoms and molecules. For example, it would be quite impossible to deduce what has happened in the story of human evolution (described in Section A) starting simply with a knowledge of the chemistry of DNA (described in Section C).

In terms of the classification of types of reduction in 6.11, the lessons to be drawn here are that:

- *it is uncontroversial within science that a constitutive reduction has been achieved between the levels of physics, chemistry and biology: there are no additional entities detectable at any of these successive levels.*

- *while conceptual-explanatory reductions are a perfectly legitimate and proper aspect of science, they should be evaluated initially on their scientific merits, which in some cases will be found lacking.*

6.13.2 Jacques Monod and the problems of cross-explanatory reductionism

In our discussion of the mechanisms of biological evolution we have noted that chance plays an important role in the evolutionary process (**6.6, 6.9** on mutation, Table 6.2 in **6.10.1**). Elsewhere we examine other ways in which chance, or more precisely indeterminacy[46] appears to be an intrinsic element in the structure of the cosmos (see **1.17, 5.11–5.13, 10.3.1, 10.9(iv)**). In his famous book *Chance and Necessity* (1972) the great French molecular biologist Jacques Monod drew the following rather bleak conclusions:

Pure chance, absolutely free but blind, [is] at the very root of the stupendous edifice of evolution ... (Monod, 1972:110)

The ancient covenant is in pieces; man at last knows that he is alone in the unfeeling immensity of the universe, out of which he emerged by chance. (Monod, 1972:167)

These much-quoted sentences provide a good illustration of the type of pre-suppositions which tend to underlie claims that evolutionary theory disproves theism. Monod starts with the observation that chance is an important ingredient in the process of evolution and jumps to the conclusion that chance is the principal metaphysical category at the root of existence. In contrast, those scientist-theologians who wish to defend a theistic account are quite prepared to acknowledge the existence of chance, indeed to see it as a positive ingredient in an unfolding creation. Polkinghorne says: 'The role of chance can be seen as a signal of the Creator's allowing his creation to make itself' (1996a:47). D.J. Bartholo-mew in his major study *God of Chance* wrote that 'chance offers the potential Creator many advantages which it is difficult to envisage being obtained in any other way' (Bartholomew, 1984:97).[47]

What we see in these quotes from Monod is a type of reductionism that underlies the position of many of those who see the relationship between science and theology in terms of a 'conflict thesis' (see **1.1**, **3.5.1**). In terms of the types of reduction outlined in **6.11** what is going on here is a version of *cross-explanatory* reductionism.

Recall that cross-explanatory reductions reduce the types of explanation that are deemed acceptable. The metaphysical conclusion that Monod draws from the existence of chance in the universe represents a ('horizontal') *narrowing* of the available explanatory types to include only the possibility of scientific, but not theological or theistic, modes of explanation.[48]

The weakness of accepting this sort of narrowing of the possibilities should be evident: it could be justified only if its particular, often unstated, presuppositions could be shown to be justified. As we noted in Chapter 3, one of the lessons from the history of the relationship between science and religion is that it is rare for a scientific theory to entail a metaphysical conclusion (3.3).

6.13.3 E.O. Wilson and sociobiology

One of the most controversial applications of reductionism in biology is to be found in the field of *sociobiology*. Edward O. Wilson, an entomologist (insect specialist) by training, is often regarded as having founded this movement in his book *Sociobiology: The New Synthesis* (1975).[49] Sociobiology derived from ideas of W.D. Hamilton in the 1960s; its essence is the idea that certain aspects of human behaviour may be explained by (i.e. reduced to) the level of evolutionary genetics. For example, sociobiologists sometimes argue that human altruism (the pro-pensity to act in ways that benefit others) can be explained in evolutionary terms.[50]

On the face of it an evolutionary explanation of altruism might seem surprising, since it may appear that the most effective way of surviving and producing the maximum number of offspring (and hence passing on one's own genes) would be to act selfishly in various respects. However, there are several possible mechanisms why altruistic behaviour might (in theory) increase one's chance of survival. To give an example, perhaps if you are programmed by your genes to (appear to) act altruistically you will be more likely to be granted a high social status by other members of your group, and hence receive benefits (e.g. food, shelter, sexual partners) denied to other individuals. Holmes Rolston III (1999) has made a compelling analysis of how sociobiological explanations of this sort can quickly become implausibly convoluted. Evolutionary biologists often refer to such explanations as 'just so' stories, after Rudyard Kipling's famous fables about how different animals came to be the way they are – the implication is that such explanations are easy to think up but notoriously difficult to substantiate.

Of particular interest from the theological point of view is the sociobiologists' claim that individuals or groups who developed religious beliefs might have had some *survival advantage* over their competitors. If religion does give rise to such an advantage then perhaps our genes are tricking us into thinking that certain beliefs are true, when the belief is in fact merely a way of (somehow) increasing our chances of survival and reproduction!

Consider this quote from Wilson:

> [W]e have come to the crucial stage in the history of biology when religion itself is subject to the explanations of the natural sciences . . . sociobiology can account for the very origin of mythology by the principle of natural selection acting on the genetically evolving material structure of the human brain. If this interpretation is correct, the final decisive edge enjoyed by scientific naturalism will come from its capacity to explain traditional religion, its chief competitor, as a wholly material phenomenon. Theology is not likely to survive as an independent intellectual discipline. But religion itself will endure for a long time as a vital force in society. (Wilson, 1995:192)

EXERCISE 6.2

What sorts of argument might a sociobiologist construct to explain how religion might confer an adaptive advantage?

Wilson's claim that religion can be explained at the level of genetics is an example of a *conceptual-explanatory reduction*. Recall that the definition of a conceptual-explanatory reduction concerns the question of whether we can explain (some of) the phenomena at one level of nature with reference only to phenomena at another level of nature. The aim is a reduction by virtue of conceptual-explanatory procedures between different ('vertical') levels of nature (6.11). Wilson claims that the appropriate level of explanation for religion is genetic adaptation. Therefore, if the truth-claims of religion were previously held to have some explanatory value a successful reduction has allegedly been performed. Fewer types of explanation are now required since theological types of explanation have been eliminated.

Wilson does see some usefulness in religion, although he regards it as nothing more than a survival-strategy which has become embedded in our genes. One way of expressing this strong sociobiological position is to say that our behaviour is still on a 'short leash', much influenced by a genetic inheritance which was almost entirely formed while humans were still hunter-gatherers.[51] Critics of socio-biology argue that many aspects of human behaviour can only be understood in economic and social terms, and have little direct relation to reproductive success and therefore little direct link to strictly Darwinian considerations (Tattersall, 1998:205f.).[52] According to this view, human behaviour is on a 'long leash' with respect to genetics. In terms of the development of different phases of Darwinism (6.6, 6.8–10), we may say that the sociobiological view corresponds most closely to 'hard' neo-Darwinism. Sociobiological explanations are *adaptationist* in that they attempt to explain specific behaviours in terms of their (alleged) adaptive advantage (6.10.3). According to the more expansive view of Darwinism that is now emerging (Table 6.2 in 6.10.1) specific behaviours are better understood as reflecting a general biological potential (in which genes play some part) rather than being the result of a tight genetic determinism (cf. 6.12).

In short, sociobiology is an ambitious form of conceptual-explanatory reduction which many scientific critics find unconvincing. As with Crick's suggestion (6.13.1) that 'the ultimate aim of biology' should be to reduce all biological explanations to the level of physics and chemistry, *the lesson here is that, while conceptual-explanatory reduction is a perfectly legitimate strategy in science – indeed the success of science depends on such reduction – it can be applied over-ambitiously ('greedily') (6.11).*

6.13.4 Richard Dawkins and the selfish gene

Perhaps the most widely known version of biological reductionism is that developed in the work of Richard Dawkins, zoologist and first Professor of The Public Understanding of Science at Oxford. Dawkins is well known for combining his particular brand of reductionism with a polemical hostility to religion and theology. At the heart of Dawkins's approach is the notion of 'the selfish gene'. Dawkins asks us to consider evolution purely from the perspective of the gene, and proposes that organisms are merely 'survival machines' which genes build in order to perpetuate themselves. Just as one might conceivably think of a chicken as an egg's way of making another egg, so Dawkins argues that 'The body is the genes' way of preserving the genes unaltered' (1989:23). Another quote from *The Selfish Gene* (first published in 1976) gives a flavour of Dawkins's vision of evolution:

> The replicators that survived were the ones that built *survival machines* for themselves to live in. . . . Survival machines got bigger and more elaborate, and the process was cumulative and progressive. . . . Was there to be any end to the gradual improvement in the techniques and artifices used by the replicators to ensure their own continuation in the world? . . . Now they

swarm in huge colonies, safe inside gigantic lumbering robots, sealed off from the outside world, communicating with it by tortuous indirect routes, manipulating it by remote control. They are in you and me; they created us, body and mind; and their preservation is the ultimate rationale for our existence. They have come a long way, those replicators. Now they go by the name of genes, and we are their survival machines. (1989:20)

Dawkins's approach is striking, and he is an accomplished popularizer of science (including his own version of it). It is therefore important to appreciate that his extreme genetic reductionism is not shared by most evolutionary biologists or philosophers of biology. Several good analyses of the difficulties with Dawkins's position are available.[33] The central problem with Dawkins's view is that genes in fact function as one part of a complex set of processes and structures which together make up the functioning cell; there is no justification for singling DNA out as a selfish manipulator of the cell or organism (see 6.12).

There is a further, apparently slightly different, way in which Dawkins attempts to undermine religious claims. This is his idea that cultural ideas may be reproduced, compete with one another, and be selected for in a way analogous to Darwinian biological evolution (recall the requirements for Darwinian evolution, listed in 6.6). Whereas in Dawkins's evolutionary scheme the 'units of selection' are genes, in his view of cultural evolution he calls the units of selection 'memes'. He writes:

> Consider the idea of God. We do not know how it arose in the meme pool. Probably it arose many times by independent 'mutation' ... Why does it have such a high survival value? ... What is it about the idea of a god that gives it stability and penetrance in the cultural environment? The survival value of the god meme in the meme pool results from its great psychological appeal. It provides a superficially plausible answer to deep and troubling questions about existence. It suggests that injustices in this world may be rectified in the next. The 'everlasting arms' hold out a cushion against our own inadequacies which, like a doctor's placebo, is none the less effective for being imaginary. (Dawkins, 1989:192–3)

At first sight it may appear paradoxical that there are two different levels to which Dawkins wishes to reduce all explanations, the genetic (in his selfish gene theory) and the cultural (in his meme theory). The underlying connection between these two different manifestations of his reductionist enterprise is evident, however, from an early stage of Dawkins's speculations in his notion of 'Universal Darwinism' (Dawkins, 1983). By Universal Darwinism Dawkins means the idea that Darwinian mechanisms (evolution by natural selection) may underlie phenomena at various levels other than genetics, including 'perhaps some unit of cultural transmission' (i.e. memes-Dawkins, 1983:422).

Two things are worth noting about Dawkins's approach in this relatively early manifesto. The first is that, having introduced this bold idea, he proceeds to outline various fairly technical details of the methods and approaches that would be required in order to develop 'a full science of Universal Darwinism'. The details need not concern us here (the idea was being presented to an audience of professional evolutionary theorists); the interesting point is that this is exactly what would be expected of a scientific proposal for a *conceptual-explanatory reduction* (6.11.1, including note on methodological issues in reduction). Dawkins has to justify to his professional colleagues the methods that he envisages using in order to pursue this particular scientific programme, the core hypothesis of which is that natural selection is a universal feature of nature (not just the mechanism of biological evolution). The 'level' of Dawkins's proposed bottom line of explanation is, in effect, not the level of genetics, or of culture, or (as paradoxically appears) both at the same time, but the mechanism of natural selection itself.

The second point of interest about Dawkins's original presentation of this idea of Universal Darwinism is that he freely admitted that 'I have not thought enough about the fantasies of the previous paragraphs to evaluate their plausibility' (1983:423). (Of course, Dawkins has thought a great deal about his proposal since then and has become convinced of its plausibility – see his later writings.[54]) For our purposes, the significance of Dawkins's reference to 'fantasies' is not that it demonstrates that his proposal is just a fantasy. Rather it illustrates the fact that the hypothesis of Universal Darwinism originated in his *imagination*. Behind the formulation of such a *conceptual-explanatory* scientific research programme, metaphysical preferences or prejudices of a *cross-explanatory* type might well have been close at hand.[55] The general nature of his conceptual-explanatory programme is very likely to have been influenced by a presupposed *cross-explanatory* narrowing of the types of explanation thought to be legitimate.[56]

The observations above help to illustrate the difference between cross-explanatory and conceptual-explanatory reductions. The reason Dawkins felt free to admit to a professional audience that his scientific programme was based on 'fantasies' was that whatever cross-explanatory, metaphysical, 'horizontal level' prejudices or presuppositions informed his proposal, ultimately it would be judged on its merits as a scientific, conceptual-explanatory, 'vertical level' reduction. From a scientific point of view it would not matter whether Dawkins first came up with the idea of Universal Darwinism at his desk or in the bath; he knows that in order to satisfy the scientific community he will eventually have to come up with the goods in terms of a convincing conceptual-explanatory reduction.

In short, cross-explanatory and conceptual-explanatory reductions often go hand-in-hand because the assumptions or hopes embodied in the former will frequently provide the ambition or motivation for the latter. However, for the reasons set out in 6.11.1, the logical structure and methodological issues involved in each of these two types of reduction are ultimately distinct.

We believe that serious confusions have often arisen when this distinction between conceptual-explanatory and cross-explanatory reductions is not recognized. These confusions may account for some of the difficulties that there have been in maintaining a dialogue between theology and science, particularly between theology and biology.

6.13.5 Religion, evolution and naturalism[57]

In this chapter we have been looking at some of the implications that evolutionary theory has for religion. There is a further complication to consider, however, which is that religion is itself a phenomenon which has arisen and developed during the course of evolution. In other words, the implications of evolutionary theory for religion are not simply that from 1859 onwards (the publication of Darwin's *Origin of Species*, **6.6**) theology has had new scientific insights to grapple with. It is also that theology must now also reassess the role and truth-claims of religion in the light of the fact that religion has itself been recognized to be a part of the evolutionary story.

The implications of this new perspective become particularly pressing if one accepts, as Drees does in his *Religion, Science and Naturalism*, a commitment to *ontological naturalism*. As we saw in our examination of types of reduction (**6.11**), ontological naturalism is an issue within the category of ontological reduction, the question of whether some 'supernatural or spiritual realm distinct from the natural world shows up *within* our natural world' (Drees, 1996:12). Whether it is ultimately coherent to affirm both theism and ontological naturalism is somewhat beyond the scope of this chapter.[58] For the purposes of the present discussion, however, the importance of Drees's approach lies (a) in his careful analysis of the implications that a commitment to ontological naturalism would have for our understanding of religion and (b) his interesting attempt to press a naturalistic programme in theology as far as it will go.

On the first of these points we can do no more here than to summarize the distinct questions that Drees identifies, which may be listed as follows:

(i) Are we currently able to give a reliable account of how and why religious behaviour and belief evolved? (1996:213). Drees is sceptical about whether this can be done at present.

(ii) Did the appearance of religion influence the subsequent course of human evolution? For example, religious rules concerning various social practices could conceivably have increased the chances of survival of religious individuals or groups (1996:210–11; cf. **6.3, 6.13.3**). Alternatively, did religion arise as a 'side-effect' of the evolution of some other trait (such as consciousness), or as an historical 'accident' (1996:250).

(iii) If religion evolved as an adaptive response to a particular environment or situation, how can it claim to be able to make truthful statements about ultimate realities? (1996:221–3).[59]

Drees's own response to the last of these questions is to doubt whether religions can claim any direct knowledge of a transcendent reality. Nevertheless, he believes that a religious naturalism inclines one to a 'more transcendent' understanding of God (1996:259), and a more religious attitude to nature: 'A naturalist view of reality does not imply that we devalue humans, but that we upgrade our view of reality' (1996:249). Drees's cautious but not dismissive view of the value of evolved religions is evident in the following passage:

Denying the adequacy of a transcendental reference of evolved religions need not imply that they are merely fictitious stories 'clothed with an aura of facticity' [so Clifford Geertz] ... Religions with their rituals and myths have arisen in certain environments and have been shaped by the challenges that humans, or their hominid ancestors if we dare to go back that far, faced. Elements of these myths can be seen as rooted in natural reality.... With the heritage of the past and with the 'capacity to "dream", however fragmentary the dreams, and to conceive of an alternative world' [Lindon Eaves], we transcend the objects that are directly present to us ..., but we do not transcend the natural world. (1996:251)

The contrast between this passage and the anti-theistic polemic of Crick, Monod, Wilson and Dawkins will be obvious. However, it must be asked whether Drees's religious naturalism delivers an account that is ultimately adequate to the specific claims of theistic religions. Our approach in this book is that, contrary to Drees's postulate of ontological naturalism, there is an aspect to reality which is not fully susceptible to a purely naturalistic description. In Chapter 10 we will consider how scientific accounts might accommodate the possibility of divine action within the natural order.

6.14 Conclusion

We have shown that Darwinism, as it has evolved through successive phases to its current state, has proved to be an enormously powerful theory for explaining how living things – including ourselves – came to be how they are. It would be fair to say that modern physics has seemed to many to be quite conducive to theism (see 1.15, 5.23), whereas Darwinism is more often regarded as posing difficulties for religious belief. (It is notable that, as the science–religion dialogue began to develop from the 1960s onwards, the first wave of scientists who made a professional move to theology more often came from the physical than the biological sciences. Conversely, the best-known proponents of anti-theistic popularizations of science have often been biologists by training). This should not serve as a discouragement to theologians to engage with biology. It could well be that the greatest gains for theology in entering into dialogue with science will be in those disciplines in whose company it feels least comfortable.[60]

Notes

1   Drafting for the first edition by CS and MRN; 2005 drafting by AR and CS.
2   There are plenty of examples of cave paintings on the World Wide Web. The reader is invited to try typing 'cave art' into a search engine.
3   This story is told in Lewis-Williams, 2002:29–31.
4   There are now *tentative* indications of human symbolic thought as early as 70,000 years ago from the Blombos Cave in South Africa. However, it does seem that vocalized speech – produced when changes in the vocal tract became combined

with the brain structures to support the production and processing of a wide range of sounds – was a decisive evolutionary advantage which made possible the extraordinary cultural leap described. The final evolutionary step, perhaps small in itself (so Tattersall, 1998:232–3), may have taken place as little as 50,000 years ago.

5   Neanderthal brains reached a size even greater than that of *Homo sapiens*. It was once suggested that the two species were so closely related that they could interbreed. However, a comparison between DNA from mitochondria (energy-producing components within cells) from modern humans and fossil bones of Neanderthals indicates that *Homo sapiens* and *Homo neanderthalis* were two entirely separate species, incapable of interbreeding, that diverged from a common stock between 550,000 and 690,000 years ago (Krings *et al.*, 1997:25).

6   There is evidence of ritual practice among at least some Neanderthal populations: the embryonic position and east–west orientation of some burials; burial with grave 'goods' such as flint tools; the possible scattering of flower blossoms – grape hyacinth, hollyhock and groundsel and boughs of pine – over the dead; the circling of a grave with six pairs of goat horns (cf. Shreeve, 1996:53). However, parts of these findings are now being disputed.

7   For a helpful analysis see Herzfeld, 2002:ch. 2.

8   Cro-Magnon is a name given to fully modern humans, after a site near the Dordogne town of Les Eyzies, where the first evidence of the replacement of Neanderthal populations by migrating *H. sapiens* populations was found.

9   See also van Huyssteen's 2003–4 Gifford Lectures, to be published in 2006. A modern description of the *imago Dei* should probably also emphasize creativity, which again is clearly an evolved characteristic.

10   Genesis 2.7, New Revised Standard Version, Hebrew terms transliterated in brackets.

11   Readers should not be confused in this regard by mention in the literature of 'mitochondrial Eve', which is a reference to our likely common ancestors in Africa, rather than to any Edenic conditions in which they might have lived.

12   The approximate length of the first edition of this book. To help get a 'feel' for the huge timescales involved, try identifying the evolutionary landmarks listed in Table 6.1 in terms of where they would occur in the book you are holding in your hands.

13   We thank Dr Robinson for permission to reproduce this table.

14   The cells shown in Figure 6.3 in 6.9, animal and plant cells, are 'eukaryotic', possessing a nucleus and other bounded substructures. Bacterial cells are 'pro-karyotic', much smaller, simpler structures. It will be seen that for a vast period (pages 70–250 in the above analogy) life on Earth was simply the history of bacterial life, just as the vast majority of organisms on the planet are bacteria. Even when the more complex eukaryotic cells appeared, these remained nothing more than single-celled organisms until about p. 390 in the story (see analogy above).

15   See 4.7 on Popper's theory of falsificationism.

16   For more detailed reflection on what may be learned from the history of evolutionary ideas, see Chapter 3.

17   For further insight into Darwin's life, see the two-volume biography by Janet Browne, 1996, 2002.

18   Darwin's hand was forced when, in June 1858, he learned that Alfred Russel Wallace (1823–1913) had arrived at a similar conclusion.

19   Quoted in Reiss, 2000:10.

20   Though theologians could and did argue for a different sort of designer God (cf. Brooke, 1991:310–17).

21   We take the title of this section from Depew and Weber (1995).

22   Lamarck believed that repeated behaviour during an organism's life passed that characteristic to its offspring. So grazing high trees would progressively stretch the necks of giraffes. We can see that this is not the usual pattern of inheritance; the son of a bad-tempered tennis star might possibly inherit a predisposition to bad temper, but would not inherit the expanded racket-forearm a tennis pro develops after years of play.

23   Those patronizing 'The Eagle' pub in Cambridge in the last fifty years may well have been told the story that in 1953 Crick burst in shouting that Watson and he had found the secret of life. Indeed the work on DNA was of the greatest importance, and did, in a sense, found a new science, and a highly successful one, called molecular biology. Watson published a popular but much contested account entitled *The Double Helix* (Watson, 1968). A recent biography of Franklin (whose X-ray crystallographs provided key evidence), and Wilkins' own auto-biography, supply different perspectives on this remarkable moment in scientific history (Maddox, 2002; Wilkins, 2003).

24   For further non-technical description of molecular biology see Woolfson, 2004 – also www.dnaftb.org/dnaftb

25   For an account of such schemes see Peters and Hewlett, 2003: ch. 4. For comment see e.g. Barbour, 1998:82–4 and notes thereon.

26   See Chapter 4 for more on the nature of scientific research programmes and the way in which scientific theories evolve.

27   We thank Dr Robinson for permission to reproduce this table.

28   Vertebrates are animals with a backbone (therefore including all mammals).

29   For other controversy with Gould see Dennett (1995:300–8) and Dawkins (1998:193–209).

30   Indeed this branch of science, effectively a subdivision of chaos theory, is often called *complexity theory*.

31   It should not be supposed that Kauffman has solved the very difficult chicken-and-egg problem of the origin of cellular life. The *details* of how a system as intricate as a self-replicating cell arose (without existing cellular machinery to make it) remain frustratingly obscure (see Conway Morris, 2003: ch. 4; also Davies, 1998, and Dawkins, 2004:464–81). What Kauffman has shown is that autocatalytic systems (where each of the components speeds up the reaction of the others) can become self-sustaining and may therefore have been the earliest self-replicators.

32   See also Bak (1997) on 'self-organized criticality'.

33   See note 45 on the physicist Erwin Schrödinger's seminal lectures on the nature of life.

34   For a study of how the language of molecular biology was also influenced by the Cold War milieu in which it developed see Kay, 2000.

35   See 6.13.4 for further discussion of Dawkins's thought.

36   Though evolved characteristics sometimes look 'maldesigned' – the human eye, for instance, has a blindspot arising from the emergence of the optic nerve from the front, rather than the back, of the retina.

37   Part of the greatness of Darwin was his ability to see that this might be a shortcoming of his theory (a particular concern of his was the evolution of the eye). However, contemporary Darwinists have little difficulty in claiming that complex structures can evolve by very gradual steps.

38   Note that the concept of levels of nature used here does not imply that a higher

level is 'better' or 'closer to God' than a lower level. The Judaeo-Christian doctrine of creation holds that the whole created order at every 'level' is created 'good' (Gunton, 1998:68–73).

39   This term is due to Daniel Dennett (1995:81–2).

40   This scheme has been designed by Dr Robinson. The terms 'constitutive' and 'conceptual-explanatory' reduction are taken from Drees's helpful classification (Drees, 1996:12–16). Note that our 'ontological reduction' is not the same as Drees's 'ontological naturalism', which is discussed above (6.13.5).

41   For example – to theists, reason-giving (motive) explanations in terms of (a) the purposes of God or (b) free choice by human agents will be congenial. Atheists will have convictions that make explanations of type (a) inadmissible. Certain neuroscientists and psychologists may be committed to working as though explanations of type (b) did not exist.

42   Note that we are not talking about *temporal* emergence – a more complex system developing *over time* from a simpler one – but to emergence with respect to different levels of description.

43   See also 14.9–14.10 on genetic reductionism considered in relation to the ethics of biotechnology.

44   We owe the analogies of the 'director's cut' and molecular 'chaperones' to Woolfson (2004: ch. 5), which offers a readable account of recent developments in genomics.

45   Crick, 1966:10. Crick was among a number of scientists who were prompted to consider questions of the chemistry of life in response to a series of lectures given by the physicist Erwin Schrödinger in Dublin in 1943, and published as *What is Life?* The remarkable success of the investigations of some of these thinkers, particularly Crick and Watson, gave momentum to this programme of attempting to redescribe biology in terms of physics and chemistry.

46   For a discussion of the various meanings of the word 'chance' see 10.3.1.

47   We take up this question of a God who works with indeterminate processes in more detail in Chapter 10.

48   Of course 'horizontal' and 'vertical' are being used metaphorically here.

49   Not to be confused with the neo-Darwinian synthesis discussed in Section C.

50   Sociobiology in its application to human behaviour is often now termed 'evolutionary psychology'.

51   Agriculture, which permitted settled societies rather than hunter-gathering, first developed in the Near East perhaps as little as 10,000 years ago.

52   See also Bowker's *Is God a Virus?* (1995) for scientific criticisms of the project of sociobiology.

53   See Poole, 1994; Goodwin, 1995:28f.; Ward, 1996b:96ff.; and Rose, 1997:213f.

54   e.g. *The Devil's Chaplain* (2003).

55   The sorts of presuppositions espoused by Dawkins are well analysed by Poole (1994) and Ward (1996b:96ff.).

56   Therefore there are essentially two prongs to Dawkins's attacks on religion: (1) criticisms of the notion of divine design (6.10.5); (2) cross-explanatory reduction of explanations to the explanatory 'complex' of Universal Darwinism (in the idea of selfish genes or memes). A recent study by McGrath (2005) is specifically devoted to evaluating and rebutting Dawkins's arguments.

57   The title of this section is a mutation of the title of Drees's book, referred to in the text.

58   Many people certainly regard the term 'theistic naturalism' as an oxymoron – they hold that to be a theist one must accept the presence of supernatural entities (such

as influences from divine action) in the world. It should be noted, however, that there are a number of theologians who question this assumption. For the purposes of the discussion in this chapter it is worth noting that ontological reductions (including ontological naturalism) are not to be confused with cross-explanatory reductions (6.11). In other words (contrary to a very common assumption) it is not the case that – a priori – an affirmation of ontological naturalism (an ontological reduction) is a rejection of theistic modes of explanation (a cross-explanatory reduction). For sure, there is much work to be done for these theistic naturalists to be able to show that truth-claiming religion can survive the ontological reduction constituted by a commitment to ontological naturalism. We acknowledge, however, that it is a possibility which some believe it to be coherent to pursue (so Knight, 2001; Robinson, 2004).

59 Drees notes that although a similar question can be asked about the status of evolved moral norms, the problem is more acute with regard to the status of evolved religion because ethical propositions do not necessary need to claim to refer to an ultimate reality outside the natural order (1996:222).

60 An interesting account by a philosopher of evolution of the question, *Can a Darwinian be a Christian?* can be found in Ruse, 2001.

Further reading

BOWKER, J. (1995) *Is God A Virus? Genes, Culture and Religion* (London: SPCK)

BROOKE, J.H. (1991) *Science and Religion: Some Historical Perspectives* (Cambridge: Cambridge University Press)

CONWAY MORRIS, S. (2003) *Life's Solution* (Cambridge: Cambridge University Press)

DARWIN, C. (1859) *The Origin of Species*, ed. J.W. Burrows (Harmondsworth: Penguin, 1985), which contains the full text of Darwin's first edition.

DAWKINS, R. (1989) *The Selfish Gene: New Edition* (Oxford: Oxford University Press)

DESMOND, A. and MOORE, J. (1992) *Darwin* (Harmondsworth: Penguin)

DREES, Willem B. (1996) *Religion, Science and Naturalism* (Cambridge: Cambridge University Press)

EDWARDS, Denis (1999) *The God of Evolution* (Mahwah, NJ: Paulist Press)

GOULD, S.J. (1991) *Wonderful Life: The Burgess Shale and the Nature of History* (Harmondsworth: Penguin)

HAUGHT, J. (2000) *God After Darwin: A Theology of Evolution (Oxford and Boulder, CO: Westview Press)*

HEFNER, P. (1993) *The Human Factor* (Minneapolis, MN: Fortress Press)

KAUFFMAN, S. (2000) *Investigations* (Oxford: Oxford University Press)

PEACOCKE, A. (2004) *Creation in a World of Science: The Re-shaping of Belief* (Oxford: Oxford University Press)

Chapter 7

Psychology and theology

Fraser Watts

7.1 Introduction

The dialogue of theology with psychology, as with most other scientific areas, tends to be a rather one-sided one. Theologians are more concerned with what scientists have to say than vice versa. Though one might regret the one-sided nature of the dialogue, this chapter will inevitably reflect the way in which the relationship between psychology and theology proceeds in practice. It will therefore be largely concerned with the theological response to psychology. The key question is whether theology can be happy with contemporary psychology. There is often a sense of conflict between psychology and religion, a feeling that psychology is saying things that the religious traditions cannot be happy with. However, I[1] will suggest that this is misconceived.

It is essential to make a distinction between what is really established by scientific research in psychology, and what is sometimes claimed by way of extrapolation from that research. I will argue that there are no securely based research findings in psychology that conflict with religious belief. However, there are many unwarranted extrapolations from psychological research which, if they were accepted, would raise conflicts with religion. It is essential to maintain this distinction between what is securely established and more speculative extrapolation. The sense of possible conflict arises, either from some psychologists saying more than, as psychologists, they really have any right to say, or from religious people assuming that psychologists are saying more than they actually are. I will be arguing that, when everything is clearly understood, there is no conflict between psychology and theology.

This implies that there are limits to what psychology can properly say, but there are two different ways of setting out such limits. One is to divide up the territory, and say that there are some things that psychology can study and other things that are outside the scope of psychology and should be left to theology. Those who advocate that approach might regard morality, aesthetics and religion itself, as being outside the scope of psychology. I reject that view. There *is* a valuable psychology of religion, morality and aesthetics. (The psychology of religion will be discussed in this chapter, though there will be no space to discuss the psychological study of morality and aesthetics). However, I *do* claim that psychology never exhausts all there is to be said about what it is studying. There are other things to be said, from other points of view. It is in that sense that psychology is inherently limited.

The dialogue between psychology and theology falls into two main areas: the first is concerned with human nature generally, the second is concerned with 'religion'. This chapter will consider both areas in turn.

SECTION A
HUMAN NATURE (7.2–7.7)

7.2 Perspectives on human nature

Even when psychology is not explicitly concerned with the religious or spiritual aspects of human nature, it often seems to be taking such a limited view of human beings that it is bound to come into conflict with the more open view of the potential of human beings in the religious traditions. A theological view of human beings emphasizes that they are made in the image of God (*imago Dei*, see 6.3.1). Sometimes this has been formulated in terms of human beings having a soul, though this terminology can cause confusion (and will be discussed later in 7.7). However, whether or not soul terminology is used, the religious traditions would want to emphasize, in some way or other, the relatedness of human beings to God. A theological view of human beings also emphasizes their potential, that they are capable of having a distinctive kind of relationship with God and to some degree growing towards the likeness of God. This is something that has been particularly important in the Eastern tradition of Christian thought. The views of the different religious traditions about being human are discussed by Ward (1998).

It is incompatible with the religious view of human nature to take a very reductive view of human beings. Such reductive views of human beings arise at various points in psychology, and they are often expressed in 'nothing but' language. For example, evolutionary psychology might suggest that human beings are nothing but survival machines for their genes. Similar issues arise when the basis of consciousness and personality in the brain is concerned; it can be suggested that we are 'nothing but' our central nervous systems. Artificial Intelligence (the enterprise of programming computers to simulate the intelligent functions of human beings) is another area where strongly reductive ideas arise, with the suggestion that the mind is 'nothing but' a computer program. Genetic reductionism has already been discussed in the last chapter. The reductionist claims of neuroscience and artificial intelligence will be reviewed here. (For a somewhat fuller discussion see Watts, 1998a, 2002; also Ward, 1992.)

Issues about reductionism have also already been considered (6.11–6.13.4). As there are no examples of reductionist explanations being carried through to a point of complete success in the biological sciences,[2] strong reductionist claims are always speculative, and no more than an act of scientific faith.

I will try to show that, though work in neuroscience and artificial intelligence is surrounded by an outer belt of speculative ideas that conflicts with the religious traditions, the core scientific work in these fields does not do so.

7.3 Brain and consciousness

Human consciousness is currently the focus of a huge amount of research activity; it is sometimes claimed to be one of the last great, unsolved mysteries. A central question is whether, and how, human consciousness can be 'explained' in terms of the functioning of the physical brain. There is a good review of the philosophical assumptions of the neurological explanation of consciousness in Flanagan (1992). More polemical, reductionist views of somewhat different kinds can be found in Churchland (1986), Dennett (1991) and Crick (1994).

The debate about the neurological explanation of consciousness is muddied by confusion over what is (or ought to be) meant by 'consciousness'. At least three different layers of meaning can be discerned (Copeland, 1993:ch. 8). First, there is a baseline sense of 'consciousness' in which it refers to the capacity to experience the external world through sense organs and to perform cognitive operations on that sense experience. Second, there is a reflexive kind of consciousness in which people monitor what they experience and know. Third, there is what Copeland calls 'the ineffable FEEL of it all', what in the technical language of philosophers are called 'qualia'. It is this last sense of consciousness that is most controversial, with some people such as Dennett (1991:ch. 12) dismissing it as a mirage. At present, science is grappling with explaining how the more basic kinds of conscious experience arise. As a matter of scientific strategy that is clearly the place to begin; the more complex issues that will arise in studying higher aspects of consciousness are hardly yet in sight.

What makes the study of consciousness such a lively area of debate at the present time is that we are not just discussing *how* consciousness can arise from the brain, but the more basic question of *whether* consciousness can be explained in physical terms at all. For a long time, it was assumed that it could not. For example, in the seventeenth century, John Locke (1632–1704), argued that because consciousness is inherently immaterial, it could not arise from matter (Locke, 1960). Certainly, the qualitative difference between consciousness and the physical brain constitutes a problem. It is a real challenge to see how the brain could give rise to something so qualitatively different from itself (e.g. Nagel, 1974). Despite the problem of seeing how the 'gap' between the nervous system of the physical brain and human consciousness could be bridged, it is hard to see how else consciousness might arise, except from the brain. The strong, contemporary presupposition is that consciousness *must* be grounded in the physical brain, and it is only a question of discovering exactly *how* it arises.

At present, we only have very speculative ideas about this. For example, Penrose (1994) has suggested that consciousness arises from quantum indeterminacy in the 'microtubules' of the brain (as discussed in 5.14). However, this is a highly speculative idea which as yet has no direct research support. In contrast, Crick (1994) has suggested that it arises from synchronized electrical rhythms in particular parts of the brain. This is perhaps a more promising idea, but also highly speculative. However, the fact that we don't yet have a convincing theory of exactly how consciousness arises from the physical brain in no way supports the conclusion that it could not do so.

7.4 Theological concerns about neuroscience

Now, the question arises of what, if anything, is at stake theologically in the attempt to explain consciousness in terms of the brain. There are some like Crick who claim that neuroscience can provide a complete explanation of consciousness, personality and soul, and that this disproves the claims of religion. However, there are many problems with this argument (see Watts, 2002). Once the exaggerated polemics of people like Crick are set aside, there is not as much at stake theologically in neuroscience as some people imagine.

As I have already indicated, one of the fundamental Christian assumptions about human beings, and indeed of most religious traditions, is that they are 'spiritual' creatures. By that I mean that they have a capacity for self-transcendence, and can form a conscious relationship with God in a way that is not possible for other creatures. Rahner (1989) is one twentieth-century theologian who has set out this view. It is a view of human nature that theology would wish to safeguard. Theology will always want to oppose any attempt to take a limited, almost demeaning, view of human beings that denies the reality of our higher attributes. In opposing such views, it is standing up for common sense, at least as much for its distinctively religious view of human nature.

Moreover, the higher aspects of human nature are not called into question simply by looking for their physical basis. This again raises issues about reductionism, and there are two further aspects of reductionism that it is important to distinguish here, one to do with explanation, the other to do with 'reality'. It is one thing to explain higher attributes in terms of lower-level processes. However, it is a quite separate (and unnecessary) further step to say that such explanation means that the higher-level phenomena are somehow not real. (The term 'real' is often the focus of philosophical confusions; and it is always wise to ask what it is being contrasted with.) The reality of the higher attributes is not called into question by explaining how they arise from lower-level ones. Provided the reality of higher human qualities of consciousness (and 'soul') is fully recognized, there is no religious objection to looking for their explanation in terms of neurological processes.

The assumption that human beings have distinctive attributes is as compatible with the investigation of their neurological basis as it is with the study of their evolutionary origin (see 6.3.1). In the course of evolution, new attributes can and do arise. Indeed, from a theological point of view, I would want to suggest that it is central to God's creative purpose that, out of the natural world, creatures such as ourselves should arise who are both natural and spiritual. Having arisen, we are capable of entering into a conscious relationship with the God from whom the natural order itself arose. Though Christianity wants to insist that human beings are spiritual creatures, in the sense of being made in the image of God and having a conscious relationship to God, it has no reason to deny that we are also natural creatures.

Another theological issue that arises here is the role of mind and brain in discerning God's revelation to us. The mind and brain sciences have been emphasizing the close intertwining of mind and brain. They are not two different things, but rather two different aspects of the same thing. We do not have any experience which is purely mental in the sense that the physical brain is not also involved; all experience is underpinned by the human brain. This also applies to our experience of God, which must be linked to brain processes as much as any other kind of experience. There is no possibility of God influencing private experience in a way that bypasses the natural processes of the brain. This underlines the point made in 4.4 about existentialism, that there is no scope for suggesting an experiential relationship to God which somehow bypasses the natural world. Human experience is, in this sense, inextricably intertwined with the natural world.

7.5 The scope of artificial intelligence

Artificial intelligence (AI) is another scientific area that sometimes seems to imply a view of human nature that is incompatible with the Christian one. It is essentially the enterprise of programming computers to simulate the intelligent activities of human beings. There is a good discussion of the philosophical assumptions of AI in Copeland (1993:ch. 9). A well-argued account of what has been achieved in AI so far can be found in Johnson-Laird (1988), and the last two chapters on the boundaries of AI in relation to consciousness, emotion and free will are especially interesting. On the other hand, a trenchant critique of AI can be found in Edelman (1992, especially the Critical Postscript).

The assumption of 'strong' artificial intelligence is that *all* intelligent human activity can be simulated in computer programs, and hence that the computers of the future will be able to do anything that human beings can do now. That seems to imply that human beings are merely machines, and not the spiritual creatures that the Christian tradition assumes. One of the key issues here is how much progress artificial intelligence is likely to make. From the outset, very bold claims have been made. Actual progress has lagged behind. However, there is no doubt that considerable progress *has* been made in AI. For example, computers are now extremely good at playing chess.

Sometimes, general arguments are advanced for why AI will or will not be able to simulate human intelligence completely. However, such arguments often turn out to be inconclusive. For example, it might be claimed that any rule-governed intelligent activity can be simulated in the computer, but that begs the question of to what extent human intelligence is rule-based. Arguing in the other direction, some, such as Penrose (1994), have tried to invoke Gödel's Theorem to show that human intelligence could not be computable. However, Gödel's Theorem is concerned with mathematical systems, and there are serious doubts about whether extrapolations from it to other areas are legitimate.

If we set aside such attempts to argue from principle, we are reduced to looking at what progress has and has not been made in artificial intelligence so far, and trying to extrapolate from that. This is a hazardous business. For example, it used to be claimed that computers could never 'learn'. However, we have already reached a point at which computers can be programmed to 're-program' themselves in the light of experience, which is a kind of learning. Moreover, that has been rendered feasible by the development of a new and radically different approach to computer programming known as Parallel Distributed Processing, or 'connectionism' (see Copeland, 1993: ch. 10). Over the decades and centuries to come, there will no doubt be many such new approaches to programming, and it would be foolish to be too dogmatic about what will and will not become possible.

However, there are certain things which at the moment look likely to remain insurmountable problems for AI. One is inner experience. An instructive example here is to consider how far a computer could go towards having emotions. Different emotions arise in human beings in fairly predictable circumstances; and there should be no difficulty in principle in programming a computer to know when a particular emotion would be appropriate. It would also be possible to program some expression of emotion. For example, appropriate sentences could be composed and spoken through a voice box. However, it is a crucial feature of human emotions that we actually *feel* angry, guilty, sad or whatever. It is hard, at present, to foresee that computers could ever have such inner experiences.

Some enthusiasts for artificial intelligence might concede this, but try to argue that 'having an emotion' consists of nothing more than being able to express an emotion in appropriate circumstances. However, we see here an example of a recurrent tendency to talk-up the achievements of computers by redefining downwards the criteria which they have to meet. There is more to intelligence than following the rules of a computer program, and there is more to being emotional than showing an appropriate emotional display.

Another limitation of computers that at present seems insurmountable is their lack of individuality. As Edelman (1992) has forcefully pointed out, computers are standard off-the-shelf pieces of hardware, and in that respect quite unlike brains, which are individual. Also, each person is the result of their quite different developmental history and social context. Computers might, through the limited learning of which they are capable, come to have some individuality in their software. However, it is difficult at present to see how computers might ever acquire the kind of radical individuality that humans possess.

7.6 Theological issues about artificial intelligence

Now let us focus more specifically on the theological issues raised by the claims of artificial intelligence. There are useful introductions to these in Puddefoot (1996), Foerst (1996) and Watts (2002).

Note, first, that it is the *claims* of artificial intelligence to which theology will particularly want to respond. The programming and use of computers, in itself, does not really cause theological debates. There may, of course, be ethical and practical issues associated with the changing lifestyle that the computer age will increasingly bring, but that is another matter.[3] Note also that it is not the computers of the present day which raise theological problems. It is the claims of artificial intelligence about the computers of the future which draw a theological response.

Let us suppose, for the sake of argument, that computers are developed which simulate all the intelligent functions of human beings (though my scientific judgement is that it is unlikely that will happen). Should Christians be concerned about the possibility of computers that simulate human beings?

There might be a feeling that, in making humanoid machines, we would be 'playing God' and usurping the functions of the creator God. However, that would not really be the case. There would still be an important sense in which God would be the 'creator' of any humanoid computers that we might build. The Christian belief is that God is creator 'of all things, visible and invisible', which implies that it would be impossible for anything to exist, even a computer, without its being dependent on God for its existence. That would not be affected by the fact that human beings had made it. MacKay (1991: ch. 8) has suggested that making such a computer would be an act of 'procreation', but would not usurp the functions of the creator God any more than biological procreation does.

One important difference, of course, between parents having a child and the making of a humanoid computer is that, in the latter case, we would be making something absolutely to our own specification. It would raise ethical issues rather like those that arise with genetic engineering (see Chapter 14), but on a much bigger scale. To many people there seems something sinister about the idea of having some kind of equivalent to a human being which was absolutely determined by its maker. However, I think the unease here stems in part from linking two ideas which are actually incompatible. Human beings are assumed to have a measure of free will and not to be wholly determined by their genes or by anything else. Either an advanced computer would have such free will or it would not. If it did not, it would be only a robot, certainly nothing like a human being. However, if we were able to build a computer that really had free will and responsibility, it would not be under our control, despite the fact that we had made it.

Nevertheless there is something disconcerting about the wilder fringes of speculation and prediction in the artificial intelligence movement, of which Moravec's book *Mind Children* (1988) is a good example. He sets out a powerful vision of computer-creatures, built by us, equivalent to us, but superior to us, which is the stuff of 'sci-fi' dreams. I think Christians are right to sense something unwholesome in the spiritual tone of such fantasies. People such as Moravec seem to be intoxicated with the hope that they will be able to 'play God'. That intoxication is something that invites theological comment, and it is a separate issue from whether they would in fact be able to accomplish all the things they boldly predict. In fact, I believe that in the wilder fringes of AI speculation, we are dealing, not with science, but with implicitly religious thinking in secular, scientistic disguise.

7.7 Immortality

A key area where the assumptions of both neuroscience and AI interface with theology is immortality. (For a general survey of religious ideas about immortality, see Hick, 1976; on resurrection in relation to modern science, see **10.10(v)**, also Polkinghorne, 1994:ch. 9.)

I suspect that one reason why some Christians are uneasy about accepting the physical basis of consciousness and personality is its implication for immortality. We have become accustomed to thinking of the Christian hope of eternal life in 'dualistic' terms, which assume the separateness of soul and body. Once you start thinking in these terms, it is natural to see eternal life in terms of the survival of the soul. Moreover, if the soul is to survive after the death of the physical body, it seems essential to assume that the soul is independent of the body, rather than being grounded in the physical processes of the brain.

While this way of thinking about immortality is indeed part of the Christian tradition, it is not the only way of thinking about eternal life. There is another strand in the tradition which emphasizes the resurrection of the body rather than the immortality of the soul. It has often been claimed that it is Greek thought that has led to the idea of the immortality of the soul, whereas Hebrew thought, which emphasized the psychosomatic unity of human beings, focused more on the resurrection of the body. However, in the Christian tradition, the two are not really alternatives; those who have maintained the resurrection of the body have usually also maintained the survival of an immortal soul as a prior step. Also, an emphasis on the resurrection of the body hardly makes the Christian tradition any easier to reconcile with modern, scientific views of the person.

I would not want to argue for the survival of a disembodied soul, but neither would I see the solution as being a strong focus on the resurrection of the body. The key corrective that needs to be entered from the Christian point of view is that eternal life is seen as a gift from God, not as the automatic consequence of how human beings are constituted. On this view, if there were no God, there would be no hope of eternal life. Theologically, the distinctive thing about human beings is that they are able to establish a conscious relationship with God in a way that does not seem to be possible for the rest of natural creation. Eternal life, I would want to suggest, should be seen arising from this relationship, rather than being the consequence of human beings possessing a potentially disembodied soul.

There is the further question of how and in what form this gift of eternal life is granted by God. One possibility is that we exist within the mind or memory of God. However, it is necessary to emphasize that our eternal life is likely to be so different from our present mortal life that the scientific investigation of mind and brain are of little relevance to understanding it. A resurrection body would be wholly unlike a mortal body; equally a continued spiritual existence in some kind of unity with God would be very different from the continuation of our present mental life without the physical body.

How we think about these things may come to be influenced by future research on 'out of the body' experiences (Ring, 1980). Of the various aspects of 'near-death' experiences, out of the body experiences are particularly interesting scientifically in that they are open to verification. If it is indeed the case that human beings, in certain unusual states of consciousness, are able to make observations that could not be made from the vantage point of the physical body, we will have to learn to think in more flexible terms about the relationship between consciousness and the body. However, the scientific investigation of these matters is still far too incomplete to enable any specific theological inferences to be drawn.

The Christian tradition has been inclined to reify the soul, i.e. to talk about it as though it were a 'thing' of some kind. Post-Second World War philosophy of mind has been helpful here in teaching us the pitfalls attendant on talking about the mind as a thing; similar lessons apply to talk about the soul. Just as it is more appropriate to say that we have mental attributes than to say that we have a thing called the mind, so it is more appropriate to say that we have spiritual qualities than to say that we have a thing called the soul (see also 10.7.1–10.7.2). There is a richer variety of thinking about soul in the Christian tradition than many people are aware of, and alongside the Platonic tradition, which can readily see the soul as disembodied, there is also the Aristotelian tradition, found for example in Aquinas, which sees the soul as the 'form' of the body (see 1.11).

Ideas about immortality have also surfaced within AI, though the issues here are quite different. One of the strange features of AI is the way in which it has taken up the 'dualistic' assumptions of separation between soul and body which have all too often become intertwined with Christianity (Cotterill, 1989). In fact, the Judaic tradition, to which Christianity is heir, is of the human being as a psychosomatic unity, an 'ensouled body'. However, Tipler interprets the Christian vision of immortality in terms of the survival of a disembodied soul, and sees computer programming as a means to achieve that. It is one of the stranger assumptions of AI that it might be possible to achieve full human mental functioning outside the context of a physical body, an assumption that sits very uneasily with contemporary neuroscience.

This strange vision of immortality realized through AI has found its most conspicuous expression in Tipler's strange book *The Physics of Immortality* (1995) (see 5.23), which holds out the vision of the personality of each one of us being immortalized by being captured in a computer program. This is pseudo-science in the guise of religion. Tipler both distorts theological thinking and strains scientific credibility in bringing the two together. It is a wild extrapolation from the current achievements of AI to claim that the essential personality of each individual could be maintained in computer form, divorced from their normal somatic and social context. It is also strange, theologically, to tie thinking about immortality so exclusively to a kind of disembodied soul, and to separate it from the gift of God.

SECTION B
RELIGION (7.8–7.12)

7.8 Psychological approaches to religion

In the second part of this chapter, we will turn from the relationship between scientific and theological views of human nature to examine more specifically how they intersect over matters of faith and the religious life.

The psychology of religion draws on many other areas of psychology. It includes, for example, the different approaches to religion associated with different personality types, the development of religious faith and understanding in children, the brain mechanisms underlying religious experience, and the group processes involved in church life. Nearly every branch of psychology can be applied to the study of religious life. A good, short introduction to the psychology of religion is Brown (1988). More thorough accounts of empirical research in the psychology of religion can be found in Hood *et al.* (1996) and Beit-Hallahmi and Argyle (1997). A survey of the various different approaches that have been taken to the psychology of religion can be found in Wulff (1991).

Whether you think that religion can be studied scientifically depends on what you mean by 'science'. There has been a growing realization that science is a family of methodologies, rather than a single methodology applied in a uniform way across different disciplines. Within the sciences, there is a broad distinction to be made between sciences that study aspects of the 'natural' world, and the human sciences that study aspects of personal and cultural life. It is one of the interesting features of psychology that it is partly a natural, biological science, and partly a social science. Different branches of psychology need to draw on and integrate different scientific methodologies.

I see no basis for trying to claim that religion is a 'no go' area for scientific study. The concern arises from the idea that if you study religion psychologically, it will all be 'reduced' to psychology and there will be nothing left. I believe that that concern is misplaced. We are here dealing again with the issues about reductionism raised earlier in the chapter (7.2). Accepting that psychology can contribute to the explanation of religious life does not mean acceptance of the strong reductionist claim that religion can be completely explained in terms of psychology.

The key point is that, at least with human beings, there is room for different explanatory discourses to be developed in parallel. We are complex, multifaceted creatures, and many human phenomena need to be approached at different levels. Depression is a good example. There are biological aspects of depression, including the genetic predisposition and the biochemistry associated with depression. There are also developmental aspects, such as the early experiences which predispose people to depression. Then there are social aspects, such as the ways in which depression can distort personal relationships, and be maintained by them. No account of depression that focuses on one of these strands alone can hope to be adequate. All are needed.

The same is true of religious life. However, I would want to claim here, not only that different psychological approaches are necessary to understand religious life, but that the theological approach is relevant too, and can sit alongside the psychological approach as a complementary perspective (see Watts, 1998b). Whereas psychological approaches generally do not concern themselves with the truth of Christian doctrine, a theological view of religious life presupposes Christian truths.

Though the relationship of theological and psychological accounts of religion to one another is somewhat analogous to the relationship between different kinds of psychological account, the analogy clearly has its limitations. It is in the nature of particular psychological approaches to religious life that they narrow the focus, and deal in detail with one particular facet of things. However, it is in the nature of a theological approach that it takes the broadest possible perspective, focusing on God who, in his nature, is seen as the source of all that there is. Theological and religious approaches to religious life are in a sense complementary, but that doesn't mean that they operate in parallel ways, or that they are concerned with exactly the same kinds of question about religion.

This assumption that psychological and theological interpretations of religious life are consistent with one another and are complementary is not universally shared. It implies a rejection of two more exclusive alternatives:

> (a) the strong reductionist view that religion can be explained completely by psychology (perhaps in conjunction with other social sciences) and that a theological view of religious life is redundant and misplaced;
>
> (b) the strong opposite view that religious life should be considered exclusively in theological terms, and that the human sciences have no contribution to make.

These exclusive views seem to rest on the assumption that phenomena can be divided up into those that are the concern of theology and those that are the concern of the human sciences such as psychology. If that assumption is accepted, the debate is about whose territory religion falls in.

There are others who try to blend psychology and theology into some kind of hybrid discipline, incorporating theological and psychological elements in a way that scarcely discriminates between them. This happens most commonly in the area of pastoral psychology. Lake's *Clinical Theology* (1966) is an example of this kind of seamless integration. In contrast I would want to suggest that psychology and theology have quite distinctive vantage points, functions and characteristics, and cannot simply be fused (see Hunsinger, 1995). Psychology and theology are distinct, but consistent with one another, and complementary to one another.

Having set out this general approach, I will now apply it to some more specific examples:

> (a) I will re-evaluate one of the best-known, and apparently 'reductionist', psychological approaches to religion, that of Freud, from this point of view; and
>
> (b) I will consider more generally how psychological and theological approaches can complement our understanding of phenomena such as religious experience.

7.9 Freud's critique of religion

Freud's is one of the best-known psychological approaches to religion. It presents a hostile critique of religion, and many have assumed that this is the form that all psychological approaches to religion must necessarily take. It is an interesting psychological approach to religion to re-examine, and we will see that it is not necessarily as hostile as at first appears. (One of the best books on Freud's psychology of religion is that of Meissner, 1984; there is also a good account in Palmer, 1997.)

In fact, Freud had several different theories of religion. However, the clearest and simplest is that set out in *The Future of an Illusion* (Freud, 1928). As the title suggests, the basic proposal is that religion is illusion. However, 'illusion' is, for Freud, a technical term, meaning wish fulfilment. The suggestion is basically that people accept religious ideas simply because they want them to be true. Freud assumes that the essence of God, in fulfilment of our wishes, is that he is both loving and all-powerful. Moreover, the need to have such a figure arises, Freud thinks, from the pervasive human experience of helplessness. He thinks that it assuages that feeling of helplessness to have a powerful, all-loving God.

A related proposal is that God is a 'projection' of the human mind. However, even in Freud's own terms, it is clearly an unusual kind of projection. Projection normally refers to the human tendency to attribute to other people, for our own psychological reasons, attributes that they do not really possess. However, in suggesting that God is a projection, Freud is assuming that we 'make up' a being who does not exist at all, and project on to him the attributes we wish him to have. It is worth noting that this theory of religion as projection was not an original idea of Freud's. Essentially the same idea can be found in Feuerbach. However, Freud develops the idea in more specific form, casting it within a detailed psychological theory which includes a general understanding of how projection and wish fulfilment operate.

Some religious believers, upset by the implications of Freud's theory of religion, want to rebut it entirely. That is not the approach I will take here. I am happy to accept that Freud's approach makes a useful contribution to the understanding of religious life. However, it is also important to understand the limitations of the theory:

(i) It should be noted that the general claims of psychoanalysis are, in fact, highly debatable, and there has been much discussion about whether it is a science and whether Freud's theories are really justified by his clinical data, or just an ill-founded and highly speculative superstructure built on top of them. (For example, see Webster, 1996.) In fact Freud's ideas about religion are some of his most speculative and least securely based on clinical observation. Even if Freud's general theory is accepted, it is not necessary to agree with Freud's conclusions about religion, for which he offers no particular empirical evidence.

(ii) As Freud admitted, the theory does not deal with the *truth* of religious claims. Strictly, as Freud makes clear, it is one thing to say that religion is 'illusion' (or wish fulfilment), but quite another whether religion is a 'delusion' (or error). What Freud is arguing is that religion arises from human wishes, and meets them. However, when being careful, he admits that it is outside the province of psychology to assess the truth of religious claims.

(iii) Freud's is not the only possible psychoanalytic theory of religion. Even Freud himself, on occasion, recognized this. It emerged in an interesting way from Freud's correspondence with Oskar Pfister, a Lutheran pastor with whom Freud apparently enjoyed a good relationship, and who early on saw the potential value of Freud's methods for the pastoral work of the Church (see Meissner, 1984). Freud wrote to Pfister, 'if I drew on analysis for certain arguments, that need deter no one from using the non-partisan method of analysis for arguing the opposite view' (Meng and Freud, 1963). That is no longer just an abstract possibility. The broad lines of alternative psychoanalytic approaches to religion are now in place.

7.10 Alternative psychoanalytic approaches to religion

One strand is a re-evaluation of the nature and function of 'illusion' (wish fulfilment) stemming from the work of the psychoanalyst and paediatrician, Winnicott (see Meissner, 1984; or, more briefly, Watts and Williams, 1988). He suggested that there was a domain of psychological life, which he termed the 'transitional', which was neither that of objective reality, nor that of subjective fantasy, but something in between. He saw the play of infants, which he observed particularly carefully, as belonging to this transitional realm. However, he also saw much adult cultural life, such as art and religion, as also 'transitional'.

Far from being an unhelpful distraction from reality, he believed that this transitional realm made an important contribution to adjustment. We have here the outline of a psychoanalytic view of religion which still sees it as wish fulfilment, but nevertheless emphasizes the constructive value of religion from the point of view of human adaptation. From this perspective, it is clear that the view that religion is wish fulfilment need not lead to a critical view of it.

Another strand in the revision of Freudian thinking about religion concerns the extent of its applicability. Even if it is accepted that *some* religion arises from wish fulfilment in the way that Freud maintains, this is not necessarily true of all religion. It was part of Freud's theory that the attributes of human parents are projected on to God. Though he sought no empirical support for this theory, others have done so, partly through statistical surveys of the attributes associated both with parents and with God, partly through very detailed clinical case studies. In some of these, there is such a far-reaching similarity between the way a particular person thinks of God and one of their human parents that it is difficult to write it off as a mere coincidence (see Beit-Hallahmi and Argyle, 1997:106–9).

However, this is not to accept that all concepts of God are 'nothing but' human projections. You can still believe in the possibility of moving away from human-based concepts of God to an apprehension of the true God that does less to distort his nature. This is, in essence, the view that Tillich (1952) takes at the end of his book, *The Courage To Be* (see also Homans, 1970). He argues for the importance of Christians moving beyond the 'transference God'.

Yet another strand in the more sympathetic application of psychoanalysis to religion emphasizes that religion at its best, far from being a symptom of poor psychological adjustment, in fact requires a high level of adjustment. This was part of Pfister's early debate with Freud, and similar views have been advanced, for example, by Lee (1948). In Freudian theory, the principle functions of the ego are love and work. It is not difficult to argue that exemplary Christians, and indeed Jesus himself, far from showing poor psychological adjustment, showed a remarkable capacity for love and work.

This leads on to the question of how such advanced levels of ego-adjustment may be facilitated by the Christian life. Meissner (1987) has sketched out one possible answer to this within the framework of what is basically a Freudian theory of personality development. However, it is one in which he sees scope for the operation of the grace of God. In simple terms, the idea is that the grace of God provides the resources to overcome obstacles to psychological development that might otherwise be insurmountable.

Since Freud's time there has been a good deal of empirical study of the mental health of religious people (Beit-Hallahmi and Argyle, 1997:189–91; Loewenthal, 1995). It turns out to be quite diverse, and to depend on the approach to religion that people have. In broad outline, the picture is that people who have a merely conventional approach to religion may have poorer mental health than average. However, those who have a particularly committed approach to religion often have better mental health than average.

These various revisionist approaches to the psychoanalytic theory of religion make use of Freud's ideas up to a point, but put them in their place, not allowing them to be paraded as a valid theory of universal application, even less a theory that determines the truth of religion. Freud's approach to religion provides a good case study of how even an apparently hostile psychological theory can be seen as compatible with the assumption of the truth of religion, once the theory is put into appropriate context and not allowed to make claims that go beyond its proper scope.

7.11 Complementary approaches to religious experience

The predominant assumption within the Christian tradition has been that there is a 'real' God, who seeks to reveal himself to humanity, and of whom it is possible for us to have some experience, however imperfect. This has been combined with an emphasis on the transcendent nature of God, and the impossibility of human beings coming to know him fully or through their own powers, but the tradition has normally maintained the possibility of some degree of apprehension of God's revelation through human experience. The main suggestion of this section will be that the available psychological data on religious experience is perfectly compatible with such assumptions, even though it does not presuppose them.

Contemporary approaches to religious experience have seen a strong emphasis on its cultural-embeddedness (e.g. Katz, 1978). The exact nature of religious experience often seems to depend on the faith-traditions of the people concerned. The tradition provides a set of expectations about religious experience, a language in which it can be described, and sometimes even a kind of 'training' that prepares people for it. Though there is clearly some validity in these points, it is also possible to argue that there are some core elements of religious experience that seem relatively universal and less shaped by tradition (e.g. Forman, 1990). Also, the empirical study of reports of religious experience indicates that descriptors of religious experience divide into two clusters, one relatively phenomenological, the other relatively belief-laden (see Hood *et al.*, 1996:258). However, we need not enter fully here into the debate about exactly how far religious experience is shaped by tradition. The main point is a more philosophical one, that the contribution of faith traditions to the shaping of religious experience is not incompatible with the assumption of a real God revealing himself through such experience.

A different kind of theory of religious experience can be advanced in terms of the unconscious 'psychodynamics' from which it arises. This is where Freud's approach to religion is relevant, directing us to look towards the role of psychological needs and wishes, the internalization of parent figures, and so on. It is a plausible claim that religious experience often arises in the context of unresolved psychological problems. Survey evidence certainly confirms that powerful religious experiences often occur in the context of stress and unhappiness, though the striking finding is that they characteristically produce a state of calm joy (e.g. Hay, 1987; Hood *et al.*, 1996:ch. 7).

Once again, different assumptions are possible. You can see religious experience as being *simply* a method of dealing with stress and unresolved psychological problems. However, it has also frequently been recognized in the Christian tradition that distress, and the accompanying sense of human inadequacy, creates a genuine sense of openness to God. It is perfectly compatible with the Christian tradition to assume that unresolved psychological problems provide a particular opportunity for God to reveal himself and bestow his grace.

Similar points can be developed in relation to various charismatic phenomena, of which much the best studied is glossolalia or 'speaking in tongues' (see Malony and Lovekin, 1985). Psychological and sociological research has given us quite a good picture of the conditions under which glossolalia is most likely to arise, though the picture is complex, and there seem to be different forms of glossolalia which arise in different circumstances. Such findings could be taken as providing a full and adequate account of why and how glossolalia arises. However, this understanding of the human context of glossolalia is by no means incompatible with the assumption that God can use this phenomenon as a particular means of bestowing his grace.

7.12 Neurological approaches to religious experience

There has also been interest recently in the neuropsychological basis of religious experience. The idea that has attracted most interest is that there is a similarity between the neural processes underlying religious experience and temporal lobe epilepsy. It was the focus of a recent newspaper report under the headline 'God Spot in the Brain'. However, the data supporting this theory are very weak (see Jeeves, 1997). Though there are some superficial similarities between religious experiences and the seizure experiences of those who suffer from temporal lobe epilepsy, the dissimilarities are very marked. For example, religious experiences are generally positive and often life-transforming, whereas seizure experiences are distressing and transitory.

The best current theory of the neurological basis of religious experience is that of d'Aquili and Newberg (1998), who see it as arising out of the operation, in a particular context, of two general-purpose cognitive operators in the brain. The first is the 'causal operator', which attributes events to causal processes and powers.

The other is the 'holistic operator', which forms a unity out of fragments of experience. D'Aquili has made a plausible argument that religious experience can be seen as arising from these two operators, one having a special application in the discernment of God's action in the world, the other underlying the powerful sense of unity that is a function of many mystical experiences.

However, once again, such a theory is neutral concerning the assumption of a real God seeking to reveal himself through religious experience. D'Aquili's theory might provide a complete and adequate explanation of the brain mechanisms from which religious experience arises. On the other hand, it can equally well be seen as a theory of the brain processes through which experience of the real God is mediated.

The assumption for which I am arguing here of the compatibility of psychological and theological views of religious experience has been formulated clearly and carefully by Meissner in his psychological study of Ignatius of Loyola (Meissner, 1992). Ignatius was concerned to identify 'uncaused consolations', i.e. religious experiences for which there was no natural explanation and which should therefore be attributed to God. Meissner argues, in contrast, that there is no incompatibility between the role of natural causes, and the assumption of a divine origin and purpose in such experiences. There is no need to assume that God's grace bypasses all natural psychological mechanisms in its operation (see also Peacocke, 1993:ch. 11).

7.13 Conclusion

This chapter has been concerned with one of the newer areas of dialogue between science and theology. The main focus in that dialogue so far has been on evolutionary biology, and the physical sciences, especially cosmology. However, it seems likely that debates about human nature and religion will now increasingly come to the fore. Psychology has been through a number of methodological twists and turns in the twentieth century as it has attempted to find a way of getting to grips with its rather elusive subject matter. However, the twin approaches of neuropsychology and cognitive science (in which the computer model of mind has been dominant) are now yielding real scientific progress.

There is certainly scope for a sense of conflict to arise between psychology and theology, both in their general assumptions about human nature and in their approach to religious life. However, it has been argued here that such conflict only arises when psychology overreaches itself. There is nothing in psychological research on neuropsychology or artificial intelligence which is incompatible with Christian assumptions about human nature. However, it is nonetheless true that these scientific activities are sometimes surrounded by an outer belt of general assumptions which do conflict with the Christian tradition. The key task in evaluating the dialogue between theology and psychology is to distinguish between what is really supported by research and what is speculative background or extrapolation.

Equally, there is no reason in principle why there should be conflict between the psychology of religion and traditional theological assumptions of the truth of religion. However, it seems likely that there will be a growing *sense* of such conflict in the years ahead, and neuropsychological theories of religion will probably be central to this. However, as has been pointed out here, such theories are in no way incompatible with traditional theological assumptions. The key point is that the explanatory perspective of the neurosciences is not the only one, and is not incompatible with other perspectives of a very different kind. The sense of conflict between theology and psychology only arises when psychology asserts that it is providing a full and adequate explanation of religion, a claim that it is beyond the competence of psychology to make. When the psychology of religion is seen as one explanatory perspective among others, it is not incompatible with the theological perspective.

Notes

1   This chapter was solely drafted by Fraser Watts.
2   Other than the merely constitutive (see 6.13.1).
3   See 13.10, 13.12.

Further reading

BROWN, L. (1988) *The Psychology of Religion: An Introduction* (London: SPCK)
HOLDER, R.D. (1993) *Nothing but Atoms and Molecules?* (Tunbridge Wells: Monarch)
JEEVES, M. (1997) *Human Nature at the Millennium* (Grand Rapids, MI: Baker Books; Leicester: Apollos)
PALMER, M. (1997) *Freud and Jung on Religion* (London: Routledge)
PUDDEFOOT, J. (1996) *God and the Mind Machine* (London: SPCK)
WARD, K. (1992) *Defending the Soul* (Oxford: Oneworld)
WATTS, F. (2002) *Theology and Psychology* (Aldershot: Ashgate)
WATTS, F. and WILLIAMS, M. (1994) *The Psychology of Religious Knowing* (London: Geoffrey Chapman)

BOOK THREE

Chapter 8

Some resources for Christian theology in an ecological age

Christopher Southgate

8.1 Introduction

In Chapter 2 we indicated something of the range of resources within the Christian tradition for expounding the relation of God to the world. Much fine theology continues to be done from that base of resources. We mentioned T.F. Torrance in 4.6 as a theologian who had applied Barth's approach to addressing the theological significance of scientific themes; Colin Gunton has also written on the theology of creation with great clarity and distinction (e.g. Gunton, 1998). The Protestant tradition has also given us such figures as Jürgen Moltmann,[1] Wolfhart Pannenberg[2] and Eberhard Jüngel.[3] Two major Roman Catholic thinkers to have written very widely in the area of systematic theology are Karl Rahner[4] and Hans Urs von Balthasar,[5] both in their different ways heirs of Thomas Aquinas. For further indication of the range of thinking in modern systematic theology see Ford and Muers (2005), which also contains essays by Philip Clayton and Celia Deane-Drummond relating theology to the physical and biological sciences respectively.

In this chapter we look in particular at the way other thinking about God has developed in areas of particular relevance to scientific themes. We recognize the strength of the continuities described in the work cited above, and yet seek to explore some of the distinctive emphases that have developed in recent theology.[6]

The twentieth century saw a variety of key challenges to the way Christian theology is formulated. These included:

    (a) the rise of Nazism in a highly civilized and traditionally Christian country, leading ultimately to the Holocaust;

    (b) the feminist movement;

    (c) the modern ecological crisis.

(as well as developments in physics, biology and psychology such as we examined in Chapters 5–7).

    (a) contributed to the growth of neo-orthodox theology, particularly associated with the towering figure of Karl Barth (see 2.4, 2.5.4, 4.6), and also to theological formulations emphasizing the suffering of God (for references see Moltmann, 8.5.6 and Fiddes, 8.5.8).

(b)   and (c) led to critiques of traditional Christian formulations of God as patriarchal and oppressive, and among feminists either to abandonment of Christianity or to modification of the images used of God.

For an exploration of whether these changes are part of a 'new paradigm' in theology see Küng and Tracy (1989), noting Küng's view that Christian theology is unnegotiably rooted in past historical events – in a *person*, and a *tradition* (Küng, 1989:32–3).

In respect of ecological theology H. Paul Santmire has constructed a taxonomy of responses to the challenge of environmental concerns (Santmire, 2000:6–9). His spectrum of responses can be applied more widely. Santmire suggests that:

(i)   some thinkers are *apologists* for the tradition, considering that it offers a strong emphasis on justice, peace and the integrity of creation;

(ii)   some are *reconstructionist*, in the sense of believing 'that a new edifice of thought must be designed, from the ground up, with new foundations and new categories. These thinkers take it for granted that traditional Christian thought offers no – or few – viable theological resources to help people of faith respond to ecological crisis and related cosmic anxieties today' (2000:6)

(iii)   between these poles are those he calls *revisionist* – working within the tradition of the Christian scriptures and ancient creeds, but 'not to abandon or defend the classical theological tradition, but to *reclaim* it, and then to *reenvision* it, for the purpose of serving the worship, the teaching, and the public witness of the church in our own time of global environmental and existential crisis' (2000:9, italics in original)

In this terminology much of our interest in this chapter falls mainly on approaches which might be called revisionist – regarding the tradition as having vital resources for understanding the relation of God to the world, but considering that significant elements are in need of reframing. We begin, however, with consideration of what many would consider more radical moves in thought which lead to a distinctly non-classical type of theology. First we treat process thought, with special emphasis on its contribution to theodicy, and second the emphasis within feminism known as 'ecofeminism'. The overall aim of the chapter is to consider what this range of resources offers in terms of the construction of a model of the relationships between God, humanity and the cosmos.

8.2 Process thought

Process philosophy arose out of A.N. Whitehead's effort to generate a radically new metaphysics which would unify the way we understand the world. In his 1927 Gifford Lectures, published as *Process and Reality*, Whitehead (1861–1947) abandoned the notion, strong in Western philosophy since Parmenides and Plato in the fifth century BCE, that what is most unchanging is most real. Instead he conceived the structure of reality in dynamic terms (an approach which goes back to Heraclitus). Whitehead set out a radical metaphysics based not on entities but on events – on an infinite series of 'actual occasions'. All entities are 'momentary constituents of the processes of reality'; unchangingness is a property of what is 'dead, past, abstract or purely formal' (Pailin, 1989:51). The emphasis is on *becoming*, on development in time, rather than on static being.

Space does not permit a detailed analysis of this way of thinking, except to say that for process thought the central metaphor for understanding the world is that of organism, rather than that of machine. The formation of each event is a function of:

- the nature of the entities involved (as in, for instance, a physicalist scheme);
- their context and interdependence on a number of levels (in a way more characteristic of biological organisms than of inanimate objects);
- their 'experience' and their effort to 'fulfil their possibilities to the full' in the given event (language deriving not merely from biology but from the analogy of human mentality).

As Barbour describes, 'Each entity is a center of spontaneity and self-creation, contributing distinctively to the world' (Barbour, 1998:285). This assignment of quasi-mental subjective experience to all entities is known as panpsychism, or sometimes panexperientialism. For brief summaries of process theology see Fiddes (1988:40–5) or Barbour (2002:94–100, 111–18).

Note that the process scheme is neither consistent nor inconsistent with experimental observations – it does not of itself give rise to any empirically testable proposals.[7] Nothing in science attributes any sort of subjectivity to an entity like an electron, nor is such a postulate anywhere supported by experiment. Whitehead's scheme is true 'meta'-physics.

8.2.1 A 'dipolar' God

In the last chapter of *Process and Reality* Whitehead turns his attention to God, and develops his concept of a dipolar deity. By this is meant that God, who in strict process thought is one entity among others – not ontologically distinct from the rest of the cosmos – is:

(a) affected by the experience of all other entities (God's 'consequent' nature); *and*
(b) constant in character as the ground both of order and of novelty (God's 'primordial' nature).

This formulation of the character of God in terms of two types of attribute in tension – responsiveness and constancy – is known as 'dipolarity' (sometimes 'bipolarity'). Charles Hartshorne (1897–2000), the greatest theological exponent of process thought, developed a somewhat different form of dipolarity. For Hartshorne God is both necessary being in himself, God's 'abstract' pole, but contingent in the particular relationships into which God enters with contingent creation, God's 'concrete' pole. This is a very helpful way of overcoming some of the intrinsic paradoxes of theism (see Pailin, 1989:ch. 4).[8] Dipolarity, then, allows God to be responsive to the world and yet remain God. The emphasis in process models of God is on a God who experiences the world's pain and struggle, and persuades it towards paths of creativity and fulfilment. In Whitehead's famous phrase God is the 'fellow-sufferer who understands' (quoted in Pailin, 1989:59).

8.3 Questions of theodicy

The fellow-suffering God, who does not coerce but merely seeks to persuade other beings in the direction of love, seems profoundly attractive in the light of the Holocaust. The massacre of Jews by a country at the heart of European Christendom stands as a devastating critique of images of God acting in power to bring his kingdom in through his chosen Church. (For indications of how theologians have tried to respond to this critique see 10.5; Fiddes, 1988:3–5; Surin, 1986:116–32 and references therein.) *Process schemes subvert the notion of the omnipotence of God*, and therefore escape some of these tensions.

The extent to which process theodicy is a satisfactory resource for addressing human-inflicted evil is crisply addressed by Surin (1986:86–92), who doubts whether it is enough to tell the victim of torture that there is a passive fellow-suffering God who understands. *Where process schemes are at their strongest is in offering a single account of human-inflicted evil and so-called 'natural evil'* (such as earthquakes) – in both cases 'evil' arises from conflicts between the desire of different entities for self-actualization. God lovingly suffers with all entities, and retains their experiences in God's eternal memory, but the process God does not 'fix' these conflicts for the benefit of one entity rather than another. Instead God tries to lure all elements towards the optimal blend of harmony and intensity. This is a particularly tempting scheme for addressing the theodicy problems of evolutionary creation, which were referred to in 6.7 and are explored in detail in 10.18–19.

Process theology has influenced many thinkers in the science-and-religion debate to a greater or lesser extent. Some have allied themselves explicitly with the process camp, in particular Ian Barbour – also others such as Charles Birch, John Cobb and Jay McDaniel.[9] Polkinghorne and Peacocke have adopted some of the rhetoric of a God who guarantees order and cooperates in the universe's exploration of possibilities, although neither theologian embraces the process scheme as a whole. We explore their concepts of God more fully in 10.10.

8.4 The critique of patriarchy

This critique has focused on the whole complex of references to God as Lord, King and Father, and to men as 'his' particular representatives, which so dominates the language of the Bible and the Christian Fathers. The aspect of the critique that most concerns us here is the strand of thinking known as 'ecofeminism'. This takes up the charge that patriarchal attitudes have led to the oppression and denigration of women, and connects this with the way humans have abused the natural world. Patriarchy, then, is seen on this view as the root of all patterns of domination and subordination. A masculine God is viewed as utterly separate and remote from the dependent believer. This dominating remoteness, it is claimed, is used to vindicate masculine power-figures dominating others deemed to be inferior and exploitable, whether they be women, or non-human creatures, or the land itself. Daphne Hampson, herself a 'post-Christian' theologian, regards the major task of feminist theology as being the reconceptualizing of God – not merely the 'renaming' but the 'reshaping' of our whole understanding of divinity (1990: ch. 5).

Ecofeminism overlaps with *the critique of anthropocentrism*, which alleges that systems of thought which emphasize the priority of humans over other species have greatly contributed to the present ecological crisis.[10] In a seminal article in 1967 Lynn White Jr described Christianity as 'the most anthropocentric religion the world has seen' (White, 1967:1205)[11] and laid the blame for humans' wholesale exploitation of the natural world on the combination of science and technology that this attitude engendered. He yearned instead for the sacramental view of the Earth he found in Francis of Assisi. White's is a (highly contentious) historical analysis, and as Colin Russell comments, it must be judged historically as well as theologically. Russell points out that 'It is a great over-simplification to posit "reverence" and "control" as mutually exclusive attitudes' (Russell, 1994:89). For an analysis of White's charge, and other factors behind the environmental crisis, see Northcott (1996: especially ch. 2).[12]

There has been much discussion in recent years as to whether patriarchy and anthropocentrism are so prejudicial to the formulation of Christianity in an age of ecological crisis as to render the faith untenable. This is a conclusion arrived at both from radical feminism by such as Hampson and Mary Daly, and from radical environmentalism by many of the followers of the 'creation spirituality' movement pioneered by Matthew Fox. Christianity will not 'work' in our present situation and we must look elsewhere for myths and rituals that will.

Those ecological theologians staying within the Christian tradition have been inclined to follow this same pragmatist line. A good example is Sallie McFague, whom we discuss in more detail in 8.5.4. Although McFague refers to herself as working within critical realism, theological as well as scientific (1987:193 note 43), her concern is to offer a plurality of models of God, based for example on the metaphors of God as Mother, Lover and Friend (McFague, 1987:97–180), and of the world as the body of God (McFague, 1993), which she hopes will *allow humanity to survive and to avoid the abuse of the Earth*.

This seems a far cry from the critical-realist approach to theology attempted by the 'scientist-theologians' Barbour, Peacocke and Polkinghorne (see Polkinghorne,

1996a:14–25), which is essentially an effort to derive consonances both between the *methods* of Christian theology and of the sciences, and also between their *cognitive-propositional claims*. In other words, an effort to derive truth-claims, rather than survival-strategies.

8.4.1 The importance of the relation between ecological theology and the science–religion debate

Divergence of approach between these two types of 'research programme' – those which attempt a pragmatically oriented remythologization of our relationship to the Earth, and those which attempt to align the traditional Christian narratives with those of science – tends to leave both on the margins of theology. *It is our contention that ecological considerations are an aspect of the world that science describes, and form an important part of the data for a critical-realist theology which takes science seriously.* (Indeed science has a particularly ambiguous role in the ecological crisis – having both (a) contributed to the technology responsible for much environmental abuse and (b) been the main source of our awareness of the extent of the crisis.)

So 'green' theology must form part of our discussion of the relationships between religious and scientific narratives, and of any formulation of a model of God, humanity and the cosmos.

8.4.2 Consideration of the relation between 'realist' and 'pragmatist' approaches

The above discussion raises an important issue concerning models of God. Is the task of theology to respond to the data of revelation in a way which is coherent, comprehensive, and fruitful of further exploration (a view analogous to critical-realist descriptions of scientific activity)? Or is it rather to propose ways of understanding our relation to the cosmos and to the divine which might allow us to survive (an essentially pragmatist view)?

That in turn raises another fascinating question: are not those two approaches, when considered in an evolutionary view of religion, actually the same? Must not adaptation to what-is-really-the-case be the most realist and at the same time the most pragmatic of cultural strategies?

8.4.2.1 An evolutionary approach to 'realism vs pragmatism'

We consider this question first from an evolutionary standpoint, in two ways:

(i) First, one might question whether religious cultures have been able to evolve far in the direction of the highest calling of their faiths. In biological evolution it is possible for there to be adaptive solutions to particular 'problems' – such as how to fly, how to see, etc. which cannot be reached because earlier patterns have locked the organism's structures into pathways from which there is no sufficiently adaptive route to the new solution. Indeed, some would argue that patriarchy, or come to that monotheism, is just such a locked pathway, which cannot now lead to a faith which would be adaptive to our present situation. Others would see the failure of New Testament faith to transform human behaviour (to a greater extent than it has) as one more restatement of the doctrine of original sin. Though a community based on self-giving and neighbour-love might be the most adaptive to ultimate reality, no paths have yet been found which allow a human society to evolve to that behaviour.

(ii) A second response is to note the sheer difficulty in evaluating the adaptiveness of a worldview. The cultural-evolutionary project of Western Christianity could have been seen, as late as 1940, as astonishingly successful – it had spread its religious, economic and political norms across a great deal of the inhabited world, and could therefore have been taken to be an evolutionary strategy of unparalleled success, and hence the strategy most closely corresponding to the way-things-actually-are.[13] Teilhard de Chardin, writing in China, could conclude that the project of Western Christianity was well on the way to flooding the Earth with 'mentality', the precursor to the final consummation of that world in Christ at the Omega Point (Teilhard, 1959; see also **10.18.1**). At the end of the century, however, although the number of Christians continued to rise rapidly across the world as a whole, the global-economic system that Western culture had produced threatened the continued survival of the human project in anything like its present form – not only through the risk of nuclear war, but through the ever-more-evident risk of radical climate change. (So James Lovelock, a kind of latter-day anti-Teilhard, writing in Cornwall, can remark that it may well be that the planet will need to discard this most troublesome of species (1988:212) – see **9.7**.)

So considerable caution has to be exercised in presuming a deep truth-content to a pragmatic scheme, and in assessing the survival-adaptedness of critical-realist approaches.

8.4.2.2 A theological approach to 'realism vs pragmatism'

It is also important to question a realist-pragmatist dichotomy on *theological* grounds. The truth of God in Christian tradition is not an idea but a dynamic being. Christianity is not about 'knowing what God is like' but about living *within* the truth of God. So Christian theology is not primarily concerned with conceptualizations for their own sake, rather it is interested in discriminating the contours of the being of God in relationship to humanity and the cosmos in particular situations, so that Christians may better live in that relationship. *Christian theology therefore seeks neither for useful but merely fictive or mythical ideas, nor for mere conceptual truth. It seeks to know the truth of God's being in order the better to live in the context of urgent practical questions.* (So Jüngel: 'the essence of Christian faith is joy in God and so concern for a more human world' (quoted in Webster, 1986:4).)

Another vital point to reassert, before discussion of particular models of God in relation to the world, is the partial, provisional, inevitably anthropomorphic and inadequate nature of all human talk about God. All the formulations that follow must be read in the light of this limitation.

8.4.3 The development and assessment of theological models

Before we begin to outline different models which have been proposed as to the relation between God, humanity and the cosmos, a comment is needed on the process of developing and assessing models. As an example, an ecologically informed critical-realist theology will need to take the data of Scriptural revelation as of central importance, but will be willing to re-evaluate these data in the light of new perceptions such as those of feminism. To return to the Lakatosian language of Nancey Murphy (4.12), belief in a God who has revealed the divine nature particularly in the events, stories, myths and wisdom of Scripture will be a core element in such a research programme; issues about whether that God is appropriately described as King, Lord and Father will be auxiliary propositions which can and should be subjected to severe testing in the light of the assembled data available to the community working in that tradition. This body of data will comprise the community's reflection on Scripture, tradition, reason (including all the fruits of scientific reasoning) and religious experience. Such a Lakatosian testing will involve the criteria Barbour lists for hypothesis-testing within science: agreement with data, coherence, scope and fertility,[14] but in particular it will major on the proposals to which a model of God, humanity and the cosmos gives rise. What proposals does it make in respect of ethics, especially environmental ethics? Are such ethics at all workable for a real human society?[15] The proposals of a programme in Christian theology will, however, be liturgical as well as ethical – they will concern the prayer and worship of the community, and will be tested by 'liturgy-assisted logic' (Polkinghorne, 1991:18–19) – by the extent to which that prayer and worship is experienced as positive, transformative and productive of distinctively moral life. They will also be progressive, exploring new data, such as a speaking of the Holy Spirit as feminine (Murphy, 1990:167f.).

It seems inevitable that in the current era Christian communities will explore a wide plurality of programmes. The history of the tradition that has given rise to modern Christianity has been typified sometimes by diversity, sometimes by the perceived need to establish orthodoxy (as in the reforms of Josiah and Nehemiah, the fourth-century patristic Councils, and, putatively, the Council of Trent). These fights for orthodoxy have continued to exert a tremendous effect on our models of God. In the reflection of peri-exilic Israel the worship of natural features (and the use of cultic prostitution) were pronounced uncreative, unhelpful to the moral and spiritual life of the community. Radical monotheism came to be insisted upon. The fourth and fifth centuries after Christ were characterized by sharp conflicts over definitions of the nature of Christ and the Trinity. Credal forms of words were set in place by ecumenical council. But there seems little likelihood that this present age will be one in which a new orthodoxy will be established.

EXERCISE 8.1

It is part of the aim of this chapter to encourage the individual student to consider what their own favoured approach, realist, pragmatic, or indeed non-realist (see 4.3, especially note 2) would be to reflection on the relationship between God, humanity and the cosmos. The aim, then, is in a sense to fill in (however cautiously and provisionally) the gaps in Figure 8.1, but it is important to note that there could be other ways to draw the diagram – as a circle, for instance, or a series of circles inside circles. What is of particular concern is not some effort to define 'God' or 'nature' in the abstract, but to characterize the *relationships* between the different entities, and how those relationships have changed and will change over the history of the cosmos.

GOD

origin of humanity?

humanity in the image of God?

fall/sin?

providence/theodicy?

incarnation?/redemption?

ultimate prospects for humans/resurrection?

creation *ex nihilo*?

making/emanation/embodiment?

autonomy/evolution of creation?

sustaining/guiding of creation?

creation's praise of/response to God?

ultimate destiny of creation?

HUMANITY   THE COSMOS

humans' understanding of cosmic history and ecological interdependence on Earth?

anthropocentrism/biocentrism/right relationship under God?

instrumental/intrinsic value of non-human creation?

human stewardship/priesthood of creation?

Figure 8.1 A framework for expressing a model of God, humanity and the cosmos

The exercise of the whole chapter is to consider how the different thinkers presented would draw the diagram in Figure 8.1 – what emphases are strongest for them – what do they omit to cover? (You will need to consult the original texts.) You should then be able to give an account of where your own model would differ from those described. One of the objectives of the exercise is that you gain a sense of the *interdependence* of doctrinal positions: what choice is made as to, for example, the nature of humanity, or the significance of the Incarnation, or the salvation of non-human creatures, influences all the other choices in the model. The most problematic and underconsidered area of Figure 8.1 is the relation of the divine to the non-human world. In considering the brief treatments 8.5.1–8.5.10 you should consider in particular their adequacy in addressing this aspect of theology.

8.5 Some models discussed

We consider two models of God stemming out of process thought, and two arising out of critiques of patriarchy and anthropocentrism. We look at three formulations of a new Trinitarianism. At the end of the chapter we consider major collections of essays on panentheism and kenosis, two themes of particular importance in current theological revisionism.

8.5.1 Model A: David Pailin in *God and the Processes of Reality* (1989)

Pailin's account is a reworking of process theism, deriving in particular from Charles Hartshorne and his concept of a Godhead containing both necessary and contingent attributes (see 8.2.1). So God is necessarily, indestructibly divine, but God's actuality as Creator is contingent on God's choice to be the Creator of this particular cosmos (Pailin, 1989:68–9). *The model is* **panentheistic** *– it regards the whole universe as contained within God, and yet considers that this does not exhaust the divine being. Pailin considers the closest analogy to be that of a human self within a body.* Although God's knowledge of the world is far greater than ours of our bodies, there is nevertheless autonomy of process within the non-divine. As in all process thought there is a strong emphasis on temporality in God (see Pailin's ch. 3 for a discussion), but Pailin's God is very much the Creator, the 'self-grounded ground of all else' (1989:127), not merely an ordering entity coexisting with the primordial chaos. This responds to a common theological criticism of Whitehead's scheme that he made creativity, rather than God, his ultimate.

As regards the narrative of Darwinism, Pailin would say that evolution illustrates the autonomy of process in the creation, and that God has not intervened within it. Divine influence on the non-conscious world is in terms of implanting 'a bias towards complexification' (1989:153) and enjoying the value of whatever emerges, rather than luring or persuading every entity towards the divine goals of harmony and creativity. This view, he says, is 'biologically tenable, metaphysically significant, theistically important and rationally credible' (1989:153). Pailin here parts company with the panexperientialism and theology of divine lure mentioned in 8.2–8.2.1. He thus deals with the great problem of the implausibility of a metaphysic based on electrons having anything akin to subjective experience, but he abandons that unity of description of God's interaction with all elements of the creation which is such a striking feature of process schemes. As Paul Fiddes has written:

> [p]rocess thinkers argue that something akin to the basic features of human experience – feeling and enjoyment – must be present everywhere. However hard it is to express the term of the analogy at the lower levels of creation ... nevertheless I believe that process thought is on to something here. Some overall vision of the 'responsiveness' and 'resistance' of creation to the Spirit of God is needed for a doctrine of creative evolution, (and) for a proper theodicy ... (1988:228)

Pailin, in trying to move process thought closer to a typically Christian emphasis on God as the ground of creation and away from the weirder aspects of Whiteheadian metaphysics, may actually have ditched something very significant. Fiddes again: 'It may be that process thought is pointing in a direction whose destination we do not yet have the conceptual tools to map; if we cannot yet define the mystery we may need "mythologies" such as universal mentality to recognise it' (1988:228).

8.5.2 Model B: Jay McDaniel in *Of God and Pelicans* (1989)

McDaniel has reflected carefully on the relation between God and the non-human world, which is in many ways more problematic for theology than efforts to articulate God's relation to humans. In particular, McDaniel considers the 'back-up chick' which some birds hatch as an 'insurance', but which is usually destroyed by its stronger sibling. The pelican is an example of a species in which such behaviour has evolved. McDaniel uses this as an illustration of the tensions involved in supposing God the inceptor and sustainer of the evolutionary process, and at the same time the one by whom nature is inexhaustibly loved (1989:23). McDaniel sees a process view as the only one which might generate a theodicy adequate to these challenges.

Like Pailin, McDaniel is a panentheist, and he makes a distinction between 'emanationist' panentheism, in which the universe is God's body, the direct expression of the divine being, and what he calls 'relational' panentheism, which regards the world as having some degree of creative independence from God. Although we may question to what extent McDaniel's relational panentheism is more than a restatement of God's immanence within all creation, his scheme does allow him to regard God as 'both agent in and patient of nature' (1989:30).

As against Pailin, McDaniel conforms more closely to the main emphases of process theology in stressing the cosmos as co-eternal with God, and advocating panpsychism. Where *he* breaks ranks with most process theologians is in following John Cobb (rather than Hartshorne) and claiming that a Whiteheadian scheme is consistent with a category of life after death (McDaniel, 1989:44–7). For Hartshorne, the ultimate purpose and consummation of life is to enrich the divine experience. McDaniel accepts this, but claims that his model is strengthened by admitting *also* some form of 'pelican heaven' – in which the products of evolution are all transformed after death to an improved state of existence (see also **10.19** and **10.20** on the redemption of the non-human creation).

McDaniel's other importance is in his pursuit of a biocentric ethic – that is, one which accords moral importance to all life and not just to human beings. He concedes that there need to be different approaches for different types of creatures – domestic animals to be considered in terms of their individual rights, other living creatures as moral patients, the rest of the non-human creation in terms of its general intrinsic value (1989:67–9).[16] He asks what theological and spiritual resources can promote the practice of such an ethic, and draws the conclusion that beyond those of process thought the most important derive from Buddhism, especially the concepts of (i) non-harming – refraining as much as possible from the violation of other creatures' interests – and (ii) emptiness.

We consider what Eastern spirituality can contribute to the dialogue between religion and science further in 9.3–9.6.1. But it is important to note the approach here – McDaniel asks: what spirituality will enable us to *act out* the theological convictions we have formed about God and the world? In this he conforms very much to the view of theology we have been articulating in this book – also to the Bossey Circle (Figure 1.2 in 1.5) Scientific and social analysis should inform contemporary theology – theology should inform ethics – theology and ethics, to be meaningful, must lead to praxis.

At the end of his book McDaniel offers the metaphor for God he feels is most helpful: God as Heart (1989:140–5). This is an image of God as the centre of the vital functions of the universe, the core of things, but also the centre of the feelings of sympathy, understanding and compassion. McDaniel's incorporations into a process-based scheme lead to an attractive model, but one which has still to meet fundamental criticisms of process thought, of which we now address three.

8.5.3 Fundamental criticisms of process thought

(i) Is dipolarity in God coherent and theologically productive? For a fierce critique see Clark, 1993:72–88, for a more careful analysis of alternatives see Fiddes, 1988:111f.

A Possible Response: It is difficult to escape the conviction that the God of the Bible has at one and the same time two types of attributes which must be held in tension, being both unchanging in character and purpose, *and* also deeply influenced by real personal relationships with humans. (See Model G, Section **8.5.10**, also Polkinghorne, 2004:105–13.)

(ii) Is the attribution of experience to the smallest entities, 'panpsychism', or more helpfully 'panexperientialism', at all meaningful?

A Possible Response: Fiddes may be correct (in the passage quoted above) in supposing that some such postulate, however difficult to articulate or substantiate, is necessary. Within a biblical theology of creation it is hard to escape the notion that the stuff of the universe is at the very least *responsive* to God (cf. Ps. 19.1; Ps. 104.27–30). See also **8.5.9**.

(iii) Is the process God enough of a God? Hartshorne has insisted that his God could be the God who raised Jesus from the dead, but the general tenor of process thought is that God and the cosmos co-develop without any guaranteed grounds for belief in God's ultimate victory over evil. It is not immediately clear how such a scheme would be reconciled with contemporary cosmological predictions about the end of the present universe, which are that either a 'Big Crunch' or an infinite expansion will eventually lead to a state quite incompatible with life.

A Possible Response: Process eschatology emphasizes the role of the divine memory. 'Our lives are meaningful because they are preserved everlastingly in God's experience, in which evil is transmuted and the good is saved and woven into the harmony of the larger whole' (Barbour, 1998:304). And since the matter of the present universe will not indefinitely support life, all eschatological schemes must depend on *some* category of existence within God (see 7.7). We take up questions of eschatology in 10.20.

8.5.4 Model C: Sallie McFague in *The Body of God* (1993)

McFague sets out first of all what she calls 'the common creation story', the account science gives us of our origins over the (approximately) 15-billion-year history of the cosmos (1993:41–2). This is, she claims, the narrative that binds all human cultures and traditions together. Nevertheless this story does not tell us how to think about ourselves in the world of the ecological crisis. It does not of itself promote 'sustainability and livability' (1993:68). Nor can the scientific narrative speak of purposes, divine or human. In the light of the use of earlier God-language for purposes of oppression we have to devise new metaphors (as McDaniel does with 'God as Heart', and as McFague did in her earlier book *Models of God* (1987), writing of God as 'Mother, Lover, Friend'). McFague explores the viability of the metaphor of the world as God's body, a 'remythologisation' with 'ethical or pragmatic concern' (1993:81) which she hopes can link the scientific narrative with the data of Christian revelation.

Again, note the nature of this approach, which emphasizes the pragmatic, the practical, the concrete, a tradition which McFague traces back to Aristotle (as opposed to the disembodied, static and absolute propositional truths of Plato). This pragmatic approach might seem to fit well with the concerns of feminism and other theologies of liberation. However, Daphne Hampson has criticized McFague's model-making as being no more than a dressed-up form of humanism, noting that 'The construction of models of God is predicated upon what one construes to be evidence for belief in God ... [McFague's] work lacks talk of such evidence' (Hampson, 1990:161). *But for McFague our function as humans is not to think true thoughts about abstractions, but 'to live appropriately and responsibly'* (McFague, 1993:89). She advocates 'attention epistemology' (1993:49), paying attention to 'inscape' – to other things in themselves and for themselves – this has similarities to McDaniel's talk of 'suchness' and to the thought of Martin Buber (for McDaniel's model see 8.5.2; for its connection to Buddhist concepts of 'suchness' see 9.6.1; on Buber and McFague see 9.2). When we pay attention to the planet we can see that it is vulnerable and fragile, and, moreover, not a hotel but our home.

Humans are seen, in this model, as utterly dependent on other parts of the 'body', and not by any means the only locus of value, but having a special role as those who know 'the common creation story', 'like it or not, the guardians and caretakers of our tiny planet' (McFague, 1993:109). It is idle to deny the differences that exist between species. Sin is defined, not as in most Christian theology in terms of deviation from the loving purpose of God, but as refusal to accept our place in the network of (embodied) relationships that is the planetary ecosystem.[17]

One recent criticism of McFague is that she does not tell the common creation story in a sufficiently Darwinian way – she is not honest enough about the competitive character of the creation (see Sideris, 2003:ch. 2 – also **10.18**).

God is understood as embodied like ourselves, as the 'prime and prior psychosomatic unity', but divine action is not only 'organic', as of the self in the body, but also 'agential', as of spirit in body. (The difficulty of this language will be evident – we cannot give a clear scientific account of what conscious agency is, still less is it easy to agree to what it might mean to be moved by spirit.) This model like the previous two is panentheistic – *the universe as God's body enlivened and empowered by the divine spirit*. McFague regards this as a model both commensurate with the scientific data, and able 'to help us to act holistically' (1993:147). Science has been used to help rule out some models, such as God as monarchical father, but is not used to try and 'rule any models in'.

Rather the traditional Jewish and Christian motif of the special concern of God for the weak and the oppressed is invoked in respect of both humanity and the non-human creation.[18]

Both the phrases italicized above, 'the universe as God's body' and 'enlivened and empowered by the divine spirit' cause McFague problems:

(a) The analogy with our own embodiedness is weakened by the fact that our 'selves' are inextricably dependent on our lower functions, from which they have arisen through evolution, whereas God for McFague is 'embodied, but not necessarily or totally' (1993:150). Polkinghorne has criticized such models on the grounds that 'the body of God' is always too much in thrall either to God or to the world (1989:18–23).

(b) The divine spirit is not identified with the Holy Spirit, except in relation to human beings. This tends to complicate the model without escaping the theodicy problems of evolutionary creation (see **10.18– 10.19**).

8.5.5 Model D: Rosemary Radford Ruether in *Gaia*[19] *and God* (1992)

Ruether's book is chiefly remarkable for the quality of its analysis of our difficulty in framing an ecological theology. She warns against trying to derive ethics purely from spirituality, which she says will tend to be a 'privatized intrapsychic activity' (1992:4) or simply trying to replace a male, transcendent deity with a female, immanent one. Rather it is important to realize how much our reception of the Hebrew accounts of creation has been influenced by Greek motifs – two in particular:

(i) the myth in Plato's *Timaeus* that the soul is a principle which aspires to become detached from its present, corrupt body;

(ii) cosmologies where the Earth is the lowest, most corrupt point (see 1.12). (Ruether, 1992:27–8)

It is easy to see how these motifs would work against our valuation of the material world.

EXERCISE 8.2

Look at the creation narratives in Genesis 1–2 and identify elements of the stories which might reinforce the motifs listed in 8.5.5, and elements which might suggest a different valuation of matter.

The ambivalence towards matter in the Christian tradition is further complicated by the New Testament emphasis on the 'Fall' of humanity (derived from Genesis 3), from which we are rescued by Christ. Humanity is somehow to blame for the world as it is, and is in need of rescue from that world; not even 'the forces that govern the universe' (Rom. 8.38, Cassirer's translation) can keep us from this rescuing love.

However, Ruether is not as naive about these 'forces' as some writers on eco-spirituality. She recognizes that the natural world was not originally benign for humans and is not capable of fulfilling our hopes for the good. Our impulse to loving care for others stands out from our mortal limits. We can promote this – to a certain extent we can even reshape the world towards this impulse, but only within the constraints imposed on us by our mortality and by the interdependence of all organisms. Ecological ethics, then, will be an 'uneasy synthesis' between 'the laws of consciousness and kindness' and 'the laws of Gaia' (Ruether, 1992:31).

Along with our impulse to kindness goes our experience that things are not as they should be, a sense of sin. Some of which, Ruether points out, is a function of humans' drive to make their own environment more favourable to their interests (a drive which of course has been, in evolutionary terms, vastly successful). But there remains a truth that our relationships to each other and to the non-human world do tend to become distorted; we assert our rights to life and power as absolutes at the expense of other beings. There are clear parallels with McFague's definition of sin (see 8.5.4 above). Ruether advocates that instead we recognize that all beings are 'covenantally related' – 'one family united by one source of life' (1992:227).[20] As we seem to be in some sense 'the "mind" of the universe, the place where the universe becomes conscious of itself' (1992:249) it is 'our urgent task to understand the web of life and live within that web as sustainers rather than destroyers' (1992:250), not absolutizing the good but recognizing that it means living within limits.

Much of Ruether's diagnosis of our crisis and the constraints that hold us back from engaging with it is very cogent, but there is a striking absence of any clear doctrine of God. The 'voices ... of God and Gaia ... are our own voices ... not in the sense that there is "nothing" out there, but in the sense that what is "out there" can only be experienced by us through the lenses of human existence ... We can ... intuit *the source of all life and thought that lies behind the whole* [our italics]. This contact, though humanly imaged, can be true. Its truth lies in the test of relationships; do our metaphors bear the fruits of compassion or of enmity?' (1992:254–5). Note again the pragmatism of the approach – theology is being tested by the ethics to which it gives rise. Insofar as there is God-talk it is of an implicitly emanationist kind: the divine is the source and matrix of what is (see the words italicized in the last quotation), but in no sense either ontologically distinct from the cosmos, or an agent within it. Ruether does approach language of a personal God when she writes:

> As we gaze into the void of our future extinguished self and dissolving substance, we encounter there the wellspring of life and creativity from which all things have sprung and into which they return, only to well up again in new forms. But we also know this as the great Thou, the personal center of the universal process, with which all the small centers of personal being dialogue. (1992:253)[21]

This is not so far from the language of a more traditional Christian theist, Keith Ward, in this passage:

> It is not that the infinite is really a person, who thinks and feels, wonders whether to create a universe, makes moral decisions, feels lonely and would like to have some friends, and wonders whether we will love God or not. It is rather that the infinite relates to us in a personal way, contracting infinity to finite form in order to bring us and all creatures capable of it to moral and intellectual maturity and lead our finite lives into fulfilling relationship with their infinite source and good. (2003:232)

For some, however, Ruether's God-talk is reconstructionist[22] – it discards too much in terms of the Christian understanding of God as personal agent to be regarded as grounded within the Christian tradition. By others it will be seen as illustrative of a key revision that disentangles God from the language of power and patriarchal oppression.

8.5.6 Model E: Jürgen Moltmann in *God in Creation* (1985)

There is, however, a significant body of theological work trying to frame Christian theology which is responsive to the ecological crisis and to feminist critique, but within a more traditionally Trinitarian framework than we have yet discussed, with the incarnation of Jesus Christ being seen as central. Moltmann has been a most eloquent exponent of this type of approach.[23] His greatest contribution has been in stressing the real suffering and chaos to which God the Trinity is exposed at the Cross (see his *The Crucified God* (1974)). He is also a great exponent of the theology of kenotic creation – God as limiting God's self in allowing creation existence and freedom to develop.[24]

Moltmann's most controversial use of this motif is in the image he uses for the first creative impulse of a Trinity which he describes in terms of a self-sufficient community of love from all eternity. In order that there *be* any other entities whatsoever the Trinity had to withdraw from a certain ontological space, to allow a primordial element of non-being. For this self-withdrawal Moltmann borrows

Luria's term *zimsum*, connoting a process of 'concentration and contraction ... a withdrawing of oneself into oneself. An inversion of God ... sets free a kind of "mystical primordial space" into which God can ... enter and in which he can manifest himself ... Here we have an act in which Nothingness is called forth' (Moltmann, 1985:87). This is attractive in terms of Genesis 1.2, which pictures a pre-creation state having some existence but 'without form and void' – also in that it sees 'letting be' as an intrinsic element in God's creative activity. Such a description of creation will be particularly consonant with scientific descriptions of the universe developing through the interplay of chance and physical law. (But see below for some criticisms of Moltmann's formulations.)

God's initial kenotic self-withdrawal leads for Moltmann to a whole series of divine self-limitations, including the creation of humans bearing God's image, and the call and election of Abraham, and culminating in the divine Son going silent to the most degrading of executions. Cross and resurrection inaugurate a new age in which evolution is *redeemed* through God's preferential love for the weak and the oppressed. (Moltmann makes this clear only in his later book *The Way of Jesus Christ* where in an important passage he takes issue with Teilhard and Rahner for interpreting the future unfolding of evolution as a *working-out* of Christ's purposes (Moltmann, 1990:292–306).) Again we see, as with McDaniel and McFague, a theologian needing to introduce an extra category of divine–human interaction – be it redemption, resurrection, or pelican heaven – beyond what parallels an evolutionary account.

Moltmann's kenotic scheme, panentheistic like Pailin's, McDaniel's and McFague's, embraces some of the advantages of both classical and process schemes. He criticizes Whitehead for making the world process co-eternal with God – and hence, in effect, itself an attribute of the ultimate. For Moltmann the world arises out of and is utterly dependent upon the love of the Trinity. But the development of the world is accomplished through the persuasive and sacrificial love of God, the God who became the Crucified One and works now through the Holy Spirit, in part within the fallible functioning of the Christian Church.

At the same time Moltmann is much firmer than any process theologian about the eventual consummation of all things in the kingdom of glory. The Sabbath, God's rest within God's creation, a concept so much neglected in Christian practice, is both the crown of creation and the foretaste of the ultimate harmony of all things at the eschaton. Some other emphases in Moltmann's ecological theology include:

(i) What can be known by us is only ever partial; we need to restore a belief in *heaven*, the unseen reality (1985:39), the 'side of creation that is open to God' (1985:163).[25] It is the kingdom of God's *energeiai*, God's 'energies'.[26]

(ii) We perceive creation not as 'very good' (Gen. 1.31) but as 'groaning in expectation' (Romans 8.19–21). 'To understand "nature" as creation therefore means discerning "nature" as the enslaved creation that hopes for liberty.' Anyone who understands this 'begins to suffer with that creation, and also to hope for it' (Moltmann, 1985:39).

(iii) Just as the Earth is thermodynamically an open system – that is to say that it receives energy from the outside, from the sun, and also gives off energy into space – so we may picture the whole universe as an open system, in communication with the 'extra-worldly encompassing milieu' of God (1985:205). And only an open system can give rise to true novelty, or experience real transformation.

Moltmann's is a powerful and persuasive model, reviewed by Bauckham (1987). Three principal criticisms can be levelled at his scheme.

8.5.7 Criticisms of Moltmann

(i) The first is a general problem with all schemes which invoke a Cross-inaugurated redemption – simply that there is so little evidence that the two thousand years since the Cross of Christ have really been transformative of human nature, or even that the Christian Church could be said to be in the forefront of what transformation there has been. Moltmann writes in fine terms of the coming kingdom, but the signs of hope and liberation for the world are few. (Hence the lure of a process scheme, or one which regards the project of redemption as still in its earliest evolutionary stages.)

(ii) The second criticism of Moltmann is that talk of *zimsum*, which forms a perfectly coherent part of Jewish Neoplatonic thought, seems at odds with the scepticism Moltmann expresses elsewhere about speculative metaphysics. And *zimsum* does raise a deep question: how *can* the all-sufficient, all-encompassing Trinity give rise to 'an annihilating Nothingness' (Moltmann, 1985:88)?

(iii) The third objection to the scheme of the writer of *The Crucified God* is that the focus of God's suffering concern for the world is so much the historical events of Incarnation and Cross. Fiddes writes: 'Clearly, if God suffers universally, we cannot speak of the being of God as first becoming suffering love at the cross. God must always have been so' (1988:7).

This leads us to the next of our models of the relationships between the divine, humans and the non-human world which start from within the Christian tradition.

8.5.8 Model F: Paul Fiddes in *The Creative Suffering of God* (1988)

This is a dense study of the coherence of the concept of kenotic creation. Fiddes rejects process thinking as making creativity the supreme value by which even God is constrained. He wants to retain a theology of God's willing the creation (and his suffering within it), but he pursues the question of the reality of change and suffering in God further than Moltmann. Further even in a sense than the process theologians, since Fiddes rejects dipolarity (1988:110–11, see 8.2.1) – his

God therefore has no perfect pole on which to fall back. Suffering is not merely an inward action of God, it is something that *happens to* the deity, something by which God is really changed (1988:62–3), something, indeed, which makes God more truly God. The world is therefore necessary to God (albeit through God's own choice). God both chooses God's self as Father, Son and Spirit, and chooses to come to fulfilment through free, open, vulnerable relation to humankind. Fiddes' contention is that these are one and the same choice.

At the same time a model of the Christian God must promise *victory* over suffering, 'he should not be overcome or defeated by suffering' (1988:100). Fiddes thus draws back from W.H. Vanstone's radical account of God's risk in *Love's Endeavour, Love's Expense*; God's risk in creation is a limited risk, because ultimately God *will* be all in all. But the character of God's eventual glory depends on the experience God shares with the creation, on a real exchange of feelings between persons.

Fiddes' main emphases, then, are twofold:

- every element in God's creative work has involved God's self-limiting and suffering love – vulnerable encounter with a creation which has some autonomy and displays some resistance to the divine will;
- the nature of God's internal nature and God's relationship with persons is one of real mutual exchange, best characterized in terms of Trinity rather than the language of process.

8.5.9 Further thoughts on fallenness and resistance in creation

To explore this further we return to the passage from Fiddes that we quoted in discussing Pailin's model – 'Some overall vision of the "responsiveness" and "resistance" of creation to the Spirit of God is needed for a doctrine of creative evolution, (and) for a proper theodicy . . .' (Fiddes, 1988:228). Fiddes is arguing that we must speak of some sort of 'free will in creation', of resistance and responsiveness, if we are to speak of God suffering in creation. This taps into Fiddes' conclusion that suffering must be something that befalls God, not a mere logical outworking of the divine plan.

This language of freely chosen resistance, and of suffering that befalls God outside the divine plan, needs further exploration, particularly in the case where it is being applied outside the sphere of human choices. The sort of creation that this is presumably *is* very much part of God's plan. Indeed it is a creation, according to St Paul in Romans 8, subjected to travail by God in order that eventually it may achieve the glorious liberty of the children of God. The language of resistance used to be expressed in the idea that the non-human creation had 'fallen' through human action at a given moment in our history. As we saw in 6.3.2, no such moment of transformation of the creation can be supported from our scientific understandings. Rather it seems clear that the non-human world has been a world of struggle and competition ever since life evolved. Fallenness is a useful short-hand description of the selfishness and violence of so much freely chosen human action, but is not appropriate to the 'travail' of non-human creation.

Instead we suggest first that the sort of universe we have, in which complexity emerges in a process governed by thermodynamic necessity and Darwinian natural selection, is the only sort of universe that could give rise to freely choosing self-conscious beings; and second that such beings are a goal of God's creation.

To realize this goal God must therefore encounter the contingency and struggle of creatures' being creatures and not-being-God. Just as the Cross, in Christian tradition, is part of God's plan (so Revelation 13.8), as the only way to bring all creation to its ultimate fulfilment, so it is part of God's plan that God encounter and bear the self-seeking and communion-denying elements in what it is to be a Darwinian creature. Immanent in all things, God must be exposed to what it is for creatures to 'be themselves', indeed to become 'selves' in the only way Darwinian creatures can, by defending their interests against competing interests. Too often theologians have adopted the description of 'fallenness' derived from a reading of Genesis 3, and then mapped this in a vague way onto the non-human creation. Process thought too uses an anthropomorphic account of the experience of all creatures. What we are endeavouring to explore here is an analysis of 'responsiveness and resistance' in terms of biological descriptions of creatures. Human selving/selfishness is only a special case of a more general picture. Every living thing has interests which it pursues,[27] indeed this is a way of defining life. This 'selving' can also be understood in biosemiotic terms (see Robinson, 2004). Von Balthasar places this tension between createdness and self-interest within a Trinitarian frame: 'The creature's No, its wanting to be autonomous without acknowledging its origin, must be located within the Son's all-embracing Yes to the Father, in the Spirit' (quoted in Fiddes, 2000:184). This formulation brings us close to the process understanding of entities' competing for fulfilment, but because we apply it in biological terms (only to living organisms and not to all entities) we bring our formulation into dialogue with the scientific narrative. All creatures are in relation to God by virtue of being creatures, *and* seek to be themselves. The 'travail' of this will only be resolved when God restores the life of those creatures in a new way at the eschaton (see **10.20**).

8.5.10 Model G: Keith Ward in *Religion and Creation* (1996)

Keith Ward provides our third Trinitarian model. His work is informed by Thomism (the system derived from Aquinas), by contemporary science, by process thought and by the theology of Barth.

In Parts III and IV of *Religion and Creation* Ward offers an important philosophical analysis of how Trinitarian faith can be combined with an account of God as active in the world the sciences describe. Ward starts from classical Western Christian formulations of the ways in which God can be described – for example Aquinas' description of God as the most perfect possible being, and Anselm's principle that God must possess every property which it is better to possess than not. But he succeeds in developing these in a direction so lacking in Augustinian–Thomist thought – towards a God who acts responsively in time to make possible the realization of values within the creation which could not have existed had creation not taken place.

Ward wrestles long and hard with the question of whether God necessarily creates. Fiddes, anxious to distance himself from too process-dominated a view, took the line that God can *choose* whether the world be necessary to God (Fiddes, 1988:135). Ward rejects that as incoherent. After some discussion he comes to the view that 'some disposition to creative activity and loving fellowship, necessarily actualized at some time, is necessary to God being what God is' (Ward, 1996a:320). This necessary disposition does not, however, generate a scheme in which the cosmos is co-eternal with God – Ward's model of creation remains *ex nihilo*, by the Father through the Son in the power of the Spirit.[28]

As was mentioned above, Ward sees dipolarity in God as a helpful insight from process thought which can be incorporated into a more traditionally Christian scheme. He discusses John Macquarrie's 'triadic' distinction in the divine nature – as primordial, expressive and unitive. But he demurs from Macquarrie's equation of these 'poles' with the persons of the Trinity. Ward has a yet grander scheme which might be called 'tetrapolar' – God is at one and the same time eternal-primordial, originative-expressive, historical-responsive and eschatological-unitive (1996a:338) – and in *each* of these God can be seen as constituted as Trinity. This is a remarkable fusion of the thought-worlds of Aquinas, Barth and Hartshorne, earthed in Ward's sense that all Trinitarian thought arises from the divine self-disclosure in the events of the New Testament.

Interestingly an article by Janet Martin Soskice (Soskice, 1998) on the naming of God stresses the same objective we see lying behind Ward's study. Soskice points out how the extent to which late twentieth-century theologians have abandoned 'the God of the attributes' – omnipotent, eternal, immutable – as 'remote and unfeeling'.[29] But she holds to the importance of not jettisoning *either* the philosophical basis of Christian theism in the utter transcendence, omnipotence and omniscience of God (towards which the tradition of negative or apophatic theology (see 1.18) makes such an important contribution) *or* the biblical conviction that God has acted and will act in the lives of human beings – that God has met us and given us names for the divine self. *Both* sets of motifs are strong in Christian revelation, reflection and worship – also in such seminal accounts of religious experience as Augustine's *Confessions*. So it is for such a fusion that a Christian model of God (containing always a measure of the unsayable) must search.

8.6 Recurrent motifs

We review now some of the key themes involved in these theological revisions and reconstructions. We have noted *the sensitivities to the language of patriarchy, power and control* that stem alike from feminist and ecological concerns and from post-modern suspicion that such language always offers a licence to oppress. We have noted also *sensitivity to the huge suffering of humanity in the twentieth century*. We have noted two types of response:

> (a) construction of a new range of metaphors for God – as Mother, Lover and Friend, as the One whose body is the world (McFague), as Heart

(McDaniel), as the matrix of all the creative energies of life (Ruether), and (much earlier, perhaps partly as a response to the suffering of the First World War) God as the fellow-sufferer who understands (Whitehead). This type of metaphorical theology begs the question as to the status of the metaphor – is it an opening to explore new possibilities in worship and prayer, is it a pragmatic device to enable us to frame new ethics, is it part of an attempted reconstruction of faith, because traditional resources are thought to have failed us? And what controls are appropriate to place on the range of metaphors used? How much continuity with the tradition should be required?

(b) re-systematizing of Christian thought around a scheme with very many classical elements, but making a major change in a particular area. This is related to Santmire's idea of revisionism (8.1). The key changes we have seen are:

   (i) exploration of panentheism, a 'metaphor with staying power' in McFague's phrase (see 1.9), which stresses God's immanent involvement in the world, but at the risk of not doing justice to the ontological divide between God and the world on which Christian theology has always insisted;

   (ii) exploration of kenosis, divine self-emptying, not just in the incarnation and passion of Christ but as a way also of understanding God's creative activity. This is in contrast to the classical understanding that God creates out of God's power and fullness.

   (iii) Closely allied to (ii), exploration of God's co-suffering with the world, in contrast to the classical understanding that God as God does not suffer.

We now explore two important collections of essays, the first on panentheism (Clayton and Peacocke (eds), 2004), the second on kenosis as creation (Polkinghorne (ed.), 2001) – as a way of evaluating these revisions.

8.6.1 Perspectives on panentheism

The book *In Whom We Live and Move and Have Our Being*, edited by Clayton and Peacocke (2004), is a major survey of the project of panentheism, drawing on the views of major proponents of the view and cautious critics, and including important perspectives from the Eastern Orthodox tradition. We now explore this survey – all references to authors and page numbers in this section are to contributions to Clayton and Peacocke (2004) unless otherwise stated.

Panentheism, as we saw in 8.5.1, may be defined with deceptive simplicity. The world is in God, but God is more than the world. So much turns, however, on how the spatial metaphor 'in' or 'within' is conceived. We raised above the question as to whether this formulation says more than that God profoundly transcends the creation, and yet is intimately immanent to every entity within it. Niels Gregersen points out that classical theism is not necessarily weak on immanence, giving examples from Aquinas. Indeed as Kallistos Ware observes, even Islam, in which the transcendence of the deity is often thought of as extreme, also teaches that the deity is nearer to the believer than his or her own jugular vein (see our Chapter 12). Ware does concede that since the seventeenth century the balance of Christian thought has leaned too much on God's transcendence. 'Above and beyond creation, God is also its true inwardness' (Clayton and Peacocke, 2004:159).

Arthur Peacocke offers a characteristically resolute defence of panentheism. He points out that, increasingly, scientific narratives offer a seamless continuity of description of the world. Rather than suggesting that God's activity is an abrogation of this law-governed naturalistic account, he advocates that we see God as 'the immanent creator creating in and through the processes of the natural order' (p. xx). Panentheism, for Peacocke, is the scheme that retains the ultimate ontological divide between God and creation but offers this intensified order of intimacy. He draws on a range of sources to defend the model: he quotes Acts 17.28 (which furnishes the title of the book); he cites Augustine's great phrase in *Confessions* 7 about the whole creation as 'some sponge, huge but bounded . . . filled with that unmeasurable sea' (of God); he draws on the *zimsum* model used by Moltmann (see **8.5.6**).

Eastern Orthodox understandings have stimulated Western-theological understandings in a number of areas. Christopher Knight quotes the understanding that creation *ex nihilo* is creation out of the depths of God's uncreated energies and possibilities, which implies a form of panentheism. Ware sees God as creating out of God's self-diffusive love — this links divine transcendence and immanence.

The 'in'/'within' metaphor is explored by Knight, who notes that it is problematically static; by Clayton, who notes that a precise formulation is elusive, and offers thirteen possible senses in which it could be understood (p. 253); and by Ruth Page, who prefers the companioning preposition 'with', a 'pansyntheistic' model (p. 228, see **10.18**).[30]

A key emphasis in panentheism is that creation and God have an impact on one another (so Denis Edwards' essay, running counter to Aquinas and most of the Christian tradition. This view leads naturally to models of divine co-suffering with creation and divine self-limitation that novelty may emerge within creation.)

Lastly, it is worth noting with David Ray Griffin that panentheism fits neatly with process thought (pp. 36–47), and that it has been resolutely opposed by (for example) Colin Gunton, 2001, and Polkinghorne, 2004:94–8.

The conclusion to which we are drawn is that the metaphor on which panentheism is based taps into a deeply important range of theological instincts, from Luke's in Acts 17 through Orthodox and ecological instincts to Peacocke's scientific naturalism. However, efforts to systematize it as an account of God's relation to the cosmos in the present, as opposed to an 'eschatological hope of a sacramental panentheism' (Polkinghorne, 2004:166) seem to fall short of the adequate (at least unless a process metaphysic has already been subscribed to).

We turn now to a closely related motif, that of divine kenosis.

8.6.2 Perspectives on divine kenosis and divine suffering, particularly in relation to creation

The book *The Work of Love: Creation as Kenosis* (Polkinghorne (ed.), 2001) was inspired in particular by the writings of Moltmann and the Anglican priest-theologian W.H. Vanstone (1924–99).[31] It takes forward the work of Moltmann (8.5.6), Fiddes (8.5.8) and Ward (8.5.10) in this area, and includes contributions from Peacocke, Polkinghorne, George Ellis and Sarah Coakley. All references to authors and page numbers in this section are to Polkinghorne (ed.), 2001 unless otherwise stated.

Moltmann discusses the way von Balthasar extends kenosis from the incarnate Christ into the whole of the life of the Trinity. It is of the essential nature of the divine Son, from all eternity, to be obedient in love and self-surrender, and of the Father to communicate himself to the Son in complete love. 'Kenotic self-surrender is God's Trinitarian nature, and is therefore the mark of all his works "outwards" (the creation, reconciliation, and redemption of all things)' (pp. 140–1).

Polkinghorne offers a helpful fourfold scheme of kenosis:

(a) kenosis of omnipotence – the divine allowing of the creation to be and to act;

(b) kenosis of eternity – God allows God's self a temporal pole which is responsive, in a way appropriate to the character of creation at that time;

(c) kenosis of omniscience – even God does not know a future which has not yet become;

(d) kenosis of causal status – God allowing divine special providence (see our Chapter 10) to 'act as a cause among causes' (p. 104), to allow providential and creaturely causalities to become interwoven. This happens most dramatically at the Incarnation.

In a careful analysis Ward argues in the converse direction – divine omniscience must mean what it says. The fact of pain and the affect of pain must be known by God. Kenotic creation, a giving-up of control to allow creatures full richness of experience, is not just a self-giving but a self-realization, which adds a new and distinctive value to the divine being. God, entering into real relationship with creation, suffers new things, and also delights in new things. Kenosis leads to enosis – God entering into the being of those who freely consent, and finally to theosis, those beings sharing in the divine life.

This is delicate ground, as David Ford commented in reviewing Fiddes' *The Creative Suffering of God*. 'God freely chooses to undergo suffering for the sake of his creation, and there is risk and uncertainty for him in this, but it is never hopeless suffering. The obvious problem here is that God is excluded from one of the most acute forms of human suffering, that of despair, and so the whole enterprise of his solidarity with humanity seems to break down' (Ford, 1990:317). The middle road between:

(i) God not genuinely affected by suffering

and

(ii) God so immured in suffering as not to be able to guarantee our hope

is very hard to walk. Perhaps Moltmann's strategy in *The Crucified God* of focusing the whole of divine suffering on the Cross of Christ, and seeing there despair, alienation and death entering the inner life of the Trinity, remains the best one. The theologian's task is then to find ways to associate all suffering, past, present and future, with the Cross, and the Resurrection. What all these theological formulations of the kenotic, suffering God stress, in different ways, is that divine suffering is not merely passive but transformative. As Fiddes puts it: 'the story of Jesus, and especially his death and resurrection, assures us that there is no greater power in the universe than empathetic love ... God will fulfil God's own purposes, not *despite* the suffering of love, but *through* it' (pp. 189–90, italics in original).

It is important to note reservations about the whole theological movement of associating kenosis with creation, and asserting the suffering of God. Sarah Coakley points out that Aquinas was familiar with the theological problems of suffering, cosmology and human freedom, and still formulated a model of God based on attributes of omnipotence, omniscience, impassibility, etc. (see Coakley, 2001; McCabe, 1987:ch. 4).[32] As McCabe shows, it is most important to understand these statements about divine attributes correctly – they are not positive statements, but negative, apophatic formulations: 'perishability, decline, dependence, alteration, the impersonality that characterizes material things, and so on – all these have to be excluded from God' (1987:41). Thomas Weinandy has made a further attempt to reassert the classical doctrine of the inability of God to suffer (Weinandy, 2000). In essence Weinandy's point is the same as McCabe's – the story of Jesus the Crucified One is 'the projection of the Trinitarian life of God on the rubbish dump we have made of the world' (McCabe, 1987:48). God does not suffer change, because what we see in the Incarnation is God's eternal nature. Peters and Hewlett question whether it is coherent for proponents of kenosis in creation to speak both of God's self-limitation and of God's suffering with the creation (2003:142–3).[33]

It should be clear that these discussions return us to the question of the 'poles' of the divine nature. There are those who stress the unchangingness of this nature, and that all that happens happens out of the inexhaustible eternal fund of the triune God's loving will. There are those who say – for a variety of reasons – that we must include description of God's responsiveness to the world in its actual flow of its temporality. God lets the world happen to God and thereby transforms the world, but also experiences new levels of self-realization.

In recognizing the tension between these views it is also important to recognize the strengths of each position.

8.6.3 Some recent contributions from evangelical theology

In the 1999 edition we questioned the extent of evangelical thought's engagement with ecological themes. What contributions did exist were sometimes mere 'apologist' restatements of the resources of biblical Christianity, not nuanced in the light of the problematics we have noted in this chapter. It is a pleasure to note significant recent contributions by Alister McGrath and R.J. Berry. McGrath has produced in remarkably short order (among other works) a book laying groundwork in science and religion (1998), a systematic trilogy in the area (2001; 2002; 2003a) and a summary of the same (2004) – also *The Re-enchantment of Nature* (2003b), looking at how underlying views of nature inform attitudes to ecological concern.[34] R.J. Berry's Gifford Lectures, published as *God's Book of Works* (2003), tie natural theology and ecological concern to Berry's experience of working with various declarations and statements on environmental matters. In *The Care of Creation* (Berry, 2000) he edits a set of essays commenting on *The Evangelical Declaration on the Care of Creation* (1994). This Declaration was produced in response to documents from the World Council of Churches that many evangelicals considered a vitiation of the distinctiveness of human beings (see e.g. Berry, 2000:43f.). Much discussion of the Declaration turns on whether humans can properly be regarded as stewards of creation.

The concept of stewardship is affirmed in recent major documents in both the evangelical and the catholic traditions (for references to these see McGrath, 2003b; Berry, 2003). Yet it has been subject to some vigorous attacks, such as Clare Palmer's denunciation of stewardship as being (in the sense in which it is popularly used) unbiblical (Palmer, 1992). Richard Bauckham confirms that the explicit understanding within the Christian tradition that humans are stewards of nature dates only to the seventeenth century (Bauckham, 2000). Anne Primavesi, writing from an ecofeminist perspective, condemns the concept of stewardship as exploitative and unecological (Primavesi, 1991:106–7). Sean McDonagh is concerned that 'within the context of this analogy the earth is reified and becomes either inert property to be cared for or financial resources to be managed in a way that gives a good return on the investment' (McDonagh, 1994:130). Edward Echlin claims that stewardship 'easily lends itself to a detached and manipulative view of creation' and that it 'has not moved hearts' (Echlin, 2004:16).

Clearly then this formulation, and behind it certain ways of expressing human distinctiveness and vocation, is under challenge. For a discussion of the relation of stewardship to Philip Hefner's created-co-creator understanding of humans,[35] and to more biocentric approaches, see Southgate (2005, forthcoming). For other appraisals of stewardship see a further volume edited by Berry (2005, forthcoming).

8.7 Conclusion

We have seen a range of ways in which Christian theologians have endeavoured to respond to vital challenges to the understanding of God.[36] We also saw how involved this discussion becomes. We would look to see development of these lines of thought in the direction of theological anthropology: what exactly, given our evolutionary origins (see 6.3.1–6.3.2), *is* this humankind with which God desires special fellowship, and what, in the light of the models of God being proposed, are the ethical (human-world) implications of human nature? A more problematic area still is that of developing a language for speaking of the non-human creation in relation to God, once notions of a human-caused 'fall' are set aside.

Notes

1   On Moltmann see Deane-Drummond, 1997c (also Bauckham, 1987, for a summary of Moltmann's thought up to 1986).

2   For a critical evaluation of Pannenberg's use of the biological and human sciences from philosophical and theological perspectives as well as from the scientific context, see Stewart, 2000.

3   See Webster (1986) for a summary.

4   See Di Noia (1997) for an introduction, also Dyck (1992).

5   See Oakes and Moss (2004).

6   We touch in 14.7(vii), 14.9(iv) on another important development, the growth of liberation theology (itself an influence on Moltmann, McFague and Ruether – see the sections following).

7   It is sometimes supposed that because Whitehead formulated his metaphysics at the time of the great developments in physics known as the second quantum revolution (Schrödinger's Equation was published in 1926, Heisenberg's Uncertainty Principle in 1927 (see 5.11)) and because both process thought and quantum theory require a somewhat unusual way of looking at the world, that therefore process schemes are particularly compatible with the new physics. But see Polkinghorne, 1994:22–3 against this view.

8   Keith Ward wants to propose a different type of theism (see 8.5.10), but sees clearly the helpfulness of dipolarity. He writes: 'The basic idea of divine dipolarity, with its associated place for temporality and possibility in God, may survive dissociation from general process metaphysics' (1996a:308).

9   See Barbour (2002); Birch and Cobb (1981); McDaniel (1989).

10   In a sense both feminist and ecological critiques of traditional formulations of Christianity are varieties of the suspicion of the 'motives' of master-narratives that is a characteristic of postmodern thought. To simplify enormously, this suspicion holds that all stories are in some respects told to serve the interests of the tellers. The New Testament texts on limiting the ministry of women can certainly be read in this way. See Walter Brueggemann's work for an effort to 'retrieve' the scriptures in full awareness of postmodernism (Brueggemann, 1993). Also see the Foreword to this volume on postmodernism and post-foundationalism.

11   See also 2.3.2. It is not hard to find biblical texts to support this: two prominent texts on human domination are Gen. 1.26, 28 and Ps. 8.6–8. Note however Brueggemann's point on Psalm 8 – that the dominion given to humans is framed in the context of doxology, the glorifying of God (Brueggemann, 1984:37–8).

12   Those referring to Northcott should note that instead of 'anthropocentric' he uses the more etymologically correct but less common term 'humanocentric'.

13   This claim has been made more recently, in a secular context, for so-called free-market economics.

14   See 1998:109, 113, for the emphases Barbour suggests are important in applying these criteria to the assessment of particular beliefs within a religion.

15   This question is especially important in 'green' theological thinking. Many fine-sounding schemes based on the radical equality of all species are questionably relevant to any real situation.

16 McDaniel's approach to animal rights is founded not on Andrew Linzey's approach, which seeks to accord 'theos-rights' to creatures (Linzey, 1994) or on Peter Singer's utilitarianism (Singer, 1990) but on Tom Regan's assertion that to be 'the subject of a life' is a sufficient criterion for the possession of moral rights (see e.g. Regan, 1990:73–87). For a summary of Singer and Regan, and a comparison with process thought as a basis for ethics, see Armstrong-Buck (1986), or more accessibly Northcott (1996:93–102, 146–7). Clare Palmer (1998) explores process thought as a basis for environmental ethics. See also Lisa Sideris (2003).

17 Definitions of sin often reveal key differences between models of the relationships between God, humanity and the cosmos.

18 Somewhat like McDaniel, McFague finds herself grafting on an extra category, resurrection, into her theological scheme, in order to associate herself more closely with 'the Christic paradigm'. So she writes (1993:179–91) of the body of God as also the Cosmic Christ in a way which seems insecurely juxtaposed with her model as a whole.

19 'Gaia', a name derived from the Greek goddess of the Earth, is used by Ruether for the whole system of interdependent living beings on the planet. See 9.7 for more exploration of this term.

20 Sideris criticizes Ruether, as she does McFague, for an excessively romantic and insufficiently Darwinian view of the creation (Sidens, 2003:ch. 2).

21 Reference to 'the great Thou' recalls the thought of Martin Buber – see 9.2.

22 That is where, by implication, Santmire himself seems to locate Ruether, 'sophisticated and substantive' though he finds her thought to be (Santmire, 2000:134 note 3).

23 Eberhard Jüngel is another very important figure in this area (see Jüngel, 1983).

24 For an explanation of kenosis see 2.5.4 note 8.

25 Moltmann here draws heavily on Barth's *Church Dogmatics* III/3 (Barth, 1960).

26 Here Moltmann invokes a distinction in Orthodox theology between God's *energeiai*, which impart the divine will to the world, and God's *ousia*, the divine being as it is in itself, utterly unchanging and unchangeable. See Gregorios (1987:57–9) and the articles by Kallistos Ware, Alexei Nesteriuk and Andrew Louth in Clayton and Peacocke (2004). See also Fiddes, 1988:111f. for an effort to get beyond this distinction.

27 Holmes Rolston III has used a similar argument to infer the intrinsic value of all creatures (Rolston, 1988).

28 Ward, like Robert J. Russell (see 1.15), is able to show that the non-singularity proposals of Hawking and others for the origin of the Big Bang need not be an obstacle to a theistic model of creation (Ward 1996a:295–9). He is also able to reject the idea that special relativity leaves God no scope to act in time (pp. 300–3).

29 Here she quotes from Moltmann's *The Trinity and the Kingdom of God* (1981).

30 It is interesting to note Herbert McCabe's emphatic rejection of such 'with' language – the immanent God is not 'with', alongside, creation: 'the creator cannot in this way ever be outside his creature . . . If the creator is the reason for everything that is, there can be no actual being which does not have the creator as its center holding it in being' (1987:44–5).

31 See Vanstone's *Love's Endeavour, Love's Expense* (1977) for his kenotic views of divine love.

32 While accepting Coakley's general point, we would note that the modern sense of the autonomy of physical process, unfolding according to the interplay of chance and law, and with an integrity respected by the God who sustains it, is much stronger now than when Aquinas wrote.

33   I am grateful to Dr Robert J. Russell for pointing me to this reservation about kenosis.
34   Also a rebuttal of Richard Dawkins (McGrath, 2005) to which we refer in Chapter 6.
35   See Hefner, 1993.
36   An imaginative addition to the range of possibilities is Andrew Robinson's use of the categories of the American philosopher C.S. Peirce in an effort to model the Trinity (Robinson, 2004).

Recommended further reading

In addition to the books that form the basis of the models described in 8.5.1–8.5.10 we recommend:

BERRY, R.J. (2003) *God's Book of Works: The Nature and Theology of Nature* (Edinburgh: T&T Clark International)

CLAYTON, Philip and PEACOCKE, Arthur (eds) (2004) *In Whom We Live and Move and Have our Being: Panentheistic Reflections on God's Presence in a Scientific World* (Grand Rapids, MI, and Cambridge: Eerdmans)

FIDDES, Paul S. (2000) *Participating in God: A Pastoral Doctrine of the Trinity* (London: Darton, Longman & Todd)

FORD, David F. with MUERS, Rachel (2005, forthcoming) *The Modern Theologians* 3rd edn (Oxford: Blackwell)

POLKINGHORNE, John (ed.) (2001) *The Work of Love: Kenosis as Creation* (London: SPCK)

SURIN, Kenneth (1986) *Theology and the Problem of Evil* (Oxford: Blackwell)

Chapter 9

Some resources for theological thinking on God and the world from outside the Christian tradition

Michael Robert Negus and Christopher Southgate[1]

9.1 Introduction

In the first section of Keith Ward's *Religion and Creation* he looks at a thinker from Judaism (Heschel), Christianity (Barth), Islam (Iqbal) and Hinduism (Aurobindo), and claims to find a common strand in their understanding of divinity (Ward, 1996a: chs 1–4, especially pp. 100–6). Each, Ward claims, wants to emphasize the dynamic quality of the relationship of the divine to the cosmos to an extent greater than is typical in their traditions. Many, however, have questioned whether all these thinkers are genuinely representative of the mainstream of their religions, and how much Ward has forced the similarity between them. Nevertheless his study points to the fact that the relation of the divine to the world is a live theological issue in a number of faiths, and that thinking in one tradition may feed theology in another. So we now consider some resources from outside the Christian tradition.

We consider (all too briefly) two Jewish philosophers, then some insights from Hinduism, Taoism and Buddhism. We end the chapter with mention of the Gaia Hypothesis, and two movements much influenced by Eastern thought – deep ecology and 'new paradigm' thinking. More detailed consideration of one religion, Islam, is offered in Chapter 12.

9.2 Two Jewish philosophers: Martin Buber and Hans Jonas

Judaism, based on its ancient Scriptures and centuries of commentary and reflection upon them, has been not only a great world faith in its own right, but also immensely influential in philosophical and religious thinking in the last two thousand years. For introductions see Solomon, 2000; Samuelson, 2003. See also Sacks, 2003.

Martin Buber (1878–1965) published in 1923 a small but very significant book called *Ich und Du* ('I and Thou', Buber, 1958). *I and Thou* is an inexhaustible study, at once poetic, mystical and philosophical. Buber's key concept was that authentic personal encounter is of a radically different character to the encounter with objects. He called these different forms of encounter 'I–Thou' and 'I–It'. All reductions and analyses of persons, as well as their use for (e.g.) economic purposes, shift them from being met as 'Thou' to being treated as 'It'. Conversely, a non-personal object such as a tree, contemplated with sufficient seriousness, can cease to be a mere 'It' (Buber, 1958:14). One Thou never becomes an It, the eternal Thou, God. God is to be addressed, not expressed; 'in each Thou we address the eternal Thou' (p. 78).

Buber wrote intriguingly about humans' relation to the non-human world, as in this passage:

> That living wholeness and unity of the tree, which denies itself to the sharpest glance of the mere investigator and discloses itself to the glance of one who says *Thou*, is there when he, the sayer of *Thou*, is there: it is he who vouchsafes to the tree that it manifest this unity and wholeness; and now the tree which is in being manifests them. Our habits of thought make it difficult for us to see that here, awakened by our attitude, something lights up and approaches us from the course of being. (1958:95)

Fascinating as it would be to trace the impact of Buber on existentialist thought in general, or to compare his contemplative encounter with the non-human world with that of a poet such as Gerard Manley Hopkins, or a Christian mystic such as Thomas Merton, our interest here is in how he is influencing contemporary ecological formulations. Sallie McFague draws, not uncritically, on Buber in proposing her 'subject–subject' model of appropriate ecological relationship (1997:97–102). H. Paul Santmire notes Buber's own struggle to say how there can be true mutuality between a human and a non-sentient creature such as a tree (Santmire, 2000:68). He proposes instead a third type of relation beyond 'I–It' and 'I–Thou' which he calls 'I–Ens'.[2] This can be between a human and a non-human creature, or even between a human and a part of fabricated nature such as a building or a city. It is a relationship which involves givenness, beauty, wonder, openness to the infinite. Santmire quotes a Hasidic saying used by Buber: 'there is no rung of being on which we cannot find the Holiness of God everywhere and at all times' (quoted in Santmire, 2000:72). These extensions of Buber's thought, particularly Santmire's, could be highly generative for theological approaches to environmental ethics.

Buber took an immensely courageous stand in Nazi Germany, staying as long as it was feasible to teach his fellow Jews. As Norbert Samuelson notes, his high reputation in Christian academic circles helped to preserve him from arrest. Eventually public teaching became impossible and he left for Jerusalem in 1938 (Samuelson, 2003:285–6). The other Jewish thinker we mention here, **Hans Jonas** (1903–93), was a pupil of Heidegger and Bultmann, trained as Buber was in existentialist philosophy, but making a profound shift into a post-Holocaust theology which also takes evolutionary biology seriously. Jonas' own mother was murdered in a concentration camp, and he formulates a very striking model of God, based on his conviction that nothing should be said theologically that could not be said to the children of Auschwitz. So Jonas writes:

> in order that the world might be, and be for itself, God renounced his own being, divesting himself of his deity – to receive it back from the Odyssey of

time weighted with the chance harvest of unforeseeable temporal experience; transfigured or even possibly disfigured by it. In such self-forfeiture of divine integrity for the sake of unprejudiced becoming, no other fore-knowledge can be admitted than that of *possibilities* ... to these, God committed his cause in effacing himself for the world. (Jonas, 1996:125, italics in original)

So we see that (from a very different starting-point) Jonas develops a model of God even more extreme than that of Whitehead, a model from which all sovereignty has vanished. God does not lure the creation on, but in divine self-abandonment allows mind to experience itself in a variety of possibilities. Any sense that evolution has an inbuilt bias towards progressiveness should be banished by consideration of what humans have done in the twentieth century.

One implication of this scheme is that human responsibility is absolutely inescapable – 'The image of God ... passes ... into man's precarious trust, to be completed, saved, or spoiled by what he will do to himself and the world' (Jonas, 1996:127). The very helplessness of God should help us to claim our responsibility. Jonas has influenced not only Jewish post-Holocaust thought but also such Christian thinkers as the Catholic theologian John Haught (see Haught, 2000:172–84 for an important discussion). He puts down a marker for all those attempting theodicy after the Holocaust. The theme of possibilities – God giving rise to them, companioning them, working with and perhaps protecting certain fruitful ones – is one we shall see woven through our exploration of God's action in the history of the cosmos (see e.g. 10.14, 10.18.1).

9.3 The contributions of Eastern thought

In recent decades there has been a considerable interest in the concepts contained in some of the religious traditions of Asia, insofar as they have seemed to offer an imaginative language for expressing some of the findings of modern science. This occurred first in physics, as a result of quantum theory, and later in biology, especially in the application of a systems approach to understanding the emergence and self-sustainability of living beings, ecosystems and the global biosphere. These seeming consonances between science and Eastern thought have in turn increased interest in these religions within Western culture.

By contrast with the concepts derived from Newton and Descartes, which present a world consisting of masses in space interacting according to fixed laws of motion in a mechanistic fashion, oriental mystical traditions emphasize fluidity, continual change and impermanence, a reality which is dynamic and alive. An early attempt to associate these ideas with twentieth-century science was Fritjof Capra's *The Tao of Physics*, first published in 1975.[3] The overarching thesis of this book is that:

The two foundations of twentieth-century physics – quantum theory and relativity theory – both force us to see the world very much in the way a Hindu, Buddhist or Taoist sees it ... Modern physics leads us to a view of the world which is very similar to the views held by mystics of all ages and traditions. (Capra, 1976:17)

Capra proceeds to assimilate modern physics to a strongly monistic (and very Western) synthesis of Eastern spiritualities. The observer-dependence of determinate observations implied by some interpretations of quantum mechanics (see 5.13) gives Capra a basis for his mystical speculations. Not only is reality-in-itself indeterminate (like his description of the One in Eastern mysticism), but the observer plays a crucial role in creating determinate reality. We create our own reality or at least affect it in a very fundamental way by what we choose to observe. Thus he concludes that 'the structures and phenomena we observe in nature are nothing but creations of our measuring and categorizing mind' (Capra 1976:292).

Capra's account of physics as a spiritual path is open to criticism at a number of levels. It is highly speculative, and dependent upon a particular interpretation of quantum mechanics which may have a short currency. Students of Eastern spirituality have attacked Capra's approach to mystical experience for presenting a misleading picture of unity among a rich diversity of spiritual traditions.[4]

There is, then, much suspicion, some of it well founded, of this association of aspects of contemporary science – quantum theory in particular – with ideas or worldviews derived from oriental religions (see Polkinghorne, 1988:93–4, and Lucas, 1996: chs 1–4). But John G. Taylor, formerly Professor of Mathematics at King's College, London, though he sees 'a large amount of vague and woolly thinking contained in Eastern mysticism', concedes that 'if these mystical ideas are used as an entrée into modern physics they have value, but only if used as stepping stones to the greater precision of the real thing' (Taylor, 1991:114–15). Without conceding that a theological idea – or indeed a mystical insight – is necessarily less precise than a theorem in physics, we wish to develop this idea of stepping-stones.

The following three sections introduce in turn aspects of Hindu, Taoist and Buddhist thought, to enable the reader to consider these as possible stepping-stones between science and theology – in *two* senses:

- from science to theology, in the sense of providing additional resources for understanding the relation of the divine to the world which science describes;
- from theology to science, in the sense of offering images and metaphors which might feed the growth of models in the science of the future.

The sections are necessarily very brief and focus upon the mystical and metaphysical aspects of the traditions rather than upon mythology, ritual or popular worship. In the case of Hinduism the emphasis is given mainly to the metaphysical system known as the Vedanta, taught by Shankaracharya and elaborated during the seventh and eighth centuries CE. A useful discussion of the Vedanta, from a Christian point of view, is to be found in Ward (1987:1–29). Many translations of the Taoist *Tao-Te-Ching* are available; the one chosen here (Bryce, 1991) is that of Fr L. Wieger which, although lacking poetic beauty, is technically very precise. There is a multitude of books on Buddhism; a very useful introductory text is that of Damien Keown (1996).

9.4 The universe as seen in Hindu metaphysics

The meaning conveyed in Hinduism by the word *Brahman* is difficult to express. It is not exactly equivalent to God, as conceived in the West. It is rather the Principle that is 'beyond all distinctions (*nirvishesha*)' and 'beyond all qualities (*nīrguna*)' that belong not only to this universe but also to the one personal God, who in Hinduism is called *Īshwara* (cf. Guénon, 1958a:25). Capra explains that the '*Rig Veda* [a collection of ancient Hindu scriptures chanted by priests] uses another term to express the dynamic nature of the universe, the term *Rita*. This word comes from the root *ri* – to move; its original meaning in the *Rig Veda* being "the course of all things", "the order of nature"' (Capra, 1976:199).

The relationship between *Brahman* and the creation is related to panentheism – indeed Peacocke makes this connection (1993:158). The panentheism of Hinduism is expressed in the words of the *Bhagavadgita*, the fifth-century BCE religious classic and 'bible' to millions of Hindus. The words of the text are the enunciations of the God Krishna attempting to inspire Arjuna, who represents each one of us in a despondent and demotivated state. Krishna speaks on behalf of the Divinity itself.

From Chapter IX

(4)   By Me all this universe is pervaded through My unmanifested form. All beings abide in Me but I do not abide in them.

(5)   And (yet) the beings do not dwell in Me: behold My divine mystery. My spirit which is the source of all beings sustains the beings but does not abide in them.

(6)   As the mighty air, moving everywhere, ever abides in ethereal space (akasha), know thou that in the same manner all existences abide in Me.

(7)   All beings O Son of Kunti (Arjuna) pass into nature which is My own at the end of the cycle; and at the beginning of the next cycle, I send them forth.

(8)   Taking hold of nature which is my own, I send forth again and again all this multitude of beings which are helpless, being under the control of nature (prakriti).

(9)   Nor do these works bind Me, O winner of wealth (Arjuna), for I am seated as if indifferent, unattached to these actions.

(10) Under my guidance, nature (prakriti) gives birth to all things, moving and unmoving and by this means, O Son of Kunti (Arjuna), the world revolves.

(*Bhagavadgita* IX.4–10, from Radhakrishnan (1958:238–42))

Hindu panentheism is a very subtle concept. The key Sanskrit expression, translated as 'divine mystery' in verse 5 above, barely translates the depth of the idea. The Sanskrit words are *yogam ais'varam*; these could be translated as 'an integrated state in which the possessions of all the divine attributes (*ais'varam*) of Being (*Īshwara*) are yoked (*yoga*) together in a unity' (cf. Radhakrishnan, 1958:239 footnotes).

It is clear from the quotation from the *Bhagavadgita* that Hinduism does not view the universe as having been created once, as in Semitic religions, with time and space coming into existence at a first moment. Rather the universe is endlessly brought into being and then destroyed, cycle after cycle, making an indefinite series of worlds. This process is sometimes described as the continual breathing of *Brahman*, each creative expiration followed by a period of persistence and then terminated by a destructive inspiration. The three phases are respectively governed by the gods *Brahmā, Vishnu* and *Shiva*, who can be regarded as the vice-regents of *Brahman*. The universe is thus lacking in permanence; in addition it has no reality independent from *Brahman*. Our apparently self-existent universe is thus the Great Illusion (*Mahā-Mohā*), because it appears to be independent from *Brahman*. This illusion is due to a 'property' called *māyā*, the illusion of separateness, which is inherent in the creative process. *Māyā* is thus the cause of the human experience of *avidyā* (literally 'non-sight', spiritual blindness, ignorance). In reality, in clear 'seeing' (*vidyā*), nothing is separate from *Brahman*. This is expressed in the metaphysical system of the Vedanta as *advaita* (non-duality), which is the state of *Brahman* and therefore the only reality of every being in the universe, including all human beings. From a more positive point of view *māyā* both veils and reveals the Divinity in nature.

One of the principal 'stepping-stones' in respect of Hinduism, then, might be in the area of developing a panentheism which emphasizes the utter dependence of the world that science describes on the divine power.

9.5 Taoism: nature's innermost reality is also the spiritual way

The fundamental text of Taoism, the *Tao-Te-Ching*, is attributed to Lao-tzu (*c.*570–490 BCE). The title of the book literally means 'The Principle (*Tao*) Its Action (*Te*) Treatise (*Ching*)'. The words *Tao* and *Te* have complex meanings in a metaphysical context. *Tao* literally means 'Way' and is sometimes translated as 'water course way' indicating that it exists naturally rather than as an artefact. *Te* is a word with complex meanings; it is often translated as 'Virtue' (see Bryce, 1991:10). René Guénon translates *Te* as 'uprightness' and writes that *Te* 'might be called a "specification" of the Way (*Tao*), in regard to a given being or state of existence; it is the direction that a being must follow in order that his existence may be accordance to the "Way", or, in other words, in conformity with the Principle (in the upward direction, whereas the descending direction is that in which the "Activity of Heaven" is exerted)' (Guénon, 1958b:40 note 4). Ninian Smart further explains the subtlety of these two important words: 'In Taoism the true nature of the cosmos was summed up as the Tao, a word that has many meanings clinging to it – the Way, or Principle, or Method. It was used in particular to mean the Way of the cosmos, the principle or spirit governing it' (Smart, 1995:55).

Taoism is *both* a description of the universe in terms of *Tao and* the proposal of a spiritual method for attaining to the reality of *Tao*.

From Chapter 21 of the *Tao-Te-Ching*

A. All of the beings *which play a role* in the great manifestation *of the cosmic theatre*, have come from the Principle [*Tao*], through its virtue (its unwinding) [*Te*].

B. Here is the nature of the Principle: It is indistinct and indeterminate. Oh how indistinct and indeterminate! In this indistinction and indetermination there are types. Oh how indistinct and indeterminate it is! In this indistinction and indetermination there are beings *in force*. Oh how mysterious and obscure it is! In this mystery, in this obscurity, there is an essence, which is reality. *That is the nature of the Principle.*

From Chapter 37

A. The Principle is always non-acting (not acting actively), and yet it does everything (without seeming to participate).

From Chapter 38

A. That which is superior to the virtue [*te*] of the Principle (the Principle itself, considered in its essence), does not act, but holds Virtue in a state of immanence within itself.

From Chapter 51

A. The Principle gives life to *beings*, then its Virtue nourishes them, until the completion of their nature, until the perfection of their faculties. Therefore all beings venerate the Principle and its Virtue.

B. No one has the eminence of the Principle and its Virtue conferred on them; they have it always naturally.

C. The Principle gives life; its Virtue gives growth, protects, perfects, matures, maintains and covers (all beings). When they are born it does not monopolize them; it lets them act freely, without exploiting them; it lets them grow without tyrannizing them. This is the action of transcendent Virtue. (From Bryce, 1991)

The ontology of the universe, in Taoist thought, starts with non-being (*Wu*) or the formless (*huan*) mystery. These words also describe the *Tao* in a state when there were no sentient beings. The state is called *hsien t'ien* ('before heaven'). Within the essence of the *Tao* were two immanent properties, or 'two determinations' called *yin* and *yang*. It is by means of the interactions between these two polar determinations that the universe comes into being. 'All natural phenomena are manifestations of a continuous oscillation between the two poles [*yin* and *yang*], all transitions take place gradually and in unbroken progression. The natural order is one of dynamic balance between yin and yang' (Capra, 1983:18).

Yang is an expansive tendency, whereas *yin* is contractive. The first manifestations of the pair were the celestial sphere or heaven and the Earth, respectively. However, in Taoist thought, there is no manifestation of pure *yang* or pure *yin*, although particular phenomena or beings have a preponderance of one property or the other, or can have a dynamic balance between the two. *Yin–yang* dominates all aspects of Taoist thought and spirituality, including the qualitative aspects of temporal cycles, especially birth and death which are seen to be two aspects of the same event. The spiritual 'task' of a Taoist is to discover the 'Invariable Middle' (*Ching-yung*) which is a state in which all the various components of the human being are harmonized. This is seen to be a permanent state and is described as *Cheng-jen* ('true man'). The human being (*jen*) in this state harmonizes within him-, or herself, heaven (*T'ien*) and Earth (*Ti*) (cf. Guénon, 1958b:122–6).

The importance of Taoism is that its paradigm of the universe is at the same time the operative context for a spiritual way. The *Tao* is *Reality*. By means of 'non-action' (*wu-wei*), which amounts to abstaining from acts that are 'out of harmony with the ongoing cosmic process' (Capra, 1983:20), the individual discovers the harmony of the *Tao*. 'Those who understand this mode of action of heaven ... concentrate themselves in meditative peace, which is the source of natural action [i.e. *wu-wei*].' 'Nothing tends more towards rest, towards equilibrium, than water.' 'Now just as rest clarifies water, it likewise clarifies the vital spirits [of the psyche], including the intelligence. The Sage's heart, perfectly calm, is like a mirror which reflects heaven and earth, and all beings' (from Chuang Tzu, ch. 13, section A, in Bryce, 1984:174).

One of the principal 'stepping-stones' in respect of Taoism, therefore, might be in the area of ecological spirituality – the power of non-action.

9.6 The contribution of Buddhism

The founder of Buddhism, Sakyamuni (d. fifth century BCE), is usually referred to as the Buddha (this word is actually a title meaning 'the awakened' or 'the enlightened one'; it describes his state of consciousness). Buddhism regards every human being as a potential buddha and provides the framework and methods that enable each person eventually to achieve full enlightenment. It is important to remember that before all else Buddhism aims firstly at clarifying the true nature of the ever-changing world (*samsāra*) and of the ordinary human state; the latter being controlled by desire, craving and consequential suffering. The unhappy state of the human being in an unfulfilling world is contrasted with a state of perfect happiness, *nirvāna*.

Buddhism seeks to identify the intrinsic cause of human suffering and explains that it can be overcome. It then provides the spiritual methods by means of which suffering gradually ceases and perfect happiness is gained. The method is set down in the Four Noble Truths:

1. The state of humans in the world is characterized by suffering (*dukkha*) relieved only by superficial, temporary pleasures.
2. The cause of *dukkha* is fundamentally an egocentric craving based

upon the double illusion that the 'world of appearances' *samsāra*, is real and that the ego is an enduring entity. The doctrine of 'absence of self', *anatta*, contrasts strongly with the doctrine of an enduring self/soul of other religions. Buddhism states that both the world and the 'I' are aggregates (*skandhas*) and are not discrete entities (cf. Nairne, 1997:19–21).

3. Egocentric craving can be overcome by the extinction of the 'poisons' of desire, hatred and illusion.

4. Buddhism provides the means, known as the Middle Way, by which *dukkha* may be overcome and *nirvāna* achieved.

The *Dhammapada* (literally the Teaching Path, which summarizes the sayings of the Buddha), explains the Four Noble Truths as follows:

He who takes refuge in the Way and journeys with those who follow it, clearly sees the great truths.

Suffering, the cause of suffering, the ceasing of suffering 'and the eightfold path' [the Middle way] that leads to an end of suffering.

Then at last he finds safety. He is delivered from suffering and is free. (Bancroft, 1997: The *Dhammapada* v. 190–2)

Buddhism stresses the need for individual effort and individual experience of its methods. The proof of Buddhism is in doing. Apart from the prescription for a life of detailed attention to morality and virtues Buddhism provides meditation to create inner peace, promote wisdom and help progress along the path to *nirvāna*.

A caring and compassionate attitude was engendered in *Mahāyāna* Buddhism by the Vow of the Boddhisattva, who refuses to enter the bliss of *nirvāna* until the last blade of grass has attained to enlightenment. So the everyday life of every Buddhist is governed by the ethical principle of *ahimsā* (non-harming), which manifests itself as a great respect for all life, total rejection of the practice of animal sacrifice and the adoption of a vegetarian diet. 'In some Buddhist cultures the practice of agriculture is frowned upon because of the inevitable destruction of life caused by ploughing the Earth. In general, however ... Buddhism ... regarded the destruction of life as morally wrong only when it was caused intentionally or as a result of negligence' (Keown, 1996:106).

Buddhist thought before the coming of the *Mahāyāna* included a view of the cosmos that included an atomic theory of matter. The fifth-century treatise known as the *Abhidharmakosha* includes a theoretical analysis of gross matter as being aggregates (*skandhas*) of atoms, called *paramanus* (literally 'extreme-minute'). These are described as the 'smallest part of matter, uncuttable, unable to be destroyed' (Sadakata, 1997:20). These atoms aggregate to form molecules (*duya-nuka*) which consist of one core atom surrounded by six others. Three such molecules produce one visible particle of matter. The main effect of this theory is that Buddhists are predisposed to accept the modern scientific particulate theory of matter. It simply confirms for them their paradigm of the impermanence and non-substantiality of matter.

For the Buddhist the 'common sense' view of the world is an illusion, as is the belief in a separate individual self. The fourteenth Dalai Lama writes: 'Ignorance, the belief that things are real, is extremely powerful. But we should remember that it is nothing more than a mistake; it is merely a misunderstanding that we cling to but which in fact has no foundation whatsoever [because all things are "composites" (*skandha* or *khandha*), and are therefore subject to disintegration and a cause of sorrow]. Its opposite, the understanding that phenomena have no reality, is based on a consistent truth that stands up to all argument. If one familiarizes oneself with this understanding, it can be developed indefinitely, since it is both true and a natural quality of the mind' (Dalai Lama, 1994:13).

Buddhism exhibits certain consonances with modern science, such as:

(i) An atomic theory of matter: thus solid matter is just an appearance, created by the way the particles are put together and by the interaction of the perceived object with the sensory and cerebral system of the observer.

(ii) A theory of the 'absence of self' (*anatta*), that the ego is not real (see below).

The assertion that there is no unitary self, no enduring ego, is affirmed by some modern psychologists (cf. Lancaster, 1991:83) and is supported in studies of some split-brain patients in the United States (Gazzaniga, 1989). In such cases it appears that the patient has two 'egos', one on each side of the brain. Gazzaniga suggests that there are several 'agents' working independently in the normal brain, but that these are dominated by the language centres in the left hemisphere, so long as the brain is intact; this gives the impression that there is only one agent, one 'I'.

9.6.1 Buddhist spirituality

The influence of Buddhism on the debate between Western science and theology is relatively small because of the non-cognitive nature of the claims of Buddhism, which is first and foremost a *practice*, rather than a metaphysics or a theology. Buddhism describes what will be experienced if the Way is followed. Nevertheless Buddhist *spirituality* has been a great influence on Christian thinkers, such as Thomas Merton,[5] Keith Ward[6] and Jay McDaniel (see 8.5.2 – also McDaniel, 1990, in which he develops the notion of God as the Zen contemplative of the world). We have already noted McDaniel's stress on the concepts of 'non-harming' and 'emptiness'. For the Buddhist 'emptiness' contains within it:

(a) the idea of 'suchness' (*tathata*), which is a sort of poetic perception of the integrity of the entity perceived. Suchness is ever-present, and becomes known to the mind when the internal ego and external physical objects become fully transparent to each other.[7]

(b) the concept of dependent origination – all entities being understood to be dependent on each other – a concept also important in deep ecology (see below);

(c) a sense of impermanence, of the beauty and transience of each moment of our lives.

(McDaniel, 1989:92–110)

The contribution of Buddhism, especially of this rich concept of non-harming, to deep ecology and to the systems thinking of Capra is touched on further in 9.9.

9.7 The Gaia Hypothesis

We turn now from the insights of ancient faiths to an idea from modern science.

(i) The Hypothesis considered in scientific terms

Rosemary Radford Ruether's use of the name 'Gaia' (8.5.5) derives from the work of the scientist and inventor James Lovelock, who since the early 1970s has been putting forward what is in its essence a scientific hypothesis – albeit a difficult one to test – that the presence of life all over the surface of the Earth has dramatically changed conditions on that surface, and caused them to remain remarkably stable in a range which allows living systems to continue.

The basic data for the Hypothesis are those seen in Table 9.1, which shows how utterly different the Earth is from a planet of the same sort of size, composition and orbit, but without life.

Table 9.1 Planetary Atmospheres: Their Composition, Temperature and Pressure (drawn from Lovelock, 1988:9) [ppm = parts per million].

Atmospheric component	*Venus*	*Mars*	*Earth without life*	*Earth as it is*
Carbon dioxide	96.5%	95%	98%	0.03%
Nitrogen	3.5%	2.7%	1.9%	79%
Oxygen	trace	0.13%	0.0	21%
Methane	0.0	0.0	0.0	1.7ppm
Surface temperature (°C)	459	−53	240–340	13
Total pressure (bars)	90	0.0064	60	1.0

Lovelock elaborates this in a particularly fascinating way in *The Ages of Gaia* (1988), tracing the proposed history of life on the planet and the way in which life might not just have altered the planet, but given rise to self-regulating mechanisms to keep it altered. This self-regulated surface to the Earth Lovelock called 'Gaia'. The science of Gaia has been much contested, but this type of thinking has now entered the general scientific consciousness, if not necessarily always by that name (Lovelock, 2004:1). For recent discussion see Schneider *et al.*, 2004.[8] Further studies of the history of the planet are revealing the big swings that have taken place in planetary environment (e.g. at the time of 'snowball

Earth', which preceded the Cambrian explosion – see 6.10.2). Gaian mechanisms did not prevent this big freeze, though biotic processes may have accelerated its thaw (McMenamin, 2004). So although life tends to stabilize the 'settings' of the planet's surface, these settings can undergo big shifts.[9] Lovelock has campaigned vigorously to emphazise the damage to 'Gaia' being done by practices which pollute the atmosphere and reduce biodiversity. He may also be timely in pointing out that the cycle of atmospheric carbon dioxide levels is at an extreme at present, and that humans' sudden stressing of the system might lead to a rapid move to a different stable state (Lovelock, 1988:158–9). Notably, he now advocates a rapid increase in nuclear power generation as the only way to avoid rapid changes associated with the build-up of greenhouse gases.[10]

EXERCISE 9.1

The issue of nuclear power offers a good opportunity for students to practise the critical use of the World Wide Web. The Web provides a rich source of accessible information. Indeed, there is more information than we can possibly handle. It is important for students to be aware that everyone has their own personal 'filtering processes', which can all too often mean focusing on the information they want to find to support a predetermined view.
Organizations, moreover, seek not only to inform but to influence those who visit their sites. The student should compare the website of the Nuclear Energy Agency with that of Greenpeace. In each case they should consider:

    (i)   what point of view the site-owner wishes them to adopt;
   (ii) how the language and images used tend to reinforce that view; and
  (iii) what hard information is being presented.

Finally, they should ask themselves whether visiting the sites changed their own point of view.

Throughout his work, Lovelock's rhetoric is of the planet as an organism, a 'living thing'. Certainly it is a bounded system far from equilibrium, one moreover which contains interacting subsystems and undergoes processes of development and change. It is more difficult to see Gaia as being capable of reproduction – unless by the 'ecopoiesis' of Mars (1988:183–202) – still less of evolving in the Darwinian sense, since there is, as far as we know, no other comparable 'organism' against which it might be selected.

(ii) The Hypothesis considered in metaphysical terms

Lovelock also shifts periodically into a somewhat different mode of writing, encouraged perhaps by the name he gave to his hypothesis.[11] Sometimes Gaia becomes personified – Lovelock suggests for instance that 'she' might 'get rid' of humans if they were a 'nuisance' to 'her'. This does make an important scientific point about the very unusual and stable conditions that pertain on the Earth. The parameters that make this a life-supporting planet (temperature, atmospheric composition, etc.) are stable to a remarkable degree, but they are not held in any absolute or lasting way within the limits that have allowed human civilization to thrive. Another ice age is not merely possible but likely. But these considerations also cause Lovelock to slide towards the language of Gaia as personal agent 'who' might 'decide' to 'punish' or 'eliminate' humans:

> Gaia, as I see her, is no doting mother tolerant of misdemeanors, nor is she some fragile and delicate damsel in danger from brutal mankind. She is stern and tough, always keeping the world warm and comfortable for those who obey the rules, but ruthless in her destruction of those who transgress. Her unconscious goal is a planet fit for life. (1988:212)

The key word here is 'unconscious', but the rhetoric of the passage makes it easy to overlook. The Gaia Hypothesis, as a scientific description couched in non-teleological terms, is a very telling proposal and a helpful way to think about the systems that make our life possible, their very long history, our ignorance of them, and our possible vulnerability to sudden shifts in their behaviour. But any extension of that proposal into describing Gaia as a purposive, personified agent would move the discussion into a different realm of explanation, in which other considerations about the nature of divinity would become important. (One very obvious example is that Gaia 'herself' is a function of this planet alone, and has no status in other parts of the universe. Another is that 'her' power is extremely limited. No Gaian feedback systems extend to the behaviour of the sun, small changes in which could completely disrupt all the systems that stabilize conditions on the Earth. So at most 'Gaia' could only be a petty deity of no great cosmic power.)

We therefore regard the Gaia Hypothesis with some caution, seeing it as a potentially helpful refinement of the scientific narrative of the development of the Earth's environment (and a reminder of how unusual and fragile that environment is), but aware that Gaia could also be the source of some ill-considered spirituality. See Lawrence Osborn (2001) for an original and thought-provoking theological 'spin' on Gaia. For further reading see Osborn (1992), Russell (1994: ch. 8) and Deane-Drummond (1996:98–114).

9.8 Deep ecology

Deep ecology is a term coined by the Norwegian philosopher Arne Naess in an article in 1972 in which he contrasted 'environmental fixes' within the existing attitudes of modern society ('shallow ecology') with a real change of mindset in relation to the planet. Characteristics of a deep-ecological mindset would be:

1. Rejection of the man-in-environment image in favour of the relational, total-field image.

2. Biospherical egalitarianism.
3. Principles of diversity and symbiosis.
4. Anti-class posture.
5. Fight against pollution and resource depletion.
6. Complexity, not complication.
7. Local autonomy and decentralization.

(Naess, quoted in Merchant, 1992:87)

The profound respect for all creatures inherent in (1), and especially in (2) – the conviction of the need for a 'biocentric' scheme which asserts that all species are of equal status[12] – has its roots in Buddhism (9.6–9.6.1). Naess, however, acknowledges that it is necessary to kill some fellow-creatures to live – this expedient should be kept to a minimum. Central to deep ecology is the concept of wilderness – areas of the planet which are as they would be if no humans ever went there. One can sense here the influence of such early American environmentalists as John Muir, and of Aldo Leopold's *A Sand County Almanac* (1949). If there is a deity of deep ecology it is wilderness.

For some writers the natural corollary of such thinking has been that there are far too many humans, and that reduction of the human population – to some notional 'carrying capacity' which the Earth could sustainably support – should be welcomed. (A figure sometimes used is 0.5 billion, as against an estimated population for the year 2000 of 6.2 billion.) There is a strain of 'environmental fascism' about some of these comments, very far from the stark but visionary tone of Naess' original article. Deep ecologists' suggestions as to how humans might live in the future are often very radical. In the standard work on deep ecology by Devall and Sessions[13] they quote Paul Shepard's: that the Earth's population be stabilized at 8 billion by 2020 and that these be positioned in cities strung around the edge of the continents, with the interior allowed to return to the wild. The contact with this wilderness, so essential to our ecological health, would all be by journeys made on foot. (This would mean feeding the world on biotechnologically- engineered microbial food (Devall and Sessions, 1985:172–4).)

Deep ecology contains many contradictions, the central one of which is that humans are to be the one species which is not to express its nature in seeking to maximize its ecological niche. Nevertheless, as a spiritual exhortation to individuals and societies whose impact on the planet is greatest (that of the *average* US citizen approaches 100 times that of the average Indian, and many Westerners' consumption is far higher) deep ecology will remain important (as McFague comments, 'for its poetic power more than its conceptual adequacy' (1993:125)).

9.9 'New paradigm' thinking

This is a concept particularly advanced by Fritjof Capra, who may be regarded as the hardest-headed and most scientifically informed speaker for deep ecology. He has strongly emphasized the importance of 'systems thinking' – 'all natural systems are wholes whose specific structures arise from the interactions and interdependence of their parts. Systemic properties are destroyed when a system is dissected, either physically or theoretically, into isolated elements. Although we can discern individual parts in any system, the nature of the whole is always different from the mere sum of its parts' (quoted in Merchant, 1992:93). This is particularly important in complex emergent systems such as life: 'while it is true that all living systems are ultimately made of atoms and molecules, they are not "nothing but" atoms and molecules. There is something else to life, something non-material and irreducible – a pattern of organisation' (Capra, 1996:81).

Capra uses the two adjectives 'ecological' and 'holistic' in explaining his worldview. This 'new paradigm' is set against the metaphor of the 'world as a machine', 'brought about by the new discoveries in physics, astronomy and mathematics known as the Scientific Revolution and associated with the names of Copernicus, Galileo, Descartes, Bacon and Newton' (Capra, 1996:19). Capra's approach to understanding the cosmos enables him to draw together several areas of modern science into a paradigm that encompasses quantum physics, systems theories, chaos theory, the mathematics of complexity, models of self-organization and Gaia theory. In each case the inadequacy of the clockwork universe, Newton's deterministic machine, is emphasized. The world in which we live is not composed of 'things', nor of 'objects', but of relationships. Thus we know that an electron is 'there' because it relates in a particular situation as a particle or as a wave. We know that a tree, a river or a table is 'there' because of the sensory and neural relationships we establish with them. The generation of these relationships is cognition (see below).

Perhaps the most interesting aspect of Capra's writings is the way in which his consideration of scientific paradigms (in for example *The Turning Point* (1983)) opens the way towards spiritual and religious considerations. In particular he has drawn heavily on Taoism and Buddhism in framing his view of reality. This is especially so when he writes about life and the nature of mind and cognition. According to the Santiago theory of cognition, proposed by Maturana and Varela (1980), life *is* cognition, in the sense that living systems operate by 'knowing' their environment. The relationships within the living system, and between the system and its environment, that are written in its patterns of organization, express the cognition that the life-form has of itself and its environment. Thus life and cognition go together. Moreover the Santiago theory rejects the idea that cognition is a representation of an objective 'out there' world. Rather each individual 'brings forth' a world that is unique to that individual of whatever species. Note that it is *not* a mind that brings forth a world; in the Santiago theory 'a world' is identical with 'a mind'.

Capra and Varela (cf. Capra, 1996:287) denote the modern human condition as being characterized by 'Cartesian anxiety'. This is a state of frustration and anxiety caused by a hopeless grasping after an exterior world of 'separate objects that we see as firm and permanent, but which are really transient and ever-changing' (Capra, 1996:186). Likewise there is an anxious grasping after an internal ego-self which does not have any independent existence but is the result of our internal structural coupling (i.e. the cognition that arises from neuronal relationships).

These points of view, which seem to be a logical development within the 'new paradigm', are very similar to the Buddhist principles of *anicca* (impermanence) and *anatta* (absence of self-essence) (see 9.6 on the illusoriness of our common-sense view of the world). The first of the Four Noble Truths in Buddhism is *dukkha*, usually translated as suffering, although a better, more generalized meaning is 'unsatisfactory and unfulfilling' (Keown, 1996:48–9) (see 9.6). Capra used the same Buddhist term *dukkha* to explain the consequences of 'trying to cling to our rigid categories instead of realising the fluidity of life', as such 'we are bound to experience frustration after frustration' (Capra, 1996:286). The solution to the problem of 'Cartesian anxiety' is to see the world as it really is, 'seeing things in their state of suchness (*tathatā*) or is-ness' (Suzuki, 1970:370). The illusory round of existence (*samsāra*) then becomes an enlightenment-experience of unlimited bliss (*nirvāna*).

Capra, then, is calling for a 'new paradigm' in which our view of reality will be altogether changed, indeed the whole idea of a realist science which discovers 'facts' about the world will be replaced by a sense of systems within systems, processes of continual mutual cognition which lose their identity when they are analysed in a reductionist way. Again, as with other deep-ecological proposals, this faces the twin dangers of (a) being seen merely as naive, unrealistic as to the way science has to be done, and six billion humans have to live, or (b) being used in an authoritarian way. Stephan Elkins has commented that 'The systems-theoretical core of Capra's ecological paradigm could be appropriated, not as a source of cultural transformation, but as an instrument for the technocratic management of society and nature, leaving the prevailing social and economic order unchanged' (quoted in Merchant, 1992:104).

9.10 Conclusion

We have seen two Jewish thinkers offer new insights into suffering and related-ness. A brief survey of insights from Hinduism, Taoism and Buddhism showed us an array of possible relationships with scientific motifs. Environmental proposals, including those suggested by the Gaia Hypothesis, included a call for equality between species, and for a holistic approach to systems. These proposals must be judged both by their faithfulness to the traditions from which they derive, and the spiritual, ethical and practical attitudes to which they lead.

Notes

1   Sections 9.3, 9.4, 9.5, 9.6, 9.6.1 and 9.9 were drafted or part-drafted by MRN. All other sections, and editing for the 2005 edition, by CS.
2   This term is the participle of the Latin verb *esse*, to be.
3   See also 3.5.4 and 9.9 on Capra.
4   However, the work does raise interesting questions about the relationship of science and spirituality. Many commentators have assumed that *The Tao of Physics* is an *apologia* for spirituality (after the fashion of nineteenth- and twentieth-century natural theologies). However, there is another possibility which becomes apparent when we consider the readership of *The Tao*. It was originally published by a firm specializing in New Age literature and its original readership would

have needed little convincing of the validity of the spiritual path detailed by Capra. On the other hand, this readership would include many people who are suspicious of physical science in general and particularly of atomic physics (with its dubious connections to the military-industrial complex). Given such a readership, *The Tao of Physics* looks more like an *apologia* for Capra's vocation. Capra presents physics in a new light as a spiritual path that can be followed with integrity to the same destination as the great mystics of the East. Unwittingly Capra has revived an important social function of older natural theologies which, while appearing to offer scientific evidence of God's existence and benevolence, actually commended science as a godly and socially valuable vocation.

5   e.g. his *Zen and the Birds of Appetite* (1968).

6   Especially in *A Vision to Pursue* (1991).

7   There are fascinating parallels between this view and the perception of nature developed by the Catholic poet Gerard Manley Hopkins, who wrote of being able occasionally to win through to a sense of the 'instress' of things, an immediate perception of the essential nature of elements of the natural world in themselves (Hopkins, 1953:xx–xxii). Within Hopkins' theology, however, the nature of a kingfisher or a kestrel was always a nature bearing the marks of its creation by the Christian God.

8   See also Lovelock, 2000 for the autobiography of a very unusual figure in science.

9   See Ward and Brownlee, 2004:chs 3–4 for some thinking on a much longer timescale, in which planetary conditions will not be nearly so favourable for the majority of present life-forms.

10   For an exploration of dilemmas as to the use of nuclear power see Southgate and Aylward, 2002:78–83.

11   The suggestion of 'Gaia', the Greek goddess of the Earth, came from the novelist William Golding.

12   Frameworks in environmental ethics may typically be divided into those which are 'anthropocentric' (humanocentric) – attributing value to entities according to their relation to humans – those which are 'biocentric', and those which endeavour to be 'theocentric' – valuing entities in terms of their value to God. The crucial question tends to be whether non-human organisms or ecosystems have value in and for themselves – 'intrinsic value', or merely instrumental value for humans. For a brief introduction see Deane-Drummond (1996:70–8); for more detail see Northcott (1996), especially ch. 4. On intrinsic natural values see Rolston (1988; 1994:ch. 6).

13   Devall and Sessions, 1985. For a more recent set of essays see Sessions (1995).

Further reading

BUBER, MARTIN (1958) *I and Thou*, transl. by Ronald Gregor Smith (London: Continuum; first edition 1937, German original 1923)

CAPRA, F. (1996) *The Web of Life* (London: Flamingo)

DALAI LAMA (1997) *The Buddha Nature: Death and Eternal Soul in Buddhism* (Woodside, CA: Bluestar)

FLOOD, G.D. (1996) *An Introduction to Hinduism* (Cambridge: Cambridge University Press)

KEOWN, D. (1996) *Buddhism: A Very Short Introduction* (Cambridge: Cambridge University Press)

LANCASTER, B. (1995) *Mind, Brain and Human Potential: A Quest for and Understanding of Self* (Shaftesbury: Element Books)

LOVELOCK, J. (1988) *The Ages of Gaia* (Oxford: Oxford University Press)

RAHULA, W. (1998) *What the Buddha Taught* (Oxford: OneWorld)

WARD, K. (1987) *Images of Eternity: Concepts of God in Five Religious Traditions* (London: Darton, Longman & Todd)

—— (1996) *Religion and Creation* (Oxford: Oxford University Press)

Chapter 10

A test case: divine action

Christopher Southgate

10.1 Introduction

So far we have seen something of the diversity of relationship that different sciences have had with theological thought. We looked in Chapter 8 at a variety of ways in which thinkers are seeking to understand the reality of God at the beginning of the twenty-first century, and commented on the cogency of different models. In this chapter we draw on all this material to address the question: How can God be considered to *act*, to *have acted*, and to be *going to act* in the course of the history of the cosmos. In a sense Chapter 8 addressed mainly the character of God as God, and the 'spatial' question of God's relation to the world. Here we address also the temporal aspect of the relationship – what, in the world, God is doing (Section A – 10.4–10.12.1), what God has done (Section B – 10.14–10.19), what God will do (Section C – 10.20).

Of the voluminous literature on the subject we particularly recommend Keith Ward's 1990 study *Divine Action*. Ward sets out a contemporary philosophical base from which to explore the subject. A very lucid, if contentious, summary of the field has been provided by Nicholas Saunders (2002).

For reasons of space we confine this discussion to the Christian tradition, but the reader is invited to explore the shape the discussion of divine action might have taken in respect of Judaism, Islam (see Chapter 12) and the Eastern religions discussed in Chapter 9.

The exploration of divine action in the Christian tradition has been taken forward by five collections of essays deriving from the Vatican Observatory Conferences, jointly organized with the Center for Theology and the Natural Sciences in 1992, 1994, 1996, 1998 and 2000. The proceedings were edited by R.J. Russell with others, and entitled *Quantum Cosmology and the Laws of Nature* (1993), *Chaos and Complexity* (1995), *Evolution and Molecular Biology* (1998), *Neuroscience and the Person* (1999) and *Quantum Mechanics* (2001), each with the subtitle *Scientific Perspectives on Divine Action*.[1] The work of 'the Divine Action Project' has been assessed by Wildman (2004).

10.2 General comments

We acknowledge the extraordinary difficulty intrinsic in even beginning to speak of the transcendent Creator of the cosmos as acting in any particular way which we can describe out of our own experience as limited, contingent beings. It may therefore be asked why there has been such a focus on this part of the debate between science and theology. Part at least of the answer must be historical. As Kaiser points out (1991:193), Newton would have subscribed to the following six ways in which God was active:

1. the creation of matter and setting of it in motion in accordance with certain prescribed laws;
2. the formation of the present world system;
3. its continued operation;
4. its occasional reformation;
5. occasional spiritual intrusions in human affairs through the agency of natural phenomena (e.g. comets and epidemics);
6. miracles.

EXERCISE 10.1

Consider the list given in 10.2 and decide in how many of these ways you believe God to act. Compare your beliefs with others you know who are exploring these issues. The combinations of beliefs will reflect different positions in the historical debate (for a discussion see Brooke, 1991: especially ch. 4).

10.3 God 'edged out'?

It is especially interesting to note that Newton himself did not hold the mechanical view of the universe to which his system led (see Brooke, 1991:144–8). Rather he thought of God directly mediating the force of gravity. Yet within a hundred years of the publication of his *Principia* in 1687 there were many who would have denied that any of these six aspects of divine action were operative. It was accepted that physical forces could act at a distance without mediation, divine or other. *Hume* had attacked the reasonableness of believing in miracles (see 10.10(iv)). *Laplace* had posited the complete determinism of a world governed by Newtonian mechanics (see 1.17). And we saw in 6.7 and 6.10.5 how the simplicity and elegance of *Darwin*'s scheme later did away with the notion that individual living creatures need be the direct products of divine design.

Over a long period in Western thought God seemed to be progressively edged out of descriptions of the development and functioning of the world – both as described by physics and by biology. *In particular it was seen how difficult it was to sustain descriptions of the physical world in which God acted as a cause complementing physical causes – filling in a gap left by scientific narratives.* The phrase 'God of the gaps', promoted by Coulson (1958:41), has become proverbial as a description of bad theologies of the activity of God. Explanation of phenomena in terms of regular, natural causes has been extremely successful since the rise of science, so the 'presumption of naturalism' (Clayton, 1997a:173) has grown in strength.

Three strategies seem to offer themselves in the face of this problem: God 'banished', God 'before', or God 'behind'. The first is to abandon talk of God's acting in the physical world. This is the strategy adopted by atheism, sometimes motivated by a form of positivism (4.2). For different reasons it was also the strategy of Bultmannian existentialism (4.4). The second strategy is some form of deism, God being described as the first cause of all things, but as not otherwise active in the unfolding cosmos. The rise of deism is discussed by Brooke (1991: especially 167–71); what is, arguably, a new form of the strategy is found in the formulations of Kaufman and Wiles (10.8(ii), 10.9(ii), see also Saunders, 2002). The third obvious strategy is to posit that God acts 'behind' the system of causation, at another level not susceptible to physical description. This goes back to Aquinas and his discussion of primary and secondary causation (Aquinas, 1956:226–35; 1975:75–9).

In the light of these 'safe' strategies, which are all forms of 'separate development' for scientific and theological description, it is striking how many recent theologians have wanted to pursue a fourth path – they have regarded the system of causation that physics offers us as *open*, containing inherent gaps which allow God to act 'through' the system, to effect particular actions within the system of natural causes without being subject to the risk that science will close the gaps. *This strategy has a great deal to do with the contemporary perception that what happens in the real universe is the result of the interplay of physical laws and an ingredient of* **chance**. *We do not live in the predictable universe of Laplace (1.17), but in one in which it is not even theoretically possible to predict in minute detail what will happen next (5.11(ii), 5.12, 5.25–5.28).* In order to proceed with our investigation we must begin to explore (a) what might be the relationship between physical law and divine action and (b) exactly what might be meant by 'chance', a word as problematic in this field as is 'nature' in ecological theology.

10.3.1 Law and chance

Law

Most accounts of divine agency within the Christian tradition are not content either with 'God banished' or with a God who is only 'before'. Rather they regard God as actively sustaining the order of the physical universe, in some way or other maintaining the regularity of the cosmos. At the same time most Christian theologians are reluctant to consider a model in which God is the only true agent, in which everything happens by the direct will of God, and physical laws are only descriptions of events which God causes. This type of model, known as 'occasionalism', is the classic position of Islamic thought (see Chapter 12). Christian thinkers tend to want to acknowledge a partial autonomy to the world, such that physical laws describe processes that happen dependent only on God's overall sustaining, and not on God's specific intervention.

So, for example, theologians of physics such as John Polkinghorne or Russell Stannard no longer regard the solar system as in need of 'occasional reformation', as Newton did (see **10.2** above), because physics no longer has the problem Newton found with his formulation of planetary orbits. But they would want to assert that God continues to sustain the laws which govern the equations by which the planets move. This sustaining activity of God is often referred to as 'general divine action'.

Chance

The word 'chance'[2] is generally used in one of three ways:

(i) *in respect of an event such as the tossing of a coin*. As Peacocke says, 'had we sufficient knowledge of the exact values of all the relevant parameters, the laws of mechanics would in fact enable us to say in any particular toss which way the coin would fall' (1979:90).[3] Thus to call such outcomes chance is to confess to the incompleteness of our *knowledge* of the relevant causative factors, it is not to deny that those factors exist or that they are sufficient to account for the event.

(ii) *in respect of combinations of events which seem to come from two different causal chains*. Peacocke again: 'Suppose that when you leave the building in which you are reading these pages, as you step on to the pavement you are struck on the head by a hammer dropped by a man repairing the roof ... the two trains of events ... are each within themselves explicable as causal chains. Yet there is no connection between those causal chains except their point of intersection' (1979:90–1).

If Laplace were right, and the whole course of the universe were theoretically predictable (**1.17**), then of course this hammer blow would also be predictable. This second meaning of chance would again be an expression of our ignorance.

(iii) *as a non-technical way of describing the outcomes of events at the quantum level* (**5.11–5.14**). Quantum mechanics, as usually understood, implies that these outcomes are *not* determinate until they occur – they can only be expressed in terms of probabilities. Not only is our knowledge of them limited by the Heisenberg Uncertainty Principle (**5.11(ii)**), but – at least in the Copenhagen interpretation of quantum theory – there is an inalienable indeterminacy about the events themselves. Polkinghorne has argued that there is indeterminacy also in the large-scale systems that are described by the mathematics of chaos (1989:28–30 – see **10.9(iv)a**).

Meaning (ii) has an enormous effect on how the world actually develops – most strikingly in the field of biological evolution. Classical Darwinism postulates that the environment, viewed as an independently changing entity, is at every moment selecting which variants (arising by a largely separate causal chain) will survive and prosper (see 6.6). Contemporary thinking would recognize the situation as much more complex than that: the environment is itself being shaped by the activities of species as they evolve (most strikingly in respect of the Gaia Hypothesis, see 9.7). But the point still has force – most dramatically in respect of the five great extinctions that have taken place in evolutionary history (see 10.18). The trajectory of the massive object that collided with the Yucatan Peninsula 65 million years ago clearly belonged to a different causal chain from the one that had given rise to dinosaurs vulnerable to the extreme conditions resulting from the collision. So the course of evolution is highly unpredictable, much influenced by this sort of chance.

But it is meaning (iii) of 'chance', the possibility of *ontological* indeterminacy, that has been of such interest to theologians. *It is vital to distinguish between what is unpredictable by humans and what is ontologically indeterministic.* The unfolding of a system might be quite beyond human prediction (indeed this is of the essence of chaotic systems) and still be constrained by a set of deterministic laws, which God would have to violate to alter the outcomes of the system. But if ontological indeterminacy exists this suggests that physical laws are not sufficient to determine the outcome of every event. It seems to offer a possibility other than God banished, before or behind: that is, the possibility of a God who is 'before' in the sense of being the initial cause of everything, 'behind' in the sense of sustaining the laws and regularities God has established, but also a God working *through* the openness and indeterminacy of the natural order.

The debate about divine action has to be taken as a whole – any Christian-theological account of God's activity must include reference to creation and to eschatological redemption – but there is a specific sub-debate, much aired in recent years, on the possibility of God's *particular* action in situations in the present, so-called special divine action. Clayton makes the important point that *any such particular action must be congruent with God's action in universal history as a whole* (1997a:177). We cannot postulate a God faithful in upholding the regularities of the cosmos, but capricious in particular providential action. God's action must also be consistent with what is believed about God's goodness and faithfulness in respect of creation. We begin, then, by taking up the question of the possibility of God's action in and through the world as it is at present (Section A). Section B will consider the 'history' of divine action since the Big Bang, and Section C questions of action in the future – eschatology and redemption.

SECTION A
WHAT GOD IS DOING: PROVIDENCE AND MIRACLE (10.4–10.12.1)

10.4 How to think about providential agency

Is it possible to speak of God acting providentially in the life of a particular person or community? Is talk of miracle coherent? In an account based on the Christian tradition this means also considering the biblical accounts of God's particular action, and what is for Christians the most central of 'actions', the resurrection of Jesus.

The first precept to note is that particular divine action cannot be discernible as such by naturalistic analysis of the world. This is axiomatic from the point of view of *science*, because such descriptions are necessarily in terms of natural systems and regularities, related at some level to the experimentally testable. Supernatural agency is methodologically excluded as an explanation of such data. It is also axiomatic from the point of view of *theology* that God is not an entity among other entities, simply a cause among causes – divine action cannot simply be described in the same terms as human action, or other forms of cause.

Other key elements in this exploration are considerations of theodicy (see also 8.3), determinism, and personal agency.

10.5 Theodicy

The theology of providence can only ever be explored alongside the problem of suffering and evil. Whenever we speak of the possibility of God's acting, we at once face the question of consistency. How is providential action consistent with so much suffering (given that most contemporary theologians are reluctant to invoke the notion that suffering is always punishment for sin).[4] The defences of God in respect of 'moral evil' (i.e. human suffering arising from human acts) have been well summarized and analysed by Surin (1986). For a different type of analysis see Fiddes, 2000: ch. 5. Typically theodicists concentrate on the suffering of humans, and distinguish between 'moral evil' – suffering caused by the acts of other humans, and 'physical' or 'natural' evil – suffering caused by phenomena in the non-human world such as earthquakes, hurricanes, etc.

We indicated in 8.2–8.2.1 that process thought conceives the balance between divine sovereignty and creaturely freedom very differently from conventional Christian theologies. God's action is always consistent, in being always a lure towards goodness and harmony, but is never overwhelming, it never decides the fate of other entities (Surin 1986:86–92).

Another important formulation of theodicy is the so-called 'Irenaean' view, also known as 'the vale of soul-making' (Surin 1986:92–6). In outline this position holds that the world needs to be as it is if humans are to *learn goodness* – they can only do this in a morally ambivalent universe.

The very popular 'free-will' formulations of theodicy (sometimes described as 'Augustinian') all limit the scope of God's action by insisting that God respects the freedom of freely choosing creatures. There is moral evil not for its soul-making potential but because God must not prevent it if humans are to *have freedom* (Surin 1986:70–8).

Polkinghorne has advanced an extension of the free-will defence in respect of 'natural evil' which he calls the 'free-process defence' (1989:66–7). Periodic destruction of human value by the natural order is a necessary corollary of God's allowing that order to be itself and to develop and change. Intellectually, that seems the most coherent response to the terrible destruction inflicted by the Indian Ocean tsunami of December 2004. The movements and collisions of continental plates have had a vast influence on the evolution of life-forms on Earth; they have helped to shape the fascinatingly diverse biosphere within which we live. Occasionally they result in huge destruction. God, who gave rise to these processes, respects their operation for the sake of the character of the creation as a whole. The theodicist, however, is unlikely to conclude that this is a sufficient account to match our conception of a God who loves and cares for every human. Two further strategies therefore tend to be enlisted to engage with the suffering of humans:

(a) suffering-God theodicy, which we discussed in **8.5.6, 8.5.8, 8.6.2**.

(b) eschatological theodicy. It is widely conceded that neither the Irenaean nor the free-will (and free-process) defence is adequate without a doctrine of 'secondary goods'. Too many humans suffer intolerably without themselves having any opportunity to express their own free will. Theodicists therefore conclude that God must offer the victims of suffering consolations beyond this life, as part of God's promise that in the end time every tear will be wiped away (Revelation 21.4).

This brief account indicates the constraints theodicy must place on views of divine action; the more special divine action is proposed, the sharper the problems posed by situations in which God seems not to have acted. We return to the issue of theodicy in **10.18–10.19** when we consider the sufferings of non-human creatures.

10.6 Determinism, compatibilism and the nature of physical law

We noted above theologians' reluctance to accept occasionalism, in which God is the only true agent. (Among other reasons, this seems to most Christian thinkers to render the problem of evil unbearable.) The natural world is seen as having some partial autonomy, though its laws are God-given. That raises the question: is the network of physical causation closed by a set of determining laws, such that every future state of the system follows directly from its present state? In such a deterministic system, it would seem that God would have to violate the same physical laws God had set in place in order to accomplish a particular providential action. It has seemed to most contemporary thinkers that that is not an appropriate model for God (which is not to say that there might not have been very occasional events which were violations of such laws, the resurrection of Jesus often being taken to be the classic case of this).

A variety of ways forward offer themselves:

(i) Some thinkers are clear that the network of physical causation is *open*, the world is non-deterministic in its unfolding.

(ii) Some hold that laws that seem deterministic do not have ontological status – they do not determine reality, but are only descriptions of regularities, or approximations to reality (see for example Cartwright,

1999; Saunders, 2002:ch. 3 gives a thorough introduction to the philosophy of physical laws).

(iii) Some hold that a *compatibilist* understanding is necessary (see 1.17). Kirk Wegter-McNelly suggests three types of compatibilism which form part of the debate:

  (a) anthropo-physical compatibilism asserts that human freedom is compatible with physical determinism
  (b) anthropo-theological compatibilism asserts that human freedom is compatible with divine determinism
  (c) theo-physical compatibilism asserts that divine freedom is compatible with physical determinism

(quoted in Wildman, 2004:39)

Position (iii) (c) is the main type of compatibilism at issue in the divine action debate, but it is noteworthy that most incompatibilists' rejection of all three types of compatibilism is fuelled by their rejection of (a), by a conviction that real human moral freedom requires more than the mere impression humans have of making choices (so Polkinghorne, 2001:188).

10.7 Personal agency

At first sight it might appear that the best way to engage with the question of divine agency is through exploring the agency of human persons. After all, most Christian formulations speak of God as in some sense personal and in some sense active in the world (for an example of non-personal metaphors for God see the discussion of Ruether in 8.5.5). Our experience of *personal* agency is of two types:

  (a) we as mental beings influence our physical bodies;
  (b) as mental-physical beings we act upon other beings and on the world around us.

Human agency is a very imprecise basis for analogies to *God*'s action. Nevertheless it seems to be the best basis we have. As Clayton puts it: '*if* one is able to conceive of human intentional action in a way that is compatible with natural scientific accounts of the physical world, then one will have done the bulk of the work necessary for a theory of divine causation' (1997a:233).

Discouragingly, however, our understanding of human agency is very partial, as the following sections indicate. Of such a simple event as my lifting my arm, we can speak of sub-atomic, atomic and biochemical events, and of nerve-impulses passing from my brain to my arm. But at the interface between neurophysiological events and conscious thought/intention our scientific understanding is very preliminary. In sections 10.7.1–10.7.2 we explore this area in more detail – the reader wishing to concentrate on the main thread of the chapter is invited to go straight on to **10.8**.

10.7.1 The mind and the brain

Nancey Murphy summarizes a range of possible relations between the mind and the brain (1999:xiii–xv). One possibility is that consciousness is an 'epiphenomenon' of the complex functioning of the brain, it is as it were the 'hum' given off by the 'machine' – not central to the brain's functioning, which could (if we knew enough) be characterized solely in terms of neurophysiological events. Another view which holds up the possibility of the conceptual-explanatory reduction[5] of mental phenomena to the neurophysiological is 'type identity theory'. This holds that mental events are real enough, but each and every one is the product of a particular state of our neurones, so if we knew the state of every neurone in a person's brain we would know the mental state of the person. The language of thoughts and feelings could be dispensed with if we knew enough about assemblies of nerve cells. A view which is less optimistic about our neurophysiological knowledge, but also attempts a reductionistic view of mental function, is a 'functionalist' approach. This view (derived in particular from thoughts about artificial intelligence – see 7.5–7.6) treats the mind/brain as a system with inputs and outputs. We might not know its internal working, but in principle its outputs could be inferred from its inputs. The views described above are sometimes described as varieties of 'eliminative materialism' or 'reductive physicalism' – descriptions at the level of matter are all we need.

Over against this type of view must be set varieties of 'non-reductive physicalism' and 'dualism'. In non-reductive physicalism mental states are acknowledged to have their own causal status – they are *emergent properties* of complex organisms; they are said to be *supervenient upon* brain processes; they affect processes in the brain and the body through *top-down causation*.

A third type of view important in the history of the debate is 'dualism'. René Descartes was convinced that the thinking essence of a human self did not belong to the physical world. Those who use the traditional language of 'immortal souls' (see 7.7) are 'substance dualists', positing like Descartes a different sort of entity in our heads other than brain-stuff. A less controversial position is 'property dualism' – the mind behaves as though it had two different sets of properties: the mental/spiritual and the physical. Property dualism can be seen as a particular sort of emphasis within non-reductive physicalism.

10.7.2 The significance of the mind–brain debate at the interface between psychology and theology

Philip Clayton has made a fascinating observation on this debate. It is that:

> the first battle for the theologian to fight is on behalf of the reality of mental phenomena, their irreducibility to the realm of the physical, and their real causal power to bring about either other mental phenomena or changes in the physical world. These are in the first place questions that arise within the disciplines that address the so-called mind/body problem: biology, physiology, cognitive science, psychology and philosophy. To the extent

that she genuinely enters into the disciplines in question, the theologian can make real contributions to this discussion. (Clayton 1997a:239–40)

So Clayton envisages the theologian as active in the dispute over models indicated above, active to assert the reality both of mental and spiritual life and of free, rational responses to the world, and hence to reject eliminative materialism.

Conversely, the neuroscientist might be active in the theological debate over the status of 'soul' language, to indicate that where that language insists on a substance-dualist view it parts company with what science has generally found it profitable to explore. As there is no evidence for 'soul-stuff', what and where it might be, how it might behave, and how it might interact with brain-stuff, substance dualism is difficult to hold,[6] and will not be discussed further here.

A fascinating, though as yet undeveloped, theory is the 'dual-aspect monism' espoused by Polkinghorne in his early work (1988:ch. 5). In this view every complex network may have a mental aspect – that aspect becomes very significant in the case of human brains, and enables us to participate in the 'noetic world'. This world is also populated by such things as the truths of mathematics, and 'active intelligences ...', which traditionally we would call angels' (1988:76, see also 2000:95–9).

This thought-aspect of the cosmos might be the medium by which God's information enters physical systems. This would be consonant with the notion that it is to human minds, the material structure with the greatest noetic aspect, that God is able to make God's most sensitive and articulate self-communication.

It is possible to question whether this noetic language actually improves on the traditional language of the spiritual, but there is a richness to the idea which merits further study. It may, for instance, have links to the Eastern Orthodox language of the *energeiai* of God (see 8.5.6). It sits intriguingly between (a) substance dualism – the mind has aspects that are parts of a realm inhabited by angels, (b) non-reductive physicalism – the spirit is only an aspect of the emergent properties of the mind, and (c) the panexperientialism of process thought.

Fraser Watts made clear in 7.4 his conviction that there is 'no possibility of God influencing private experience in a way that bypasses the natural processes of the brain', though equally he holds that 'it is as *persons* that God relates to us, not as mere minds, brains, souls or spirits' (Watts, 2002:79). So our understanding of the action of God in the world must take into account both God's relating personally to persons,[7] and God's relating to the physical stuff of which the world is made. Even a view of divine action which restricted God's activity to interaction with the human spirit would still have to account for divine engagement with the brain-stuff within whose functioning 'mind' and 'spirit' are emergent properties.

10.8 Various views of God's action in the world: a classification

Acknowledging, then, our difficulty in understanding personal agency, we return to the problem of God's action in the world the sciences describe. The ground of the discussion of providential action has been 'staked out' by various 'camps'. We begin by classifying these, then explore their approach to the 'causal joint' between God's activity and the physical world (10.9). We then compare in detail the views of Arthur Peacocke and John Polkinghorne (10.10). Finally we summarize the main positions in the field of special divine action (10.11–10.12).

A classification of views

   (i) *theistic naturalism*
Willem B. Drees has surveyed the field with characteristic insight (1996:93–106), but is reluctant to speak of particular divine action because this might seem to undermine the adequacy of naturalistic explanations, to which he is committed.[8] For different reasons Bultmann and his school also insisted on the adequacy of the scientific description of events (see 4.4).

  (ii) *general providential action without particular gaps in the causal order*
This view is espoused by Gordon Kaufman (1972) and even more radically by Maurice Wiles (1986).

 (iii) *particular providential action without gaps in the causal order*
In different ways this is proposed by
   (a) neo-Thomists, such as Austin Farrer;
   (b) those strongly committed to the image of the cosmos as the body of God; and
   (c) Arthur Peacocke with his concept of 'top-down' or 'whole–part' causation.

 (iv) *particular providential action employing particular gaps in the causal order*
Again there are three camps here:
   (a) John Polkinghorne, locating the relevant 'gap' as being the one offered (supposedly) by non-linear systems such as give rise to the phenomenon of chaos;
   (b) those such as George Ellis, Nancey Murphy, Robert J. Russell and Thomas Tracy who follow a suggestion of Pollard's that quantum theory offers the pertinent gaps; and
   (c) process theologians who postulate that the course of development of every entity is particularly exposed to the divine persuasion in a way which is outside the descriptions of science.

The classification above is based on Thomas Tracy's essay in *Chaos and Complexity* (1995:289–324) – his relatively non-technical summary of the different positions is a good introduction to their intricacies. Clayton offers a careful analysis of the metaphysics of divine action (1997a:esp. ch. 6). On Peacocke and Polkinghorne see 10.10.

10.9 The causal joint

One important way in which to investigate the different positions is by asking the question: What is the 'causal joint' at which God as a transcendent, immaterial cause interacts particularly with causative factors in the material world?

(i) Drees

His view would be that to search for an extra ingredient at a causal joint is to neglect the self-sufficiency of naturalistic accounts, one of the premises he sets out so clearly at the beginning of *Religion, Science and Naturalism* (1996:12–21).

(ii) Kaufman and Wiles

These both reject descriptions of divine action as particular to individual situations. God's relation is to the-world-as-a-whole, and history-as-a-whole, the relation of creating and sustaining the cosmos from moment to moment. As Tracy points out, this is essentially to subsume providence into creation, and pays a heavy theological price in so doing (1995:301–4).

(iii)(a) Neo-Thomists

Thinkers of this school speak of 'double agency', a concept developed by Aquinas and rearticulated in twentieth-century theology in particular by Austin Farrer (1966; 1967). God is the primary cause of all that is; in effecting the divine purposes God works always through secondary causes, through the laws of the universe and the activities of human agents. Our experience of God's activity is *always* mediated. God can work through these secondary causes to bring about particular results. But it is quite impossible to give an account of the causal joint, because (i) divine causation differs from any other kind – we should not expect to be able to characterize it within our own terms – and (ii) we have no 'pure-secondary causes' to look at – everything is informed by divine causation. We have no 'control experiment' by reference to which we might characterize the added causal ingredient of the divine.[9]

Anyone giving an account of divine action must respect these two points. But double agency has been much criticized, not least because of the difficulty in offering any satisfactory analogy which would illustrate it.[10] Polkinghorne, the most vocal representative of position (iv) above, has gone as far as to call Farrer's account 'theological doublespeak' (1994:82). Clayton suggests that if this model of divine agency claims any more than the mere sustaining of natural causes then 'it envisions a type of continuous divine intervention in the world that is no weaker than the classical accounts of miracles' (1997a:177). These criticisms are not altogether fair – what is clear from Kathryn Tanner's careful piecing-together of the 'rules' for this sort of discourse (1988:90–8) is that double agency cannot be abstracted from the intricate Thomistic reasoning from which it arose. It thus profits from the strengths of that system and suffers from its weaknesses. One of the latter relates to God and time (see our discussions at 5.5–5.9 and in Chapter 8). Any system based on the Augustinian–Thomist conception that God gave rise to the whole time-span of creation in the 'moment' of its divine inception runs into great difficulty in describing real freedom in other agents with whom God might enter into relation.

(iii)(b) The world-as-the-body-of-God

The use of this image is the one which makes strongest use of the analogy of human action, as mental beings 'on' physical bodies (see 10.7–10.7.1 above). But in the case of human action, descriptions in terms of the mental, the intentional, are *grounded in the physical*. The human 'intender' is not an autonomous entity existing independently of nerves and muscles; it is a body containing a brain. And as soon as we ground God in the physical world by making that world God's body we run into the problems touched on in 8.5.4. Again Polkinghorne is a pithy critic, pointing out that pressing this analogy either places God too much in thrall to the world (unable to act autonomously because God is dependent on the inputs from a body, as human action is) or the world too much in thrall to God (humans could no more act freely than an organ of the body can).[11]

(iii)(c) Peacocke

Arthur Peacocke wants to use this same mind–body analogy, but with a very proper caution – 'in a human body, the "I" does not transcend the body onto-logically in the way that God transcends the world' (1995:285). He is also very cautious about explicating the causal joint – such a description of the problem 'does not do justice to the many levels in which causality operates in a world of complex systems interlocking in many ways at many levels' (282). He does not find any theologically relevant gaps in the causal order, and is temperamentally most reluctant to contemplate anything smacking of divine *intervention* in the natural order (see 10.10(iv) on miracles).

So Peacocke follows Kaufman and Wiles in postulating that God's action is on the-world-as-a-whole, but he goes further than either in that:

(i) he offers a metaphor for divine action in terms of the way in which the properties of a whole system, such as a chemical system far from equilibrium, or a biological ecosystem, affect the behaviour of individual parts. The nature of the whole, and of its environment, exerts constraints on the behaviour of the parts. This he originally called 'top-down causation' but now prefers to call 'whole–part influence' (Peacocke, 1999:221). Brain function may also be of this kind – our mental life being the highest emergent property (see 6.11.1) of the brains in our bodies. The material world, on this model, has God as its boundary or environment; relationship with God is the highest emergent property of any physical system.

(ii) Peacocke allows the possibility that this general action of God on the-world-as-whole might have particular effects – just as a boundary constraint in one of the systems described above might generate a particular, localized pattern. This is perhaps the most criticized element in his scheme, since he gives no indication as to exactly how this might take place (cf. Clayton, 2004:262–3).

Peacocke's God, then, is the environment of the cosmos.[12] His God's interaction with the world, by means of the input of information – is the highest-level emergent property of the cosmos as system, a system within which God is radically and totally immanent, as well as transcendent. For a diagram of Peacocke's sense of God's activity pervading the cosmos see Peacocke, 2004b:148–9.

As Drees points out (1995:236), speaking of the environment of the whole universe can never be more than a metaphor, but it is the strength of panentheism that it can offer such a telling metaphor. Tracy also takes Peacocke to task for stretching a concept too far – he points out that the examples of 'top-down' causation we know about are all analysable in 'bottom-up' terms.[13] Top-down causation is a purely explanatory procedure, it is a bold strategy to invoke it for ontological purposes, and to suppose that a 'whole' can be invoked as an actual cause within a system (Tracy, 1995:note to 307).

(iv)(a) Polkinghorne

If Peacocke's carefully nuanced account can be seen as bold, then Polkinghorne's must be thought that much bolder. In *Science and Providence* (1989) Polkinghorne seemed not only to *locate* the causal joint of particular divine action but also to suggest a *means* by which God might effect such action. His account of providential action, moreover, included not only such classic instances in the Christian tradition as the virginal conception and empty-tomb-raising of Jesus, but even the validity of prayer for rain.

The key scientific observation for Polkinghorne is that non-linear systems of the sort that exhibit chaos are exquisitely sensitive to the conditions in which they develop (see **5.25–5.27**), and hence their development very rapidly becomes unpredictable.[14] That much is generally accepted. But Polkinghorne has gone further and proposed that these large-scale systems are ontologically indeterminate, not only unpredictable in terms of our knowledge but genuinely open to the future, and that God can therefore influence each one of them by an input of 'active information' (without energy input, which could be detectable). God respects the regularities of the physical laws God has created and holds in being, but nevertheless has freedom to work through these indeterminacies.

Polkinghorne is famous, or notorious, for possessing a sweatshirt bearing the slogan 'Epistemology models Ontology'. This reflects his view that the unpredictability of complex non-linear systems is a clue to their ontological indeterminacy. He has been very much criticized for this view (see e.g. Murphy, 1995:327–9), given that the equations that model these systems are entirely deterministic (see **5.27**). However, as Saunders indicates, Polkinghorne's position has often been misunderstood. Polkinghorne does not deny the deterministic character of the equations of chaos, rather he says that our mathematics here is an approximation to a richer reality (Polkinghorne 1998:ch. 3; Saunders, 2002: ch. 7). He would agree with Lawrence Osborn's view in **5.28** that 'the equations are maps, not the reality'. Within this reality, presumed to be indeterministic, God may impart 'active information', without input of energy, to move a system between equienergetic pathways through its 'attractor',[15] thereby influencing, perhaps very markedly, the outcome of real systems in the macroscopic world. Saunders, however, goes on to indicate a further problem with Polkinghorne's view, namely that strange attractors are themselves a property of deterministic mathematical frameworks.

(iv)(b) Murphy, Russell, Tracy and Ellis

Another approach to asserting particular providence through gaps in the causal order is to follow a suggestion first made by Arthur Compton as long ago as 1935, and developed in detail by William Pollard in 1958. This is to locate theologically productive indeterminacy at the quantum level, rather than at the macroscopic level. This is the approach (with differences) of Nancey Murphy, Robert J. Russell, Thomas Tracy and George F.R. Ellis and is reviewed by Russell in *Quantum Mechanics* (Russell *et al.*, 2001).[16] At first sight it is an enormously tempting line of argument:

> real freedom in agents, human and divine, requires an open future – genuine, ontological indeterminacy. The main (though not the only) interpretation of contemporary physics is that quantum systems possess such indeterminacy. Therefore, this is where divine agency can operate without detection, or interference in the autonomy of natural (particularly living) entities. There seems a real consonance, or at least compatibility, between quantum theory – the most imaginative, ingenious and counterintuitive element in natural science – on the one hand, and the demands of theology on the other.

Tracy gives the following five types of divine agency, in addition to the initial creation:

1. 'God acts directly in every event to sustain the existence of each entity that has a part in it.' (*Conservation*, see **10.3.1**)
2. 'God can act directly to determine various events which occur by chance on the finite level.' (*Quantum-level intervention*)
3. 'God acts indirectly through causal chains that extend from God's initiating direct actions.' (*Amplification of effects at quantum level*)
4. 'God acts indirectly in and through the free acts of persons whose choices have been shaped by the rest of God's activity in the world.' (*Persuasion* (presumably a function of 2. and 3.))
5. 'God can also act directly to bring about events that exceed the natural powers of creatures, events which not only are undetermined on the finite level, but which also fall outside the prevailing patterns and regular structures of the natural order' (*Miracles*, see **10.10(iv)**)
   (The Tracy quotations and the basis of the titles are taken from Clayton 1997a:215.)

EXERCISE 10.2

Compare Tracy's list in **10.9(iv)** with the divine actions of Newton's God listed in **10.2**. After considering the material so far, decide which of these five modes of divine action you believe in. Note that Clayton comments: 'all but the last of these five can be accepted without affront to natural law' (1997a:215).

Note the key elements of this proposal – genuine ontological indeterminacy at the quantum level, and amplification of these effects to make a significant difference to events in the macroscopic world. The indeterminacy is presumed to be to do with the collapse of the wave-function (see **5.13**) since the Schrödinger Equation (**5.11.1**) itself is deterministic. These thinkers differ as to the question – does God interact with every quantum event (Murphy), with every event until entities with a degree of consciousness arise (Russell), with only selected events (Tracy) or with only selected events focusing on human brain states (Ellis). Murphy's account poses questions about the status of free will, Tracy's raises issues of theodicy. For further analysis see **10.12** below and Saunders 2002:chs 5–6.

Both Peacocke and Polkinghorne reject quantum indeterminacy as a candidate for the causal joint. The link between the probabilistic world of quantum mechanics and the macroscopic world is still poorly understood (see **5.13**), nor is it known if there can be any equivalent to chaotic behaviour (where large effects are caused by small changes in initial conditions) within quantum systems. Except in devices designed to amplify them, the effects of quantum fluctuations tend to cancel out – the 'amplification' suggested by mode 3 above is therefore questionable.[17]

Among Peacocke's objections are:

(a) his sense that ontological indeterminacy has to be taken seriously – God could not logically have the knowledge to determine the precise result of a quantum event, and if God were to alter such an event, God would have to alter a great number of others simply in order to hide divine activity behind the observed statistics.

(b) a conviction that this picture of God continually determining the outcome of processes established in creation is at variance with the very fruitful emphasis in the scientist-theologians that God has created processes which *themselves* can, when sustained by God, give rise to the novelty, diversity and complexity we so celebrate (see Peacocke, 1998).

Setting aside this quantum proposal for the present we consider in more depth the differences between Peacocke and Polkinghorne. Among the impressive range of their writings, texts particularly suitable for comparative purposes are: Peacocke, 1993:chs. 9, 11; 1995; 1998; 1999; 2001a; 2004b; Polkinghorne, 1989; 1995a:ch. 6; 1995b; 1996a:ch. 3; 1996b; 1998a; 2000, 2004 and they merit careful study.

10.10 Peacocke and Polkinghorne compared

(i) Introduction

These two thinkers stem from different scientific traditions and, though both Anglicans, reflect two different theological instincts. This reinforces the point made in 1.5 that there is not one simple relation between science and Christian theology (let alone theologies derived from other faiths). Different sciences suggest different relations with theology, and different theological preconceptions lead to different approaches to the same data. Polkinghorne is a physicist, at heart one who analyses the mechanisms by which the material world operates, and theologically somewhat conservative, much influenced by Moltmann. Peacocke's science was the biology of macromolecules, the ideal vantage-point from which to consider different levels of description and the existence of irreducible levels of complexity. Theologically he belongs to a more liberal Anglican school, much influenced by Geoffrey Lampe.

(ii) Approaches to panentheism and theodicy

This difference can be seen in their two approaches to *panentheism*. Polkinghorne remains suspicious of the concept. His theology holds the world at a distance from God, stressing divine transcendence. His God seems always in some sense an operator on the physics of the world. Panentheism, he thinks, *will be* the condition of the creation at its culmination at the eschaton (Polkinghorne, 2004:166). Peacocke wants to stress divine immanence. The creativity of the world, of which biology is so eloquent, is for him a sign of the divine omnipresence. And Peacocke is, as we have seen, willing to consider a range of metaphors for God in relation to the world. He finds panentheism a helpful member of this range.

They differ too in their approach to *theodicy*, Peacocke inclining to an 'Irenaean' approach which sees the world of suffering as a necessary context for the growth of free beings towards God, Polkinghorne to a 'free-will defence' – if beings are genuinely free they will be free to inflict suffering – augmented by a free-process argument in respect of natural evil (see 10.5).

(iii) Models of divine action

However, the positions of Peacocke and Polkinghorne on divine action are not as dissimilar as has sometimes appeared. Polkinghorne writes:

> It is important to recognize that, in this scheme, the significance of the sensitivity of chaotic systems to the effects of small triggers is *diagnostic* of their requiring to be treated in holistic terms and of their being open to top-down causality through the input of active information. It is not proposed that this is the localized mechanism by which agency is exercised. *I do not*

suppose that either we or God interact with the world by the carefully calculated adjustment of the infinitesimal details of initial conditions so as to bring about a desired result. The whole thrust of the proposal is expressed in terms of the complete holistic situation, not in terms of the clever manipulation of bits and pieces [emphasis ours]. It is, therefore, a proposal for realizing a true kind of top-down causality. It may fittingly be called *contextualism*, for it supposes the behavior of parts to be influenced by their overall context. (1995b:154)

and:

It seems entirely conceivable that God also interacts with the creation through the input of active information into its open physical process. We glimpse, in a rudimentary way, what might lie behind theology's language of God's 'guiding' and 'drawing on' creation, language often associated with talk of the Spirit working immanently on the inside of creation. (1996b:248)

This is close to Peacocke's emphases on divine immanence, whole–part influence, and God as the ultimate boundary condition. It is the difference in emphasis between these two careful and committed thinkers that remains fascinating. Polkinghorne's stress is still on the question – why do certain things happen and not others? Hence his interest in God choosing the paths of systems through chaotic attractors. Peacocke still wants to stress God's respect for the freedom of the systems God has created. However, Polkinghorne's system-open-to-God-as-overall-context is very similar to Peacocke's whole–part-influence-on-the-world-as-a-whole, given that they both agree that (a) the future is not known to God – God is working with at least a genuine epistemic openness – and (b) divine action can have *particular* effects.

(iv) The question of miracle

We have seen that Polkinghorne still sticks to his emphasis on the possibility of particular, revelatory divine acts in a way which Peacocke strives to avoid. So it is to their approach to 'miracle' that we now turn. The first point to make about miracle is that definition is all-important. The eighteenth-century philosopher David Hume's famous attack on miracle can be summarized as follows:

1. A miracle is a violation of the laws of nature.
2. We have uniform experience that the laws of nature are never violated.
3. 'no testimony is sufficient to establish a miracle, unless the testimony be of such a kind, that its falsehood would be more miraculous, than the fact, which it endeavours to establish' (Hume, 2000:431).

As C.S. Lewis commented:

Now of course we must agree with Hume that if there is absolutely 'uniform experience' against miracles, if in other words they have never happened, why then they never have. Unfortunately we know the experience against them to be uniform only if we know that all the reports of them are false. And we can know all the reports to be false only if we know already that miracles have never occurred. In fact we are arguing in a circle. (Lewis, 1947:123)

In other words, we would reject testimony to a miracle unless it convinced us, by reference to our previous experience, that the witnesses were not deluded (point 3), but by definition our experience will always tell us otherwise (point 2). Hume's argument remains influential, particularly as taken up by Antony Flew (1997). This Humean approach, however, is based on a premiss which the new science no longer has on offer. As Flew says, [Christians] 'have to presuppose the existence of a strong natural order' (1997:54). But even granted a strong natural order, it is very clear from the science of unpredictability in non-linear dynamic systems (including the human brain) that it is inconceivable that the behaviour of a real-life system involving human beings could be the subject of a totally comprehensive scientific explanation. If we do not know – precisely – what the laws of nature prescribe in a particular situation we cannot be sure what would constitute a 'violation'. We have therefore to define miracle in theological terms rather than in terms of scientific regularities.

A possible definition would be:

> **an extremely unusual event, unfamiliar in terms of naturalistic explanation, which a worshipping community takes to be specially revelatory, by dint of the blessing or healing it conveys, of the divine grace.**[18]

As Clayton emphasizes, such a theological definition does *not* mean 'This event *could* not have occurred, that is without divine assistance, given what we know about the natural world' (1997a:178).

Polkinghorne has an extensive discussion of miracle in his *Science and Providence* (1989), and takes a very positive view of the possibility of such events. Again this is a reflection of his sense of the openness and flexibility of physical processes. God does not violate the regularities God has put into place (1996b:248f.), but God still has scope for working within the natural processes to generate remarkable results.

Peacocke takes a much more cautious view, questioning 'whether such direct "intervention" is compatible with and coherent with other well-founded affirmations concerning the nature of God and of God's relation to the world' (1993:183).

(v) The resurrection and virginal conception of Jesus

The normative Christian miracle of the resurrection of Jesus[19] finds our two theologians, again, close in many respects, but with differences of emphasis. Polkinghorne sees the New Testament accounts as, overall, offering a self-consistent account of a bodily resurrection that left a tomb empty and that led to appearances of the risen Lord in a transformed type of body. 'The empty tomb is of great importance, "with its proclamation that the risen Lord's glorified body is the transmutation of his dead body; that in Christ there is a destiny not only for humanity but also for matter"' (Polkinghorne, 1996a:55). Peacocke would agree that something happened which was no mere trick within the psyches of the disciples, but he is much more reluctant to accept either the emptiness of the tomb, or indeed the theological desirability of an empty tomb (1993:279–88). Clearly other human tombs are not empty. The atoms that were 'us' become dispersed at our death. If we are resurrected with any sort of embodied status, it is because the pattern that was most distinctively ourselves has been held in God. Jesus' resurrection body was also of a different order, not easy to recognize, able to pass through walls. This must surely also reflect a pattern transmuted in God. So the atoms of Jesus' body are, for Peacocke's theological naturalism, much better left to disperse in the tomb.

Likewise Peacocke is very little disposed to accept the virginal conception of Jesus. In a careful analysis he points out how strange it would be if God's action in the world amounted in this particular case to supplying a complete set of chromosomes as from a human father. The old images of God's relation to living things: the pre-Darwinian specific designer of creatures, the pre-Humean cosmic tinkerer, would return with a vengeance in such a scenario. For Peacocke 'it is theologically imperative that the birth stories and the doctrine of the virginal conception of Jesus be separated from the doctrine of the incarnation' (1997:38). Whereas Polkinghorne, without concerning himself too much with the biological details, considers that 'the dual origin of the X and Y chromosomes ... seems a possible physical expression of the belief, in the words of the Nicene creed, that Jesus "by the power of the Holy Spirit became incarnate of the Virgin Mary and was made man". In other words, his conception was an act of divine–human co-operation' (1996a:79).

So two highly trained scientist-theologians, both pursuing programmes of critical realism in science and theology, reveal how junctures arise when one has to accord one programme, the scientific or the theological, priority over the other. Both thinkers agree that the scientific data necessitate dispensing with an Edenic paradise from which humans 'fell' (see 6.3.2), but they disagree over miracle, empty tomb and virginal conception.

10.11 Process schemes and double agency

We conclude this section by considering briefly two other influential descriptions of divine action. It is not difficult to see that *process schemes* can accommodate divine activity in particular situations, since divine persuasion or lure is present in every interaction between entities. Close consideration, however, shows that process thought is in a similar position to that of the *neo-Thomists* – both introduce a type of influence which is at a remove at once both from our ordinary experience *and* from the scientific accounts:

- Neo-Thomists posit a divine influence which (a) knows the results of its actions already through the atemporal omniscience of God's action and (b) executes its purpose by being the particular primary cause behind secondary causes, and yet allegedly (c) still allows creatures their freedom.
- Process thinkers posit a sort of panexperientialism which allows all entities, however inanimate, to be aware of the divine will and to respond to it (or not).

Indeed Settle considers a process metaphysic to be the natural result for a search for an appropriate account of double agency (Settle, 1996).

Those convinced for other reasons of the rightness of either of these positions will accept the version of divine providence that the account offers – but neither account offers any purchase on discussing a model of God in relation to the physical world as science describes it.

Where neo-Thomism and process thought differ so sharply is in terms of *theodicy*. The great problem with an account of providence in terms of primary and secondary agency is that the most evil of persons becomes a secondary agent of God.

The merits of process theodicy were pointed out in 8.3, but we noted at 8.5.3 the question it raised – whether the process God is God enough to be the ground of hope. The neo-Thomist God, then, is so much God – omniscient, omnipotent – as to pose great problems for theodicy: the process God, in contrast, cannot be held to account for evils from which the divine fellow-sufferer has laboured to dissuade the entities concerned. Between these poles come the accounts of providential action, general and special, undertaken by a self-limiting God to whom the future remains not wholly known, that we have discussed in the rest of the chapter.

10.12 Conclusion to the debate on special divine action

Wildman's analysis of the state of the divine action debate in his 2004 article is interesting. He gives his view that those who press special divine action in its strongest way, as

(i) objective
(ii) incompatibilist
(iii) non-interventionist in respect of the laws of nature, and
(iv) regarding those laws as having strong ontological force – genuinely prescribing what events will occur –

are indeed pressing for the strongest 'traction' with scientific descriptions. They are opening up to the full the possibility that science itself will rule out mechanisms of divine action. *But the effort to push divine freedom into a box causes it to vanish.*[20] One of the achievements of the Vatican/CTNS Project may have been to clarify this conclusion. Every proponent of special divine action has somehow to relax one of these conditions. We have seen Peacocke, in effect, relax theo-physical incompatibilism (10.9(iii)(c)) by invoking panentheism – a system which might appear mathematically deterministic is open to the future because it has its being within God (2001a:ch. 5). God is described as working 'in, with and under' the explorations of created entities – this is also, in different ways, the approach of neo-Thomism and process thought. We have seen Polkinghorne take a particular strategy towards condition (iv), regarding the laws describing dynamic systems as only approximations to a more complex and open reality. Wildman shows that the proponents of special divine action at the quantum level all relax condition (iv) in one way or another, regarding the laws as *descriptions* of a world in which God is always active (Murphy, also in a different way Russell, see 10.12.1), or as *having only statistical force at the quantum level* (Tracy, Ellis).

The discussion of the theology of divine action now seems to be resolving itself into a debate between quantum indeterminacy, contextualism (of which in their different ways Polkinghorne and Peacocke can be seen as representative) and some sort of metaphysical account of double agency – along either neo-Thomist or process lines. It is hard to avoid concluding that efforts to derive a particular consonance between the new physics and accounts of divine action have met with very limited success. Theologians have been forced either into *pressing* quantum indeterminacy further than seems satisfactory (Tracy, Ellis and Murphy), or into *guessing* that epistemological indeterminacy in chaotic systems somehow models a real openness, to which scientific descriptions only approximate (Polkinghorne), or back to speaking of God as the 'context' of the physical universe, *asserting* that systems must be regarded as indeterminate because they unfold in the context of a personal God (Peacocke).

Perhaps the most interesting ways forward come from those who want to try and combine elements from the different camps. It is interesting that Nancey Murphy, in an essay of exemplary clarity, extends a quantum-indeterminacy-based account towards a new metaphysics of causation in which chaos theory and top-down causation both find a place (1995:338–57). Philip Clayton, working from Peacocke's panentheistic whole–part model of divine action, also makes room for special action at the quantum level (Clayton, 1997a:chs. 7 and 8). Even Murphy, however, concedes that she does not know how much of a 'window' for special divine action quantum indeterminacy provides. Tracy writes: 'what is needed is not so much a theory of divine action as an array of coherent possibilities that can be called upon as needed to articulate the claims of a particular religious tradition' (Tracy, 2004:196). It is best not to limit God's action to a particular locus – or indeed to focus on efficient causation as the sole way of thinking of God acting.[21]

10.12.1 The contribution of Robert J. Russell

We reserve a special mention for Russell's work, partly because he has been so much the inspiration and constant factor in the exploration of divine action over many years, partly because his grasp of physics and philosophical theology has enabled him to analyse the possibility of non-interventionist special divine action at the quantum level in great detail, but also because of three insights of his which lead us into our discussion of God's activity through the history of the cosmos. Russell sees:

(a) that the evolutionary process is directly susceptible to possible quantum non-interventionist special divine action, because certain mutations (see 6.9) are caused by single events at the sub-molecular level (Russell, 1998)

(b) that the extent of divine action may well have altered profoundly over the history of the cosmos – before life began God may have acted in every event to ensure the possibility of a fruitful universe, but once conscious entities arose which had their own lives and interests, it may be that God withdrew to a great extent in order to respect those entities' freedom (Russell, 1998:215–16)

(c) that even before humans evolved there were issues of theodicy associated with God's providential action within a world full of creaturely suffering (Russell, 2001:318–20). We address this in 10.18–10.19; Russell's own response is to invoke a Trinitarian engagement with divine redemption at the eschaton (see 10.20).

SECTION B
WHAT GOD HAS DONE: THE HISTORY OF THE UNIVERSE (10.13–10.19)

10.13 The Big Bang and 'before'

We saw in 1.15 that contemporary speculations on the origin of the universe suggest that it may have developed out of a quantum event of some kind, a chance fluctuation in a situation which contained no matter or energy, but only possibilities.

Just as Darwinian evolution pushed theological reflection on biology away from the notion of God designing individual creatures, so these quantum-cosmological speculations are, even before they are substantiated, tending to push theological reflection on physics further and further away from thought of the Big Bang as a precisely divinely controlled instant. That is not to say that God is not the ultimate cause of there being anything rather than nothing – as Ward says, the doctrine of *creatio ex nihilo*, while hardly given direct warrant by the Christian scriptures, is nevertheless 'implicit in the Biblical doctrine that God is the creator of heaven and Earth, that he can do all things, that nothing is beyond his power' (1990:6). Nor is it to say that the laws and parameters governing the field of possibility were not set by God – again, the tradition has always presumed that whatever rationality governed the behaviour of the universe was a reflection of the rationality of God. Rather the presence of this ineradicable element of chance in the development of the universe calls forward images of God's creative action other than the merely mechanical.

For example, the biblical image of God as the potter (Isaiah 64.8; Jeremiah 18.6; Romans 9.21 – all with the stress on the absoluteness of God's power) bears further thought. Is not the activity of the potter at her or his wheel sometimes with a definite objective, but sometimes freer, more improvisatory? At those times the potter has set up the possibilities, and then allows shapes to appear, with which she or he then works. Or again (an image of which Arthur Peacocke is especially fond), God could be pictured as a composer of fugues who has set up the rules which circumscribe the form, but waits for the particular inspiration of the moment to dictate how the particular fugue will arise and grow.[22] The Hebrew Bible offers a haunting image of the primordial universe – however Genesis 1.1–2 are interpreted,[23] verse 2 does suggest two elements, a structureless primordium (*tohu-va-bohu* in the Hebrew) and a mighty or divine wind (*ruach elohim*). God, then, might be pictured as brooding on a sea of possibility, a contemplation which gave rise to the heavens and the earth. We are not in any way attempting to project onto the biblical author any anachronistic cosmological awareness, merely to notice a mythic depiction which has some resonances with the newest physics. Peter Van Inwagen has suggested that God, faced with an infinity of different but equally acceptable possible initial states of the universe, might simply decree 'Let one of this set be.' Van Inwagen considers that this form of creation, again consonant with the newest science, might be describable in a way which was free both of divine caprice and of divine dice-tossing carelessness.[24]

10.14 Anthropic considerations

In **5.20–5.24** we mentioned the apparent fine-tuning of the universe and identified different forms of the anthropic principle. What concerns us here is what Polkinghorne has called the 'moderate' and Drees the 'theistic' anthropic principle. Polkinghorne considers that the apparent fine-tuning of this universe so as to be precisely such as could produce life is 'a fact of interest calling for an explanation' (1991:78). Against this it is important to note Drees' objection that it is perfectly possible that these 'tunings' of the physical constants could disappear as our understanding grows (1996:271). It is fair to suppose, however, that it will still be worthy of comment that the origin of the universe was such an exceptionally-low-entropy-event, occupying such an infinitesimally tiny part of the apparent space of possibilities (Penrose, 1989:445).

Of the various explanations considered in **5.21–5.24** the most coherent seem to be either that this is the one universe – out of a huge number – which has the particular parameters that allow life to exist, or that this universe has been fine-tuned by a designer.

Although it is not possible to choose definitively between these possibilities, 'the design hypothesis has a great deal to say for it' (Murphy, 1993:432). We agree that, to someone already committed to a theistic research programme, apparent anthropic fine-tuning provides previously unexpected confirmation. A programme which has as its core a conviction that God created a meaningful and life-producing universe would generate an auxiliary hypothesis to the effect that the conditions of the very early universe would be found to be those which would be likely to give rise to life at least within a portion of that universe. 'Anthropic' observations seem to confirm that hypothesis and to extend it by suggesting divine design by fine-tuning. *But this research programme continues to be in competition with others*, for instance the many-universe interpretation of quantum theory (5.13(iii)), which makes this anthropic universe only one of an almost infinite number, and hence regards its properties as being of no special interest.

Divine 'tuning' of the Big Bang, if we were to accept it, might be envisaged as being as follows: *God creating the possibilities that have led to life, by setting the laws and parameters of the universe*. We must accept that our knowledge here is very fragmentary – we can only guess at whether there could be matter based on other laws and physical constants. An astrophysicist could note that the stabilities of the elements hydrogen, helium, carbon and oxygen are such as to allow stars to develop and generate a whole range of other elements. A life scientist's sense would be that in this universe complex life could only have arisen roughly as it did – based on macromolecules made largely from carbon, hydrogen and oxygen.[25] We have no means of knowing if other elemental systems are possible in other, 'differently tuned' universes. However, the universe we know has clearly been productive – of stars, of heavy elements and of second-generation stars around which planets containing those elements could cohere and, at least in one case, be a breeding-ground for life.

The presence of laws and physical constants which look fine-tuned is in no sense a proof of God's existence or activity. As indicated above, however, it seems unlikely that all the anthropic coincidences will be accounted for scientifically, since they deal with the 'givens' of astrophysics, the laws and physical constants of the universe.

10.15 The early universe

Adherents of a theistic research programme, who see the coincidences as suggestive of a way in which God created the possibilities that have led to life, might press further and ask if the course of the very early universe might not also have involved a second type of divine tuning, that of: *God preserving a certain amount of structure during the very early universe's rapid expansion*, its so-called 'inflation'. The theories of inflation developed in particular by Guth and by Linde (see 5.19) are in a sense hypothesis-savers; they came about to rescue a theory in difficulties. So they must be handled with more than usual theological care. It remains the case that the present universe is extraordinarily uniform – as though indeed it had been blown up like a balloon – but not *quite* uniform. Some structure survived and enabled galaxies to form – again, an essential prerequisite for a life-producing universe.

However, as we move into the development of the universe it becomes very hazardous to assign particular events to the result of divine activity as one cause among others. A theistic-creation programme would predict that the Creator would have to preserve some structure in an inflating universe. We do observe such structure. Note that this prediction is not about the *creation* of possibilities, but about the actual chronology of development of this universe, and *God selecting, or perhaps better protecting, certain possibilities so that life could occur*. There is a possible meeting-point between this theory and the discussion of quantum divine action above – Greene notes that the structure that survived inflation may have been the quantum fluctuations of the pre-inflation state (2004:305–10). God might therefore have interacted with them without violating the physical laws God had created.

However, there is every prospect that astrophysics will generate its own explanation of the persistence of structure during inflation. So a postulate of this sort of divine action can only be held very tentatively.

Those with a strong view of providence might go further and note how important the formation of the Moon may have been for the development of life on Earth – especially in slowing and stabilizing the Earth's orbit and stimulating the mixing of nutrients through the action of the tides. They might suggest that, given that the very early Earth had become a place where the precious possibility of life had arisen, God might, again, have protected that possibility by allowing a massive collision to generate a satellite moon.[26] Such an action could no doubt have been effected through the input of 'active information' into a complex dynamical system, along the lines of Polkinghorne's proposals. But the suggestion advances the theistic research programme still less than the comment on inflation above, since present-day astrophysics could give an entirely adequate account of how the moon arose, as a chance event in the first two senses described in 10.3.1.

10.16 The origin of life

The distinction between living and non-living things has, historically, been regarded as a very evident and profound one.[27] This distinction is not so easy to maintain as might be thought. Moreover, recent consideration of the sorts of systems that may have given rise to life on Earth (such as the edges of hot mineral springs or the 'black smokers' at hydrothermal vents in the deep ocean) suggests that in those sorts of conditions some sort of self-replicating system would be quite likely to develop (see **6.10.3** and Kauffman, 1995:60–9). There are a great many unanswered questions in this area. But the emphasis within the science has moved from supposing that there must have been a very extraordinary coincidence for life to be generated to thinking some sort of proto-life a likely consequence of certain conditions. Not that it is easy to draw a theological inference from this change in scientific perception. As John Polkinghorne perceptively states:

> If the evolution of life is seen to be almost inevitable, the atheists say that naturalism reigns and there is no need for a Creator, while the theists say that God has so beautifully ordained the order of nature that creation is indeed able to make itself. If life is so rare as to make its occurrence on Earth seem a fortuitous event, the atheists say that it shows that humans have emerged by chance in a world devoid of significance, while theists are encouraged to see the hand of God behind so fruitful but unpredictable an occurrence. Science influences metaphysical understanding but it certainly does not simply determine it. In the end, metaphysical answers are given for metaphysical reasons. (Polkinghorne, 1998c:79)

As was emphasized in looking at Big Bang cosmology in **1.15**, theology does well to track these developments in fundamental questions with caution. Even

Darwin seems to have been uneasily aware that the very beginning of systems subject to evolution by natural selection was a possible 'gap' for God, a place in the unfolding of the natural world where the divine breath might have been specially breathed. With the development of our understanding of self-organizing systems, that 'gap' has gone, surely for ever. Rather attention focuses once again on the remarkably promising system that the Earth was for the origin of life. Certain parameters seem to have been particularly favourable – the distance from the Sun, a chemically reducing environment, the presence of abundant water, high carbon dioxide levels which kept the early Earth warm enough to keep surface water liquid (and later provided the oxygen which higher organisms breathe) – and certain chance events seem to have been particularly propitious, such as the formation of the Moon (see above).

Can we then advance a fine-tuning argument as to God's action in respect of the early Earth? Not with nearly the force that it is advanced in respect of the universe as a whole. The notion that this planetary environment arose by 'chance' in our sense (ii) (10.3.1) – a purpose-free intersection of causal chains – is an eminently reasonable conjecture. Again, a 'many-planets' view – the notion that an Earth-type environment was quite probable given the number of stars in the universe – is much more convincing than the many-universes argument, since we are dealing with an observable and to some extent even testable proposition.[28] What remains of the tuning proposal is no more than the argument above about the whole universe, that it seems remarkable that its laws and its matter should be just such as to engender life *somewhere* within it.

So any sense that God acted particularly to engender this planetary environment would have to lead to a proposal about the second type of providential action discussed above (10.15) – God acting to select or protect a particular set of possibilities.

10.17 The evolutionary development of life

As soon as organisms of any complexity arise, the universe acquires additional properties – the behaviour, experience (at however basic a level) and interaction of these organisms. If Polkinghorne's 'scientist-theologians' are right to insist that:

> God's act of creation involves a kenotic act of self-limitation, truly allowing the other to be. It is therefore necessarily a costly and vulnerable action in which divine almightiness is qualified by the loving gift of an appropriate degree of independence to the beloved creature. (1996a:45–6)

then it may be imagined that emergent properties related to the development of entities as delicate and complex as living organisms would impose further constraints on particular divine action to steer creation. As we saw in 10.12.1 this is an implication of Russell's work. The fugue, to go back to Peacocke's metaphor, acquires other motifs, which even the master improviser must respect. At the same time the range of possibilities for development is enormously increased. Eventually organisms caused a major alteration in the conditions of the Earth's surface (see the Gaia Hypothesis, 9.7). With the further growth of biological complexity came more intricate systems for responding to the environment. Peacocke has pointed out that this of itself must mean the development of pain and suffering, as well as the decay, death and indeed extinction which are necessary concomitants of the evolutionary process.

10.18 Questions of theodicy in respect of evolution

We mentioned in 6.7 that speaking of an evolutionary creation gives rise to severe problems for theodicy – the task of justifying God in the face of all the suffering caused to creatures of all kinds over more than a billion years. This implies the need to consider a category of evil outside those normally discussed in theodicy. Beyond 'moral evil' arising out of the activities of human beings, and 'natural evil', suffering caused to *humans* by the non-human creation (earthquakes, etc.), there is 'evolutionary evil', the suffering and seeming futility within the non-human creation as a result of natural selection.

If elements of the non-human creation are judged to have any intrinsic value (9.8 note 12), then the evolutionary evil of their being created as part of a process which *necessarily involves* a great deal of suffering must be laid at God's door. A vast number of species, moreover, may have had a 'role' in creation at one time but are now extinct. Some extinction, admittedly, reflects moral evil, or at least questionable ethical choices. Indeed the rate of human-induced extinction is currently estimated at over 100,000 times the background rate (Leakey and Lewin, 1996:241). But there have been five great extinction events in the past (1996:44–56). The most recent and most famous is the one 65 million years ago which may have been triggered by an asteroid or comet, 15km across, colliding with the Yucatan Peninsula, and which eliminated an extraordinarily successful evolutionary 'project' called the dinosaur. But the previous event in the Permian era was much more extensive – it is thought that only 4 per cent of species survived. The cause is unknown.

Theologically this raises the question whether we have to envisage the God of this creation designing, or at least permitting, a process which has used millions of species merely as a means to an end, and then tossed them aside. Peacocke is content to say that God, while taking delight in every aspect of creation, suffers 'in, with and under the creative processes of the world' because 'God purposes *inter alia* to bring about a greater good thereby, namely, the kingdom of free-willing, loving persons in communion with God and each other' (Peacocke, 1998:372). The evolutionary costs are justified, for Peacocke, by the 'vale of soul-making' that the Earth ultimately becomes.

If so, our response might be analogous to the one famously given to the character Ivan Karamazov by Dostoevsky, that:

> Listen: if all have to suffer so as to buy ... harmony by their suffering, what have the children to do with it – tell me, please? It is entirely incomprehensible why they should have to buy harmony by their sufferings. Why should they, too, be used as dung for someone's future harmony? ... I don't

want harmony ... too high a price has been placed on harmony. We cannot afford to pay so much for admission. And therefore I hasten to return my ticket of admission ... It's not God that I do not accept, Alyosha. I merely most respectfully return him the ticket. (Dostoevsky, 1958:286–7)

Might we not, on behalf of the millions of discarded species and the billions of creatures brutally predated upon or parasitized, want to substitute the word 'humanity' for 'harmony' and 'creatures' for 'children' and with Ivan return our tickets?

This is in effect the approach taken by Ruth Page in her *God and the Web of Creation* (1996, see also Page, 2004). Not only does she mount a massive attack on anthropocentrism (see 8.3) – she also protests against any significant notion of divine activity in creation at all. Her God is the creator of possibilities, a theme we have taken up in this chapter, but for Page God does not steer creation nor does creation's unfolding serve some long-term divine purpose. To say either would in her view create unbearable problems of theodicy (Page, 1996:91–105). Rather God is a God of letting possibilities be (*Gelassenheit*, in the terminology of the philosopher Heidegger) and keeping company (*Mitsein*) with those possibilities as they unfold. There are some contradictions in Page's account,[29] and at times it smacks of an uneasy mixture of deism and process thought, but nevertheless she has marked out important ground. Creation of possibilities does as we have seen have interesting consonances with the newest theories of the origin of the universe (see 1.15, 10.13). Moreover, such a radically non-teleological account of God the 'Creator' goes a long way towards solving the theodicy problems of evolutionary evil.

EXERCISE 10.3

Compare Page's view of God's relation to evolution with that of Keith Ward in his *God, Chance and Necessity*. Ward not only affirms that God has used evolution for the long-term purpose of giving rise to sentient life-forms, he also implies that this outcome did not have sufficient a-priori probability for God to 'leave evolution to it', and that therefore part of the divine role was to adjust the course of evolution to steer it towards God's chosen goal (1996b: chs 4 and 7; also 1998:ch. 6).

10.18.1 The probability of the early life on this planet evolving to give rise to freely choosing self-conscious beings

This is a vital issue, which we digress to examine, in order to formulate a theology of divine action in respect of evolution. The first thing to note is that – scientifically – we have no more sense of the size of this probability than we do of the probability of there being intelligent life elsewhere in the universe. In both cases estimates vary from close to zero to close to one (a probability of one reflects an outcome which is certain). This has not, however, restricted either scientific or theological speculation!

One important guess is that of Pierre Teilhard de Chardin, the French theologian and anthropologist who remains the most ardent embracer of evolution as a working-out of God's purposes in the world (see especially his *The Phenomenon of Man*, 1959).[30] Teilhard regarded the progress of evolution as leading by a near-inevitable sequence from the 'hylosphere', a world containing only inanimate matter, to the 'zöosphere', the world of living organisms. (Thus far Teilhard seems to foreshadow in a remarkable way recent thinking on the self-organizing properties of matter.) He thought this process of 'intensification' had then led to the 'nöosphere', the realm of consciousness and cultural information, which would spread throughout the world and become more and more dominant until mind became the central reality, and all creation would converge on the 'Omega Point', which he identified with the consummation of the cosmos in Christ (as in Colossians 1.20). Again, one might say that part of Teilhard's vision has been fulfilled in the development of the Internet, a very rapidly growing web of information which is starting to cover the surface of the planet.

However, Teilhard has had very many critics – not merely in the Roman Catholic hierarchy which for many years proscribed his work. In a famously denunciatory review Peter Medawar rejected the scientific validity of any equation of evolution with inevitable progress (1996:1–11). Arguably, Teilhard's model is not about evolution at all, but about the redemptive process by which God gradually draws the world to its consummation (Haught; 2004; also Grumett, 2005).

Teilhard's celebration of Western technology, even to the extent of praising the advent of nuclear weapons (see Hefner, 2003:2–3), rings hollow now. And passages like:

> Should the planet become uninhabitable before mankind has reached maturity; should there be a premature lack of bread or essential metals ... should any of these conditions occur, then, there can be doubt that it would mean the failure of life on earth ... So far as [these] conditions ... are concerned, it does not seem that we have any particular need to fear the possibility of defeat. (Teilhard, 1966:118–19)

indicate a thinker whose perceptions were formed before it was evident just how endangered the 'human project' had become. Theologically, too, Teilhard seems to neglect the 'evolutionary evil' that we have been discussing, and the issue of theodicy that it raises (see **10.18**).

For our purposes the other important guesses about the probability of the evolutionary process giving rise to organisms like ourselves are those of Keith Ward in *God, Chance and Necessity* (1996), Stephen Jay Gould in *Wonderful Life* (1991), and Simon Conway Morris in *Life's Solution* (2003). Ward and Gould both put the probability as very low: Conway Morris, fascinatingly, regards the probability of there being a life-bearing planet such as Earth as very low, but *given* the formation of such a planet, he thinks complex, intelligent life a very likely outcome.[31]

Ward supposes that:

> Taking natural selection alone, it seems to me highly unlikely that rational beings should ever come to exist in a universe like this ... To make it likely that rational beings should emerge, there would have to be some weighting of the probabilities of events occurring which would make the emergence of rationality inevitable, sooner or later ... I regard evolution by natural selection as a much more insecure and precarious process than seems compatible with the theistic idea of a goal-directed process ... a continuing causal activity of God seems the best explanation of the progress towards greater consciousness and intentionality that one sees in the actual course of evolution of life on earth. (1996b:77–8)

This is both to overestimate our knowledge of the probability, and to misunderstand the nature of probability itself. Evolution had to give rise to some outcome or other, and the 'experiment' has only run once, in this solar system at least. We simply cannot state that another outcome would have been more likely, and that therefore God had to tweak the system to make it run the right course. There is no parallel with the possible anthropic 'tuning' of physical constants we noted above. All we can do is note that the systems that have led to life do exhibit a certain tendency to lead to greater complexity, environmental factors permitting.

We have, however, to acknowledge the force of Gould's argument (see 6.10.2) that other outcomes to evolution, not involving freely choosing self-conscious beings, were also perfectly possible, and that particular historical circumstances, especially those of the great extinctions, contributed enormously to the particular biosphere we have today. For instance, Gould stresses that of all the different taxa of creatures found in the fascinatingly diverse Burgess Shale none seemed a much more probable survivor than another, but only the worm *Pikaia* led to present-day vertebrates.

So once again those with a strong view of providence may want to suppose that God, while respecting the freedom offered to the creation in the interplay of chance and law, went so far as to protect the possibility of freely choosing self-conscious beings at certain key junctures. Conway Morris, however, reaches a very different conclusion, with different implications for theology – he believes the situation and composition of the Earth made complex life extremely likely. So God might be pictured as giving rise to that favourable locus and then allowing its processes to unfold. At a time when scientific opinion seems so divided theologians may do well to suspend judgement.

10.19 Possible theologies of divine action in respect of evolution

It is our view that Ruth Page is correct, to the extent that if God is described as imparting any direction to evolutionary creation with a long-term purpose, beyond the good of those creatures existing at that time, then the problems of theodicy *are* severe. This is a problem which was already puzzled over by Darwin and his friend Asa Gray (Brooke, 2003:198, 206), but it has received all too little discussion until recently. The subject is reviewed by Southgate (2002, and references therein; also by Peters and Hewlett, 2003:chs 6–7).[32] Other important contributions include those of Tracy (1998) and Russell (1998), Edwards (1999, 2006), Peacocke (2001b), Haught (2000) and Rolston (2003). The account that follows is based on Southgate, 2002:811–21. Key moves include:

(i) Tracy's extension of the free-process defence (**10.5**) to the interests of all organisms. The free-process defence cannot be used in its usual sense, that of the suffering-inducing operation of the natural world being necessary to the free choosing of creatures, since as Niels Gregersen writes, 'What can possibly be the benefit of freedom for nonhuman creatures if they can never be in a position to accept or reject the offer of divine love, because they don't know what it means?' (Gregersen, 1999:133). Tracy wants to make a slightly different case. Conceding that non-human creatures do not have the possibility of freely chosen personal relation to God, he affirms that they have their own experience, and express their own capacity for life in their own particular way. Pain and suffering are part of the system that makes this possible.

This bold extension of the free-will defence into the arena of natural process and non-human experience falls short because the free-will defence, even as normally deployed *in re* moral evil, does not succeed of itself. The weight of innocent human suffering, the abundance of situations in which humans are deprived of their free will, these corrode the straightforward defence. It is not sustainable except in combination with a theory of secondary goods, an eschatological perspective which, while not devaluing the present, emphasizes that the sufferings of this world are indeed as nothing compared with the glory about to be revealed to us (Romans 8.18). Likewise, because intrinsic to evolutionary creation are casualties for which there is only pain, and no expression of their experience, Tracy's defence fails unless there is some ultimate good that will actually *redeem* the individuals and extinct species concerned, not just other individuals and species which benefit from their suffering and extinction (see below).

(ii) Edwards' response along the lines of Job 38–42 – our knowledge of God's ways and purposes must be limited (though we can trust in God as we see God in the self-limiting and sacrificial love of Jesus) (Edwards, 1999:36–42).

(iii) Peacocke – 'God suffers in and with the sufferings of created humanity and so, by a natural extension, with those of all creation, since humanity is an evolved part of it. The suffering of God, which we could glimpse only tentatively in the processes of creation, is in Jesus the Christ concentrated to a point of intensity and transparency which reveals itself to all who focus on him' (Peacocke, 1998:372). Fascinatingly, Peacocke's more recent essay alters this to '... intensity and transparency that reveals it as expressive of the perennial relation of God to the creation' (Peacocke, 2001b:42).

(iv) R.J. Russell's model of the progressive withdrawal of divine action as complex organisms develop (**10.12.1**) (and his response to the theodicy issues in terms of a developed eschatology – see **10.20**).

(v) Haught's emphasis is also eschatological, emphasizing the unfinished character of the creation, and based on a 'metaphysics of the future' – the creation drawn onwards by God the ground of its hope and potentiality. Haught writes of

God's kenotic 'letting-be' of the creation, of a love 'willing to risk the disorder and deviation that actually occur in the evolution of cosmic beauty' (Haught, 2000:137). Consciousness is not the goal of creation for Haught: the goal is beauty, which will persist even when consciousness passes away. He is aware too of the problem of the casualties of evolution. He recognizes that an evolutionary theology must refigure Christian thinking not only on creation, revelation and divine action but also on redemption. So for Haught 'Everything whatsoever that occurs in creation – all the suffering and tragedy as well as the emergence of new life and intense beauty – is "saved" by being taken eternally into God's feeling of the world ... In God's sensitivity to the world, each event is redeemed from absolute perishing and receives the definitive importance and meaning that religions encourage us to believe in' (Haught, 2000:43). This view of redemption is all of a piece with a process-theological view that the only resurrection life is as part of the memory of God. It sits, however, less easily with the more traditional Christian affirmation that humans have some bodily resurrection which restores to them some autonomy of personality.

(vi) Mark Wynn, reviewing Holmes Rolston's work in the context of natural theology, summarizes his view as follows: 'Decay and predation, and pain, are also ecosystemic preconditions for various forms of flourishing' (Wynn, 1999:110). Wynn notes that this counts against the notion that nature is clumsy, or 'merely' cruel. Rolston and Wynn are surely right that our view of the goodness of the world needs to be informed by a holistic, ecosystemic perspective. But Rolston's scheme does not directly attend to the loss of value in the lives of the victims of evolution. He has famously described nature as 'cruciform'; he even notes in a recent essay that 'Each of the struggling creatures is delivered over to preserve a line ... We have a kind of "slaughter of the innocents" ... In their lives ... they share the labor of the divinity' (Rolston, 2001:59). This is very telling. The suffering of the children slaughtered by Herod at the time of the birth of Jesus is not redeemed by the survival of Jesus alone, it is redeemed, presumably, by his voluntary self-surrender for all at the Cross, *and* by the resurrection life of the children. Jesus *chose* the cruciform life; the casualties of evolution have it imposed on them for the longer-term good of others, and their individual redemption remains in question (see below). So to call nature cruciform only sharpens the question of evolutionary theodicy.

The evolutionary theodicist's choices are two:

(a) to posit God merely as the passive, suffering companion of every creature (so Page), a view self-consistent but dubiously faithful to the Christian tradition; or

(b) to mount a defence of teleological creation using a *combination* of the theological resources we began to map out in Chapter 8. Southgate offers this proposal for the evolutionary theodicist:
- acknowledge the pain, suffering, death and extinction that has been intrinsic to the evolution of creation;
- affirm God's co-suffering with every sentient being in creation;
- take the Cross to be indicative of this compassion, *and* to inaugurate the transformation of creation.

- if divine fellowship with creatures such as ourselves is in any sense a goal of evolutionary creation, then advocate *a very high doctrine of humanity*, supposing that indeed humans are of very particular concern to God. That does not in any way exclude a sense that God delights in every creature which emerges within evolution, but it leads to the possibility that humans have a crucial and positive role, co-operating with their God in the healing of the evolutionary process.
- *give some account of the redemption of the non-human creation* such as the 'pelican heaven' of Jay McDaniel (8.5.2). A God of loving relationship could never regard any creature as a mere evolutionary expedient.

(cf. Southgate, 2002:820–1)

Such considerations as 'pelican heaven' lead us naturally to consider the fate of the universe as a whole, which we do in Section C.

SECTION C
WHAT GOD WILL DO (10.20)

10.20 Eschatology

A central element in the Christian tradition has always been the sense that God will ultimately effect the consummation of all creation (whatever that might mean). This eschatological category of divine action must therefore be included in any comprehensive account.[33] The resurrection of Jesus is often regarded as being the inauguration of the eschatological transformation (e.g. 1 Corinthians 15.20).

We have already noted (8.2.1) that process thought pictures the eternal co-development of God and the world. *One of the clearest conclusions of contemporary cosmology, however, is that this universe will not persist for ever – it will either collapse in on itself (the so-called 'Big Crunch'), or expand away to infinity (so-called 'heat death').*[34] *(Long before that this solar system will be uninhabitable.*[35]*) Any continuation of the matter or information in the present universe will have to be in a different form.* Ted Peters emphasizes the importance of the question when he writes: 'Should the final future as forecasted by the combination of big bang cosmology and the second law of thermodynamics come to pass ... then we would have proof that our faith has been in vain. It would turn out that there is no God, at least not the God in whom followers of Jesus have put their faith' (Peters, 1993:175–6).

Willem B. Drees, addressing eschatology in his *Beyond the Big Bang* (Drees, 1990: ch. 4), chooses to rule consideration of the distant future out of court as more than a 'thought-experiment': 'It is not realistic to relate the future on a cosmological scale, counted at least in billions of years, to perspectives for humankind' (1990:117). His own interest in eschatology is oriented much less towards some conceivable long-term immortality than towards 'the call to conversion for the sake of a more just future' (1990:154). Indeed the yearning for justice, and a conviction that a greater sense of God's presence will be transformative in this direction, is a most important element in Christian eschatology.

However, it is no less reasonable to do 'thought-experiments' about God's relation to the billions-of-years distant future than to speculate about the divine relation to the Big Bang. As Peters implies, the scientific conclusion italicized above demands a theological response. Polkinghorne and Russell are the scientist-theologians who have done most to develop this important area of the interface of science and theology. (For introductions to their views see Polkinghorne, 2004:ch. 6; Russell, 2002). It is intriguing to contrast the approach of Drees with that of Russell. Drees as we saw earlier (6.13.5) wants to treat scientific naturalism with all possible seriousness, and then see what ground there might be for theology to work on: Russell wants to explore the 'worst-case', scientifically most challenging, most 'dissonant', theological account of resurrection and eschatology, and then see what purchase there might be from there on a dialogue with scientific cosmology. So he is in the process of exploring the implications of a view of the resurrection of Jesus as an objective transformation of matter, a mighty act of God going far beyond the constraints of non-interventionist special divine action in the present age, and the beginning of a final act which will transform the character of all creation. This wide-ranging eschatological vision, embracing all creation, is vital to Russell for reasons of evolutionary theodicy (10.18) – it is only thus that an evolutionary creation can be vindicated.

Polkinghorne's formulation is as follows:

> It seems to me that it is of the essence of humanity to be embodied and that the soul is the immensely complex 'information-bearing pattern' in which the ever-changing atoms of our bodies are arranged. It is surely a coherent hope that the pattern that is me will be remembered and re-embodied by God in his eschatological act of resurrection. The 'matter' of that resurrected world will be the transformed matter of this dying universe, transmuted by God in his faithful action of cosmic resurrection. It will have new properties, consistent with the end of transience, death and suffering, because it will be part of a new creation, now no longer standing apart from it(s) Creator as the 'other', and so paying the necessary cost of an evolutionary world's making of itself, but fully integrated with the divine life through the universal reconciliation brought about by the Cosmic Christ. (1996a:54–5)

This, however, is not the only recourse in this highly speculative area. For instance, someone committed to speaking of an eternal co-development of God and the world might take refuge in a many-universes view (see 5.13(iii), 5.22). The heat death of this universe would leave all that was of value in the memory of God, where it would achieve at least an 'objective immortality' (Barbour, 1998:304),[36] but ongoing relationship with physical entities would take place in other universes.[37]

It will be observed that scientifically-informed eschatology tends to be more at home thinking of consummation over the very long timescales suggested by cosmology, the many billions of years this universe has before it, than with the imminent end of things implied by apocalyptic elements of the New Testament.[38]

But there is a consonance between cosmology and Christian tradition to the effect that this universe will end, and anything which is to do with humans and their values would have to depend on God rather than presently existing physical processes for its continuation.

Is heaven, then, a place for God and humans, or a broader redemption of all creation? What are we to make of certain 'cosmic-Christological' texts which speak of the reconciliation of all creation taking place in Christ (e.g. Colossians 1.20; Ephesians 1.10). There is an urgent need for a re-exploration of these texts and their implications for our understanding of our relation to the non-human creation. Gunton makes an important point when he writes:

> [T]here is in the Bible no redemption, no social and personal life, apart from the creation. It is therefore reasonable, especially in the light of Old Testament witness to the creation, to hold that the Bible as a whole is concerned with the future of creation ... But the fact that it is Israel and Jesus who are at the centre of God's action in and towards the world means that it is the personal that is central, the non-personal peripheral. That does not rule out an ecological concern, but it cannot be of independent interest. (Gunton, 1992:33–4)

Human personhood, then, is of the first importance theologically (see 10.9) but humanity will be redeemed, ultimately, as *part* of a new creation rather than *away* from contact with the rest of creation. It is interesting to contrast the approach of Russell and Polkinghorne with that of a theologian like Kathryn Tanner, who works from classic Christian resources to formulate a new systematic theology, rather than starting from a scientific background. Tanner draws a parallel with the need to see creation *ex nihilo* in terms of ontological dependence upon God. So also, the future fate of the universe is most centrally related to its belonging to God rather than to its physical end (Tanner, 2003:ch. 4). Tanner develops this by reference to the understanding that a human being 'in Christ' is already part of eternal life. As Gunton implies, transformation of persons, a process which cannot be destroyed by physical death, is central. But Tanner lacks that concern for the future fate of matter as a whole which comes so naturally to physicists such as Russell and Polkinghorne. Scientifically-informed eschatology must try and give some sort of account of what might be continuities and discontinuities between this creation and the new one. Polkinghorne's proposal is along the following lines:

Table 10.1

CONTINUITY	DISCONTINUITY
Embodiment	No transience, pain or suffering
Temporality – since this is so fundamental to our experience	No tendency to disorder[39]
Process – God will still draw us on into the fullness of the divine life	
Personhood – the 'real me' will persist, though it can only do so through being held, at death, within the love of God	

Continuities and discontinuities at the eschaton, according to John Polkinghorne (2004:154–63; cf. 2002:103–34)

Scientifically-informed eschatology must also try and relate the great trans-forming act of God, of which the resurrection of Christ is the beginning, to the rest of our understanding of God's relation to living creatures other than humans. Polkinghorne indeed rebukes other theologians for too anthropocentric an atti-tude, and yet he himself limits the involvement of animals in the eschatological sphere. They will be there as types rather than as individuals (pets being an arguable exception – so Polkinghorne, 2004:152). This runs the risk of not doing full justice either to the richness of individual animal experience, or to the theodicy problems that evolutionary creation poses. Simple organisms may be agreed to be types rather than individuals, but it is individual animal centres of experience that are subject to intense suffering, individual animal lives that sometimes fulfil little or nothing of their potential, which surely call for redemption by the God who gave rise to the evolutionary order (see 10.18; McDaniel, 1989; Southgate, 2002).

Many contemporary theologians have moved away from any sort of static pic-ture of heaven to one which is dynamic, richly exploratory of relationships, an emphasis strong in Moltmann and also found in the passages just cited from Gunton and Polkinghorne. So in eschatology too we find the emphasis on a network of relationships, and on the inseparability of humans from their context in the cosmos, which has informed our search for models throughout the last nine chapters.

10.21 Conclusion

We have explored the vigorously debated territory of the compatibility of divine agency with the world described by contemporary science. Numerous possibilities lie between the trite materialist assertion that such action is impossible, and the over-optimistic assumption that the 'new physics' provides easy openings for models of the causal joint. Which possibility is adhered to will depend as much on the theological assumptions of the adherent as on the status of the science.

Whatever position is adopted, construction of a coherent model of God's relation to the cosmos will rest on a coherent account of God's relation not only to the present world, but to the origin and development of the cosmos, and its final end.

Notes

1   The conference series ended with a 'capstone' meeting in September 2003, which will be published as Russell *et al.*, 2005. Summaries of the five books so far published are available on www.ctns.org/books.html.

2   The subject of a major study from David Bartholomew, *God of Chance* (1984).

3   Whether we could *ever* possess such knowledge of even the simplest real system is highly doubtful, as shown by the example we give in **5.26** of a snooker table.

4   Though as fine a theologian as John Wesley gave this as the explanation for the terrible earthquake and tsunami that devastated Lisbon in 1755.

5   See **6.11**.

6   Though experimentation on out-of-body experiences (see **7.7**) *may* show that the human being has physically demonstrable properties not yet understandable within physicalist understandings.

7   For a very thoughtful study of personhood see Habgood, 1998.

8   See **6.13.5** for a study of Drees's naturalism.

9   See Stoeger's essay in *Chaos and Complexity* (Stoeger, 1995:239–61).

10 Perhaps the most pleasing attempt, at least for double agency involving humans as secondary agents, is Tom Settle's of a ballroom dancer (a human agent) being 'led' by her partner (God) – though she also exercises her own technique and creativity (Settle, 1996).

11 Polkinghorne (1989:18–21). The difficulty is illustrated by the fact that Sallie McFague, one of the most eloquent exponents of the 'embodiment image', is able to give no account of divine action, beyond some vague talk of 'spirit'. She *describes* her model in *The Body of God* as being 'agential-organic' (1993:140f.), but the agential side is never given substance.

12 A description which tallies with Moltmann's writing of the world as a system open to the creative energies of God (see **8.5.6**). In earlier writing Peacocke used the image of the cosmos as a developing child in the womb of its mother (1979:142). As he would be very well aware, this analogy is strictly limited – foetuses and mothers are, after all, composed of exactly the same material. Another favourite analogy of Peacocke's is that of God as an improvisatory composer, like J.S. Bach generating his fugues (1993:174–5).

13 And the one system we don't at all understand is the human brain. Drees has elsewhere criticized thinkers for using top-down causation to explain the relation of the mind and the brain, and the mind–brain relation to explain top-down causation (1996:101–2).

14 Real situations of human interest are full of such systems – it is not only the great red spot of Jupiter but the human heart itself which is thought to exhibit chaotic dynamics in its normal functioning.

15 Systems in mathematical chaos often show a surprising ordering of behaviour around a complex pattern known as a strange attractor.

16 It is important to stress that none of these thinkers supposes that this is the only mode of action open to God. But they do want to press the question – could the quantum level be appropriately regarded as a key locus of special divine action?

17   Though it may be significant that two important candidates for loci of particular divine action – mutations in genetic material and neuronal events in the human brain – may both be instances where such amplification is possible. See Russell, R.J. (1998) on mutation. On quantum events in the brain see Penrose, 1994: ch. 7.

18   An alternative is simply to avoid the term altogether and speak as Murphy does of 'special' and 'extraordinary' divine acts (1995:330–2).

19   See also 7.7 on resurrection and immortality.

20   … leaving, Wildman might have added, thinking of Lewis Carroll's Cheshire Cat, nothing but a grin.

21   So Robinson 2003:332–3, drawing on Rahner, 1999:23.

22   See Peacocke, 1993:174–5.

23   See Westermann, 1984:93–110 for a thorough examination of the exegetical options.

24   Quoted in Tracy (1995:note to 321–2).

25   Indeed Howard van Till claims that: 'It is not simply the *numerical values of certain parameters* that must be "just right" in order for life to develop. No, it's the entire formation economy of the universe that must be "just right". The full menu of the universe's formational capabilities must be sufficiently robust to make possible the actualization of carbon-based life' (quoted in Conway Morris, 2003:327, italics in quotation).

26   This idea first came to our attention in an unpublished talk by Professor Owen Gingerich. See also Conway Morris, 2003:87–92 on just how unusual a satellite the Moon may be, and Comins, 1993:1–49 for an account of the implications of there being no moon.

27   One of the great developments in nineteenth-century chemistry was when Wöhler succeeded in producing a compound characteristic of living things, urea, from one which appeared characteristically *in*organic, ammonium isocyanate.

28   Considerable evidence has now emerged of planets around other stars; interestingly Simon Conway Morris can still hold that there may only ever have been one planet as favourable for life as Earth (2003: ch. 5).

29   As in Page's sudden acceptance of resurrection (1996:61), after she has gone so far to minimize the potency of divine action.

30   For a brief, if critical, summary of Teilhard's work see Santmire (1985:155–71); for new studies see Grumett (2005) and Fabel and St John (2003).

31   See 6.10.2 for the disagreement between Gould and Conway Morris on the Burgess Shale.

32   The subject was also treated in R.J. Russell's 2004 Witherspoon Lecture – and see Williams, 2005.

33   See however 5.22, 7.7 for our rejection of claims that physics itself can supply such a description via Frank Tipler's 'physical eschatology'.

34   At the time of writing the latest calculations suggest that heat death is the more likely.

35   For a vivid account of the prospects for life in the solar system see Ward and Brownlee, 2004.

36   Process thinkers are divided as to whether to postulate any 'subjective immortality', in which entities continue to experience themselves in this new state. McDaniel, as we have seen, postulates a 'pelican heaven' (8.5.2) – others follow Hartshorne in not seeing any need for this. On the latter view it is enough for entities to enrich the consequent nature of God.

37   Some cosmologies imagine that there may be a process by which new universes

frequently (on a cosmic timescale) bud off from existing ones. What remains unclear, however, is whether structure or information could possibly survive from one universe to the next.

38 As to the possibility of an imminent apocalypse precipitated by a clash of spiritual powers, science can of course say nothing.

39 The idea that the eschatological state will be characterized by a suspension of the second law of thermodynamics is an idea particularly developed by Russell – see his 1984 paper; also Worthing, 1996:ch. 4.

Further reading

CLAYTON, P. (1997) *God and Contemporary Science* (Edinburgh: Edinburgh Academic Press)

PAGE, R. (1996) *God and the Web of Creation* (London: SCM Press)

PEACOCKE, A. (2001) *Paths from Science towards God: The End of All our Exploring* (Oxford: Oneworld)

POLKINGHORNE, J. (1989) *Science and Providence* (London: SPCK) (2000) *Faith, Science and Understanding* (London: SPCK)

RUSSELL, R. J. *et al.* (eds) (1995) *Chaos and Complexity: Scientific Perspectives on Divine Action* (Vatican City: Vatican Observatory; Berkeley, CA: Center for Theology and the Natural Sciences)

—— (1998) *Evolutionary and Molecular Biology: Scientific Perspectives on Divine Action* (Vatican City: Vatican Observatory; Berkeley, CA: Center for Theology and the Natural Sciences)

WARD, K. (1990) *Divine Action* (London: Collins) (1996) *God, Chance and Necessity* (Oxford: OneWorld)

WARD, Peter D. and BROWNLEE, Donald (2004) *The Life and Death of Planet Earth: How the New Science of Astrobiology Charts the Ultimate Fate of Our World* (New York: Owl Books; first publ. 2003)

WILDMAN, Wesley J. (2004) 'The Divine Action Project, 1988–2003', *Theology and Science* 2 (1), 31–75

BOOK FOUR

Chapter 11

Science and education

Michael Poole

11.1 Introduction to Book Four

The fourth part of this volume moves beyond our focus on the interaction between the sciences and Christian theology to look at:

- science as it is considered in education, and the contribution science education can make to the dialogue (Chapter 11)
- science as it stands in relation to Islam, a monotheism at once similar to and very different from Christianity (Chapter 12)
- science's relation to the growth of technology and its effects on society (Chapter 13)
- the challenges posed by the technological possibilities raised by the new genetics (Chapter 14)

11.2 Science education and the science–religion dialogue

Within society, the view that science and religion are at loggerheads is still a significant component of popular folklore. The view persists in spite of the scholarship developing in two major domains. The *history of science* has indicated the inadequacy of the idea of conflict as a generalization about the ways in which science and religion have interacted in the past (Bowler, 2001:5; Brooke, 1991:36f.; Cantor, 1991:289–95; Russell, 1985:5). The *philosophy of science* over the last half-century has highlighted deficiencies in those views of science which put it on a pedestal as the final judge of truth in every sphere of human action.

Furthermore, the need to make judgements about the applications of science has underlined the role of values in principled decision-making. *If research in these value-laden areas is taken seriously, there is a place for science education to make a major contribution to an understanding of the interplay between science and religion.*

11.3 Meeting-points

Four areas in which science education might make a contribution to understanding issues of science and religion lie in the ways it treats:

1. The content of science
2. The nature of science (philosophical issues)
3. The applications of science (includes moral issues)
4. How science operates as a social activity (historical and sociological issues)

I shall sketch out these areas in turn. Then, because it is not possible to treat each in detail in a single chapter, I shall major on teaching about a key area – *the nature of science*. It will be apparent that I shall be writing from the perspective of a *critical realist* (see 1.7).

11.3.1 The content of science

The content of the science that is taught may raise issues of science and religion if:

(i) the scientific picture and specific religious texts are both *making apparent reference to the same subject*.
(ii) the content of the science prompts wonder and questions beyond the capabilities of science to answer.

(i) Making apparent reference to the same subject

Instances where the scientific picture and religious texts both *appear* to be referring to the same subject are found in cosmology, evolutionary biology and psychology. Some of the interactions are explored in Chapters 5, 6, 7 and 10 of this book. Particular examples would be the astronomical issues of Galileo's time and the Darwinian controversies (see 1.12, 3.2.1–2). A third example concerns the origins of the universe (see 1.15, and Poole, 1995:chs 5–7).

Attempts to read modern science into ancient religious texts, such as the book of Genesis, have proved counterproductive. These texts were written long before modern science and for a very different purpose than to satisfy cosmological, biological or geological curiosity. In the time of Galileo, efforts to drag astronomical theories out of Bible texts prompted his famous quotation of 'an ecclesiastic of the most eminent degree: "That the intention of the Holy Ghost is to teach us how one goes to heaven, not how heaven goes"' (Seeger, 1966:273).

At issue here was the hermeneutical[1] question about the meaning of particular Bible passages that might appear to be confirmed or denied by scientific discoveries. Many supposed puzzles disappear when the 33 or so literary *genres*[2] of the ancient writings are taken into account. The problems generated by reading one's own ideas into a text (*eisegesis*), rather than understanding what the text is seeking to say (*exegesis*), sometimes arise from a mistaken view of what loyalty to the Bible involves. To lose sight of the literary *genres* employed results in failing to treat the text seriously or carefully enough.

(ii) Wonder and questions beyond the capabilities of science to answer

Our remarkable world often prompts awe and wonder, something recently highlighted in the *National Curriculum for England* under the category 'spiritual'. Richard Dawkins describes the way good science can intensify these feelings of awe and wonder, while seeking to strip them of religious associations (Dawkins, 1998). But although awe and wonder do not necessarily have specific religious associations, religious factors are often involved (see 15.5.3).

The apparent 'fine-tuning' of the universe for the existence of life-as-we-know-it is an example of how the content of science prompts questions which lie beyond the capabilities of science to answer. Islam places a strong emphasis on the possible religious implications of this 'fine-tuning' and Christians also see these 'cosmic coincidences' as entirely consistent with a purposeful Creator. The topic is explored in 5.20–5.24 and 10.14.

A realization that there were questions which science was unable to answer went hand in hand with the beginnings of modern Western science some four centuries ago (Russell, 1987). The same is true today and numerous organizations exist to encourage dialogue about matters of science and traditional religions.[3] However, alongside such discussions there has been a resurgence of mysticism in what is loosely termed the New Age Movement. We touch on this in discussing *The Tao of Physics* in 9.3 and a more detailed examination of this heterogeneous collection of ideas is found in Lucas (1996).

11.3.2 The nature of science

It is most important that science education should address the nature and scope of the subject in which it seeks to educate (Woolnough, 1992). Two illustrations of how the nature of science may impinge on matters of science and religion are raised by the following complex questions:

- Does science, in assuming the uniformity of nature, rule out the miraculous? (see 10.10(iv))
- Does science indicate a deterministic world, perhaps thereby precluding religious teaching about free will and human responsibility? (see 1.17, 5.11–5.14, 5.25–5.27)

But there are various questions in addition to these; questions about the status and the scope of science as a way of knowing about, and constructing a view of, the world. Extravagant claims about the status of Science with a capital 'S' have been made in which the scope of Science has been viewed as all-encompassing. The philosophy of science probes attempts like these. It also sets out demarcation criteria for (i) what distinguishes science from non-science and (ii) for what kinds of questions science can hope to answer (see e.g. Trigg, 1993).

11.3.3 The applications of science

As will be seen in Chapter 13 there has been a growing concern about the uses to which science and technology are put and their effects on our environment (Houghton, 1994; Russell, 1994; Berry, 2003). Although moral codes may be formulated without reference to religion, the world's religions have a great deal to say about how we *ought* to act. Their teachings inform and influence moral decision-making. Medicine in particular is a growth area with respect to ethical decisions, concerning issues like organ transplants, the use of transgenic materials, abortion, euthanasia, cloning and so forth. The escalation of *nanotechnology* in addition has opened up a huge new area of ethical decision-making (Bryant *et al.*, 2002). The applications of science feature extensively in science syllabuses and specifications.

11.3.4 How science operates as a social activity

Here we are concerned with the many ways in which science and religion *have been* and *are* perceived to have interacted in society, often with several different ways operating simultaneously. It needs constantly to be borne in mind that there is no such thing as 'the' relationship between science and religion (Brooke, 1991:2ff.).

Within the sociology of science there has been a movement by some of science's detractors to adopt an opposite position to that of the logical positivists who almost deified Science (see 4.2). That has been to treat the findings of science as simply the (empty) outcomes of the social conditioning of its practitioners. Such a view is in contrast to the general view of scientists, who see themselves as making provisional and corrigible attempts to describe and classify a real world, one that exists largely independently of its observers. The position encounters the problem of *reflexivity* because if this is so, then the findings of *social* science also are the outcomes of the social conditioning of its practitioners, raising questions as to their credibility.

11.4 Some educational questions

As we consider the contribution science education can make to the dialogue between science and religion, a number of supplementary questions need to be asked and answered for particular educational situations. For example:

1. What conceptual demands will be made in examining how science relates to religious beliefs? Will all pupils/students be able to cope with them and if so at what ages, bearing in mind what developmental psychology has to tell us?
2. What contributions does/can science education make to cross-curricular studies, specifically to religious studies?
3. What level of science education is to be considered, is it primary, secondary or tertiary?[4]

11.5 A *modus operandi*

Since the first edition of this book was published (1999) it has become apparent that it is being used in a variety of countries with different strategies for science education. Furthermore, the English scene is changing,[5] so I shall not repeat the detailed account of developments in England that was a feature of this chapter in the first edition. Rather I shall concentrate on general principles, although I do wish to use examples from the English educational system to illustrate the second and third of the three questions.

There appear to be three ways (11.6.1–3) in which science education can make contributions to the dialogue between science and religion, depending on whether such issues can be/are introduced into science lessons. Science education in avowedly atheistic countries may be used as a 'stick to beat religion' and any mention of religion is likely to be derogatory. Some governments, adopting a more moderate position, nevertheless wish to present a secularist image and do not make any place for such considerations in the classroom. The USA, with its 1st Amendment setting out the separation between church and state, occupies a rather special position since, despite strong religious adherences within the American population, religion is not allowed to be taught in public schools. On my understanding, however, this does not prevent historical studies of, say, the Galileo Affair or the Darwinian controversies from being treated in the classroom.

11.6.1 One way for science education to make a contribution

Where issues of science and religion are not, for one reason or another, introduced into science lessons, **science education can still make a contribution to the dialogue**. This is by teaching the nature, content and applications of science well, so as not to promote and perpetuate the sort of imperialistic view of science which has, in the past, contributed to a popular view of a necessary conflict between science and religion. There is nothing inherently atheistic about the scientific enterprise. After all, in the early growth of Western science there were many who found in the biblical mandate to manage the Earth an incentive for doing science. Arguably if one better understood how the world worked one could do a better job of management. Added to that it seemed that gaining knowledge of the workings of the world could show the glory of the Creator and offer means of alleviating human suffering.

So, from the point of view of good science education alone, I offer the following list of what I consider to be sound practice in teaching about the nature of science:

Science teaching should make it clear that:

Science ...

1. ... requires certain assumptions (presuppositions) to be made before the scientific enterprise can begin.
2. ... 'maps out' *laws* which are *descriptive of* the *normal* behaviour of the natural world.
3. ... has its limitations as well as its strengths.
4. ... is one way of looking at the world; but it is not the only valid way.
5. ... sometimes raises questions which science itself cannot answer.
6. ... involves *values* but cannot tell us whether particular actions are morally right or wrong; only what the likely consequences of those actions will be.
7. ... offers certain *types* of explanation but these are not the only valid *types* of explanations.
8. ... results in knowledge which is provisional and corrigible; it is not 'absolute truth'.
9. ... is not the final arbiter of *meaning* or of *truth* in every domain.
10. ... has its own concepts and its own 'language and grammar' for communication.
11. ... employs *reductionism as one of its methods* but does not imply *reductionism as metaphysics*.
12. ... makes use of *direct, indirect* and *cumulative* evidence to justify its conclusions.
13. ... does not have one, single, *the* 'scientific method' which will deliver the required answers.
14. ... operates within a tacit methodological agreement that the *causes* it refers to are *proximate*, not *First* causes.
15. ... involves chance and randomness but does not entail the *metaphysical* conclusion that the universe is accidental.

Since the above list is all about good science education, no mention has been made of religion. But now there follow comments on each of the 15 points, suggesting some

Implications for teaching about science and religion

1. Science requires certain assumptions (presuppositions) to be made before the scientific enterprise can begin

Rationality
This presupposition underpins, not just science, but all meaningful discourse. Without it, speech is just noises and writing is just squiggles on paper.

Intelligibility

Without the assumption that the universe is capable of being understood, the scientific enterprise would not begin.

Orderliness

If the world were not assumed to be orderly there would be no reason to look for *patterns of regular behaviour* that could be embodied in *scientific laws*.

Uniformity

The presuppositions of uniformity and orderliness are closely allied, but the idea of the *uniformity of nature* is the basis for trust in *repeatability* and *prediction*.

It is upon these presuppositions that the practicability of engaging in science is based. They have been seen by Christians and members of some other religions as reflecting the non-capricious nature of a God who is the guarantor that the scientific endeavour is meaningful and worthwhile. The particular presupposition of the *uniformity of nature* is a generalization about what is normally the case. It does not preclude the possibility of miracles (a topic which is treated in 10.10(iv)).

2. Science 'maps out' *laws* which are *descriptive of* the *normal* behaviour of the natural world

These laws are not *prescriptive* of what is *bound* to happen; only prescriptive of our expectations, based on precedent. That is the reason for using the metaphoric phrase 'Science "maps out" *laws*'. Science is like map-making in that its practitioners search out what is there and construct shorthand ways of expressing what they find. Scientific laws tell us nothing about whether miracles can or cannot take place, only that they are not normally to be expected.

3. Science has its limitations as well as its strengths

The strengths of science include giving understanding of the world, predicting, utilizing knowledge gained for technological purposes and exercising control. Science is, nevertheless, a mixed human activity, being the cause of some problems and the solution of others. The next six sections spell out some of its limitations:

4. Science is one way of looking at the world; but it is not the only valid way

> Order: Passeriformes; Family: Turdidæ; especially *Luscinia megarhynchus*. Length 16 cm; summer migrant.

This may be a partial scientific description of a nightingale, but it is not in competition with

> Thou wast not born for death, immortal Bird!
>   No hungry generations tread thee down;
> The voice I hear this passing night was heard
>   In ancient days by emperor and clown:[6]

5. Science sometimes raises questions which science itself cannot answer

Science reveals the apparent 'fine-tuning' of the universe for the emergence of life-as-we-know-it. Differences in the physical constants, sometimes of as little as 1 in 10^{60} (see 5.20.1–5.20.2), would mean that we would not be here. This is quite astonishing and raises *metaphysical* questions which science is not competent to answer, questions like 'Is the universe a cosmic accident or was it planned?' 'Does life have any meaning or purpose?' and 'Why is there something, rather than nothing?'

6. Science involves *values* but cannot tell us whether particular actions are morally right or wrong; only what the likely consequences of those actions will be

Values such as *truth-telling* and avoiding *plagiarism* are integral to science. Other values are involved in the applications of science in well-publicized areas like nuclear fission, the environment and medicine, values like responsibility, care for life and trust. Values depend on *beliefs*, and *beliefs* can be true or false. Science investigates what *is*. Moral discourse is about what *ought* to be.

7. Science offers certain *types* of explanation but these are not the only valid *types* of explanations

For example, the question 'Why am I here?' is logically capable of being answered with the following three *compatible* explanations:

  1. *Explanation in scientific terms*
     Big Bang; stellar evolution; chemical evolution, organic evolution; pair bonding, sperm uniting with the ovum, etc.
  2. *Explanation in terms of human agency*
     Parents' desires; their falling in love
  3. *Explanation in terms of divine agency*
     God's purpose and plan for us

The above illustrates the ambiguity of 'Why?' and cautions about pressing too hard the distinction, 'Science is concerned with "How?" while religion is concerned with "Why?" questions.'

  To offer an explanation of one *type* when another type is requested/intended is to commit an *explanatory type-error*. A court of law might conclude that the explanation of why Mr Bloggs died was that Mrs Bloggs killed him. A pathologist involved in the case might conclude that the explanation of why Mr Bloggs died was that he swallowed a lethal dose of potassium cyanide. A detective questioning the pathologist would expect her to give an explanation of the second *type*, *qua* pathologist. It would be a *type error* for her to give, in her professional capacity, an explanation of the first *type*, whatever she might say in everyday conversation after the case was over.

The infamous, and counterproductive apologetic device of the *God-of-the-gaps* is a classic example of an *explanatory type-error*. Apologists who thought they were maintaining a place for God amid ever-advancing scientific explanations of the world, pointed to whatever had not yet been explained scientifically and said 'that's God'. In so doing they overlooked the logical compatibility between explanations of *mechanisms* and explanations of *agency and purpose*. One does not have to choose between 'In the beginning God created the heavens and the Earth' and 'The universe originated in a Big Bang.'

8. Science results in knowledge that is provisional and corrigible; it is not 'absolute truth'

Nevertheless, the aim of science, from a critical realist position, is *truth* about the world. The *truthlikeness* (Popper) of a theory is the extent to which that theory corresponds to reality or has more *verisimilitude* than another one. Scientists, in general, believe themselves to be developing progressively more truthlike theories, but ones which are always corrigible in the light of further work. The philosophical complexities of deciding the extent to which any given theory corresponds to reality are explored in Chapter 4. Sensory data can often be interpreted in a variety of ways depending on the presuppositions that are brought to the observations.

9. Science is not the final arbiter of *meaning* or of *truth* in every domain

The last of the above six limitations of science concerns the attempt of the logical positivists (see 4.2) to make science into a golden image. But the feet of clay could not bear the weight put upon them. They demanded empirical/scientific tests for all meaningful propositions and that these should be either *analytic* or *synthetic*. The demand turned out to be *self-referentially incoherent* in the face of the wording of the Verification Principle and the necessary presuppositions of science.

10. Science has its own concepts and its own 'language and grammar' for communication

Examples of scientific concepts are *atom, bonding, wave, photosynthesis, field, isomorphism*. This brief list indicates a number of factors about the ways language is used in science. Some words, like *atom*, are coined often from other languages, because the original meaning of the words used tell us something about the concept. *Atom* comes from a Greek word meaning indivisible, reflecting early beliefs that matter was composed of small 'particles' that could not be further subdivided – a belief now understood to be wrong. Other words like *force* and *work* are common words that have been borrowed from everyday life and given a special meaning.[7] Still other terms like *wave, flow* and *current* point to how common words about water are employed as metaphors to enable us to be articulate about what would otherwise render us speechless. *Light, radio, X-rays* and *heat* all belong to what is known as the *electromagnetic spectrum* and they all show properties like amplitude, frequency and velocity which characterize waves. In an electrical circuit something seems to move round in a similar way to the *flow* of water in a pipe, where the *current* depends on the bore of the pipe or the thickness of the wire. Finally the words *bonding* and *isomorphism* indicate, like other uses of language than scientific ones, that the context determines the meaning or, as Wittgenstein put it, we must look at language 'when it is doing work', not when it 'is like an engine idling' (Wittgenstein, 1967:51[e]). The meaning of *bonding* is very different when it is *chemical bonding* from when it is biological *pair bonding*. The word *isomorphism*, which in chemistry refers to similar structures, in psychology refers to 'the parallelism between phenomenal experience and neural processes'.

Some *metaphors* that are employed in science turn out to be particularly fruitful as aids to understanding phenomena. The flow of water to illustrate electricity and the use of water waves to illustrate light, mentioned above, are examples. These metaphors are *systematically developed* and renamed *models*. Science postulates these conceptual models and tests them. Over recent years science education has emphasized the valuable role of models (see 1.9) in helping to understand phenomena that may be *invisible, new* or *conceptually difficult* to grasp (Association for Science Education, 1994). Other examples are the 'billiard-ball' model used in the kinetic theory of gases and the 'solar-system' model for atoms. But many models go far beyond pictorial representations.

Religious thought, like science, makes extensive use of models in referring to the *invisible*, the *novel* and the *conceptually difficult*. The concept of *spirit*, for example, is compared with *wind*, which, although invisible and mysterious in its starting and finishing, is *effective* (John 3.8). The topic of language in general, and of conceptual models in particular, forms an excellent way into teaching about the interplay between science and religion. Understanding the role of models can help to dispel the facile view, often encountered by teachers of religious education, that 'science deals with the hard facts, while religion is full of vague talk about shepherds, harvests and thrones in the sky'! Chapter 8 explores different models for God that have been developed in recent dialogue.

11. Science employs *reductionism as one of its methods* but does not imply *reductionism as metaphysics*

Reducing matter to its simpler components (constitutive reductionism, see 6.11) is a tested and successful approach to understanding the world. But it is a huge and unjustifiable leap to move from 'human beings are highly complicated chemical mechanisms' to 'human beings are *nothing but* highly complicated che-mical mechanisms'. Even at the chemical level, such sloppy talk – dubbed *nothing-buttery* – fails to recognize that *emergent properties* arise because of the way those atomic components are assembled.[8] It is possible that consciousness is one such *emergent property*. Could *spiritual nature* (made in the 'image of God') (6.3.1) be another?

12. Science makes use of *direct, indirect* and *cumulative evidence* to justify its conclusions

There are substantial differences between scientific evidence and religious evidence although both make use of *indirect evidence* and the building up of a *cumulative case* to establish what is not amenable to *direct* sensory tests. The Christian religion is founded on the unique and amazing claim that Jesus Christ was resurrected from the dead to the power of an endless life. The *direct evidence* of sight, touch and sound could only have been available to the witnesses whose testimonies can be read and evaluated. To these can be added the evidence of religious experience and answered prayer, but these, while persuasive to the believer, are not publicly available tests. Much of the test procedure must be of an historical nature, seeking to make a coherent and persuasive explanation for difficulties encountered in naturalistic accounts of the empty tomb, the change in the lives of a small group of disillusioned people and, shortly afterwards, millions more. To these must be added the arising of the Christian Sunday from the jealously guarded Jewish Sabbath and the testimonies of countless millions since. The request 'prove to me scientifically that God exists', though not so commonly heard these days, is a strange one and reflects the entrenchment of logical positivist ideas many decades after the weakness of its central tenets were exposed.

13. Science does not have one, single, *the* 'scientific method' which will at the turn of a handle deliver the required answers

It involves creative insight, lucky guesses, dreams and serendipity. The well-known stories of Archimedes[9] and Kekulé[10] illustrate these other aspects of sci-entific discovery. In this context it is important to note the well-tested differ-entiation between the *context of discovery* and the *context of justification* of what is believed. Tests for the truth of what is discovered use evaluative criteria like *comprehensiveness, consistency, coherence* and *congruence* (Poole, 1995:47).

14. Science operates within a tacit methodological agreement that the *causes* it refers to are *proximate*, not *First* causes (e.g. God)

This was not always so, but the policy enables those with different religious beliefs or none to work together in a common enterprise. It also reflects the under-standing that science is the study of the *natural* world. It is important, however, to distinguish between a commitment to this study, and a further commitment to a reductionistic 'naturalism', a metaphysical position which asserts that ultimately everything is amenable to explanation by the methods of the natural sciences (see cross-explanatory reductionism, 6.11, 6.13.1–6.13.4).

15. Science involves chance and randomness but does not entail the *metaphysical* conclusion that the universe is accidental

In recent decades, the processes of evolutionary biology (*chance/randomness + selection*) have been mimicked (Ger. *Evolutionstrategie*) to find solutions to complex problems in engineering and elsewhere. The strategy has been dubbed 'Darwinian design', and alongside it a more sophisticated tool known as *genetic algorithms* was invented and developed. It arose through investigating the processes involved in adaptation in nature and how they might be mimicked in computing systems. The purpose was to seek out solutions to complex problems, using an iterative process and parallel processing, problems which would otherwise require impracticable amounts of computing time. The tool has been ever more widely used in biology, social science engineering and logistics and is particularly applicable to solving *optimization* problems.

Thus intelligent (human) designers are purposefully employing *chance/randomness + selection* to achieve desired outcomes. It is superfluous to spell out the theological parallel.

11.6.2 A second way for science education to make a contribution

If there are no prohibitions against treating issues of science and religion where they may naturally arise in teaching the science curriculum, this offers an additional way for science education to contribute. Two factors that militate against this are the pressures of time in teaching overcrowded science syllabuses and the inadequacy felt by many science teachers in teaching material fraught with historical and philosophical pitfalls. The first indicates the need for concise but nontrivial treatments of issues. The second signals the need for published material and taught courses to help teachers whose studies have not prepared them for such an undertaking. There is already a considerable quantity of published material, including some prepared for secondary school use.[11] As the closing remarks of this chapter indicate, there are already many courses on science & religion available globally. An additional resource arises from a survey of Science in the National Curriculum (1995) for topics where issues of science-and-religion might arise.[12] The content of the subsequent (1999) version of *Science* in *The National Curriculum for England* is little changed and the survey remains relevant. There is, however, a significant additional stipulation that is of relevance to our current concerns:

> In *Science: The National Curriculum for England* (DfEE/QCA 1999), the new section entitled 'Ideas and evidence in science' in Sc1: Scientific enquiry . . . has made a significant shift in what teachers are required to teach. It now

requires treatment of various aspects of the nature of science, a topic which many think should never have been omitted.

Ideas and evidence in science

Pupils should be taught:

a. how scientific ideas are presented, evaluated and disseminated [for example, by publication, review by other scientists]
b. how scientific controversies can arise from different ways of interpreting empirical evidence [for example, Darwin's theory of evolution]
c. ways in which scientific work may be affected by the contexts in which it takes place [for example, social, historical, moral and spiritual]
d. to consider the power and limitations of science in addressing industrial, social and environmental questions, including the kinds of questions science can and cannot answer, uncertainties in scientific knowledge, and the ethical issues involved.

Science teachers now have to address matters which had previously been considered the province of teachers of history, PSHE and even religious education, following the statutory requirement of the Education Reform Act that *The curriculum for a maintained school ... promotes the spiritual, {our emphasis} moral, cultural, mental and physical development of pupils at the school* (Education Reform Act 1988, page 1). (Bausor and Poole, 2003:117, 120; & 2002:18–32)[13]

Although this requirement has been implicit ever since 1988, here it is spelt out. At the time of writing, the most recent revision of the science curriculum for England (programme of study at Key Stage (KS) 4 (14–16 years) is available and will come into operation in September 2006). One quotation of particular note for our present concerns is the requirement that 'Pupils should be taught: ... that there are some questions that science cannot currently answer, and some that science cannot address.' (p. 37)

11.6.3 A third way for science education to make a contribution

This can be through cross-curricular links with, say, the history department and, in particular, the religious education/religious studies department, depending on national education policy and provision. Such inter-departmental cooperation can be of mutual benefit, especially in the likely event (in England) that the religious education department also has science & religion on its syllabus. I say *likely* in view of the interest in issues of science & religion indicated by a survey of Local Education Authority (LEA) Agreed Syllabuses in religious education in England.[14] Two-thirds of the Agreed Syllabuses of the 154 LEAs were searched and about two-thirds of these included references to such issues. There was a commonality of topics, these being clustered under the general headings of

- creation and origin of the universe/Earth;
- origin of life, evolution, Darwinism;

- miracles, laws of nature/scientific laws;
- medical ethics;
- value of animals;
- environmental issues.

... Three issues featuring in the science–religion debates, which we deemed significant, received almost no mention in the syllabuses searched:

- **Use of language.** A comparison of how language is used in science and in religion, e.g. in metaphors and models. Of the 104 Agreed Syllabuses searched, only about half a dozen made mention of this topic.
- **Nature of explanation.** A common area of confusion in popular literature on science-and-religion results from a failure to recognise that more than one explanation may be both logically possible and appropriate. Less than half-a-dozen mentions of explanation were made.
- **'Conflict' view of science-and-religion.** Without some understanding of the social forces which fostered this phenomenon – stretching from the latter part of the nineteenth century throughout much of the twentieth century – it is difficult to understand the context of the science–religion debates, but few syllabuses mentioned it.

(Bausor and Poole, 2003:118ff.)

11.7 Recent developments in England

In religious education

Because of the special nature of religious education in England, it has seemed that there could be benefit from some help being provided nationally through a *Non-Statutory National Framework for Religious Education* (Qualifications and Curriculum Authority www.qca.org.uk/re/). A Feasibility Study Group of the QCA (www.qca.org.uk/ages3–14/subjects/3655.html) reported favourably, and a writing group produced a *Draft Framework* (www.qca.org.uk/ages3–14/subjects/7150.html). The final version was launched by the Secretary of State for Education and Skills in October 2004. The importance of treating issues of science & religion are clearly set out, as indicated by the following extracts, selected from numerous others in the Framework:

Religious education provides opportunities to promote:

...

- *effective contributions to scientific, medical and health issues* through exploring philosophical and ethical questions of the origin, purpose and destiny of the cosmos and life within it, exploring the nature of humanity and human interaction with the world, exploring developments in genetics and medicine and their application and use and exploring concepts of health and well-being and their promotion

. . .

religion and science: issues of truth, explanation, meaning and purpose

. . .

exploring the connections between religious education and other subject areas such as the arts, humanities, literature, science.

(QCA, 2004:16, 29)

In science education

The most recent revision of the science curriculum for England (KS 4, referred to in 11.6.2) is framed in more general terms than earlier versions. It puts the nature, methods and implications of science at the very core of learning, with key ideas in biology, chemistry and physics (the *content*) providing a wide range of contexts for so doing. Thus the curriculum is freed up for more variety of approaches, giving more time to issues like the nature of explanations and the ethical implications of scientific work. In practice, this is most likely to be constrained by the way qualifications like GCSE are specified, in order to meet the curriculum requirements.

Finally, I turn to some brief comments on some earlier educational questions raised in 11.4, about conceptual demands and the age ranges concerned.

11.7.1 Primary education

In starting to shape pupils' subsequent thinking about science and religion, the major factor at work at the primary level is the view of the scope and capability of science that pupils pick up from the teacher. Since *Science in the National Curriculum* envisages no specific lessons on the nature of science at secondary, let alone primary level, ideas about science will be conveyed to primary pupils implicitly. Thus teachers of primary science need to understand enough about the nature of the scientific enterprise to present accurate ideas about the scope of science. They also need some knowledge of the history of science if pupils are to

- understand how scientific theories may be overturned, and
- be disabused about the unbroken success and progress of science.

11.7.2 Secondary education

What has already been said about primary science education continues to apply, with additions, at secondary level. But here the *content* covered is likely to raise issues of science and religion in a way that would be much less likely at primary level. When references are made to Galileo and Darwin, great care is needed since, as C.A. Russell has pointed out (1989), these two historical episodes have constantly been rewritten, adapted and edited to further the desire of certain pressure groups to present science and religion as in conflict. Tendentious historiography and extravagant claims for science have been major factors in promoting and perpetuating the so-called *warfare model* of science and religion.

11.7.3 Tertiary education

First degree science courses in the UK (with notable exceptions) are generally content-based and many of them pay little attention to the history and philosophy of science (HPS). One educational consequence of this pattern is that teachers of school science are initially unlikely to have encountered much about the history or philosophy of their subject to pass on to their pupils – implicitly or explicitly. Hence the status quo tends to be perpetuated and appropriate introductory ideas about HPS are often under-represented within schools. There are moves to rectify this situation.[15]

Science Studies at universities cover a huge range of topics, many of which have connections with science-and-religion issues in their content, historical development and philosophical underpinning. In addition to the subjects that have already been mentioned, geology, physics (relativity, quantum mechanics and chaos theory) and the behavioural sciences raise issues of this kind. For instance, geology is germane to the recent amazing resurgence of religious belief in a 'geologically young' Earth. Quantum mechanics features in debates about God's action in the world, while the behavioural sciences include psychological studies of religious belief and studies of the mind–brain problem.

The same points made earlier, about the presuppositions with which we approach our studies, apply at tertiary level as well as the others. As at primary and secondary levels, the implicit attitudes and worldviews of teachers, lecturers and tutors influence their teaching. Science curricula, too, reflect particular worldviews. It is useful to identify these worldviews, especially when they are not made explicit, and in particular it is important to recognize our own!

What has already been said will have indicated the considerable range of educational aspects of issues in science and religion. The literature of studies in this area is already large and is growing rapidly. The educational significance of this developing cross-disciplinary area is best encapsulated by indicating the growth in numbers of courses on science & religion in universities and colleges around the world. The Center for Theology and the Natural Sciences (CTNS) in California for instance, had an extensive Science and Religion Course Program, supported by a grant from the John Templeton Foundation. Awards were made for setting up and supporting such courses, and the number that was funded by this organization alone was in excess of seven hundred.

Notes

1   *Hermeneutics* see 1.11 note 25.
2   Literary *genre* is the term used for an established category of composition that is

characterized by distinctive language or subject matter. Poetry is one example of a particular literary *genre*. The 'elevated prose' of the initial chapters of Genesis is another.

3   e.g. Christians in Science (CiS), the Science and Religion Forum (S&RF) and the Society of Ordained Scientists (SOSc) in the UK, the South African Science and Religion Forum, the Institute for the Study of Christianity in an Age of Science and Technology (ISCAST) in Australia and, in the USA, the Templeton Foundation, the Center for Theology and the Natural Sciences (CTNS) and the American Scientific Affiliation (ASA). Then there is the European Society for the Study of Science And Theology (ESSSAT), while at the time of writing, the recently formed International Society for Science and Religion (ISSR) has circulated its members with a list of 120 Local Societies worldwide.

4   In England, primary pupils' ages range from 5 to 11 years. Secondary students' ages range from 11 to 16 years (16 being the statutory school-leaving age). Two more years of 'sixth-form studies' bring the students who take them to about 18 years of age. Tertiary education includes undergraduate and postgraduate studies.

5   Readers may refer to the following for details: Cerini, B., Murray, I. and Reiss, M. (2003) *Student Review of the Science Curriculum* (London: NESTA); Department for Education and Employment/ Qualifications and Curriculum Authority (1999) *Science: The National Curriculum for England* (London: DfEE/QCA) Hollins, M. (2004) 'Modernising science for the 21st century: Reform of GCSE', *Education in Science* 210, 8f.; Osborne, J.F., Simon, S. and Collins, S. (2003) 'Attitudes towards science: a review of the literature and its implications', *International Journal of Science Education* 25 (9), 1049–79; Osborne, J.F., Erduran, S. and Simon, S. (2004) *Ideas, Evidence and Argument in Science (IDEAS) Project* (London: King's College); University of York and Oxford, Cambridge and RSA (OCR) Examinations (2003) *Science for the 21st Century* (a collection of pilot GCSE courses).

6   From *Ode to a Nightingale* by John Keats. See Midgley, *Science and Poetry* (2001) for further discussion of the relation between explanations.

7   A *force* is that which tends to produce motion in a body. The *work* done by a force may be defined as the product of the force and the distance moved in the direction of the force.

8   For a thorough treatment of reductionism see **6.11–6.13.4**.

9   Archimedes (290/280–212/211 BCE) was said to have discovered his 'Principle' through causing water to overflow from his bath.

10   Friedrich August Kekulé (1829–96) conceived the structure of the benzene ring while dreaming.

11   Science and Religion in Schools Project, 9 Park End Street, Oxford OX1 1HH, UK, www.srsp.net, + 44 (0)1865 248844.

12   The survey was conducted, both with respect to content and methodology, within the Science Education section of the Church and Associated Colleges Project, *Engaging the Curriculum: A Theological Programme*. This project, involving the 26 Church and Associated Colleges, was based at Liverpool Hope University College, Liverpool L16 9JD. Publication: Poole (1998) (available from Christian Education, 1020 Bristol Road, Selly Oak, Birmingham B29 6LB).

13   PSHE stands for Personal, Social and Health Education.

14   'Religious education is unique in that it is nationally required, but its syllabuses are locally determined. Each of the 154 Local Education Authorities in England has the duty of setting up a Standing Advisory Committee for Religious Education (SACRE), and every five years its **Agreed Syllabus** for religious education

has to be reviewed by an Agreed Syllabus Conference' (Bausor and Poole, 2003:118).

15　Two such moves in England concern the AS Level courses 'The Public Understanding of Science' and 'Perspectives on Science'.

Further reading

ASHRIF, S. (1998) 'Science teaching, culture and religious values', *School Science Review* **79** (288), 51–4

ASSOCIATION FOR SCIENCE TEACHING (1998) *Values and Science Education*, policy statement (Hatfield: ASE)

BERRY, R.J. (2003) *God's Book of Works: The Nature and Theology of Nature* (Edinburgh: T&T Clark)

BOWLER, P. (2001) *Reconciling Science and Religion: The Debate in Early-Twentieth-Century Britain* (Chicago, IL: University of Chicago Press)

CHARIS (1997) *Charis Science* (Nottingham: Stapleford Centre)

FULLICK, P. and RATCLIFFE, M. (1996) *Teaching Ethical Aspects of Science* (Southampton: Bassett Press)

McCLUNE, R. (1998) 'Science education for the year 2000 and beyond', *Education in Science* **176**, 17–20

MILLAR, R. and OSBORNE J. (eds) (1998) *Beyond 2000: Science Education for the Future: Report with Ten Recommendations* (London: Nuffield Curriculum Projects Centre)

POOLE, M.W. (1998) *Teaching about Science and Religion: Opportunities within Science in the National Curriculum* (Abingdon: Culham College Institute)

QUALIFICATIONS AND CURRICULUM AUTHORITY (2004) *The Non-Statutory National Framework for Religious Education* (London: QCA)

WRIGHT, A. (2000) *Spirituality and Education*, Master Classes in Education Series (London: RoutledgeFalmer)

Chapter 12

Islam and science

Michael Robert Negus

12.1 Introduction

Sections 12.2 to 12.4 of this chapter provide a brief insight into the nature of Islam, in particular the concept of God, the role of the Prophet Muhammad and the origin and significance of the Qur'ān. In section 12.5 the past scientific developments of Islam are briefly examined. In section 12.6 we see how the doctrine of *tawhīd* (Oneness) and the sin of *shirk* are central to an understanding of a Muslim's concept of self, and of relationship to God and to the created universe. Sections 12.7 to 12.9 briefly explain some of the many ways in which Muslims have tried to integrate modern science with Islam. Finally, in section 12.10 the particular difficulty of the interaction of Darwinism and Islam is examined. For basic information about Islam the book by Karen Armstrong (2000) is a readable chronological arrangement of the origin and development of Islam. It is written by a non-Muslim but is sympathetic and accurate.

12.2 The concept of God

Islam sees itself as the last of the three 'Abrahamic monotheisms'. It completes the sequence of revelation from Judaism through Christianity, then finally to Islam. It regards itself as the restorative revelation which seals the sequence. Islam also sees itself as a restatement of the primordial, 'Adamic' monotheism, and moreover goes as far as stating that every human being is born a Muslim but may become something different as a result of the environment in which he or she is raised.

For Muslims God is Allāh; this is not a title, it cannot be translated as 'God'. Allāh is a personal name, often referred to as The Name of Majesty. Linguists suggest that it is derived from *al-llāh*, 'the divinity', although the word for 'god' in Arabic is *al-ilāh* and has a plural form. There is clearly a common root but the word Allāh is a personal name; it is regarded as a revelation from God and has a sacramental value, both in its written and spoken forms.

Allāh acts with an absolute freedom of will, this being the ultimate reason why things are as they are, why things exist and why events happen as they do. He is the Creator of everything, of both good and evil, not just good alone. Allāh punishes those who involve themselves in evil, even though he is responsible for the existence of evil. He punishes those who disobey his command. The correct state of a human is to be a slave (*'abd*) to Allāh, who is his or her Master (*Rabb*). This attitude, of servanthood or more correctly slavery, is manifest in the physical posture of the prayer rite, in which each Muslim touches his or her head on the ground before the majesty of God. Nothing escapes the will or the knowledge of Allāh – yet human beings seem to act with free will and are open to the punishment of hell if they attempt to turn against the will of God. The paradox between predetermination and free will is a serious problem in most religions, but has an elevated importance in Islam. The main reason for this is the assertion that only God can act, hence the human will can only acquiesce to the act that God makes in the individual's mind. Thus the effective will of God precedes the human will. If God wills something evil in the mind then the mind cannot avoid it even though, as a result of God's command, he or she must not acquiesce to it. By acquiescing the human will takes the responsibility for the evil upon itself, hence the Qur'ān (Koran) says, 'Whatever good happens to you is from Allāh; but whatever evil happens to you, is from your own soul' (Qur'ān 4:79, Sūra, *An-Nisā*, 'Women'). Some recent Islamic philosophers, for example Muhammad Iqbal, have emphasized the degree of freedom given to creatures, so ameliorating the 'fatalism' that is commonly attributed to Islam. For a discussion of the classical view of predestination in Islam and the thinking of Iqbal, see the third chapter of Ward (1996a:59–76).

There is no doctrine of original sin in Islam. Adam and Eve are regarded as being deceived by Satan, and because of that the guilt is upon Satan, not upon the first human pair. In fact Adam is regarded as the first Prophet in Islam, the last being Muhammad. In Islam the primary human faculty is the intelligence (*'aql*). Intelligence is required to see the truth, which is regarded as self-evident, that there is one Divinity, one Creator of the universe and of all living things. This truth is expressed in the principal confession of faith *Lā ilaha illā Llāh*, 'no divinity except Allāh'. The greatest sin in Islam is to deny this truth by 'associating' something with Allāh, indicating that it has divine or implicitly divine status. Thus a Muslim scientist would accept that Newton's laws are an expression or summary of the will of Allāh with regard to motion, but would reject the suggestion that Newton's laws determine motion.

The merciful nature of God in Islam is often misunderstood by non-Muslims. Each prayer, each act and each verse of the Qur'ān starts with the words *Bismi Llāhi r-Rahmā ni r-Rahīm*, 'in the name of Allāh, Absolutely Merciful-in-Himself, Infinitely Compassionate-to-His creatures'. The two 'Names of Mercy' *Rahmān* and *Rahīm* are derived from the root *rhm* which has the meaning 'matrix' or 'womb' and expresses maternal protection. The womb is taken as a prototype for the good mother who nourishes, protects and cares for her offspring. (It may be surprising that two of the greatest names of Allāh express maternal qualities, since the God of Islam is usually thought of, by Westerners, as being utterly masculine.) Human beings are required to turn away from a state of *ghaflah*, 'heedlessness' towards Allāh. This act is called *tawbah* and is the spiritual act that redeems the individual. Then in a state of worship as a 'slave' of Allāh, the Muslim receives the fullness of Allāh's Mercy and total forgiveness.

The importance of intelligence as a gift from Allāh no doubt explains the development of knowledge in general and science and technology in particular in

Islam. This is expressed in the often quoted *hadīth* (saying) of the Prophet Muhammad: 'The quest for knowledge is obligatory for every Muslim.'

Islam justifies natural science by regarding it as a process of studying the acts of the Creator. It therefore goes easily with an attitude of worship. The practising Muslim can, in principle, be a good scientist. This possibility and some of the difficulties involved are discussed in 12.5, 12.7 and 12.8 below. Technology is regarded as justified because it brings benefit and relief from toil for the community. The problems that arise from the application of science and technology in the modern world are only too well known both inside and outside of the Islamic world. Technology in a broader context will be discussed in the next chapter. To some extent the contemporary problems are caused by the energy sources that are used to drive modern industry, but other problems arise from biotechnology such as genetic engineering and, more recently, cloning (see Chapter 14). Such problems did not, of course, apply in the traditional Islamic world.

Islam has an ecological perspective which is based upon one of the functions that Allāh bestowed upon mankind. Adam and his seed were each given, by God, the role of *khalīfah*, 'vicegerent', and each individual was endowed with the duty and the power to care for and manage the Earth and its resources on behalf of the Creator. In principle this provides for the possibility of a full Islamic 'green' policy which includes the management and the conservation of ecological diversity. The role of vicegerent is obligatory upon every Muslim individual as well as upon government and organizations. Moreover there is a price to be paid for neglect or failure of this duty since each individual will have to give an account of his/her function as *khalīfah* on the day of judgement.

12.3 The religious dimensions of Islam: God, the Prophet and the Qur'ān

Islam resounds with the message of God's unity:

> Say: He, Allāh is One.
> Allāh the Infinitely Resplendent.
> He begetteth not, nor is He begotten.
> And there is none like unto Him
> (Qur'ān 112:1–4, Sūra *al-ikhlās*, 'Purity of Faith')

The significance of the Islamic consciousness of the oneness and uniqueness of God cannot be overestimated. It is not simply a doctrine but an active organizing principle which permeates religious thought and religious practice. It also provides the underlying axiom that explains Islam's scientific worldview.

The place of the Prophet Muhammad in Islam is often misunderstood by Christians. Muhammad is human, not divine. He had both a human mother and a human father. He is a prophet, not an incarnation. He died and his grave is in Medina. Although human he is often said to be a 'jewel among men' and is always referred to with respect; thus after mention of his name a Muslim says 'upon him be blessing and peace'. The Prophet is the channel through whom the Qur'ān was revealed to the world. He listened to the Qur'ān being read by the angel Jibrā'īl (Gabriel) and then himself recited exactly what he had heard. The Qur'ān is therefore precisely the word of God, with nothing added and nothing taken away. This is why it is the absolute truth and this is why Muslim scientists treat it so seriously.

The Qur'ān, then, is regarded by Muslims as the literal, spoken words of God. It is in essence a 'recitation' rather than a book, and at its inception Muhammad was commanded by the angel to recite: 'Recite in the Name of thy Lord!' (Qur'ān 96:1, Sūra *iqra'*, 'Recite!'). The Qur'ān as written down consists of 114 sūras or chapters, ranked, more or less, in order of length, not in chronological order. The notable exception to the ordering is the first sūra *al-fātihah* ('The Opening'), which, because of its special ritual character and usage, is placed at the beginning and written or printed in a highly decorated form. The Qur'ān was the first Arabic text to employ vowel signs and other notations to ensure correct recitation. The Qur'ān has played a principal role in many respects: it is the key text for classical Arabic, it is the source of the legal system (*sharī'ah*) of Islam, it has been used as a source of mystical knowledge and it has a sacramental role during recitation. Since the Qur'ān is the spoken word of God, to recite it is to be very close to God. The Qur'ān is therefore given great respect and reverence. The traditional exegesis of the Qur'ān is very different from the exegesis of the Gospels. Commentaries on the Qur'ān seek to explain the circumstances that provoked the 'sending down' (*tanzīl*) of the verses; there is also a methodology for employing one or more verses axiomatically in the development of Islamic Law. By way of extension and because God spoke the Qur'ān in Arabic, it is also true that the Arabic language, both spoken and written, has a sacred nature. Thus the form of the Arabic Name of Allāh is sacred. The ability of the language to act as a vehicle in some sense for the 'presence' of its Author is so great that in June 1997 the sportswear manufacturing company Nike withdrew 38,000 pairs of trainers from its worldwide market because of an objection from Muslims that a new logo design, printed on the underside of the soles, resembled too much the Arabic Name of God.

12.4 The universe and its Creator

Numerous verses of the Qur'ān repeatedly affirm that God is the Creator of the universe.

> The Originator of the heavens and the earth;
> When He decreeth a matter He says unto it: 'Be', and it is.
> (Qur'ān 2:117, Sūra *al-baqarah*, 'The Heifer')

In some respects the Qur'ān expresses itself in a way similar to the book of Genesis. Thus the heavens and the Earth and all that is between them are said to have been completed in six days (Qur'ān 50:38). The Earth itself was completed in two days (Qur'ān 41:9). Having finished this creation God withdrew and took His place upon a throne.

Allāh it is Who created the heavens and the earth,
and all that is between them, in six days.
Then He mounted the Throne.
He directeth the ordinance from the heaven unto the earth,
then it ascendeth unto Him in a Day, whereof the measure
is a thousand years of your reckoning.

(from Qur'ān 32:4–5, Sūra *as-sajdah*, 'The Prostration')

The above verses are typical of the way in which the Qur'ān often refers to a previous 'revelation' (in this case the 'days' of Genesis), adds a further previously unrevealed detail (the Throne of Ordinance), and reveals a mystery, the descent of ordinance and the ascent of confirming concordance (cf. Qur'ān 2:231), together with a comment on the difference between time as experienced by humanity and as experienced by God.

Some verses of the Qur'ān give details of processes involved in creation or of the intentions of the Creator. Six verses are listed below to give a sample of the sort of problems encountered by a Muslim scientist who wants to reconcile modern scientific knowledge with statements found in various parts of the Qur'ān.

(a) Do not the unbelievers see that the heavens and the earth
were joined together [literally the two were one patch] before
we parted them.
We made from water every living thing.

(Qur'ān 21:30, Sūra *al-anbiyā'*, 'The Prophets')

(b) Then He turned His will to the heavens,
and it was smoke.
He said to it and to the earth:
Come you two willingly or unwillingly.
They said: we come obediently.

(Qur'ān 41:11, Sūra *fussilat*, 'They are Expounded')

(c) We created not the heavens and the earth
and all that is between them save with truth [*illā bil-haqq*],
and for a term appointed.

(Qur'ān 46:3, Sūra *al-ahqāf*, 'Wind Curved Sandhills')

(d) And We created not the heavens and the earth and all that is between
them in play.
We created them not save with truth [*al-haqq*]
but most of them know not.

(Qur'ān 44:38–9, Sūra *ad-dukhān*, 'The Smoke'; compare with 38:28)

(e) Allāh created the heavens and the earth with truth [*al-haqq*]
Lo! therein is indeed a sign [*āyāt*] for believers.

(Qur'ān 29:44, Sūra *al-'ankabūt*, 'The Spider')

(f) And He it is Who created the heavens and the earth
      ... that He may try you, which of you is best in conduct.
                                                    (Qur'ān 11:7, Sūra *hūd*)

In many verses of the Qur'ān (see quotation (a) above) there is a challenge to 'the unbelievers' that they are unable to discern the obvious evidence of the Creator's work. Another assertion in the Qur'ān is that the creation was effected with and endowed with 'truth' (*haqq*) (see quotations (c), (d) and (e) above). Also in numerous verses (e.g. Qur'ān 6:97–9 and quotation (e) above) the Qur'ān describes the works of the Creator as 'signs' (*āyāt*) for 'those who understand' (*yufqahūn* – literally those who use *fiqh*, the deductive process of rational thought). Al Ghazzālī (1058–1111), the highly respected theologian and logician of Tūs, who is still revered by Muslims, encouraged the application of intelligence (*'aql*) to the texts of the Qur'ān as well as to all aspects of life. He wrote against *naql*, which is the process of simply 'copying' the thoughts of precedents. Bagley explains that

> for Al-Ghazzālī, as for others of his day, 'intelligence' meant deductive reasoning, from premises given by divine revelation; not inductive reasoning, through which new knowledge might be sought. He favoured the use of intelligence in support of religion, as well as for practical purposes, though he thought that religious discussion should not be excessive and that it should only be carried on by qualified persons. (Bagley, 1964:xxxiv)

Since the Qur'ān contains sections that have a quasi-scientific significance and because the verses are regarded as the direct words of Allāh and are therefore absolutely true, the Muslim can only apply deductive reasoning to them. Remember that the words are believed to be eternal truths, independent of the time or age in which they were first revealed. A Muslim scientist might, for example, attempt to link modern science and the Qur'ān with reference to quotation (a) in the following way:

- The Qur'ān says that the 'heavens and the earth', i.e. the whole of physical existence, were originally a single entity that was split apart. Thus, through science we would not be surprised to discover that the fundamental particles found in the 'heavens' (the 'out-there' universe), and in the matter from which the Earth is made, are identical.
- The Qur'ān says that Allāh made all living things from water. Hence the intimate and necessary relationship we observe between water and all plants and animals is readily understood in terms of their origin. It is reasonable to deduce, from the verse, that all living forms will be composed of a high proportion of water, and this is what science has confirmed.

In addition to statements about the universe, animals and plants, the Qur'ān contains statements of epistemological significance. The Creator is said to have made all things 'with truth' (quotations (c), (d), and (e)). This explains, for a Muslim, why it is possible to understand creation by rational thought and intelligence, and why science aims at finding the elusive truth. Islamic metaphysics explains the intelligibility of creation as a dynamic interaction within the triad of the intelligent subject (*al-'āqil*), the intelligible object (*al-ma'qūl*) and intelligence (*al-'aql*), the latter being common to both subject and object (cf. Burckhardt, 1988:142). One of the differences between secular science and Islamic science is that the ability of science to gain knowledge through reason is taken as a presupposition without question or comment in the secular sphere (see Poole, 1990:26–9 and cf. Poole, 1995), whereas in Islam it is recognized and explained as existing because of the nature of God and of His creative act.

The status of scientific knowledge in Islamic thought is therefore very different from that in modern Western thought. Science is seen as providing only relative and provisional knowledge. It cannot be compared with the absolute truth spoken infallibly by God and recorded faultlessly in the Qur'ān. Thus, if there is a contradiction between science and the Qur'ān, then the science is likely to be assumed to be wrong. Science is also seen as a component of the social phenomenon of mankind; it arose in society and should therefore be regulated by the legal system (*sharī'ah*) that regulates society. Science in Islam does not have the autonomy, or the exclusive claim on truth, that it is often taken to possess in modern Western society.

12.5 The flourishing of science and technology in the Golden Age of Islam

The development of science in Islam is inseparably bound up with the expansion of the Islamic Empire. After the death of Muhammad, in 632, the four Caliphs established the *dār al-islām*, the 'Territory of Islam'. Very soon the territory ruled by Islam included Persia, Syria, Egypt and Mesopotamia. By the year 750 the territory had expanded to an empire stretching from Spain to India and including extensive parts of northern Africa. The Empire was held between the ninth and the twelfth centuries as a single vast unifying power. Its significance cannot be overestimated in constituting a foundation for the development of much of modern science. During the seventh to the ninth centuries Islamic scholars, working with the immense collection of Greek, Egyptian and Oriental documents in Alexandria (cf. Nasr, 1976:9), made a vast number of translations and compilations into Arabic. This effectively opened up the whole of the extant knowledge of the ancient worlds and, very importantly, ensured its eventual survival for the West and for us today.

During the tenth and eleventh centuries of the Christian Era the developments that took place in the *dār al-islām* led to this period being named the 'Golden Age'. A group of *hukamā* (singular *hakīm*), 'natural philosophers', developed medicine, astronomy and mathematics. They refined algebra, improved and popularized arithmetic, founded plane and spherical trigonometry and developed the physics of optics. Their influence on the West was so great that many Arabic words are still used in these disciplines, words such as algebra, algorithm, zenith, azimuth, nadir; other words such as alcohol and alkali came into the English language in the context of the chemical processes involved in alchemy, itself an

Arabic word. During the course of the twelfth century scholars working in Sicily and Toledo translated the manuscripts that had been written during the Golden Age from Arabic into Latin. These included translations of philosophical works. Thus Thomas Aquinas (d. 1274) was able to read translations of the works of Plato and Aristotle as well as the thoughts of tenth-century Ash'arite theologians. Moreover Aquinas employed a secretary who could translate from Arabic into Latin.

An example of a *hakīm* working in the tenth and eleventh centuries is Ibn al-Haytham (965–1039). In the West, his name, like those of all the Islamic scholars, was transliterated as a single Latin word. In his case he became known in the West as Alhazen. He was outstanding in astronomy and in mathematics. His special success was in optical studies of lenses and mirrors. He compiled tables of the angles of incidence and refraction of light rays (published in his book *kitāb al-manādhir*) and so had the data required to discover Snell's Law. He extended his studies to determine the angle of refraction of the sun's light as it passed through the atmosphere (see Nasr, 1987), and thereby estimate the height of the atmosphere. He applied his studies of refraction to explain the optical properties of the eye. Another *hakīm*, named Abū Rayhān al-Bīrūnī (973–1051), in his astronomical studies, described the Earth as a sphere after observing the shadow of the Earth in lunar eclipses; by means of observations and trigonometric calculations he was able to calculate with some accuracy the circumference and radius of the Earth. These sophisticated observations were provoked because, for the *hukamā*, science was integral to Islam and equivalent to piety. Some of the best and most eloquent praises of science ever written come from the pens of Muslim scientists who considered their works to be acts of worship; an example is the great Andalusian scholar Abū Umar Yūsuf al-Qurtubī (d. 1071), whose book *The Comprehensive Account of the Enlightenment and Virtue of Science and the Prerequisites of Telling its Truths and of Carrying its Mission* 'has no contemporary parallel' (Sardar, 1980:88). The material presented in this chapter can only hint at the quality of science in Islam during the Golden Age; those wishing to read further are recommended the two excellent volumes by Nasr (1968; 1976) referenced in the Bibliography.

Given the links between science and technology it is not surprising that the Golden Age of Islam also gave rise to the invention of a great variety of machines and devices to make life easier. These range from simple tools such as scissors to complex automatic, water-powered machines which were used to lift water into aqueducts for distribution in cities. Machines were also developed for technical commercial purposes, for example weighing machines using Archimedes' Principle to determine automatically the density – and hence the purity – of metals.

The evidence that we gain from a study of the Golden Age of Islam is that human intelligence is regarded as a sacred gift from the Creator; its specific use to gain knowledge and to understand is positively encouraged in Islam. The main purpose of the study of the universe is to perceive the work of the Creator and thereby to enhance respect and an attitude of adoration.

The Qur'ān contains admonitions to provoke the acquisition of such knowledge and includes numerous axiomatic statements that Muslim scholars have employed to support deductive reasoning in their attempts to understand Nature. It is very important to note, however, that the work of the natural philosophers of the Golden Age included the use of inductive reasoning. The data on refraction gained by Ibn al-Haytham allowed him to look for a general law to describe the phenomenon, which he unfortunately failed to achieve because he used chords, rather than sine values, in an attempt to find what we now know as Snell's Law. Likewise al-Bīrūnī used a number of astronomical observations to infer a model of the Earth and the moon which then enabled him to calculate the size of the Earth. Such procedures, among several others carried out by the two scientists, show that inductive, empirical reasoning was quite natural to them, and apparently compatible with their concept of the relationship between the deductive reasoning that starts from the statements in the verses of the Qur'ān and their own observational investigations of nature. Traditional Islamic science at its best in the Golden Age was a blend of deductive and inductive reasoning, although the latter was much rarer than the former.

12.6 The Islamic paradigm of the universe

The doctrine of *tawhīd* is central to the Islamic understanding of the nature of the universe. *Tawhīd* means 'being one' or 'making one'. Manzoor (1984:155) defines the doctrine as the 'metaphysical and theological doctrine *par excellence* which gives the religion of Islam its unique profile and distinctive morphology'. Ayatullah Mutahhari (1985:74) comments on *tawhīd* as expressing the essential nature of the universe: the universe has for its essence 'from Him-ness' (*innā lillāh* [literally 'truly we belong to God']) and 'to Him-ness' (*innā ilayhi raji'ūn* [literally 'truly to Him we are returning', Qur'ān 2:156]). This relates to the idea referred to earlier in this chapter that the ordinance of God 'descends' to the Earth and, having accomplished its purpose, the knowledge of its effect returns back to God. The universe has its origin from God and to God it will return. The commands that govern the universe are given by God and the knowledge of their concordance sent back to Him. Mutahhari writes that the doctrine of *tawhīd* means that the universe is 'unipolar and uniaxial' (Mutahhari, 1985:74).

The doctrine of *tawhīd* is without doubt the principial axiom of the Islamic worldview. In a scientific context this doctrine seems to be intuitively true and inductively supported. Thus, for example, the fact that the Moon, the Earth and the Earth's oceans are moving in a gravitational system with a *single* centre of gravity is a confirmation of the axiom. Similar confirmations are seen in the *unifying* logic of the Periodic Table or the dynamic *integrity* of an ecosystem. The search for a theory of everything (GUT, the Grand Unifying Theory) and the proposal that the universe is derived from a singularity (see 1.15) should also find easy acceptance as confirming the deductions that can be made from the doctrine of *tawhīd* (although many Muslims are uneasy with the apparent atheism and implied evolutionism of the Big Bang Theory). It is interesting to note the close match that exists between the deductive implications of *tawhīd* and the modern, inductive interpretation of the characteristics of the universe. Paul Davies writes that 'another highly relevant feature of the world's orderly contingency concerns the nature of that order, which is such as to bestow a rational unity on the cosmos.

Moreover, this holistic orderliness is *intelligible* to us' (Davies, 1993:170). This conclusion, in the words of a respected modern scientist, is a succinct expression of what a Muslim could derive from a combination of the key doctrines of *tawhīd* and *al-'aql*, that is Unity and Intelligibility, by deduction from the Qur'ān and no other knowledge.

Tawhīd is the essence of the Islamic faith. In fact 'the unity of all reality (*tawhīd*) and the balance of nature (*mīzān*) *as recognised by Islam constitutes an important basis for religious ecology and environmental ethics*' (Amin, 2003:xxxiii). The opposite of *tawhīd* is *shirk*, which is the cardinal sin in Islam, meriting the punishment of hell. *Shirk* literally means 'association', although it is often translated as 'polytheism'. In this religious sense the word describes the belief or supposition that there are 'partners' with God. Surty (1990:119) concludes that the mission of all the prophets 'was the emancipation of humanity from the shackles of *al-Shirk*. Sirriyeh (1990:157) traced the meaning and interpretation of *shirk* from its mention in the Qur'ān until modern times. She concludes,

> 'the concept of shirk has shown a remarkable adaptability in different circumstances and may yet be developed in new directions'. Shirk in a scientific sense would be applied to any statement or assertion that suggested that the universe, either in part or in its totality, did not depend entirely upon God. Clearly it is possible to discover unity in the universe experimentally, as well as for a Muslim to believe a priori that the unity has its cause in the Creator. The important point to make here is that *shirk* is essentially an attitude, conveyed perhaps by a theory, that ascribes to something that has been created the attributes of the Creator upon whom the existence of that thing depends. From an Islamic point of view it is possible for every phenomenon that is studied by science, whether Western or Islamic, to be described in such a way that it can be integrated into a world-view that preserves tawhīd and prevents shirk. This is fundamental to the Islamic understanding of the natural environment and ecology, since 'humans and nature are one and are at peace in the consciousness of tawhīd. When tawhīd is forgotten, the relationship becomes unpeaceful. Through exploring the nature of peace in Islam, we gain a special approach to the Islamic understanding of ecology. (Said and Funk, 2003:155–6)

12.7 Islam and modern science

Science is apparently opposed to Islam if 'by science we understand a rational and empirical method of studying the phenomenon of nature' (for its own sake, without any control). 'The pursuit of knowledge is not an end in itself; it is only a means of acquiring an understanding of God and solving the problems of the Muslim community' (Sardar, 1984:22–3). Nasr adds to this the positive perspective that: 'the aim of all the Islamic Sciences ... is to show the unity and interrelatedness of all that exists, so that, in contemplating the unity of the cosmos, man may be led to the unity of the Divine Principle, of which the unity of Nature is an image' (Nasr, 1987:22).

Kurt Wood has proposed that the interactions between the statements found in the Qur'ān and modern science fall into four categories or 'theses'. These are:

1. The Compatibility Thesis – the Qur'ān and modern science are not mutually contradictory in any respects, because the same God is the origin of both.
2. The Concordist Thesis – the Qur'ān contains scientific teaching.
3. The Veiled Reference Thesis – scientific statements are found in the Qur'ān that science does not yet understand.
4. The Verification Thesis – modern science proves that the Qur'ān has a divine origin.

(Wood, 1993:91–4)

These four theses are outcomes of a strong tension which exists between Islam and modern science. The tension exists because modern science never refers to God as creator, contains no explicitly God-based value system, and proposes, in the theory of evolution, that humanity is not a special creation. Abdullah Omar Nasseef, Professor of Geology at King Abdulaziz University, writes that 'modern science does not want to speak of the Will of God or the attributes of God'. 'Religion teaches us that the universe, in fact the entire creation is for man and God wants man to behave as His representative on Earth. Nature is not a blind force evolving mindlessly on its own' (Nasseef and Black, 1984:6–8).

One of the bizarre, but actually tragic, consequences of the tension is the manifestation of a pseudoscience. Hoodbhoy comments that: 'fundamentalists often claim that every major discovery of modern science was long anticipated in the holy scriptures of their faith. Read the text carefully, they say, and you will find it there. But if you do not find it, either you have not done a good job at reading or the so-called scientific fact is a fake' (Hoodbhoy, 1991:65). This pseudoscience claims to show that the Qur'ān describes the chemical composition of milk, the effect of high altitude on humans, the nature of cumulo-nimbus clouds, that Adam and Eve 'fell' from another planet, predicts the incandescent light bulb, the atom bomb, the Sargasso Sea, the Hubble expansion of the universe, the structure of atoms, special relativity, aeroplanes, UFOs and so forth. References to these will be found in Wood (1993) and Hoodbhoy (1991). The driving force for these bewildering ideas is explained by Wood's theses 2, 3 and 4 listed above. They constitute a wonderful example of the misuse of deductive reasoning and of the fantasy that arises when a scholar loses genuine scholarship and seeks to prove what he or she *wants* to be true, rather than respecting truth as something refreshing, challenging and waiting to be discovered. Hoodbhoy rejects the notion of an 'Islamic science'. Other Muslims, such as Waghid (1996:90), propose a rationale for Islamic science that constitutes 'creative order, truth and justice'. Negus (1995:31) proposes that a better approach would be to 'define the Muslim scientist rather than Islamic science', using, as a role model, a great *hakīm* like al-Bīrūnī. Butt, after reviewing the opinions of several Muslim authors about the nature of the best expressions of Islamic science, writes:

the practice of Islamic science creates an atmosphere that encourages the remembrance of Allah, motivates behaviour according to the dictates of the sharia and promotes the conceptual values inherent in the Qur'ān. It is a living dynamic entity able to provide contemporary solutions to contemporary problems within the most humane and ethical framework in perfect harmony with man and nature. It is a science truly international in character. (Butt, 1991:64)

Wood has analysed the Compatibility Thesis. He suggests that the thesis 'seems to be an eminently reasonable operating principle for the believer'. He offers three possible approaches within the thesis:

a *compartmental* approach that completely decouples 'spiritual' and 'scientific' kinds of knowledge, limiting scripture to the former; a *phenomenological* approach to the text which seeks to understand the Scriptural texts referring to natural phenomena in the context of the common knowledge bank of the original recipients of the word; and a *scientific exegesis* approach which seeks detailed scientific information in Scriptural texts. (Wood, 1993:92)

These three approaches present a range of possibilities. The most dangerous is undoubtedly the third, because it has a tendency to *force* a scientific interpretation upon verses of the Qur'ān.

Seyed Ali Ashraf reaffirms the traditional position that science should operate within 'basic limits set by the Qur'ānic revelations'. Nasseef and Black consider that 'As the Muslim society is still dominated by the religious code of life, and as the acceptance of the religious code for all spheres of life is still a basic social assumption, it is possible for the Muslims to use scientific discoveries within the Islamic code of life and redirect technology for the benefit of mankind. The greatest problem is the theory of evolution' (Nasseef and Black, 1984:2–3). Seyed Ali Ashraf goes as far as stating four 'basic limits' with reference to evolution. These are, in a simplified form, that God is the only Cause, that the laws governing the universe are given by God, that Adam was a completely new species and did not evolve from a pre-existing species, and that Adam was the first Prophet.

There are about half a dozen Muslim writers who seem to support the theory of evolution and who have gone as far as trying to find evidence to support it in the verses of the Qur'ān. Shaikh Abdul Mabud, the Deputy Director-General of the Islamic Academy based at Cambridge, refers to this group (he lists the members of the group) as 'theistic evolutionists'. He writes: 'no matter what the theistic evolutionists think, the truth and authenticity of the Qur'ān does not lie in its being compatible with modern science' (Mabud, 1986:19).

Maurice Bucaille, a French surgeon and a convert to Islam, is a typical example of the 'theistic evolutionists'. His main book *The Bible, the Qur'ān and Science*, has been translated into ten different languages, including English. Another book, *What is the Origin of Man?*, supports human evolution. The final chapters of his book contain numerous quotations from the Qur'ān, which he claims refer to evolution. But Bucaille *bends the meaning* of the Arabic words to suit his own ideas.

Wood comments that 'Bucaille proposes new meanings for Qur'ānic words to bring them into accord with modern scientific knowledge, without requiring any standard philological justification' (Wood 1993:90).

The theory of evolution is without doubt the scientific theory most rejected by Muslims. The author once advised a master's degree student, who was a practising teacher from Kuala Lumpur, on the teaching of science in primary schools. During the conversation she said, 'we accept all science in Islam, there is no problem; but we reject completely Darwinism, because we believe what it says in the Qur'ān, that man was made by God'. Muslim students in Western countries are taught evolution in schools and colleges. They know the theory, will answer examination questions on it, but privately reject it totally.

12.8 Identifying problems and recognizing points of agreement

There is, then, without doubt a tension between Islam and modern science. One thing which needs to be resolved is the conflict that appears to exist between the scientific-like statements in the Qur'ān and the discoveries and paradigms of modern science. There is the belief among Muslims that the Qur'ānic verses are absolutely true; it is also commonly held that the truth conveyed by the verses is independent of time and setting. There is an unwillingness to accept that some statements are true in a contextual rather than universal sense. This reluctance seems unnecessary. For example, when the Qur'ān refers to the universe it seems that a pre-Copernican or Ptolemaic model of the universe is assumed. Such a model, based upon Earth-centred appearances, does not impugn the integrity or truth of the Qur'ān as long as one remembers the cultural and historical context in which the revelation was received, recited and heard. The prime purpose of the Qur'ān is to provoke a response that leads to salvation. The Qur'ān is surely not a scientific treatise, and science is not indispensable for salvation. The two approaches identified by Wood within his Compatibility Thesis, namely the 'compartmental' and 'phenomenological' approaches, seem to offer a hopeful way forwards. It would make sense for Muslims to reflect upon the importance of the fact that the occasions of the 'piecemeal revelation' (*tanzīl*) of the Qur'ān were frequently context-specific and couched in a language that was for the immediate benefit of those hearing them. Such an approach would prevent the extravagant interpretations made by authors such as Bucaille, mentioned in section 12.7 above.

There are two very positive and constructive points of interaction between modern science and Islam, the first stemming from the definition of God as the One (*al-Ahad*) and the other from a definition of the human being, the vicegerent (*khalīfah*) of God.

The doctrine of *tawhīd* ('oneness'), which is so central to Islam, has a parallel that resonates through much of the thinking of modern science. This principle of unity-in-multiplicity is seen universally, in individual organisms, natural systems and in the mathematical formula used to describe their behaviour. Without doubt *tawhīd* is the strongest link between the essence of Islam and the discoveries of modern science. Özdemir (2003:28–9) has proposed a set of eight principles that

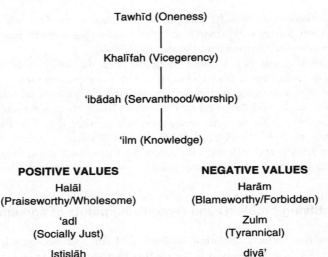

Tawhīd (Oneness)

|

Khalīfah (Vicegerency)

|

'ibādah (Servanthood/worship)

|

'ilm (Knowledge)

POSITIVE VALUES	NEGATIVE VALUES
Halāl (Praiseworthy/Wholesome)	Harām (Blameworthy/Forbidden)
'adl (Socially Just)	Zulm (Tyrannical)
Istislāh (In the Public Interest)	diyā' (Wasteful)

Figure 12.1   Ten Islamic concepts for the development of Islamic policies on science

can be deduced from the Qur'ān and which define the relationship between God and nature, the integration and biodiversity of the ecosystems as expressions of God's will, and the role of human beings with regard to nature – including the need to prevent 'the appearance and emergence of corruption in ecosystems' since to 'prevent corruption on earth (*fasād fi 'l-ard*), is one of the primary responsibilities of all believers'.

In recent years, it has become more and more apparent that our planet is suffering from the damaging effects of some kinds of technology and that, unless corrective measures are taken, the future of the human species, and perhaps other forms of life, are threatened. In this context the concept of mankind as *khalīfah*, as being responsible for the stewardship of the world, is very apposite (see 12.2 above). In addition, as new developments take place in science, such as genetic engineering and cloning, many secular as well as religious people are asking for scientists to recognize a value-system and apply it, rather than naively believing that their work is neutral and that moral responsibility does not apply to them. The regulation of science by society is something natural to Islam, which has always seen science and technology as justifiable so long as they are for the service of the community and not a threat. Science cannot escape from the value context in which it exists, neither can it ignore the consequences of new discoveries.

12.9 Proposals for the regulation and Islamization of science

In 1980 a comparative study of Islamic and Western science and technology was inaugurated within the International Federation of Institutes for Advanced Studies (IFIAS) in Solna, Sweden. This was also supported by Islam and the West

International in Geneva. In September 1981 a seminar entitled 'Knowledge and Values' took place in Stockholm, organized within IFIAS. Descriptions of the outcomes of the seminar are given by Butt (1991:43–64) and Sardar (1985). The Muslim scientists who gathered for the seminar identified ten 'Islamic concepts', which they put together in a hierarchic structure that would serve as a model of what is distinctive about Islamic science, and which might act as a guide for the development of policies for Islamic science throughout the Muslim world. The model is shown in Figure 12.1.

The pairs of contrasted social values at the bottom of the diagram are self-explanatory. The descending sequence of four concepts at the top of the diagram needs some explanation, especially for Christians. The highest concept in this paradigm of Islamic science is *tawhīd*, the Unity of the universe that we have already discussed above. It is important to remember that *tawhīd* also means 'making one'. It is thus a kind of constructive principle for the model. Ultimately, in practice, it means a refusal to see any object, process or law existing as independent from God, the One. To do so is to commit the sin of *shirk* ('association' – i.e. ascribing to a created object a divine attribute, such as independent existence). *Khalīfah* is the divinely ordained function of humanity on Earth. Humans were given the trusteeship of the Earth, indeed of the universe, by God. They must not therefore exploit or pollute the planet. Each man and woman will be required to give an account of their trusteeship, to God at the Last Judgement. The concept of *'ibādah* indicates that a human is a 'slave' (*'abd*) before God, and so is required to worship Him. The same concept applies in fact to the whole creation, which according to the Qur'ān, praises its Creator and 'prostrates itself' (Qur'ān 55:6). After this comes knowledge (*'ilm*), where the application of science begins. The operation of science within society, its funding and the licensing of what it can or cannot do, is regulated by the three pairs of positive and negative principles. The model could, with some modification and development, be incorporated into the Islamic legal system or *Sharī'ah*. Whether or not this will ever happen is, however, another thing altogether.

An alternative approach to the Knowledge and Values IFIAS seminar is shown by the publications of the International Institute of Islamic Thought (IIIT). This was founded in 1981 and is based in Herndon, Virginia. In 1987 a workshop on the Islamization of Attitudes and Practices in Science and Technology was held at Herndon. A paper by the president of IIIT (al-'Alwānī, 1989:11), identified three major guidelines to effect Islamization. Expressed in a simplified form these are:

1. Muslims should accept legitimately proven scientific facts.
2. All knowledge must be integrated into the Islamic (Qur'ānic) scheme of things.
3. Anything in modern science that is contrary to Islam must be rejected.

EXERCISE 12.1

Consider the following: if the three precepts listed in 12.9 were adopted by Christian theologians, how would the debate with science look in terms of Ted Peters' classification in 1.4?

Islam is a worldwide religion and the Muslim *Ummah* constitutes about one-fifth of humankind. There have been a number of conferences in various parts of the *dār-al-Islām*, 'the house of Islam', which are intended to have global influences, affecting the Islamic expression of science and technology in all countries where the religion is found. These include the Organization of Islamic Conferences Standing Committee on Scientific and Technological Co-operation (COM-STECH). This was established by the Islamic Summit in 1981 at Islamabad, Pakistan, and it is composed of all the member states of the Organization of Islamic Countries. 'COMSTECH aims at assessment of human and material resources, building on indigenous capabilities in the fields of science and technology, promotion and continuing co-operation and co-ordination in scientific and technological areas of its member states and creation of effective institutional structure for planning research, development and monitoring of scientific and technological activities at Ummah level' (ur-Rahman, 1995). Another example of pan-Islamic coordination of science is the conference held at Riyadh in Saudi Arabia in 1981. This conference led to the publication of a number of texts in English which focus on education as well as the 'Islamization' of science. One of the texts, edited by Faruqi and Nasseef (1981) includes a chapter by al-Hashimi (1981) that deals with the problems of the 'Islamization' of psychology. The author concludes that 'psychology can be studied in the light of Islamic Studies' (1981:67); he recommends that courses should be provided so that students and lecturers in psychology can gain 'a grounding in Islamic spiritual education, along with a detailed and scientific explanation of the Islamic concept of the human psyche'.

Islam recognizes its strong heritage of science, developed during the Golden Age, and in modern times sees the importance of science and technology for economic benefit. Abdus Salam, the 1979 Nobel Prize winner in Physics, wrote:

> so far as the Sciences are concerned, the Muslim Ummah [world-wide Community] has a proud past. For 350 years, from 750 CE to 1100 CE, the Ummah had an absolute world ascendancy in Sciences. From 1100 CE for another 250 years, we shared this ascendancy with the emerging West. From the fifteenth century onwards – the period paradoxically coinciding with the great Empires of Islam (Osmnali in Turkey, Safvi in Iran, Mughal in India) – we progressively lost out. There is no question, but today, of all the civilizations on this planet, science is the weakest in the lands of Islam. The dangers of this weakness cannot be overemphasised since honourable survival of a society depends directly on strength in Science and Technology in the condition of the present age. (Salam, 1987)

Islam has, however, reacted against the way that Western science has developed. Western science, until relatively recently, has shown little if any concern for religion or the social consequences of its activity. The Islamic system, based on the *Sharī'ah*, described above, could perhaps control the more unruly developments of science, although there is no intention in Islamic countries to incorporate such changes into the *Sharī'ah* at the present time. The second reaction, to 'Islamize' Western science, which is perhaps the most popular option among many Muslim scientists, is more likely to be successful since it can operate freely in the academic world without the need for action by governments.

12.10 Islam and Darwinism

Finally there is the problem of the theory of evolution. In spite of those who write against it, and who argue that the theory is actually unscientific, because it cannot be falsified (see 6.4), the theory is supported by overwhelming evidence. The theory of evolution may be generally true without the proposed mechanisms being complete descriptions of the way evolution has occurred. The main objection by Muslims is the apparent contradiction by evolutionists of the special creation of humanity. The Qur'ān, like the book of Genesis, says that humans were created from clay or soil (see Qur'ān 15:26; 23:12; 55:14). The Qur'ān states that 'He created man from argillaceous clay, like pottery' and, more precisely, the creation was from: the 'quintessence of clay' (23:12) and the creative act was completed by a divine breath, thus 'when I have fashioned him and breathed into him of my Spirit, fall ye [the angels] down in obeisance unto him'. Given our modern knowledge, which was not available to the first recipients of the revelation during the seventh century in Mecca, we could interpret these mysterious words in a metaphorical way. However, the idea that humans came into being through the means proposed by Darwin is almost universally rejected by Muslims. The underlying reason for this is that evolutionary theory assumes continuity between the species, in this case between higher apes and humans, whereas special creation emphasizes discontinuity and therefore the pre-eminence of humans. It would seem that with regard to organic evolution there is an irreconcilable difference between Islam and modern Western science. As a result of their rejection of Darwinism some Muslims find themselves allied to the special creationist movements, such as the Institute for Creation Research, an academic and research organization based at Santee, California. For an exposition of the criticisms aimed at evolutionary theory from a Muslim point of view see Bakar (2003).

This section has dealt with an apparent stalemate in the interaction of Islam and the main paradigm of modern biology. Perhaps the way out of the dilemma is to re-examine the nature of each component, the nature and *raison d'être* of the Qur'ān and the nature of provisional 'truth' in empirical science. If the Qur'ān and modern science have different objectives then the conflict between them may be more apparent than real. The following quotation from al-Hashimi (1981:58) seems to be a very balanced and constructive point of view which gives respect to both Islam and science; its perceptive simplicity might provide a way forward: 'There can be no doubt that the Qur'ān is *not* [our emphasis] a book of psychological, scientific, geographical or cosmic theory. It is essentially a book of guidance.'

12.11 Conclusion

Muslims regard the Qur'ān as absolutely true. Moreover one of the most important names of Allāh is *al-Haqq*, 'the True'. Modern science attempts to discover
the truth about the universe, but defines truth in a provisional sense. That which
is 'true' is from a scientific point of view simply more complete and more universally applicable than some other, usually earlier, provisional scientific statement. *The meanings of truth in Islam and modern science are therefore quite different.* If
the Qur'ān describes the rising of the Sun or the apparent movements of the
planets around the Earth then these are certainly true statements because the
Qur'ān is referring to the human perception of these events. al-Hashimi's remark
(in section 12.10) about the nature and purpose of the Qur'ān as a book of
guidance is very apposite – since the Qur'ān uses the context of human understanding, in every respect and in every historical context, to make its points,
which are always aimed at the destiny of humans who must one day come face to
face with their Lord. Sufficient evidence has been presented in this chapter to show
that it is possible for a Muslim to find a way through many of the difficulties in
the encounter between modern science and Islam. Each needs to be treated with
respect and understood in its own context. The flourishing of science in mediaeval
Islam shows how supportive Islamic society can be to scientific developments.
There is evidence that similar developments in the areas of science and technology
continue today. It is also possible, at least in theory, for an Islamic society to
control the destructive problems that may arise from some scientific discoveries
and techniques, by means of a system based upon the *Sharī'ah*. However, we note
finally that in the interaction between modern science and Islam one striking
contradiction remains: that is the question of the origin of humans.

Bibliographical note

Two texts and translations of the Qur'ān are given below. The translations chosen
are mostly from Pickthall's bilingual version, although this author (MRN) has
also used the Yusuf 'Ali version. In some cases MRN offers his own translation of
certain words using, for authority, J. G. Hava's *Al-Faraid: Arabic–English Dictionary* (Beirut: Catholic Press, 1964) and Hans Wehr's *Dictionary of Modern
Written Arabic* (Ithaca, NY: Spoken Language Services, 1976).

Qur'ān *The Holy Qur'ān. Text, Translation and Commentary by 'Abdullah Yusuf 'Ali.*
(Brentwood, MD: Amana Corporation)
Qur'ān *The Meaning of the Glorious Qur'ān translated by M.M. Pickthall* (Karachi:
Taj Company, undated bilingual edition)

Further reading

AMIN, A.Z. (2003) 'Preface to Islam and Ecology', in *Islam and Ecology: A Bestowed Trust*, ed. R.C. Foltz, F.M. Denny and A. Baharuddin (Cambridge, MA: Harvard University Press, for the Center for the Study of World Religions, Harvard Divinity School), xxxiii–xxxv

ARMSTRONG, K. (2000) *Islam: A Short History*. (Reading: Ithaca Press)

BAKAR, O. (2003) 'The nature and extent of criticism of evolutionary theory', in *Science and the Myth of Progress*, ed. M. Zarandi (Bloomington, IN: World Wisdom) ch. 8

BUTT, N. (1991) *Science and Muslim Societies* (London: Grey Seal Books)

FOLTZ, R.C., DENNY, F.M. and BAHARUDDIN, A. (eds) (2003) *Islam and Ecology: A Bestowed Trust* (Cambridge, MA: Harvard University Press, for the Center for the Study of World Religions, Harvard Divinity School)

AL-GHAZZALI (1983) *Inner Dimensions of Islamic Worship*, translated from the Ihya' by Muhtar Holland (Leicester: Islamic Foundation)

LINGS, M. (1985) *Muhammad: His Life based on the Earliest Sources* (London: Islamic Texts Society and George Allen & Unwin)

NASR, S.H. (1980) *Living Sufism* (London: Unwin Paperbacks)

ÖZDEMIR, I. (2003) 'Towards an understanding of environmental ethics from a Qur'anic perspective', in *Islam and Ecology: A Bestowed Trust*, ed. R.C. Foltz, F.M. Denny and A. Baharuddin (Cambridge, MA: Harvard University Press, for the Center for the Study of World Religions, Harvard Divinity School), 3–37

SAID, A.A. and FUNK, N.C. (2003) 'Peace in Islam: an ecology of the spirit', in *Islam and Ecology: A Bestowed Trust*, ed. R.C. Foltz, F.M. Denny and A. Baharuddin (Cambridge, MA: Harvard University Press, for the Center for the Study of World Religions, Harvard Divinity School), 155–83

SARDAR, Z. (1989) *Explorations in Islamic Science* (London: Mansell)

SCHUON, F. (1995) *Understanding Islam* (Bloomington, IL: World Wisdom Books)

SIRRIYEH, E. (1990) 'Modern Muslim interpretations of shirk', *Religion* 20, 139–59

SURTY, M.H.I. (1990) *The Qur'ān and Al-Shirk*. (London: TaHa)

WARD, K. (1996) *Religion and Creation* (Oxford: Clarendon Press)

ZARANDI, M. (ed.) (2003) *Science and the Myth of Progress* (Bloomington, IN: World Wisdom)

Chapter 13

Technology and Christianity

Jacqui Stewart[1]

13.1 Introduction

The relation between science and Christianity has been extensively explored by contemporary authors, particularly in relation to the physical sciences, astronomy, evolution and genetic engineering. The relation of technology to Christianity has been less well covered, and there are relatively few books in university libraries on the subject.

This apparent neglect of the subject cannot be defended in a technological age, where education, industry, government, health, agriculture and communication all affect and are affected by technology. An enormous proportion of UK government expenditure is on technological development, and an increasing number of UK university staff in science faculties are engaged in technological research. No discussion of the compelling issues of today – the environment and pollution, health, war and weapons, famine and poverty, leisure and creativity – can take place without reference to technology. And yet despite the formidable resources of technology, humans cannot agree about what is to be done about these problems. This chapter is an attempt at the difficult task of introducing the relation between technology and Christianity. It would take a whole book, rather than a single chapter, to do justice to the subject, and therefore only selected aspects can be presented. This chapter concentrates on some of the contemporary and controversial theological approaches to technology.

13.2 What is technology?

The general public, and many scientists, draw a distinction between so-called pure science and technology. Pure science is seen as the pursuit of truth for its own sake, whereas technology is thought of as the application of science to practical problems. Unfortunately, the history of science and technology shows that this is not what has actually been going on. For example, the steam engine was developed by trial and error prior to the Industrial Revolution in Britain, and was in widespread use before there was any satisfactory theory of thermodynamics to predict power output or other aspects of the machines' properties. (A good discussion of this area is given by Mathias, 1972.) Similarly, Marconi's development of the wireless telegraph anticipated the elaboration of a complete relevant physical theory (Basalla, 1988:102). In order to understand technology's relation to science and to religion, we must first define it. Basalla does so in terms of the devices or artefacts produced. He says:

> The artefact – not scientific knowledge, not the technical community, nor social and economic factors – is central to technology and technological change ... the final product of an innovative technological activity is typically an addition to the made world; a stone hammer, a clock, an electric motor. (Basalla, 1988:30)

However, modern technology often involves the novel use of existing devices, so that a more general definition is needed. Further, Basalla's approach does not consider the goal-directed nature of technology. A more satisfactory approach is that of Ravetz (1971), who defines a technological problem as an investigation directed at finding a way of making a specified practical change in the world. This may or may not require the assistance of new pieces of scientific theory, or result in a new physical device. However, the success of the technological project always depends on meeting the practical needs posed by the initial problem. A scientific project, on the other hand, is not tied to any particular outcome, as illustrated by, for instance, the discovery of penicillin.

However, when we speak of technology, we speak of more than a technical problem whose solution is some kind of means, or way of doing things. Technology in agriculture may call to mind, not a plough, but tractors and combine harvesters. The term technology implies an increase in power over the physical environment which humanity has experienced only in the last century and a half. It also implies improvement or progress of some kind. Western societies tend to consider that modern technologies provide the 'best' of a range of possible ways of doing things. It is important to notice that in fact the choice is not made in the laboratory or the factory. When domestic refrigeration was first developed, both gas and electric refrigerators were made. Gas refrigerators were cheaper to construct and run. They would have been the technology of choice, were it not for the economic factors that gave the electrical companies in the USA at the time the power to limit research and promotion of gas 'fridges, and to fund the development of electric 'fridges instead. The result is the world dominance of electric 'fridges.

Technology in modern society is, then, a phenomenon in which perceived practical problems are solved by increasingly powerful means, chosen by complex social processes. It is clear that values and goals must be implicated in those processes. Religions promote certain values and goals, and we may therefore expect to find relationships between the practice of religion and the use of technology in society.

13.3 Is technology good or bad?

Many historians and social scientists have examined the role of technology in modern society, and have come to differing conclusions about its value. The general public in Western Europe is ambivalent about technology. On the one hand, we applaud the technological contribution to modern healthcare; what we eat is dependent on food technology and what we wear is produced via textile technology. We welcome the progress brought by the electronic revolution. We recognize that technology benefits poorer parts of the world. Clean water, improved transportation and communication enable better education, healthcare and economic development. An optimistic view of technology stresses that such physical benefits lead to a reduction in human suffering and an increase in human happiness. They also bring an increase in human freedom and power which is seen as good in itself. Authors such as E. Mesthene (1967) are quite clear that technology is benign and makes the world a better place.

On the other hand, there is public concern that, for example, the global environment is being damaged by modern technology. Pollution by the enormous number of motor vehicles, by large-scale industrial operations releasing dangerous chemicals, and by radioactivity from the nuclear industry, all contribute to environmental damage. There are many other anxieties about technology. The public is suspicious of medical technology applied to human reproduction. There has been a lot of controversy about test-tube babies and the new genetics (on the latter see Chapter 14). Authors such as Langdon Winner (1977) have claimed that technology is out of control and is threatening to be destructive for humanity.

The existence of these two kinds of view makes it plain that questions of value surround technology. Religions are sources of value in our society, both historically and in terms of present-day interactions. We may therefore ask what kind of historical interactions there have been between technology and Christianity, before we look more closely at the question of technology today.

13.4 Technology and Christianity in the history of Western Europe

Two examples will be sufficient to show the breadth of the connections between technology and Christianity in Western Europe. The twelfth century was remarkable for a tremendous surge and development in one area of technology — that of building. The evidence for this still stands in the form of the great cathedrals of Europe. These building projects occupied much of the energy and effort of the cities and towns where they took place. Local craftsmen and labourers were employed directly, and artisans received commissions of various kinds, so that the church authorities acquired a degree of social control over the community via such projects. However, the cathedrals were more than monuments to church power. They were also vehicles for the extension of technical possibilities. Arnold Pacey has provided particularly acute analyses of social and religious aspects of technology, in both historical and contemporary contexts. In his book *The Maze of Ingenuity* (1992), Pacey refers to the pursuit of a *technical ideal*, and gives as an example some of the issues in the building of Durham Cathedral, begun in 1093. The practical problem at Durham was to construct a space that was both high and wide out of stone. Islamic builders of the period knew how to construct stone domes, but their techniques were not known to the builder of Durham. Previous buildings had often had wooden roofs, but stone was more fireproof and aesthetically more satisfying. The problem was solved by the construction of a network of stone ribs to support the curved stone vault that covered the space between the vertical piers of the nave. This provided the necessary additional strength to hold the vault in place, and made scaffolding easier since the vault could be filled in section by section. The networked ribs formed arches, which crossed the building diagonally and transversely. The diagonal ones were traditionally shaped, and semicircular. But the transverse ones had to be pointed to fit, and proved to be the precursor to the famous Gothic arch. However, the weight of the roof thus supported was too great to be held by the existing design of vertical piers, partly because the rib vault introduces a greater force thrusting outward, and the building was buttressed from the outside, with the first flying buttresses. The building of this cathedral, a project of religion, resulted in technological innovations which then spread rapidly through Europe.

The means by which such technology was disseminated were also connected closely to the religion of the period. Between 1112, when he came to the little-known abbey of Cîteaux, and 1153, when he died, St Bernard presided over a movement that founded 340 Cistercian abbeys in the period. Building methods were included in the information that was passed from the mother house to the new foundations, so that tunnel vaulting was built in Fountains Abbey only seven years after its appearance in 1140 at Clairvaux. The abbeys also used water mills, and harnessed water power for hammer forges and textile fulling mills. All of these technologies were passed on from place to place, spreading into local economies, by the agency of the monks. The reasons for their use of technology did not initially include a profit motive. They had a practical way of life, based on rules of conduct drawn up for spiritual reasons, which emphasized work as an activity valued by God. St Benedict's famous dictum was *Labore est Orare* – to work is to pray. Monastic technology served spiritual ideals. But there were others in society, merchants, farmers, craftsmen, for whom a profit was a significant requirement and who were under economic pressure to utilize technological improvements. In particular, the cloth trade of northern Europe and Italy demonstrates such groups. Pacey asks whether the technological advances in Europe from the eleventh to the fourteenth centuries derive from the idealism of the Church or the needs of commerce. In the great push to build cathedrals following Durham, he sees the evidence as pointing to religious idealism as the major factor. As increasing wealth lead to the emergence of an educated class apart from the clerical and monastic leaders of society, so the number of cathedral-building initiatives grew. Between 1150 and 1280, eighty cathedrals were built or rebuilt in France, many in the wealthier cloth towns. If the *motive* was religious idealism, rather than profit, what were the *effects* on the technology employed? There were enormous advances in the capacities of the builders. Buildings were developed to be taller than ever before. The techniques of using the flying buttresses were refined and extended. The introduction of window tracery enabled bigger and bigger windows to be constructed. Pacey observes that the builders were never satisfied, always trying, for the glory of God, to better their handiwork. He suggests that this spirit of questing, and continuous innovation in pursuit of improvement, came to be infused into the technology to which we are heirs in the present age.

Interesting examples of other interactions between religion and technology can be seen later, in the sixteenth and seventeenth centuries. Pacey gives an illuminating account of mining and mineral technology after the Reformation. Martin Luther's father was a miner, and the region of Saxony where Luther lived was an important mining area. Attempts at giving mineral technology intellectual respectability had already been made, particularly by George Bauer, writing as Georgius Agricola (1494–1555). Bauer wrote, in scholarly Latin, the definitive account of his time of metal assaying and smelting techniques. He anticipated the emerging scientific approach of the seventeenth century with his emphasis on actual observations. But his work was not directly accessible to the miners of his time, since they did not read Latin. However, there is evidence that it was popularized, not by any obvious industrial or commercial interest, but by Lutheran pastors. Johann Mathesius included comments on mining and minerals in a book of sermons, and Pacey quotes a miner's hymn of the time. Pacey accounts for this by referring to the Reformation understanding of the 'priesthood of all believers', which consecrated the most humble human activity as a vocation of equal value to God, and which sought to remove religion from its association with abuses of wealth and privilege. Hence the need to value and improve mining technology, in order to recognize and enhance the contribution of the miners. Similar ideas for practical improvement in technologies generally were put forward by Francis Bacon (1561–1626), and Comenius (1592–1671) and Glauber (1604–70) in Eastern Europe and Germany. They represent a new tendency in Western intellectual life, which stemmed from the religious motive of benefiting the 'ordinary people'. Their lives would be bettered if they had improved technical education. Pacey observes that many of the subsequent attempts to bring this about were associated with Protestant groups opposed to excessive privilege in society. This motive of service to the community gives way to nationalist and mercantile ideals in the eighteenth century, only to reappear in some of the philanthropy of the nineteenth century.

Religion, then, can be shown to have provided motives for the development of technologies in Europe long before the Industrial Revolution, and to have influenced the kinds of developments taking place, as well as shaping attitudes to the practical transformation of the world.

13.5 The technical ideal: does technology have inherent values?

We normally think of technology as being, like science, about 'facts'. Since technology is concerned with producing defined practical changes in the material world, we suppose that it is about practical facts. However, on close examination, the situation is more complicated. For example, the technology involved in the construction of passenger aircraft cabins has been extended in recent years following a serious fire on an aircraft at Manchester Airport. The discussion of this reveals two sets of assertions. The first set are uncontested and agreed by everyone. Plastic burns, producing toxic smoke. Smoke is dark and impairs visibility. Plastic is lightweight, reducing the load needed to be lifted for flight. And so on. The second set of assertions cause disagreements. Wool is a better upholstery fabric because it burns less easily – but it is heavier, more difficult to clean and more expensive. Smoke hoods would enable passengers to breathe during a fire – but they are bulky, difficult to put on and would slow people's movement. The first set of agreed assertions are 'facts'; the second set are not. It turns out to be the case that we have already gone through some process of evaluation and agreeing about a situation before we pronounce it to be a 'fact'. They include all kinds of things that we would normally take for granted, such as, in the example above, the concept that if smoke is 'toxic' then it is bad to expose people to it. Hidden in the 'facts' are assumptions that seem quite obvious in a simple example (the idea that humans are desirable, that it is not good to poison or kill them), but which are not mere observations about the world. These assumptions are related to values, the scales of desirability or worth by which we judge our activities.

Value can be understood as monetary worth, or as someone's ultimate reason for the actions of their life, or as a particular feature by which alternative courses of action can be chosen. Sociologists observe that what is valued is closely related to what is understood as good. Objects can also be valued, whether artistic, technological or religious, whether simple or complex. The process of realizing values is difficult, since we may well want several good things at once. It may be necessary for practical reasons to put things in order of goodness or desirability, and only then begin the process of evaluation or judgement. Sociologists describe the way in which different groups of people organized in different societies can also have values that are shared within a group, but which may differ between groups. This feature of shared value is the basis of culture, and our values are culturally conditioned to the extent that we are exposed to values as practised and shared by the community we live in.[2]

The facts of modern technology are shaped by the values of culture just as those of the old cathedral builders were. The significant values we may note include most obviously the concept of efficiency. This is difficult to define, but implies increasing power; we can do more with less. Closely related is speed; a new technology is always faster in performing its task. A technology may embody negative values; every feature of a land mine is engineered in line with its purpose as an agent for maiming and killing humans. A 'better' land mine is one that kills more people more often. Other values are less obvious; the microwave and television are both devices that tend to reduce human interaction. It is not possible to cook a complete meal for a family faster in a microwave than by conventional means. The microwave is sold primarily as a quick means of cooking. Consequently, any group of people who rely on one for their meals develop the habit of eating sequentially, at separate times, rather than together. The conversation and interaction associated with a shared meal is reduced. Similarly, the use of a television in the main social space of a house may lead to a loss of conversation between people, because their visual attention and hearing are claimed by the television.

13.6 The 'defining' role of technology

Many authors have pointed out that a particular technology may change human perceptions of possible behaviour. Lewis Mumford (1895–1990), in *Technics and Civilization* (1946) famously asserted that the invention of the mechanical clock, not the steam engine, was the key to the industrial age. Mumford argued that this was because the clock permitted human behavioural organization that had not been possible before it, and this was because it redefined the human sense of time. Before the widespread use of reliable clocks, time was defined mostly in terms of the cycle of night and day, with its interaction with human biology, and the seasons. People experienced time in terms of time to eat, time to sleep, time to plough, time to make preserves, and so on. Time was structured by human activity – patterns of births, marriages and deaths. There was no feeling that each day or week should have the same quantity of activity arranged in it; people were variably active as the time and place demanded. The times of the seasons were perceived in terms of their interaction with human activity, so that spring, for a shepherd, was when the lambs appeared. This was not always on the same date, and so time was 'historical', about sequences of meaning which were both cyclical and cumulative. Periods of birth, growth, decay and death succeeded each other, and each passing layer of memory built upon the previous one. The clock disrupted this by introducing a regular, measured concept of time, not in step with the natural world, and independent of human activity. People no longer ate when they were hungry, but at the clock-determined 'meal-time'.

This new measured time allowed an enormous development in technology in terms of moving devices. The concept and means of regular measurement of time permits synchronization of processes, reproducibility and standardization of processes and regularity. A windmill provides numerous examples of this. For instance, mechanical synchronization allows the hoppers to the stones to open as the sacks of grain are inverted at the top of the hoist, and timed grinding produces an equal particle size so that all sacks of flour are standardized and have similar cooking properties. Mumford claimed that the exploitation of these aspects of mechanically measured time was essential to the Industrial Revolution, and its inception had further effects on the human appreciation of time. With the advent of factory labour, time became something that could be bought or sold. The concept of free time, or leisure, appeared as the time that the labourer kept back for him- or herself, and did not sell to the employer. Thus the new piece of technology, the clock, is associated with an alteration in human concepts which could not have taken place otherwise. This is referred to as the 'defining' role of a technology, which is to say, the way in which that technology causes human activity to be redefined.

The other particularly significant defining technology in Western Europe has been the invention of printing. Marshall McLuhan (1911–80) characterized the stage of Western culture prior to printing as 'hearing humanity'. Words were immediately ephemeral, an instantaneous experience, and there could be no developed sense of history. Printing changed this radically. Language became associated with writing, which, being permanent, could be analysed, pondered on, categorized and generally become the object of intellectual activity. McLuhan claimed that this caused a cultural explosion, in which the ear and eye were dissociated, and in parallel with this, there was a separation of the emotions and the intellect. In the twentieth century, the medium of the television and video screen call for a reintegration of the senses. The two-dimensional, indistinct image they project, smaller than the objects represented, require the viewer to participate in imagination, to fill up the gaps and make the shapes real in the mind. The input for this is both visual and aural, so that once again, the emotional impact of sights and sounds becomes significant. The act of intellectual analysis becomes harder and may be perceived as irrelevant. The controversy surrounding McLuhan's many contributions does not detract from the value of the observations he made on the defining roles of these everyday technologies.

If we look at the changes in human lives in Britain between the beginning of the nineteenth and the end of the twentieth centuries, we can see numerous examples of the defining effects of new technologies. The pedestrian-oriented street plan of the old city centres, with narrow closes and little marketplaces interspersed, has been replaced with huge ring roads and out-of-town shopping centres, because the car has become a major defining technology. We shop, eat and socialize at a distance from our homes, in a manner that would have been unrecognizable to Jane Austen's characters, for instance. The advent of electricity, and lighting in the home and street, has changed the character of night completely. Our generation 'goes out' at night, when any sensible Victorian would have gone to bed. Our homes have changed, under the influence of the technologies of war and building. This is because the craftsman-built homes of the nineteenth-century middle classes, which accommodated large families with grown-up children and servants, were mostly located in the cities and took the brunt of the extensive bombing in the Second World War. A large proportion of British housing stock was damaged or destroyed. In the post-war period, there was a concerted attempt to rehouse those affected by this, and modern building technology, with prefabricated and standardized components, was used. This gave rise to the small, two- or three-bedroom semis and the blocks of flats that are part of our urban landscape today. But the new houses have no room for an ageing grandparent, or an adult child. They have no large parlour to accommodate a Sunday gathering of the extended family, or even a piano. So many of the social patterns of the previous generation are now an impossibility, and society has to struggle to find new ways of providing social contact for old people, or housing for young single people. Later on we will look at some of the theological implications of the defining role of technology, and look at some other examples.

13.7 Does the origin of a technology have implications for its effects?

A major part of the definition of technology includes the solving of a given practical problem. Does the nature of the problem set control the particular values implicit in the means for its solution? Several authors have looked at this issue, and many have noted that the origin of a technology can be closely associated with particular defining effects. That is to say, the kind of problems to be solved are indeed associated with specific ways of revaluing aspects of humanity.

David Lyon has referred to the way in which modern electronics began in wartime (1988:26–7). The principles behind the silicon semiconductor emerged during work on radar. Later, the need to process information from radar became pressing. British radar stations were initially linked by voice and manual systems to military headquarters. In the USA in the Cold War, digital processing equipment was installed to speed up telephonic transfer. The needs of wartime code-breaking also contributed to the development of computation. The early valve-operated computers that were developed for these kinds of task were structured from the beginning with speed and security as prominent features. When the Bell Laboratories developed the transistor, they recognized its defence potential straightaway. Even today, the largest proportion of government funding for electronics research and development goes to the defence industry. The computers of the present still retain the initial capacities for speed and secrecy. However, this has proved to be at the expense of intelligence and inter-communication. It is still very difficult to get different computers to communicate, and fortunes have been made in the computer industry by those who have introduced simple 'networking' approaches. The great speed with which computers operate can now be either beneficial or detrimental, depending on the outcome. We may be glad that a police computer in the UK can pick out the alias of a confidence trickster in minutes, permitting his arrest and detention, but the same kinds of computer system allow police in countries under tyranny to pick out the names of political opponents or human rights activists. People then go quickly not to justified trial but to unjust detention or worse. Is such speed always a good thing? We may at least begin to question some of the values that seem to be associated with the adoption and promotion of new technologies in our society.

13.8 How do the values uncovered in contemporary technology relate to religious values? Mumford, Tillich and Reinhold Niebuhr

Lewis Mumford drew some explicitly religious conclusions from his work on the emergence of technology. He concluded that by the twentieth century, the accumulated effects of technology were redefining previous religious ideals in new terms, in terms of the machine. He asserted:

> The machine was the substitute for ... the Christian ideals of grace and redemption. The machine came forth as the new demi-urge that was to create a new heaven and a new earth: or at least, as a new Moses, that was to lead the barbarous humanity into the promised land. (1946:58)

Mumford claims that the religious reasons for human activity, such as had motivated the mediaeval monks and the cathedral builders of Europe, have been replaced by a belief in technology as a good in itself. This is often linked with a belief in 'progress' as an inevitable and beneficial consequence of the introduction of technology.

Certainly, these issues were controversial in the first part of the twentieth century, but relatively few theologians addressed the issues of theology and technology as such. Some were very positive about the benefits of technology, such as those associated with the Social Gospel movement, in line with the general religious optimism of the USA.

Paul Tillich (1886–1965) saw technology as an integral part of human culture. He gave culture and human experience a significant role in his theology, because it provided the questions and problems to which biblical revelation provided correlative answers. This does not mean that he endorsed all technological thinking in an unqualified way, but he did see it as constitutive of human experience. Nevertheless, he spoke of the open nature of technical possibility as being the root of conflict, because the possibility of doing something, the means, could be disconnected from the reasons for doing it, the ends. He wrote:

> This leads to tension from which many conflicts of our contemporary culture arise: the perversion of the relation of means and ends by the unlimited character of technical possibilities. Means become ends simply because they are possible ... Such distortion may affect a whole culture in which the production of means becomes the end beyond which there is no end. This problem, intrinsic in technical culture, does not deny the significance of technology but shows its ambiguity. (Tillich, 1978:61–2)

This concern for the proper relation of ends and means is also found in theological writers as different as William Temple and Jacques Ellul (see **13.9** below).[3]

The other significant American theologian to have commented on technology is Reinhold Niebuhr (1892–1971).[4] He is sometimes cited as having a positive assessment of technology. He was opposed to pacifism in the Cold War, and argued for the moral legitimacy of nuclear weapons. But this information in itself does not tell us about the criteria Niebuhr used in his assessment of such technology, and his actual arguments were theological. He certainly took science and technology seriously, and in an essay on history and science, he remarked:

> Christian culture was wrong in insinuating the specific insights and prejudices of a particular age into the 'credo', while modern science was wrong in assuming that its descriptions of detailed historical sequences in nature and history offered an adequate insight into the meaning of life. Thus we have been subjected for centuries to a conflict between a theology which had become a bad science, and a science which implied an unconscious theology ... a theology of propositions about the ultimate meaning of life. (Quoted in Tinsley, 1973:89)

Niebuhr regarded science and technology as part of the contemporary culture which he believed should be subjected to theological critique. His attitude to technology was not therefore one of inevitable approval, and he was sometimes quite pessimistic about it.

13.9 Ends and means: Ellul and William Temple

However, the most extensive and important writer on theology and technology in the twentieth century is probably the French theologian, Jacques Ellul (1912–94). He was very much influenced by the theology of Karl Barth (see 4.6). He has therefore a very clear view of the world and humanity as created by and dependent upon God. The purpose of all creation is to serve and glorify God, and to be redeemed by God. This redemption is effected by the life, death and resurrection of Jesus Christ, which manifests in human history the fulfilment which God promises for the universe at the end of time. Jesus Christ is both the mechanism, or 'means' of redemption, and the purpose or 'ends' of it. This is very important for Ellul's understanding of the difference between means (how things are done) and ends (why things are done). The shortest account of his theological views on this can be found in his book, *The Presence of the Kingdom* (first published in 1948). He says:

> The first truth which must be remembered is that for Christians there is no dissociation between the end and the means. It is a Greek ethical idea which has caused this division. The point at which we ought to start is that in the work of God the ends and the means are identical. Thus when Jesus Christ is present the Kingdom has 'come upon us' ... Jesus Christ in his incarnation appears as God's means, for the salvation of man and for the establishment of the Kingdom of God, but where Jesus Christ is, there also is this salvation and this Kingdom. (Ellul, 1989:64)

Ends and means, goals and the ways to them, are central concerns in theology. Christian theology supplies a framework within which Christians and their communities, the churches, can assess how well they are living out their traditions and witness. This involves discussing and defining the goals of the Christian community, as well as setting out criteria for their attainment.

Ellul argues that technology has provided a transformation of worldview, and has given modern society a new basis in terms of such ends and means. He says:

> The first great fact that emerges from our civilization is that today everything has become 'means'. There is no longer an 'end'; we do not know whither we are going. We have forgotten our collective ends, and we possess great means: we set huge machines in motion in order to arrive nowhere. (1989:51)

This new set of assumptions governs social, political and economic life, and he refers to it as 'La Technique'; I think the best translation would be 'Technological Worldview'. These assumptions are in no sense identical with any technology itself; they are the sum of the conceptual changes resulting from the defining and formative effects of technology. Ellul has devoted several books to discussing this, the most important of which are *The Technological Society* (1964) and *The Technological Bluff* (1990). According to Ellul, the Technological Worldview is the set of values initially ushered in by and associated with technology, but now detached from it, and providing an independent basis for value in the modern world. He describes several features characteristic of it. It includes assumptions that:

- normalization or standardization is desirable;
- increased speed is desirable;
- increased power is desirable;
- change is good in itself;
- growth or extension is good in itself;
- only rational or calculating logic is acceptable;
- all claims to value should be excluded – argument should be disinterested.

All of these assumptions are commonly linked to ideas of efficiency or effectiveness, and are recognizably part of public discussion about all aspects of society. Subjects such as government initiatives to bring certain kinds of technology into education, plans to reorganize aspects of the health service, or enquiries into road and rail transport services, are debated against a background of these assumed values.

These are all implicit values in technology that have been noted by other authors, such as those cited in the previous section. However, Ellul goes further than other authors in the claims he makes for the interaction between these values. Ellul argues that the grouping of these assumptions into this Technological Worldview is not a random process, but can be described with significant aspects. He claims that it is:

- rational;
- artificial or constructed;
- autonomous with respect to value or authority;
- self-determining but not directed to an end.

In other words, the set of assumptions is not drawn from nature or given in any sense, but is a human creation. It does not allow for critique by any value system, such as religion, or for control by any authority, such as the state.

From a theological perspective, Ellul has serious objections both to the content of the Technological Worldview and to its constitution and function in the modern world. These objections centre on this question of ends and means. The question asked is always 'Why?' 'Why do we do this – for what reason, or purpose, to what end?' The end can then be evaluated; we ask, is it good or bad, desirable or undesirable, because for Christianity, only the good is desirable. The effect of the Technological Worldview is to replace such debate and evaluation of the ends with a discussion of the means. The question 'How?' replaces the question 'Why?' Evaluation – the weighing up of issues on a scale of good and bad – is specifically excluded from the Technological Worldview. The search for power is unrestricted. Christianity restricts it by claiming that only God has ultimate power, and it is wrong for humans to seek it. We see terrible results whenever they do. The unqualified acceptance that greater speed, complexity and growth is always desirable in technology has obvious problems in relation to environmental concerns. Complex technologies consume energy and physical resources which could be better conserved if slower, simpler ways of doing things were used. The assumption that logical or calculation rationality is objective, scientific and 'better' than reasoning which includes value judgements is also a problematic one. Such rational arguments have been used, for instance, to argue for compulsory euthanasia for the mentally retarded, and indeed, this has been put into practice on such grounds. But society clearly cannot be organized on such amoral principles, because they quickly become immoral.

Ellul is easily misunderstood. It is essential to see the theological basis for his approach. He is not arguing for the abolition of technology, but for the reintroduction of the concepts of purpose, goal and value into the way we debate and use technology.[5]

It is worthy of note that William Temple (1881–1944), the Anglican Archbishop of Canterbury who had a great influence on the development of the British Labour Party during the Second World War, expressed some related ideas in his short book *Christianity and Social Order*, first published in 1942. He was dealing with the practical consequences of Christianity in terms of contemporary political, social and economic organization. Nevertheless, the principles he invoked are still, if not even more, relevant in our present society, accustomed as we are to the technical fix as a solution for all ills. Temple asserted that all Christian claims or comments on society had to begin with an understanding of God as Creator, as having a divine purpose of love for all creation, and as having created humanity as part of that purpose. Consequently, humanity has a role to play and a destiny with God. All social organization exists to empower humans in working towards that destiny. Consequently, he wrote:

> the means (industry, commerce) is to be judged by its success in promoting or facilitating the true ends of human life ... above all, happy human relationships. (Temple, 1976:83)

He commented on the effect of the nineteenth-century expansion of technology:

> The immense possibilities opened up by the application of 'power' – water, steam and electricity – to industrial production so fascinated men that they ceased to ask what was the purpose of this vast mass of production. It tended to be an end in itself. It was no longer subordinated to the general scheme of a complete human life in which it should be a part. (1976:85)

It is interesting that his remarks converge so much on the theological position of Ellul.

13.10 Current issues: technology and the information revolution

Technology has advanced even further since Temple's time, and the electronic revolution in computing and information technology has led to our age being described as the 'silicon society'. There may be quite specific theological implications associated with this. David Lyon has commented, from a Reformed perspective close to that of Ellul, about the possible redefinition of what it means to be human by the advent of electronic and computer technology, particularly in his book *The Information Society* (1988). This may be happening in several ways. The widespread model of the computer has given rise to words which are now applied to humans – children particularly have been observed to do this. They speak of being 'programmed' to do something; of 'interfacing' with someone; they define themselves in terms of the similarities and differences between themselves and the computer. Computers also limit possibilities; even educational programmes will only display certain information, and only in a certain way; the Web pages of the Internet contain material that may or may not be true, but the use of the computer makes investigation of claims much more difficult. Computers may permit the previously unpermissible; the violent war games and interactive pornography now available separate the viewers' experience from the possible consequences of their actions.

David Lyon also sees important political consequences from the widespread use of the new technology, because it is not actually available to everyone. Poor underclasses are being created in the wealthier West, and developing countries are excluded more completely from participation in the electronic revolution. Computers distance those in powerful bureaucracies, looking at a screen in an office, from those whom they are meant to serve, enable or protect. There is the separation of the end, the recipient, whether a bank customer or a job seeker, from the means, the decision-making person, by the interposing of the machine. Lyon points to a reduction in human interaction as a significant consequence of this technology, and like Ellul, he sees this as negative in terms of the Gospel. He takes the work of bringing in the Kingdom very seriously. He argues that hope in God's future fulfilment and redemption of the world is a key feature of Christianity. Because of this, it follows that Christians cannot place their hope in technology itself, as he fears many societies are doing, but must hope in God. The consequence of this will be that Christians will be free to evaluate technology, to use it as a good servant, but not to allow it to become their master.

John Habgood, the former Archbishop of York, has also raised some concerns about the concept of information, particularly in the context of the Internet, in his Priestland Lecture for radio in 1994. Text and figures can be transmitted at speed and over distance; it can be edited or altered at will; it can be seen by anyone with sufficient economic power to gain access. However, such information is not subject to any process of critique and evaluation, such as takes place in conventional education. There is no guide present when such information is encountered. In a word, wisdom is absent, because mere possession of knowledge is not enough. Skills of assessment and judgement are required for wisdom, and they have to be learned through human interactions. Lord Habgood suggests that an increasing dependence on electronic means of communication may make us better informed, but we risk not being any wiser.[6]

13.11 Two contemporary theologians' responses to technology: Barbour and Susan White

There have been accounts of technology and theology which have been less critical than those cited so far; Ian Barbour provides one such view in *Ethics in an Age of Technology* (1992). Much of the book is devoted to a discussion of particular areas of technology such as agriculture, energy and electronics. He reviews a wide range of topics, and therefore does not have time to explore specific issues very deeply. The book attempts an objectivist stance; it begins with a survey of attitudes to technology as either favourable or unfavourable, but it does not address the difficulty of treating such a subject from a context-free position. Hence it tends throughout to the social optimism that was a feature of earlier American thought. Barbour does consider biblical contributions to the critique of technology alongside philosophical and humanist perspectives, but does not offer any evaluation of these different perspectives. He commends process theology as particularly relevant to present crises, and this kind of theology is very different from any of the other Christian theological approaches mentioned in this article. In particular, process thought does not understand the role of Jesus Christ as pivotal in the ways that Tillich, Niebuhr, Ellul or Temple would. It has a much more positive view of human activity than other strands in Protestant theology. It sees more of a philosophical basis to religious truth than other theologies, and is usually associated with a universalist approach to other religions or value systems.

The difficulty with Barbour's use of this approach is that his overall optimism prevents engagement with the issues raised by other authors. He summarizes his concerns in terms of the requirement for means by which technology can be directed to meet basic human need, research can be prioritized for the benefit of the majority, technology can be made environmentally friendly, work can be made satisfying, and democratic control of technology ensured (1992:243–4). These ideals are assumed to be attainable without qualitative changes in technological thinking. But this very point is itself contested by the other authors I have cited. To be fair to Barbour, he intended *Ethics in an Age of Technology* to be a text appropriate for use in engineering schools (Barbour, 1996:108), hence the paucity of its engagement with specifically theological issues, and, arguably, its lack of radical edge in regard to technology. For a dialogue between Barbour and his critics see the articles by Shinn, Stivers, Gerhart and Ferré in the March 1996 issue of *Zygon*, and Barbour's response there. For evaluations of Barbour's long engagement with areas of ethical and environmental concern see Scoville, 2004; Shinn, 2004; and Southgate, 2004:239–44.

A more recent contribution to the question of theology and technology comes from Susan White, who has written from the interesting perspective, not of systematic or philosophical theology, or political theology, but of the liturgy. Since this is of immense practical importance to Christianity, her book *Christian Worship and Technological Change* (1994) is significant. White asks what kind of challenges to Christian worship are being presented by the pervasive technology of our period. She argues that the conventional view of the liturgist is dominated by the problems of the historic transmission of text, and the role of ritual in liturgy.

Both of these areas present obvious problems of cross-cultural understandings from the perspective of the technological society, and White notes:

> If the 'modern technological person' is discussed at all in the current climate, he or she tends to be discussed as a liturgical or ritual 'problem' ... many theologians would subscribe, at least implicitly, to this idea that modern technology and technological ways of thinking are unalterably opposed to the nature of the religious quest. (1994:31)

White observes that while Christian mission has taken up the concept of inculturation, the expression of religious value in the symbols and practices of specific local cultures, this has not been extended to a recognition of the technological nature of present Western culture. Few hymns mention coal, steel or electricity; God's world is one of green hills with sheep on, and the factories are 'dark Satanic mills'. She proposes three issues through which this situation might be addressed. The first is the question of what technologies have actually affected or changed worship and liturgy. For example, the building of the great cathedrals and the invention of printing mark two obvious historical irruptions of technology into liturgy. Her second issue is the question of how these technological developments have shaped the subsequent forms of liturgy. Her third question is related to the concerns expressed by Lewis Mumford. She asks whether human technological self-understanding and social practice allows participation any more in a liturgy that developed with a pre-technological understanding of what it means to be human. Susan White gives details of some of the answers to these questions. She notes that the introduction of written script was associated with a decline in extempore community prayer. The introduction of the printing press has had an enormous effect on Western societies. White summarizes its effects on worship:

> The press was an indispensable agent in the fracture of the Church's liturgical tradition. In the early years of the Reformation, print technology made possible ... the dissemination of increasingly diverse and distinctive worship traditions ... But print technology also made possible the strong conservative reaction to the Reformation ... For the next four hundred years, the Tridentine rites remained virtually unaltered and were imposed almost universally, and the task of the Roman Catholic liturgist became almost entirely interpretative rather than creative. (1994:47)

She also looks at the effects of the computer revolution in the twentieth century. She notes three possible effects:

(i)   a great increase in source material for liturgy without appropriate selection;
(ii) the encouragement of transient liturgical practice;
(iii) the covering-up of the origins of liturgical practice.

It is interesting that these effects depend on features of technology questioned by other authors I have already cited. Further, Susan White sees an effect of 'bureaucratization' of liturgy as it becomes shaped by technologically-based management and distribution systems. Among other questions, she asks if a liturgy passed down by experts in church management structures can properly address itself to the needs of socio-economically diverse congregations. In the past, liturgy has certainly been reactive to technology. White uses Mumford's concept of the 'myth of the machine' to explore the question of how present-day Christian worship can intersect with a technological understanding of humanity. She focuses on the requirement for uniformity – the loss of play in both an engineering and a creative sense, the drive for progress to perfection or absolute control, and mechanistic logic as particular features of this model. How have these views, as transferred to humanity, affected worship?

Certainly the nineteenth century saw the emergence of religious revivalism which stressed the need to build a better world. Self-improvement became a moral imperative, and technology was an important part of that. This included the application of technique to religious practice – easy, rousing hymns, the 'mercy seat' for repentant sinners, short sermons directly appealing to the hearer's background. All these features were collected in manuals and circulated as necessary aids to the establishment of thriving churches. The more churches were managed on these ideal lines, the more they approached the perfect organization on a mechanical model, the better they would be. Similarly mechanistic thinking caused a deference to expertise, argues Susan White, so that ministers were expected to have appropriate training in special areas – hospital chaplaincies, religious education, and so on. Such models also shaped the experience of the worshippers to some degree. Expectations of worship are now that it should be responsive to the needs of the congregation; ministers are required to evaluate their own work and form corporate links with others. Susan White quotes a recent book on parish work, and points out that in the text she cites, the word minister may be replaced by 'worker', the word worship by 'product' and the word parish by 'factory'. The text still makes perfect sense, and is identical with the kind of technological manual produced by nineteenth-century exponents of technical progress and efficiency in industry. This kind of rethinking of parish life needs to be recognized, and its implications examined theologically.

Susan White concludes with an assessment of the challenges of modern technology, both in itself and as a factor shaping society, to present-day Christian worship. She notes the contribution of what she calls 'technological evil', in the shape of the Holocaust, to the loss of credibility of public prayer. She notes the effect of the electronic media on human expectations of corporate worship – 'good' television attracts a large audience and leaves a warm glow; do modern Christians expect the same thing in worship? She concludes that attempts to exclude technology from worship are doomed to failure, and a purely negative condemnation of technology will be an ineffective measure. She argues:

> To the extent that worship can embody and sustain Christian love, hope and charity, then the dehumanizing, fragmenting, death-dealing elements of technology will be called into question. To the extent that technology can enhance the sense of human freedom, the unity of the global family, and the possibility of self-transcendence, then the irrelevant, individualist and

repressive elements of worship will be called into question. In other words, if technology and worship can enter into a relationship of mutual critique, there is the possibility that both may undergo genuine renewal. (1994:122)

White does acknowledge that there are dangers in the present role of technology, but she seems to feel that there can be some mutual rapprochement of theology and technological thinking. Her difference with, for instance, Ellul, on this point may be more apparent than real. It may result from her making a less precise distinction between technology itself and the thought processes and ideologies that have come to accompany its use, than has been made by other authors. Nevertheless, White's contribution is novel and original.

EXERCISE 13.1

Examine a piece of modern liturgy from a major religious group. Consider in what cultural situation the liturgical imagery is grounded. Try to rewrite one prayer or passage in the light of White's insights, and the technological culture in which you live.

13.12 *Technosapiens*

The themes of freedom and self-transcendence that we noted in White find eloquent expression in Philip Hefner's *Technology and Human Becoming* (2003). Hefner picks up a question posed by Teilhard de Chardin (see 10.18.1) – what are we *becoming* with our technology? Hefner stresses how closely humans (at least, he might have added, modern Western humans) are coupled to technology, through prosthetic aids like spectacles and hearing aids, through the drugs we take, increasingly through various forms of implant and through genetic technologies – also through our intense reliance upon, and relationship with, computers. We are becoming, in Donna Haraway's term, 'cyborgs', hybrids of human being and technological aids – put another way, we are becoming 'Technosapiens'.[7]

We are able to become this because of the power of our imagination – technology can be seen (like liturgy) as in some sense the performance or realization of our imagination. And because humans themselves are evolved creatures within the natural world, technology and the advent of the cyborg is itself natural, is part of the journey of exploration of the species that is described in Genesis as being in the image and likeness of God. God, for Hefner, is 'the One who speaks the word of possibility to the creation and sustains its drive towards that possibility' (2003:83).[8] We are created co-creators; restlessness is the medium of our exploration; technology can be seen as a sacred space, a means of grace, a medium of divine action.

This is very creative ground, though it perhaps does not take sufficiently seriously humans' capacity for idolatry, for stretching our imaginations towards desires that are ultimately unwholesome. As Hefner himself says, 'to be so free is a fearful thing' (2003:68). Christopher Southgate observes that the positive theological evaluation of technology in created co-creator thinking rests on an underlying conviction that the future should be better than the past or the present (Southgate, 2005; cf. Peters, 2003:213), whereas much talk of stewardship is based on a hope that the future will be no worse than the present, and much biocentrism looks romantically back to a notional past that was better than either.

Where Hefner and Haraway make important contributions is in eroding any demarcation between what is 'natural' and 'given', and what we can or should alter, a distinction which is ever decreasingly helpful. We have reached a stage at which we can affect most phenomena on the surface of the Earth, and it is natural (in the sense of being a product of evolution) that we have this ability and use it. Indeed Southgate has tried to argue for humans as created co-redeemers with God, that we should stretch our imagination and ingenuity towards the healing of nature (2002:818–20; 2005).[9] Robert J. Russell offers a related perspective, advocating a view of the human as 'eschatological companion' to nature in a way which rejects technological utopianism and accepts its intrinsic limits (Russell, 2003).

13.13 One technologist's reflection

Reflections on technology and religion or theology are not only originated by theological thinkers. Illustrative of contributions from practitioners of technology is that from the engineer Professor George Bugliarello in a useful collection edited by Matthews and Varghese (1995). President of the Polytechnic University of New York from 1973 to 1994, and a member of numerous national bodies in the USA, he is well known for promoting such discussion. His concerns are fairly typical. He notes a present-day crisis of public confidence in technology, and argues that this relates to questions about several features of technology.

He is concerned first of all about the concept of technological progress. Early technology was accompanied by an optimism that power over the physical world could bring nothing but good for humanity; things would, as a result of the increasing use of technology, get better and better; humanity would progress. The destruction wrought by technological warfare, the environmental catastrophes of the second half of the twentieth century, and the increasing cultural questioning of the power of the electronic media, suggest that 'further good' is only a possible result of technology; it can also bring evils. Public confidence in technology cannot be restored, argues Bugliarello, until there has been some serious examination of how progress to good can be secured, and how evil as a technological consequence can be avoided.

Closely related to this is the question that he raises about the reason for science and technology. Why is it done? He argues that modern technology does not seem to have a clearly defined goal or end. Bugliarello thinks this also can and should be made clear. He feels that it cannot be done without a new accountability, a new sense in which science and technology can be seen to be answerable to society at large, with reciprocal responsibilities between the technologists and the communities that utilize their creations. He argues that all of these discussions about the goals and values of science must include a religious dimension, not least because science itself is global and therefore multicultural; the principles and ethics of the world religions must come into play in the working out of any new compact between technology and society.

13.14 Conclusion

Technology has been a feature of human life since its beginnings, from the first wood and stone spears to the silicon complexities of today. Humans have always felt the need to alter their physical environment, and from early on, religion has supplied explanations and motives for this. Theological evaluation of those motives has been less common. There might be good Christian theological grounds for distinguishing between the monastic applications of technology, which attempted to enact some practical good, and the building of the cathedrals. Some authors see no reason to attempt evaluation, and some see no theological difficulties with the situation. However, it is clear that the introduction of technology has always been associated with changes in human behaviour, attitudes and values. Since the Industrial Revolution, there have been an increasing number of theological voices urging caution, and suggesting that the Church might not be faithful to its witness if it adopts the aspects of technological thinking that accompany the new technology. Such caution is supported by historians and sociologists, who point to common features of concern in technological thinking. Promotion of the value of speed, efficiency, increased power and growth, progress and the overt exclusion of value have all been repeatedly connected with the use of technology in modern societies. Even the practices of Christian worship can be shown to be affected by this. The problems do not seem to lie in particular technologies as such. Rather, the fundamental Christian understanding of the purpose, meaning and goal of humanity and the universe is seen to be at risk. These are the true 'ends', for which all human activity should be organized. From a theological perspective, the methods and mechanics, the means, of that activity, must not be allowed to replace its proper end, which is the calling of humanity to fellowship with God.

Notes

1   1999 text all drafted by JS. 2005 editing by Christopher Southgate.
2   See also **1.20**, **14.10–14.12** on values.
3   See also **1.20** – 'can', the possible, does not imply 'ought', the imperative.
4   For an assessment of Niebuhr see Tinsley (1973).
5   We take up this theme in our discussion of the use of biotechnology in Chapter 14.
6   Again, we take up the theme of wisdom in Chapter 14, especially **14.11–14.1.1**.
7   'Creating Technos@piens' was the theme of the European Society for the Study of Science and Theology meeting at Nijmegen in 2004. See Görman *et al.*, 2004 for the proceedings, and *The Haraway Reader* (Haraway, 2003) for a conspectus of her work.
8   Note again the theme of God's working with possibility, which we touched on in

Eastern Orthodox thought in 8.6.1, in the Jewish thinker Hans Jonas at 9.2, in the radical Christian theologian Ruth Page at 10.18, and in our own thinking on divine action (e.g. at 10.13, 10.15).

9   This concept is also used, in a slightly different sense, by Ronald Cole-Turner (1993:96–7).

Further reading

ELLUL, J. (1989) *The Presence of the Kingdom* (Colorado Springs, CO: Helmers Howard) (1990) *The Technological Bluff* (Grand Rapids, MI: Eerdmans)

HEFNER, PHILIP (2003) *Technology and Human Becoming* (Minneapolis, MN: Fortress Press)

LYON, D. (1988) *The Information Society* (Oxford: Polity Press and Basil Blackwell)

MACKENZIE, D. and WAJCMAN, J. (1985) *The Social Shaping of Technology* (Milton Keynes: Open University Press)

PACEY, A. (1983) *The Culture of Technology* (Cambridge, MA: MIT Press)

TILES, M. and OBERDIECK, H. (1995) *Living in a Technological Culture* (London: Routledge)

WHITE, S. (1994) *Christian Worship and Technological Change* (Nashville, TN: Abingdon Press)

ZIMAN, J. (1995) *An Introduction to Science Studies* (Cambridge: Cambridge University Press)

Chapter 14

Biotechnology: a new challenge to theology and ethics

Celia Deane-Drummond

14.1 What is biotechnology?

The last chapter made it clear that technology, as the application of science, is not as cleanly separated from science as one might suppose. Biotechnology is no exception to this and can be defined as the general application of biology to commercial practice. Biotechnology encompasses the application of genetic engineering for a variety of purposes – industrial, agricultural and medical. Biotechnology raises in a sharp way questions about whether our human nature is being undermined (Fukuyama, 2002), or whether we are expressing more of God's image as co-creators, technology serving to define who were are as human beings (Hefner, 2003). We will be focusing on genetic engineering in this chapter, as it presents a particularly sharp challenge to theology and ethics.

14.2 Genetic engineering in medicine

There is a vast literature on the medical use of genetic engineering. In general, genetic engineering is portrayed in a positive way in having particular medical advantages over other forms of chemical intervention. Most of the examples in the literature that stress the positive benefits of biotechnology focus on the medical advantages of human genetic engineering for the treatment and diagnosis of various genetically related diseases. Unfortunately, there is insufficient scope here to discuss these particular examples in any detail. We will mention them here as a way of introducing the relevance of both theology and ethics to biotechnology.[1] We offer here a relatively critical stance on recent developments in biotechnology, indicating that these technologies pose a number of problems from theological and ethical perspectives. For more positive appraisals, see Peters 1997b, Bryant *et al.*, 2002.

14.3 Genetic engineering and screening in humans

The prospects for genetic engineering in humans were given a boost at the start of the millennium by the announcement that the draft sequence of human genes had been completed in the Human Genome Project (HGP) (see Sulston and Ferry, 2002).[2] A surprisingly paltry 30,000 genes were identified, far less than expected.

In general, the introduction of missing genes into somatic (body) cells, 'somatic gene therapy', is portrayed in a positive way in having particular medical advantages over other forms of chemical intervention. There have been doubts raised over controversies surrounding the death of Jesse Gilsinger, who died in September 1999 from an adverse immune reaction to the adenoviral carriers used as vectors to carry the genes for ornithine transcarbamylase deficiency. In December 2002 two children developed leukaemia during a French trial to test the efficacy of gene therapy for an immune deficiency syndrome. Some scientists believe that we should accept some failures as a matter of course, but in both the examples cited prior studies in primates had indicated there might be a risk involved. The ethical issues raised include informed consent, the merge of scientific and commercial interests, and lack of due precaution.

The increasing commercial availability of diagnostic kits for genetic screening also raises a number of issues that are of theological and ethical significance. Some genes, such as that for Tay-Sachs disease, are always fatal. Other genetic diseases, such as phenylketonuria, can be treated at birth. Other genes predispose offspring to developing disease, for example a gene called BRCA1 involved in breast cancer. Attempts to insert genes to address inherited diseases constitute one new medical strategy. Somatic gene therapy continues to undergo trials, with disappointing results to date. Implantation of embryos fertilized in the laboratory (IVF embryos) in which a gene has been modified – 'inherited genetic modification' (IGM) – remains illegal at present. The emphasis in genetic technologies has moved away from the possibility of IGM to preimplantation genetic diagnosis (PGD), which screens IVF embryos with faulty genes prior to implantation in the mother's womb, so that only embryos that will give rise to babies free of the relevant genetic defect are implanted.

In the UK licences for PGD have been issued by the Human Fertilization and Embryology Authority for screening for about forty inherited diseases, including, for example, thalassaemia, cystic fibrosis, fragile X, and Duchenne muscular dystrophy. The level of expression of a gene will depend on its penetrance; some genes when present always lead to effects at the level of the organism ('phenotypic effects'), while others do not. Those diseases selected for PGD would be expected to have a high level of penetrance, that is, they are almost inevitably expressed in those carrying the genes. There are, however, other diagnostic tests that are given to adults or children suspected of carrying a disease gene where the penetrance may not be so high. In these cases it is worth asking if the anxiety caused by knowing a faulty gene is present is worth the knowledge that the test brings. Other genes, such as the one that causes Huntington's chorea, may only be expressed later on in life. For late onset diseases not all those who carry such genes will want to know that they are at risk.

From a theological point of view we need to consider the assumptions about human nature that lie behind genetic screening. Are we stigmatizing even further those with congenital variations? Are those mothers who refuse to have prenatal tests going to be refused medical treatment of their children? Will insurance be denied those who refuse such tests or who are diagnosed as carriers of disease? As with other instances in biotechnology we need to ask, who really is to benefit? Does the know-how necessarily support its application? Most diagnostic methods are heavily patented, but what limits should be placed on patenting where human genes are involved? What are the risks involved? Who is really in control? For example, do the patients have access to adequate counselling and how is this presented? Should PGD be used to allow parents to choose the sex of their child? More controversial still is the idea that those who are deaf should be granted access to PGD in order to *select for* deaf children. The argument in this case is that a child born into the hearing community would not be part of the parental deaf community, except by imitation, e.g. learning sign language.

Another area that is likely to expand rapidly in the future is the use of targeted drug treatment (pharmacogenetics) based on individual genetic profile of patients. There are implications of such genetic knowledge for insurance and employers, both of whom would stand to gain from such information. Some of those on the forefront of new developments in biotechnology believe that the Church's role will primarily be to counsel patients who have gained knowledge from genetic screening methods. But should the Church assume that such a development is always desirable and necessary?

So far there are relatively few people affected by genetic diagnostic testing programmes, though this may be set to change in the coming years. A national genetic database collection using a sample of those resident in the UK was initiated in the summer of 2003. In addition, the UK Government White Paper on genetics published in the same year stipulated that all women over the age of 36 should have access to prenatal screening for Down syndrome.

EXERCISE 14.1

What is your initial response to the idea of biotechnology for (a) medical purposes; (b) food production; (c) commercial purposes (as in, for example, manufacture of soap powder)? Can you identify principles lying behind these initial reactions?

EXERCISE 14.2

Should parents who are deaf be allowed to *select for* deaf children using pre-implantation genetic diagnosis? How would this differ ethically from deliberately deafening a hearing child?

14.4 Genetic engineering in the production of food

Medical applications of biotechnology will, in the first instance, affect only a small proportion of the population, even in countries wealthy enough to exploit them. However, the application of biotechnology for agricultural purposes affects all consumers of food. Furthermore, such applications have *global* consequences in terms of the human community and the wider natural environment.

(i) Background to the initiative in agriculture

In the late 1960s a 'green revolution' spawned an optimistic attitude to genetic engineering as applied to agriculture. Traditional plant breeding methods were used by scientists to develop high-yield varieties. When this was combined with more intensive use of fertilizer, there were vast increases in yield, especially in Third World countries. In India, for example, the wheat crop was doubled in six years. However, the dream that the Green Revolution could solve the world food crisis ran up against some unexpected difficulties. Small farmers and the rural communities were ousted by wealthier landowners who could afford the costly fertilizers.

(ii) Reduction in fertilizer use

More recently, there has been a drive for the development of crops that require *less* fertilizers. Much of the task of genetic engineering has been no more than to complement that of traditional breeding methods. However, instead of taking several years to develop a new crop, it now takes a matter of months. In this respect genetic engineering could be seen as *a liberation* from time constraints imposed by slow-growing crops. There are one or two examples where genetic engineering has had a positive impact on the environment and represents few difficulties in terms of social justice (Deane-Drummond, 2004a). For example, nematode worms can be controlled effectively by introducing a rice gene called cystacin into potato and banana crops. This gene has no side-effects, in contrast to nematicides that are highly toxic to both humans and animals. Nematodes are most prevalent in poorer countries such as Bolivia, who can ill afford to lose their crop in this way. In a hungry world few would wish to legislate against the development of crops that could flourish in the poorer areas of the world where there are pests that are hard to control, as well as being hampered by dry, salty or nutritionally poor conditions.

(iii) Introduction of patents

While the Green Revolution was directed towards the needs of the Third World, at least in its original intention, contemporary genetic engineering is more often conducted in the West under industrial contracts requiring expensive *patents* for new varieties. The perceived novelty of genetic engineering techniques and the organisms they produce has allowed researchers to patent living organisms, and/or their parts or processes. Peters has suggested that the fear of patenting in many cases is an emotional fear based on the misconception that life is controlled and determined entirely by genetic material (Peters, 1997b:115–41). While we would agree that the initial reaction to patenting in some quarters was highly exaggerated, Peters fails to consider adequately the wider social and environmental *consequences* of patenting. In the human sphere patenting is equally ambiguous, since it leads to the possible exploitation of human societies for their 'rare' genes, as well as forcing those in the Third World to comply with patent regulations stipulated by the TRIPS (Trade Related Intellectual Property Rights) Agreement. This agreement was devised largely because the USA was concerned that its intellectual ideas were being stolen by 'piracy' initiatives in other parts of the world, but it had the negative effect of preventing the use of generic drugs on poor communities, who could ill afford the expensive patent rights. Hence it is highly doubtful that patenting of biotechnology always works for the public good in a manner that would be consistent with Christian ideas about the common good (Clague, 2005). A good example of the way that this has worked against the interests of the poorer communities in the world is the Neem tree in India. In this case US and Japanese multinationals have taken out patents on the uses of its oil and its derivatives. Yet this tree was used for its medicinal properties in traditional medicine, so arguably it is the Western countries that have exploited native knowledge, not the other way round. In the case of crop plants, patenting has accelerated the trend towards monopolies in seed production by one or two large companies. Unfortunately, this has the overall effect of leading to the loss of genetic diversity. Sean McDonagh argues that the only response consistent with Christian ethics is to campaign against patenting of life forms (McDonagh, 2004).

(iv) Maximization of profits

In common with other commercial practices, the development of genetically modified organisms (GMO research) generally aims at maximum profits, so that those projects that are less profitable are not funded (see 1.5.1 note 15 and 1.20 for comment on choices about funding and their relation to the scientific enterprise). Projects such as the genetic engineering of bacteria to synthesize prescription drugs, or the modification of tomato, soybean and strawberry crops for the Western market, all have a commercial aim. We only hear in the media about a small fraction of these developments.

An engineered tomato known as FLAVR SAVR was the first genetically engineered whole food launched in the USA. This tomato has the gene that leads to softening 'scrambled', so that the tomatoes ripen without going squashy during transportation, which is to the commercial advantage of the producers. The worry that the tomato might not be 'safe' is largely illusory in this particular case. It is the social consequences of the technology that raise more issues, for example, oil seed rape can be genetically modified so that it produces oil that is similar in type to that normally found in palm trees, grown in Southern climes (Bruce and Bruce, 1998: 38–40). It does not take much imagination to realize the likely knock-on effects on trade.

Figure 14.1 The production of Dolly: the first cloned sheep (adapted from Bruce and Bruce, 1998:18, Fig 1.5)

(v) The particular case of animal cloning

The ability of scientists to clone sheep promises to allow unlimited production of sheep having identical genetic make-up. The breakthrough for *science* was that up until this time mammals could not be cloned. Ian Wilmut, working at the Roslin Institute in Edinburgh, led a team that discovered it was possible to insert the genetic material of a sheep's somatic cell into an egg cell that had its nucleus removed (Wilmut *et al.*, 1997) (see Figure 14.1). In most cases hybrid cells failed to survive. However, in a small fraction of cases an embryo developed which was then implanted into a surrogate mother. In one case a normal lamb developed.[3]

Dolly, produced just six months later, was genetically engineered with some unnamed human genes. The announcement made in *The Independent* on 4 March 1998 stated that PPL Therapeutics were now able to produce the human blood clotting protein Factor IX in transgenic cloned sheep. Movement of genes from one species to another is known as *transgenic* manipulation. Factor IX is necessary for the treatment of haemophiliacs. The level of production was sixty times that from human extracts. The benefit of such a technique is that it will solve the problem of obtaining sufficient quantities for medical needs. Nonetheless, since these announcements, the commercial development of using cloned animals has come up against some difficulties, in that the overall success rate of cloning is not really sufficient for this to be viable as an ongoing commercial project. This may be one reason why companies have turned their attention to the prospects offered by using therapeutic cloning in humans (see 14.8).

14.5 What are the dangers?

(i) The threat to animal welfare

For the above example, what are the risks for animal welfare? What many do not realize is that it took over 250 attempts to get just one cloned sheep. The unsuccessful attempts showed a range of abnormalities, especially enlarged size with concurrent risk to the mother. We might see this as a threat to animal welfare for the sake of human interests.

Transgenic manipulation raises further issues of importance to animal welfare. For example, pigs have been injected with human growth hormone genes, and sheep with genes from bacteria. How many genes can we introduce before it becomes a new species? Is it right to violate the 'pigness' of a pig? Those pigs that were engineered with a human growth hormone grew slightly faster than normal, but they were arthritic, had ulcers and were partially blind. This was caused by excess production of growth hormone. In other words, although the gene could be introduced into the pig genome, *there was no regulation of the expression of this gene*. This example illustrates one of the risks of transgenic manipulation, that there is no way of knowing in advance how far such genes will be able to be regulated in the recipient organism. It is also becoming increasingly clear that the regulatory aspects of the genome are far more complicated than was once thought, hence the possibility of a risk-free approach to inherited genetic modification in either animals or humans is very unlikely. Scientists have found that the genetic code is insufficient in order to specify gene function; a hidden regulatory system lurks behind the gene sequences (see 6.12), and so far these regulatory processes are only poorly understood.

(ii) Environmental risk assessment

Environmental risk factors associated with genetic engineering are related to the power of the technology to bring about irreversible change in the hereditary material of plants, animals and bacteria. For example, it is now possible to genetically engineer crop plants which are resistant to chemical herbicides. Genetically engineered rapeseed and maize which contain resistance to herbicides have increased production over the last ten years since their first release, with the majority of the crop grown in the USA, though a significant portion is grown in Canada, Argentina and parts of Europe. The genetic modification allows the farmers to control weeds in fields of oil seed rape which would normally die on exposure to the herbicide. In many cases there were no public consultations prior to the release, which may be one reason why there has been a backlash in Europe, and increasing resistance in the USA.[4] In the UK the consultation that took place in 2003 seems to have been ignored by Government policy makers (see below). While the companies concerned deny any risk to the environment, it is not proven that the engineered rapeseed will have no harmful environmental effects. If anything, the *science* suggests the opposite, since rapeseed can cross-fertilize with wild mustard plants and even become a weed on roadside verges.

(iii) The threats to human well-being

The long-term effects of herbicide-resistant crops to human health are unknown, though they are very unlikely to be significant. The relative certainty in making such a claim relies on the knowledge that many plants contain far higher levels of natural herbicides and pesticides which are consumed regularly in much higher doses. Scare stories that promote the idea that GMOs will impact negatively on human health are therefore not well founded in current knowledge. Nonetheless, any effects on, for example, allergic reactions, need to be monitored carefully (see below). The increased dependence of the farmers on herbicides for weed control encourages an equal dependence on the *hybrid seed* sold by the same company as one package. Hybrid seeds do not breed true to the next generation, which means that the next generation of plants is not uniform. The traditional method of saving seed for the next year's crop is now impossible, or rather only possible with loss of yield. The farmers are forced to buy new seed and herbicide every year. The impacts of these stipulations are of particular significance for farmers in the poorer communities in the world, where recycling seed is seen as an integral part of their lifestyle.

(iv) Loss of genetic diversity

Another indirect risk, which is also characteristic of conventional plant breeding, is the overall loss in genetic diversity. Crops which grow from wild strains have a much greater variability that protects them naturally from pests and disease. When a crop is genetically engineered (or bred) the resultant uniformity brings the desired increase in yield, but also carries a greater vulnerability to disease. This loss of variability within one species is irreversible. In order to find new sources of variation researchers have sought wild strains that have retained their genetic variability. These wild strains are on the whole confined to the poorer Southern continents. There are also *indirect* effects on genetic diversity by environmental impacts over and above that resulting from conventional agriculture. Some field research conducted in the UK and published in 2003 has indicated that biodiversity is reduced when GM oil seed rape and GM sugar beet are grown in place of conventional intensive agriculture, but not when GM maize is grown. These results reflect changes in agricultural practices and herbicide use, rather than direct impacts of genetic engineering as such. However, the research gave the British Government ammunition to argue for the introduction of GM maize, in spite of widespread public resistance to such a development in a survey conducted in the same year that was known as the GM Nation Report (Deane-Drummond, 2004a).

(v) Potential allergic reactions to modified food

Another risk of manipulations across species is that new proteins in the transgenic food may cause potentially lethal reactions in humans. The US seed company Pioneer Hi Bred, for example, was forced to drop development of genetically engineered soybeans containing Brazil nut genes. Extracts of the genetically engineered soybeans reacted with human blood serum from individuals who suffered from nut allergy. While it might be possible to exclude certain plants that are known to cause allergic reactions, many foods are allergenic to a small number of people. Given the difficulty of labelling GM food and keeping agricultural products free from contamination, monitoring of global movements of GM sources becomes increasingly difficult to attain.

14.6 Some hidden agendas

In order to assess the impact of biotechnology we need to address the question of the overall direction of the research to date. This is a relatively young science, but as it is primarily a commercial enterprise, in the West at least, so market forces drive it. We may like to ponder the fact that more money has been spent on the development of strawberries that can withstand frost conditions for the spring USA market than on improving the yield of basic subsistence crops, such as cassava, maize or bean plants in the Third World.

Could this technology be used more effectively to help those in deprived parts of the world? Many scientists have argued that GM is necessary in order to counter food shortages. The introduction of any new product would require careful planning and consultation with the local communities; there is much to suggest that Southern nations do not necessarily want what they see as 'Westernized' agriculture. It becomes, in spite of well-meaning intentions, a form of colonialism. In addition, there is the issue of patent payments, which would almost inevitably lead to a transfer of capital back to Western societies. While there might be some limited examples where the technology could be used for the public good, so far the bulk of such developments have not served the needs of those that are on the margins of the global economy. One might also be somewhat suspicious of the altruistic gloss given to developments to introduce Vitamin D into rice, for example, when it is clear from a nutritional point of view that this supplement is only effective in combination with other vitamins. Other rapidly expanding technologies include the development of tissue culture grown in laboratory conditions that have been engineered to produce 'synthetic' products. It may be only a matter of time before a biotechnological means is found to produce substitutes for substances such as vanilla or cocoa. If this were to take place we would witness a collapse in the economy of Madagascar, which relies on vanilla bean exports, and in the economy of West Africa, which relies on cocoa. For more exploration of the ethical issues around application of biotechnology in the developing world see Martin-Schramm and Stivers, 2003: ch. 12, and Bharathan *et al.*, 2002.

We mentioned above that loss of genetic diversity can be exacerbated through biotechnology (see 14.5(iv)). As a result it is only those parts of the world that are supposedly less 'developed' which have a reserve of 'wild' strains that still contain natural variability. The cash payment for the patent of these strains is far less than the potential benefit to its recipients. Vandana Shiva has called this and other similar practices 'biopiracy' (Shiva, 1997). Biotechnology is becoming a means of oppressing Third World economies and could be part of the deepening of the divide between rich and poor nations.

14.7 Public responses to genetic engineering

There has been a gradual realization in recent years that the public's perception of risk has its own value and can contribute to the overall assessment of particular technologies (see Porritt, 2000: ch. 3; Deane-Drummond and Szerszynski, 2003). The acceptance or otherwise of a particular technology is ultimately dependent on public approval. Hence the public response to genetic engineering is a vital ingredient in its further development. The Centre of the Study of Environmental Change based at Lancaster University investigated public perceptions of risks associated with technologies such as the genetic modification of organisms. Unilever and a number of non-government organizations sponsored one of the more recent reports, *Uncertain World* (Grove-White *et al.*, 1997). The research is significant in and of itself as it demonstrates the way *some* large companies may be starting to show a more responsible attitude to the impact of new technologies. A research method known as *focus groups* involved guided discussions with nine small groups of people from different parts of the UK and with different social characteristics. The results overall showed very little public enthusiasm for biotechnology. Public perception identified commercial interest as lying behind many of the new proposed products, especially those related to food. Their concern seemed to be exacerbated by certain kinds of information, rather than reduced. A similar finding arose out of the results of the more recent GM Nation debate that covered an even wider range of different groups, and used different methods in order to collate the results of the survey.[5]

14.7.1 Religious dimensions to the public response

The *Uncertain World* report did not address the issue whether the public responses to genetic engineering had any religious dimension, whether implicit or explicit. However, close examination of the original data used to produce the document has revealed the following results (see Deane-Drummond *et al.*, 2003:17–38).

(i) The ordering of nature

Almost all respondents were anxious or worried about the idea that genetic engineering amounted to a 'messing about with nature'. Their sense of risk arising from such 'tampering' was related to possible effects both on their own health and of damage to the environment. Furthermore, a strong sense of order in the natural world prevails: 'I don't think we should mess with nature. Nature was designed for specific reasons. We mess with it. We have no right'; 'It's actually broken the natural order.' A deep sense of order in the natural world, with humanity having a special place, followed by animals and then plants, has its basis in the theological doctrine of creation. While the idea of the Creator as the divine Designer has gone out of fashion ever since the demise of natural theology (1.3.1, 6.7, 6.10.5), a sense of design in the natural world does seem to prevail in the public mind. In some cases a more explicit reference to theism surfaces. For example one respondent believed that interference with nature goes beyond permissible boundaries, for 'I'm not sure whether man should play God and change things for the better, for the lucre, at the end of the day.' For many, the idea of God *as such* is hidden, but the sense of ordering prevails.

(ii) Natural is good

Another theme which surfaced is the idea that what is present in nature and untouched by human interference is good. Overall the *reason* for changing the natural to something else was questioned. While a form of biotechnology has been going on for centuries in cheese and beer-making etc., any attempt to try and persuade us that this is the same as genetic engineering was dismissed. The irreversible nature of genetic change is such that the original 'natural' form may be lost and this seems threatening. Most philosophers argue that equating the natural with value, that is what is natural is automatically good, is a weak philosophical argument. It has been dubbed the 'naturalistic fallacy'. Reiss and Straughan argue against the fear of genetic engineering as 'unnatural' for this reason (Reiss and Straughan, 1996:60–1).

However, it is more likely that the public insistence on the natural is less a philosophical premiss than a theological one. By this we mean that there is an implicit *religious* concept that what is created is good. Again God's blessing of creation in Genesis and affirmation of the natural order in other scriptural texts, especially the wisdom literature, affirms this as a core element of the Christian tradition. Nonetheless, a romantic affiliation with the natural world is unnecessary and at times unhelpful in view of the realities of the harshness of the natural world (Page, 1991:7; see also Sideris, 2003). Yet it would be odd to regard diseases themselves 'sinful' in any sense. Overall there is in the public mind a 'yes' to creation as a gift from God. This sense of affirmation prevails as an implicit, rather than an explicit, theology.

(iii) The special place of humanity

In almost all cases there was a mixed reaction to the idea of transgenic experiments with human genes transferred to pigs or sheep. The reaction was particularly strong in cases where it was proposed that *human* genes enter the food chain. Common language such as 'it's disgusting', 'horrible', 'cannibalism', 'no, not that', and so on, reflect an abhorrence at the idea that we might be consuming something of another human being. This is not a logical response to facts, but a deep-seated intuition about the special place of humanity and our distinction from the rest of creation. When one respondent was reminded of the very tiny fraction of material that was of human origin, which might even share the same chemicals as bacteria, the reaction was the same.

Overall the theological notion that humans are made in the image of God prevails, albeit in a hidden form. Nonetheless, some were more prepared to object from explicitly religious grounds. Of fundamental concern was the source of the human gene; would it have come from a foetus? There was a sense that religious (in this case explicitly Roman Catholic) boundaries had been crossed by other medical research and that this may well happen again. Was this going to lead to an infringement of human dignity, especially in the case of an unborn child?

(iv) The place of animals

The response to experimentation with animals was cautious and in some cases caused concern as to whether the animals would be fairly treated. Measures to counter bovine spongiform encephalopathy (BSE, so-called 'mad cow disease') were cited as an example of unnecessary slaughter of animals. Others were worried that experiments done on animals were the 'thin end of the wedge'. In general this was a weaker theme, but there was a greater sense of respect for animals compared with plants, for example. One group was concerned about introducing genes from animals that were not accepted as food on religious grounds. How many genes from a pig could be transferred to a sheep before it is no longer a sheep? Are looks alone an adequate guide? If there is repugnant distaste about eating even a gene of human origin, the same could be said for those who express distaste over eating pork or cows. The logic might suggest otherwise, but consumers do not necessarily respond to 'logical' analyses.

(v) Environmental value

What was somewhat surprising was a tendency in all groups to look at the wider environmental consequences of genetic modification. The long-term and latent effects of BSE served as an example of how hidden dangers could surface much later. When soap powder was modified, for example, the immediate thought in many minds was: what about the effect on the ecosystems? Furthermore, questions surfaced regularly about the Third World, and possible effects on poorer communities. Such global and broad ecological concerns perhaps reflect an implicit green theology which is holistic and integrates human need with the wider interests of the environment.

(vi) Recognition of human sin

While the notion of 'sin' was never mentioned, another clear theme was an underlying sense of mistrust of the motives of those involved. There were strong statements like 'it's all for human greed', 'it's for profit'. BSE again served as an example that reinforced the suspicion that the full story is never really made explicit. One participant commented: 'I think if I'd read that before BSE my thoughts might have been more positive ... Sometimes we meddle too much ... You can never be sure what the effects are going to be at the end of the day.' There was little belief in the underlying values of the organizations, especially supermarkets and the Government. While the former was suspected to encourage such developments for pure self-interest and profit, the 'filthy lucre', the Government was viewed with suspicion as those out of touch with the needs of ordinary people.

(vii) A liberation theology

Human weakness on an individual level has been recognized by Christian theologians throughout the centuries, drawing on the Augustinian notion of 'original sin'. A more recent development has been the recognition, through the development of liberation theology,[6] of sinfulness at a structural and organizational level. What is of particular interest is the overall sense of powerlessness expressed in the focus groups. There is a feeling of inevitability about the development of agricultural biotechnology and that such development will benefit a few. While 'oppression' is not a word that is used, at least some of the anxiety comes from this sense of being dominated by negative forces wielded by powerful minority groups such as the Government and multinational companies.

Are there any signs of hope in this somewhat negative assessment? There are certainly signs that hope is still present, but sadly it does not seem to be the lot of the Church to be bearers of this hope. One group mentioned the idea that the Church *might* be able to become bearers of moral and ethical values, in other words, somehow act as a 'moral voice'. However, this was undermined by the perception that the Church was also a landowner, which would compromise its impartiality. Groups that did come over very strongly as bearers of an alternative vision were Greenpeace, Friends of the Earth and other non-government consumer organizations such as Watchdog. They were seen as those who could balance the discussion by presenting an alternative view that was unsullied by desire for profit. This is a somewhat naive view, since the political agenda of campaign organizations is far from neutral, hence it sets up polarities that may or may not be helpful in reaching decisions. Since the survey was written, the Church of England has made the decision not to facilitate the commercial testing of GM crops; they have banned such testing on their own land. This decision could be seen as the successful outcome of the work of Christian Ecology Link.

14.8 The possibility of human cloning

In the light of the overall public distaste for genetic modifications of animals involving human genes, it is hardly surprising that there has been an overall negative public reaction to the possibility of human cloning. In January 1998 the Human Genetics Advisory Commission produced a consultation document on Cloning Issues in Reproduction, Science and Medicine. They invited public responses to this document, but their further deliberations were not published until the end of 1998. Selections of this consultation document are reproduced here, along with parts of this author's own response taken from a letter sent to the Secretariat in April 1998. Additional comments are now made by this author in December 2004 in the light of further discussions, especially in the light of more recent controversies over stem cell research. See also Exercise 14.3, following Box 14.1.

BOX 14.1

EXTRACTS FROM CONSULTATION DOCUMENT ON CLONING

The UK has effectively banned cloning for the deliberate creation of whole human beings under the Human Fertilisation and Embryology Act 1990.

1.3 For the purposes of this consultation we draw the distinction between two types of cloning: on the one hand, human reproductive cloning, where the intention is to produce identical fetuses or babies; and on the other hand, what may be broadly called therapeutic cloning, which ... includes other scientific and medical applications of nuclear replacement technology.

Response

My first concern is that although you, quite correctly, distinguish between reproductive and therapeutic cloning, the presentation is such

---

that the link is not assessed or evaluated. I am concerned that giving the green light to all so-called 'therapeutic cloning' could open the door to reproductive cloning in a way that this document does not really consider adequately. For example in section 5.3 you note that one of the 'therapeutic' uses of cloning is in the treatment of infertility.

Additional note. Since that was written the language of therapeutic cloning has been replaced by a more innocuous sounding rhetoric of 'stem cell research'. Of course, in those cases where adult stem cells are used, this raises relatively few ethical issues. However, where stem cells are derived from cells created by cloning methods, which seems to be the preferred method for the development of disease treatments, due to the greater pluripotency[7] of embryonic stem cells, then this raises important ethical issues concerned with the status of the human embryo (Waters and Cole-Turner, 2003). In addition, scientists have now managed to produce sperm cells and egg cells from cloned embryos in rats, hence offering the prospect of an alternative route to fertility treatment that bypasses the need for donated eggs or sperm. Such a scenario could lead to men becoming the source of eggs for the first time in living history (see below).

7.2 Nuclear replacement research can improve our knowledge about physiological processes and the genotype. For example, it is hoped that this work will offer a greater insight into the origins of cancer and other cellular development processes such as aging and cell commitment.

Response

What is the evidence that this research has additional benefits compared with other types of physiological research already taking place?

Additional note: This technique, that is cloning technology, is also going to be the method of choice for the possible development of IGM (see section **14.3**)[8] that is currently under discussion. Stem cells are themselves closely related to cancer cells, and were historically derived from teratocarcinomas. The risk of such stem cell lines becoming cancerous is not widely aired in public debates.

7.4 ... The Committee went on to conclude that the special status of the embryo would permit some embryo research up to the fourteenth day of development provided the research was strictly controlled and monitored ... Would the use of nuclear replacement techniques or embryo splitting to create embryos raise any new issues in relation to the special status of the human embryo?

Response

I would argue that the answer to this is yes, by permitting human embryonic nuclear replacement to take place the whole concept that the human embryo does have a special status starts to sound shallow and empty of meaning. ... Even given the fourteen-day-old restriction, what would prevent such modified embryos being taken and used elsewhere where restrictions are not enforced?

Additional note. This response is sometimes known as the 'slippery slope' argument in ethics. The gradual slackening of regulation in contested areas is in evidence in the approval by the HFEA of the use of PGD for HLA[9] tissue typing, rather than in conjunction with diagnosis of genetic disease. The point here is not so much as to whether this shift is ethically justifiable, but the likely pressure always to push beyond the current ethical limits by those who are working at the forefront of knowledge. In these situations, it would be difficult to speak of 'respect' for the embryo when its fate is destruction. A commitment to lack of 'trivial use' is hardly sufficient as an ethical guide in such contested areas. A less ethically problematic source of embryonic stem cells would be from IVF embryos that are known not to be suitable for implantation due to poor quality (see Deane-Drummond, 2004b:124–9).

SECTION 8

HUMAN REPRODUCTIVE CLONING THE ETHICAL IMPLICATIONS

8.3 There are a number of situations where it has been suggested that cloning technology could be applied to make a 'copy' of another human being ... none of the activities suggested in these scenarios are permitted in the UK ... For example:

Parents might wish to replace an aborted fetus, dead baby or child killed in an accident ...

An individual might seek to use cloning technology in an attempt ... to cheat death.

Response

None of these supposed arguments in favour of reproductive cloning seems to have any real weight. From an ethical perspective it is abhorrent that those who have lost a child would be denied the grieving process on account of a 'replacement'. As noted throughout the text, the chances of such individuals having an identical personality and character is very slim, leading to further disappointment, false hopes and a waste of resources.

Additional note: Such a view also reflects an unwarranted genetic determinism, which is also used as a means of support for cloning by proponents (Harris, 1998:9–42). This is one area where there seems to be some agreement that this technology is unnecessary and should be resisted.

8.4 There are many general questions about intervention and reproductive technology, which are not unique to cloning. For example, what limits are there on the role of prior choice of characteristics of offspring, where this is scientifically made possible?

Response

The idea that parents can have designer babies implied by 8.4 seems highly objectionable and by no means reliable, leading to the marginalisation of all but so called 'perfect' individuals defined as such by the subjective opinion of the parents.

Additional note. Although some have argued that the use of HLA typing in order to treat a sibling who is dying of a particular disease amounts to a 'designer baby', we suggest that the elements of chance in this case are sufficient for this not to be an appropriate label. What would be more concerning would be those scenarios where specific characteristics of children were positively selected for in order to satisfy the whim of parents, such as enhanced intelligence or aesthetic appearance. Cloning specifies the genetic make-up completely, hence eliminates the elements of contingency that many have argued is necessary for the human person to be 'free'. Of course, this is not intended to imply in any way that such a person would be 'determined' by the genetic profile being known in detail.

8.5 A potential application of human reproductive cloning by nuclear replacement might be used to assist human reproduction. A lesbian couple might wish to have a child ... Another scenario might be where both individuals of a couple are infertile. ... Would the use of nuclear replacement techniques be beyond the limit of what is ethically acceptable to resolve a couple's fertility problem?

Response

The possibility that children might be born to lesbian couples using this technique is objectionable. The ethical effects on the child seem to have been ignored in the overall quest for parental choice. Who would the child look to as his/her father? The short answer to the question raised is yes, it is beyond the limits of what is ethically acceptable. Infertility as such seems to have been raised to a reified status, so that any action is considered to be acceptable if only this problem is solved ... it seems to ignore the potential disadvantages both to the individual born in this way, the community and the couple concerned.

NOTE: Professor Harris has argued in favour of cloning for infertile couples (Harris, 1998:9–42). Other philosophers, such as Hilary Putnam from Harvard University, have put the case for an alternative view, insisting that cloning to gratify parents' needs is wrong (Putnam, 1998).

Additional note. John Harris has argued in favour of using cloning technology in order to generate sperm and egg cells from embryonic stem cells, which are pluripotent (Testa and Harris, 2004). Harris has approved the possibility that this method could be effective in allowing homosexual couples to produce their own genetically related child. However, it seems to me that such attention to genetic linkage betrays the sort of genetic essentialism that Harris seems keen to deny. Resistance would be based on common sense towards 'political correctness' and resource allocation, rather than a reaction against the 'unnaturalness' of such intervention.

8.5 The nuclear replacement technology used to produce Dolly is still in its early stages. We do not know whether the work which created Dolly is repeatable in animals, nor is it known whether it can be replicated in humans. We should bear in mind that Dolly was the only normal lamb born from 276 similar attempts. Only 29 resulted in implantable embryos, all of which, except the one leading to Dolly, resulted in defective pregnancies or grossly malformed births ... human cloned reproduction might be associated with similar 'wastage' rates and uncertainties about malformations.

How does this case differ from the experiments that first led to successful in vitro fertilisation (IVF) procedures?

Response

The possible malformations and failures, which are inevitable in developing human reproductive cloning, just add more weight to the argument against such technology being developed.

There are wide differences between human reproductive cloning and IVF. The first holds potential for abuse and manipulations, which would amount to eugenics. The second (while tests are, in theory, possible to screen out 'abnormal' embryos) is reliant on the natural process, albeit taking place outside the human body. Philosophers have for a long time argued that 'natural' is not necessarily the good, but the opposite is not true either – this argument cannot be used to justify blatant artificial interference.

Additional note Reproductive cloning also generates the full genetic make-up of a future child in a way that removes any 'chance' aspects in reproduction. While those who claim that inherited genetic modification, or for that matter use of PGD for HLA typing, inevitably leads to 'designer babies', such levels of selection where there is considerable room for chance are a far cry from the detailed stipulation rendered possible by human cloning technology.

EXERCISE 14.3

Make your own response to the statements of the Consultation Paper before reading further. What issues do you find particularly significant?

14.9 Theological issues

(i) Biotechnology and models of God

Given the implicit theology emerging from public discussions of genetic engineering, it is relevant to ask: how far does the above pose a specific challenge to theology? Public religious intuitions need to be taken into account in developing an adequate theology. We could ask ourselves which models of the God–world relationship are adequate in the light of the rapid changes taking place in our social fabric and our creaturely environment brought about by biotechnology. Some of the models suggested in Chapter 8 will be briefly assessed below.

Process-theological models (8.2–8.3, 8.5.1–8.5.3) tend to liken the world to an 'organism', rather than a 'machine'. At first sight, then, any idea of the natural world as a mechanism, which is presupposed in biotechnology, is rejected. Process theology would reject the reductionism at the heart of biotechnology (see 14.10(i)). Another concept in process thought is the notion that everything has a *telos* or goal, which is directed towards greater enrichment. Biotechnology suppresses this goal at the heart of all living things.

However, there are other strands in process thinking that might suggest a more positive appraisal. For example, the drive towards human enrichment and creativity is a strong element. Some theologians suggest that the ability of humans to manipulate genes is just one more example of human creativity (Hefner, 2003; cf. 13.12). Indeed, some leading exponents of biotechnology have suggested as much, that such a science is the flowering of our human potential. It can be used or abused, just like any other application of science (Reiss and Straughan, 1996:7). A similar view that stresses the power of human creativity is taken by the theologian Ted Peters, who insists that giving humans more freedom does not weaken the freedom of God (Peters, 1997b:159–62; see also Cole-Turner, 1993). On this view the new genetics should be seen less as a threat than as an opportunity to exercise our freedom. Any moratorium on genetic engineering assumes that genetic determinism is in control, rather than humanity. However, we suggest that human freedom needs to include the *capacity* to reject, as well as affirm, latest developments in science. In other words, in order to be human we need to know when to say *enough*, as Bill McKibben suggests in his provocative book on human genetics (McKibben, 2003). In general it is the positive appraisal of our human abilities that seems to win through in process thought. The increase in novelty possible through genetic engineering would also suggest that, in some contexts, process thinking would favour this approach. We might ask ourselves how the God who lures all of creation towards its fullness could respond to the radical shifts in genetic make-up induced by transgenic transformations. In other words the positive assumption that seems to be behind process thinking does not seem to deal adequately with drastic genetic changes that are radically different from the 'natural' evolutionary process. The only response might be that God suffers with the creature, but the overall process will lead to ultimate good. As was noted in **8.5.2** and **9.6.1**, McDaniel's modified process scheme is more Buddhist in flavour. From his perspective, biotechnology could not be supported in any form. The above confirms our conclusion that some strands of process theology tend to support biotechnology, while others oppose it.

Ecofeminist theology (see **8.4**, **8.5.4–8.5.5**) is clearer-cut. In general, it is more sceptical about the benefits of science. Theologians such as Rosemary Radford Ruether link the oppression of women by men with men's domination of the natural world (Ruether, 1992:173–201; 1996:1–8). Biotechnology becomes one more example of the oppressive abuse of the natural world. The same attitude would be characteristic of those who support creation spirituality, as McFague indicates (McFague, 1997:5–25). If the world is the body of God and shot through with the spirit of God, then domination of any aspect of the creaturely world for human benefit would be totally unacceptable. Other feminist writers have a more specific *political* agenda and are particularly concerned with the global injustices incurred by biotechnology (Shiva, 1997).

Moltmann, in common with feminist theologians, has argued that our under-standing of God influences the way we treat the Earth (Moltmann, 1985:1–7). God is no longer a God characterized primarily in terms of power, but in terms of love and response. His view shares some of the characteristics of process and feminist thinking, but he also takes into account perspectives from Eastern Orthodoxy. For Moltmann, technology has become a web into which we are caught up and trapped. This entrapment would apply equally to biotechnology. Moltmann's stronger sense of political justice in comparison with process thought allows his theology to be more directly sensitive to the social issues raised by biotechnology.

(ii) A theological future for creation

Moltmann's emphasis on the *future* is also of relevance to the problem we are discussing. Does his understanding of the future of creation encourage us to engage in genetic engineering? For Moltmann the new creation will be one where God will be 'all in all'. The world becomes transfigured by the presence of God through the participation of creation in God's infinite creativity (Moltmann, 1969:34; 1973:41). This echoes the Eastern Orthodox concept of participation of creation in the *energeiai* of God (Zizioulas, 1990). Karl Rahner, similarly, insists that it is God's intention to give creation a supernatural end, which has an effect on the essence of being itself (Rahner, 1965:302–17). For Rahner, the natural knowledge of God as perceived in creation is not sharply distinguished from the revelation of God. However, the Christological dimension in Rahner's thought tends to detract from the themes of the future glory of creation. Moltmann, similarly, insists that while on the one hand the Cross of Christ reminds us that the future of creation is not utopia on Earth, on the other hand the Resurrection inaugurates a new creation which carries with it elements of the old creation. The promise of biotechnology is tempered by the realization of human sinfulness, and the need for the redemptive initiative of God.

(iii) Facing human sinfulness

The theological concept of sin is equally relevant to biotechnology as it faces squarely the possibility of human error of judgement. First, the Cross of Christ reminds us both of the reality of the suffering of creation and the very real temptation of humans to sin in identifying their human enterprise with absolute value. Genetic engineering can never achieve utopia on Earth. Moreover, God's love for all creation demands a respect for the interests of all creatures, whether they are produced by genetic engineering or traditional breeding methods. The Creator's intention is towards future glorification. Hence the human motivation to develop new varieties and transgenic species needs to be carefully scrutinized.

It would be inappropriate to lay the blame for the abuse of genetic engineering on the scientists alone. We are all implicated in the social web of which scientists are a part. In seeking for a change in attitude among those more directly involved, a wider transformation of heart and mind, or *metanoia*, is needed which incorporates sensitivity to creation in every aspect of our lives. This *metanoia* includes an attitude of humility and respect for all members of the human and non-human community. We cannot avoid sacrificial effort on our part. The words of the Ecumenical Patriarchate on the ecological crisis are relevant in this respect: 'This is a new situation, a new challenge. It calls for humanity to bear some of the pain of creation as well as to enjoy and celebrate it. It calls first and foremost for repentance, but of an order not previously understood by many' (1990:11).

(iv) Perspectives from liberation theology

A Christian theological perspective would insist on examining the long-term consequences to poorer nations, communities and the environment, in other words a commitment to the public good. It is this broader view that is essential to keep in mind when dealing with decisions about the validity of particular biotechnology and genetic engineering projects. In this way the wider human and cosmic contexts act as twin points of reference.

For some years, questions to do with development were considered in a way that was detached from environmental issues. Development workers tended to despise environmentalists as those who seemed to pay more attention to the survival of animals, rather than people. More recently, there has been a greater appreciation of the interrelationship between environmental problems and development issues. This linkage is of special relevance to the particular questions surrounding genetic engineering, as highlighted in the case studies above. Boff has argued that technology does not exist in and for itself, but is adopted within a particular model of development, which is causative of the ecological crisis (Boff, 1997:65–70). The disruption of our basic connectedness with the universe is counter to the religious and spiritual traditions of humankind. He argues, further, that the relationship between ecology and poverty is a direct one, for the poor and oppressed belong to the natural world (Boff, 1997:107). What is striking in this most recent liberation theology is a shift towards a greater emphasis on mysticism as a way of generating the energy necessary for change. The theological outline of this mysticism is unclear, but it seems to bear a resemblance to the radical cosmic eco-spirituality of Thomas Berry (Berry, 1987; 1999). Elsewhere Boff has suggested that 'the organ best fitted to comprehend this mystery is the heart and what Pascal called the esprit de finesse – intuition' (Boff, 1995:145). This bears some resemblance to the idea of wisdom to which we will return in the final section.

EXERCISE 14.4

Given the range of theological models available (see Chapters 2, 8 and 9), which one(s) do you consider the best equipped to meet the problems posed by biotechnology? How might this theology influence ethics?

14.10 Ethical questions

Given the theological perspective we have been outlining, what are the implications for environmental ethics? The possibility of dishonesty in the use of environmental language to cover up materialist or power-craving instincts has to be exposed. The latter raises questions about human justice.

(i) The ambiguous promise

The extent to which we perceive genetic engineering as a threat or a promise reflects our own divided perceptions. On the one hand, we are anxious to solve the immediate problem; on the other hand, we search for the broader, more holistic 'visions'. The beneficial effects of genetic engineering in the development of new medicines, and the protection of animals and plants – and in some cases humans – against disease, are often cited by genetic engineers to justify their work and achievements. However, in some cases the root cause of the disease may be overlooked. For example, overcrowding and other unhealthy conditions foster many of the diseases in animal husbandry. To engineer the animals against disease does not get at the root of the problem. Genetic engineering is inevitably the fruit of a reductionist methodological approach (cf. 6.11–6.12). The unashamedly anthropocentric (that is, human-centred) philosophy that is behind these developments is anthropocentrism at its worst: namely use of a particular technique purely for individual commercial benefit. On the other hand, the wider impact of genetic engineering leads to the anxiety that it is to the detriment of life and the planet as a whole.

(ii) Is it 'natural'?

It might be possible to argue against any genetic engineering on the basis that it is somehow unnatural, which we have already mentioned in the section above on public issues. However, it is important here to distinguish between the use of genetic engineering to speed up what would be possible in normal breeding methods and its use in transgenic experiments. There are those who object to genetic engineering on the basis that it is an invasion of biological integrity. However, according to biologists' understanding of evolution, biological integrity *as such* does not exist. We share many of the same genetic, biological and physiological processes as other life-forms, as exemplified in the results of the human Genome Project. It seems questionable whether natural selection is any more beneficial for the species than artificial breeding or genetic engineering. The philosophical basis for regulation and constraints in genetic engineering needs to be sought in avenues other than a vague notion of biological integrity.

In all breeding methods there is a tendency to treat animals and plants as commodities. Genetic engineering allows, then, an even greater detachment from the animal or plant in such a way that they can become highly vulnerable to exploitation. The philosopher Martin Heidegger rejects the idea that technology is neutral and is simply a means to an end (Heidegger, 1969:1–14). He suggests that modern technology has failed to 'bring forth' what was the original intention of the natural environment. Instead technology is confrontational and challenging. As such, *this is an unreasonable demand placed on the natural world.* He believes that the greatest illusion for human beings is to see everything as their own construction, since it drives out other forms of revealing from *within* the natural world. Heidegger did not exactly reject technology, but was acutely aware of its ambiguities for a genuinely human existence. The same attitude could be taken to the biotechnology revolution.

(iii) The need for respect

Paul Taylor has suggested that respect for the natural world is a key paradigm in the development of a theory of environmental ethics. We are all part of a single biotic community (Taylor, 1986:72–90). The question is whether recognition of mutual dependence constitutes a moral relationship as well. Robin Attfield argues against the idea that interdependence strengthens moral relationships, preferring the notion that all species that have interests have *moral standing* (Attfield, 1983:158). He believes that 'rights' are not the only basis of moral concern; something can lack 'rights' but still have moral standing. What does it mean for a species to have interests? This seems to be related to the idea of what constitutes respect. Immanuel Kant believed that if we treat people as a means to our own ends and do not recognize their ends, we are failing to show respect. Genetic engineering has to treat living things in a mechanistic way in order to achieve its goals. However, there is a distinction between treating a living thing purely as a means for our own ends, disregarding the creature's ends, and bringing our interests into line with that of the creature. This echoes the idea of Heidegger that we need to become sensitive to the 'revealing' within the natural world. However, it still requires *human* judgement and a form of empathy to decide exactly what the interests of the creature mean in practice.

There seems to be no need to reject all genetic engineering in principle, as long as we take into account the interests of the creatures concerned. It is clear that the extent of genetic manipulation that is acceptable must be qualified by existing knowledge of the evolutionary complexity of the organism. In other words, while it might be acceptable to genetically engineer bacterial species and relatively simply organisms, it becomes more problematic ethically to genetically engineer those species that are more complex in evolutionary terms, such as mammals, primates and humans.[10]

The mixed reaction to *cloning* underlies a fear that this might be applied to humans, alongside a concern by scientists that public panic should not be allowed to stem research (Butler and Wadman, 1997). The hope is that the particular ethical problems raised by cloning can be clarified. The need to respect the dignity of humans has been used by some scientists to argue against human cloning (Kahn, 1997). As we have seen, Harris believes that cloning does not amount to an affront to human dignity (Harris, 1998:31). He compares cloning with IVF, arguing that those who support this cannot logically object to cloning, that cloning can do 'some good', so should be welcomed. However, the notion of respect *does* seem to be relevant in this context. As we have argued above, cloning raises issues as to the motives *behind* such a cloning process. Are we really giving due respect to an individual if she or he has no 'natural' father, unless we assume that he is the 'grandfather'? What are the consequences socially and in a religious sense? While the papal ban on all IVF and cloning is clear-cut, many would urge that a distinction can and should be made to differentiate the two processes. Furthermore, the concept of *human* dignity is founded as much on the theological principle of humanity as made in the image of God as on the philosophical Kantian notion of treating all creatures as worthy of respect (rather than simply as means to one's ends).

(iv) Environmental consequences

As well as the above concern for the interests of the creature, we need to take into account the long-term interests of the environment as a whole, as well as the interests of the whole human community. For example, if we take the example of herbicide resistance introduced by genetic engineering, there seems to be little evidence that this causes immediate harm to the species involved. If anything, the crop benefits as now it is resistant to herbicides. Nonetheless, as we showed above, the potential effects on the ecosystem and the farming community could be very harmful.

Holmes Rolston III has argued for the idea of systemic value as a way of taking into account the worth of the whole ecosystem(s) (Rolston, 1989:188; 1994: ch. 6). This could possibly be a useful concept as applied to the above example. However, the idea needs some qualification, as it can lead to an overly romanticized view of the biological integrity of the system, which is a highly debatable topic among ecologists (see Sideris, 2003). Ecosystems emerge in a more random way than is implied by some 'deep green' philosophers. Having said this, there is no guarantee that the new ecosystem that would develop after human interference would be either desirable or subject to human regulation. It is ironical, perhaps, that genetic engineering, which seeks to assert human power over the natural environment, can lead to situations which could, potentially, become uncontrollable. The utopian dream of a custom-made world is supposed to lead to a fully controlled environment for human habitation. Charges of sentimentality abound, both against genetic engineers and, in return, against the animal liberationists.

The philosopher A.A. Brennan suggests that one of the main problems in making decisions about the environment is our lack of honesty (Brennan, 1992:18). The first myth he highlights is that of 'restoring nature', after human interventions such as mining, industrialization, etc. There is a strong belief that, given the right technology, we could restore nature to the original condition. We could add here the myth of 'improving nature' as applied to genetic engineering. A good example would be the attempt by scientists, so far unsuccessful, to transfer nitrogen-fixing genes from legumes, such as clover and peas, to cereal plants, such as wheat. Such transgenic experiments promise to improve nature by giving wheat plants the potential to fix gaseous nitrogen so that they would become less dependent on artificial fertilisers. More often than not projects are given an environmental gloss as a way of appropriating funds.

(v) The concept of 'wild' nature

Another common myth is that of 'wild' nature. This is sometimes used to support preservation of biodiversity, and hence indirectly to argue against genetic intervention. Rolston has used this idea as a paradigm for his philosophy of environmental ethics (Rolston, 1989:221). Attached to this myth is the concept that all 'wild' ecosystems are both *stable* and *diverse*. While the characteristic of biodiversity does apply to the tropical rainforest, this is not true for all other ecosystems. We are not saying that the preservation of biodiversity is mistaken, rather it cannot be supported by reference to 'wild' nature.

The myth that the ecosystem is in a perfect state of balance which inevitably leads to the preservation of biological diversity is important for 'deep green' philosophers, as it seems to provide a biological basis for non-interference. However, absolute non-interference is not really an option for humans, any more than any other species. It is the *form* of meddling that raises moral, aesthetic and policy issues. The biodiversity of *species* in this context needs to be carefully distinguished from the variability in a given species that we mentioned above (14.5(iv)). Natural variability in one species is an in-built mechanism for protection against disease. But the loss of species *themselves* through loss of highly diverse ecosystems, as in the tropical rainforests, cannot be desirable either. There is a case for the careful cultivation of national parks and other 'artificial' natural systems as places with inherent value, in addition to a simple preservation of 'wilderness', which in Europe at least is virtually non-existent (Attfield, 1994). While we would argue the case against some of the extremes of genetic engineering practice as applied to agriculture, humanity still has a responsibility to work with the natural world in creative cultivation and 'sustainable' development.

14.11 A rediscovery of wisdom: some lessons from biotechnology

A theological critique requires a radical change of attitude in formulating the goals of biotechnology – from one based on consumerism and the individual pursuit of happiness to a more community-based view that includes respect for the whole environment.

There need to be much tighter controls on transgenic experiments, the results of which are not obtainable by conventional breeding, but to ban all genetic engineering is unrealistic and most likely to be dismissed by those who are already in power. Peters has argued convincingly that we need to avoid shrinking back from genetic engineering through fear that genes *alone* control the destiny of life. However, his stress on human freedom is still highly anthropocentric and has a tendency towards the individualism of the Enlightenment. One of his main arguments for supporting genetic engineering is to reduce suffering of those humans with genetic disease (Peters, 1997b:58; cf. also Cole-Turner, 1993). No one would deny that some advances have positive benefits for humans. However, Peters also refuses to accept the idea of the natural world as in any way sacred (Peters, 1997b:13). While Christian theology does not regard the natural world as divine in the pantheistic sense, we still need to place love and respect at the heart of our approach to the natural world. Awareness of the presence of God in creation can become the lens through which we seek out our responsibilities in caring for the Earth. The most common mindset among genetic engineers is to fix on a particular problem or goal and then to find ways of achieving this goal. *A theological approach encourages those who are involved to see the wider social and religious consequences of these decisions.* There seems to be no real philosophical basis for complete abstinence from genetic engineering as applied to agriculture. Rather, following Heidegger, *we need to work towards the transformation of genetic engineering so that it comes to represent a more fully humane enterprise, in touch with the immediate and long-term effects.*

How can this shift come about? Few would reject the idea that the quality we need to foster and develop in formulating new directions for science is that of *wisdom*. Science can no longer afford to focus on short-term commercial interest at the expense of the wider interest of the community. The public face of science is damaged by the portrayal of biotechnology as a mindless machine, bent on its own discoveries regardless of the consequences. The insights of ordinary people carry their own wisdom, the wisdom of the non-specialist. Even here we see an implicit religious language emerging which is part of our own particular cultural heritage. Again, from the margins of the human community other voices are raised in protest against lop-sided practices and policies.

14.11.1 Wisdom in theology

However, wisdom in the *theological* sense can take us further into an understanding of an adequate relationship between God, humanity and the cosmos. It can become the basis for an eco-theology that takes into account the insights of contemporary feminist thinkers, but finds echoes back to the ancient writings of the early Church Fathers and Eastern Orthodox Christianity (Deane-Drummond, 2000). This marriage of East and West is important, as it serves to challenge the reductionist presuppositions of Western culture as expressed in science. It is, nonetheless, a marriage rather than a replacement. To reject *all* the technology we have developed thus far seems unrealistic and naive. Instead the goals and aims of this technology need to be redirected in the light of the whole picture.

Hardy has also suggested that wisdom is closely connected with our understanding of God and God's relationship with the world (Hardy, 1998:136). Wisdom is the dynamic interwovenness of God, the whole cosmos and humanity. Wisdom is the means through which we discover how far our purposes are matched with those of God. It is the 'dynamic of human knowledge, understanding and practice on the one hand, and God and the fulfilment of God's purposes on the other' (Hardy, 1998:137). Theological wisdom is thus both within and beyond human understanding. It challenges all human arrogance and shows the proper ordering of things in their relationship to each other. We need to ask ourselves how far this sense of ordering has become distorted in the transgenic and cloning practices emerging in modern biotechnology. The ancients saw both the sciences and theology as having a place within an overarching wisdom. The temptation today is to identify wisdom with knowledge. Goodness is subordinated to what is known. This dimension of wisdom seems particularly relevant for modern biotechnology. The truncated view of wisdom as 'know-how' needs to be replaced by a fuller idea of wisdom as carrier of beauty and goodness. The Russian Orthodox theologian Bulgakov describes wisdom as truth and beauty, reflecting the divine glory (Bulgakov, 1993:89; see also Deane-Drummond, 2000:88–9). Luther and Calvin portrayed the Wisdom of God as the transcendental contradiction to all worldly wisdom, but said wisdom was now radically separated from its source. Those who practised science resisted this description of wisdom, so that wisdom instead became reduced to knowledge alone, detached from 'the dynamics of the truth and goodness of the multi-dimensional world from and to God . . . this in turn produced an inability to deal with the moral implications of the knowledge which was achieved, and a blindness to consequences' (Hardy, 1998:142).

Hardy suggests further that the re-opening of wisdom that we desperately need today comes through worship. Nonetheless, he does not spell out how this worship might find expression. Is this confined to the Christian community? We would prefer to advocate a shared search for the beauty and goodness of wisdom within the particular religious traditions of individuals and their communities. This would lead to the possibility of dialogue between different cultures and religious groups. The possibility of a global ethic, suggested by Hans Küng, is attractive in this respect (Küng, 1990:56–62). The difficulty with this view and any which seek alliance across cultures is that we tend to end up with the lowest common denominator, which has no real impact in practice.

14.11.2 Wisdom in practice

The future of ethical practice through the lens of wisdom looks to the Ultimate Wisdom of God, which achieves its realization on Earth both now, and 'not yet'. In this way wisdom can challenge those projects which assume that the future is one which just emerges from the present. Practical wisdom or prudence (*phronesis*) is concerned with the development of the threefold deliberation, judgement and action, orientated towards the good. One way where this could start would be in the design and implementation of science policy. Those responsible for making decisions for funding need to ask not just, 'Does this fit in with the logic of our current state of knowledge?' or, more insidiously, 'Will this make a profit?' but 'Is this wise?' 'What are the long-term as well as the short-term benefits?' 'What effect will this have on the social and cultural context as well as the environmental context?' This would apply particularly to the whole issue of the possibility of human cloning which we discussed above. It is getting a grip on the complexity of each problem which can seem daunting; it is tempting to ignore the complexity in favour of one or other factor. The pressure just to look at one issue, to the exclusion of all others, is a legacy of scientific method which has conditioned us to think in this way in our ethical decisions as well.

One of the failures in biotechnology seems to be a failure to address the issue of who takes responsibility. Furthermore, we need to be clear about what these responsibilities are and who takes account of positive responsibilities, that is, duties that are specific to this profession. A clarification and demarcation of responsibilities, including protecting the environment, keeping a check on the advantage in the marketplace and consumer interests and concerns, all require proper use of wisdom. Busch *et al.* have suggested that we need adequate assessment of:

- future health risks associated with biotechnology;
- future environmental consequences;
- future burdens and benefits associated with the transformation of institutions;
- an assessment of decrease in quality of life associated with shift in nature and focus of science resulting from biotechnology research and development.

(Busch *et al.*, 1992:191–2)

We would like to add a fifth, namely *an assessment of the social and cultural impact arising directly out of the new technologies*. While it is linked to the last element on Busch's list, it puts emphasis on cultural and social impact, rather than 'quality of life', which could imply restriction to material good, or restriction to quality as defined from a Western perspective.

14.12 Conclusion

To conclude: overall we have shown that the promise of biotechnology is an ambiguous one and that the latest advances present new challenges for theology and ethics. On the one hand biotechnology promises, for example, to assist medical science in its search for the diagnosis and treatment of disease, while on the other hand it has the potential for profoundly negative environmental and social consequences. Issues such as patenting, transgenic experimentation, the loss of genetic diversity and particular threats to human and environmental well-being through direct and indirect influences all require careful consideration. The belief that all life is entirely defined by genetics needs to be challenged, but the consequences of the use of the technology have to be assessed carefully and with appropriate caution. The theological approach that may be best suited to assisting the struggle to find a future for biotechnology is that of *wisdom*. Wisdom incorporates the science of the Enlightenment, but looks to reshape it along different lines. It is a gathering up of what is positive in all our history, rather than ignoring what has taken place. Facing up to the difficulties of the present also means facing up to the negative, a *metanoia* from old attitudes that have been damaging and destructive. A theological approach to wisdom has no room for arrogance and a false utopia. Rather, it admits the reality of suffering and evil, but refuses to give them the last word. The God of Wisdom takes on the suffering and evil and challenges all human attempts to find wisdom as if it is a possession to be grasped and used for human aggrandizement. Wisdom can, furthermore, increase our capacity to wonder: to be full of awe at the beauty of the cosmos, in celebration of life as individuals and in community with the natural world.

Notes

1   For further examples and more detailed discussion of ethical issues see Deane-Drummond, 2005.

2   Interestingly, Sir John Sulston, who led the British team in the HGP, is a vigorous opponent of many of the current systems by which biomedical knowledge becomes commercialized.

3   Note that strictly speaking this was *nuclear cloning*, rather than complete cloning since the maternal egg that was subsequently enucleated prior to cloning came from a different sheep compared with the mammary gland somatic cell line that supplied the nucleus that was then inserted. Egg cells contain mitochondria that *also* contain genetic material. But the idea that 'Dolly' was a clone is a reasonable approximation to what happened. The technique is also called somatic cell nuclear

transfer (SCNT) to make this clearer. Dolly died unusually young in 2003 with early-onset arthritis.

4   See Gaskell *et al.* (1999) for exploration of the different responses of the public in Europe and the USA.

5   See http://www.gmpublicdebate.org, accessed 9 December 2003. Further discussion is in Deane-Drummond, 2004a.

6   Liberation theology takes its roots from the particular situation of political and economic oppression, mostly in Latin America, and a theological agenda that stresses a preferential option for the poor, and liberation for those who suffer oppression.

7   The more cell-types a cell-line can give rise to, the more 'pluripotent' it is. Very early embryonic cells are clearly capable, under the right stimuli, of giving rise to every cell type in the adult body. Cells from umbilical cords retain a high degree of pluripotency.

8   Inherited genetic modification (IGM) is generally preferred as a term over 'germ line therapy', since the latter only refers to gametes, while the former covers all aspects of genetic modification that might have impacts on the hereditary material. Older literature generally uses 'germ line therapy'.

9   Human Leukocyte Antigen (HLA) typing allows tissue type to be identified, and hence prevents a negative immune response where HLA is matched.

10   For further discussion see Deane-Drummond, 1997b:90–1.

Further reading

BARBOUR, I.G. (1992) *Ethics in an Age of Technology* (London: SCM Press), 85–115

BRUCE, D. and BRUCE, A. (eds) (1998) *Engineering Genesis: The Ethics of Genetic Engineering in Non-human Species* (London: Earthscan), 77–109 (2005 edition forthcoming)

BRYANT, John, BAGGOTT LA VELLE, Linda and SEARLE, John (eds) (2002) *Bioethics for Scientists* (Chichester: John Wiley & Sons)

DEANE-DRUMMOND, C. (1997) *Theology and Biotechnology: Implications for a New Science* (London: Geoffrey Chapman), 79–101, 133–56

(2005, forthcoming) *Genetics and Christian Ethics* (Cambridge: Cambridge University Press)

FUKUYAMA, F. (2002) *Our Posthuman Future* (London: Profile Books)

PETERS, T. (1997) *Playing God? Genetic Determinism and Human Freedom* (London: Routledge), 1–26

REISS, M. and STRAUGHAN, R. (1996) *Improving Nature: The Science and Ethics of Genetic Engineering* (Cambridge: Cambridge University Press), 43–89

SHIVA, V. (1995) 'Biotechnological development and the conservation of diversity', in V. Shiva and I. Muser (eds), *Biopolitics: A Feminist and Ecological Reader on Biotechnology* (London: Zed Books), 193–293

BOOK FIVE

Chapter 15

A look to the future

Christopher Southgate

15.1 Introduction

We have shown that there is a conversation between different sciences and religion which need not be on the basis of conflict. We have stressed throughout the diversity of the relationships involved and their dynamic quality. Both scientific and theological models are frequently in a state of flux. Because of the complexity of the issues we do not offer a summary here – the ongoing exercise of the book has been that the reader make his or her own summaries. Instead this chapter will be given over to a consideration of how this 'special relationship' we have been studying might develop in the future.

15.2 One-way traffic

But before we do so we note one preconception which all our explorations have not overturned. We have rejected John Updike's caricature (1.1) that each science in turn has 'harried' theology out of a different sphere of influence. We have worked from the Bossey Circle (Figure 1.2) which calls on theology to learn from scientific insights and give rise to ethics and praxis, and we have encouraged readers to develop models to that effect. We have noted the possibility that the insights and images of different religions might feed the imagination of scientists. Both Willem B. Drees and Philip Clayton imply that theological preferences might influence a scientist in her/his choice of model (Drees, 1990:67–8, see 1.15; Clayton, 1997a:239, see 10.7.2).

It is true that the innovative proposals of Copernicus and Kepler (1.12) were both informed by aesthetic, quasi-religious ideas from Greek thought. And Thomas Kuhn's work (see 4.10) emphasized the limits that exist on what 'can be thought' in a particular scientific field – all sorts of factors influence this, including the symbolism of religion, and the metaphysics to which theology gives rise. But our wide-ranging survey of the sciences has turned up only two modern cases where a major scientist's choice of model was strongly influenced by theological inclination:

    (a)   Albert Einstein's vigorous opposition to the mainstream of quantum physics on the grounds that 'God does not play dice' (see 5.11(iii)).

Reality could not, in Einstein's view, be probabilistic in its ultimate character. This provided quantum theory with its keenest critic, but the weight of opinion continues to be greatly against Einstein.

(b) Fred Hoyle's development of the steady-state theory of the universe in opposition to the Big Bang. As we indicated in 1.15 Hoyle's resistance to the idea of a 'Genesis-like' beginning led him to develop (with others) a very sophisticated counter-theory. But again, the weight of scientific evidence and opinion has run strongly against his view.

So these cases seem to be rare, and, even in the case of the most distinguished of scientists, religiously informed insights need not necessarily be vindicated. We continue to grant the possibility that religion might have this sort of influence, but concede that overwhelmingly the traffic is in the other direction. A single issue of the magazine *New Scientist* reveals the vigour and pace of scientific advance in areas of interest to theologians. 22 January 2005 reported early results from the Huygens probe that had landed on Titan, a moon of Saturn, eight days before. Analysis of the chemistry of Titan may well reveal whether life may be expected to be common in the universe (see 10.16).[1] Individual nerve cells from rats and cats have been visualized in action for the first time, furthering the possibility of understanding brain processes in detail (see 7.3). And a new hypothesis about black holes may allow testing of that most elusive cosmological proposal, string theory (see 5.19).

We can only agree with Fraser Watts that: '[t]heologians are more concerned with what scientists have to say than vice versa' (7.1). New scientific narratives continue to inform and constrain what can be thought theologically, as we saw particularly with the doctrine of the Fall (6.3.2).

15.3 Looking to the future

It is relatively unusual for a book in either science or religious studies to spend time on guesswork about how the subject will develop beyond the date of publication. Such 'crystal-ball gazing' tends to be stimulated only by particular anniversaries or landmarks.[2] Inevitably the end of the millennium was seen as a point at which to take stock. Thus it gave rise to books with titles like *The End of History* (and, indeed, *The End of Science*!). The new century is also a time to try and look forward. However, it is enormously difficult to predict how interdisciplinary dialogues, such as those between sciences and religions, will unfold. Of necessity this unfolding will be a function of innovative developments in each particular science, and in theology in all its branches – from the scriptural to the systematic. Again, a very influential book on the *dialogue* can alter the whole way the relationships between subjects are viewed.

Holmes Rolston III has offered his gaze into the crystal ball (Rolston, 1996:61–82). He predicts, in effect, that cosmological physics is likely to continue to enjoy something of a 'special relationship' with monotheism, since so many physicists have seemed to discern a place for (at the least) a law-giving agent. He acknowledges that there is by no means the same link between evolutionary biology and monotheism and wonders if further understanding of the science underlying increases in biological complexity (see 6.10.3) will bring a rapprochement between biology and theology. We are not clear that it will – a more comprehensive scientific explanation of complexification will not of itself promote a sense of divine immanence 'in, with and under' (to use Arthur Peacocke's much-copied phrase) biological processes. If anything it may serve to fuel a sense that the only sort of God that can function as an explanation is a God of initial conditions. A God who fine-tuned what we know as the anthropic coincidences (5.20–5.24, 10.14) is not *necessarily* more than a deist God. The God of the-tendency-of-complex-systems-to-move-to-the-edge-of-chaos could belong to the same stable.

Indeed, we regard some sort of fault-line between, on the one hand, models of the transcendent God who makes laws and 'designs' processes, and on the other models of the immanent God who sustains life through the messiness and contingency of evolution, as in a sense inevitable. (The need to develop the former will keep company with developments in cosmological physics and complexity theory; the need to develop the latter will further the investigations of kenosis and panentheism to which we referred in Chapter 8.)

The question we want to ask is: were this book to be rewritten in ten or twenty or thirty years, what would be its emphases? The besetting concern with divine action in the light of contemporary science, the main theme of the Vatican Observatory Conferences, seems to be running its course – at least in its initial form as a debate about determinacy, indeterminacy and the causal joint. We have reviewed the current impasse in Sections 10.6–10.9. We expect the debate to revive in some years' time, fuelled by developments in cognitive science (see below).

15.3.1 Exploration across a range of religions

A marked development in the last few years has been *the general interest in exploring the relation of science to religions other than Christianity*. This is already of value (not least to the Christian) for a number of reasons:

(a) looking at a range of religions challenges the constructs too easily put on Christianity as being the sole or necessary context for the development of knowledge about the natural world. We refer to the Golden Age of Islam at 12.5. Chinese medicine provides a sophisticated system for describing health having only tangential contacts with the Western system for describing disease. And while Eastern religions have not given rise to a system as successful in interpreting physical regularities as Western science, it could be argued that they have been just as successful in promoting human wisdom (the need for which is so evident from our discussions in Chapters 13 and 14).

(b) the exploration of many-religions dialogue with scientific themes provides important common ground on which adherents of different religions can meet without some of the squabbling that inter-religious meetings have sometimes engendered. The self-confidence and general integrity of the scientific enterprise can provide a ground of mutual respect and hope from which inter-religious dialogue can take new steps towards understanding.

(c) Different religious views of the world provide, as was suggested in Chapter 9, a new set of images and metaphors which may feed the imagination of scientists and hence broaden the range of models that can be generated.

We expect comparative studies involving different religions, and comparisons between the spiritualities of working scientists, to continue to be in the forefront of the debate. For introductions to these themes see Peters and Bennett, 2002: chs 7–13, and Richardson and Slack, 2001.

15.4 Three key areas of scientific advance

15.4.1 The implications of the new genetics

There seems little doubt that the full completion of the Human Genome Project (at present still only in draft form), though it represents no major conceptual advance, will nevertheless be a landmark in the development of scientific knowledge of the human person. We mention the possibility of the growth of genetic reductionism at 6.12 and again in Chapter 14. At the very least the possibility of obtaining a one-dimensional string of letters which could be encoded on a 'smartcard' or chip and which would describe the complete genetic inheritance of a human, including their propensities to contract certain diseases – not just the 'classic' genetic disorders present from birth such as haemophilia or cystic fibrosis but diseases typical of later life such as breast cancer – will challenge humans to attend closely to the nature of human being.

At the same time questions will continue to arise as to when human life can be considered to begin and end, and what procedures may be used to give rise to life, or to terminate it. These questions in medical ethics will require further intensive theological reflection on the person – also on the respective creative roles of God and humanity.

The possibilities offered by new genetics and new medicine will be a vastly important area in which theologians must understand the science, and question the values that prompt the directions in which it searches, in order to formulate ethical principles which are both relevant to the moment and faithful to the traditions from which the principles derive.

15.4.2 The status of animals and the uniqueness of *Homo sapiens*

Allied to genetic progress will be developments in our understanding of the capacities and experiences of non-human animals and their abilities. These seem likely further to shade the distinctions between humans and the most intelligent and social of the other mammals (see 6.2). Again the doctrine of humanity will be challenged by this, as will our understanding of the appropriate treatment of domesticated animals. Other figures will emerge alongside Andrew Linzey, who has been the pioneer in trying to provide ethical prescriptions in this area with a theological basis (see Linzey, 1994).

Palaeoanthropology is a notoriously difficult area in which to predict the future, since the finding of hominid remains is so much a matter of chance, and the record so incomplete. But if, for instance, *H. Floresiensis* were confirmed as a new species (see 6.2), and DNA were obtainable from its remains, that would provide significant insight (albeit only at a certain level of explanation) as to human uniqueness. In time this would be coupled with our gradually increasing understanding of the particular subset of genes that code for characteristically human functions. We think in particular of human children's extraordinary language-learning ability. However, a satisfactory explanation of the remarkable explosion of human abilities referred to in 6.2 is likely to continue to elude us.

15.4.3 The science and theology of consciousness

We see the rise of consciousness studies – in the broadest sense – as the most important likely development in those areas of science in most active dialogue with theologians. We mentioned in 1.5 the rapid rise in neuroscience, and cognitive psychology will surely also develop apace, together with the understandings of intelligence provided by computer simulations of various sorts. But, as Watts emphasizes, the study of *emotions* will be just as important as the study of computation-like problem-solving – possibly more so as leading to a more holistic picture of 'the brain minding the body' (cf. Damasio, 1995:159). This picture will in turn be complicated by the markedly cyborg-like relationship humans are beginning to develop with certain technologies (see 13.12).

Not only will an increased understanding of consciousness, self-awareness and human agency affect our sense of our relation to other animals, it will also have a crucial effect on our understanding of human interaction, of sin, and ultimately of divine agency, to which human agency remains our principal analogy (10.7–10.7.2).

15.5 Three theological projects

15.5.1 Eschatology in conversation with science

It is significant that Robert J. Russell, who did so much to steer the divine action debate, has turned his attention to eschatological issues. We expect vigorous thinking in this direction over the next ten years, driven on by Russell's 'worst case' approach (see 10.20). Proposals in eschatology will rest on which elements of the new creation will be continuous with our old nature, and of the old creation in general, and which will be radically transformed. One of the issues impelling this exploration will be that of evolutionary theodicy, a fraught issue but one which is at last beginning to receive proper attention.

15.5.2 Further investigations of theological anthropology

A perennial issue for theology is the human being, its distinctiveness and relation to God, what relationship it should assume with the non-human creation. What, for instance, constitutes *appropriate* co-creativity in the 'created co-creator' of Hefner's phrase? (Hefner, 1993; see also Peters, 2003). Does human cloning? Can Hefner's insight be held together with an appropriate understanding of stewardship, and of what we hold in common with other species?[3]

As we indicated above questions will continue to arise in biomedical ethics, propelled by our ever-increasing command of technologies in areas which previously were 'givens' of nature. These continue to challenge us as to when human life can be considered to begin and end, and what procedures may be used to give rise to life, or to terminate it. These classic questions in medical ethics will require further much theological reflection on the human person. A great deal of ethical attention has been lavished on beginning-of-life issues; we anticipate more attention going in the future into dementing diseases such as Alzheimer's, probing the difficult question as to what happens to an individual's relationship with God in such a disease.

15.5.3 The role of wonder

It is intriguing that the theme of awe and wonder links a range of writers otherwise coming from very different perspectives. As we indicated in Chapter 11, the notion that good science evokes a sense of wonder is of great importance to Richard Dawkins (e.g. his *Unweaving the Rainbow* – to know the science of a rainbow is not to have lost sight of its poetry, but to have one's wonder enhanced, cf. Dawkins, 1998:chs 2–3). Wonder is immensely important too for R.J. Berry, writing as an evangelical Christian. He devotes a chapter of his Gifford Lectures to exploring profound reactions to the natural world – 'ecologies of the heart' – and the significance of wilderness (Berry, 2003:ch. 10). Wonder at the universe is crucial for Brian Swimme and Thomas Berry – writing without a theistic basis, they depict the universe 'birthing itself' in a way which seems to cry out for recasting as the wondrous work of the Creator (Swimme and Berry, 1992). We have already seen wonder linking the 'attention epistemology' of Sallie McFague with the perception of 'suchness' in Jay McDaniel and 'inscape' in Gerard Manley Hopkins (8.5.4 and 9.6.1). Indeed Hopkins' metaphysics of 'inscape' may provide a way of accommodating the wonder both of the scientist and of the poet, in a way which may offer the possibility of a unified view of these diverse perceptions.

15.6 Physics

It may seem surprising that in this gaze into the future so little has been said about physics. There may indeed be, in twenty years, a unified account of physical forces, a 'Theory of Everything'. But cosmological physics is a field already aware of its limits, aware that in considering such questions as to whether there is one universe or many, and whether this universe had a cause, the science presses up against metaphysical assumptions which it cannot itself dictate. That is why our guess is, like Rolston's, that there may be little change in the relationship between physics and theology.

An exception would be if a radically new understanding were to develop of the nature of quantum mechanics, or of its relation to the macroscopic world. We have shown how important quantum indeterminacy has been in the argument over the real, ontological openness of the world to the future – a change in our understanding of that would be of the greatest philosophical and theological significance. Equally, the implications of quantum non-locality, the continuing relations of quantized particles once they have interacted (see **5.11(iii)**) have yet to be fully worked out.[4] And a new consensus on 'the measurement problem' (see **5.13**) would have a great influence on our understanding of the macroscopic world. It is because these advances seem so elusive that we give them little prominence here.

15.7 The integration of science, technology, religion and ethics

Rolston ends his predictions with a consideration of the ethics of science and of the new technologies which grow around it. His plea is that science be applied more equitably to the question of how over six billion persons can live on this planet. That it be recognized that scientific knowledge confers power, that religious values are necessary if just and appropriate use is to be made of that power. Sustainability in human activity can arise only if science gives us the data by which we can know the resources we are wasting, and religion and ethics give us a new sense of justice and wisdom in their use. The issue of climate change, and the possibility that planetary systems are being destabilized much more quickly than was at first realized, adds a sharp edge to this. Highly sophisticated science is necessary in order to understand the effects and offer possible solutions, but it cannot provide the willpower or mutual understanding necessary to effect change. 'The dialogue between science and religion', Rolston concludes, 'is likely to continue. There will be a humane future only if we can integrate the two' (1996:78).

In ending on such a prophetic note we do not suppose that this integration can come easily, or be any freer of disputes and squabbles than any other 'special relationship'. But the momentum for increased dialogue *is* there, and the stakes, as the new millennium begins, could hardly be higher.

Notes

1   A fascinating suggestion of Ward and Brownlee is that Titan, the surface of which is currently at around -200 degrees C, may be the last place in the solar system where life evolves and survives. The expansion of the sun in its red giant phase will wipe out life on all the inner planets (2003:212–13).

2   Thus the conference celebrating the fiftieth anniversary of Schrödinger's *What is*

Life? led to a book entitled *What is Life? The Next Fifty Years: Speculations on the Future of Biology* (Murphy and O'Neill, 1995).
3   Southgate begins to explore this in his forthcoming article (Southgate, 2005).
4   The subject of a thesis by Kirk Wegter-McNelly (2003).

Further reading

CHAPMAN, A. (1998) 'The greening of science, theology and ethics', in *Science and Theology: The New Consonance*, ed. Ted Peters (Oxford: Westview Press), 211–27
HARDY, D. (1998) 'The God who is with the world', in *Science Meets Faith*, ed. Fraser Watts (London: SPCK), 136–53
MURPHY, M.P. and O'NEILL, L.A.J. (1995) *What is Life? The Next Fifty Years* (Cambridge: Cambridge University Press)
ROLSTON III, H. (1996) 'Science, religion and the future', in *Religion and Science*, ed. by W. Mark Richardson and Wesley J. Wildman (London: Routledge), 61–82

Appendix: A note for teachers

Quite a difference may be found between teaching the science–religion debate to science students and to those in the humanities with little or no science background.

Science students may have a strong grasp of the factual claims of contemporary science, and the mathematical and experimental basis on which those claims are arrived at. They are sometimes less strong at adopting a critical attitude to the sciences, or at seeing that science is one among a range of types of rational enquiry. So particular attention may be given to the philosophical material in Chapter 4. It may be helpful to point out that a highly sceptical empiricism, such as lay behind logical positivism, would make it next to impossible to advance science, as well as to contemplate any sort of theological scheme.

Students specializing in the humanities, in contrast, often lack confidence in addressing the conclusions of science. Indeed there are problems in expounding these conclusions without the use of mathematics. Much, however, can be done by means of diagrams and analogies.

One way in which it may be possible to catch the imagination of certain students (especially those who declare themselves 'allergic' to science) is through reference to literary works which raise scientific topics. It may be helpful to start a discussion of the Copernican revolution using *Paradise Lost* VIII. 117f., or of the anthropic principles using Dante's *Paradiso* X. 7–21. Tennyson's *In Memoriam* LV–LVI (interestingly published before *On the Origin of Species*) provocatively raises issues about the relations between God and evolution.

To cite a few more recent sources: Tom Stoppard has a fascinating comedy *Hapgood* using the paradoxes of quantum mechanics as a metaphor for espionage. Graham Swift's novel *Ever After* turns in part on the struggles of a nineteenth-century thinker who realizes he must accept the conclusions of Darwin. And the title poem of R.S. Thomas' *Mass for Hard Times* is one of many in which the poet uses the language and concepts of science to probe the question of humans' wisdom, or lack of it. Teachers will no doubt call their own favourite examples to mind.

Another useful stratagem is to bring into the class a practising scientist in the field being studied at the time. Not because that person is necessarily the best conveyer of the basic information the students need, but because it helps them to see the cast of mind of that particular type of researcher, and the ways they articulate their subject.

It is helpful to emphasize that students will know more than they think – if only from having heard reports of new scientific breakthroughs in the media – and that they will already have preformed opinions, however little articulated, about the relation between sciences and the claims of religion. So although it may be that a certain amount of factual material has to be provided (as we have done in Chapters 5–7 in particular) a conversation needs to develop in which these pre-existing views are tested and honed.

We have provided a very extensive bibliography of printed sources, and referred from time to time to three major journals in the area – *Zygon*, *Science and Christian Belief* and *Theology and Science*. Other organizations and educational resources were mentioned in Chapter 11. More and more, however, fast-moving academic debates will draw on the World Wide Web as the primary means of communication. As a way in, we mention two developing resources which promise to be important in this connection: the organizations Counterbalance (www.counterbalance.org) and Metanexus (www.metanexus.net). Both publish an expanding range of valuable resources, including lectures and interviews with leading scholars. Portions of *God, Humanity and the Cosmos* appear on the Counterbalance site. We encourage you to train your students in the critical use of the Web (as in Exercise 9.1) and wish you well with all your explorations.

References and Bibliography

AL-'ALWĀNĪ, T.J. (1989) 'Islamization of attitudes and practices in science and technology', in *Islamization of Attitudes and Practices in Science and Technology*, ed. M. A. K. Lodhi (Herndon, VA: Association of Muslim Scientists and Engineers)

AMIN, A.Z. (2003) 'Preface to Islam and ecology', in *Islam and Ecology: A Bestowed Trust*, ed. R.C. Foltz, F.M. Denny and A. Baharuddin (Cambridge, MA: Harvard University Press for the Center for the Study of World Religions, Harvard Divinity School), xxxiii–xxxv

AQUINAS, Thomas (1956) *On the Truth of the Catholic Faith: Summa Contra Gentiles, Book III: Providence*, trans. V.J. Bourke (Garden City, NY: Doubleday & Co.)

(1964a) *Summa Theologiæ, Volume I: Christian Theology (Ia.1)*, trans. T. Gilby OP (London: Eyre & Spottiswoode)

(1964b) *Summa Theologiæ, Volume II: Existence and Nature of God (Ia.2–11)*, trans. T. McDermott OP (London: Eyre & Spottiswoode)

(1964c) *Summa Theologiæ, Volume III: Knowing and Naming God (Ia.12–13)*, trans. H. McCabe OP (London: Eyre & Spottiswoode)

(1964d) *Summa Theologiæ, Volume IV: Knowledge in God (Ia.14–18)*, trans. T. Gornall SJ (London: Eyre & Spottiswoode)

(1965) *Summa Theologiæ, Volume VI: The Trinity (Ia.27–32)*, trans. C. Velecky OP (London: Eyre & Spottiswoode)

(1967) *Summa Theologiæ, Volume VIII: Creation, Variety, and Evil (Ia.44–49)*, trans. T. Gilby OP (London: Eyre & Spottiswoode)

(1975) *Summa Theologiae, Volume XIV: Divine Government (Ia.105.5)*, trans. T.C. O'Brien (London: Eyre & Spottiswoode)

ARMSTRONG, Karen (2000) *Islam: A Short History* (Reading: Ithaca Press)

ARMSTRONG-BUCK, S. (1986) 'Whitehead's metaphysical system as a foundation for environmental ethics', *Environmental Ethics* 8, 241–59

ASSOCIATION FOR SCIENCE EDUCATION (1981) *Science in Society* (London and Hatfield: Heinemann and ASE) (consisting of a Teacher's Guide and twelve Readers and suitable for a General Studies course for sixth forms)

(1983) *Science In a Social CONtext (SISCON)-in-Schools)* (Hatfield: ASE) (eight booklets providing for a General Studies course for sixth forms)

(1986–) *Science and Technology in Society (SATIS)* (Hatfield: ASE) (contains materials for 14–16-year-olds, 16–19-year-olds and 8–14-year-olds)

(1994) *Models and Modelling in Science Education* (Hatfield: ASE)

(1998) *Summary of Policies* (Hatfield: ASE)

(1998) *Values and Science Education*, policy statement (Hatfield: ASE)

ASTLEY, J., BROWN, D. and LOADES, A. (eds) (2003) *Problems in Theology, I: Creation: A Reader* (London and New York: T&T Clark)

ATKINS, Peter W. (1981) *The Creation* (Oxford: Freeman)

ATTFIELD, R. (1983) *The Ethics of Environmental Concern* (Oxford: Blackwell)
(1994) 'Rehabilitating nature and making nature habitable', in *Philosophy and the Natural Environment*, ed. R. Attfield and A. Belsey (Cambridge: Cambridge University Press), 45–58

AUGUSTINE OF HIPPO (1961) *Confessions*, trans. R.S. Pine-Coffin (New York: Penguin)

AYALA, Francisco (1985) 'Reduction in biology: a recent challenge', in *Evolution at a Crossroads*, ed. D.J. Depew and B.H. Weber (Cambridge, MA: MIT Press), 65–79

AYER, A.J. (1971) *Language, Truth and Logic* (Harmondsworth: Penguin; first published 1936)

BAGLEY, F.R.C. (trans.) (1964) *Ghazzali's Book of Counsel for Kings (Nasihat al-Muluk)* (Oxford: Oxford University Press)

BAK, P. (1997) *How Nature Works* (Oxford: Oxford University Press)

BAKAR, O. (2003) 'The nature and extent of criticism of evolutionary theory', in *Science and the Myth of Progress*, ed. M. Zarandi (Bloomington, IN: World Wisdom), ch. 8

BALL, I. *et al.* (eds) (1992) *The Earth Beneath* (London: SPCK)

BANCROFT, A. (ed.) (1997) *The Dhammapada* (Shaftesbury: Element)

BANNER, Michael C. (1990) *The Justification of Science and the Rationality of Religious Belief* (Oxford: Clarendon Press)

BARBOUR, Ian G. (1966) *Issues in Science and Religion* (New York: Harper & Row)
(1974) *Myths, Models and Paradigms: A Comparative Study in Science and Religion* (San Francisco: Harper & Row)
(1990) *Religion in an Age of Science* (London: SCM Press)
(1992) *Ethics in an Age of Technology* (London: SCM Press)
(1996) 'Response to critics of *Ethics in an Age of Technology*', *Zygon* **31** (1), 101–10
(1998) *Religion and Science: Historical and Contemporary Issues* (London: SCM Press)
(2000) *When Science Meets Religion: Enemies, Strangers or Partners?* (London: SPCK)
(2002) *Nature, Human Nature and God* (London: SPCK)

BARR, J. (1992) *The Garden of Eden and the Hope of Immortality* (London: SCM Press)

BARRETT, Peter (2000) *Science and Theology since Copernicus: The Search for Understanding* (Pretoria: Unisa Press, University of South Africa)

BARROW, J.D. and TIPLER, F.J. (1986) *The Anthropic Cosmological Principle* (Oxford: Clarendon Press)

BARTH, Karl (1936) *Church Dogmatics, Volume I, Part 1*, trans. G. T. Thomson (Edinburgh: T&T Clark)
(1957) *Church Dogmatics, Volume II, Part 1*, trans. T.H.L. Parker, W.B. Johnston, H. Knight and J.L.M. Haire (Edinburgh: T&T Clark)
(1958) *Church Dogmatics, Volume III, Part 1*, ed. G.W. Bromiley and T.F. Torrance, trans. J.W. Edwards, O. Bussey and H. Knight (Edinburgh: T&T Clark)
(1960) *Church Dogmatics, Volume III, Part 3*, ed. G.W. Bromiley and T.F. Torrance, trans. G.W. Bromiley and R.J. Ehrlich (Edinburgh: T&T Clark)
(1961) *Church Dogmatics, Volume IV, Part 3, I*, trans. G.W. Bromiley (Edinburgh: T&T Clark)
(1968) *The Epistle to the Romans*, trans. by E.C. Hoskyns (Oxford: Oxford University Press)

BARTHOLOMEW, D.J. (1984) *God of Chance* (London: SCM Press)

BASALLA, G. (1988) *The Evolution of Technology* (Cambridge: Cambridge University Press)

BAUCKHAM, Richard (1987) *Moltmann: Messianic Theology in the Making* (Basingstoke: Marshall Pickering)

(2000) 'Stewardship and relationship', in *The Care of Creation: Focusing Concern and Action*, ed. R.J. Berry (Leicester: Inter-Varsity Press), 99–106

BAUSOR, J. and POOLE, M.W. (2002) 'Science-and-religion in the agreed syllabuses: an investigation and some suggestions', *British Journal of Religious Education* 25 (1), 18–32

(2003) 'Science education and religious education: possible links?', *School Science Review* 85 (311), 117–24

BEHE, Michael (1996) *Darwin's Black Box: The Biochemical Challenge to Evolution* (New York: Free Press)

BEIT-HALLAHMI, B. and ARGYLE, M. (1997) *The Psychology of Religious Belief, Behaviour and Experience* (London: Routledge)

BERG, P. and SINGER, M. (1992) *Dealing with Genes* (Mill Valley, CA: University Science Books)

BERGER, K. (2003) *Identity and Experience in the New Testament* (Minneapolis, MN: Fortress Press)

BERNSTEIN, R.J. (1983) *Beyond Objectivism and Relativism: Science, Hermeneutics and Praxis* (Oxford: Blackwell)

BERRY, R.J. (2003) *God's Book of Works: The Nature and Theology of Nature* (Edinburgh: T&T Clark International)

BERRY, R.J. (ed.) (2000) *The Care of Creation: Focusing Concern and Action* (Leicester: Inter-Varsity Press)

(2005, forthcoming) *Environmental Stewardship: A Primer* (London: T&T Clark International)

BERRY, Thomas (1987) 'The Earth: a new context for religious unity', in A. Lonergan and C. Richards (eds), *Thomas Berry and The New Cosmology* (Mystic, CT: Twenty-Third Publications), 27–39

(1999) *The Great Work* (New York: Bell Tower)

BHARATHAN, Geeta, CHANDRASHEKRAN, Shanti, MAY, Tony and BRYANT, John (2002) 'Crop biotechnology and developing countries', in *Bioethics for Scientists*, ed. John Bryant, Linda Baggott la Velle and John Searle (Chichester: John Wiley & Sons), 171–98

BIRCH, C. and COBB, J.B. (1981) *The Liberation of Life* (Cambridge: Cambridge University Press)

BIRCH, C. and VISCHER, L. (1997) *Living with the Animals: The Community of God's Creatures* (WCC Publications: Geneva)

BIRCH, C., EAKIN, W. and MCDANIEL, J. (eds) (1990), *Liberating Life: Contemporary Approaches to Ecological Theology* (Maryknoll, NY: Orbis Books)

BLACKBURN, Simon (1994) *The Oxford Dictionary of Philosophy* (Oxford: Oxford University Press)

BOFF, L. (1995) *Ecology and Liberation: A New Paradigm*, trans. John Cumming (Maryknoll, NY: Orbis Books)

(1997) *Cry of the Earth: Cry of the Poor*, trans. by P. Berryman (Maryknoll, NY: Orbis Books)

BOHM, D. (1980) *Wholeness and the Implicate Order* (London: Routledge & Kegan Paul)

BOWKER, J. (1995) *Is God A Virus? Genes, Culture and Religion* (London: SPCK)

(1998) 'Science and religion: contest or confirmation?' in *Science Meets Faith*, ed. Fraser Watts (London: SPCK), 95–119

BOWLER, P. (2001) *Reconciling Science and Religion: The Debate in Early-Twentieth-Century Britain* (Chicago, IL: University of Chicago Press)

BRAITHWAITE, R.B. (1971) 'An empiricist's view of the nature of religious belief: the ninth Arthur Stanley Eddington Memorial Lecture', reprinted in *The Philosophy of Religion*, ed. B. Mitchell (Oxford: Oxford University Press), 72–91

BRAY, G. (1998) *The Personal God: Is the Classical Understanding of God Tenable?* (Carlisle: Paternoster)

BRENNAN, A.A. (1992) 'Environmental decision making', in *Environmental Dilemmas: Ethics and Decisions*, ed. R.J. Berry (London: Chapman & Hall)

BROGLIE, Louis de (1949) 'A general survey of the scientific work of Albert Einstein', in *Albert Einstein: Philosopher Scientist*, ed. P.A. Schilpp (La Salle, IL: Open Court), 107–27

BROOKE, J.H. (1991) *Science and Religion: Some Historical Perspectives* (Cambridge: Cambridge University Press)

(1996) 'Science and theology in the Enlightenment', in *Religion and Science: History, Method, Dialogue*, ed. W.M. Richardson and W.J. Wildman (London: Routledge), 7–27

(2003) 'Darwin and Victorian Christianity', in *The Cambridge Companion to Darwin*, ed. J. Hodge and G. Radick (Cambridge: Cambridge University Press), 192–213

BROOKE, J.H. and CANTOR, G. (1998) *Reconstructing Nature: The Engagement of Science and Religion* (Edinburgh: T&T Clark)

BROWN, L. (1988) *The Psychology of Religion: An Introduction* (London: SPCK)

BROWN, P. (1993) *The Body and Society: Men, Women and Sexual Renunciation in the Early Church* (New York: Columbia University Press)

BROWN, P. *et al.* (2004) 'A new small bodied hominin from the late Pleistocene in Flores, Indonesia', *Nature* 431, 1055–61

BROWNE, Janet (1996) *Charles Darwin, Vol. I: Voyaging* (London: Pimlico, first published 1995))

(2002) *Charles Darwin, Vol. II: The Power of Place* (London: Jonathan Cape)

BRUCE, D. and BRUCE, A. (eds) (1998) *Engineering Genesis: The Ethics of Genetic Engineering in Non-human Species* (London: Earthscan; 2005 edition forthcoming)

BRUEGGEMANN, Walter (1984) *The Message of the Psalms: A Theological Commentary* (Minneapolis, MN: Fortress Press)

(1993) *The Bible and Postmodern Imagination: Texts under Negotiation* (London: SCM Press)

BRÜMMER, V. (1984) *What Are We Doing When We Pray? A Philosophical Inquiry* (London: SCM Press)

BRUNNER, E. (1952) *The Christian Doctrine of Creation and Redemption: Dogmatics*, Vol. II (London, Lutterworth)

(1953) *Eternal Hope* (London: Lutterworth Press)

BRYANT, John, BAGGOTT LA VELLE, Linda and SEARLE, John (eds) (2002) *Bioethics for Scientists* (Chichester: John Wiley & Sons)

BRYCE, D. (1984) *Wisdom of the Taoist Masters (a translation from the French of Leon Wieger's Les Pères du Système Taoiste)* (Lampeter: Llanerch Enterprises)

—— (1991) *Tao-Te-Ching*, translated from the Chinese by L. Wieger – English-language version by D. Bryce (Felinfach: Llanerch Publishers)

BUBER, Martin (1958) *I and Thou*, trans. by Ronald Gregor Smith (London: Continuum; first edition 1937, German original 1923)

BUCAILLE, M. (1986) *What is the Origin of Man?* 4th edn (Paris: Seghers)

—— (1989) *The Bible, the Quran and Science* 6th edn (Paris: Seghers)

BUCKLEY, M.J. (1987) *At the Origins of Modern Atheism* (New Haven and London: Yale University Press)

BUGLIARELLO, G. (1995) 'Science at the crossroads', in *Cosmic Beginnings and Human Ends*, ed. C.N. Matthews and R.A. Varghese (La Salle, IL: Open Court), 109–28

BULGAKOV, S. (1993) *Sophia: The Wisdom of God: An Outline for Sophiology* (Hudson, NY: Lindisfarne Press)

BULTMANN, R. (1983) 'The Meaning of God as Acting', in *God's Activity in the World: The Contemporary Problem*, ed. O.C. Thomas, (Chico, CA: Scholars Press)

(1985) 'New Testament and mythology: demythologizing the New Testament proclamation', in *New Testament and Mythology and Other Basic Writings*, ed. and trans. by S.M. Ogden (London: SCM Press), 1–43

BURCKHARDT, T. (1988) *An Introduction to Sufi Doctrine*, trans. by D. M. Matheson (Lahore: Sh. Muhammad Ashraf)

BURNEY, C.F. (1925–6) 'Christ as the *Archē* of Creation' *Journal of Theological Studies*, 27, (1925–6), 160–77

BURRELL, D.B. (1993), *Freedom and Creation in Three Traditions* (Notre Dame: University of Notre Dame Press)

(2004) 'Act of creation with its theological consequences', in *Aquinas on Doctrine: A Critical Introduction*, ed. T.G. Weinandy, D.A. Keating and J.P. Yocum, (Edinburgh: T&T Clark International), 27–44

BURTT, Edwin A. (1954) *The Metaphysical Foundations of Modern Science* (Garden City, NY: Doubleday & Co.)

BUSCH, L., LACY, W.B., BURKHARDT, J. and LACY, L.R. (1992) *Plants, Power and Profit: Social, Economic and Ethical Consequences of the New Biotechnologies* (Oxford: Blackwell)

BUTLER, D. and WADMAN, M. (1997) 'Calls for cloning ban sell science short', *Nature* **386**, 8–9

BUTT, N. (1991) *Science and Muslim Societies* (London: Grey Seal Books)

BUTTERFIELD, Herbert (1965) *The Origins of Modern Science 1300–1800* (New York: Free Press)

CAIRNS-SMITH, A.G. (1990) *Seven Clues to the Origin of Life*, rev. edn (Cambridge: Cambridge University Press; first published 1985)

CAMPBELL, D.T. (1976) 'On the conflicts between biological and social evolution and between psychology and moral tradition', *Zygon* 11, 167–208

CANTOR, G. (1991) *Michael Faraday: Sandemanian and Scientist: A Study of Science and Religion in the Nineteenth Century* (Basingstoke: Macmillan)

CAPEK, M. (ed.) (1976) *The Concepts of Space and Time* (Dordrecht: Reidel)

CAPRA, Fritjof (1976) *The Tao of Physics* (London: Fontana)

—— (1983) *The Turning Point* (London: Flamingo)

—— (1996) *The Web of Life* (London: Flamingo)

CARTWRIGHT, Nancy (1999) *The Dappled World: A Study of the Boundaries of Science* (Cambridge: Cambridge University Press)

CASSIRER, H. (1989) *God's New Covenant: A New Testament Translation* (Grand Rapids, MI: Eerdmans)

CERINI, B., MURRAY, I. and REISS, M. (2003) *Student Review of the Science Curriculum* (London: NESTA)

CHAMBERLAIN, J. Knox (1993) 'Psychology', in *Dictionary of Paul and His Letters*, ed. by G.H. Hawthorne *et al.* (Downers Grove: IVP), 765–74

CHARIS (1997) *Charis Science*: Unit 1 The Value of Life (Sc2), Unit 2 Body Matters (Sc2), Unit 3 It's All in the Balance (Sc2), Unit 4 Watch Your Waste (Sc2), Unit 5 A Brief History of Atoms (Sc3), Unit 6 Metals (Sc3), Unit 7 Most Noble Nobel (Sc3), Unit 8 Continental Drift (Sc3), Unit 9 There's No Place Like Home (Sc4), Unit 10 The Big Bang (Sc4), Unit 11 Fuel Consumption (Sc4) (Nottingham: Stapleford Centre)

CHURCHLAND, P.S. (1986) *Neurophilosophy: Towards a Unified Science of the Mind / Brain* (Cambridge, MA: MIT Press)

CLAGUE, J. (2005, in press) 'Patently unjust? Biotechnology, commercialisation and the common good', in *Capabilities and Justice: Towards Structural Transformation* ed. Séverine Deneulin, Mathias Nebel and Nicholas Sagovsky (Dordrecht: Kluwer)

CLARK, S.R.L. (1993) *How to Think about the Earth* (London: Mowbrays)

CLAYTON, Philip (1997a) *God and Contemporary Science* (Edinburgh: Edinburgh Academic Press)

(1997b) 'Inference to the best explanation', *Zygon* **32** (3), 377–91

(2004) 'Panentheism today: a constructive systematic evaluation', in *In Whom We Live and Move and Have our Being: Panentheistic Reflections on God's Presence in a Scientific World*, ed. Philip Clayton and Arthur Peacocke (Grand Rapids, MI, and Cambridge: Eerdmans), 249–64

CLAYTON, Philip and PEACOCKE, Arthur (eds) (2004) *In Whom We Live and Move and Have Our Being: Panentheistic Reflections on God's Presence in a Scientific World* (Grand Rapids, MI and Cambridge: Eerdmans)

CLINES, D.J. (1998) 'Humanity as the image of God', in *On the Way to the Postmodern: Old Testament Essays, 1967–1998*, [DW1] Vol. II, JSOTS 293 (Sheffield: Sheffield Academic Press)

COAKLEY, Sarah (2001) 'Kenosis: Theological Meanings and Gender Connotations', in *The Work of Love*, ed. J. Polkinghorne (London: SPCK; Grand Rapids, MI, and Cambridge: Eerdmans), 192–210

COBB, J.B. and GRIFFIN, D.R. (1976) *Process Theology: An Introductory Exposition* (Philadelphia: Westminster Press)

COHEN, I.B. (1985) 'Three notes on the reception of Darwin's ideas on natural; selection (Henry Baker Tristram, Alfred Newton, Samuel Wilberforce)', in *The Darwinian Heritage*, ed. D. Kohn (Princeton: Princeton University Press), 589–607

COLE-TURNER, Ronald (1993) *The New Genesis: Theology and the Genetic Revolution* (Louisville, KY: Westminster/John Knox Press)

COMINS, N. (1993) *What if the Moon didn't Exist?* (New York: HarperCollins)

CONWAY MORRIS, Simon (1998) *The Crucible of Creation* (Oxford: Oxford University Press)

(2003) *Life's Solution: Inevitable Humans in a Lonely Universe* (Cambridge: Cambridge University Press)

COOK, Alan (1998) ' Uncertainties of science', in *Science Meets Faith: Theology and Science in Conversation*, ed. Fraser Watts (London: SPCK), 25–41

COOPER, J.W. (2001) 'Biblical anthropology and the body–soul problem', in *Soul, Body and Survival*, ed. K. Corcoran (Ithaca: Cornell University Press), 218–28

COPELAND, J. (1993) *Artificial Intelligence: A Philosophical Introduction* (Oxford: Blackwell)

COTTERILL, R. (1989) *No Ghost in the Machine* (London: Heinemann)

COULSON, C.A. (1958) *Science and Christian Belief* (London: Fontana)

CRAIG, William Lane (1991) *Divine Foreknowledge and Human Freedom: The Coherence of Theism-Omniscience* (Leiden: Brill)

(2003) 'Design and the anthropic fine-tuning of the universe', in *God and Design: The Teleological Argument and Modern Science*, ed. Neil A. Manson (London: Routledge), 155–77

CRAIG, W.L. and SMITH, Q. (1993) *Theism, Atheism and Big Bang Cosmology* (Oxford: Clarendon Press)

CRICK, Francis (1966) *Of Molecules and Men* (Seattle, WA: University of Washington Press)

(1994) *The Astonishing Hypothesis: The Scientific Search for the Soul* (London: Simon & Schuster)

CRUTCHFIELD, J.P. *et al.* (1995) 'Chaos', in *Chaos and Complexity: Scientific Perspectives on Divine Action*, ed. R.J. Russell, N. Murphy and A. Peacocke (Vatican City: Vatican Observatory; Berkeley, CA: Center for Theology and the Natural Sciences), 35–48 (reprinted from *Scientific American* 225 (6), (1986), 46–57

DALAI LAMA (14th: Tenzin Gyatso) (1994) *A Flash of Lightning in the Dark of Night: A Guide to the Bodhisattva's Way of Life* (Boston: Shambala)

—— (1997) *The Buddha Nature: Death and Eternal Soul in Buddhism* (Woodside, CA: Bluestar)

DAMASIO, A. (1995) *Descartes' Error* (London: Picador; first published 1999)

D'AQUILI, E. and NEWBERG, A. (1998) 'The neuropsychology of religion', in *Science Meets Faith*, ed. F. Watts (London: SPCK), 73–91

DARWIN, Charles (1859) *On the Origin of Species by Means of Natural Selection, or the Preservation of Favoured Races in the Struggle for Life* (London: John Murray). The 1985 edition, ed. J.W. Burrows (Harmondsworth: Penguin) contains the full text of Darwin's first edition.

(1860) Letter from Darwin to J.D. Hooker, 20? July 1860, in *The Correspondence of Charles Darwin*, ed. F. Burkhardt, vol. VIII, p. 293

(1871) *The Descent of Man, and Selection in relation to Sex*, 2 vols. (London: John Murray)

(1958) *The Autobiography of Charles Darwin*, ed. N. Barlow (London: Collins)

DAVIES, John (2001) *God at Work: Creation Then and Now: A Practical Exploration* (Norwich: Canterbury Press)

DAVIES, Paul (1974) *The Physics of Time Asymmetry* (Leighton Buzzard: Surrey University Press)

(1982) *The Accidental Universe* (Cambridge: Cambridge University Press)

(1990) *God and the New Physics* (Harmondsworth: Penguin)

(1993) *The Mind of God* (Harmondsworth: Penguin)

(1995) *About Time* (Harmondsworth: Penguin)

(1998) *The Fifth Miracle* (Harmondsworth: Penguin)

DAVIS, S.T. (1983) *Logic and the Nature of God* (Grand Rapids, MI: Eerdmans)

DAWKINS, R. (1983) 'Universal Darwinism', in *Evolution from Molecules to Men*, ed D.S. Bendall (Cambridge: Cambridge University Press), 403–25

(1989) *The Selfish Gene*, new edition (Oxford: Oxford University Press; first published 1976)

(1991) *The Blind Watchmaker*, reprint with appendix (Harmondsworth: Penguin; first published 1986)

(1998) *Unweaving the Rainbow: Science, Delusion and the Appetite for Wonder* (Harmondsworth: Penguin)

(2003) *The Devil's Chaplain: Selected Essays* (London: Weidenfeld & Nicolson)

(2004) *The Ancestor's Tale* (London: Weidenfeld & Nicolson)

DEWEESE, G.J. (2004) *God and the Nature of Time* (Aldershot: Ashgate)

DEACON, Terrence (1998) *The Symbolic Species: The Co-evolution of Language and the Human Brain* (Harmondsworth: Penguin; first published 1997)

DEANE-DRUMMOND, Celia (1996) *A Handbook on Theology and Ecology* (London: SCM Press)

(1997a) 'Sophia: the feminine face of God as a metaphor for an ecotheology', *Feminist Theology* 16, 11–31

(1997b) *Theology and Biotechnology: Implications for a New Science* (London: Geoffrey Chapman)

(1997c) *Ecology in Jürgen Moltmann's Theology* (Lewiston, NY: Edwin Mellen Press)

(2000) *Creation Through Wisdom: Theology and the New Biology* (Edinburgh: T&T Clark)

(2004a) 'Genetic interventions in nature: perspectives from a Christian ethic of wisdom', in *Biodiversity and Ecology: An Interdisciplinary Challenge*, ed. D. Edwards and M.W. Worthing (Adelaide: ATF Press), 30–44

(2004b) *The Ethics of Nature* (Oxford: Blackwell), 86–135

(2005, forthcoming) *Genetics and Christian Ethics* (Cambridge: Cambridge University Press)

DEANE-DRUMMOND, C. and SZERSZYNSKI, B. (eds) (2003) *Re-Ordering Nature: Theology, Society and the New Genetics* (London: T&T Clark/Continuum)

DEANE-DRUMMOND, C., B. SZERSZYNSKI and R. GROVE-WHITE (2003) 'Genetically modified theology', in *Re-Ordering Nature: Theology, Society and the New Genetics* ed. C. Deane-Drummond and B. Szerszynski (London: T&T Clark), 17–38

DEMBSKI, William A. (1998) *The Design Inference: Eliminating Chance through Small Probabilities* (Cambridge: Cambridge University Press)

DEMBSKI, William A. and RUSE, Michael (eds) (2004) *From Design to DNA* (Cambridge: Cambridge University Press)

DENNETT, D.C. (1991) *Consciousness Explained* (Harmondsworth: Penguin)

——(1995) *Darwin's Dangerous Idea* (Harmondsworth: Penguin)

DEPARTMENT FOR EDUCATION/WELSH OFFICE EDUCATION DEPARTMENT (1995) *Science in the National Curriculum* (London: HMSO)

DEPEW, D.J. and WEBER B.H. (eds) (1985) *Evolution at a Crossroads* (Cambridge, MA: MIT Press)

——(1995) *Darwinism Evolving* (Cambridge, MA: MIT Press)

DERKSE, W. (1993) *On Simplicity and Elegance: An Essay in Intellectual History* (Delft: Eburon)

DESMOND, A. (1997), *Huxley: From Devil's Disciple to Evolution's High Priest* (Reading, MA: Addison Wesley)

DESMOND, A. and MOORE, J. (1991) *Darwin* (London: Michael Joseph)

DEVALL, B. and SESSIONS, G. (1985) *Deep Ecology* (Salt Lake City, UT: Peregrine Smith)

DI NOIA, J.A. OP (1997) 'Rahner', in *The Modern Theologians: An Introduction to Christian Theology in the Twentieth Century*, ed. David F. Ford (Oxford: Blackwell)

DIAMOND, Jared (1991) *The Rise and Fall of the Third Chimpanzee* (London: Hutchinson Radius)

——(1995) 'The evolution of human inventiveness', in *What is Life? The Next Fifty Years: Speculations on the Future of Biology*, ed. M.P. Murphy and L.A.J. O'Neill (Cambridge: Cambridge University Press), 41–55

(2004) 'The astonishing micropygmies', *Science* 306, 2047–8

DOSTOEVSKY, Fyodor (1958) *The Brothers Karamazov*, trans. by D. Magarshack (Harmondsworth: Penguin)

DRAPER, J. (1874) *History of the Conflict between Religion and Science* (London: Kegan Paul)

DREES, Willem B. (1990) *Beyond the Big Bang: Quantum Cosmologies and God* (La Salle, IL: Open Court)

(1995) 'Gaps for God?' in *Chaos and Complexity: Scientific Perspectives on Divine Action*, ed. R.J. Russell, N. Murphy and A. Peacocke (Vatican City: Vatican Observatory; Berkeley, CA: Center for Theology and the Natural Sciences), 223–37

(1996) *Religion, Science and Naturalism* (Cambridge: Cambridge University Press)

DUHEM, Pierre (1954) *The Aim and Structure of Physical Theory*, trans. by P.P. Weiner (Princeton, NJ: Princeton University Press; first French edn 1906)

DYCK, William (1992) *Rahner* (London: Continuum)

ECHLIN, Edward P. (2004) *The Cosmic Circle: Jesus and Ecology* (Blackrock, Co. Dublin: Columba Press)

ECUMENICAL PATRIARCHATE (1990) *Orthodoxy and the Ecological Crisis* (Gland: World Wide Fund for Nature)

EDELMAN, G. (1992) *Bright Air, Brilliant Fire: On the Matter of the Mind* (Harmondsworth: Penguin)

EDUCATION REFORM ACT (1988) (London: HMSO)

EDWARDS, Denis (1999) *The God of Evolution: A Trinitarian Theology* (Mahwah, NJ: Paulist Press)

    (2006, forthcoming) ' "Every sparrow that falls to the ground": the cost of evolution and the Christ-event', *Ecotheology*.

EINSTEIN, Albert (1923) 'On the electrodynamics of moving bodies', in A. Einstein *et al.*, *The Principle of Relativity: A Collection of Original Papers on the Special and General Theory of Relativity* (New York, NY: Dover), 35–65

ELDREDGE, N. and GOULD, S.J. (1972) 'Punctuated equilibrium: an alternative to phyletic gradualism', in *Models in Paleobiology*, ed. T.J.M. Schopf (New York, NY: Freeman Cooper & Co.)

ELLIS, G.F.R. (ed.) (2002) *The Far Future Universe: Eschatology from a Cosmic Perspective* (Radnor, PA: Templeton Foundation Press)

ELLUL, J. (1964) *The Technological Society* (New York: Random House)

——(1989) *The Presence of the Kingdom* (Colorado Springs, CO: Helmers Howard; first published in French, 1948)

——(1990) *The Technological Bluff* (Grand Rapids, MI: Eerdmans)

ENDLER, J.A. (1986) *Natural Selection in the Wild* (Princeton, NJ: Princeton University Press)

FABEL, Arthur and ST JOHN, Donald (eds) (2003) *Teilhard in the 21st Century: The Emerging Spirit of Earth* (Maryknoll, NY: Orbis)

FANTOLI, A. (1996) *Galileo: For Copernicanism and for the Church*, 2nd edn, trans. G. Coyne (Vatican City: Vatican Observatory)

FARRER, Austin (1966) *A Science of God?* (London: Geoffrey Bles)

    (1967) *Faith and Speculation* (London: A&C Black)

FARUQI, I.R. and NASSEEF, A.O. (eds) (1981) *Social and Natural Sciences: The Islamic Perspective* (Sevenoaks: Hodder & Stoughton)

FEINGOLD, M. (2002) 'Science as a calling? The early modern Dilemma', *Science in Context* 15, 79–119

FERGUSSON, D.A.S. (1998) *The Cosmos and the Creator: An Introduction to the Theology of Creation* (London: SPCK)

FEYERABEND, Paul (1993) *Against Method: Outline of an Anarchistic Theory of Knowledge*, 3rd edn (London: Verso)

FIDDES, Paul S. (1988) *The Creative Suffering of God* (Oxford: Clarendon Press)

    (2000) *Participating in God: A Pastoral Doctrine of the Trinity* (London: Darton, Longman & Todd)

FINOCCHIARO, M.P. (ed.) (1989) *The Galileo Affair* (Berkeley and San Francisco: University of California Press)

FLANAGAN, O. (1992) *Consciousness Reconsidered* (Cambridge, MA: MIT Press)

FLEW, A. (1955) 'Theology and falsification', in *New Essays in Philosophical Theology*, ed. A. Flew and A. MacIntyre (London: SCM Press), 96–9

——(1997) 'Neo-Humean arguments about the miraculous', in *In Defence of Miracles: A Comprehensive Case for God's Action in History*, ed. R.D. Geivett and G.R. Habermas (Leicester: Apollos), 45–57

FLOOD, G.D. (1996) *An Introduction to Hinduism* (Cambridge: Cambridge University Press)

FOERST, A. (1996) 'Artificial intelligence', *Zygon* 31, 681–93

FOLTZ, R.C., DENNY, F.M. and BAHARUDDIN, A. (eds) (2003) *Islam and Ecology: A Bestowed Trust* (Cambridge, MA: Harvard University Press for the Center for the Study of World Religions, Harvard Divinity School)

FORD, David F. (1990) Review of *The Creative Suffering of God* by Paul S. Fiddes, *Journal of Theological Studies* 41 (1), 316–18

FORD, David F. with MUERS, Rachel (eds) (2005, 3rd edn) *The Modern Theologians* (Oxford: Blackwell)

FORMAN, R.K.C. (ed.) (1990) *The Problem of Pure Consciousness* (New York, NY: Oxford University Press)

FOSTER, M.B. (1934) 'The Christian doctrine of creation and the rise of modern science', *Mind* 43, 446–68

FOX, M. (1983) *Original Blessing: A Primer in Creation Spirituality* (Santa Fe, NM: Bear & Co.)

FREUD, S. (1928) *The Future of an Illusion*, trans. by W.D. Robson-Scott (London: Hogarth Press)

FUKUYAMA, F. (2002) *Our Posthuman Future* (London: Profile Books)

FULLICK, P. and RATCLIFFE, M. (1996) *Teaching Ethical Aspects of Science* (Southampton: Bassett Press)

GASKELL, George, BAUER, Martin W., DURANT, John, and ALLUM, Nicholas C. (1999) 'Worlds apart? The reception of genetically modified foods in Europe and the US', *Science* 285, 384–7

GAZZANIGA, M.S. (1989) 'The organisation of the human brain', *Science* 245, 947–52

AL-GHAZZALI (1983) *Inner Dimensions of Islamic Worship*, trans. from the Ihya' by Muhtar Holland (Leicester: Islamic Foundation)

GILKEY, Langdon B. (1963) 'The concept of providence in contemporary theology', *Journal of Religion* 43, 171

GINGERICH, Owen (1982) 'The Galileo Affair', *Scientific American* 247, 132–43

(1993) *The Eye of Heaven: Ptolemy, Copernicus, Kepler* (New York: American Institute of Physics)

GLEICK, J. (1988) *Chaos: Making a New Science* (London: Cardinal)

GOODWIN, Brian (1995) *How the Leopard Changed Its Spots* (London: Orion Books)

GOODWIN, C. (1860) 'On the Mosaic cosmogony', in *Essays and Reviews*, ed. F. Temple, 5th edn (London, 1861)

GÖRMAN, Ulf, DREES, Willem B. and MEISINGER, H. (eds) (2004) *Creating Technos@piens? Values and Ethical Issues in Theology, Science and Technology*, Studies in Science and Theology 9 (Lund, Sweden: Centre for Theology and Religious Studies)

GOSLING, David (1992) *A New Earth* (London: CCBI)

GOULD, Stephen Jay (1991) *Wonderful Life: The Burgess Shale and the Nature of History* (Harmondsworth: Penguin; first published 1989)

——(1996) *Life's Grandeur: The Spread of Excellence from Plato to Darwin* (London: Cape)

(2002) *Rocks of Ages: Science and Religion in the Fullness of Life* (London: Vintage; first published 1999)

GRANBERG-MICHAELSON, Wesley (ed.) (1987) *Tending the Garden: Essays on the Gospel and the Earth* (Grand Rapids, MI: Eerdmans)

GRAY, A. (1860) 'Natural selection and natural theology', in *Darwiniana*, ed. A. Hunter Dupree (Cambridge, MA: Harvard University Press, 1963), 121–2

GREEN, J.B. (2002) 'Eschatology and the nature of humans: a reconsideration of pertinent biblical evidence', *Science and Christian Belief* 14, 33–50

GREEN, J.B. (ed.) (2004) *What About the Soul? Neuroscience and Christian Anthropology* (Nashville, TN: Abingdon)

GREENE, Brian (2004) *The Fabric of the Cosmos: Space, Time and the Texture of Reality* (Harmondsworth: Penguin)

GREGERSEN, Niels H. (1999) 'Autopoiesis: less than self-constitution, more than self-organization', *Zygon* 34 (1), 117–38

GREGERSEN, Niels H., DREES, Willem B. and GÖRMAN, Ulf (eds) (2000) *The Human Person in Science and Theology* (Edinburgh: T&T Clark)

GREGERSEN, Niels H. and GÖRMAN, Ulf (eds) (2002) *Design and Disorder: Perspectives from Science and Theology* (Edinburgh: T&T Clark)

GREGERSEN, N.H., and VAN HUYSSTEEN, W. (eds) (1998) *Rethinking Theology and Science: Six Models for the Current Dialogue* (Grand Rapids, MI: Eerdmans)

GREGORIOS, P.M. (1987) *The Human Presence* (Amity, NY: Amity House)

GROVE-WHITE, R., MCNAGHTEN, P., MAYER, S. and WYNNE, B. (1997) *Uncertain World: Genetically Modified Organisms, Food and Public Attitudes in Britain* (Lancaster: Centre for the Study of Environmental Change)

GRUMETT, David (2005, forthcoming) *Teilhard de Chardin: Theology, Humanity and Cosmos* (Leuven: Peeters)

GUÉNON, R. (1958a) *Man and his Becoming According to the Vedanta* (New York: Noonday Press)

(1958b) *The Symbolism of the Cross* (London: Luzac & Co.)

GUNTON, Colin (1992) *Christ and Creation* (Carlisle: Paternoster Press)

(1998) *The Triune Creator: A Historical and Systematic Study* (Edinburgh: Edinburgh University Press)

(2001) *Becoming and Being: The Doctrine of God in Charles Hartshorne and Karl Barth*, 2nd edn (London: SCM Press; first published 1978)

GUTH, A.H. (1997) *The Inflationary Universe: The Quest for a New Theory of Cosmic Origins* (Reading, MA: Addison-Wesley)

HABGOOD, John (1998) *Being a Person: Where Faith and Science Meet* (London: Hodder & Stoughton)

HAMPSON, Daphne (1990) *Theology and Feminism* (Oxford: Blackwell)

HANSON, N. (1958) *Patterns of Discovery* (Cambridge: Cambridge University Press)

HARAWAY, Donna J. (2003) *The Haraway Reader* (London: Routledge)

HARDY, D.W. (1996) *God's Ways with the World: Thinking and Practising Christian Faith* (Edinburgh: T&T Clark)

(1998) 'The God who is with the world', in *Science Meets Faith*, ed. F. Watts (London: SPCK), 136–53

HARE, R.M. (1955) 'Theology and falsification B', reprinted in *New Essays in Philosophical Theology*, ed. A. Flew and A. MacIntyre (London: SCM Press), 99–103

HARRIS, J. (1998) *Clones, Genes, and Immortality* (Oxford: Oxford University Press)

HARRISON, P. (1998) *The Bible, Protestantism and the Rise of Natural Science* (Cambridge: Cambridge University Press)

HASEL, G. (1974) 'The polemic nature of the Genesis cosmology', *Evangelical Quarterly* 46, 81–102

AL-HASHIMI, A.H. (1981) 'Islamizing the discipline of psychology', in *Social and Natural Sciences: The Islamic Perspective*, ed. I. R. Faruqi and A. O. Naseef (Sevenoaks: Hodder & Stoughton), 49–70

HASKER, W. (1999) *The Emergent Self* (Ithaca, NY, and London: Cornell University Press)

HAUGHT, John F. (1995) *Science and Religion: From Conflict to Conversation* (Mahwah, NJ: Paulist Press)

(2000) *God After Darwin: A Theology of Evolution* (Oxford and Boulder, CO: Westview Press)

(2004) 'Darwin, design and the promise of nature', The Boyle Lecture, 2004 (available on the World Wide Web)

HAWKING, Stephen W. (1988) *A Brief History of Time* (London: Bantam)

HAY, D. (1987) *Exploring Inner Space*, 2nd edn (Harmondsworth: Penguin)

HEALY, N.M. (2003) *Thomas Aquinas: Theologian of the Christian Life* (Aldershot: Ashgate)

HEFNER, Philip (1993) *The Human Factor* (Minneapolis, MN: Fortress Press)

(1996) 'Theological perspectives on morality and human evolution', in *Religion and Science*, ed. W.M. Richardson and W.J. Wildman (London: Routledge), 401–23

(2003) *Technology and Human Becoming* (Minneapolis: Fortress Press)

HEIDEGGER, M. (1969) *The Question Concerning Technology and Other Essays*, trans. by W. Lovitt (London: Harper Torchbooks), 3–35

HERZFELD, Noreen L. (2002) *In our Image: Artificial Intelligence and the Human Spirit* (Minneapolis, MN: Fortress Press)

HESSE, M. (1980) 'In defence of objectivity', in *Revolutions and Reconstructions in the Philosophy of Science* (Brighton: Harvester Press), 167–86

(1998) 'Is science the new religion?' in *Science Meets Faith*, ed. Fraser Watts (London: SPCK), 120–35

HICK, J. (1971) 'Theology and verification', reprinted in *The Philosophy of Religion*, ed. B. Mitchell (Oxford: Oxford University Press), 53–71

——(1976) *Death and Eternal Life* (London: Macmillan)

HOLDER, R. (1993) *Nothing But Atoms and Molecules?* (Tunbridge Wells: Monarch)

HOLLINS, M. (2004) 'Modernising science for the 21st century: Reform of GCSE', *Education in Science* 210, 8f.

HOLTON, Gerald (1956) 'Johannes Kepler's universe: its physics and metaphysics', *American Journal of Physics* 24, 340–51

HOLTON, G. and ROLLER, D. (1958) *Foundations of Modern Physical Science* (Reading, MA: Addison-Wesley)

HOMANS, P. (1970) *Theology After Freud: An Interpretative Inquiry* (Indianapolis, IN: Bobbs-Merrill)

HOOD, R.W., SPILKA, B., HUNSBERGER, B. and GORSUCH, R. (1996) *The Psychology of Religion: An Empirical Approach* (New York, NY: Guilford)

HOODBHOY, P. (1991) *Islam and Science* (London: Zed Books)

HOOYKAAS, R. (1972) *Religion and the Rise of Modern Science* (Edinburgh: Scottish Academic Press)

HOPKINS, Gerard Manley (1953) *Poems and Prose*, ed. W.H. Gardner (Harmondsworth: Penguin)

HOUGHTON, J. (1994) *Global Warming* (Oxford: Lion Publishing)

HOWELL, K.J. (1996) 'Galileo and the history of hermeneutics', in *Facets of Faith, Volume IV: Interpreting God's Action in the World*, ed. J. van der Meer (Lanham, MD: University Press of America), 245–60

HOYLE, F. (1982) *Facts and Dogmas in Cosmology and Elsewhere* (Cambridge: Cambridge University Press)

HUME, David (2000) 'Why we should disbelieve in miracles', in *Philosophy of Religion: A Guide and Anthology*, ed. Brian Davies (Oxford: Oxford University Press, 2000), 430–6

HUNSINGER, D. van D. (1995) *Theology and Pastoral Counselling: A New Inter-disciplinary Approach* (Grand Rapids, MI: Eerdmans)

HUNSINGER, G. (1991) *How to Read Karl Barth: The Shape of His Theology* (Oxford: Oxford University Press)

IRENAEUS of LYONS (1967) *Against the Heresies*, The Ante-Nicene Fathers 1, trans. and ed. A. Roberts and J. Donaldson (Grand Rapids, MI: Eerdmans)

IRONS, W. (1996) 'Morality, religion, and human evolution', in *Religion and Science*, ed. W.M. Richardson and W.J. Wildman (London: Routledge), 375–99

ISHAM, C.J. and POLKINGHORNE, J.C. (1993) 'The debate over the block universe', in *Quantum Cosmology and the Laws of Nature*, ed. R.J. Russell, N. Murphy and C.J. Isham (Vatican City: Vatican Observatory and Berkeley, CA: Center for Theology and the Natural Sciences), 135–44

JAKI, Stanley L. (1978) *The Road of Science and the Ways to God* (Edinburgh: Scottish Academic Press)

(1980) *Cosmos and Creator* (Edinburgh: Scottish Academic Press)

JEEVES, M. (1997) *Human Nature at the Millennium: Reflections on the Integration of Psychology and Christianity* (Grand Rapids, MI: Baker Books)

JOHN PAUL II (1988) 'A message to the Revd George V. Coyne SJ, Director of the Vatican Observatory', in *Physics, Philosophy and Theology*, ed. R.J. Russell, W.R. Stoeger SJ and G.V. Coyne SJ (Vatican City: Vatican Observatory), MI–14

JOHNSON-LAIRD, P.N. (1988) *The Computer and the Mind* (London: Fontana)

JONAS, Hans (1996) *Mortality and Morality: A Search for the Good after Auschwitz*, a collection of essays edited by Lawrence Vogel (Evanston, IL: Northwestern University Press)

JÜNGEL, Eberhard (1983) *God as the Mystery of the World: On the Foundation of the Theology of the Crucified One in the Dispute Between Theism and Atheism*, trans. by D.L. Guder (Edinburgh: T&T Clark)

KAISER, C. (1991) *Creation and the History of Science* (London and Grand Rapids: Marshall Pickering and Eerdmans)

(1996) 'The laws of nature and the nature of God', in *Facets of Faith, Volume IV: Interpreting God's Action in the World*, ed. J. van der Meer (Lanham, MD: University Press of America), 185–97

KAHN, A. (1997) 'Clone mammals: clone man?', *Nature* **386**, 119

KATZ, S.T. (ed.) (1978) *Mysticism and Philosophical Analysis* (New York, NY: Oxford University Press)

KAUFFMAN, S. (1995) *At Home in the Universe* (Harmondsworth: Penguin)

(2000) *Investigations* (Oxford: Oxford University Press)

KAUFMAN, Gordon (1972) *God the Problem* (Cambridge, MA: Harvard University Press)

KAY, Lily E. (2000) *Who Wrote the Book of Life? A History of the Genetic Code* (Stanford, CA: Stanford University Press)

KEARNY, H. (1971) *Science and Change 1500–1700* (New York: McGraw-Hill)

KEOWN, D. (1996) *Buddhism: A Very Short Introduction* (Oxford: Oxford University Press)

KINGDON, Jonathan (1993) *Self-Made Man and His Undoing: The Radical Reworking of Evolution Theory* (London: Simon & Schuster)

(2003) *Lowly Origin: Where, When, and Why Our Ancestors First Stood Up* (Princeton, NJ: Princeton University Press)

KNIGHT, Christopher C. (2001) *Wrestling with the Divine: Religion, Science and Revelation* (Minneapolis, MN: Fortress Press)

KOBE, D.H. (1998) 'Copernicus and Martin Luther: an encounter between science and religion', *American Journal of Physics* **66**, 190–6

KRAGH, Helge (1996) *Cosmology and Controversy: The Historical Development of Two Theories of the Universe* (Princeton, NJ: Princeton University Press)

KRINGS, M. *et al.* (1997) 'Neanderthal DNA sequences and the origin of modern humans', *Cell* **90** (1), 19–29

KUHN, T.S. (1957) *The Copernican Revolution* (Cambridge, MA: Harvard University Press)

(1962) *The Structure of Scientific Revolutions* (Chicago, IL: University of Chicago Press)

(1970a) 'Logic of discovery or psychology of research?' in *Criticism and the Growth of Knowledge: Proceedings of the International Colloquium in the Philosophy of Science, London 1965, Volume IV*, ed. I. Lakatos and A. Musgrave (Cambridge: Cambridge University Press), 1–23

(1970b) *The Structure of Scientific Revolutions*, rev. edn with postscript (Chicago, IL: University of Chicago Press)

(1970c) 'Reflections on my critics', in *Criticism and the Growth of Knowledge: Proceedings of the International Colloquium in the Philosophy of Science, London, 1965, Volume IV*, ed. I. Lakatos and A. Musgrave (Cambridge: Cambridge University Press), 231–78

(1971) 'Notes on Lakatos', in *In Memory of Rudolf Carnap: Proceedings of the 1970 Biennial Meeting of the Philosophy of Science Association*, ed. R.C. Buck and R.S. Cohen, Boston Studies in the Philosophy of Science 8 (Dordrecht: Reidel), 137–46

KÜNG, Hans (1989) 'Paradigm change in theology: a proposal for discussion', in *Paradigm Change in Theology: A Symposium for the Future*, ed. Hans Küng and David Tracy (Edinburgh: T&T Clark), 3–33

(1990) *Global Responsibility* (London: SCM Press)

KÜNG, Hans and TRACY, David (eds) (1989) *Paradigm Change in Theology: A Symposium for the Future* (Edinburgh: T&T Clark)

KVANVIG, J.L. (1986) *The Possibility of an All-Knowing God* (London: Macmillan)

LAKATOS, Imre (1970) 'Falsification and the methodology of scientific research programmes', in *Criticism and the Growth of Knowledge: Proceedings of the International Colloquium in the Philosophy of Science, London, 1965, Volume IV*, ed. I. Lakatos and A. Musgrave (Cambridge: Cambridge University Press), 91–196

LAKE, Frank (1966) *Clinical Theology: A Theological and Psychiatric Basis to Clinical Pastoral Care* (London: Darton, Longman & Todd)

LAMBERT, W.G. (1965) 'A new look at the Babylonian background of Genesis', *Journal of Theological Studies* 16, 294

LANCASTER, B. (1991) *Mind, Brain and Human Potential: The Quest for an Understanding of Self* (Shaftesbury: Element)

LASH, Nicholas (1979) 'Can a theologian keep the faith?' in *Theology on Dover Beach* (London: Darton, Longman & Todd), 45–59

(1986) 'Ideology, metaphor and analogy', in *Theology on the Way to Emmaus* (London: SCM Press), 95–119

(1992) *Believing Three Ways in One God: A Reading of the Apostles' Creed* (London: SCM Press)

LAUDAN, Larry (1977) *Progress and its Problems* (London: Routledge & Kegan Paul)

LEAKEY, R. and LEWIN, R. (1996) *The Sixth Extinction: Biodiversity and its Survival* (London: Weidenfeld & Nicolson)

LEE, R.S. (1948) *Freud and Christianity* (Harmondsworth: Penguin)

LEOPOLD, Aldo (1949) *A Sand County Almanac* (Oxford: Oxford University Press)

LEWIS, C.S. (1947) *Miracles: A Preliminary Study* (London: Geoffrey Bles)

LEWIS-WILLIAMS, David (2002) *The Mind in the Cave: Consciousness and the Origins of Art* (London: Thames & Hudson)

LINDBERG, D. (1992) *The Beginnings of Western Science* (Chicago: University of Chicago Press)

LINDBERG, D. and NUMBERS, R. (eds) (2003), *When Science and Christianity Meet* (Chicago: University of Chicago Press)

LINGS, M. (1985) *Muhammad: His Life based on the Earliest Sources* (London: Islamic Texts Society and George Allen & Unwin)

LINZEY, Andrew (1994) *Animal Theology* (London: SCM Press)

LIVINGSTONE, D. (1992), 'Darwinism and Calvinism: The Belfast–Princeton connection', *Isis* **83**, 408–28

LLOYD, G. (1993) *Being in Time: Selves and Narrators in Philosophy and Literature* (London: Routledge)

LOCKE, John (1960) *An Essay Concerning Human Understanding* (London: Collins; originally published 1690)

LODHI, M.A.K. (ed.) (1989) *Islamization of Attitudes and Practices in Science and Technology* (Herndon, VA: Association of Muslim Scientists and Engineers)

LOEWENTHAL, K.M. (1995) *Mental Health and Religion* (London: Chapman & Hall)

LOVELOCK, James (1988) *The Ages of Gaia* (Oxford: Oxford University Press)

(2000) *Homage to Gaia: The Life of an Independent Scientist* (Oxford: Oxford University Press)

(2004) 'Reflections on Gaia', in *Scientists Debate Gaia*, ed. Stephen H. Schneider *et al.* (Cambridge, MA: MIT Press), 1–5

LUCAS, Ernest (1996) *Science and the New Age Challenge* (Leicester: Apollos)

(2001) *Can we Believe in Genesis Today?* (Leicester: IVP)

LUSCOMBE, Philip (2000) *Groundwork of Science and Religion* (Peterborough: Epworth Press)

LUTHER, M. (1958) *Luther's Works, I: Lectures on Genesis Chapters 1–5*, ed. J. Pelikan (St Louis: Concordia)

(1983) 'Sermon for Trinity Sunday; Romans 11:33–36', in *The Sermons of Martin Luther* (Grand Rapids, MI: Baker Book House)

LYON, D. (1988) *The Information Society* (Oxford: Polity Press / Blackwell)

MABUD, Shaikh M. (1986) 'Theory of evolution: an assessment from the Islamic point of view', *Muslim Educational Quarterly* 4 (1), 9–56

MCCABE, Herbert (1987) *God Matters* (London: Geoffrey Chapman)

MCCORMACK, B. (1995) *Karl Barth's Critically Realistic Dialectical Theology: Its Genesis and Development, 1909–1936* (Oxford: Clarendon Press)

MCDANIEL, J. (1989) *Of God and Pelicans* (Louisville, KY: Westminster / John Knox Press)

—— (1990) 'Revisioning God and the self: lessons from Buddhism', in *Liberating Life: Contemporary Approaches to Ecological Theology*, ed. C. Birch, W. Eakin and J. McDaniel (Maryknoll, NY: Orbis Books), 228–58

MCDONAGH (1994) *Passion for the Earth: The Christian Vocation to promote Justice, Peace and the Integrity of Creation* (London: Geoffrey Chapman)

(2004) *Patenting Life: Stop* (Blackrock, Co. Dublin: Columba Press)

MCFAGUE, S. (1982) *Metaphorical Theology: Models of God in Religious Language* (Philadelphia: Fortress Press)

—— (1987) *Models of God: Theology for an Ecological, Nuclear Age* (London: SCM Press)

—— (1993) *The Body of God: An Ecological Theology* (London: SCM Press)

—— (1997) *Super, Natural Christians: How We Should Love Nature* (London: SCM Press)

MCGRATH, Alister E. (1998) *The Foundations of Dialogue in Science and Religion* (Oxford: Blackwell)

(2001) *A Scientific Theology, Vol. I: Nature* (Grand Rapids, MI: Eerdmans)

(2002) *A Scientific Theology, Vol. II: Reality* (Grand Rapids, MI: Eerdmans)

(2003a) *A Scientific Theology, Vol. III: Theory* (Grand Rapids, MI: Eerdmans)

(2003b) *The Re-enchantment of Nature: Science, Religion and the Human Sense of Wonder* (London: Hodder & Stoughton)

(2004) *The Science of God* (London: T&T Clark International)

(2005) *Dawkins' God: Genes, Memes and the Meaning of Life* (Oxford: Blackwell)

MCGREW, Timothy, MCGREW, Lydia and VESTRUP, Eric (2003) 'Probabilities and the fine-tuning argument: a skeptical view', in *God and Design: The Teleological Argument and Modern Science*, ed. Neil A. Manson (London: Routledge), 200–8

MACKAY, D.M. (1991) *Behind the Eye* (Oxford: Blackwell)

MACKENZIE, D. and WAJCMAN, J. (1985) *The Social Shaping of Technology* (Milton Keynes: Open University Press)

MACKEY, J.P. (1983) 'Trinity, Doctrine of the', in *A New Dictionary of Christian Theology*, ed. A. Richardson and J. Bowden (London: SCM Press), 581–9

MCKIBBEN, Bill (2003) *Enough: Genetic Engineering and the End of Human Nature* (London: Bloomsbury)

MACKIE, J.L. (1971) 'Evil and omnipotence', reprinted in *The Philosophy of Religion*, ed. B. Mitchell (Oxford: Oxford University Press), 92–104

—— (1982) *The Miracle of Theism: Arguments For and Against the Existence of God* (Oxford: Clarendon Press)

MACKINNON, Donald (1968) 'Philosophy and Christology', in *Borderlands of Theology and Other Essays* (London: Lutterworth Press), 55–81

MCMENAMIN, Mark A.S. (2004) 'Gaia and glaciation: Lipalian (Vendian) environmental crisis', in *Scientists Debate Gaia*, ed. Stephen H. Schneider *et al.* (Cambridge, MA: MIT Press), 115–27

MACQUARRIE, John (1977) *Principles of Christian Theology*, 2nd rev. edn (London: SCM Press; first published 1966)

MADDOX, Brenda (2002) *Rosalind Franklin: The Dark Lady of DNA* (London: HarperCollins)

MALONY, H.N. and LOVEKIN, A.A. (1985) *Glossolalia: Behavioural Science Perspectives on Speaking in Tongues* (New York, NY: Oxford University Press)

MANSON, Neil A. (2000) 'There is no adequate definition of "fine-tuned for life"', *Inquiry* 43, 341–52

MANSON, Neil (ed.) (2003) *God and Design: The Teleological Argument and Modern Science* (London: Routledge)

MANZOOR, S.P. (1984) 'Environment and values', in *A Touch of Midas: Values and Environment in Islam and the West*, ed. Z. Sardar (Manchester: Manchester University Press)

MARGENAU, H. and VARGHESE, R.A. (eds) (1992) *Cosmos, Bios, Theos* (La Salle, IL: Open Court)

MARSONET, M. (1996) *The Primacy of Practical Reason: An Essay on Nicholas Rescher's Philosophy* (Lanham, MD: University Press of America)

MARTIN-SCHRAMM, James B. and STIVERS, Robert L. (2003) *Christian Environmental Ethics: A Case Method Approach* (Maryknoll, NY: Orbis)

MATHIAS, P. (1972) *Science and Society, 1600–1900* (Cambridge: Cambridge University Press)

MATTHEWS, C.N. and VARGHESE, R.A. (eds) (1995) *Cosmic Beginnings and Human Ends* (La Salle, IL: Open Court)

MATURANA, H. and VARELA, F. (1980) *Autopoiesis and Cognition* (Dordrecht: Reidel)

MAY, G. (1994) *Creatio Ex Nihilo: The Doctrine of 'Creation out of Nothing' in Early Christian Thought*, trans. by A.S. Worrall (Edinburgh: University of Edinburgh Press)

MEDAWAR, Peter (1996) *The Strange Case of the Spotted Mice* (Oxford: Oxford University Press)

MEISSNER, W.W. (1984) *Psychoanalysis and Religious Experience* (New Haven, CT: Yale University Press)

(1987) *Life and Faith* (Washington DC: Georgetown University Press)

(1992) *Ignatius of Loyola: The Psychology of a Saint* (New Haven, CT: Yale University Press)

MENG, H. and FREUD, E.L. (eds) (1963) *Psychoanalysis and Faith: The Letters of Sigmund Freud and Oskar Pfister* (New York, NY: Basic Books)

MERCHANT, Carolyn (1992) *Radical Ecology* (London: Routledge)

MERTON, Thomas (1968) *Zen and the Birds of Appetite* (New York, NY: New Directions)

MESTHENE, E. (1967) *Technology and Social Change* (Indianapolis, IN: Bobbs-Merrill)

MEYERSON, E. (1985) *The Relativist Deduction: Epistemological Implications of the Theory of Relativity* (Dordrecht: Reidel)

MIDGLEY, Mary (1996a) 'One world, but a big one', *Journal of Consciousness Studies* 3 (5–6), 500–14

——(1996b) 'Science in the world', *Science Studies* 9 (2), 49–58

(2001) *Science and Poetry* (London: Routledge)

MILLAR, R., and OSBORNE J. (eds) (1998) *Beyond 2000: Science Education for the Future: Report with Ten Recommendations* (London: Nuffield Curriculum Projects Centre)

MILLER, P.D. (2004) 'What is a human being? The anthropology of Scripture', in *What About the Soul? Neuroscience and Christian Anthropology*, ed. J.B. Green (Nashville, TN: Abingdon), 63–74

MITCHELL, B. (1973) *The Justification of Religious Belief* (London: Macmillan)

MITHEN, Steve (1999) *The Prehistory of the Mind: The Cognitive Origins of Art and Science* (London: Thames & Hudson; first published 1996)

MOLTMANN, Jürgen (1967) *Theology of Hope: On the Grounds and Implications of a Christian Eschatology*, trans. by J.W. Leitch (London: SCM Press)

(1969) *Religion, Revolution and the Future*, trans. by M.D. Meeks (New York, NY: Charles Scribner's Sons)

(1973) *Theology and Joy*, trans. by R. Ulrich (London: SCM Press)

(1974) *The Crucified God*, trans. by R.A. Wilson and J. Bowden (London: SCM Press)

(1981) *The Trinity and the Kingdom of God*, trans. by M. Kohl (London: SCM Press)

(1985) *God in Creation*, trans. by M. Kohl (London: SCM Press)

(1990) *The Way of Jesus Christ*, trans. by M. Kohl (London: SCM Press)

(1996) *The Coming of God: Christian Eschatology*, trans. M. Kohl (London: SCM Press)

(2003) *Science and Wisdom*, trans. by M. Kohl (London: SCM Press)

MONOD, Jacques (1972) *Chance and Necessity*, trans. by A. Wainhouse (London: Collins)

MOORE, J. (1979) *The Post-Darwinian Controversies: A Study of the Protestant Struggle to Come to Terms with Darwin in Great Britain and America, 1870–1900* (Cambridge: Cambridge University Press)

MORAVEC, H. (1988) *Mind Children: The Future of Robot and Human Intelligence* (Cambridge, MA: Harvard University Press)

MUMFORD, L. (1946) *Technics and Civilization* (London: Routledge)

MURPHY, M.P. and O'NEILL, L.A.J. (1995) *What is Life? The Next Fifty Years* (Cambridge: Cambridge University Press)

MURPHY, Nancey (1990) *Theology in the Age of Scientific Reasoning* (Ithaca, NY: Cornell University Press)

——(1993) 'Evidence of design in the fine-tuning of the universe', in *Quantum Cosmology and the Laws of Nature: Scientific Perspectives on Divine Action*, ed. R.J. Russell, N. Murphy and C.J. Isham (Vatican City: Vatican Observatory; Berkeley, CA: Center for Theology and the Natural Sciences), 407–35

——(1994) 'What has theology to learn from scientific methodology?' in *Science and Theology: Questions at the Interface*, ed. by M. Rae, H. Regan and J. Stenhouse (Edinburgh: T&T Clark), 101–26

——(1995) 'Divine action in the natural order: Buridan's ass and Schrödinger's cat', in *Chaos and Complexity: Scientific Perspectives on Divine Action*, ed. R.J. Russell, N. Murphy and A. Peacocke (Vatican City: Vatican Observatory; Berkeley, CA: Center for Theology and the Natural Sciences), 325–57

——(1996) 'On the nature of theology', in *Religion and Science: History, Method, Dialogue*, ed. W.M. Richardson and W.J. Wildman (New York, NY: Routledge), 151–9

(1997) *Anglo-American Postmodernity: Philosophical Perspectives on Science, Religion, and Ethics* (Boulder, CO: Westview Press)

(1999) 'Introduction', in *Neuroscience and the Person: Scientific Perspectives on Divine Action*, ed. Robert J. Russell *et al.* (Vatican City: Vatican Observatory; Berkeley, CA: Center for Theology and the Natural Sciences), i–xxxv

(2000) 'Science and Society', in *Systematic Theology, Vol. III: Witness*, ed. J.W. McClendon and N. Murphy (Nashville, TN: Abingdon), 99–131

MURPHY, Nancey and ELLIS, George F.R. (1996) *On the Moral Nature of the Universe: Theology, Cosmology, and Ethics* (Minneapolis, MN: Fortress Press)

MURRAY, Paul D. (1998a) 'Theology after the demise of foundationalism', *The Way* 38, 160–9

——(1998b) 'Theology in the borderlands: Donald MacKinnon and contemporary theology', *Modern Theology* 14, 355–76

(2003) 'Epistemology', in *Encyclopedia of Science and Religion*, ed. J.W. Van Huyssteen (New York: Macmillan), 266–8

(2005) *Reason, Truth and Theology in Pragmatist Perspective* (Leuven: Peeters)

MUTAHHARI, M. (1985) *Fundamentals of Islamic Thought* (Berkeley, CA: Mizan Press)

MYERS, D.G. and JEEVES, M.A. (2002) *Psychology through the Eyes of Faith* (San Francisco: Harper)

NAGEL, Thomas (1974) 'What is it like to be a bat?' *Philosophical Review* 83, 435–50, reprinted in T. Nagel (1979) *Mortal Questions* (Cambridge: Cambridge University Press)

(1986) *The View from Nowhere* (Oxford: Oxford University Press)

NAIRNE, R. (1997) *Tranquil Mind: An Introduction to Buddhism and Meditation* (Kalk Bay, SA: Kairon Press)

NASR, S.H. (1968) *Science and Civilization in Islam* (Cambridge, MA: Harvard University Press)

(1976) *Islamic Science: An Illustrated Study* (London: World of Islam Publishing)

(1980) *Living Sufism* (London: Unwin Paperbacks)

(1987) *Science and Civilization in Islam*, 2nd rev. edn (Cambridge, MA: Islamic Text Society)

NASSEEF, A.O. and BLACK, P.J. (1984) *Science Education and Religious Values* (Cambridge: Islamic Academy)

NEGUS, Michael Robert (1995) 'The concept of Islamic science and the thought patterns of a Muslim scientist', *Muslim Education Quarterly* 12 (4), 30–6

NEWTON, Isaac (1713) General Scholium to the Second Edition of the *Principia*, in *Newton's Philosophy of Nature: Selections from his Writings*, ed. H.S. Thayer (New York: Hafner, 1953), 42

NORTHCOTT, Michael (1996) *The Environment and Christian Ethics* (Cambridge: Cambridge University Press)

NUMBERS, R.L. (1992) *The Creationists: The Evolution of Scientific Creationism* (New York: Knopf)

OAKES, Edward T. SJ and MOSS, David (eds) (2004) *The Cambridge Companion to Hans Urs von Balthasar* (Cambridge: Cambridge University Press)

OAKLEY, F. (1961) 'Christian theology and the Newtonian science: rise of the concepts of the laws of nature', *Church History* 30, 433–57

OSBORN, E. (2001) *Irenaeus of Lyons* (Cambridge: Cambridge University Press)

OSBORN, L. (1992) 'The machine and the mother goddess: the Gaia Hypothesis in contemporary scientific and religious thought', *Science and Christian Belief* 4, 27–41

(2001) 'Archetypes, angels and Gaia', *Ecotheology* 10, 9–22

OSBORNE, J.F., ERDURAN, S. and SIMON, S. (2004) *Ideas, Evidence and Argument in Science (IDEAS) Project* (London: King's College)

OSBORNE, J.F., SIMON, S. and COLLINS, S. (2003). 'Attitudes towards science: a review of the literature and its implications', *International Journal of Science Education* 25 (9), 1049–79

OYAMA, Susan (2000) *The Ontogeny of Information: Developmental Systems Theory and Evolution*, 2nd edn revised and expanded (Durham, NC.: Duke University Press; first published 1985)

ÖZDEMIR, I. (2003) 'Towards an understanding of environmental ethics from a Qur'anic perspective', in *Islam and Ecology: A Bestowed Trust*, ed. R.C. Foltz, F.M. Denny and A. Baharuddin (Cambridge, MA: Harvard University Press for the Center for the Study of World Religions, Harvard Divinity School), 3–37

PACEY, A. (1983) *The Culture of Technology* (Cambridge, MA: MIT Press)

(1992) *The Maze of Ingenuity*, 2nd edn (Cambridge, MA: MIT Press)

PADGETT, A.G. (1992) *God, Eternity and the Nature of Time* (New York: St Martins)

PAGE, D. (1998) 'Hawking's timely story', *Nature* 333, 742–3

PAGE, Ruth (1991) 'The animal kingdom and the kingdom of God', in *Occasional Paper No. 26, The Animal Kingdom and the Kingdom of God* (Edinburgh: Church and Nation Committee of the Church of Scotland and the Centre for Theology and Public Issues), 1–9

(1996) *God and the Web of Creation* (London: SCM Press)

(2004) 'Panentheism and pansyntheism: God in relation', in *In Whom We Live and Move and Have Our Being: Panentheistic Reflections on God's Presence in a Scientific World*, ed. Philip Clayton and Arthur Peacocke (Grand Rapids, MI, and Cambridge: Eerdmans), 222–32

PAILIN, David (1989) *God and the Processes of Reality* (London: Routledge)

PALEY, William (1802) *Natural Theology: Or, Evidence of the Existence and Attributes of the Deity Collected from the Appearance of Nature*, 2nd edn (Oxford: J. Vincent)

PALMER, Clare (1992) 'Stewardship: a case study in environmental ethics', in *The Earth Beneath*, ed. I. Ball *et al.* (London: SPCK), 67–86

(1998) *Environmental Ethics and Process Thinking* (Oxford: Clarendon Press)

PALMER, M. (1997) *Freud and Jung on Religion* (London: Routledge)

PANNENBERG, Wolfhart (1976) *Theology and the Philosophy of Science*, trans. by F. McDonagh (London: Darton, Longman & Todd)

(1989) 'The doctrine of creation and modern science', in *Cosmos as Creation*, ed. Ted Peters (Nashville, TN: Abingdon)

(1991–4) *Systematic Theology*, trans. G.W. Bromiley (Edinburgh: T&T Clark)

(1993) *Towards a Theology of Nature: Essays on Science and Faith*, trans. by W.C. Linss, ed. Ted Peters (Louisville, KY: Westminster John Knox Press)

PARSONS, S.F. (1996) *Feminism and Christian Ethics* (Cambridge: Cambridge University Press)

PASCAL, Blaise (1966) *Pensées*, trans. by A.J. Krailsheimer (Harmondsworth: Penguin)

PEACOCKE, Arthur (1979) *Creation and the World of Science* (Oxford: Oxford University Press)

—— (1986) *God and the New Biology* (London: Dent)

—— (1993) *Theology for a Scientific Age*, expanded edn (London: SCM Press)

—— (1995) 'God's interaction with the world: the implications of deterministic "Chaos" and of interconnected and interdependent complexity', in *Chaos and Complexity: Scientific Perspectives on Divine Action*, ed. R.J. Russell, N. Murphy and A. Peacocke (Vatican City: Vatican Observatory; Berkeley, CA: Center for Theology and the Natural Sciences), 263–87

—— (1997) *The Idreos Lectures* (Oxford: Harris Manchester College)

—— (1998) 'Biological evolution: a positive theological appraisal', in *Evolutionary and Molecular Biology: Scientific Perspectives on Divine Action*, ed. R.J. Russell, W.R. Stoeger and F.J. Ayala (Vatican City: Vatican Observatory; Berkeley, CA: Center for Theology and the Natural Sciences), 357–76

—— (1999) 'The sound of sheer silence: how does God communicate with humanity?' in *Neuroscience and the Person: Scientific Perspectives on Divine Action*, ed. R.J. Russell, N. Murphy, T. Meyering and M. Arbib (Vatican City: Vatican Observatory; Berkeley, CA: Center for Theology and the Natural Sciences), 215–47

(2001a) *Paths from Science to God: The End of all our Exploring* (Oxford: Oneworld)

(2001b) 'The Cost of New Life' in *The Work of Love: Creation as Kenosis* ed. John Polkinghorne (London: SPCK; Grand Rapids, MI and Cambridge: Eerdmans), 21–42

(2004a) *Creation and the World of Science: The Re-Shaping of Belief*, updated edn (Oxford: Oxford University Press; first published 1979)

(2004b) 'Articulating God's presence in and to the world unveiled by the sciences', in *In Whom We Live and Move and Have Our Being: Panentheistic Reflections on God's Presence in a Scientific World*, ed. Philip Clayton and Arthur Peacocke (Grand Rapids, MI, and Cambridge: Eerdmans), 137–54

PENROSE, Roger (1989) *The Emperor's New Mind: Concerning Computers, Minds and the Laws of Physics* (Oxford: Oxford University Press)

(1994) *Shadows of the Mind: A Search for the Missing Science of Consciousness* (Oxford: Oxford University Press)

(1997) *The Large, the Small and the Human Mind* (Cambridge: Cambridge University Press)

PETERS, Ted (1993) *God as Trinity: Relationality and Temporality in the Divine Life* (Louisville, KY: Westminster John Knox Press)

(1997a) 'Theology and natural science', in *The Modern Theologians*, ed. D. and F. Ford (Oxford: Blackwell), 649–68

(1997b) *Playing God: Genetic Determinism and Human Freedom* (London: Routledge)

(1998) 'Science and theology: toward consonance', in *Science and Theology: The New Consonance*, ed. T. Peters (Oxford: Westview Press), 11–39

(2003) *Science, Theology and Ethics* (Aldershot: Ashgate)

PETERS, Ted and BENNETT, Gaymon (eds) (2002) *Bridging Science and Religion* (London: SCM Press)

PETERS, Ted and HEWLETT, Martinez (2003) *Evolution from Creation to New Creation: Conflict, Conversation and Convergence* (Nashville, TN: Abingdon)

PIKE, N. (1970) *God and Timelessness* (London: Routledge & Kegan Paul)

PINNOCK, C.H. (2001) *Most Moved Mover: A Theology of God's Openness* (Grand Rapids, MI: Baker)

PLANTINGA, A. (1987) 'On Ockham's way out', in *The Concept of God*, ed. Thomas V. Morris (Oxford: Oxford University Press), 171–200

POLANYI, M. (1958) *Personal Knowledge: Towards a Post-Critical Philosophy* (London: Routledge & Kegan Paul)

(1967) *The Tacit Dimension* (London: Routledge & Kegan Paul; first published 1966)

POLKINGHORNE, John (1988) *Science and Creation* (London: SPCK)

(1989) *Science and Providence* (London: SPCK)

(1990) *The Quantum World* (Harmondsworth: Penguin)

(1991) *Reason and Reality* (London: SPCK)

(1994) *Science and Christian Belief: Reflections of a Bottom-up Thinker* (London: SPCK)

(1995a) *Serious Talk* (London: SCM Press)

(1995b) 'The metaphysics of divine action', in *Chaos and Complexity: Scientific Perspectives on Divine Action*, ed. R.J. Russell, N. Murphy and A. Peacocke (Vatican City: Vatican Observatory; Berkeley, CA: Center for Theology and the Natural Sciences), 147–56

(1996a) *Scientists as Theologians* (London: SPCK)

(1996b) 'Chaos theory and divine action', in *Religion and Science: History, Method and Dialogue*, ed. W.M. Richardson and W.J. Wildman (London: Routledge), 243–52

(1998a) *Belief in God in an Age of Science* (New Haven, CT: Yale University Press)

(1998b) 'Beyond the Big Bang', in *Science Meets Faith*, ed. F. Watts (London: SPCK), 17–24

(1998c) *Science and Theology: An Introduction* (London: SPCK)

(2000) *Faith, Science and Understanding* (London: SPCK)

(2001) 'Physical process, quantum events, and divine agency', in *Quantum Mechanics: Scientific Perspectives on Divine Action*, ed. Robert J. Russell *et al.* (Vatican City: Vatican Observatory; Berkeley, CA: Center for Theology and the Natural Sciences), 181–90

(2002) *The God of Hope and the End of the World* (London: SPCK)

(2004) *Science and the Trinity: The Christian Encounter with Reality* (London: SPCK)

POLKINGHORNE, John (ed.) (2001) *The Work of Love: Creation as Kenosis* (London: SPCK; Grand Rapids, MI and Cambridge: Eerdmans)

POLKINGHORNE, J. and WELKER, M. (eds) (2000) *The End of the World and the Ends of God: Science and Theology on Eschatology* (Harrisburg, PA: Trinity Press International)

POOLE, Michael W. (1990) 'Beliefs and values in science education: a Christian perspective (Part 1)', *School Science Review* 71 (256), 26–9

(1994) 'A critique of aspects of the philosophy and theology of Richard Dawkins', *Science and Christian Belief* 6 (1), 41–59

(1995) *Beliefs and Values in Science Education* (Buckingham: Open University Press)

(1998) *Teaching about Science and Religion: Opportunities within Science in the National Curriculum* (Abingdon: Culham College Institute)

(2002) 'Explaining or Explaining Away? – The Concept of Explanation in the Science–Theology Debate', *Science and Christian Belief* 14(2), 123–42

POPPER, Karl (1959) *The Logic of Scientific Discovery* (London: Hutchinson)

——(1963) *Conjectures and Refutations: The Growth of Scientific Knowledge* (London: Routledge & Kegan Paul)

——(1972) *Objective Knowledge: An Evolutionary Approach* (Oxford: Oxford University Press)

PORRITT, Jonathan (2000) *Playing Safe: Science and the Environment* (London: Thames & Hudson)

PRANCE, G. (1996) *The Earth Under Threat: A Christian Perspective* (Glasgow: Wild Goose Publications)

PRIGOGINE, I. and STENGERS, I. (1984) *Order Out of Chaos: Man's New Dialogue With Nature* (London: Heinemann)

PRIMAVESI, Anne (1991) *From Apocalypse to Genesis: Ecology, Feminism and Christianity* (Tunbridge Wells: Burns & Oates)

PUDDEFOOT, J.C. (1996) *God and the Mind Machine* (London: SPCK)

PUTNAM, Hilary (1981) *Reason, Truth and History* (Cambridge: Cambridge University Press)

——(1998) 'Why fraternity cannot be cloned', *The Times Higher Educational Supplement*, 30 January, 18–19

QUALIFICATIONS AND CURRICULUM AUTHORITY (2004) *The Non-Statutory National Framework for Religious Education* (London: QCA)

QUINE, Willard V.O. (1953) 'Two dogmas of empiricism', in *From a Logical Point of View: Nine Logico-Philosophical Essays*, 2nd edn (Cambridge, MA: Harvard University Press), 20–46

RADHAKRISHNAN, S. (1958) *The Bhagavadgita: With an Introductory Essay, Sanskrit Text, English Translation and Note* (London: Allen & Unwin)

UR-RAHMAN, A. (1995) Standing Committee on Scientific and Technological Cooperation (COMSTECH). Conference Papers of the International Conference on Science in Islamic Policy in the Twenty-first Century, March 26–30, 1995. 3 Constitution Avenue, G-5 / 2 Islamabad-44000, Pakistan

RAHNER, Karl (1965) *Theological Investigations*, vol. I, trans. by C. Ernst (London: Darton, Longman & Todd)

(1989) *Foundations of the Christian Faith*, trans. by W.Y. Dych (New York: Crossroad)

(1999) *The Trinity*, trans. Joseph Donceel (New York: Crossroad Herder; first published 1967)

RAHULA, W. (1998) *What the Buddha Taught* (Oxford: OneWorld)

RASMUSSEN, D.T. (ed.) (1993) *The Origin and Evolution of Humans and Humanness* (Boston, MA: Jones & Bartlett)

RAVETZ, J.R. (1971) *Scientific Knowledge and its Social Problems* (Oxford: Oxford University Press)

REGAN, T. (1990) 'Christianity and animal rights: the challenge and promise', in *Liberating Life*, ed. C. Birch, W. Eakin and J. McDaniel (Maryknoll, NY: Orbis Books), 73–87

REISS, Michael J. (2000) 'The ethics of genetic research on intelligence', *Bioethics* 14 (1), 1–15

REISS, M. and STRAUGHAN, R. (1996) *Improving Nature: The Science and Ethics of Genetic Engineering* (Cambridge: Cambridge University Press)

RESCHER, Nicholas (1973) *The Coherence Theory of Truth* (Oxford: Clarendon Press)

——(1992a) 'Idealism', in *A Companion to Epistemology*, ed. J. Dancy and E. Sosa (Oxford: Blackwell), 187–91

——(1992b) *A System of Pragmatic Idealism, Volume I: Human Knowledge in Idealistic Perspective* (Princeton, NJ: Princeton University Press)

——(1993a) *A System of Pragmatic Idealism, Volume II: The Validity of Values* (Princeton, NJ: Princeton University Press)

——(1993b) 'In matters of religion', in *Philosophers Who Believe: The Spiritual Journeys of 11 Leading Thinkers*, ed. K.J. Clark (Downers Grove, IL: InterVarsity Press)

——(1994) *A System of Pragmatic Idealism, Volume III: Metaphilosophical Inquiries* (Princeton, NJ: Princeton University Press).

——(1995) 'Pragmatism', in *The Oxford Companion to Philosophy*, ed. T. Honderich (Oxford: Oxford University Press), 710–13

RICHARDSON, W. Mark and SLACK, Gordy (2001) *Faith in Science: Scientists Search for Truth* (New York and London: Routledge)

RICHARDSON, W.M. and WILDMAN, W.J. (1996) *Religion and Science: History, Method, Dialogue* (London and New York: Routledge)

RIDLEY, M. (1993) *Evolution* (Oxford: Blackwell Scientific)

RING, K. (1980) *Life After Death: A Scientific Investigation of Near-Death Experience* (New York, NY: Coward McCann & Geoghegan)

ROBINSON, Andrew J. (2003) 'A semiotic model of the Trinity: God, evolution and the philosophy of C.S. Peirce', Ph.D. thesis, University of Exeter.

(2004) 'Continuity, naturalism and contingency: a theology of evolution drawing on the semiotics of C.S. Peirce and Trinitarian thought', *Zygon* 39 (1), 111–36

ROLSTON, Holmes, III (1988) *Environmental Ethics: Duties to and Values in the Natural World* (Philadelphia: Temple University Press)

(1989) *Philosophy Gone Wild: Environmental Ethics* (Buffalo, NY: Prometheus Books)

(1990) 'Joining Science and Religion', in *John Paul II on Science and Religion: Reflections on the New View from Rome*, ed. Robert John Russell, William R. Stoeger SJ and George V. Coyne SJ (Vatican City: Vatican Observatory), 83–94.

(1994) *Conserving Natural Value* (New York, NY: Columbia University Press)

(1996) 'Science, religion and the future', in *Religion and Science*, ed. W.M. Richardson and W.J. Wildman (London: Routledge), 61–82

(1999) *Genes, Genesis and God: Values and their Origins in Natural and Human History* (Cambridge: Cambridge University Press)

(2001) 'Kenosis and nature' in *The Work of Love: Creation as Kenosis*, ed. John Polkinghorne (London: SPCK; Cambridge and Grand Rapids, MI: Eerdmans), 43–65

(2003) 'Naturalizing and systematizing evil', in *Is Nature Ever Evil? Religion, Science and Value*, ed. Willem B. Drees (London: Routledge), 67–86

RORTY, Richard (1979) *Philosophy and the Mirror of Nature* (Princeton, NJ: Princeton University Press)

ROSE, Steven (1997) *Lifelines: Biology, Freedom, Determinism* (Harmondsworth: Penguin)

ROSS, S.A. (1998) *Extravagant Affections: A Feminist Sacram* (London: Continuum)

RUETHER, Rosemary Radford (1992) *Gaia and God* (London: SCM Press)

RUETHER, Rosemary Radford (ed.) (1996) *Women Healing Earth* (London: SPCK)

RUPKE, N. (1983) *The Great Chain of History: William Buckland and the English School of Geology, 1814–1849* (Oxford: Clarendon Press)

RUSE, Michael (2001) *Can a Darwinian be a Christian? The Relationship between Science and Religion* (Cambridge: Cambridge University Press)

(2003) *Darwin and Design: Does Evolution Have a Purpose?* (Cambridge, MA: Harvard University Press)

RUSSELL, C.A. (1985) *Cross-Currents: Interactions between Science and Faith* (Leicester: InterVarsity Press)

—— (1987) 'Some founding fathers of physics', *Physics Education* 22 (1), 27–33

—— (1989) 'The conflict metaphor and its social origins', *Science and Christian Belief* 1 (1), 3–26

—— (1994) *The Earth, Humanity and God* (London: UCL Press)

RUSSELL, Robert J. (1984) 'Entropy and evil', *Zygon* 19 (4), 449–68

(1993) 'Finite creation without a beginning: the doctrine of creation in relation to Big Bang and quantum cosmologies', in *Quantum Cosmology and the Laws of Nature: Scientific Perspectives on Divine Action*, ed. R.J. Russell, N. Murphy and C.J. Isham (Vatican City State: Vatican Observatory and Berkeley, CA: Center for Theology and the Natural Sciences), 293–329

(1996) 'T=0: Is it theologically significant?' in *Religion and Science: history, method, dialogue*, ed. W.M. Richardson and W.J. Wildman (London: Routledge), 201–24

(1998) 'Special providence and genetic mutation: a new defence of theistic evolution', in *Evolutionary and Molecular Biology: Scientific Perspectives on Divine Action*, ed. R.J. Russell, W.R. Stoeger and F.J. Ayala (Vatican City: Vatican Observatory; Berkeley, CA: Center for Theology and the Natural Sciences), 191–223

(2001) 'Divine action and quantum mechanics: a fresh assessment', in *Quantum Mechanics: Scientific Perspectives on Divine Action*, ed. R.J. Russell, P. Clayton, K. Wegter-McNelly and J. Polkinghorne (Vatican City: Vatican Observatory; Berkeley, CA: Center for Theology and the Natural Sciences), 293–328

(2002) 'Eschatology and physical cosmology: a preliminary reflection', in *The Far-Future Universe: Eschatology from a Cosmic Perspective*, ed. George F.R. Ellis (Radnor, PA: Templeton Foundation Press), 266–315

(2003) 'Five attitudes toward nature and technology from a Christian perspective', *Theology and Science* 1 (2), 149–59

(ed.) (2004) *Fifty Years in Science and Religion: Ian Barbour and his Legacy* (Aldershot: Ashgate)

RUSSELL, Robert J. *et al.* (eds) (1988) *Physics, Philosophy and Theology: a common quest for understanding* (Vatican City State: Vatican City Publications)

(1990) *John Paul II on Science and Religion: Reflections on the New View from Rome* (Vatican City State: Vatican City Publications)

(1993) *Quantum Cosmology and the Laws of Nature: Scientific Perspectives on Divine Action* (Vatican City: Vatican Observatory; Berkeley, CA: Center for Theology and the Natural Sciences)

(1995) *Chaos and Complexity: Scientific Perspectives on Divine Action* (Vatican City: Vatican Observatory; Berkeley, CA: Center for Theology and the Natural Sciences)

(1998) *Evolutionary and Molecular Biology: Scientific Perspectives on Divine Action* (Vatican City: Vatican Observatory; Berkeley, CA: Center for Theology and the Natural Sciences)

(1999) *Neuroscience and the Person: Scientific Perspectives on Divine Action* (Vatican City: Vatican Observatory; Berkeley, CA: Center for Theology and the Natural Sciences)

(2001) *Quantum Mechanics: Scientific Perspectives on Divine Action* (Vatican City: Vatican Observatory; Berkeley, CA: Center for Theology and the Natural Sciences)

(2005, forthcoming) *Scientific Perspectives on Divine Action: Fourteen Years of Problems and Progress* (Vatican City: Vatican Observatory; Berkeley, CA: Center for Theology and the Natural Sciences)

SACKS, Jonathan (2003) *The Dignity of Difference: How to Avoid the Clash of Civilizations*, revised edn (London and New York: Continuum; first published 2002)

SADAKATA, A. (1997) *Buddhist Cosmology: Philosophy and Origins* (Tokyo: Kosei)

SAID, A.A. and FUNK, N.C. (2003) 'Peace in Islam: an ecology of the spirit', in *Islam and Ecology: A Bestowed Trust*, ed. R.C. Foltz, F.M. Denny and A. Baharuddin (Cambridge, MA: Harvard University Press for the Center for the Study of World Religions, Harvard Divinity School), 155–83

SALAM, A. (1987) 'The future of science in Islamic countries', A paper given at the Islamic Summit held in Kuwait in January 1987

SAMUELSON, Norbert M. (2003) *Jewish Philosophy: An Historical Introduction* (London: Continuum)

SANDERS, J. (1998) *The God Who Risks: A Theology of Providence* (Downers Grove: IVP)

SANTMIRE, H. Paul (1985) *The Travail of Nature: The Ambiguous Ecological Promise of Christian Theology* (Philadelphia: Fortress Press)

(2000) *Nature Reborn: The Ecological and Cosmic Promise of Christian Theology* (Minneapolis, MN: Fortress Press)

SARDAR, Z. (1980) 'Can science come back to Islam?' *New Scientist* 88 (1224), 212–16

(1985) *Islamic Futures: The Shape of Things to Come* (London: Mansell)

(1989) *Explorations in Islamic Science* (London: Mansell)

SARDAR, Z. (ed.) (1984) *A Touch of Midas: Science, Values and Environment in Islam and the West* (Manchester: Manchester University Press)

SAUNDERS, Nicholas (2002) *Divine Action and Modern Science* (Cambridge: Cambridge University Press)

SCHEFFLER I. (1967) *Science and Subjectivity* (Indianapolis, IN: Bobbs-Merrill)

SCHILPP, P.A. (ed.) (1949) *Albert Einstein: Philosopher-Scientist* (La Salle, IL: Open Court)

SCHNEIDER, Stephen H. *et al.* (eds) (2004) *Scientists Debate Gaia* (Cambridge, MA: MIT Press)

SCHRÖDINGER, Erwin (1969) *What is Life?* (Cambridge: Cambridge University Press; first published 1944)

SCHUON, F. (1968) *In the Tracks of Buddhism*, trans. M. Pallis (London: Allen & Unwin)

—— (1995) *Understanding Islam* (Bloomington, IL: World Wisdom)

SCOVILLE, Judith N. (2004) 'Ethics, technology and environment', in *Fifty Years in Science and Religion: Ian G. Barbour and his Legacy*, ed. Robert John Russell (Aldershot and Burlington, VT: Ashgate), 225–38

SEEGER R.J. (1966) *Galileo Galilei: His Life and Works* (Oxford: Pergamon)

SEGERSTRÅLE, Ullica (2000) *Defenders of the Truth: The Battle for Science in the Sociobiology Debate and Beyond* (Oxford: Oxford University Press)

SELLARS, W. (1963) *Science, Perception and Reality* (London: Routledge & Kegan Paul)

SESSIONS, G. (ed.) (1995) *Deep Ecology for the 21st Century* (Boston, MA: Shambhala)

SETTLE, T. (1996) 'The dressage ring and the ballroom: loci of double agency', in *Facets of Faith and Science, Volume IV: Interpreting God's Action in the World*, ed. J. van der Meer (Lanham, NY: University Press of America), 17–40

SHANKS, Niall (2004) *God, the Devil, and Darwin: A Critique of Intelligent Design Theory* (Oxford: Oxford University Press)

SHINN, Roger L. (2004) 'Technology requires ethical decisions', in *Fifty Years in Science and Religion: Ian G. Barbour and his Legacy*, ed. Robert John Russell (Aldershot and Burlington, VT: Ashgate), 213–24

SHIVA, Vandana (1997) *Biopiracy: The Plunder of Nature and Knowledge* (USA: South End Press)

SHIVA, Vandana and MUSER, I. (eds) (1995) *Biopolitics: A Feminist and Ecological Reader on Biotechnology* (London: Zed Books)

SHREEVE, J. (1996) *The Neandertal Enigma* (London: Viking)

SIDERIS, Lisa H. (2003) *Environmental Ethics, Ecological Theology, and Natural Selection* (New York: Columbia University Press)

SINGER, Peter (1990) *Animal Liberation*, rev. edn (London: Cape)

SIRRIYEH, E. (1990) 'Modern Muslim Interpretations of Shirk', *Religion* **20**, 139–59

SLOAN WILSON, David (2003) *Darwin's Cathedral: Evolution, Religion and the Nature of Society* (Chicago, IL: University of Chicago Press; first published 2002)

SMART, N. (1995) *Worldviews: Cross-Cultural Explorations of Human Beliefs*, 2nd edn (Englewood Cliffs, NJ: Prentice-Hall)

SMOOT, G. and DAVIDSON, K. (1993) *Wrinkles in Time* (London: Little, Brown)

SOLOMON, Norman (2000) *Judaism: A Very Short Introduction* (Oxford: Oxford University Press)

SORABJI, R. (1983): *Time, Creation and the Continuum: Theories in Antiquity and the Early Middle Ages* (London: Duckworth)

SOSKICE, Janet Martin (1985) *Metaphor and Religious Language* (Oxford: Clarendon Press)

—— (1993a) 'Bad language in science and religion', in *Explorations in Science and Theology: The Templeton London Lectures at the RSA* (London: RSA), 69–78

—— (1993b) 'The truth looks different from here, or: on seeking the unity of truth from a diversity of perspectives', in *Christ in Context: The Confrontation Between Gospel and Culture*, ed. H.D. Regan and A.J. Torrance (Edinburgh: T&T Clark), 43–59

(1998) 'The gift of the Name: Moses and the burning bush', *Gregorianum* 79 (2), 231–46

SOUTHGATE, Christopher (2002) 'God and evolutionary evil: theodicy in the light of Darwinism', *Zygon* 37 (4), 803–21

(2003) 'Research in science and religion', in *The Encyclopaedia of Science and Religion*, ed. J. Wentzel van Huyssteen (New York: Macmillan), 768–76

(2004) 'Environmental ethics and the science–religion debate: a British perspective on Barbour', in *Fifty Years in Science and Religion: Ian G. Barbour and his Legacy*, ed. Robert John Russell (Aldershot and Burlington, VT: Ashgate), 239–48

(2005, forthcoming) 'Stewardship and its competitors: a spectrum of relationships between humans and the non-human creation', in *Environmental Stewardship: A Primer*, ed. R.J. Berry (Edinburgh: T&T Clark International)

SOUTHGATE, Christopher and AYLWARD, Alex (2002) 'Environmental ethics: further case-studies', in *Bioethics for Scientists*, ed. John Bryant *et al.* (Chichester: John Wiley), 73–83

SPITZ, Lewis W. (1971) *The Renaissance and Reformation Movements, Vol. II* (Chicago: Rand McNally)

STANESBY, D. (1985) *Science, Reason and Religion* (London: Croom Helm)

STANNARD, Russell (1991) *Black Holes and Uncle Albert* (London: Faber & Faber)

(1996) *Science and Wonders: Conversations about Science and Belief* (London: Faber & Faber)

STENMARK, Mikael (2004) *How to Relate Science and Religion: A Multi-Dimensional Model* (Grand Rapids, MI, and Cambridge: Eerdmans)

STEWART, Jacqui A. (2000) *Reconstructing Science and Theology in Postmodernity: Pannenberg, Ethics and the Human Sciences* (Aldershot: Ashgate)

STOEGER, W.R. (1995) 'Describing God's action in the light of scientific knowledge of reality', in *Chaos and Complexity: Scientific Perspectives on Divine Action*, ed. R.J. Russell, N. Murphy and A. Peacocke (Vatican City: Vatican Observatory; Berkeley, CA: Center for Theology and the Natural Sciences), 239–61

SULSTON, John and FERRY, Georgina (2002) *The Common Thread: A Story of Science, Politics, Ethics and the Human Genome* (London and New York: Bantam Press)

SURIN, KENNETH (1986) *Theology and the Problem of Evil* (Oxford: Blackwell)

SURTY, M.H.I. (1990) *The Qur'ān and Al-Shirk* (London: TaHa)

SUZUKI, D.T. (1970) *Mysticism: Christian and Buddhist* (London: Allen & Unwin)

SWIMME, Brian and BERRY, Thomas (1992) *The Universe Story: From the Primordial Flaring Forth to the Ecozoic Era: A Celebration of the Unfolding of the Cosmos* (San Francisco: HarperSanFrancisco)

SWINBURNE, Richard (1979) *The Existence of God* (Oxford: Clarendon Press)

—— (1993) 'The vocation of a natural theologian', in *Philosophers Who Believe: The Spiritual Journeys of 11 Leading Thinkers*, ed. K.J. Clark (Downers Grove, IL: InterVarsity Press), 179–202

(1997) *The Evolution of the Soul* (Oxford: Clarendon)

TANNER, Kathryn (1988) *God and Creation in Christian Theology: Tyranny or Empowerment?* (Oxford: Blackwell)

(2003) *Jesus, Humanity and the Trinity: A Brief Systematic Theology* (Minneapolis, MN: Fortress Press; first published 2001)

TATTERSALL, Ian (1998) *Becoming Human: Evolution and Human Uniqueness* (New York: Harcourt Brace)

TAYLOR, J.G. (1991) Chapter 7 of *The Ghost in the Atom*, ed. P.C.W. Davies and J.R. Brown (Cambridge: Cambridge University Press), 106–17

TAYLOR, P. (1986) *Respect for Nature: A Theory of Environmental Ethics* (Princeton, NJ: Princeton University Press)

TEILHARD DE CHARDIN, Pierre (1959) *The Phenomenon of Man*, trans. by B. Wall (London: Collins)

(1966) *Man's Place in Nature*, trans. by R. Hague (London: Collins)

TEMPLE, William (1976) *Christianity and Social Order* (London: SPCK; originally published 1942)

TESTA, G. and HARRIS, J. (2004) 'Ethical aspects of ES cell-derived gametes', *Science* **305**, 1719

THEISSEN, Gerd (1984) *Biblical Faith: An Evolutionary Approach*, trans. by J. Bowden (London: SCM Press)

TILES, M. and OBERDIECK, H. (1995) *Living in a Technological Culture* (London: Routledge)

TILLICH, Paul (1952) *The Courage to Be* (London: Fontana)

(1978) *Systematic Theology, Vol. III* (London: SCM Press)

TINSLEY, E.J. (ed.) (1973) *Reinhold Niebuhr* (Peterborough: Epworth Press)

TIPLER, F.J. (1995) *The Physics of Immortality: Modern Cosmology, God and the Resurrection of the Dead* (London: Macmillan)

TORRANCE, Thomas F. (1969) *Theological Science* (Oxford: Oxford University Press; reissued Edinburgh: T&T Clark, 1996)

(1976) *Space, Time, and Resurrection* (Edinburgh: Handsel; reissued Edinburgh: T&T Clark, 1998)

(1980) *Christian Theology and Scientific Culture* (Belfast, Dublin and Ottawa: Christian Journals)

(1985) *Reality and Scientific Theology* (Edinburgh: Scottish Academic Press)

(1996) *The Christian Doctrine of God: One Being, Three Persons* (Edinburgh: T&T Clark)

TOULMIN, S. (1990) *Cosmopolis: The Hidden Agenda of Modernity* (Chicago: University of Chicago Press)

TRACY, Thomas F. (1995) 'Particular providence and the God of the gaps', in *Chaos and Complexity: Scientific Perspectives on Divine Action*, ed. R.J. Russell, N. Murphy and A. Peacocke (Vatican City: Vatican Observatory; Berkeley, CA: Center for Theology and the Natural Sciences), 289–324

(1998) 'Evolution, divine action, and the problem of evil', in *Evolutionary and Molecular Biology: Scientific Perspectives on Divine Action*, ed. Robert J. Russell *et al.* (Vatican City: Vatican Observatory; Berkeley, CA: Center for Theology and the Natural Sciences), 511–30

(2004) 'Scientific perspectives on divine action? Mapping the options', *Theology and Science* **2** (2), 196–201

TRIGG, Roger (1993) *Rationality and Science: Can Science Explain Everything?* (Oxford: Blackwell)

——(1998) *Rationality and Religion* (Oxford: Blackwell)

TYNDALL, J. (1874) 'Presidential Address to the British Association for the Advancement of Science', in *Science and Religion*, ed. T. Coslett (Cambridge: Cambridge University Press, 1984)

UNIVERSITY of York, and Oxford, Cambridge and RSA (OCR) Examinations (2003) *Science for the 21st Century* (a collection of pilot GCSE courses)

UPDIKE, John (1986) *Roger's Version* (New York, NY: Ballantine)

VAN HUYSSTEEN, J. Wentzel (1989) *Theology and the Justification of Faith: Constructing Theories in Systematic Theology*, trans. by H.F. Snijders (Grand Rapids, MI: Eerdmans)

(1997) *Essays in Postfoundationalist Theology* (Grand Rapids, MI: Eerdmans)

(1998) *Duet or Duel? Theology and Science in a Postmodern World* (London: SCM Press)

(1999) *The Shaping of Rationality: Towards Interdisciplinarity in Theology and Science* (Grand Rapids, MI: Eerdmans)

(2003) 'Fallen angels or rising beasts? Theological perspectives on human uniqueness', *Theology and Science* 1 (2), 161–78

(2006, forthcoming) *Alone in the World? Science and Theology on Human Uniqueness* (Grand Rapids, MI: Eerdmans)

VAN HUYSSTEEN, J. Wentzel (ed.) (2003) *Encyclopedia of Science and Religion* (New York: Macmillan)

VAN TILL, H.J. (1996) 'Basil, Augustine, and the doctrine of creation's functional integrity', *Science and Christian Belief* 8, 21–38

VANSTONE, W.H. (1977) *Love's Endeavour, Love's Expense* (London: Darton, Longman & Todd)

WAGHID, Y. (1996) 'Creative order, truth and justice: the rationale of Islamic science', *Journal of Islamic Science* 12 (1), 87–101

WARD, Keith (1982) *Holding Fast to God: A Response to Don Cupitt* (London: SPCK)

(1987) *Images of Eternity: Concepts of God in Five Religious Traditions* (London: Darton, Longman & Todd)

(1990) *Divine Action* (London: Collins)

(1991) *A Vision to Pursue* (London: SCM Press)

(1992) *Defending the Soul* (Oxford: OneWorld)

(1996a) *Religion and Creation* (Oxford: Oxford University Press)

(1996b) *God, Chance and Necessity* (Oxford: OneWorld)

(1998) *Religion and Human Nature* (Oxford: Clarendon Press)

(2003) *God: A Guide for the Perplexed* (Oxford: Oneworld; first published 2002)

WARD, Peter D. and BROWNLEE, Donald (2004) *The Life and Death of Planet Earth: How the New Science of Astrobiology Charts the Ultimate Fate of Our World* (New York: Owl Books; first published 2003)

WARE, B.A. (2000) *God's Lesser Glory: The Diminished God of Open Theism* (Wheaton, IL: Crossway Books)

WATERS, B. and COLE-TURNER, R. (2003) *God and the Embryo: Religious Voices on Stem Cells and Cloning* (Washington: Georgetown University Press)

WATSON, James D. (1968) *The Double Helix: A Personal Account of the Discovery of the Structure of DNA* (London: Weidenfeld and Nicolson)

WATTS, Fraser (1994) 'Are we really nothing more than our neurones?' *Journal of Consciousness Studies* 1, 275–9

(1998a) 'Brain, mind and soul', in *Science Meets Faith*, ed. F. Watts (London: SPCK), 59–72

(1998b) 'Science and theology as complementary perspectives', in *Rethinking Theology and Science: Six Models for the Current Dialogue*, ed. N. Gregersen and W. van Huyssteen (Grand Rapids, MI: Eerdmans)

(2002) *Theology and Psychology* (Aldershot: Ashgate)

WATTS, Fraser (ed.) (1998c) *Science Meets Faith* (London: SPCK)

WATTS, F. and WILLIAMS, M. (1988) *The Psychology of Religious Knowing* (Cambridge: Cambridge University Press; reissued London: Geoffrey Chapman, 1994)

WEBSTER, J.B. (1986) *Eberhard Jüngel: An Introduction to his Theology* (Cambridge: Cambridge University Press)

WEBSTER, R. (1996) *Why Freud Was Wrong: Sin, Science and Psychoanalysis* (London: Fontana)

WEGTER-MCNELLY, Kirk (2003) 'The world, entanglement and God', Ph.D. thesis, Graduate Theological Union, Berkeley, California

WEINANDY, Thomas (2000) *Does God Suffer?* (Edinburgh: T&T Clark)

WEINER, J. (1994) *The Beak of the Finch* (London: Cape)

WELCH, C. (1996) 'Dispelling some myths about the split between theology and science in the nineteenth century', in *Religion and Science*, ed. W.M. Richardson and W.J. Wildman (London: Routledge), 29–40

WERTHEIM, Margaret (1995) *Pythagoras' Trousers: God, Physics and the Gender Wars* (New York, NY: Times Books)

WESTERMANN, Claus (1984) *Genesis 1–11*, trans. by J.J. Scullion (London: SPCK)

WEYL, H. (1949) *Philosophy of Mathematics and Natural Science* (Princeton, NJ: Princeton University Press)

WHEELER, John A. (1977) 'Genesis and observership', in *Foundational Problems in the Special Sciences*, ed. R.E. Butts and K.J. Hintikka (Dordrecht: D. Reidel, 3–33)

WHITE, A.D. (1960) *A History of the Warfare of Science with Theology in Christendom* (New York: Dover; first published 1896)

WHITE, Lynn, Jr (1967) 'The historic roots of the ecologic crisis', *Science* 155, 1203–7; also reprinted in *The Care of Creation: Focusing Concern and Action* ed. R.J. Berry (Leicester: InterVarsity Press, 2000), 31–42

WHITE, Susan (1994) *Christian Worship and Technological Change* (Nashville, TN: Abingdon Press)

WHITEHEAD, A.N. (1967) *Process and Reality: An Essay in Cosmology* (New York: Macmillan; first published 1929)

WHITROW, G.J. (1980) *The Natural Philosophy of Time* (Oxford: Clarendon Press)

WILDMAN, Wesley J. (2004) 'The divine action project 1988–2003', *Theology and Science* 2 (1), 31–75

WILES, Maurice (1986) *God's Action in the World* (London: SCM Press)

WILKINS, Maurice (2003) *The Third Man of the Double Helix: The Autobiography of Maurice Wilkins* (Oxford: Oxford University Press)

WILKINSON, D. (2002) *The Message of Creation: Encountering the Lord of the Universe* (Leicester: IVP)

WILLIAMS, B. (1978) *Descartes: The Project of Pure Enquiry* (Harmondsworth: Penguin)

WILLIAMS, Patricia (2001) *Doing Without Adam and Eve: Sociobiology and Original Sin* (Minneapolis, MN: Fortress Press)

(2005, forthcoming) 'How evil entered the world: an exploration through deep time', in *The Evolution of Evil*, ed. Ted Peters and Martinez Hewlett

WILLIAMS, Rowan (2000) *On Christian Theology* (Oxford: Blackwell)

WILMUT, I., SCHNIEKE, A.E., MCWHIR, J., KIND, A.J. and CAMPBELL, K.H.S. (1997) 'Viable offspring derived from fetal and adult mammalian cells', *Nature* 385, 810–13

WILSON, E.O. (1975) *Sociobiology: The New Synthesis* (Cambridge, MA: Harvard University Press)

(1995) *On Human Nature* (Harmondsworth: Penguin; first published 1978)

(1999) *Consilience: The Unity of Knowledge* (London: Abacus; first published 1998)

WINNER, L. (1977) *Autonomous Technology* (Cambridge, MA: MIT Press)

WITTGENSTEIN, Ludwig (1967) *Philosophical Investigations*, 3rd edn, trans. by G.E.M. Anscombe (Oxford: Blackwell; repr. 1968)

(1969) *The Blue and Brown Books: Preliminary Studies for the Philosophical Investigations*, 2nd edn (Oxford: Basil Blackwell)

WOLTERSTORFF, N. (2000) 'God and Time', *Philosophia Christi* 2, 5–10

WOOD, K.A. (1993) 'The scientific exegesis of the Qur'an', *Perspectives on Science and Christian Faith: Journal of the American Scientific Affiliation* 45 (2), 90–4

WOOLFSON, Adrian (2004) *An Intelligent Person's Guide to Genetics* (London: Duckworth)

WOOLNOUGH, B. (1992) *Science and Religion: Friends or Foes?* SATIS 16–19, No. 125 (Hatfield: Association for Science Education)

WORTHING, M.W. (1996) *God, Creation and Contemporary Physics* (Minneapolis, MN: Fortress Press)

WRIGHT, A. (2000) *Spirituality and Education*, Master Classes in Education Series (London: RoutledgeFalmer)

WULFF, D.M. (1991) *Psychology of Religion: Classic and Contemporary Views* (New York: John Wiley)

WYATT, P. (1996) *Jesus Christ and Creation in the Theology of John Calvin* (Allison Park, PA: Pickwick)

WYNN, Mark (1999) *God and Goodness: A Natural Theological Perspective* (London, Routledge)

YOUNG, Frances (1991) 'Creatio ex nihilo: a context for the emergence of the Christian doctrine of creation', *Scottish Journal of Theology* 44, 139–51

ZARANDI, M. (ed.) (2003) *Science and the Myth of Progress* (Bloomington, IN: World Wisdom)

ZILSEL, E. (1942) 'The genesis of the concept of physical law', *Philosophical Review* 51, 245–79

ZIMAN, J. (1978) *Reliable Knowledge* (Cambridge: Cambridge University Press)
(1995) *An Introduction to Science Studies* (Cambridge: Cambridge University Press)

ZIMMERLI, W. (1978) *Old Testament Theology in Outline*, trans. by David E. Green (Edinburgh: T&T Clark)

ZIZIOULAS, John D. (1990) 'Preserving God's creation: Three lectures on theology and ecology. I', *King's Theological Review* 12, 1–5
(1990) 'Preserving God's creation: Three lectures on theology and ecology. III', *King's Theological Review* 13, 1–5

Index

Individuals and organizations referenced in the Bibliography appear in bold.